Accounting and Food

The interrelations between accounting and food have been hitherto neglected at an international level. This regret is particularly meaningful with regards to Italy, where 'Food', besides being a physiological need to satisfy, is one of the main pillars of the 'Made in Italy' industry, and the so-called Italian lifestyle, which has become a part of the popular culture.

Accounting and Food seeks to explore the accounting, business and financial history of some of the most prestigious Italian food producers. Moreover, given that 'Food' has been at the center of production and trade throughout the history of mankind, food production and commerce will be investigated from the critical angles of accounting, accountants and merchants. Relatedly, the interconnected history of the food fairs and expositions of the major Italian trade centers will be also unveiled.

Accounting and Food examines the role of accounting, accountants and merchants in food production and international trade (e.g., grain, wine), and considers the history of food producers, paying particular attention to the role played by women entrepreneurs over time.

Finally the book explores the interrelations of accounting, food and state, local authorities and social institutions, in particular insofar as these latter institutions were involved in the political economy, regulation, allocation and distribution of food to populations and societies.

Accounting and Food will be of particular interest to researchers and scholars in the field of accounting history but also to those working in the areas of regional development, regional economics, food and sociology and other related disciplines.

Luciano D'Amico is Professor of Business Economics at the Faculty of Communication Sciences and Rector of the University of Teramo, Italy. He is a past President of the Italian Society of Accounting History.

Roberto Di Pietra is Professor of International Financial Accounting and Head of the Department of Business and Law of the University of Siena, Italy. He is President of the Italian Society of Accounting History.

Massimo Sargiacomo is Professor of Business Economics in the Department of Business Administration at the University G. d'Annunzio of Chieti-Pescara, Italy. He is a past President of the Academy of Accounting Historians and chairman of the 2016 World Congress of Accounting Historians.

Routledge New Works in Accounting History

Series Editors: John Richard Edwards, Richard Fleischman, Garry Carnegie, Salvador Carmona

For a full list of titles in this series, please visit www.routledge.com

This innovative series contains volumes on accounting history, auditing, bibliography, development of accounting principles and standards, education and ethics, financial reporting, law and regulations, management accounting and the theoretical works of leading scholars. Providing students, teachers and researchers with the opportunity to learn more about the discipline of accountancy and its past, this series is a vital addition to any accounting library.

38 **Accounting Research, 1948–1958**
David Solomons, Stephen A. Zeff

39 **Management Control in a Voluntary Organization**
Peter Booth

40 **Leonard M. Savoie**
Edited by Donald E. Tidrick

41 **Making the Australian Chartered Accountant**
Chris Poullaos

42 **Commerce, Accounts, & Finance**
Edited by Paul J. Miranti Jr

43 **A History of Canadian Accounting Thought & Practice**
Edited by George J. Murphy

44 **The History of the Financial Control Function of Local Government Accounting in the United Kingdom**
Richard Brief

45 **Local Authority Accounting Methods**
Hugh J. Coombs, John Edwards

46 **Curtis Jenkins Cornwell & Company**
S. V. Cornwell

47 **Contributions of Limperg & Schmidt to the Replacement Cost Debate in the 1920s**
Frank L. Clarke, Graeme Dean

48 **Accounting and Food**
Some Italian Experiences
Edited by Luciano D'Amico, Roberto Di Pietra and Massimo Sargiacomo

Accounting and Food

Some Italian Experiences

Edited by
Luciano D'Amico, Roberto Di Pietra and Massimo Sargiacomo

Routledge
Taylor & Francis Group
LONDON AND NEW YORK

First published January 2016
by Routledge

2 Park Square, Milton Park, Abingdon, Oxfordshire OX14 4RN
711 Third Avenue, New York, NY 10017

Routledge is an imprint of the Taylor & Francis Group, an informa business

First issued in paperback 2018

Library of Congress Cataloging-in-Publication Data
CIP data has been applied for.

ISBN: 978-1-138-65245-3 (hbk)
ISBN: 978-1-138-61659-2 (pbk)

Typeset in Sabon
by Apex CoVantage, LLC

Contents

Figures

Tables

Foreword

When we thought about the idea of this volume, and the preliminary organization of a workshop held in Milan on June 13, 2015—during the Expo Food Fair—we had the perception that in the accounting and accounting history literature, there was a general paucity of research on the interrelations between accounting and food. The first thing that came to our mind was that the history of searching for food, as well as bartering, record-keeping, and market transactions, coincided more or less with the history of humankind. In prehistoric times, the act of counting and enumerating was closely associated with the allotment of animals captured or killed as a result of hunting and fishing activities and the operation of markets for food products. In this sense, sets of stones, legumes, knots in ropes of different color and length, or engravings on pieces of wood or bones were used as counting and recording devices (Besta, 1910, 414). For the ancient Mesopotamian and Egyptian civilizations, the object of account and enumeration, often reported on clay tablets and tokens (e.g. Schmandt-Basserat, 1981a, b), was often the trade of goods (Ezzamel, 2012) related to food (Melis, 1950, 133; Ezzamel, 1994, 221; Ezzamel and Hoskin, 2002, 333). Similar practices emerged along the "Spice Road" and the trade between historical civilizations in Asia, Northeast Africa and Europe, which began to flourish in the fifteenth and sixteenth centuries (likewise, the 'Salt Road' during the Roman Empire). Indeed, whilst scholars have shown that throughout history accounting data has concerned transactions related to food (Melis, 1948, 33; Coronella, 2014), there is still much to say about the history of food, markets, merchants and recordkeeping. Such connections have been explored only with regards to very few merchants, as, for example, Fabio Besta has done for the well-known Jachomo Badoer (Peragallo, 1977, 1981) and the Barbarico family ledgers (Sargiacomo, Servalli and Andrei, 2012).

If we think that the above economic relationships are worthy of deeper study, so are the relations between food culture and accounting in different societies. Undoubtedly, accounting records contain events, values, meanings, symbols and traditions connected to food. Bookkeeping "codifies" those stories according to the accounting systems and methods adopted. The knowledge of those systems and methods enables us to decode and narrate such stories after centuries have gone by, passing on to the present the original cultural content related to the food object of those records (Catturi, 2003). Accounts and accounting not only incorporate the memory of the specific administrative fact that they intend to narrate but also the value system of the same period. Possessing the knowledge that allows the decoding of the cultural characteristics reflected in accounting (that is to say, in its objectives, theoretical foundations, logic of redaction, mechanical functioning) enables us to go back to that moment and interpret it through its cultural characteristics (Catturi, 1995).

In addition to being the means for satisfying basic nutritional needs, food has represented for centuries one of the most vivid expressions of human cultures, that is the specific cultures that animate and characterize the populations and the particular human communities at all times and geographical areas. Food is a universal and essential aspect of human existence. Life without nutrition cannot be conceived, and food is central as a focus for communication, sociability and conviviality. Being omnivorous (thus not specialized in the type of nutrition they consume), humans experience towards food on the one hand, a natural form of Neophobia (that is to say, of fear of eating an unknown substance) and on the other hand, a natural form of Neofilia (that is to say, of desire to taste new flavors). In this dynamic between Neophobia and Neofilia, human beings anchor their choices about food in a cultural influence based on traditions, that is on the experiences and knowledge accumulated and handed down over time (Rozin, 1976). Food is, therefore, a cultural vehicle that spans space and time; it is able to be, at the same time, global and local, that is to say an international cultural landmark but also an element related to a specific territory and its geophysical and microclimatic features (Counihan and van Esterik, 2013).

Food is a cultural factor both when it is referred to as a specific product and when it is referred to as the process that led to its production, and thus realization, preservation, ripening, maturation, aging, etc. Food is culture because in a product it is possible to find the elements, also symbolic, that characterize a certain cultural environment, with the related moments of fruition and aggregation of people (Fernandez-Armesto, 2010). Food is culture because in the process that leads to its realization it is possible to identify the underlying (economic and social) human activities, from the ancient and primordial (haunting, fishing and harvesting), to the agricultural, handicraft, manufacturing, industrial and commercial. Food as a cultural container is one of the first economic goods to become the subject of economic activities and, therefore, the subject of the most ancient forms of accounting records. Food can be recognized, thus, as a "cultural container" that contributes to the formation of culture and, to some extent, of the identity of a certain community of individuals, whether they are organized in a single family, tribe, clan, religious group or ethnic group (Montanari, 2006).

One of the most startling examples of the cultural significance of food is provided by "pasta", whose consumption and production origins go back several millennia (Houyuan, Xiaoyan, Maolin, et al., 2005), and whose products, like macaroni, vermicelli and lasagna, have more recently entered the global Anglophone dictionaries, thus penetrating international lifestyles, and becoming a cultural symbol of well-being, celebration and hospitality. Therein, it is interesting to note that the plea raised by Anthony Hopwood to study "accounting and everyday life" (1994) has already triggered several works by different authors on the interrelations between accounting and culture. Seminal studies have investigated the relations between accounting and the movies (Beard, 1994; Jeacle, 2009), the fashion industry (Jeacle and Carter, 2012), the household engineering and budgeting (Walker, 1998, 2003), and the beauty industry (Jeacle, 2006), as well as whisky as a part of popular culture (Jackson, Paterson, Pang, and Scarparo, 2012). Nevertheless, despite such wealth of research, there remains much to be said on the intersection of accounting and the cultural aspects of food production and consumption.

Another potential research avenue connecting food and accounting is the agri-business industry. Agriculture accounting (e.g., Paolone, 1990; Paolini, 2000) was and still is an under-investigated field of research. Too much time has passed since the publication of the paper in *Abacus* by John Freear on Robert Loder's on farm accounts (Freear, 1970). There are few publications among the generalist and specialist accounting history literature on accounting and agricultural production (e.g., Carnegie 1995, Juchau and Hill, 1998; Macve, 2002; Ji, 2003; Bryer, 2006). The paucity of extant research, which inspired the recent special issue on "Histories of accounting and agriculture" in *Accounting History Review*, suggests a possible research avenue on the accounting, business and financial history of food-agribusiness industry producers. Indeed, glancing through the accounting and accounting history literature, with the exception of the much analysed brewing industry (e.g, Clarke, 1898; Corran, 1981; Gourvish, and Wilson, 1985; Thornton, 1913; Quinn, 2014), show us that there is a need for further research.

The last, but not least, future strand of research that we see is the interplay between accounting and the role played by the state, politics and local authorities in the broad government and administration of food for the sustainability of populations. Admittedly, a major strand of Foucauldian-supported accounting research has been associated with the "governmentality" frame (Foucault, 1988, 1991), which has underpinned seminal studies focused on the public sector (e.g., Miller, 1990; Miller and Rose, 1990). In this context, if we think that each year there is a World Food Exposition (in 2016 it will be held in Russia), whose food related topics are also partially linked to economic life and the sustainability of populations, this invites both historical and contemporary studies on the interplay between accounting and the roles played by state, regional and local governments to deploy effective politics on food-related experimentations, production, cultivations, calculations, administration and trade. In this context, only very recently seminal studies have appeared which explore related topics. Indeed, Walker (2014) highlighted that accounting featured prominently, at diverse levels of government, in what has been identified as the most significant attempt to address rural poverty in 1930s–1940s American history. At the same time, he revealed the role of accounting in an attempt to preserve an ideal (ruralism) and an institution (the family farm) as central to the American way of life (2015). Despite the emergence of such seminal studies in agriculture and rural related studies, food will feature significantly on the agendas of politicians and international organizations in the future, and we think that the accounting community has an important contribution to make to debates, especially in so far as they emphasize the role of government in food production, distribution and consumption and its role in rural poverty alleviation, sustainability, and the feeding of human beings across the globe.

With the above premises, this volume has sought to answer, even to a miniscule extent, to the above highlighted research agenda. The contributions we propose in this book aim to stimulate the debate in and around accounting and food. All the chapters in this volume refer almost completely to the Italian context. All the "stories" we have related on accounting and food cover a broad spectrum of periods from the sixteenth to the twentieth century. Among the chapters, we have included histories of entrepreneurs, merchants, families, companies, non-profit organizations, religious institutions and also various kinds of foods such as cereals, pasta, rice, wine, beer, etc.

Notwithstanding this multiplicity of histories, and considering the earlier illustrated research avenues to date uncovered or not fully explored in the existing literature, we have been able to group the seventeeen chapters in three sections. The first six chapters are grounded on the specificity of a food "industry" and will deal with the accounting, business and financial histories of food companies. A second group of chapters is centred on "Society and Culture" , which is the main background to which is anchored the story related by the authors on the linkages between accounting and food. In the third group of chapters, the focus is on the interrelations between accounting, food and "State, Politics and Local Government".

Among the six chapters that refer to a specific food industry, we have included a study on the contexts, organization and accounting practices of the brewers Birra Peroni. The aim of the authors (Antonelli, D'Alessio and Cafaro) is to highlight the strategic responses and accounting system of one of the most important Italian brewers between 1896 and 1946. By applying "New Institutional Sociology" to a private company change, the manuscript shows the importance of change and the establishment of accounting rules and routines in legitimising and corroborating the company's strategies in response to environmental pressures and the building of a corporate institution and its operational approach.

Cantino, Pollifroni, Cortese and Longo in the subsequent chapter examine the branding strategies and accounting in the wine production of Fontanafredda (1858–1932). The objective is to understand, through the analysis of accounting sources, the results of successful strategies or bad practices during the period under observation, perceiving dynamics and consequences of company's choices in its lifecycle.

In the third chapter, the authors (Consorti, D'Amico and Sargiacomo) cover the neglected history of the pasta industry, providing a longitudinal investigation of the business history of a well-known Italian pasta producer—De Cecco—focusing the analysis on the 1886–1955 time span. The chapter first highlights the early origin of pasta as popular culture, and then it identifies the key choices that confronted the senior management of the this successful Italian extra-refined pasta producer. Finally, it addresses a tentative analysis of the internal business and production management, at the same time exploring the ways in which the general partnership, since before World War I, had already organized its sales and distribution management both in Italy and well beyond the national borders.

The main goal of the study in Chapter 4 is the genetic and evolutionary analysis of the company Birrificio Angelo Poretti—Carlsberg Italia within the brewery industry in Italy over the period 1877–1980. In this case, the authors (Doni, Frausin and Gasperini) adopted a longitudinal thematic analysis with the aim of understanding how the content of the documents changes according to the different institutional settings experienced by the company.

In the fifth chapter, Rubino, Mazzotta and Veltri address the call for a contextualized and interdisciplinary approach to analyse the Amarelli accounting practices. Giving relevance to the logic of the practice, they have adapted Bordieu's framework distinguishing between contextual and firm-specific factors to investigate which factors more greatly affected the way in which Amarelli held its accounts.

Magli and Nobolo focus their attention on the features in organizational models, administration and accounting systems at Caffarel from 1900 to 1979. Through an analysis of the innovations and changes in the habits and customs over time, this investigation offers some reflections on the company's ability to achieve excellence in this industry. The conclusions show that the company's success was mainly due to entrepreneurial spirit and an ability to adapt to environmental and social changes.

In the second sections of this volume, we grouped seven chapters in which the focus is on the relevance of "Society and Culture".

This is the case of the study in Chapter 7, in which the authors (Andrei, Balluchi, Furlotti, Marchini and Tibiletti) have related the history of the Parma Ham Consortium. This study,drawing on the financial statements and other documents disclosing accounting and governance matters, highlights the main elements that have characterized the evolution of the role played by the Consortium and the impact it has had on the production and sale of Prosciutto Parma.

Chapter 8 is on the "herstory" literature. Bellucci, Mari, Picciaia and Terzani analyse the role played by Luisa Spagnoli in the development of the world famous Perugina chocolate company. This study aims to highlight Spagnoli's entrepreneurial characteristics: how and why she developed these characteristics despite the adverse social context and the dominant culture in the period, focusing on one of the most interesting periods in Perugina's history (1924–1935).

In Chapter 9, Tiziana Di Cimbrini compares the accounting system of the storehouse of Pinerolo workers in the late nineteenth century to that of its parent organization, the mutual aid society of Pinerolo workers (1864–1906). She explores the power of the logical food-health combination to affect the accounting system of an organization, focusing on different competitive isomorphic pressures This author also compares the same storehouse to that generally used in the industry of consumer cooperatives, under the hypothesis, consistent with previous literature, that the isomorphic pressure exerted by the parent organization is prevalent.

The tenth chapter is on the role played by English merchants in Sicily in the nineteenth century. Benjamin Ingham was the most successful merchant and Vincenzo Florio learned from him how to become a successful entrepreneur. In this chapter, Di Pietra highlights evidence of the business relationship between Ingham and Florio and the characteristics of the Ingham business accounting system and practices. Ingham has exported Marsala wine throughout the world and has imported accounting practices to Sicily the British accounting environment.

In Chapter 11, Arianna and Simone Lazzini examine the different forms and methods by which the Sarzana Cathedral Chapter managed its properties and privileges in the eighteenth century. The aim of the study is to highlight the relationships between the clergy and the rural world in the seventeenth and eighteenth centuries.

Chapter 12 concerns the D'Agata Company, a business enterprise that originated in Catania in the first half of the nineteenth century and developed in the last century in Avola (Siracusa), becoming one of the leading companies in the production of almonds. The authors (Pulejo and Centorrino) aim to understand how this firm worked from 1939 to 1956 and why, after having established business relations all over the world and having received positive results as a supplier of major agribusiness companies, this firm suddenly declined.

In Chapter 13, the authors (Avallone, Zanini, Ramassa and Quagli) analyse the original accounting records of Nicolò Di Negro, a Genoese grain trader operating as a commission agent in the second half of the sixteenth century. This study puts the observed accounting practice into its historical perspective and shows how an ancient "agency relationship" translated into accounting terms. The analysis also reveals the combined nature of the accounting approach used by Nicolò, as a mix of cash and accrual accounting, and the authors seek to demonstrate that this approach was functional to Nicolò's objective to prove his honesty and trading capacity to his principal.

The third section of this volume includes four studies based on the intersection between accounting, food and "State, Politics and Local Governments".

In Chapter 14, the authors (Dell'Osa and Lippolis) investigate the main environmental and social pressures that influenced the operations of the merchant companies of the Republic of Ragusa (today Dubrovnik) in the second half of the sixteenth century. Then, through the analysis of the accounting books of the Stefani company, much attention has been paid to the importance of the diffusion of the double-entry technique in the Balkans, and to the fact that the accounting technique—extremely advanced and sophisticated in the context of the Italian Renaissance—had induced a spontaneous process of imitation among merchant companies in Ragusa.

The authors (Magliacani and Pepe) of Chapter 15 have studied the case of the "Azienda Annonaria di Vigevano" (1915–1920). Their aim is to extend knowledge on the relation between accounting and the state during that period in order to demonstrate how food accounting reflected and created the socio-economic and political environment.

In the sixteenth chapter, the authors (Servalli and Gitto) explore the case of the Bergamo Municipality during the period of the Venetian domination, considering the sixteenth and seventeenth centuries. The control on cereals, exercised by the Cereals Board, was investigated adopting the Foucauldian "governmentality". In the light of this framework, the contribution unveils how accounting operated in its role of technology of government offering the municipality a macro- and micro-knowledge for reshaping actions.

In Chapter 17, the authors (Zuccardi Merli and Bonollo) point their attention on the Ente Nazionale Risi (National Rice Institution), a key public organization established to support policies for the Italian rice production. This study aims to analyse how the state monitored the activities of Ente Nazionale Risi in the 1945–1980 period by highlighting the role played by the Supreme Audit Institution (SAI), through the examination of audit reports and its regulatory framework.

They way in which we decided to group the studies included in our volume represents just an example of the richness and the narrative elements that are possible to get from the relationship between accounting and food. Several other stories are waiting to be identified, examined, related and categorized adopting different perspectives. There is a world that is waiting to be discovered and studied. This book is a first move in this direction, but much more can be done in the near future, especially in terms of comparisons between different countries within same or similar observation periods.

Being at the end of the publication process, we wish to thank the forty-five authors who have enthusiastically joined us in this scientific project, participating at the "Accounting and Food" Milan Conference of June 2015, and reviewing papers and providing feedback for each other in a cooperative and stimulating academic community. In a related manner, we acknowledge the helpful and generous support provided by our colleagues Tiziana Di Cimbrini and Luca Ianni in order to achieve the homogenization of the content of the volume to the publisher templates and guidelines, as well as to complete the comprehensive and exhausting proofreading of this book.

Now we have finished working on this volume. Let us think about the next one!

17 January 2015

Luciano D'Amico Roberto Di Pietra Massimo Sargiacomo

REFERENCES

Beard, V. (1994), Popular culture and professional identity: Accountants in the movies, *Accounting, Organizations and Society*, 19 (3), 303–18.

Besta, F. (1910), *La Ragioneria*, Vol. II. Milan: Casa Vallardi.

Bryer, R. A. (2006), The genesis of the capitalist farmer: Towards a Marxist accounting history of the origins of the English agricultural revolution, *Critical Perspectives on Accounting*, 17 (4), 367–97.

Carnegie, G. D. (1995), Pastoral accounting in pre-Federation Victoria: A contextual analysis of surviving business records, *Accounting, Auditing & Accountability Journal*, 8 (5), 3–33.

Catturi, G. (1995), *Comunicazione ed informazione aziendale*, Quaderno n. 4. Viterbo: Documenti di Strategia e Politica aziendale.

Catturi, G. (2003), *L'Azienda Universale*. Padua: Cedam.

Clarke, E. W. (1898), *Brewery Bookkeeping: A Practical Treatise on Brewery Accounts and Office Management*. Chicago: H. S. Rich & Company.

Coronella, S. (2014), *Storia della Ragioneria Italiana, Epoche, Uomini e Idee*. Milan: Franco Angeli.

Corran, T. H. (1981), James Deady, Henry Meux, and the Griffin Brewery: Fraud in an early-nineteenth-Ccntury business, *Business History*, 23 (3), 327–45.

Counihan, C., and van Esterik P. (2013), *Food and Culture. A Reader*, (Third Edition). New York: Routledge.

Ezzamel, M. (1994), The emergence of the 'accountant' in the institutions of ancient Egypt, *Management Accounting Research*, Vol. 5, no. 3-4, 221–46.

Ezzamel, M. (2012), *Accounting and Order*. Routledge, Taylor & Francis: New York.

Ezzamel M. and Hoskin, K. (2002). Retheorizing accounting, writing and money with evidence from Mesopotamia and ancient Egypt. *Critical Perspectives on Accounting*, 13 (3), 333–67.

Fernandez-Armesto, F. (2010), *Storia del Cibo*. Milan: Mondadori.

Foucault, M. (1988), The political technology of individuals, in: L. Martin, H. Gutman and P. Hutton (Eds), *Technologies of the Self: A Seminar with Michel Foucault*, pp. 145–62, Amherst: University of Massachusetts Press.

Foucault, M. (1991), Governmentality, in: G. Burchell, C. Gordon and P. Miller (Eds), *The Foucault Effect: Studies in Governmentality*, pp. 87–104, Hemel Hempstead: Wheatsheaf.

Freear, J. (1970), Robert Loder, Jacobean management accountant. *Abacus*, 6(1), 25–38.

Gourvish, T. R. and Wilson, R. G. (1985), Profitability in the brewing industry 1885–1914, *Business History*, 27 (2), 146–65.

Hopwood, A. (1994), Accounting and everyday life: An introduction, *Accounting, Organizations and Society*, 19 (3), 299–301.

Houyan, L., Xiaoyan, Y., Maolin, Y., et al. (2005), Culinary archaeology: Millet noodles in late Neolithic China, *Nature*, 437 (7061), 967–8.

Jackson, W. J., Paterson, A. S., Pong, C. K., and Scarparo, S. (2012). "How easy can the barley brie". Drinking culture and accounting failure at the end of the nineteenth century in Britain. *Accounting, Auditing and Accountability Journal*, 25 (4), 635–58.

Jeacle, I. (2006), Face facts: Accounting, feminism and the business of beauty, *Critical Perspectives on Accounting*, 17 (1), 87–108.

Jeacle, I. (2009), Going to the movies: Accounting and twentieth century cinema, *Accounting, Auditing and Accountability Journal*, 22 (5), 677–708.

Jeacle, I. and Carter, C. (2012), Fashioning the popular masses: Accounting as mediator between creativity and control, *Accounting, Auditing and Accountability Journal*, 25 (4), 719–51.

Ji, X. (2003), Concepts of cost and profit in Chinese agricultural treatises: With special reference to Shengshi Nongshu and Pu Nongshu in the seventeenth century, *Accounting, Business & Financial History*, 13 (1), 69–81.

Juchau, R. and Hill, P. (1998), Agricultural cost accounting development in Britain: The contributions of three men from Wye—a review note, *Accounting, Business & Financial History*, 8 (2), 165–74.

Macve, R. H. (2002), Insights to be gained from the study of ancient accounting history: Some reflections on the new edition of Finley's The Ancient Economy, *European Accounting Review*, 11 (2), 453–71.

Melis, F. (1948), *La Ragioneria nella Civiltà Minoica. Dalle Iscrizioni Venute alla Luce in Creata (XIX–XIV a.C.)*. Rome: RIREA.

Melis, G. (1950), *Storia della Ragioneria*. Bologna: Zuffi.

Miller, P. (1990), On the interrelations between accounting and the state, *Accounting, Organizations and Society*, 15 (4), 315–340.

Miller, P. and Rose, N. (1990), Governing economic life, *Economy and Society*, 19(1), 1–31.

Montanari, M. (2006), *Food is culture*. New York: Oxford University Press.

Paolini, A. (1999), *L'azienda Agricola. Aspetti di Gestione e Controllo*. Torino: Giappichelli.

Paolone, G. (1990), *L'economia dell'impresa agricola: profili e condizioni di equilibrio*. Torino: G. Giappichelli.

Peragallo, E. (1977), The ledger of Jachomo Badoer: Constantinople September 2, 1436 to February 26, 1440, *The Accounting Review*, 52 (4), 881–92.

Peragallo, E. (1981), Closing procedures in the 15th century ledger of Jachomo Badoer, a Venetian merchant, *The Accounting Review*, 56 (3), 587–95

Quinn, M. (2014), Stability and change in management accounting over time—A century or so of evidence from Guinness, Management Accounting Research, 25, 76–92.

Rozin, P. (1976), The selection of foods by rats, humans and others animals, in: J. S. Rosenblatt, R. A. Hinde, E. Shaw, and C. Beer (Eds), *Advances in the Study of Behaviour*, Vol. 6, pp. 21–73, New York: Academic Press.

Sargiacomo, M., S. Servalli and P. Andrei. (2012), Fabio Besta: Accounting thinker and accounting history pioneer., *Accounting History Review* 22 (3), 249–67.

Shmandt-Basserat, D. (1981a), Tablets and token: A re-examination of the so-called "Numerical Tablets", *Visible Language*, 15 (3), 321–44.

Shmandt-Basserat, D. (1981b), Decipherment of the earliest tablets, *Science*, 211 (4479), 283–5.

Thornton, F. W. (1913), *Brewery Accounts*. New York: Ronald Press.

Walker, S. P. (1998), How to secure your husband's esteem: Accounting and private patriarchy in the British middle class household during the nineteenth century, *Accounting, Organizations and Society*, 23 (6), 485–514.

Walker, S.P. (2003), Professionalisation or incarceration? Household engineering, accounting and the domestic ideal, *Accounting, Organizations and Society*, 28 (8), 743–72.
Walker, S.P. (2014), Accounting and rural rehabilitation in New Deal America, *Accounting, Organizations and Society*, 39 (3), 208–35.
Walker, S.P. (2015), Accounting and preserving the American way of life, *Contemporary Accounting Research*, 32 (4), 1676–1713.

1 "I Will Be Your Beer!" Contexts, Organization and Accounting Practices of Birra Peroni

An Institutional Perspective (1896–1946)

Valerio Antonelli, Raffaele D'Alessio and Emanuela Mattia Cafaro

INTRODUCTION

In Italy, accounting history literature has very rarely dealt with the food industry, despite Italy being known in the cliché that is most popular outside its boundaries, as the "home of pizza and spaghetti" (i.e., centuries-old cooking, food and winemaking traditions).

The food industry covers a wide range of areas, addressed herein as an industrial food and beverage-making process in which Italian products are unrivalled: pasta, cheese, chocolate, liquorice, sweets, olive oil, wine and champagne. Of such industrial products, one of those that may be most relevant to accounting history is certainly beer. In Italy, the "brewing culture" only caught on in the late nineteenth century and especially in the twentieth century, as it had to compete with the centuries-old wine-drinking tradition. Therefore, brewers had to understand and adapt to the environment to assert their rights and prevail over their domestic and international competitors. From this perspective, this chapter will look into the strategies and accounting practices adopted by Birra Peroni, a company that sells one of Italy's most popular beer brands, mainly known for its TV commercials on "Carosello," a popular prime-time advertising show that was broadcast for many years on Italian State television after the Second World War.

Founded in 1846 in Vigevano, Birra Peroni moved to Rome in 1864 and then gradually grew, peaking at the turn of the century when it took over a number of beer and frozen food companies. After the First World War, which deprived the company of its best engineers—German ones, from the enemy country—and under the Fascist regime, the new company was the first to concentrate its businesses. Over those years, it expanded its productive capacity and opened three plants, in Bari, Naples and Livorno. With the Second World War and Allied occupation, Birra Peroni came into contact with U.S. tastes and technology, so it changed its formulas and plants accordingly. Birra Peroni enjoyed prosperity after the Second World War and the following two decades, spurred by Italy's economic miracle. Finally, in 1988, it was taken over by the multinational corporation Danone.

Of this 170-year history, we have cut out the middle—from 1896 to 1946—not only for its time-defining momentum but also because that was the time the company produced the greatest (and sometimes the only) archival evidence of its accounting system. In the period covered by this chapter, the accounting system went hand in hand with the company's strategic response to environmental pressure, especially when it introduced cost accounting and reporting systems in its Italian plants and changed the corporate financial reporting system. This eased the institutional work required to build the company's identity and strengthen the institutional approach that the organisation was beginning to embrace.

The purpose of this chapter is to contribute to accounting history literature in several respects:

1. It provides a picture of the history of the context, the response strategies and the institutional dynamics of one of Italy's most important food companies.
2. It adds archival evidence to the many other papers that have already been written about the brewing industry, very popular in the United Kingdom.
3. It applies new institutional sociology (NIS) to private companies, which is not the favourite domain of this approach, as has been done before, with another Italian company, by Sargiacomo (2008).
4. It shows the importance of change and the establishment of accounting rules and routines in legitimising and corroborating the company's strategies in response to environmental pressure and the building of a corporate institution and its operational approach.

The chapter is organised as follows. The second section describes the research method, based on a literature review of accounting history studies in brewing, outlines a NIS-based theoretical framework and describes the main primary and secondary sources for the chapter. The third section reviews the life of the company, briefly as to the first (1846–1896) and third (1946–1996) half-centuries, and more extensively as to the second one (1896–1946). The fourth section is focussed on Birra Peroni's accounting system, its organisation, its change and its role, from our theoretical perspective. The last section offers conclusions, summarises the results and reveals the limits of the chapter and points to the potential developments thereof.

RESEARCH METHOD

Literature Reviews

In Italy, the food industry has been all but forgotten by Italian-language accounting history papers (Capellaro, 1996; Cavazzoni, 1998; Mari et al., 2008). With the exception of all chapters published in this volume, Italian papers published in international refereed journals have neglected this industry too.

This is not the case with international economic history, business history and accounting history literature. There are very many, and varied, historical papers about food and beverage, and they cover several countries in Europe, America, Asia and Oceania. In this vast scenario, attention may be focussed on papers that specifically deal with accounting history in the brewing industry. Such papers may be divided into three groups.

The first group is that of textbooks and articles published at the time between the late nineteenth century and the Second World War. This group provides an extremely interesting portrait of accounting practices in the brewery industry as reported by the current affairs press of the time (Clarke, 1898; Harris, 1899; Lanham and Northcott, 1906; Allen, 1912; Thornton, 1913; De Payer, 1916; Goettsche, 1934; Hamilton, 1939), as well as a helpful secondary source (Mutch, 2008).

The second group of papers is about the "strange case" of brewing, nationalised in the UK during the First World War, as strategic for the British Army, then privatised only 60 years later (Talbot, 2002, 2005a, 2005b, 2007).

Finally, the third group of papers reviews the accounting systems adopted and developed by the world's key breweries (Wilson and Gourvish, 1998), such as Guinness (Quinn, 2014; Quinn and Jackson, 2014), as well as breweries in the United States (Stack, 2000; Walter et al., 2014), Canada (Felton and Mann, 1990), Spain (Moreno, 2011; Moreno and Càmara, 2014), Australia (Wilson and Shailer, 2007) and Britain (Corran, 1981; Gourvish and Wilson, 1985; Mason, 1992; Talbot, 2006; Higgins and Verma, 2009).

Multiple approaches and issues are addressed, but they are all focussed on the brewing industry. They are also similar in quite a few respects, which are also relevant to this chapter, such as market and production issues, the relationship between beer and the national culture and the complexity of the accounting systems, especially cost accounting.

Theoretical Framework

The theoretical framework of the chapter is the aforementioned NIS. The research perspective, based on the institutional features of organisations, relative to their context on the one hand, and developments in multiple decision centres on the other hand, began over 30 years ago (Meyer and Rowan, 1977; DiMaggio and Powell, 1983; Scott, 1987; Zucker, 1987; Powell and DiMaggio, 1991).

Today, the new institutionalism applied to sociology and organisational research is best represented as an extended family of scholars who share a broadly defined theoretical approach. Within this framework, researchers differ in their conceptualisation of institutions (specific legal or resource relationships versus a wider culture), the focus of causal arguments (top-down versus bottom-up) and the focal feature of organisations (formal structures versus practices and behaviour) (Greenwood et al., 2008; Powell and Bromely, 2015).

We particularly refer to institutional work, that is, examining the practices of individual and collective players aimed at creating, maintaining and disrupting institutions (Lawrence et al., 2011); institutional approaches, defined as the socially constructed, historical pattern of material practices, assumptions, values, beliefs and rules by which individuals produce and reproduce their material subsistence, organise time and space (Thornton and Ocasio, 1999); and strategic response to institutional pressure, classified into acquiescence, compromise, avoidance, defiance and manipulation (Oliver, 1991). These three concepts, and their related theories, help us explain the organisation and entrepreneurial behaviour of Birra Peroni over time.

Within the institutional framework, management and accounting scholars face many problems concerning the way organisations adapted to cope with external pressure and to reduce variety in knowledge, routines, techniques and accounting systems as part of their structures (Scott, 1995; Covalenski et al., 1996; Abernethy and Chua, 1996). At the same time, many forces push enterprises to adjust to the outside world (Goodstein, 1994). Finally, the legitimacy of accounting tools or innovation comes from experiences, rules or values shared by a community of professionals or scholars (Covalenski and Dirsmith, 1988; Carpenter and Feroz, 2001); at the same time it bolsters the image and reputation of the organisation (Carruthers, 1995). One of the most influential patterns of research based on the institutional approach attempts to explain the ways, forces and the shapes connected with stability (Granlund and Lukke, 1998; Granlund, 2001; Lukka, 2007) and change in management accounting (Burns and Scapens, 2000; Brignall and Modell, 2000; Hussain and Hoque, 2002; Siti-Nabiha and Scapens, 2005; Seal, 2006), as well as financial accounting and financial reporting systems (Ansari and Euske, 1987; Mezias, 1990; Greenwood and Suddaby, 2006; Tsamenyi et al., 2006; West and Carnegie, 2010; Goretzki et al., 2013).

As to accounting history research, NIS is applied especially in order to explain accounting change. Most cases refer to State-owned firms, such as the Spanish monopolies in the eighteenth century examined by Carmona et al. (1998), Carmona et al. (2001) and Núñez (2002); Japanese aviation between the world wars, investigated by Noguchi and Boyns (2012); the Japanese local government in the last 30 years by Yamamoto and Noguchi (2013); public sector organisations, such as the Portuguese Royal Treasury in the eighteenth century, analysed by Gomes et al. (2008); and finally private firms, with the contributions of Ahmed and Scapens (2000) on the evolution of cost accounting practices and Sargiacomo (2008) on the history of the Italian firm Brioni after the Second World War.

Sources for the Chapter

This chapter is based on many primary and secondary sources. Primary sources come from the Archivio Storico Peroni (Peroni's historical archives), located in Rome, Via Birolli 8, whose evidences were inventoried and listed in Brignone (2001). Our sources consist of the articles of the association (1898) and all account records made available by the firm: annual reports (1900; 1907–1920), a journal (1903), preparatory documents to the annual reports (1915), a ledger (1942), a report on the Naples plant (1929), a report on production management (1929), a memorandum on the Bari plant by Alberto Canali (1925–1932), revenue and expense reports on the Bari and Naples plants (1933), a memorandum on the Naples plant (1933) and the 1934 financial statements of Società Toscana Paszkowski and the beer- and malt-testing sheets of Società di Livorno (1933). No account records are listed in the official archive list with reference to the period 1846–1896 and the period 1946–1979 (Brignone, 2001).

Secondary sources come from books about the history of the company, of brewing and of the industries in Rome, as well as a wide international literature about brewing and its accounting system, covering the period addressed in this chapter.

BIRRA PERONI: INSTITUTIONAL WORK, INSTITUTIONAL APPROACH AND STRATEGIC RESPONSE

First Period (1846–1896)

The firm Birra Peroni was established in mid-nineteenth century Italy, still divided and fighting for unity. In 1846, Francesco Peroni (1818–1894) decided to split from the shop of his father, Giovanni Battista, and set up his own factory in Vigevano (Anonymous, 2015). The reason for this choice is that there were no competing breweries in that area (Brignone, 1995). Because of this, Francesco Peroni felt he would stand a chance to expand faster and easier.

At that time, a number of events led to the unification of Italy. In 1848, an attempt was made to declare Rome as the new capital of Italy. Such attempt was thwarted by the French troops who came to defend Pius IX. Most of the troops were left stationed in Rome afterwards. The idea of boosting sales by selling to the French soldiers, who were more used to drinking beer, along with the worsening of the economic and social conditions of Vigevano, probably led Francesco Peroni to open up in a city that would soon become the economic and social hub of the new Kingdom of Italy (Corfield, 2015).

So, in 1864, Francesco Peroni opened new headquarters in Rome and founded a new company (Racheli, 1993; Milano, 1994). Francesco's son Giovanni was appointed at the helm of the new Rome premises, while the

Vigevano unit worked on for a few more years under Ercole Peroni's management. In 1896, the Lombardy-based plant was wound up once and for all, having been sold to Natale and Vandone & Compagni (ASP, 1898).

Second Period (1896–1946)

The period 1896–1946 was a time of dramatic political, social and economic change. The belle époque, the First World War, Fascism and the Second World War, in quick succession, inevitably shook up and disrupted Birra Peroni as well (Peroni, 2008).

We reviewed the events that Peroni went through in these years—the prime of its life—in an attempt to understand which strategic responses to institutional pressure made the company so successful. Figure 1.1 shows this pattern.

Economic pressure: As the First World War broke out, Birra Peroni, which had just recently merged with Società del Ghiaccio (Ice Company) and had thrived and grown in the early twentieth century, was confronted with a steep rise in brewing costs (Racheli, 1978). This increase, compounded by a

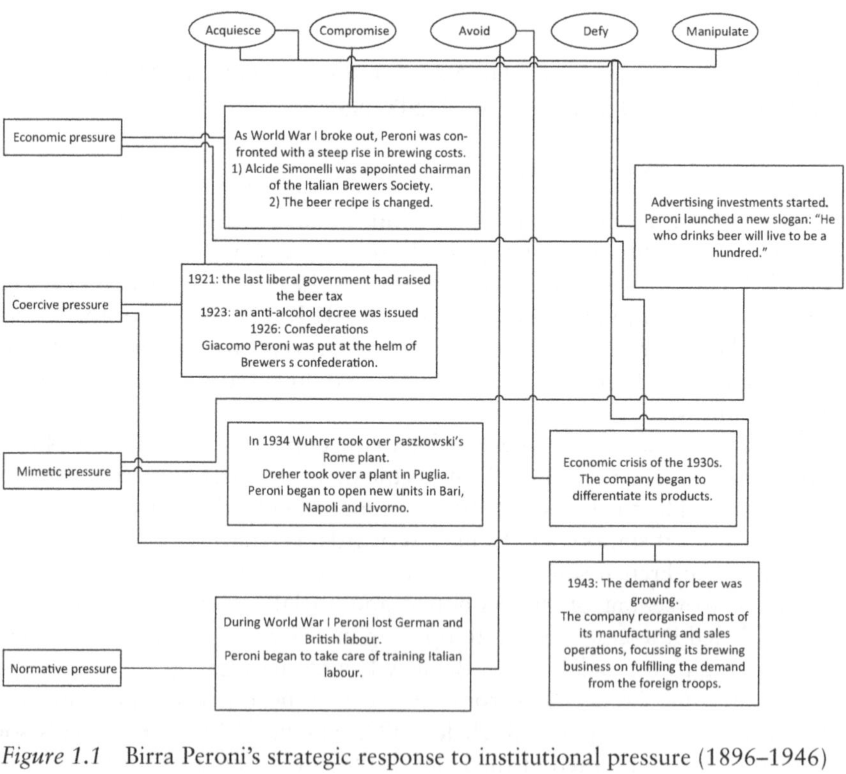

Figure 1.1 Birra Peroni's strategic response to institutional pressure (1896–1946)

Source: Brignone (1995, adapted); Sargiacomo (2008, p. 226)

50% rise in the manufacturing tax, was probably due to Italy's deep dependency on foreign exports of brewing ingredients (Colli, 1995). Italy's inadequate domestic production and dependency on foreign countries became even worse during the war, resulting in a rise in sales prices that, given the circumstances, a growing demand could not adequately sustain (Colli, 1997).

In those circumstances, the company went in two directions, adopting a strategic response that seemed to be as compromising as it was manipulative. First, the management decided to reduce production costs by changing the brewing recipe and using cheaper and more ordinary ingredients. The sugar content of the beer was reduced from 13.5 degrees to 12 degrees, and such ingredients as rice, chestnuts and figs were added to the recipe to make up for the lack of barley and malt (Brignone, 1995).

Meanwhile, by the end of 1915, Alcide Simonelli, then manager of the Rome plant with Cesare Peroni, was appointed chairman of the Italian Brewers' Society. As chairman, he negotiated exports, imports and supplies of raw materials with the governmental authorities (ASP, 1915).

Normative pressure: A rise in the cost of raw materials was not the only consequence of the First World War; another key productive factor disappeared: labour (Toscano, 2002). In those years, most of the company's labour and skilled technicians were British and German nationals. So, when the war broke out, they were inevitably called up. From then on, Birra Peroni trained Italian labour in an attempt to fill the gap left by the war (Brignone, 1995).

Coercive pressure: In 1921, the last liberal government had raised the beer tax: the tax burden rose from 3 to 4 Italian Lire per hectolitre (Colli, 1998). After 1922, the Fascist government enacted a number of rules that were somewhat detrimental to the brewing industry. In 1923, an antialcohol decree was issued. The purpose of the antialcohol decree was to reduce the number of public licences and limit the time of day during which alcoholic beverages could be bought and sold (Ponzano, 1924). Finally, in 1926, the "Confederazione generale fascista dell'industria italiana" ("Comprehensive Fascist Confederation of Italian Industry") was established to protect and rationalise the Italian industry in all respects (Colli, 1995). At this stage, the institutional change came as a sort of structural overlap, as the organisations used to working separately were forced to get together.

From then on, trade associations began to spring up to defend the interests of the different businesses. It is in that climate that the "Federazione nazionale delle industrie delle acque gassate, della birra e del freddo" ("National Federation of Sparkling Water, Beer and Frozen Product Companies") was born (Brignone, 1995). In this way, the Fascist government tried to control production and balance demand and supply by controlling the supply side. This involved a coercive reduction in a company's production volume, so as to adjust it to market requirements (Ciocca and Toniolo, 1976).

In this context, the company's strategic response may be viewed as a compromise. Giacomo Peroni, former president of the earlier Unione Italiana Fabbricanti di Birra (Italian Brewers' Union) was put at the helm of the new association. As the manager of the new association, Giacomo could act as an institutional entrepreneur and therefore bend the institutional change to his own and his company's interests. In fact, despite the need to reduce the company's production volume as imposed by the Fascist government, in his role Giacomo Peroni managed to avoid such cuts and toss them off on his competitors. This is suggested by the fact that it was precisely in those years that the company increased its production volume and sales (Brignone, 1995).

Mimetic pressure: From 1920 to 1940, all of the key brewers, especially Dreher and Wührer, began to expand in the national territory by opening new plants and taking over new units (ASP, 1933).

In the 1920s, Birra Peroni too began to open new units in order to strengthen its local leadership. The first move was the opening of a plant in Bari in 1924. That city was chosen for its strategic location in the south of Italy, in the Puglia region. The opening of the Bari plant was followed by the opening of a plant in Naples in 1929, also chosen for its strategic location (ASP, 1929).

In 1934, one of Birra Peroni's key competitors, Wührer, took over Poszkowski's Rome plant (ASP, 1934). The company's strategic response may be regarded as acquiescence, especially imitation (Oliver, 1991). This is therefore a case of mimetic isomorphism, which drives companies working in the same line of business to respond by imitating the assumedly successful ones. Actually, in those years, all leading breweries tried to strengthen their national leadership by expanding from the north to the south of the peninsula.

Once taken over by Wührer, in 1939, Birra Peroni set up a new plant in Livorno (ASP, 1934b).

Mimetic pressure: Advertisements of alcoholic beverages, especially beer, began to catch on as early as the late nineteenth century. By the end of the twentieth century, many alcoholic beverage factories had begun to make investments in advertising. In other words, they were becoming aware of the importance of making their products visible on the market (Rentini and Zanelli, 2005). This is the direction that some companies took to advertise their products, such as Fernet Branca, Cynar and other bitters producers. Birra Peroni did not want to be outdone. As early as 1929, it launched the slogan for its advertisement: "Chi beve birra, campa cent'anni" ("He who drinks beer will live one hundred years") (Rentini and Zanelli, 2005). In 1935 the company progressively increased its investments in advertising (Brignone, 1995). It was by increasing such investments that the company managed to overcome the Crash of 1929.

Economic pressure: The Crash of 1929 began to be felt in the early 1930s. In those years, the company went through an economic crisis, as did most national businesses (Ciocca and Toniolo, 1976). In an attempt to face the crisis, the company began to differentiate its products. This behaviour may be called an avoidance strategy, in which an organisation attempts to shirk institutional rules by avoiding them. In particular, an escape strategy occurs when an organisation "escapes" environmental pressure by changing its purposes and goals. In the1930s, Birra Peroni started to produce lemon soda, orange soda and a tamarind drink. These new drinks, which were in increasing demand, helped make up for the drop in the demand for beer (BAICR, 2007).

Coercive pressure: The Second World War brought back the same problems as in 1915. In fact, since the first few years of the war, there had been problems finding raw materials and labour. However, the demand for beer was growing, mainly for the troops. So, in this case, what helped the company survive was the implementation of an acquiescing strategy. The company reorganised most of its manufacturing and sales operations, focussing its brewing business on fulfilling the demand from the foreign troops stationed in Italy (Brignone, 1995).

Third Period (1946–1996)

The end of the Second World War marked a recovery for Birra Peroni, as well as the Italian economy in general. After the end of the war, the company worked straightaway to become independent of German labour and hired Italian skilled engineers, who went abroad for training courses (Brignone, 1995).

The company continued expanding in Italy, and in those years took over some key competitors. In 1952, it absorbed the Udine-based Dormisch brewery and, a few years later, the Taranto-based brewery of Nicola Raffo (Gourvish and Wilson, 1995).

In the 1960s, the company began strengthening its distribution network, which made it more easily available: first in Italy, and by the nineties the rest of the world as well. The company became a powerful international brand. The new Nastro Azzurro beer, launched in 1963, soon became a hit in 50 countries (Villa, 2011).

In 1974, one of Birra Peroni's main competitors, Dreher, was sold to the multinational corporation Heineken. From then on, Birra Peroni felt the need to have closer contacts with multinational corporations. In 1988, the company, which until then had been a family-run business, decided to sell part of its shares to I.F.I., Fiat Group's financial institution and to the multinational corporation Danone. Through this merger, Birra Peroni managed to take hold of a historical competitor: Wuhrer (Brignone, 2001).

THE ACCOUNTING SYSTEM AT BIRRA PERONI

The historical reenactment of Birra Peroni accounting systems is strictly based on the (scarce) archive evidences we found. Such evidences are scattered and some inferences are necessary in order to depict a complete scheme of the accounting mechanisms.

During the period we examined (1896–1946), the accounting system at Birra Peroni was based on double entry bookkeeping. Financial and cost accounting were integrated into one system, as was also the case at the large majority of Italian firms at this time. To this purpose, the journal (ASP, 1903) and the ledger (ASP, 1942) were adopted in order to keep records in a systematic way. The former focussed on transactions and the latter on calculating costs and determining gross profits of main products (i.e., beer, ice and snow, and beer houses).

The annual reports of 1900–1920 have been largely reviewed. In this period, the annual report was composed of a board of directors' report, an auditors' report, a balance sheet and a profit and loss account (ASP, 1900, 1907a, 1907b, 1907c, 1908a, 1908b, 1908c, 1909a, 1909b, 1909c, 1910a, 1910b, 1910c, 1911a, 1911b, 1911c, 1912a, 1912b, 1912c, 1920). An example of an annual report is provided in Figure 1.2.

In those years, the only rule for drawing a balance sheet was laid down by the Italian Commercial Code of 1882; the code did not set forth any strict rule, and said nothing about the contents and form of the balance sheet or of the profit and loss account. Articles 176 to 182 of the Code

Assets		Liabilities	
Property	1,542,305.70	Share capital	2,300,000.00
Plants, machinery and equipment	1,004,433.30	Creditors	498,911.34
Expenditures to construct plants	12,189.60	Reserves	38,211.68
Inventories	104,457.90	Other reserves	5,598.61
Receivables	266,361.44	Deposits	65,030.88
Receivables from shareholders	68,256.15	Escrows	511,168.54
Bills receivable	101,552.31		3,418,921.06
Cash	19,257.03	Net Profit	288,413.87
Financial instruments	55,525.00		
Deposits	20,623.25		
Escrows	511,165.54		
Total	3,707,334.92	Total	3,707,334.92

Expenses		Revenues	
Overhead costs	166,891.63	Ice and snow gross profit	361,981.42
Production cost	2,301,291.78	Brewery gross profit	2,420,375.33
Taxes	37,854.78	Beer houses gross profit	16,711.35
Brewery expenses	24,699.34	Property rents	47,831.73
Buildings taxes	8,338.23		
Maintenance	11,912.98		
General expenses	6,497.22		
	2,557,485.96		
Net profit	288,413.87		
Total	2,845,899.83	Total	2,845,899.83

Figure 1.2 Birra Peroni 1911 balance sheet and profit and loss account

Source: ASP (1911)

covered the balance sheet, but did not go into the details of its form or contents. Article 176 stated the balance sheet should "clearly and truthfully" show the profits and losses, as well as the actual capital stock and any payment made, either on time or late. So, there being no strictly defined rules for drawing up a balance sheet, it could be drawn up in the way that best fulfilled a company's need. At Birra Peroni, where most of the shares belonged to the Peroni family, the key role played by the balance sheet was that of determining the distributable profits. This is clearly shown by a schedule summarising the profit-distribution methods. The need to determine the distributable profits was, then, more important for minority shareholders than keeping control over the company's management. Profits were distributed, as shown in Figure 1.3, after allocating 5% of profits to the reserve requirement (under Article 182 of the Commercial Code) and 10% to the board of directors.

The fact that profit distribution was such a sore problem, especially for minority shareholders, who were keen on receiving higher dividends, is also suggested by the profit calculation method. On the one side, accounting for fixed assets was adopted, but on the other side, in the ledger, there is no trace of a closing procedure to supplement the running costs and therefore reduce the distributable profits (ASP, 1903). There are no entries for depreciation, the only costs associated with the plants being servicing and repairs, as also shown by the ledgers (ASP, 1942).

The balance sheet plays a key role in reconciling power relations between majority and minority shareholders, with the former—essentially all members of the Peroni family—interested in producing income to be reinvested in the company's management, and the latter more interested in receiving the dividends. Furthermore, loans and bonds were not so relevant in financing the company, and thus the annual report was not involved in managing relationships with the credit market.

Profits	288,414.00
5% To Reserve	14,420.70
10% To Board of directors	28,841.40
Remaining profit	245,151.90
Last year profits	5,598.00
	250,749.90
To shareholders	230,000.00
To extraordinary reserve	20,000.00
	749.9

Figure 1.3 Distribution of profits, 1911
Source: ASP (1911)

Cost Accounting and Reporting

It is the review of cost accounting that provides most of the evidence, through the tight interconnections existing between such accounting practices and the corporate strategy.

At Birra Peroni, management accounting served two of its key purposes: steering the corporate strategies and providing economic control over the management. Examples of cost accounting have been found in the annexes to the report on the Bari plant for 1925–1932. In 1924, mimetic pressure led Birra Peroni to expand by opening a new plant in Bari, then one in Naples and one in Livorno. As a consequence of such expansion, the company's need to keep local production and distribution under control substantially increased.

People were sent to the company's further plants to inspect and report on how the industrial and commercial operations were carried out. In particular, the report on the Bari plant by Birra Peroni's general manager, Alberto Canali, investigated the reasons for the sales decrease and cost increase experienced between 1925, the year the plant began operating, and 1932 (ASP, 1933).

Canali found a sales decrease in that period; above all he found that the sales volume was inadequate for the production volume. The amounts produced by the Bari-based plant outnumbered the amounts sold. In his report, his solution to such problems was opening new stores and reducing the retail price whenever possible (ASP, 1933).

To reduce the price, special care had to be taken of the costs, which had increased as a result of the decreasing production volumes. As production dropped, the effect of economies of scale, and the attendant reduction of unit costs, disappeared. That is why Canali focussed his attention on calculating the cost of brewing. To do this, costs were divided into fixed, semi-variable and variable costs (Figure 1.4).

The schedules enclosed with the report included other management costs, advertising costs and contributions under the "fixed production costs" entry. "Semi-fixed costs" included labour, maintenance and repairs, power, lighting, water and fuels. Finally, "variable costs" included raw materials, manufacturing tax, transport and loss of containers. Such grouping was instrumental to establishing the full cost of brewing. Such full-costing accountancy could be used to estimate the cost of beer in each factory and relate it to the cost of production in other factories—in this case, the one in Rome.

As to this, Canali found that the general costs of the Bari plant were not in line with the general accounting records (ASP, 1933). In addition, his report included a schedule that matched each group of expenses with brewing and icemaking.

As to sales, in his report on the factory, Canali reviewed the sales trends of different areas of southern Italy, such as Puglia, Lucania, Campania and Calabria. The sales schedule of these areas and the overview suggested that sales had decreased over that period (ASP, 1933c).

General cost of production in the Bari factory							
Year	Production		Total cost of production	Coefficient of proportionality between produced beer and total costs	Coefficient of proportionality between produced beer and costs categories		
	Beer	Ice			Fixed costs	Semi-fixed costs	Variable costs
1925	22,664	3,450	4,555,492	4.5	0.39	6.9	25.25
1926	30,168	4,480	6,570,112	4.53	0.95	7.9	21.15
1927	30,213	13,560	6,669,466	4.52	0.45	8.9	20.85
1928	29,504	24,615	6,015,248	4.89	0.71	8.89	19.9
1929	28,658	24,713	6,115,677	4.64	1.08	8.65	18.85
1930	23,499	25,478	5,362,916	4.38	1.35	8.05	14.1
1931	18,262	26,993	4,317,328	4.24	1.1	6.7	10.5
1932	9,987	21,245	2,857,906	3.48	0.81	3.94	5.25

Categories of exp	1925	1926	1927	1928	1929	1930	1931	1932
Fixed costs								
Other expenses	53,540.15	53,666.65	221	63,593.55	77,815.25	108,356.50	52,476.40	108,609,05
Advertising	25,184.00	43,283.30	149.85	36,744.70	11,871.40	139,045.45	109,410.30	56,100.60
Contribution	706.5	113,672.30	152.65	46,563.80	44,633.25	69,450.55	59,424.40	69,506.45
Semi-fixed costs								
Wages	630,508.05	731,072.05	8,599.00	936,748.20	951,908.15	946,876.05	840,038.75	681,738.40
Mantainence	407,998.65	523,402.50	6,458.40	465,229.45	454,999.80	448,503.50	366,931.90	196,512.48
Driving force	171,281.30	258,126.50	2,788.80	204,849.60	200,712.85	152,305.85	152,305.85	89,487.70
Lighting	27,364.80	30,745.50	558.9	35,993.70	44,577.10	41,760.75	41,760.75	24,460.60
Water	59,066.75	66,416.80	255.8	104,326.05	119,561.80	151,945.75	131,329.05	100,577
Fuels	83,785.95	118,619.40	269.1	71,765.60	85,949.10	52,568.40	52,568.40	35,293.70
Variable costs								
Raw materials	1,335,583.05	1,887,298.20	15,062.85	1,255,943.70	1,171,325.85	797,648	582,040	317,013.20
Production tax	1,291,161.80	1,692,248.20	1,836.35	1,772,156.20	1,723,354.55	1,353,864.30	1,132,256.85	716,424.90
Transport	244,333.15	794,520.60	9,806.95	824,475.35	889,298.90	806,061.35	549,894.35	345,765.55

Figure 1.4 Production costs in the Bari factory, 1925–1932

Source: ASP (1933b)

The strategic response to environment changes—consisting of locating production near consumption in order to avoid most problems related to distributing beer at a distance (bottling, freezing, transporting, insuring etc.)—needed a significant cost accounting change. Whereas in the previous 30 years Birra Peroni had a one-site production plant and an integrated accounting and reporting system, the addition of three plants—at a distance of ca. 200 km each—implied a segmental cost accounting and reporting system. What is more, the Peroni family could not exercise a direct control on production quality and financial performance. As a consequence, accounting tools should support control at distance in order to maintain the corporate image, to improve quality and to pursue the ever-increasing size of the firm. By monitoring variable costs and sales, an incentive to reach such objectives was maintained.

Accounting Practices from a NIS Perspective

The institutional environment affects all of the corporate strategy, and with it the accounting practices that are an extension of that strategy. Therefore, any strategic choice made by the company in response to external pressure must necessarily be supported by proper accounting practices that may enable it to implement that strategy.

Double entry bookkeeping and financial reporting practices were intended to enforce the institutional identity and to consolidate the relationship with the shareholders and, on the other side, to safeguard the company's secret from external stakeholders. In fact, the profit calculation method was adapted to ensure a satisfactory payout. Furthermore, the profitability of each business unit—such as ice and snow production, beer production and the distribution of beverages—was shown in the profit and loss account, but without details. In doing so, the company's management prevented external stakeholders from analysing the most important characteristics of each activity.

One of the most far-ranging strategic choices, and one that had the greatest impact on the accounting practices, was the opening of the new plants. They needed to be kept under control from a distance in an attempt to prevent fraud and measure the performance of each plant. An example was found in the accounting records of the Bari factory, where production costs and sales trends had been thoroughly reviewed since its foundation. The clear distinction between fixed and variable costs and its use in estimating cost behaviour shows how such information was used to implement corporate strategy as a response to institutional pressure. In addition, the practice of classifying cost into fixed and variable enforced ex post the strategic response to the environment. In fact, the analysis of cost behaviour could demonstrate how increasing production capacity and multiplying production sites was the best way to ensure a clear success for a leader in the Italian brewing industry.

Archival evidence also suggests that the company's accounting practices were very similar to breweries located in different areas of the Northern Hemisphere, above all in the Anglo-Saxon countries. This seems to substantiate the assumption that organisations working in the same line of business have a deep influence on each other, an influence that makes them behave similarly, not just in terms of strategic conduct but also in terms of accounting practices.

For example, in describing the accounting practices of U.S. breweries, Thornton (1913, p. 66) tells about the formal structure of the ledgers as well as the patterns and distinctive entries of the profit and loss accounts. By collating the company's balance sheets for the same years, we find that such entries and structures are very similar to those he described. We discovered further similarities analysing the handbook of Clarke (1898).

As to Italy, the *Enciclopedia Rota* was a large series of accounting handbooks covering all kinds of organisations and contained over one hundred volumes. Such books were all printed in the first 30 years of the twentieth century. Among them is a 400-page monograph on brewery activities and accounting by Ponzano (1924), in which he describes some aspects of Italian breweries' accounting practices in those years, and shows how production processes, account books, financial statements, statistical data, cost sheets and many other calculative tools could be adopted (p. 152–165). Once again, the structure and type of documents, for instance the cost analysis methods or the balance sheet form, matched those implemented by Birra Peroni.

The imitation strategy, which leads organisations to standardise their accounting practices, is strong here as well. This happened because, by being part of the same institutional context, such organisations responded to the same pressure, they affected each other and their accounting practices inevitably reflected such influence.

Thus, Birra Peroni's accounting policies show how the "best practices" emerging in the brewery sector were adopted in order to support the institution's image, especially towards internal actors, to enforce its identity as an emergent leader of the industry, and to favour the strategic response to institutional pressure. The legitimacy of new accounting tools and innovation came from experiences, rules or values largely shared by the community of brewing entrepreneurs and accounting professionals, both in Italy and abroad. This also bolstered the image and reputation of the organisation. In fact, Birra Peroni had a prominent role during the Fascist era, and Giacomo Peroni became the president of the national association of brewery producers. In this perspective, Birra Peroni had to justify and corroborate its prominent role by showing its supremacy also in accounting practices, adopting all the management tools known. The adoption of such techniques was not only motivated by a decision-making or control purpose but also by a desire to build its reputation. In fact, the leader of the brewery sector had to enforce its own institutional identity and its societal role also by modernising and dominating all kinds of calculative devices.

The interplay between the financial reporting, the cost accounting and the reporting, on the one side, and the institutional work done inside the firm by the family Peroni, the institutional approach to the company identity and image, and the strategic responses to environment changes, on the other side, confirms the role of accounting as a social practice and its importance in Birra Peroni's success in the Italian context we examined.

CONCLUSIONS

Accounting history studies about Italian companies, published in international refereed journals, have never addressed the role played by accounting in food companies, and there are still very few Italian-language studies on the subject.

This chapter reviewed the case of Birra Peroni, one of Italy's most important and famous breweries, in the years 1896–1946, focussing on the role played by accounting at that stage, from an NIS perspective.

Birra Peroni was founded in 1846 by Francesco Peroni and was originally located in Vigevano. Since 1864, a new site had been producing beer in Rome. Giovanni Peroni, the son of Francesco, moved the business to Rome at the end of the nineteenth century. Ice- and snowmaking was added to brewing.

At the beginning of the twentieth century, the company dramatically grew and became a market leader through takeovers and vertical integration processes. With the outbreak of the First World War, the firm had to face two problems. First, an unpredictable lack of qualified personnel occurred because all technicians came from Germany, an enemy of Italy. Second, there was increased demand, mainly from the Italian army because of industrial mobilisation.

After the First World War, the Italian brewing industry became progressively concentrated, and in 1925 Giacomo Peroni was appointed chairman of the national brewery producers' association under Fascism. The mergers and the growing demand for beer put pressure on the organisation, leading it to open three additional plants, in Bari (1924), Naples (1929) and Livorno (1939).

Because the only surviving account records in the firm archive are for the period 1896–1946, this chapter's historical re-enactment was limited to those years.

At the end of the nineteenth century, the accounting method consisted of a double entry bookkeeping system, based on a journal and a ledger. A capital- and income-oriented accounting system emerged. In the following years, a variety of managerial tools, including cost sheets, cash budgets, subsidiaries reports, were added in order to manage the growing complexity of the organisation. It is particularly interesting to go into the details of the accounting and reporting systems when the factories were located outside

Rome. Quality and efficiency had to be controlled and fraud had to be avoided.

In response to market change after the First World War, Peroni's strategy and structure changed, too. In turn, the accounting system was bound to change, even if such a change cannot be clearly analysed. Cost accounting and control were systematically put in place from afar, in order to face mass production problems and manage the plants around Italy. At the same time, some stability may be observed in the accounting practices, especially in the annual reports and in the journals and ledgers, set up in organisational routines and rules.

From an NIS perspective, the chapter shows first that the accounting system is an integral part of the organisation as a set of rules, routines and artefacts. Then, the accounting system is a key part of the institutional work of creating an entrepreneurial identity and business, the institutional approach that makes the company work that defines its values, its decision-making rules and its monitoring mechanisms. Finally, the accounting system is an essential support to Peroni's strategic response to environmental pressure.

The contribution of the chapter to accounting history literature is threefold: (1) it sheds light on the history of one of Italy's most famous family-run food businesses; (2) it adds evidence to the NIS approach to accounting history, extending the only one concerning an Italian firm, the one by Sargiacomo (2008), and the history of brewing, quite well developed in the English-speaking academic world; and (3) it demonstrates the importance of the accounting system in supporting the company's growth and in legitimating the company's choices inside and outside the organisation. Furthermore, Peroni's cost sheets and their purpose were additional evidences to the controversial debate on the origins and development of cost accounting in Italy (Antonelli et al., 2009).

The limits of the chapter include the scarcity of accounting records preserved in Birra Peroni's archives for the period immediately after the Second World War up to the 1970s. In fact, no ledgers, journals, annual reports, cost sheets or any other documents are indexed in the official archive list for the aforementioned period.

This chapter paves the way to many prospective research options. First, it would be extremely interesting to extend the period of the review to the time of greatest development and competitive pressure that followed the Second World War, when Peroni became one of Italy's best-known brands. During this period, the firm advertised its beer with the extremely famous slogan—said by its star, German actress Solvi Stubing, for whom this chapter has been named—"I'll be your beer!" Second, other Italian breweries could be reviewed too, before and after the twentieth-century concentration of the business. Third, the NIS perspective could be applied to research into the accounting practices of other Italian companies with the same distinctive traits, in terms of environmental pressure, organisational response, stability versus change of accounting systems and so on.

ACKNOWLEDGEMENTS

We would like to warmly thank Daniela Brignone, manager of Rome's Archivio Storico Peroni, for her kind help and extensive knowledge of the company's life, which she so kindly provided to us when we visited the archives and the museum.

REFERENCES

Primary Sources

Archivio Storico Peroni, Rome, Via Birolli 8

ASP (1898) Documentazione relativa alla costituzione della società romana.
ASP (1900) Bilancio 1900.
ASP (1903) Libro giornale della "Società riunite fabbriche di ghiacci e neve e ditta Francesco Peroni."
ASP (1907a) Bilancio e conto profitti e perdite esercizio 1907.
ASP (1907b) Relazione del consiglio di amministrazione.
ASP (1907c) Relazione dei sindaci.
ASP (1908a) Bilancio e conto profitti e perdite esercizio 1908.
ASP (1908b) Relazione del consiglio di amministrazione.
ASP (1908c) Relazione dei sindaci.
ASP (1909a) Bilancio e contro profitti e perdite esercizio 1909.
ASP (1909b) Relazione del consiglio di amministrazione.
ASP (1909c) Relazione dei sindaci.
ASP (1910a) Bilancio e conto profitti e perdite esercizio 1910.
ASP (1910b) Relazione del consiglio di amministrazione.
ASP (1910c) Relazione dei sindaci.
ASP (1911a) Relazione del consiglio di amministrazione all'assemblea ordinaria degli azionisti tenuta il 20 marzo 1911.
ASP (1911b) Bilancio e conto profitti e perdite esercizio 1911.
ASP (1912a) Relazione del consiglio di amministrazione all'assemblea ordinaria degli azionisti tenuta il 29 febbraio 1912.
ASP (1912b) Relazione dei sindaci all'assemblea ordinaria degli azionisti tenuta il 29 febbraio 1912.
ASP (1912c) Relazione del consiglio di amministrazione all'assemblea straordinaria degli azionisti tenuta il 29 febbraio 1912.
ASP (1915) Documenti preparatori al bilancio.
ASP (1920) Bilancio e conto profitti e perdite esercizio 1920.
ASP (1929) Breve relazione circa l'andamento dello stabilimento di Napoli nei primi mesi della nuova gestione, 20 settembre.
ASP (1933a) Stabilimento di Bari. Esercizio industriale, Marzo.
ASP (1933b) Spese generali di produzione dal 1925 al 1932.
ASP (1933c) Riepilogo vendita in città e provincia dal 1925 al 1932. Lucania. Campania. Zone varie. Riepilogo generale.
ASP (1934a) Allegato al bilancio Società Toscana Paszkowski.
ASP (1934b) Moduli per le analisi della birra e del malto effettuati per la società De Giacomi di Livorno da laboratori vari.
ASP (1942) Libro maestro.

Secondary Sources

Abernethy, M. and Chua, W. (1996) A field study of control system 'redesign': The impact of institutional processes on strategic choice. *Contemporary Accounting Research* 13(2): 569–606.

Ahmed, M.N. and Scapens, R.W. (2000) Cost allocation in Britain: Towards an institutional analysis. *European Accounting Review* 9(2): 159–204.

Allen, R.S. (1912) Twentieth-century brewery accounting. *The Western Brewer* November: 238.

Anonymous (2015) Francesco Peroni. Available at: http://www.treccani.it/enciclopedia/francesco-peroni/

Ansari, S. and Euske, K.J. (1987) Rational, rationalizing and reifying uses of accounting data in organizations. *Accounting, Organizations and Society* 12(6): 549–570.

Antonelli, V., Boyns, T. and Cerbioni, F. (2009) The development of cost accounting in Italy, c. 1800 to c. 1940. *Accounting History* 14(4): 465–507.

BAICR (2007) *Musei del gusto. Mappa della memoria enogastronomica*. Milan: Carsa Edizioni.

Brignall, S. and Modell, S. (2000) An institutional perspective on performance measurement and management in the 'new public sector'. *Management Accounting Research* 11(3): 281–306.

Brignone, D. (1995) *Birra Peroni: 1846–1996, centocinquanta anni di birra nella vita italiana*. Rome: Electa.

Brignone, D. (2001) *Archivio della Società Birra Peroni: inventario*. Rome: Ministero Beni e Attività Culturali.

Burns, J. and Scapens, R.W. (2000) Conceptualizing management accounting change: An institutional framework. *Management Accounting Research* 11(1): 3–25.

Capellaro, I. D. (1996) *L'azienda vitivinicola Sella & Mosca. Il più importante complesso produttivo del settore nel contesto economico sardo*, in Atti del III Convegno nazionale di storia della ragioneria '*Vita economica e storia della ragioneria in Sardegna dalla seconda metà del Settecento*', Alghero, 20–21 ottobre 1995, Pisa: Pacini, pp. 373–380.

Carmona, S., Ezzamel, M. and Gutiérrez, F. (1998) Towards an institutional analysis of accounting change in the Royal Tobacco Factory of Seville. *Accounting Historians Journal* 25(1): 115–147.

Carmona, S., Macías, D. and Pilar, M. (2001) Institutional pressures, monopolistic conditions and the implementation of early cost management practices: The case of the Royal Tobacco Factory of Seville (1820–1887). *Abacus* 37(2): 139–165.

Carpenter, V.L. and Feroz, E.H. (2001) Institutional theory and accounting rule choice: An analysis of four US state government's decisions to adopt generally accepted accounting principle. *Accounting, Organization and Society* 26(7–8): 565–596.

Carruthers, B. G. (1995) Accounting, ambiguity, and the new institutionalism. *Accounting, Organizations and Society* 20(4): 313–328.

Cavazzoni, G. (1998) *La Buitoni-Perugina*, in Atti del IV Convegno nazionale di storia della ragioneria. '*Storia di imprese tra il XVI ed il XIX secolo*', Perugia, 2–3 ottobre 1997, Rome: Rirea, pp. 121–128.

Ciocca, P. and Toniolo, G. (1976) *L'economia italiana nel periodo fascista*. Bologna: Il Mulino.

Clarke, E. W. (1898) *Brewery bookkeeping: A practical treatise on brewery accounts and office management*. Chicago: H.S. Rich & Company.

Colli, A. (1995) Per una storia del settore birrario italiano. Dalle origini alla seconda guerra mondiale. *Quaderni di ricerca dell'Istituto di storia economica dell'Università Commerciale L. Bocconi* 3(12): 21–40.

Colli, A. (1997) Produzione e consumo di birra in Italia dall'Unità alla seconda guerra mondiale. *Rivista di storia economica* 13(3): 283–326.

Colli, A. (1998) The Italian brewing industry, c. 1815–1990. In: Wilson, R.G. and Gourvish, T.R. (eds.), *The dynamics of the international brewing industry since 1800*. London: Routledge, pp. 32–58.

Corfield, J. (2015) Peroni. In: Martin, S.C. (ed.), *The SAGE encyclopedia of alcohol: Social, cultural, and historical perspectives*. London: Sage, p. 312.

Corran, T.H. (1981) James Deady, Henry Meux, and the Griffin Brewery: Fraud in an early-nineteenth-century business. *Business History* 23(3): 327–345.

Covaleski, M.A. and Dirsmith, M.W. (1988) An institutional perspective on the rise, social transformation, and fall of a university budget category. *Administrative Science Quarterly* 33(4): 562–587.

Covalenski, M.A., Dirsmith, M.W. and Samuel, S. (1996) Managerial accounting research: The contributions of organizational and sociological theories. *Journal of Management Accounting Research* 8(1): 1–36.

De Payer, E.C. (1916) Brewery accountancy and income tax. *The Journal of the Federated Institute of Brewing* XXIL: 2–46.

DiMaggio, P.J. and Powell, W.W. (1983) The iron cage revisited: Institutional isomorphism and collective rationality in organizational fields. *American Sociological Review* 48(2): 147–160.

Felton, S. and Mann, H. (1990) Accounting for a brewery at Louisbourg. *Contemporary Accounting Research* 7(1): 261–277.

Goettsche, H.C. (1934) *Brewery accounting; Complete system and forms*. Crawfordsville: R.R. Donnelley & Sons Co.

Gomes, D., Carnegie, G.D. and Rodrigues, L.L. (2008) Accounting change in central government: The adoption of double entry bookkeeping at the Portuguese Royal Treasury (1761). *Accounting, Auditing & Accountability Journal* 21(8): 1144–1184.

Goodstein, J.D. (1994) Institutional pressures and strategic responsiveness: Employer involvement in work-family issues. *Academy of Management Journal* 37(2): 350–382.

Goretzki, L., Strauss, E. and Weber, J. (2013) An institutional perspective on the changes in management accountants' professional role. *Management Accounting Research* 24(1): 41–63.

Gourvish, T.R. and Wilson, R.G. (1985) Profitability in the Brewing Industry 1885–1914. *Business History* 27(2): 146–165.

Granlund, M. (2001) Towards explaining stability in and around management accounting systems. *Management Accounting Research* 12(2): 141–166.

Granlund, M. and Lukka, K. (1998) It's a small world of management accounting practices. *Journal of Management Accounting Research* 10(2): 153–179.

Greenwood, R., Oliver, C., Suddaby, R. and Sahlin-Andersson, K. (2008) *The SAGE handbook of organizational institutionalism*. London: Sage.

Greenwood, R. and Suddaby, R. (2006) Institutional entrepreneurship in mature fields: The Big Five accounting firms. *Academy of Management Journal* 49(1): 27–48.

Hamilton, G.S. (1939) *Brewery accounting*. London: Gee & Co.

Harris, W. (1899) *Brewers' accounts*. London: Howard & Jones.

Higgins, D.M. and Verma, S. (2009) The business of protection: Bass & Co. and trade mark defence, c. 1870–1914. *Accounting, Business & Financial History* 19(1): 1–19.

Hussain, M. and Hoque, Z. (2002) Understanding non-financial performance measurement practices in Japanese banks: A new institutional sociology perspective. *Accounting, Auditing & Accountability Journal* 15(2): 162–183.

Lanham, W. and Northcott, W.C. (1906) *Brewers' and bottlers' accounts*. London: Gee & Company.

Lawrence, T., Suddabby, R. and Leca, B. (2011) Institutional work: Refocusing institutional studies of organization. *Journal of Management Inquiry* 20(1): 52–58.

Lukka, K. (2007) Management accounting change and stability: Loosely coupled rules and routines in action. *Management Accounting Research* 18(1): 76–101.

Mari, L.M., Cavazzoni C., Bellucci A. and Cardoni A. (2008) *La storia della Perugina (1907–1985). La vicenda imprenditoriale attraverso l'analisi dei bilanci societari*, Paper Presented at the IX Convegno Nazionale Società Italiana di Storia della Ragioneria '*Dalla rilevazione contabile all'economia aziendale*', Perugia, 27–28 settembre 2007 (.pdf version on CD-ROM).

Mason, J. (1992) Accounting for beer: An investigation into the accounting practice of three Northamptonshire breweries, 1882 to 1914. In: Boys, P. and Freear, J. (eds.), *Accounting history, 1976–1986. An anthology*. Abingdon: Routledge, pp. 187–204.

Meyer, J.W. and Rowan, B. (1977) Institutionalized organizations: Formal structure as myth and ceremony. *American Journal of Sociology* 83(2): 340–363.

Mezias, S.J. (1990) An institutional model of organizational practice: Financial reporting at the Fortune 200. *Administrative Science Quarterly* 35(4): 431–57.

Milano, L. (ed.) (1994) *Drinking in ancient societies: History and culture of drinks in the Ancient Near East*. Papers of a Symposium held in Rome, May 17–19, 1990, Padova: Sargon.

Moreno, A. (2011) Desarrollo de una cervecera en una región poco desarrollada a la luz de sus documentos Contables: El Alcázar (1928–93). *De Computis Revista Española de Historia de la Contabilidad* 15(2): 160–204.

Moreno, A. and Càmara, M. (2014) Evolution of information content from an institutional perspective: El Alcázar brewery (1928–1993). *Accounting History* 19(3): 369–398.

Mutch, A. (2008) C. Howard Tripp and brewery management: The emergence of service sector management 1850–1914. *Management & Organizational History* 3(2): 161–175.

Noguchi, M. and Boyns, T. (2012) The development of budgets and their use for purposes of control in Japanese aviation, 1928–1945: The role of the state. *Accounting, Auditing & Accountability Journal* 25(3): 416–451.

Núñez, M. (2002) Organizational change and accounting: The gunpowder monopoly in New Spain, 1757–87. *Accounting, Business & Financial History* 12(2): 275–315.

Oliver, C. (1991) Strategic responses to institutional processes. *Academy of Management Review* 16(1): 145–179.

Peroni, R. (2008) *La bionda della mia vita: ritratto della famiglia che ha creato la birra in Italia*. Milan: Sperling & Kupfer.

Ponzano, A. (1924) *Le fabbriche di birra e le malterie*. Turin: Utet.

Powell, W.P. and Bromely, P. (2015) New institutionalism in the analysis of complex organizations. In: Wright, J.D. (ed.), *International encyclopedia of social and behavioural sciences*, second edition. Amsterdam: Elsevier.

Powell, W.P. and DiMaggio, P.J. (eds.) (1991) *The new institutionalism in organizational analysis*. Chicago: The University of Chicago Press.

Quinn, M. (2014) Stability and change in management accounting over time. A century or so of evidence from Guinness. *Management Accounting Research* 25(1): 76–92.

Quinn, M. and Jackson, W.J. (2014) Accounting for war risk costs: Management accounting change at Guinness during the First World War. *Accounting History Review* 24(2–3): 191–209.

Racheli, A.M. (1978) L'opificio della Birra Peroni nel quartiere Salario in Roma. *Ricerche di storia dell'arte* 7: 61–78.

Racheli, A.M. (1993) *Recupero edilizio e archeologia industriale: la fabbrica della Birra Peroni a Roma (1901–1992)*. Rome: Marsilio.

Rentini, S. and Zanelli, L. (2005) Alcol e pubblicità. *Alcol etilico* 7(1): 31–39.

Sargiacomo, M. (2008) Institutional pressures and isomorphic change in a high-fashion company: The case of Brioni Roman Style, 1945–89. *Accounting, Business & Financial History* 18(2): 215–241.

Scott, W.R. (1987) The adolescence of institutional theory. *Administrative Science Quarterly* 32(3): 493–511.

Scott, W.R. (1995) *Institutions and organizations*. London: Sage.

Seal, W. (2006) Management accounting and corporate governance: An institutional interpretation of the agency problem. *Management Accounting Research* 17(4): 389–408.

Siti-Nabiha, A.K. and Scapens, R.W. (2005) Stability and change: An institutionalist study of management accounting change. *Accounting, Auditing & Accountability Journal* 18(1): 44–73.

Stack, M. (2000) Local and regional Breweries in America's brewing industry, 1865 to 1920. *The Business History Review* 74(3): 435–463.

Talbot, P.A. (2002) Accounting for taste: The government pint. *Journal of the Brewery History Society* 108: 4–28.

Talbot, P.A. (2005a) Accounting for the nationalised brewery (1916–1974) and the public good. *Journal of Finance and Management in Public Services* 4(2): 57–71.

Talbot, P.A. (2005b) Costing the state pint (1916–1974). *Journal of Finance and Management in Public Services* 5(2): 9–30.

Talbot, P.A. (2006) Sir John Barleycorn, Miss Hop and their only child Master Beer: Accounting for malt 1700–1939. *Journal of the Brewery History Society*, 129: 1–30.

Talbot, P.A. (2007) The privatisation of the state management scheme: Evaluating the financial arguments. *Journal of Finance and Management in Public Services* 9(1): 31–45.

Thornton, F.W. (1913) *Brewery accounts*. New York: Ronald Press.

Thornton, P. and Ocasio, W. (1999) Institutional logics and the historical contingency of power in organizations: Executive succession in the higher education publishing industry, 1958–1990. *American Journal of Sociology* 105(3): 801–843.

Toscano, P. (2002) *Le origini del capitalismo industriale nel Lazio: imprese e imprenditori a Roma dall'unità alla seconda guerra mondiale*. Cassino: Edizioni dell'Università degli studi di Cassino.

Tsamenyi, M., Cullen, J. and González, J.M.G. (2006) Changes in accounting and financial information system in a Spanish electricity company: A new institutional theory analysis. *Management Accounting Research* 17(4): 409–432.

Villa, K. (2011) Peroni brewery. In: Oliver, G. (ed.), *The Oxford companion to beer*. Oxford: Oxford University Press, p. 647.

Walter, L.A., Edelman, L.F. and Hatten, K.J. (2014) The US brewing industry, strategic windows and survival. *Journal of Management History* 20(4): 434–458.

West, B. and Carnegie, G.D. (2010) Accounting's chaotic margins: Financial reporting of the library collections of Australia's public universities, 2002–2006. *Accounting, Auditing & Accountability Journal* 23(2): 201–228.

Wilson, M. and Shailer, G. (2007) Accounting manipulations and political costs: Tooth & Co Ltd, 1910–1965. *Accounting and Business Research* 37(4): 247–266.

Wilson, R.G. and Gourvish, T.R. (1998) *The dynamics of international brewing industry since 1800*. London: Routledge.

Yamamoto, K. and Noguchi, M. (2013) Different scenarios for accounting reform in non-Anglophone contexts: The case of Japanese local governments since the 1990s. *Accounting History* 18(4): 529–549.

Zucker, L.G. (1987) Institutional theories of organizations. *Annual Review of Sociology* 13(4): 443–64.

2 Branding Strategies and Accounting in Wine Production

A Historical Analysis of Fontanafredda (1858–1932)

Valter Cantino, Massimo Pollifroni, Damiano Cortese and Mariangela Longo

INTRODUCTION

This chapter aims to study the results of the business activity of the wine producer, Fontanafredda, between 1858 and 1932, by analysing company records and other administration documents. Admittedly, the wine industry—together with pasta and high-fashion goods—has long made an important contribution to the Italian economy, as part of the "Made in Italy" lifestyle (Porter, 1998; Sargiacomo, 2008). The chapter is linked to the manifesto of the Società Italiana di Storia della Ragioneria (Italian Society of Accounting History): the objective is to understand the dynamics and consequences of entrepreneurial choices made over a period of time. This was made possible by analysing both the accounting and nonaccounting records that reflect the misfortunes that befell Fontanafredda.

Research began with the examination of historical documents preserved on the premises at Fontanafredda, in particular:

- The will of Count Emanuele Guerrieri di Mirafiore e Fontanafredda[1]
- The Inventory Failure Report of the company Anonima Mirafiore—Vini Italiani[2]
- The Statement of Transferral of Ownership, which Fontanafredda received from the Istituto di Credito Fondiario Monte dei Paschi di Siena.[3]

Work proceeded with the verification of the sources found in the State Archives in Turin, especially:

- Files containing documents relative to the financial years 1872 and 1873
- Estimates and bills regarding the sales over certain periods
- The inventory for the year 1876
- Business correspondence

Finally, the bibliographical review focussed on works that have been published on the subject of Fontanafredda, which are particularly rich in detail regarding documents, sources and interviews, in particular:

- Tablino L., Fontanafredda. *125 anni tra vigneti e cantine. Testimonianze, immagini documenti* (2004).
- Tablino, L., Fontanafredda. *125 anni tra vigneti e cantine. Immagini e documenti, MPS Tenimenti s.p.a.* (2005).
- Tablino L., Fontanafredda. *125 anni tra vigneti e cantine (1922–1973). Testimonianze, immagini, documenti, MPS Tenimenti s.p.a.* (2006).

In order to have a clear picture of the most significant phases of the evolution of the company, it is important to mention the milestones that this work focusses on:

- 1858: Vittorio Emanuele II purchased the land;
- 1860: the land was registered under the private estate of Vittorio Emanuele II and made over to the children resulting from his morganatic relationship with Rosa Vercellana;
- 1872–73: the first sales of wine were recorded;
- 1878: the "E. di Mirafiore" winery was founded;
- 1919: the "Società Anonima Mirafiore—Vini Italiani" was founded;
- 1930: the firm failed;
- 1932: the property was taken over by the Istituto di Credito Fondiario Monte dei Paschi di Siena.

The choice of concluding the chapter with the transferral of the property to the Monte dei Paschi di Siena was made due to the fact that this event was a significant turning point, which transformed the winery from a simple business concern into a crowning glory for the bank. The transferral influenced the business model over the years, until the company's recent acquisition by the purchasers, who have established new strategies.

1858–1876: FROM THE PURCHASE OF THE LAND TO THE SALE OF WINES

Fontanafredda is an Italian hamlet where the winery that bears its name is situated, in Serralunga d'Alba, on the hills of the Langhe. The winery is currently a limited company. According to the deeds dated 1700, the name comes from the existence of a "cold spring."

In 1858, Vittorio Emanuele II bought the land from Giacomo Roggeri with an "atto di comando del regio delegato" ("royal decree") to the town of Serralunga d'Alba. The land was composed of just over 52 hectares.

In 1860, the land was registered under the private estate of Vittorio Emanuele II in the name of Emanuele Alberto Guerrieri, Count of Mirafiori, and his sister, Maria Vittoria, born from the morganatic relationship with Rosa Vercellana [10079 (1816–1875) Pratiche riguardanti affitti, vendite, acquisti e permute di beni immobili tra i privati e la Real Casa].

The following year, various expenses were recorded, which served to increase and improve the property. Expenses included those for the purchase of "fixed assets" and money spent on "the cultivation of land, especially the planting of vines," for a total amount of 24,060,14 Italian Lire.[4]

There is a record from 1863 of a bill for the work of Paolo Gallo, the master builder at Fontanafredda. It is stated that he worked on the "farmhouse," the "manor house" and the "lodge," as well as the canal, the aqueduct and the building of a new road. The bill is for a sum of 68,879.18 Italian Lire.[5]

From the works of Tablino (2004), it is known that in the years following the agricultural reforms introduced by Cavour around 1850, Fontanafredda was also adapted to comply with the new standards and methods.

In order to better understand the extent of the work that was carried out, there is a request for clarification, "on 31 December, 1850," for the fact that the management was "continuing to receive bills for the Fontanafredda estate." This request interpreted the intentions of His Majesty who "regarding 30–8–1863 established the sum of said expenses at 73,266.68 Italian Lire which will be paid by the private estate." There follows the request "to be authorised to pay all the sums owed" that "will be distributed and classified according to the above-mentioned register" (Tablino, 2004). For these reasons, Giovanni Quaglia, an agent of the King, was appointed comptroller of the accounts the following year.

In 1872, the financial year closed with an expenditure of 8,681.08 Italian Lire and a revenue of 7,040,70 Italian Lire, of which wine accounted for 831 Italian Lire and grapes for 6,403.70 Italian Lire. These are considered to be the first sales, which increased the following year, turning Fontanafredda from a producer and retailer of the fruit from the harvest into a wine-producing concern.

At this point reference must be made to the technical phase regarding the typology of planting of the vines. Records show that in this period at Fontanafredda there were *alteni*, a type of cultivation that involved other plants and trellises. This kind of cultivation had been used in ancient Rome, "where the vine was grown on trees, or on trellises, in order to facilitate the ripening of the fruit grown on flat land."[6] It is clear that this type of cultivation was still present from the times of the previous owner, Roggeri, rather than a choice of the estate at that time. Furthermore, Tablino underlines the fact that the output at that time was equal to 60%, and there was an indiscriminate inclusion of nongrape material, such as wheat, in the rows.

The technical solutions and innovation in the management of the vineyard, as well as the attention to quality resulting in success on the market, which are clearly visible to anyone visiting the hills of the Langhe, are indeed a long way off at this stage.

Tablino notes that 78 hectolitres of wine were produced in 1873: 58 bottles of Barolo, "Patrimonio di sua Maestà" ("from His Majesty's estate") for the value of 1 lira each and 60 bottles of Nebbiolo at 0.8 lira each.

The first file of documents analysed in the State Archive in Turin contain details regarding the income and expenditure from 1 January to 31 March 1873 for Tenuta Reale di Fontana Fredda [11122 (1872–1878) Contabilità delle vigne di Barolo e Fontanafredda].[7] Some of the items are of particular interest:

- The provision of bundles of vines for the price of 50 centesimi (cents) for a total sum of 24 Italian Lire from Parrusso Caterina, as well as the payment made to Destefanis Maurizio for the sum of 371 Italian Lire for the purchase of "140 dozen Nebioli (sic) vine shoots and 84 of Barbera";
- The purchase of "24 dozen Barbera vine shoots" from Baldi Giuseppe;
- The "planting of posts in the vineyards from the 2nd to the 15th March," which employed 21 agricultural labourers, costing 156.95 Italian Lire, and, in the same period, "19 women to tie the vines" (for a cost of 60.25 Italian Lire). The tying procedure is carried out again, this time with 20 women, until the end of the month, for a cost of 79.50 Italian Lire. At the same time 15 agricultural labourers were being paid to set up the trellises. A payment was also made in this period to the Secretary "Treasurer of the Regia Mandria for the purchase of 6,700 chestnut posts," for the sum of 1,129.10 Italian Lire, whereas Sandrone Giuseppe had already been paid 5.50 Italian Lire for his work on the trellises supporting the vines and digging 880 ditches for the planting of the vines.

The estate was investing heavily in the vines, which can be seen by the employment of a specialist, Raimondo Giuseppe, who received an annual salary of 366 Italian Lire, a quarter of which was paid in the month of February. The documents also reveal that pruning work was carried out as well as the digging of other ditches.

The quarter closes with an expenditure of 4,377.84 Italian Lire and the sale of 50 litres of "substandard quality wine," for the sum of 16 Italian Lire. A total of 1,620 litres of Dolcetto were delivered to the Regia Mandria from the estate for a sum of 874.80 Italian Lire (0.54 Italian Lire per litre) and 115 Italian Lire for 360 other wines, earning a total of 1,260.20 Italian Lire at the end of the quarter.

It is also interesting to note the amount of tax that was paid:

- 21.99 Italian Lire to the "Diano Tax Revenue agency for land tax in 1873 on the property owned in the district of Diano"

- 88.25 Italian Lire "for the first tax instalment on land and buildings in the district of Serralunga"
- 16.55 Italian Lire "to the Monforte Tax Revenue agency for tax on land owned in the district of Castiglione for the current year."

The final balance of the second quarter closes 19 July 1873, with an expenditure of 5,695.22 Italian Lire and revenues of 3,259.33 Italian Lire. The sale of wine accounts for 1,536.35 Italian Lire of the total revenue.

The third file of documents regarding the month of July shows that there are numerous payments for the reaping and threshing of wheat, as well as work carried out on the vines. There was an expenditure of 2,529.55 Italian Lire and revenues worth 185.47 Italian Lire, but none came from wine. For the period spanning 4 August to 31 October 1873 (fourth file), some of the most significant payments were made for the hoeing and stripping of the vines, harvesting[8] and destemming, as well as the building of trellises in the vineyards and the cleaning and levelling of ditches. Included in the expenditure is the cost of the removal of the vats in preparation for the new production. There is also an item for the transport costs borne by Icardi—agent of the estate[9]—"to go to Turin to negotiate with the highly esteemed Director for the sale of the grapes." The sale of Dolcetto accounts for 1,090.20 Italian Lire of the total revenue of 2,340.75 Italian Lire.

The fifth file contains documents that show an expenditure for 1,514.31 Italian Lire and revenues of 1,002.26 Italian Lire, 607 coming from the sale of wine.

The sixth file, which is a supplementary file, regards the period from January to February 1874, with revenues of 3,650.34 Italian Lire and an expenditure pertaining to the previous year, and shows revenues of 4,342.90 Italian Lire, 1,441 of which were for the sale of wine.

In June 1873—as can be seen in the work of Tablino (2004)—the yearly production was recorded:

- 5,000 litres of Dolcetto, including 1,000 litres that were given to the casual wage agricultural labourers employed on a daily basis with a half measure of water;
- 1,200 litres of second quality Dolcetto, given in lieu of payment to the cowhands and the casual agricultural labourers;
- 2,000 litres of third quality wine;
- Top quality wine, Nebbiolo and Freisa—made specifically for the King;
- 250 litres of white wine.

These records show that wine production was increasing, and that the winery was employing a considerable number of agricultural labourers and was a source of income for the surrounding area. Data regarding 1874 shows that 18,982 litres of wine were produced and sold,[10] bringing in an income of 4,811.94 Italian Lire.

A substantial part of the production was reserved for the Royal Court, and the general superintendent paid a great deal of attention to the quality and quantity of the wines. For example, on 2 February 1875[11] the office wrote a note saying:

> would Agent Icardi be so kind as to send [. . .] samples of the best quality wines produced from the grapes ripened at Fontanafredda in 1874, including Barbera and Dolcetto wines, specifying on each bottle the number available for each type of quality.

In the same year, note 971 made the "request" to "know the quality and quantity of the wines of this estate [. . .] that have already been sold."[12]

An order from the superintendent is registered on 17 September 1875, which approves the proposed sales terms, and also states:

> However, the wine that this agency must produce for the Royal Court must be around the same quantity and quality as that of the previous year, 1874, as well as five or six casks of top quality Barbera wine made from choice grapes and with the utmost care, even if the cost of said procedure should be high.[13]

Therefore the type of product was the most important aspect, no matter how much it would cost.

Further confirmation of this situation can be found in the document, "Destination of the wines produced in 1875"[14] which provides the agent of the estate with indications regarding the production of the previous year:

> Of the wine produced from the waste material of the grapes, having deducted the quantity necessary for the use of the estate, the Agent must remain at the disposal of the Superintendent, so that in due course, around 2/3 of the total amount delivered last year to Valdieri must be sent to the mountains, and this amount must be selected from the finest qualities: the remaining amount must be sold by you at the best possible price.

The King preferred Barbera and Grignolino.

In a private act dated 1875 , the estate

> sells and relinquishes to [. . .] Sebastiano and Matteo Ferreri, hotelier brothers at the Villa in Bra and to the Manassero brothers [. . .] owners and shopkeepers, the entire production of the harvest of this estate [. . .] of top quality Barbera, for the sum of six *brente*[15] of wine, as well as waste material.[16]

It seems as if there is a return to the previous sales strategies, but actually, as well as the instructions regarding the number of casks to produce, other conditions imposed restraints that show a constant change in strategy. In fact, the estate reserved the right to keep as much waste grape material[17] it deemed fit to produce the amount of wine needed for the estate. A further obligation for the Ferreri and Manassero brothers is that of "producing, as far as possible, the wine in vats and placing it in the barrels of that Estate."

The prices of the Dolcetto, Nebbiolo and blends stated in the contract are based on those used on the Alba market, whereas the prices of Barbera and muscatels are based on the Asti market.

The following extract is particularly interesting, as it shows the close ties between Fontanafredda and the private estate of the King: "payments shall be made to the General Superintendent of the Private Estate of the King or the Office at the Fontana Fredda estate."

On the other hand, regarding purchases, there is a clear distinction between the actual production and the royal property, which can be seen in the following note:[18]

> With regards to the wine delivered to the Royal Palace of Sant'Anna di Valdieri, the bills issued in the month of September were returned, so that the costs incurred for transportation could be charged to the Royal Court, in order not to reduce the income deriving from the "fixed value of the wines."

An important issue is raised here: expenses are borne by the royal estate,[19] "which obviously drew upon the money obtained from the annual sum conferred to the King by the legitimate Government,"[20] but the management of the profits was carried out from a purely profit-making point of view.

In order to fully understand the market at the time, it is interesting to see the average price of the grapes, recorded by the municipal district of Asti, on 20 October 1875: Barbere "2 centesimi 28 millesimi 111," Grapes "1 centesimo 58 millesimi 234." Prices differ in the municipal district of Alba:

- Dolcetti: 1.9961 Italian Lire
- Neirani 2.0473 Italian Lire
- Barbere 2.0925 Italian Lire
- Nebioli 3.1160 Italian Lire
- Grape varieties 1.7708 Italian Lire.[21]

The first mention of a sensory analysis of the Fontanafredda wines can be found in a document contained in the files of the State Archives in Turin, dated 10 April 1876. In fact, there is a reference to the Nebbiolo of the Barolo vine of the previous year, where it is described as "good, but you can smell the sulphur." This was caused by the sulphuration process used for the barrels. This problem was no longer present in the wine tasted after bottling. This may not seem to be relevant for this chapter, but in fact it helps to understand the production process, in particular the organoleptic aspect of the products, in the year when a new "factory" was being built near the new vats. This can be considered as proof that Fontanafredda was working towards increasing both the quality and quantity of the production. In 1887 the cement barrels made by Borsarti-Zollikon (Tablino, 2004) were introduced.

Continuing the perusal of the documents found in the Archive, bill 1202, dated 1876, states that 650 litres of wine were sent to the "Guardaroba" in Rome.[22] Moreover, there is the[23] "Inventory of the Estate of Fontana Fredda 11 November 1876," carried out by Icardi Giuseppe—"Agent of the Estate of Fontanafredda—[with the help of Mr. Borgna Pietro] on behalf of the Intendant of the private estate of H.M. Count Carmagnola," recorded on 19 February 1877.

There is also the list of the agricultural equipment used for the vine and the cellar, as well as the cattle and existing supplies at 11 November. Even the haylofts and granaries were itemised in the inventory,[24] whereas for the cellar and wines there is a reference to the barrels, both old and new, for a sum of 5,089.50 Italian Lire. Other objects, including a *brenta*, a grape press, "a second-hand press in good condition," for a total of 5,752.50 Italian Lire.

As far as the wines are concerned, the list includes:

- Wine in the cellar: old wine of 1875, Grignolino, Barbera pomace, Uvaggio (blend) pomace;
- Wine produced in 1876: Dolcetto, Barbera, Uvaggio (blend), Freisa, Nebbiolo, Uvaggio pomace (low quality blend), "good" Grignolino, white Moscato, good light wine for a sum of 27,715 Italian Lire;
- Records of bottles in the wine cellar of 1866 Barbera, 1871 Nebbiolo, wine from the estate and mature Dolcetto, and empty bottles, for a sum of 291,60 Italian Lire.

The total sum recorded in the document is 47,046.60 Italian Lire.

The "summary of the management at 30 September 1877" is stated in the file from 11 November to 31 December 1876, with an income of 324 Italian Lire, corrected to 24, and an expenditure of 1,493.44 Italian Lire, corrected to 1,491.44. The income (at September 1877) deriving from agriculture amounts to 14,445.81 Italian Lire and there is an expenditure of 17,112.31 Italian Lire.[25]

At the same time, there is a receipt regarding the "wine sold," for a sum of 2,543 litres and a revenue of 584.8 Italian Lire for the months of May and June 1876. A further 950 litres were sold throughout the year, while the list of the wines "destined to the Royal Castle of Pollenzo, upon the order of Her Highness the Countess of Mirafiori" including "Nebbiolo pomace and other wines," shows a further amount of 3,513 litres, which must be added to the 950 delivered to Turin and to the Guardaroba in Alba and Rome.

All this goes to show that in this early period Fontanafredda seems to be a developing business concern. The winery is taking advantage of market opportunities and is no longer simply a cost for the superintendent of His Majesty's personal estate but is also generating revenue and an income for the area of and around Serralunga, thus becoming a positive direct and indirect economic force for the whole area.

FROM E. DI MIRAFIORE WINERY TO SOCIETÀ ANONIMA MIRAFIORE—VINI ITALIANI

The estate continued its development that led to the natural evolution of a truly consolidated establishment fully integrated on the market and with business strategies.

In 1877 there is the receipt "for the wine sent by the Fontana Fredda Estate to the Royal Palace of S. Anna di Valdieri," for 7,134 litres of Dolcetto at a price of 0.80 Italian Lire per litre. In total, 329 litres of blends were delivered at 0.70 Italian Lire per litre, whereas 320 bottles of Freisa were delivered at a cost of 1 lira each. White wine totalling 166 bottles was sold at the same price; 85 bottles of Grignolino for an amount of 1.25 Italian Lire each; and finally, 50 bottles of Barbera at the same price. The sum is 6,642.25 Italian Lire, "reimbursed to the Ministry Office of the Royal Palace on 24 October 1877."[26]

There are still close ties with the royal household and the cash flows deriving from it—although between 16 April and 13 July 1877 a total of 381 litres of wine, for the sum of 187.16 Italian Lire, was sold to Mr. Bo Pittore;[27] and the sum of 1,343.94 Italian Lire was paid for other wine sold between May and September, as can be seen in receipt 1,639.

In receipt 637, dated 4 May 1877, Vignola, the intendant, tells Mr. Giuseppe Icardi, agent of the Fontanafredda estate,

> to duly go the appropriate tax revenue office to remove yourself from the list of tax payers eligible for Wealth tax, for the financial year 1878, the correct authorisation issued by the Administration of the Royal household in this city is attached, due to which, through the Ministry of His Majesty's household, the amount of tax will be paid to the State coffers in Rome and will be deducted from your monthly salary from 1 January 1878.

The following provides further evidence: "His Excellency the Minister expresses the intention that from the first day of February [1878] . . . the Fontana Fredda Estate shall cease to be administered by this Tax office."

Finally, the letter written by the Intendant on the subject of the "Purchase of property pertaining to the Fontanafredda Estate,"[28] dated 5 July 1877, states:

> the undersigned informs the Agent, Icardi that soon Mr. Ruetta, a surveyor, operating at the Opera Pia Barolo, will proceed to measure the

> property belonging to the Estate and is authorized by the competent Authorities to sell the property to the Countess of Mirafiore.[29]

These are clear signs that things were changing, leading to a new milestone in the evolution of the business model. In fact, in 1878 Emanuele Alberto Guerrieri, Count of Mirafiori, son of the King and Rosa Vercellana—called "la Bela Rosin" (Farinetti, 2011)—founded the "E. di Mirafiore" winery, which he then left to his son Gastone, with his wife Margherita Boasso Sella.

This is proof of how the entrepreneurial and family history—as will be seen later on—are so closely linked in Fontanafredda. In the "Secret will of the Illustrious Count Emanuele Guerrieri of Mirafiore and Fontanafredda" dated 24 December 1894, it is stated:

> I entrust my children with the Estates of Mirafiori, Fontanafredda, Barolo and Sommariva Perno, which I do not wish to be ceded, because I spent my life trying to improve the first three at great personal sacrifice, and two of them bear the name of our family.

This was an important constraint for the future generation, which, however, did not prevent the future phases of the firm, also due to the circumstances it found itself in. It is, nonetheless, a very particular scenario.

After the constitution in 1878 there are no accounting records, as the only personal property of the King remaining were the Barolo vines, for which documents exist.

From 1880 onwards, the estate also began to trade abroad, also thanks to the crisis that was affecting the French wines due to phylloxera (Tablino, 2004). The production was successful and widely acclaimed. A catalogue of the estate dating back to the beginning of the 10th century (Tablino, 2004) shows the "Diploma d'onore" e "Gran Medaglia d'oro" in Brussels (1888) ("Certificate of Honour" and "Gold Medal"), then again in Cologne the following year and in 1890 in Edinburgh. The "Gran Diploma di eccellenza" e "Grande medaglia d'oro" ("Diploma of Excellence" and "Gold Medal") were awarded in Chicago in 1892, and similar awards were given in San Francisco (1894) and London (1904). This period is significant for Barolo wines, and at the end of the 19th century the price to 1.5 Italian Lire per litre.

On 25 May 1919, the Società Anonima per Azioni "Mirafiore—Vini Italiani" was founded in Sommariva Perno, with a share capital of 3 million Italian Lire, divided into 30,000 shares with a value of 111 Italian Lire each. The Count Gastone di Mirafiori bought 12,500 shares.

The board of directors was composed of a minimum of three up to a maximum of seven directors (the period of office was four years, according to Article 124 of the Commercial Code) and the Count of Mirafiori, the lawyer Luigi Murialdi and the lawyer Luigi Parodi were chosen for the first year of operation. The elected president was Gastone di Mirafiori. The board of statutory auditors was composed of three statutory auditors and two substitutes.

From that year onwards, as specified in the deed dated 25 June 1919—the contract determining the purchase of the cellars and vineyards of the Opera Pia Barolo—the partnership between Gastone and Luigi Parodi was in place. The only person to benefit from this partnership, thanks to the future sale of the land, was Parodi, and the phase of instability (Servalli, 2006) began, as the fortunes of Fontanafredda began to go downhill.

If, under the leadership of Gastone, the years between 1900–1914 had proved to be those of expansion, "for Fontanafredda the decade from 1920–30 was dominated by financial experts, land speculators and middlemen with the usual entourage of promissory notes, verbal promises, false hopes and scams" (Tablino, 2006, p. 109).

The new owner of Fontanafredda in the next phases, Romualdo Tartara di Tortona, ceded his shares to an engineer from Turin, Mr. Messina. This is how this change in ownership was described:

> in this period trade decreased, there was a great drop in exportation and production, as well as in the workforce [. . .]. Administrative mismanagement, a direct consequence of the complicated events which were taking place, both from a moral and technical point of view, together with a lack of assets.

The article from the magazine *Rivista Le Vie d'Italia* in 1927 continues thus:

> today there is the renaissance of the Società Anonima Mirafiore. All the shares have been recently purchased by a strong group of financial experts that are led by the engineer, Paolo Attilio Messina, a man of exceptional qualities and superb temperament.[30]

However, the trend continued to be negative for the descendants of the royal family. On 18 January 1927 in Alba, Gastone definitively left the company during an extraordinary meeting of "Mirafiore vini italiani." The minutes of the meeting state:

> the vendor, Count of Mirafiori issues a full and final receipt and acknowledges that, as a result of this sales contract, he no longer has any claim to ownership of this property, land or buildings that are part of the Fontanafredda estate.
>
> (Tablino, 2006, p. 111)

Tablino states that Gastone also "burnt some documents before dying: perhaps they held the solution to the many mysteries surrounding Mirafiore's failure?"; this highlights the numerous unanswered questions regarding the disastrous management. Gastone's huge commitment to politics probably played a part: he was elected as a member of parliament in 1913, 1924 and

1929. He then became a senator in 1934, and therefore he had less time to dedicate to running the company.

On 28 January 1929, the chancellor of the Court of Alba issued an injunction for the payment of over 1 million Italian Lire. This sum was too high for the company to pay, so bankruptcy was inevitable. The company was declared bankrupt on 6 December 1930 and the accounting data shows liabilities for the sum of 14,000,105 Italian Lire (Tablino, 2006).

BANKRUPTCY

The sentence by the Court of Cuneo on 24 September 1930 involved the following parties: the Istituto di Credito Fondiario Monte dei Paschi di Siena, the Società Anonima Mirafiori vini Italiani, the Nuova Cassa di Risparmio di Mondovì, the Banca di Mirafiore and the Fratelli Trani, Vittorio Del Piano and Cavallero Natalina. The sentence stated that "the settlement regarding the prices the buildings will be sold at is now open" and "authorisation is given for the public auction of the estate." Following the proposal of the Monte dei Paschi, the assets were divided into two lots, worth 200,000 Italian Lire each. The second lot referred to "Fontana Fredda." All the parties involved agreed to the proposal made by the Monte dei Paschi.

The inventory[31] of the bankruptcy provided an extremely detailed list of all the assets pertaining to the estate, even including "faulty bottles," buildings, the agricultural land and the productive capacity. Information was also given regarding the quality of the wines and potential yield, the mechanical and oenological machinery installed, for a total sum of 3,739,811.30 Italian Lire.

In 1932, Monte dei Paschi purchased the estate, which became part of its assets, whereas the Gancia family, well known in the industry, became the owners of the Mirafiori brand.[32] In fact, on 4 July, the Court of Cuneo recorded the statement of transferral of ownership for the possession of the "estate known as Fontanafredda with the Manor house and annexed buildings for the production, conservation and trade of wines," with a surface area for the Serralunga d'Alba estate of just over 59 hectares.

CONCLUSIONS

The period from the purchase of the Fontanafredda estate, in 1858, until the transferral of ownership to the Monte dei Paschi di Siena, in 1932, represents the most important phase of wine production in Piedmont (Comba, 1994; Berta and Mainardi, 1997; Gambera, 2014) and other more traditional business models that were found in the period of the unification of Italy.

During this period there was a change from a relatively limited capacity of production of poor quality to a substantial amount of wine of a better

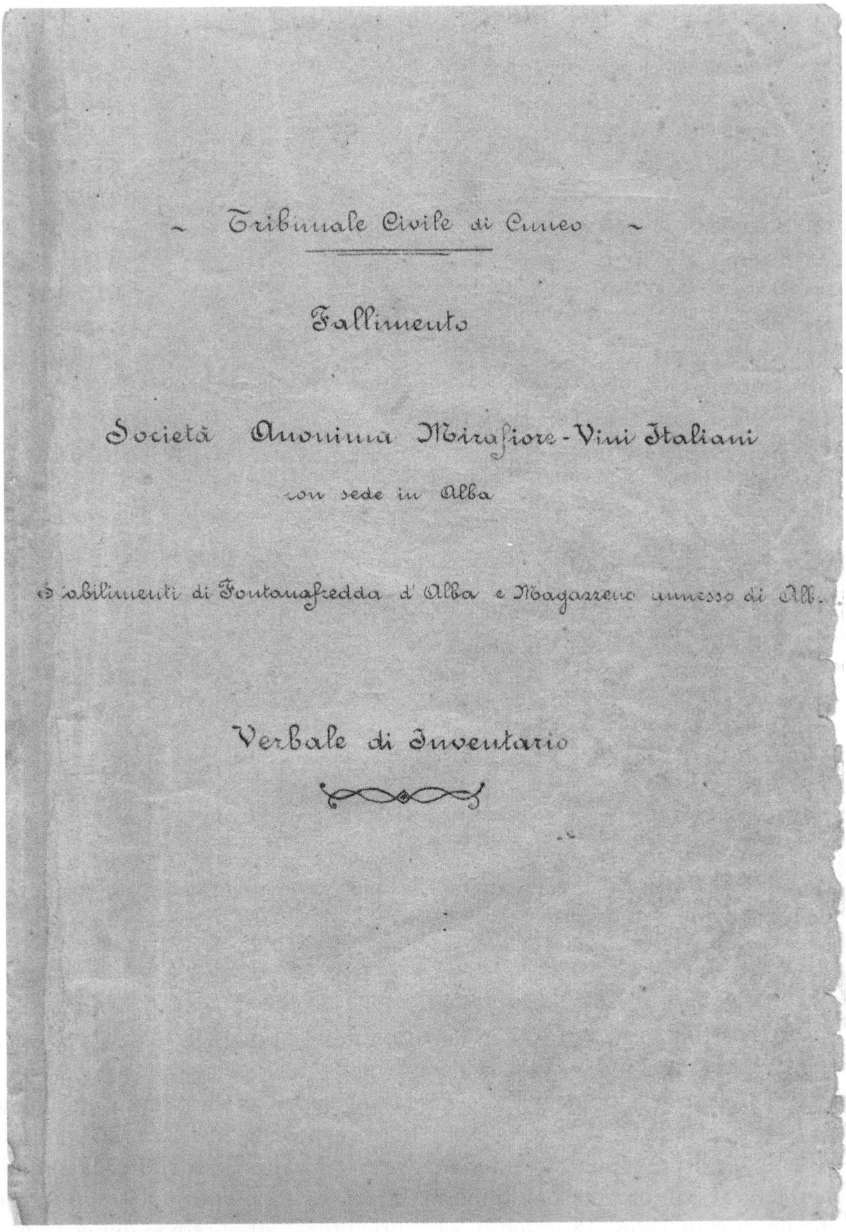

Figure 2.1 Inventory of the bankruptcy

RIASSUNTO D'INVENTARIO

1)	Materiali vari di magazzino e scorte			£	44.106,10
2)	Macchinario			£	62.514,==
3)	Impianti meccanici ed enologici			£	464.300,==
4)	Attrezzi			£	46.543,60
5)	Mobilio			£	121.875,75
6)	Recipienti ed imbelli			£	47.878,30
7)	Botti			£	101.149,95
8)	Vini			£	289.166,30
9)	Bestiame			£	14.647,==
10)	Scorte agrarie			£	15.601,==
11)	Terreni agrari			£	1.380.390,==
12)	Febricati rursli, civili ed indust.			£	1.349.700,==
13)	Gestione Seli e tabacchi			£	2.337,70
14)	Varie			£	470,==
				£	3.940.649,70
	Beni di terzi de detrarre:				
1)	Botti	£	8.822,70		
2)	Vini	£	179.515,70		
3)	Bottiglie	£	12.500,==		
		£	200.838,40	£	200.838,40
	Valore riassuntivo d'inventario				
				£	3.739.811,30

=========
======

Figure 2.2 Inventory of the bankruptcy: final summary/inventory of the bankruptcy: signatures (first part)

quality: "from 38 hl in 1870, in barrels, to 390 hl in 1876, total sales cask wine" (Tablino, 2004, p. 113). This was made possible by the technical and technological development that was taking place at the time in the area, as well as strategies that were being implemented to foster expansion and comply with the structural standards regarding the vines and cellars. One of the pieces of information found in the work of Tablino supports this: for the harvest in 1866, 18 casual wage agricultural labourers employed on a daily basis (Tablino, 2004) were used, whereas in 1878 as many as 58 were required.[33] Therefore the market had increased and was also expanding on an international scale, broadening the image of the brand and increasing sales. At the same time, the reputation of Barolo was increasing greatly, becoming one of the finest wines, acclaimed in Italy and also abroad (Frank, 2010; O' Keefe, 2014).

Il Curatore si rende depositario a norma di Legge dei sopra elencati beni di spettanza del Fallimento.

Nulla essendovi più da inventariare presso gli Stabilimenti di Fontanafredda d'Alba ed annesso Magazzeno di Alba, il presente Verbale viene chiuso alle ore I9 del giorno I7 Gennaio I93I - IX°, dando atto che le operazioni del presente inventario, iniziatesi alle ore I5,30 del giorno 24 Dicembre I930, vennero continuate dal giorno stesso sino ad oggi, dalle ore 8 alle I2 e dalle ore I4 alle I9, con interruzione nei giorni 25 e 29 Dicembre I930 e I Gennaio I93I.

Previa lettura e conferma, il presente Verbale viene sottoscritto in ciascun foglio dagli intervenuti:

Rappr.dei Creditori

Rappr.Ing.Mario Fossati

Amministratore unico

Perito

Curatore

=&=&=&=&=&=&=&=

=&=&=&=&=

=&=

Figure 2.3 Inventory of the bankruptcy: final summary/inventory of the bankruptcy: signatures (second part)

On the other hand, this was a period when negative performances and results were also present due to the close ties between ownership and management, which was geared towards the family-run business model. Here the presence of the royal family was strongly felt, and some of the choices that were taken were not always the right ones from an entrepreneurial point of view.

The changeover to a privately run company, where the expenses were no longer borne by grants from the royal household, together with Gastone's private life, weighed heavily on the company. Its debts became increasingly heavy and eventually led to bankruptcy.

The innovation that was introduced in the productive processes was a positive factor, from a modern point of view. In fact, some of the by-products of the winemaking process at Fontanafredda were added, such as distillation, in particular Cognac and acquavite. However, the generational change (Dell'Atti, 2007; Vallone, 2009) proved to be a negative factor and did not work harmoniously with innovation. This certainly also happened because of external factors and speculation, not just mismanagement.

Even though the history of Fontanafredda did not end positively, it is important to chart the positive factors of the history of the estate and how important it was for the area of the region it represented. A firm must also be judged for its capacity to generate income for the local economy, both directly and indirectly, thanks to a high-profile product that is able to convey the value of a local product on an international market, too. Proof of this combination[34] is provided by Tablino when he describes the management of Gastone and Margherita during the years immediately prior to the bankruptcy: "their main aim" was "to give employment to many people" and the information that follows backs this up: "the rise in employment figures of the firm is surprising, reaching two hundred employees in 1915" (Tablino, 2004, p. 118).

Nowadays, the situation is the same even with the new ownership. There are 153[35] employees and an annual turnover of approximately 9 million euro (production and sale of wine), a sign that the history and tradition of the past are still a fundamental factor in the success of today.

NOTES

1. Dated 24 December 1894 and recorded on 2 January 1895.
2. Dated 24 December 1930.
3. Dated 4 July 1932.
4. The value of the fixed assets was 1,948.04 lire. A total of 8,092.10 lire was spent on cultivation and the vineyards. Further money was spent on cattle, hay and straw (Sovrintendenza Generale del Patrimonio Particolare di S.M. [1810–1865], 10075 [1831–1865] Fontanafredda: Miscellanea).
5. Supplies and work carried out by Gallo Paolo—"*Deconto finale di Fontana Fredda* (1863)—Riassunto Generale delle opere eseguite a Fontana Fredda dal Capo mastro sig. Gallo Paolo di Pollenzo dal 1° gennaio 1862 a tutto giugno

1863" (Ibid., n. 903–1863). [General summary of the works carried out at Fontana Fredda by the master builder, Mr. Gallo Paolo from Pollenzo, from 1 January 1862 until June 1863.]

6. Ibid., p. 68.
7. Sovrintendenza Generale del Patrimonio Privato di S.M. (1866–1887, 1920–1946), 11123 (1872–1878) Documenti contabili relativi alla R. tenuta di Fontanafredda, n. 1044–1873. [Accounting reports relative to Fontanafredda, first quarter.]
8. Fifty items for casual wage agricultural labourers employed on a daily basis, men and women, for a cost of 289.40 lire between 14–27 September.
9. Sig. Giuseppe Icardi, appointed by patent issued 3 April 1876.
10. Sovrintendenza Generale del Patrimonio Privato, n. 1720 dated 1875.
11. Sovrintendenza Generale del Patrimonio Privato, n. 243 dated 1875.
12. Following this request, on 7 June 1875, Icardi replied "regarding the quality, it is entirely wine, of all types and blends" and specifies the amount available.
13. Sovrintendenza Generale del Patrimonio Privato, n. 1901 dated 1875.
14. Dated 16 March 1876.
15. Ancient unit of measure for wine.
16. Sovrintendenza Generale del Patrimonio Privato, n. 1533, dated 20 September, registered on 28 September.
17. Inferior quality was "perfectly normal in those years: science and techniques were a thing of the future" (Tablino, 2004, p. 74), at least throughout 1878. After 1890, an oenologist, Catoni, is recorded to have been working at Fontanafredda.
18. Sovrintendenza Generale del Patrimonio Privato, n. 156 dated 4 October 1875.
19. An example is given by bill number 267 issued by the superintendent on 25 February 1876—similar to many others (a similar document can be found for the months of May through September)—authorizing the expenditure for the month of March upon receipt of an estimate sent by the estate, with a reminder to the administration "to send two copies of the estimate." In fact, the office checked each expense, and either approved it or requested further details before giving the go-ahead. This highlights the degree of attention paid to the management of the resources at Fontanafredda.
20. Tablino (2004, p. 117). Tablino states how right from the start

    > it is difficult to understand how such a transformation took place from a legal point of view, that is to say, from the administration of the private estate of the King [. . .] to a private administration, even if it was carried out by the natural children of the King. [. . .] The matter becomes even more complex in that the entire parcel of land [. . .] was [. . .] made out to the children born from the relationship between the King and Rosa Vercellana. (Ibid., pp. 116–117)

21. City of Alba, average price of grapes sold on the public market in 1875 (31 October).
22. For the year, Tablino indicates a production of 39,000 litres, 2,000 of which were bottled—equal to 2,392 bottles (Tablino (2004), p. 107).
23. Sovrintendenza Generale del Patrimonio Privato, quote.
24. For a sum of 1,470 and 1,029.50 lire, respectively.
25. Another document, the final balance of the year, dated 31 December, states the "note of the sums that remain to be paid due to lack of funds at the Fontanafredda Estate": 1,371.08 lire.
26. Sovrintendenza Generale del Patrimonio Privato, n. 1286 dated 1877. The "receipt for the wine in litres and in bottles given to His Majesty's Guardaroba

from the month of February until 20 September 1877," paid on 12 February 1878, show a sale for the value of 3,179.90 lire.
27. Ibid., n. 1695 dated 14 July 1877.
28. Ibid., n. 902 dated 1877.
29. The letter continues that even "if there should be an error regarding the size of the designated land for a few ares, this shall not hinder the implementation of the entire contract." For the land that at the time was rented, expiring on 11 November, the feast of San Martino, 1879, compensation was found that was deemed to be "fair and justified" for the tenants.
30. *Il progresso dell'industria vinicola italiana*, Rivista mensile del T.C.I. "*Le Vie d'Italia*," April 1927.
31. Società Anonima Mirafiore—Vini Italiani with the headquarters in Alba. Estate of Fontanafredda d'Alba and Magazzeno [*sic*] annexed to Alba.
32. The current management is the new owner of the brand.
33. Tablino (2004, p. 110). Pay is 1 lira per day for the labourers and 0.60–0.70 lira for the women, depending on their age.
34. An interesting letter on the link between firm and territory can be found in Baldarelli et al. (2009).
35. Final balance, year 2014.

REFERENCES

Primary Sources

State Archives in Turin

Inventory Failure Report of the company Anonima Mirafiore—Vini Italiani.
Sovrintendenza Generale del Patrimonio Particolare di S.M. (1810–1865):
———10075 (1831–1865) Fontanafredda: Miscellanea.
———10079 (1816–1875) Pratiche riguardanti affitti, vendite, acquisti e permute di beni immobili tra i privati e la Real Casa.
———10081 (1824–1865) Acquisti e permute in Pollenzo e vicinanze nell'interesse dell'azienda del Patrimonio Particolare di S.M.
Sovrintendenza Generale del Patrimonio Privato di S.M. (1866–1887, 1920–1946):
———11122 (1872–1878) Contabilità delle vigne di Barolo e Fontanafredda.
———11123 (1872–1878) Documenti contabili relativi alla R. tenuta di Fontanafredda.
Statement of transferral of ownership which Fontanafredda received from the Istituto di Credito Fondiario Monte dei Paschi di Siena.
Will of Count Emanuele Guerrieri di Mirafiore e Fontanafredda.

Secondary Sources

Baldarelli, M.G., Ferrone, C. and Medei, R. (2009) Dialogo, Fiducia e reciprocità in economia aziendale: un caso di scuola e prime riflessioni teoriche. *Contabilità e Cultura Aziendale* IX, n. 2.

Berta, P. and Mainardi, G. (1997) *Storia regionale della vite e del vino in Italia. Piemonte*. Milan: Accademia Italiana della Vite e del Vino—Regione Piemonte—Unione Italiana Vini.

Capaldo, P. (2013) *L'azienda. Centro di Produzione*. Milan: Giuffré.

Carosso, V. (1951) *California wine industry: A study of the formative years, 1830–1895*. Berkeley and Los Angeles: University of California Press.

Comba, R. (1994) *Vigne e vini nel Piemonte antico*. Alba: Famija Albeisa.
Coronella, S. (2009) *Agli albori delle ricerche di storia della ragioneria in Italia. Il contributo degli studiosi del XIX secolo*. Rome: Rirea.
Coronella, S. (2014) *Storia della ragioneria italiana. Epoche, uomini, idee*. Milan: FrancoAngeli.
Dell'Atti, A. (2007) *Il passaggio generazionale nelle imprese familiari*. Bari: Cacucci.
Farinetti, G. (2011) *Regina di cuori: la donna che Vittorio Emanuele amò tutta la vita*. Venice: Marsilio,
Frank, M.G. (2010) *Barolo*. Lincoln and London: University of Nebraska Press.
Gambera, A. (2014) *Le colline del Barolo al tempo dello zolfo*. La Morra: Agorà.
Monte dei Paschi di Siena (1953) *Le aziende agricole del Monte dei Paschi di Siena*. Florence-Milan: Electa.
O' Keefe, K. (2014) *Barolo and Barbaresco: The king and queen of Italian wine*. Berkeley: University of California press.
Porter, M.E. (1998) *The competitive advantage of nations*. NewYork: Macmillan.
Sargiacomo, M. (2008) Institutional pressures and isomorphic change in a high-fashion company: The case of Brioni Roman Style, 1945–89. *Accounting, Business & Financial History* 18(2): 215–241.
Servalli, S. (2006) *Fondamenti di economia aziendale*. Turin: Isedi.
Tablino, L. (2004) *Fontanafredda. 125 anni tra vigneti e cantine. Testimonianze, immagini, documenti.*
Tablino, L. (2005). *Fontanafredda. 125 anni tra vigneti e cantine. Immagini e documenti*, MPS Tenimenti s.p.a.
Tablino, L. (2006) *Fontanafredda. 125 anni tra vigneti e cantine (1922–1973). Testimonianze, immagini, documenti*, MPS Tenimenti s.p.a.
Vallone, C. (2009) *Il passaggio generazionale nel family business e i fattori strategici di successo per la continuità aziendale: analisi comparata tra Italia e Gran Bretagna*. Milan: Giuffré.

3 Accounting and Management in the Pasta Industry

The De Cecco Case (1886–1955)

Augusta Consorti, Luciano D'Amico and Massimo Sargiacomo[1]

Maccarone, m'hai provocato e io ti distruggo adesso, maccarone! Io me te magno . . .!

[Maccarone, you have provoked me and now I destroy you, maccarone! I eat you . . .!]

—Alberto Sordi, "An American in Rome," 1954

INTRODUCTION

Despite Italy's undisputed place in the history of pasta civilization, together with China (Rovetta, 1951), and its reputation as a focal point of the dried industrial-made pasta tradition (Serventi and Sabban, 2000), a longitudinal investigation of the business history of Italian pasta producers has been to date neglected in the international accounting and management literature. This regret is even more meaningful if we think that *pasta, macaroni* and/or *vermicelli* are terms that for centuries have permeated the mass popular culture, thus fostering and inculcating a certain habitus of social conviviality among different populations and societies.

Admittedly, the plea raised by Anthony Hopwood on studying "Accounting and Everyday Life" (1994), has triggered works of different authors who have, for example, developed studies on the relations between accounting and the movies (Beard, 1994; Jeacle, 2009), the fashion industry (Jeacle and Carter, 2012), home expense engineering (Walker, 1998, 2003), the beauty industry (Jeacle, 2006) and whisky as a part of popular culture (Jackson et al., 2012). Despite such wealth of research, while there already exist several studies on the broad agribusiness history, like the brewing industry (e.g., Clarke, 1898; Thornton, 1913; Corran, 1981; Gourvish and Wilson, 1985), to the knowledge of the coauthors there are no international accounting or business history case studies regarding well-known pasta enterprises.

With these premises, this chapter seeks to provide a historical analysis of the De Cecco Pasta Italian company. Based on a tradition of superior craftsmanship, the pasta industry has long made an important contribution to the Italian economy. The label "Italian Macaroni" or "Italian Pasta," besides being a part of the popular culture, has always been a source of competitive advantage in the international extra-refined pasta market. The long-standing success of the De Cecco company in the global market has depended on competitive strategies (Porter, 1985, 1987) and entrepreneurial choices undertaken at significant moments by key actors of the De Cecco family in response to environmental opportunities and threats. Starting the pasta production activities in 1886 by the founder Filippo, the joint-stock-company now directed by Filippo Antonio De Cecco represents an iconic brand that embodies the values and aspirations of a group or culture (Kapferer, 2004), and competes in a world market among the top three leading competitors.

The objects of the study are threefold:

1. To highlight the historical early origin of pasta as popular culture, as well as of the much later birth and spread of the pasta industry;
2. To identify the key choices that confronted the senior management of successful Italian extra-refined pasta producers;
3. To conduct a tentative analysis of the internal business and production management, at the same time exploring the ways in which the general partnership since before World War I had already organized its sales and distribution management both in Italy and beyond.

The chapter thus seeks to address the portrayed lacunas by drawing on a range of primary sources to explore the birth and development of the De Cecco Pasta company, focusing the analysis in the 1886–1955 time span.

These objects of investigation are developed in the chapter through an extensive review of internal company archival material and a variety of secondary sources. Primary sources located at Fara San Martino company historical archive include, but are not limited to: the founding deeds of incorporations stipulated by notaries in Casoli 1914, 1924 and later in 1927; Fara San Martino and Chieti town historical archives; the cadastral and architectural plans of Fara and Pescara factories; invoices, 1914–1951; registers of money orders and cheques, 1937–1941; letters, 1914–1925; 1936–1938; cash register (scattered years), 1938–1939; clients data sheet, 1939–1940; register of manufacturing accounts, 1905–1928; register of expenses and sales, 1938–1941; registers of wages, scattered years until 1957. Primary data has also been collected on the Register and Bulletin of the Chamber of Commerce of Pescara, at the National Institute of Statistics (Istituto Nazionale di Statistica), High Commission for Nutrition (Alto Commissariato dell'Alimentazione). The results of our searches are analyzed through interpretative lenses and narrated as a case study (Yin, 2014).

In order to pursue the research objectives, this chapter is organized as follows. The next section portrays the social and economic scenario of post-unification Italy. The subsequent section provides additional contextualization, unveiling the early origin and diffusion of pasta popular culture, and the much later nineteenth-century birth and spread of the pasta industry until the 1950s. The following section highlights both the launch of the new venture in the late nineteenth century, and the entrepreneurial role played by the founding key actors, as well as the continuous will to maintain the guidance and governance of the company firmly in the hands of the broad De Cecco family. The section thereafter unveils the company's pasta production, by analyzing the Fara and Pescara premises as portrayed by pictures and incorporation deeds, at the same illustrating the accounting, financial and labor evidences provided by the surviving accounts. The penultimate section elucidates the sales management of the company, mainly by analyzing the content of the letters of the company to sales agent in Italy and in the world—and especially in the United States—and at the same time using the information contained in the registers of money orders and cheques, as well as in the invoices. Concluding observations and opportunities for further research are outlined at the end of the chapter.

THE MAIN FEATURES OF POSTUNIFICATION ITALY

Italy's economy after the unification was in serious difficulty. Industrialization had not yet become extensive, with the exception of some northern regions, located inside the so-called industrial triangle: Lombardy, Piedmont and Liguria. In the year of unification (1861), despite the earlier birth of Ansaldo (1853), Italy had produced about 30,000 tonnes of iron and cast iron, versus the roughly four million tonnes of Great Britain, one million tonnes of France and 600,000 tonnes of Germany. The country's economy was mainly based on agriculture, trading and craftsmanship but huge differences between the north and the south emerged over time. The economy of the south still remained mainly tied to the management of "latifundium." The differences in wealth between the different regions became more and more clear (Ciccarelli and Fenoaltea, 2010).

The (slow) growth of the Italian industry was favoured by an economic policy marked by the intervention and the protection of industry by the government. From the 1870s, the State started financing industry and adopting customs protection measures. This fostered heavy industry and the big agricultural concerns that grew cereals, but harmed the rest of the agricultural world that was based on specialized cultures. The first ones were mostly located in the north, the others in the south. In 1900, the production of iron and cast iron reached 190,000 tonnes (Fenoaltea, 2002).

Although the peninsula was now formally united from a social and political perspective, socially and culturally it was not. "We have made Italy. Now we must 'make' the Italians" (D'Azeglio, 1899, preface) was the very famous quote by Massimo D'Azeglio that became a must, especially at the end of the 1880s. In the scenario, in 1875, emigration started to achieve big data. Until the end of the century, it almost entirely involved emigrants from the north (Dingelstedt, 1910).

Italy's economy in the early twentieth century was still mainly agricultural, but the Italian industrial revolution was quickly becoming a reality in the north (especially in the textile, chemical and engineering and metal working industries) (Toniolo, 1977). The gap between the north and south (still largely based on agricultural latifondism and small handicraft businesses) was widening, as almost only northern Italy was experiencing significant industrial development. The most renowned companies established in this period were: Cartiere Burgo (1905); Lancia (1905); Alfa Romeo (1906); Italcementi (1906); Falck's Acciaierie and Ferriere Lombarde (1906); and Dalmine (1906). Important companies established earlier continued to thrive as well, such as Pirelli (1872), Edison (1884), Breda (1886), Montecatini (1888) and Fiat (1899) (Ciccarelli and Fenoaltea, 2010).

Italy was definitely going through hard times from the social and political point of view. The phenomenon of emigration, which had already started in the last 20 years of the nineteenth century (De Michelis, 1925), progressively intensified. However, starting in the twentieth century, emigration almost only involved people from the south (Foerster, 1924). In the early twentieth century, the government started implementing a policy aimed at increasing public works, reclamation and road works in the south of the country, also by granting tax reductions and empowering agricultural credits. In those years, railways were put under State control (Fenoaltea, 1970), the first modern labour law reform was passed (holidays, prohibition of night work for women and children, etc.) and the State monopoly on life insurance was enforced.

In the next section we will briefly portray the early diffusion and spread of pasta popular culture, as well the birth of the Italian pasta industry, which will be embedded in the earlier illustrated postunification Italian scenario.

THE DIFFUSION OF PASTA POPULAR CULTURE AND THE BIRTH OF THE ITALIAN PASTA INDUSTRY

Admittedly, the history of pasta consumption dates back many millennia. Early signs of the handmade pasta fabrication and consumption can be found in China at least around 3800 B.C. (see Houyuan et al., 2005). In Italy, the presence of pasta makers is partially documented since the start of the second millennium, as provided by inscriptions and figures in tombs (e.g., the Etrurian "Grotta Bella" tomb at Cerveteri), as well as by the content of different notary deeds (e.g., Genova State Archive, twelfth century, notarius Giovanni Scriba; see Laurioux, 1995, p. 205). Well-known philosophers like Cicero(ne), or later Horace (Orazio), often hinted at the Latin *laganum*, corresponding to the actual "lasagna" (Serventi and Sabban, 2000, p. 33).

Clearer startling evidences of the presence of pasta in Italian culture and society are recorded in the fourteenth century, when—for example—Boccaccio in his *Decameron* was already talking about "macaroni" (i.e., first page of the third novel in the "Eighth Day"chapter). Importantly, in the same century the *laganum* preparation was portrayed by Marco Gavio Apicio—a well-known Latin philosopher and culinary expert—in his book entitled *De re coquinaria*, which is considered the first book ever written on culinary instructions and tradition (Andre, 1974). Records and figures of women preparing "vermicelli" pasta are also enshrined in the fourteenth century "Tacuinum Sanitatis" (Cogliati Arano, 1979, pp. 86, 138). Importantly, it is in the fourteenth and fifteenth centuries that in several Italian cities like Rome, Naples, Savona, Milan and Palermo, there appeared the first corporations of Italian pasta makers (i.e., Corporazioni di Pastai Italiani), which were supposed to protect and defend the rights of pasta makers and bakeries, thus unquestionably witnessing how pasta was already considered a part of the Italian culture and society. Subsequent corporations, and respective statutes, appeared in the sixteenth century, like the Neapolitan "Arte dei Vermicellari," and were later renamed into "Arte dei Maccaronari" (Majetti, 1885). With these premises, not surprisingly, day by day, terms like pasta, macaroni and vermicelli (and much later spaghetti) began to enter the mass popular culture.

Despite these early clues, it is unanimously considered that the pasta industry—as identified by industrial production process and sale—had not been launched before the nineteenth century (Rovetta, 1951, p. 9), where—as said in the preceding section—most of Italian industries began to develop. Indeed, it was the drying of pasta the main issue that limited the possibility of entrepreneurs to fabricate and sell pasta on a continuous commercial basis, especially in locations where bad, cold weather conditions were prevailing, thus being not favorable for pasta desiccation and conservation (Ceschina, 1907). The Neapolitan lands, Liguria, Sicily and Abruzzi, were the best emergent sites for pasta fabrication, and this fostered also the launch of the Italian industry of pasta machinery (D'Onofrio, 1924; Rovetta, 1951, p. 15).

In postunification Italy, pasta acquired an even more distinctive symbolic social and unifying value, and therein, echoing those times, a well-known commentator argued:

> Our country is a collection of population. But when lunch time is stricken, the Peninsula inhabitants, seated in front of a spaghetti dish, recognize themselves as Italians. Neither the military service, nor the universal suffrage, exert an equal unifying power . . . Italy's unification, dreamt by our Renaissance's father, now it is called pastasciutta.
>
> (Marchi, 1990, p. 77)

With the explosion of emigration from Italy, especially in the fourth quarter of the nineteenth century the number of pasta-eaters were improving outside Italy, thus fostering the numbers of consumers, at least in the many "Little Italy" neighborhoods located in many pivotal cities in the U.S. (e.g., New York, Boston, Philadelphia) and elsewhere. Italians emigrants making pasta were already present in the U.S. at least in the second quarter of the nineteenth century, as Antonio Zerega founded the A. Zerega & Sons company, which is said to be the first pasta establishment in the U.S. (Carleton, 1901, p. 19). The increasing number of Italian emigrants at the end of the nineteenth century fostered increasing demand for pasta abroad, and a kind of verbal propaganda, although Italian emigrants were usually associated to bad social stereotypes constructed in different languages around words like *Maccaronì*, *Pastar*, *Pasta-eater*, *Spaghettifresser*, *Espaguetis* and so forth. The so-called Mangia-Pasta, or pasta-eater, or the equivalent concept in other languages, was always a pejorative nickname, either associating Italian emigrants with a social class of poor consumers or identifying them with members of the mafia families (e.g., think to "Sopranos eat your manicotti" in the well-known television series).

When, at the end of the nineteenth century, it was clear that pasta was incredibly well known in the U.S., whose territories have also to defend the production and sale of wheat and their own pasta establishments, American trade associations aptly tried to reverse the stereotype of the bad pasta consumer into an elitist group of consumers, promoting its culture and diffusion. Therein, it is interesting to note the birth of the National Association of Macaroni and Noodle Manufacturers of America in 1904, which was later renamed into the National Pasta Association (NPA) (Donna, 1946, p. 15). Importantly, they also later launched the *Macaroni Journal*, published by an American-Canadian association of entrepreneurs. Indeed, they used romantic stories through comic strips and cartoons to sustain the cultivation of wheat, at the same time emphasizing the concept of pasta as elitist international food, thus fuelling the building of a new culture, and eliminating the old ideas connected to Italian ghettos diffused in foreign cities.

Before World War I, in 1913, there was the best-ever record of Italian pasta export, which nearly reached 71 million kg; on the contrary, in 1928 they cascaded down to 1.2 million kg (Rovetta, 1929, p. 17). Indeed, the interwar period, and the Italian fascist political protectionist economy, had limited the export of wheat and pasta for national consumption, thus fuelling the internal production of competing countries, such as the U.S., which in 1929 boasted already 550 establishments (Rovetta, 1929), 377 of which had an industrial dimension, according to the U.S. Department of Commerce (Carr, 1932, p. 7).

The block of food-producing exports ended after 1945;not surprisingly, immediately after World War II the Italian production and sale of pasta skyrocketed again (Portesi, 1957). Indeed, the production capacity of Italian pasta enterprises more than doubled in a 17-year period, shifting from 569,700 tonnes of pasta in 1936, to 1,374,500 tonnes in 1953–1954 (Alto Commissariato dell'Alimentazione, 1953).

This improvement of production capacity was sustained by a flourishing pasta industry, which was made up by a widespread number of establishments located in different regions, and employing a good number in the workforce, as portrayed by Table 3.1.

Table 3.1 Establishments and employees per region and macro-region in 1951

	Establishments per region and macro-region 1951		Employees per region and macro-region 1951	
	N	%	N	%
Northern Italy	877	39.0	8618	33.8
Central Italy	349	15.5	5272	20.6
Southern Italy	1023	45.5	11630	45.6
Total	2249	100.0	25520	100.0
Abruzzo-Molise	171	16.7	1128	9.7
Basilicata	6	0.6	47	0.4
Calabria	31	3.0	756	6.5
Campania	164	16.0	4454	38.3
Puglia	104	10.2	1535	13,2
Sardegna	43	4.2	651	5.6
Sicilia	504	49.3	3059	26.3
Southern Italy	1023	100,0	11630	100.0

Source: National Institute of Statistics, 1951.

Importantly, the great improvement recorded by pasta factories was led not only by export requests, but also by domestic production. Indeed, by 1955, annual consumption of spaghetti in Italy doubled from 14 kg (30.9 lbs.) per person before World War II to 28 kg (61.7 lbs.) (Salerno, 1956). Accordingly, by the mid-1950s Italy had reassumed its position as the world's top pasta producer (Serventi and Sabban, 2000, p. 257).

More than ever before, pasta in the mass popular culture meant an occasion of conviviality, thus acting as a joining conductor of different members of the same family nuclei, friends, people at work or on holidays. Relatedly, the tragedy of World War II had offered to all the world the views of the beauties of Italy, pasta included, thus increasing the attractiveness of Italian products in the world.

NEW VENTURING, ENTREPRENEURSHIP AND FAMILY GOVERNANCE

New Venturing and Entrepreneurship

When, on 20 May 1886, the 32-year old Filippo Di Cecco[2] went to declare the birth of his daughter Annantonia in front of the Fara San Martino town officer (Fara Town Archive), he declared himself to be a "pastaio"—that is, a "pasta maker" or "pasta entrepreneur"—thus officially witnessing at least the first year of industrial pasta activities (Certificate of birth of Annantonia De Cecco, 1886). We therefore argue that several endogenous and external factors presided over the decision of the De Cecco founding father Filippo to be a "pasta maker" at least from 1886, given that in the preceding years he always stated that he was a "miller." First, although Abruzzi was a rural region boasting one of the worst industrial outputs in postunification Italy (Sabatini, 1996), it showed a strong concentration of activities and employees occupied in the food industry, most of which were activities organized as artisanal laboratories (Archivio Storico Industria Italiana, 1895; Paolini, 1996). Second, the stimuli provided by the 1884 abolishment of the prior 1868 tax on wheat milled, triggered throughout Italy an impetus towards new pasta ventures (Sabatini, 1996). Third, and undoubtedly, the De Cecco family already owned a mill (bought in 1878), and Filippo was working as a miller. Accordingly, he was asked to extend his prior existing experiences to "pasta industrial entrepreneur," having already in his hands the "milling pipeline," synergies and working experiences. Fourth, the localization at Fara San Martino—and the "genius loci" there connected—was pivotal both for the richness of raw materials and for its proximity to the Verde River, which permitted the exploitation of hydro-energy.

This latter point held pivotal importance for the pasta factory for a number of reasons. Indeed, while hydro-energy was already used in Abruzzi, especially in the wool industry, Filippo Di Cecco was already exploiting it for the mill, and beginning in 1907 he would be involved in an energy venture.[3] This revealed to be an incredible advantage in order to provide power to the factory and support production. Indeed, the location of Fara San Martino could not be considered "strictly convenient" for the moist mountain weather, which rendered more difficult the pasta drying, which in most factories in South Italy was done under the sun. On the contrary, the presence of the hydro-energy allowed the development of new hot-air drying facilities—whose patent was ascribed to Filippo Di Cecco in 1889 (Treccani Encyclopedia, 1935; Serventi and Sabban, 2000, p. 191)—as well as to fuel the kneader and press pasta machines. Relatedly, hydro-energy allowed the subsequent industrial development that generally affected the Italian pasta making industry (Rovetta, 1951). Importantly, through De Cecco's localization in Penne, with the increasing prosperity of the company, both it and the town began to flourish. There developed the birth and growth of a "company town" relationship, similar to that portrayed within nineteenth-century British literature, such as the growth of the cotton industry in the Oldham district (see, e.g., Smith, 1962; Hunt and Garr, 1985).

If the new production cycle needed a few years to be ameliorated and obtain high-quality pasta, much of the entrepreneurial attention was also devoted to the search of new national and foreign markets. Undoubtedly, the national and international industrial exhibitions, which started in the eighteenth century as technical competitions, became increasingly important during the nineteenth century, both as reviews of the production activities of a country and, from the business point of view, to attract public attention to the award-winning products. They became the best opportunities to compete with the market, to get out of localism and provincialism. They were an opportunity for businesses to meet traders, to know and be known, to launch their products on the international market, to compare the quality of their goods with those of competitors. Exhibitions were set up in all parts of the world and enjoyed extraordinary success with their visitors.

The first exhibition in which De Cecco participated as a pasta producer was held in L'Aquila (Italy) in 1888, and he received a bronze medal (Clementi, 1998, pp. 215–217). There were many industrial exhibitors—784 from the provinces of Abruzzo—but the vast majority of them were small craft firms. It is no exaggeration to call it a disappointing event. In 1892, at the National Exhibition held in Palermo, the founder Filippo Giovanni was awarded the silver medal. In 1893, De Cecco was in Rome, where he received a gold medal, for the exhibition of industrial progress. It was evidenced by an article in the weekly magazine entitled *I 3 Abruzzi* dated 1 May 1893. It is said that at the exhibition of Rome, long and small pasta manufactured by De Cecco were likely to go unnoticed to the public accustomed to luxury and major equipment because they were placed in a small window, with a simple sign with the printed name of the producer. Nevertheless, in the same year, a much more important opportunity was given to the young pasta Italian producer, as Chicago was celebrating the fourth centenary of the discovery of America in 1892–1893, and organized a major World's Fair. Filippo De Cecco decided to participate, and shipped a few boxes of pasta from the port of Naples. At the fair, the De Cecco's "macaroni" and "vermicelli" received a gold medal and the Diploma of Merit "for superior manufacture, color, and firmness of form after cooking."[4]

This was followed, again in 1893, by the Grand Diploma of Honor and Gold Cross at the World's Fair held in Monaco. The fame of pasta from Fara San Martino was consolidated. In 1894, it received a Gold Medal in San Francisco (California). In 1898, the general Italian Fair was held from April to October in Turin to commemorate the fiftieth anniversary of the Statuto Albertino. Again, Mr. De Cecco did not remain empty-handed, as he received the Bronze Medal and the corresponding Diploma. At the turn of the century, then, Filippo De Cecco presented his pasta in numerous national and international exhibitions. Again in 1898, in Hamburg, he received a Diploma and Gold Medal, and later in 1903 in L'Aquila the Grand Diploma of Honor. The growing reputation and celebration of Pasta De Cecco culminated with the decoration received by the founder Filippo De Cecco in 1905 as Knight of the Order of Labor, thus witnessing the entrepreneurship of a pasta producer whose knowledge surely left the limited municipal boundaries and disseminated its "macaroni" well out of the region where it was based, and also at an international level.

The Establishment of Family Governance through General Partnerships

Considering the paramount success that the pasta producer began to achieve at the start of the twentieth century, it is not surprising that Filippo De Cecco, aiming at regularizing his entrepreneurial activity, decided to establish a general partnership (S.n.C.) at the end of 1914. The analysis of primary sources many years after the business was established suggests that several reasons motivated this step. Initial motivation came from the need for his sons' participation, some of whom began to play a significant role in the management of activities. The eldest, Saturnino, was 37 years old and managed the business of the pasta factory in full autonomy with his father, as reported by documents in the company's files. A de facto, but formally irregular, company involved great limits and did not correspond to the cases of trade regulations. This does not mean that it could not operate, as the legislation provided the opportunity to establish a business with no written and official contract support. In simple words, in order to get a complete management discipline, it was necessary for the business to have a registered and legally valid incorporation. Indeed, the Commercial Code of 1882 was introduced precisely to fill (it would be more correct to use the word "refine") this legislative gap of the Italian Civil Code of 1865, by introducing four different company organizations in their formal aspects and content: S.n.C. (general partnership), S.a.S. (simple limited partnership), S.a.A. (partnership limited by shares) and S.A. (public limited company). To give a practical example to understand the peculiarities of the different organizations, all members of a general partnership would be unlimitedly accountable for all debts, while the members of a simple limited partnership would be accountable only to the extent of their contribution. This explains the second reason: the founder demanded accountability of his children in the business.

A third set of explanations must be sought in the growth of De Cecco factories. In the late nineteenth century, the production volume remained stable at 150 kg daily, saturating local consumption, while with the acceleration of business contacts with foreign countries that figure increased. It is easy to understand that it was no longer feasible to continue an activity with limited rules at most. A simple partnership, although actually established, could not carry out any business. The final reason identified is much more practical. In case the founder passed away, the next generation would have stumbled into red tape to protect their rights, as any legal act of succession was missing, until that day. In practice, only with the foundation of the general partnership Cav. Filippo De Cecco & figli (Knight of the Order of Labor Mr. Filippo De Cecco and his sons) could the next generation ensure protection of their interests.

On 31 December 1914, in Lama dei Peligni, in the office of lawyer Giuseppe Cocco, located in Largo del Mercato 5, the notary Esculapio De Cinque drew up the Deed of Incorporation of the general partnership

Cavalier Filippo Di Cecco & figli. The document of the Deed of Incorporation, enshrined in the company archive, is divided into two complementary parts of 23 pages. The first seven pages describe a donation of goods and are followed by the actual Deed of Incorporation consisting of nine pages and forming the first part of it. The last pages (17 to 23, the second part attached) are the valuation of buildings and equipment mentioned in the pages of the donation and, until then, the exclusive property of Mr. De Cecco. Before a notary and two witnesses there were the entrepreneur Filippo De Cecco and all his sons: Saturnino, Giuseppe, Onofrio, Giovanni and Adolfo. Although all defined as "industrial" businessmen, Adolfo was not 21 years old and thus underage. He had to be authorized, as confirmed by the documentation, by the magistrate of Lama dei Peligni on 14 November of the previous year. This latter information confirmed that, at least from the previous year, Filippo De Cecco began to think of a corporate act and donation, since the authorizations for his underage son were obtained in advance. In a related manner, this conforms to the introductory hypotheses about the importance and protection of the new generation, which was fully employed in the family industry. The name "industrial entrepreneur" used for all the sons further confirms this, and in the development in size of the factory, which was going to be industrially organized due to the increasing demand. Mr. De Cecco said he wanted to donate half of all property described in the document to all his children; soon after, the reason for the deed was described, thus confirming all that was analyzed earlier.

Far from being interpreted as an investiture from above, the words of the founder emphasize the responsibility, results and active role of the past, present and future of the second generation of entrepreneurs, with the hope of exceeding and enhancing the performance achieved until that moment. The confirmation of these intentions is offered at the end of the donation, in which the working capital consisting of pasta, flour, semolina, bran, wheat, receivables and cash is excluded from the donation. This suggests that it was the will of the father Filippo that in his sons, the immediate availability of cash and receivables, might have fomented the desire to leave and spend what had already been collected.[5]

In the deed of foundation of the company there are 20 rules, whose main points will be now summarized. The first item, the corporate purpose, reports the manufacture of pasta products, production of flour and semolina, and their wholesale and retail sale. The name of the company Cavalier Filippo Di Cecco & figli and consolidation of the plant in Fara San Martino follow. However, they are followed by the hope and vision about all branches to be established in Italy and abroad, revealing a strong will of expansion over three decades, given the term of the company set from 6 January 1915 to 31 December 1944. The regulation of rights on corporate signature is the scope of the third item. In this case, exclusivity belongs to Mr. De Cecco who, however, will not make any use of it in any business unrelated to the company. As concerns the delegation of corporate signature, the next item sets precise rules—that is, any operation, whether performed by proxy, may not exceed 1,000 Italian Lire; otherwise, a specific authorization from the second delegated shareholder is required. The fifth item establishes the lack of compensation to the managing partner and its delegates.

Importantly, through an operation that we might label a "liability operation," Mr. De Cecco established his own limitation in all matters of buying and selling of real estate, machinery, and signing of all contracts with terms exceeding one year. Unanimous consent was required for this type of operation, considering that the managing partner of the company, Mr. De Cecco (as a sort of sole CEO), was entitled to five votes, and each of his sons had one vote. For important decisions, the unanimity rule was in force, while for ordinary issues absolute majority was accepted. In case of a tie, the decision was made by the senior partner. Seniority, defined as greater responsibility and experience, will always have a prominent place in the company. Proceeding with the eighth item, after deciding that the share capital amounted to 230,982.28 Italian Lire as total assets described in the donation, the roles and obligations in the company were regulated.

Another interesting aspect that deserves attention is about profits and losses: the division will take place in the shares due (five-tenths and one-tenth per child). The legislation allowed operating in different ways, but the will remained firm on the fair division of duties and honors. In fact, in case Mr. De Cecco passed away, the company would have continued with the remaining five children. From that moment, all the decisions, profits and losses would be of their exclusive interest (item 13). In the last part of the contract (items 20 and 21), two rules of merit and demerit are explained, which clearly summarize the general spirit in which the founder decided to expand the company. Work, commitment, sacrifice, merit and accountability are the pillars that support the entire corporate system, thanks to the work of the founder Mr. De Cecco who wanted to define them clearly in an official document.

The passing of the reins to Filippo's sons is recorded on 22 August 1924, when some modifications were introduced to the prior incorporation deed. Indeed the company's name shifted from Cav. Filippo De Cecco & figli (Knight of the Order of Labor Mr. Filippo De Cecco and his sons) to F.lli De Cecco di Filippo Fara San Martino snc (De Cecco Brothers [sons] of Filippo, general partnership [located in] Fara San Martino). The change in the company name mirrored more equity in the distribution of votes among Filippo and his sons, thus ensuring a smooth generational transition from of the founding father to his sons.

Moreover, the merger of the towns of Pescara and Castellamare Adriatico, and the constitution of the Province of Pescara, paved the way to the launch of a new company, "La Società Anonima Molino De Cecco Pescara" (i.e., Anonymous partnership De Cecco Mill, Pescara), made up by the De Cecco brothers—Saturnino, Giuseppe, Onofrio, Giovanni and Adolfo, all acting as co-CEOs—and headed by the old Filippo. The new venture boasted 5 million Italian Lire as share capital and was located close to the railway station named "Porta Nuova"; its act was stipulated at Filippo's house in Fara San Martino on 18 January 1927[6] (i.e., notaries archives of Casoli-Lama dei Peligni), a few weeks after the proclamation of the new Pescara province. Thus, on one hand, this marked a new pivotal step of the De Cecco success, while on the other hand, the opening of a new company, with a new factory, proved important for the Province of Pescara as an economic and trade center from then onwards. The aforementioned pasta production premises at Fara and Pescara, and their respective bookkeeping systems, will be portrayed in the next section.

THE PASTA PRODUCTION PREMISES IN FARA SAN MARTINO AND PESCARA

Admittedly, the industrial climate in which the founder of the company operated was influenced by a permanent technical evolution in order to increase production volumes and profits (Rovetta, 1951) on the one hand, while enriching and expanding the pasta market beyond the local area on the other to the. Accordingly, all the operations carried out by Filippo De Cecco between the end of the nineteenth century and early twentieth century followed two related and interdependent directions, which unfolded their strength in the following decades. The attention of the founder to production management and the experience gained in the choice of raw materials is tangible from the earliest years. The same can be said about the broad area of sales management and advertising of the company. In this section we will provide an analysis of the former, and in the next section we will discuss the latter.

In the 1914 incorporation deed, after the presentations of the contracting parties and some cadastral information, the properties of Mr. De Cecco were listed, consisting of real estate and industrial equipment; these were then listed specifically in the report. The founder stated he owned an industrial plant used as a mill and pasta factory. He emphasized how he exploited the waters of the Verde River to obtain hydro-energy (the plant was driven by hydraulic power by channeling river water on the right bank, where the plant was located in a single block of buildings). It is no coincidence that in a list of the most important equipment, the first to appear was a hydraulic turbine, which was able to produce 130 horsepower.[7]

In describing the factory as a whole, we note that it was composed of three buildings, each with an intended use, but also interdependent. Figure 3.1 shows an image of the two main parts, on the right and left of the road, separated by a bridge, as described in the document.

The group of three buildings forming the entire plant is thus described in the incorporation deed. The first, the largest of the three, had four levels: a basement containing the turbines, dynamos and pulleys for the generation

Figure 3.1 Postcard showing the De Cecco premises at the start of the twentieth century

Source: De Cecco folder: cadastral and architectural plans of Fara San Martino premises; various documentation of different years (De Cecco company archive at Fara San Martino)

of electricity; the first level, with three wide rooms containing the mixers, kneaders, presses and other equipment needed for production of pasta, as well as other machines for adjustment of power and thermal needs of the plant (regulating turbines and boilers); a second level with five rooms used to warehouse, store and dry the pasta; and the third level with four rooms only for drying by electric fans. The second building, smaller in terms of square footage, was used as a mill and had five levels: a basement with loading channels; a ground floor with machinery to process flour; and three additional levels including an attic for milling work. The third building contained a basement and three floors for storage and drying of pasta. The total area described covered 2,730.10 square meters with an estimated value of 1,365.05 Italian Lire; the addition of the buildings and real estate brought the total value to 111,622.28 Italian Lire.

By analyzing the list of equipment, we can get an idea of the company's production capacity in the first and second decades of the twentieth century. The four double-chamber presses had a capacity of 40–50 kg, and the reaction turbine could generate 130 horsepower. The 16 electric drying fans, along with the three machines described earlier—the most expensive ones at the time—indicate that the volume of production increased since the end of the nineteenth century. Importantly, primary sources suggest that in 1916 the founding father sent a request to Ministry of Public Works, asking for a new authorization for the diversion of the Verde River in order to increase the power yield to 262 horsepower. This being said, assuming that the four presses worked at least 10 daily cycles, we arrive very quickly to the estimation in a few years of a daily capacity of 30 tons of pasta.

Unfortunately, we have not found precise surviving evidences on the production cycle, but as it was already supposed, it is possible to consider the aforementioned estimation of the 1920s, considering that World War I did not damage the plant but only slowed down its activities. The estimated value of all separate equipment, including the machinery of the pasta factory, machine shop, furniture, mill and semolina mill, flour production department and all ancillary machines was 119,360 Italian Lire, which when added to the previous real estate estimation, is the company's capital of 230,982.28 Italian Lire described earlier in the items of the deed of incorporation.

As said in the third section, while the Italian international pasta export trade was damaged by the economic downturn caused by the Great War, the De Cecco company's pathway to success seemed not to be slowed down too much by this external major factor. Indeed, a new De Cecco partnership factory opened in 1927, and according to primary sources the new venture closed its first financial year with a balance of 350,000 Italian Lire. Figure 3.2 offers an image of the huge six-floor Pescara plant, which at

Figure 3.2 The six-floor Pescara plant of the Società Anonima Molino De Cecco, from 1920

Source: Relazione Statistica sull'andamento economico della provincia durante l'anno 1929, con riferimento agli anni precedenti, Consiglio e Ufficio Provinciale dell'Economia di Pescara (Pescara, 1930, pp. 108–109)

the start of 1930s was already said to daily manage 60 tons of wheat. It later produced about 12 tons of pasta, which were addressed to national and international markets. The incorporation deed, stipulated with the Act n. 251, 18 January 1927, again in Casoli—like the 1914 Fara one, but by the notary Nicola Travaglini—reveals that the Pescara premises also included wide rooms leading to the market, considering also that the new plant was in front of the railway station of "Pescara Porta Nuova."

The accounting system for the two factories was not sophisticated. The archives of the company reveal rudimentary bookkeeping for the exchange of items on cash or credit, as well as for recording sales and expenses. For example, there are lists of debtors and creditors; very detailed cash reports; registers of salaries; and some reports on a charge and discharge inventory system. A certain attention on cash and credit is also suggested by the evidences provided by the register of money orders and cheques, by the data sheets compiled per each client, as well as by the cash registers and invoices. On the contrary, there is no clear evidence of accountings for individuals, groups or activities. In fact the archival sources suggest an absence of costing and productivity artifacts.

Nevertheless, the surviving 1905–1928 register of manufacturing accounts shows great attention was devoted to the debit credit/movements of wheat, coarse-grained products, pasta, packaging, transports and brans, thus highlighting the most important product accounts, together with personnel. The absence of accounting for individuals, for groups or for spaces is witnessed by the manpower accounts, where there are no traces of a disciplinary gratification-punishments apparatus, or accounting for precise pipeline teams in the manufacturing supply chain, but rather items that underline that a certain sum "has been paid to the workers at the end of February," or March, April, etc.

World War II brought great destruction to both the Fara San Martino and Pescara factories that at that time employed about 600 people. Indeed, the Journal of the Pescara Chamber of Commerce reported that in the 1943 the German occupation caused damage to the factories:

> Fara San Martino premises, including the electric energy power station, were firstly stripped of machines, devices and stocks, and later fully devastated by fires and mines . . . At Pescara everything was ravaged, and whilst nothing was possible to salvage from the pasta factory, 60% of the mill machines was recovered. . . . After the Liberation, executives and employees, coming down from the mountains were they sought refuge from the Nazi, immediately started the reconstruction works.
> (1947, p. 95)

The journal then warmly concludes that

> Today, the re-building endeavours, always animated by the determined and painstaking initiative of the De Cecco's family, has reached a good

> point; nevertheless, there is still much to do in order to bring back the factories to ancient splendour. The De Cecco hard-working spirit, the harmony that has always reigned between executives and workers, together with the hope to have a better future, are surely early clues of a prompt, complete and brilliant upswing.
>
> (1947, p. 95)

De Cecco's spirit succeeded in rebuilding the factories and reinforcing production management, paving the way to other successes achieved in the subsequent decades. Nevertheless, the increase in production volumes highlighted in this section, as well as the funding and building of a new huge factory in Pescara, ought to be matched with the capability of being on the market, otherwise failure would be everyday around the corner. By understanding this basic principle and assuming that his market had not to be confined to the local area, Mr. De Cecco and his sons were to be known at the national and international levels.

SALES AND DISTRIBUTION MANAGEMENT

As said earlier, after the unification of Italy, in fact, and as the historical research has revealed, few were the points of reference that—according to Massimo D'Azeglio—were supposed to unite the north with the south of the country, that is, military service, public education and religion. Nevertheless, recent behavioral and cultural strands of research on mass consumption (Capuzzo, 2006) have tended to highlight the role played by pasta in social grouping processes. How can we argue that pasta did not contribute to the Italian culture and, by extension, to the unity of ideals and nation of Italy? The tradition of pasta consumption remains thoroughly embedded in the Italian society from Milan to Palermo, and it is certainly not a coincidence that the spread of pasta factories has occurred according to a patchy distribution, ignoring the economic framework conditions of the individual parts of Italy.

Moreover, the food "language" was one of the strong items that characterized and united the Italian communities both in Italy and abroad. Thus, pasta, spaghetti and pizza were perhaps the pivotal ingredients of the family lexicon that characterized the emerging Italian communities, that is the various "little Italy" districts in every American city. It is likely that Filippo De Cecco realized that the demand for pasta by the Italian immigrants from Abruzzo and in the U.S. initially would have significantly expanded the boundaries of the market for pasta products.

Therein, the surviving primary sources at the Fara San Martino archive portray that Mr. De Cecco's strategy can be considered a real and modern attempt to do marketing and sales/distribution management before its time. The decision to participate in fairs and exhibitions since the 1880s and 1890s, especially at the international level, meets and met two pivotal needs. In general, the choice was verging on the one hand to identify, create and deliver value to a new and growing market, and this applies to Italy as well as abroad. On the other hand—and herein lies the real insight of a true entrepreneur—it is possible to illuminate one of the first attempts of brand management linked to "Made in Italy" products aimed at the international markets, like what occurred in parallel in the fashion industry (Sargiacomo, 2008).

We can be certain that, on the date of incorporation of the general partnership, the pasta produced by the plant in Fara San Martino was known at the regional and national levels. The contacts with the American market, thanks to the direct contacts of people with Abruzzo who migrated in the late nineteenth century, privileged the market of Philadelphia, where Frank Angelucci, from Lama dei Peligni, played a key role in the marketing and sales of De Cecco pasta.[8]

The overseas exhibitions, Chicago in 1893 in particular, were a springboard to broadening the market. In fact, Italian exports became regular only after 1904 and reached their peak during the period immediately preceding the outbreak of World War I. A 1911 letter sent to Frank Angelucci in Philadelphia provides a vivid and immediate insight into trade relations with U.S. buyers:

> We enclose an invoice for 800 boxes of pasta that will be shipped from Naples today, if everything goes well, barring unforeseen circumstances. The invoice shows our credit of 13,418.50 Lire. The bank of Lama, after the payment dated 12 July, did not make any other payment to us. With the next shipment, we will exclude completely third quality pasta. We will also send more of the pasta numbers 4, 5, 6, 7, 12, 15, 16, and the other kinds of pasta of which now there are a few. About third quality pasta, if you want to increase its sale, we are willing to reduce the price by 5 Lire every 100 kg, and you should sell it at 75 cents per kilogram; that is to say: you have to accept little profit on it. About you complaint for the sizes of "zitone", "mezza vita", you are absolutely right. No pasta maker is able to dry these large macaroni without any veins. When we put it in the boxes, we are very careful and discard the ones that have veins which then produce the grit. However, when they stay in the boxes for a long time, they end up breaking anyway, especially in hot weather. So a customer who wants large macaroni must accept to eat them a little chopped, or buy "penne", which are also large cut macaroni. It is not true that the boxes are big; when packed, they are forced to hold 25 kilograms; then, with the journey, they settle down, and when they arrive there, it seems that pasta is long in the box. This is all for today, kind regards.
>
> (Letter to Frank Angelucci, 9 August 1911)

This excerpt illustrates how Mr. Filippo De Cecco dealt with some of the issues he encountered in export. First, the quantity shipped, as reported in the letter, of 20 tons shows a significant industrial production. If we consider the cost of transportation, the average price of 68 cents per kilo was not much higher than the price in Italy. For example, in 1913, a small shipment to L'Aquila required 63 cents per kilo. The bank of Lama is probably the cooperative bank of Lama dei Peligni, active since 1886, which provided directly for the payment of money coming from the U.S. through a trustee. The complaints, which are answered in the letter, focus on the special pasta: in summary, the shape determines the taste. Unfortunately, the old catalogs of 1911 are not kept, but we can assume, according to today's cataloging, reference is made to long pasta shapes. The primary sources provides evidences that during the years 1910–1912, 2,700 boxes of pasta were shipped to Philadelphia every month, for a total value of about 47,000 Italian Lire. Other information that comes from this letter is that pasta was classified, produced and sold according to different qualities, and respective prices. This chimes with what a well-known commentator—Renato Rovetta—wrote in 1929, when he argued that only the so-called extra-refined or sublime pasta are made using "dorum wheat flours." On the contrary, the remaining other typologies, entitled either of "fine or first quality," or "of commercial or second quality, as well as of "third or local quality," are made using mixtures of "common soft wheat flours," having proportions that sometimes overcome 50% (Rovetta, 1929, p. 28–32).

The quality classification into different typologies—and respective prices—is confirmed by the invoices. An example is provided in Figure 3.3, showing an invoice issued on 22 November 1922 to Mr. Remigio Consalvi. On the left side, the invoice refers to the shipping by railway of "Casse" (i.e., big boxes) and "Sacchi" (i.e., sacks), and to I, II and III quality of pasta, the first of which is referred to as "tipo extra," that is to say "extra-refined pasta." On the right side the invoice portrays "Quantita" (quantity), "Prezzo" (price) and "Importo" (amount of money).

Importantly, the De Cecco pasta dried with hot air lasted a long time and could make long journeys to reach not only Sulmona—the Abruzzi town where Mr. Consalvi was located—but also the U.S. or even more distant locations. Indeed, the preceding letter to Mr. Angelucci and invoice to Mr. Consalvi hint at big transportation boxes and sacks, and at that time 25-kilo wooden boxes were used to store pasta of various shapes and ship them to any shop in the world.

In the U.S. the contacts were Frank Angelucci in Philadelphia, Raffaele Romano (from Fara San Martino) in New York and Angelo Merlino (from the Valle Peligna) in Seattle. Mr. Merlino initially received products from Philadelphia. From 1912, he asked to receive the pasta without the intermediation of Mr. Angelucci, perhaps as a consequence of interbuyer competitions and conflicts. Indeed, as evidenced by a letter dated 17 May 1912, the order request was accepted with the commitment that the goods were not delivered to the department of Philadelphia, where they had agreements with Frank Angelucci (letter dated 17 March 1912 to Angelo Merlino). Relations

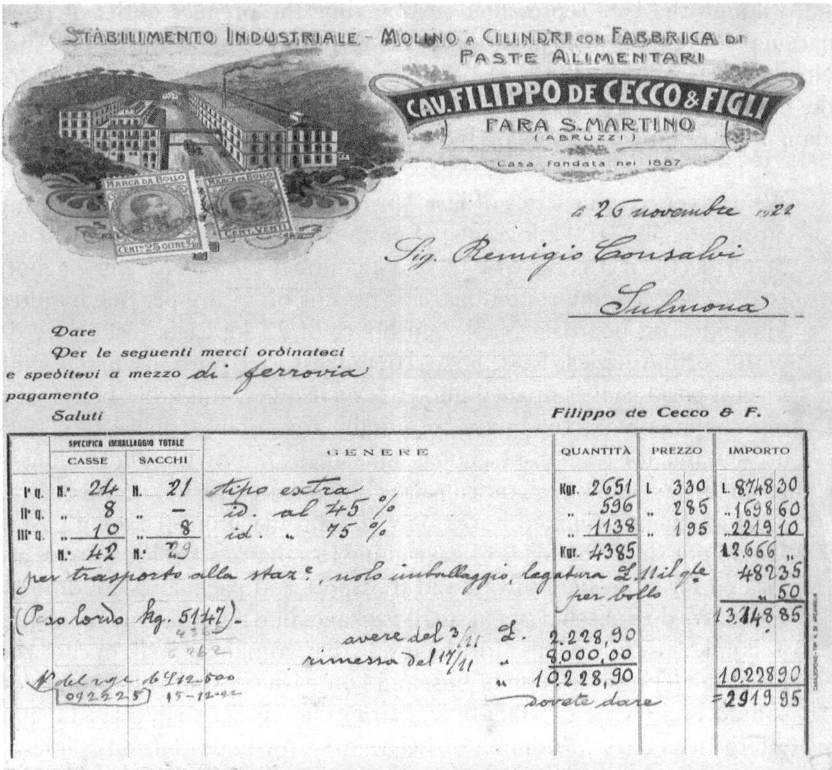

STABILIMENTO INDUSTRIALE - MOLINO A CILINDRI CON FABBRICA DI PASTE ALIMENTARI

CAV. FILIPPO DE CECCO & FIGLI

FARA S. MARTINO (ABRUZZI)

Casa fondata nel 1887

lì 26 novembre 1922

Sig. Remigio Consalvi

Sulmona

Dare

Per le seguenti merci ordinateci e speditevi a mezzo di ferrovia

pagamento

Saluti

Filippo de Cecco & F.

	Casse	Sacchi	Genere	Quantità	Prezzo	Importo
I° q.	N. 24	N. 21	tipo extra	Kgr. 2651	L. 330	L. 8748 30
II° q.	8	—	id. al 45 %	596	285	1698 60
III° q.	10	8	id. 75 %	1138	195	2219 10
	N. 42	N. 29		Kgr. 4385		12666 ..
			per trasporto alla staz., nolo imballaggio, legatura L. 11 il q.le			482 35
			per bollo			50
			(Peso lordo kg. 5147)			13148 85
			avere del 3/11	L. 2.228,90		
			rimessa del 17/11	8.000,00		
				10.228,90		10228 90
			dovete dare			2919 95

Figure 3.3 The invoice issued by the De Cecco partnership to Mr. Remigio Consalvi on 26 November 1922

Source: De Cecco company archive at Fara San Martino

with the U.S. were consolidated and proved so fruitful that in 1914 the founder asked a family member to move to New York, in order to take care of the U.S. market, which had become vital for the company (on 2 May 1914, Filippo De Cecco sent a letter to Mr. Angelucci about his intentions).

Due to adverse events, no brother moved to America. The transfer of a child to America would have meant the beginning of the commercial management directly in the hands of the parent company. This strategy would be implemented very late in the history of the company. Mr. De Cecco, however, had already realized that this choice would have meant better performance in terms of profit. The final sale price would have been established by the company, not by the individual distributors who, once they bought wholesale product, decided independently about selling prices and could make any profit they wanted, despite the pleas raised by the founders, like the one showed in the preceding 9 August 1911 letter to Mr. Frank Angelucci.

Although the U.S. represented at that time the premier outlet of international sales, the foresight of the founder did not stop at the conquest of North America. Indeed, in 1914, the De Cecco pasta was also shipped for the first time to Argentina, as evidenced by a letter sent in 1914 to Mr. Casalanguida residing in Tucuman. In its central part it is said:

> We answer to your letter of last April 1914 . . . We will accept to ship 5 tons (i.e. 50X 100 kilograms) of pasta to you as a test, so that you can better decide if it is the case to sign a contract with us for one or more years. These are the conditions. The price is of 74 lire per one hundred kilograms on board in Naples, in boxes of 25 kg each, just as we do with North America. These boxes contain assorted portions, that is, with several pasta shapes divided into paper packages, and other boxes with one shape only. Mixed boxes are suitable for families; one-shape boxes are suitable for restaurants, hotels, and small shops with retail selling of pasta. Boxes with one shape can also contain cut pasta (e.g. gnocconi and pastine), whereas mixed boxes only contain macaroni (i.e. long pasta). We do not ship wooden boxes weighing less than 25 kg, because we are located far from the railway, and transport and packaging are difficult for us. We do not sell pasta in small packages like Buitoni. Our packaging is simple, just like we use for the inside that you know well. In case you meet our represented conditions, and you wish we ship you 5 tons, you should pre-pay us £3,700,00, and from the day we cash the said sum, after fifteen days we commit ourselves to ship you pasta from Naples.
>
> (Letter to Mr. Casalanguida, 16 May 1914)

What stands out in the details, as in the previous cases, is the problem related to the transportation of pasta, much felt by the company since it operated in an area where slow and difficult communication imposed narrow roads for trade, notably foreign trade. It is very interesting to read about the packaging associated with the use of *cartate*," or true blue sheets of paper used in the old Italian grocery stores, and the reference to competitors (Buitoni), which is opposed in the packaging methods. In the letter, paying attention to the regional-language value, it is noted that *macaroni* means long pasta. Why this clarification? At the beginning of the twentieth century, macaroni referred to two totally different types of pasta: in the north of Italy, for centuries, gnocchi were first made with wheat flour and then potatoes, while in the south all long thread-like pastas, were cut in strips or hollow sticks (such as bucatini). The sale price, as is clear from the statements of the company's founder, is slightly higher than that applied in North America. It is likely that the costs of transportation to Argentina were a little higher and were charged to sold products. Relatedly, the financial aspects of the transaction is also touched on in the letter, as the company asked for a prepayment of a good amount of money (i.e., 3,700 Italian Lire), underlining that only after 15 days from the cashing of the money it would have shipped the products. This prepayment perhaps is due to the fact that Mr. Casalanguida was a new wholesaler while, on the contrary, in the case of Mr. Angelucci, it is certain that this latter was the best U.S. buyer/distributor at that time. Nonetheless, the founder underlined in the former 1911 letter that "the bank of Lama, after the payment dated 12 July, did not make any other payment to us," thus emphasizing the focus on cash management, which was discussed in the preceding section.

The buoyancy of exports in the period immediately preceding the outbreak of World War I was not limited to this company, but it was a common *trend* all over Italy. Indeed, in 1913, Italian exports touched 71,000 tons (63% of which were imported by the U.S.) and then barely exceed 12,000 tons in 1928 (Rovetta, 1929, p. 818). The aforementioned key choices made by De Cecco management enabled the company to substantially increase the production and sales of pasta. These were primarily—but not exclusively—destined to the U.S. market, and America seemed increasingly intrigued by the company. The success obtained in the U.S. through many fairs since Chicago in 1893 indeed fostered a high degree of brand loyalty (Czerniawsky and Maloney, 1999), despite strong competition from Italian companies like Barilla or Buitoni, as well as by major U.S. producers. Nevertheless, during both the World Wars many Italian manufacturers lost a large market share, especially in the U.S., where the rise of large local manufacturers stole the scene from Italian companies (Portesi, 1957).

Primary sources suggest that after the devastation of World War II and the subsequent reconstruction of the company factories at the end of the 1940s, by the 1950s De Cecco started to distribute its products in the U.S. through either concessionary firms, like La Fara Imported Macarony Company in Philadelphia (see Figure 3.4), or large wholesalers like D. Lampariello & Sons in New York. This was a selling strategy common among top European luxury companies at the time, like Christian Dior or Gucci (Dior, 1957; Forden, 2001). This created a stronger link with American department stores, buyers and agents in order to gain a wide and stable market quota and defend against Italian, French and American producers.

CONCLUSIONS

This chapter has developed a longitudinal investigation of the business history of a well-known Italian pasta producer. Admittedly, despite the general interest of accountants in "Accounting and Everyday Life" (Hopwood, 1994), and the existence of several studies on the broad agribusiness history, like the brewing industry (e.g., Clarke, 1898; Thornton, 1913; Corran, 1981; Gourvish and Wilson, 1985), to date there are no international accounting or business history case-studies regarding well-known pasta enterprises. This chapter has sought to address these lacunas.

Figure 3.4 Packaging of Pasta De Cecco: end of 1940s, 1950s

The manuscript initially sought to illustrate the ancient origin of pasta as popular culture, as well as to highlight more recent rise and diffusion of pasta industry. Then, focusing on the De Cecco case 1886–1955, the chapter identified the key choices that confronted the senior management since its new venturing in 1886, as well as the entrepreneurial role played by the founder Filippo De Cecco and his sons. Therein primary sources have enabled the co-authors to portray the establishment of the family governance through different partnerships, as well as to conduct a tentative analysis of the internal business and production premises. In the chapter sales and distribution management have been also illustrated by referring to existing commerce both inside Italy and well beyond the national borders.

Future strands of research into the history of the De Cecco, especially during the 1956–1989 period, will consider two related subjects. First, an analysis of the evolution of cost accounting procedures, unveiling their relation to the contribution margin, and the determination of the price lists using numerous foreign currency units. The second focus will be on the practices of production management and quality assurance employed in the production facilities.

A comparative study with other pasta producers, in Italy or abroad, might also be very fruitful in order to elucidate similarities, or differences, in the managerial behaviors of such companies during recent decades, as well as in the more recent and sophisticated management accounting practices. This hitherto unexplored issue of the "pasta" industry would deserve closer attention of the accounting community in the immediate future.

NOTES

1. Augusta Consorti and Massimo Sargiacomo are Full Professors of Economia Aziendale at G. d'Annunzio University of Chieti-Pescara. Luciano D'Amico is Full Professor of Economia Aziendale and Rector of the University of Teramo.
2. Please note that "Di/De Cecco" are used indistinctively in the legal and official documents (e.g., Certification of Birth in the Town Office, 1886; Knight of the Order of Labor Certificate, 1905; Deed of Incorporation 1914).
3. Indeed, since 1907 Mr. Filippo Di Cecco appeared as shareholder in the "Società Elettromeccanica Zecca-Cauli" located in Lanciano, which was supposed to produce and distribute energy throughout Lanciano and neighboring territories (Benegiamo and Nunziato, 1996). Therein see Pierucci (2003).
4. The authors during their visits at the company historical archive located inside Fara San Martino headquarters saw the awards, certifications, diplomas and medals.
5. The will of Mr. De Cecco, as highlighted by the 1914 incorporation deed, seem to echo the words that a French silk manufacturer, Alexandre Colcombet, wrote in 1894 to his children:

   > You would be making a mistake if you thought that my business, which I have from my father, which he had from his father, is a property that belongs to you by right of birth. . . . I shall leave you factories that will ruin you or enrich you, depending on whether you're ready to work diligently and tenaciously. It becomes your business; my responsibility ends.
   >
   > (quoted in Lands (2008)

6. Interestingly from a governance perspective, one of the members of the board of auditors of the new Pescara jsc was the Notary Esculapio De Cinque, who had stipulated the first 1914 Fara incorporation deed. Relatedly, another member was the Lama dei Peligni lawyer Giuseppe Cocco, whose office hosted the mentioned notary when he drew up the deed of incorporation of the general partnership Cavalier Filippo Di Cecco & figli.
7. Primary sources suggest that in 1905 Mr. DeCecco already requested the authorization for the derivation of the Verde river, thus installing an electrical junction box and obtaining 19 horsepower.

8. Since the arrival forms of all who landed at Ellis Island between the end of the nineteenth century and the beginning of the twentieth are contained in a public database (which is available online), it is possible to argue that Frank Angelucci is Francesco Angelucci, 27 years old, who arrived at Ellis Island on 10 July 1902 on the ship *Aller*, which sailed from the port of Naples.

REFERENCES

Primary Sources

Archive of Notaries—District of Lanciano

Founding deed of incorporations stipulated by notary Esculapio De Cinque in 1914 and 1924 with regard to Fara San Martino De Cecco partnership and premises.
Founding deed of incorporations stipulated by notary Travaglini in 1927 with regard to Pescara De Cecco partnership and premises.

Chamber of Commerce of Pescara

Register and Bulletin of the Chamber of Commerce of Pescara, 1947.

Chieti Town Historical Archive

De Cecco folder: cadastral and architectural plans of Fara San Martino premises; various documentation of different years.

De Cecco Historical Archive at Fara San Martino

Cash Register: scattered years until 1938–1939.
Clients data sheet: 1939–1940.
Invoices: 1914–1951.
Letters: 1914–1925, 1936–1938.
Register of Expenses and Sales: 1938–1941.
Register of Manufacturing Accounts: 1905–1928.
Registers of Money Orders and Cheques: 1937–1941.
Registers of Wages: scattered years until 1957.

Fara San Martino Town Historical Archives

Certificate of birth of Annantonia De Cecco, 1886.

Secondary Sources

Alto Commissariato dell'Alimentazione (High Commissioner for Nutrition), Rapporto 1953–4, (Roma).
Andre', J. (a cura di) (1974) *De re coquinaria. L'Art culinaire*. Paris: Les Belles Lettres.
Archivio Storico dell'Industria Italiana (1987) *Le condizioni industriali dell'Abruzzo-1895*. Bologna: Analisi.
Beard, V. (1994) Popular culture and professional identity: Accountants in the movies. *Accounting, Organizations and Society* 19(3): 303–318.
Benegiamo, M. and Nunziato, P. (1996) Gli elettrocommerciali abruzzesi in età giolittiana: La società Zecca-Cauli & C. *Abruzzo Contemporaneo* 2: 135–155.

Carleton, M.A. (1901) *Macaroni wheats,* Bulletin n.3. Washington: Government Printing Office.
Capuzzo, P. (2006) *Culture del consumo.* Bologna: Il Mulino.
Ceschina, G. (1907) *Primo contributo allo studio dell'essiccazione delle paste alimentari.* Milan: Tip. degli Ingegneri.
Ciccarelli, C. and Fenoaltea, S. (2010) *Throughout the magnifying glass: Provincial aspects of industrial growth in post-unification Italy.* Rome: Banca d'Italia.
Clarke, E.W. (1898) *Brewery bookkeeping: A practical treatise on brewery accounts and office management.* Chicago: H.S. Rich & Company.
Clementi, A. (1998) *Storia dell'Aquila.* Bari: Laterza.
Cogliati Arano, L. (a cura di) (1979) *Tacuinum Sanitatis.* Milan: Electra.
Consiglio e Ufficio Provinciale dell'Economia. (1930) *Relazione Statistica sull'andamento economico della Provincia di Pescara durante l'anno 1929 con riferimenti agli anni precedenti.* Pesara: Duval.
Corran, T.H. (1981) James Deady, Henry Meux, and the Griffin Brewery: Fraud in an early-nineteenth-century business. *Business History* 23(3): 327–45.
Czerniawsky, R.D. and Maloney, M. (1999) *Creating brand loyalty.* New York: Hudson House Publishing.
D'Azeglio, M. (1899) *I miei ricordi.* Florence: Tip. G. Barbera.
De Michelis, G. (1925) *Italian emigration and the remittances of emigrants.* Rome: Provveditorato generale dello Stato.
Dingelstedt, V. (1910) Italian emigration. *The Scottish Geographical Magazine* July: 338–353.
Dior, C. (1957) *Christian Dior and I.* Boston: Dutton.
Donna, M.J. (1946) History and aims of national macaroni manufacturers association. *The Macaroni Journal* XXVII(12): 15. Minneapolis: National Macaroni Manufacturers Association.
D'Onofrio, G. (1924) *L'Industria delle conserve alimentari.* Milan: Hoepli.
Fenoaltea, S. (1970) *Railroads and Italian industrial growth, 1861–1913: Discussion paper no. 177.* Presented at the Second World Congress of the Econometric Society, Cambridge England, 8–14 September 1970. Philadelphia: University of Pennsylvania.
Fenoaltea, S. (2002) *Production and consumption in post-unification Italy: New evidence, new conjectures.* Rome: Banca d'Italia.
Foerster, R.F. (1924) *The Italian emigration of our times.* Cambridge: Harvard University Press.
Forden, S.G. (2001) *The house of Gucci: A sensational story of murder, madness, glamour, and greed.* New York: Harper.
Gourvish, T.R. and Wilson, R.G. (1985) Profitability in the brewing industry 1885–1914. *Business History* 27(2): 146–65.
Houyan, L., Xiaoyan, Y., Maolin, Y., Kam-Biu L., Zhengkai X., Xiaoyan R., Linhai C., Naiqin W. and Tung-Sheng L. (2005) Culinary archaeology: Millet noodles in late Neolithic China. *Nature* 437(7061): 967–968.
Hopwood, A. (1994) Accounting and everyday life: An introduction. *Accounting, Organizations and Society* 19(3): 299–301.
Hunt, J. and Garr, D. (1985) *The cotton mills of Oldham.* Oldham: Oldham Leisure Services.
I 3 Abruzzi (1893) 17, 1st May. Lanciano: Tipografia Tomassini.
Jackson, W.J., Paterson, A.S., Pong, C.K.M. and Scarparo, S. (2012) "How easy can the barley brie". Drinking culture and accounting failure at the end of the nineteenth century in Britain. *Accounting, Auditing and Accountability Journal* 25(4): 635–658.
Jeacle, I. (2006) Face facts: Accounting, feminism and the business of beauty. *Critical Perspectives on Accounting* 17(1): 87–108.
Jeacle, I. (2009) Going to the movies: Accounting and twentieth century cinema. *Accounting, Auditing and Accountability Journal* 22(5): 677–708.

Jeacle, I. and Carter, C. (2012) Fashioning the popular masses: Accounting as mediator between creativity and control. *Accounting, Auditing and Accountability Journal* 25(4): 719–751.
Kapferer, J.N. (2004) *The new strategic brand management.* London: Kogan Page.
Lands, D. (2008) *Dynasties: Fortune and misfortune in the world's great family businesses.* London: Penguin Books.
Laurioux, B. (1995) *Des lasagnes romaines aux vermicelles arabes: quelques rèflexions sur les pâtes alimentaires au Moyen Age.* Paris: Publications de la Sorbonne.
Majetti, R. (1885) Associazioni di arti e mestieri nel diritto romano: *corporazioni di arti e mestieri napolitani dal 14. al 19. secolo.* Napoli: La Cava.
Marchi, C. (1990) *Quando siamo a tavola.* Milan: Rizzoli.
National Institute of Statistics, 1 1951, Roma.
Paolini, T. (1996) L'industria abruzzese nell'800. *L'Abruzzo nell'Ottocento.* Pescara: Istituto Nazionale di Studi crociani, pp. 73–92.
Pierucci, P. (2003) L'industria della pasta in Abruzzo fra Otto e Novecento. In: Barciela, C. and Di Vittorio, A. (eds.), *Las industrias agroalimentarias en Italia y Espana durante los siglos XIX y XX.* Palma De Mallorca: Publicaciones de la Universidad de Alicante, pp. 442–456.
Porter, M.E. (1985) *Competitive advantage. Creating and sustaining superior performance.* NewYork: Free Press.
Porter, M.E. (1987) From competitive advantage to corporate strategy. *Harvard Business Review* 65(3): 43–59.
Portesi, G. (1957) *L'industria della pasta alimentare.* Rome: Molini d'Italia.
Rovetta, R. (1929) *Industria del pastificio o dei maccheroni.* Milan: Hoepli.
Rovetta, R. (1951) *Industria del pastificio o dei maccheroni.* Milan: Hoepli.
Sabatini, G. (1996) L'agricoltura abruzzese tra Otto e Novecento. *L'Abruzzo nell'Ottocento.* Pescara: Istituto Nazionale di Studi crociani, pp. 61–71.
Sargiacomo, M. (2008) Institutional pressures and isomorphic change in a high-fashion company: The case of Brioni Roman Style, 1945–89. *Accounting, Business & Financial History* 18(2): 215–241.
Serventi, S. and Sabban, F. (2000) *La pasta: Storia e cultura di un cibo universale.* Bari: Laterza.
Smith, R. (1962) An Oldham limited liability company, 1875–1896. *Business History* 4(1): 34–53.
Thornton, F.W. (1913) *Brewery accounts.* New York: Ronald Press.
Toniolo, G. (1977) *Effective protection and industrial growth: The case of italian engineering, 1898–1913.* Rome: Banco di Roma.
Walker, S.P. (1998) How to secure your husband's esteem: Accounting and private patriarchy in the British middle class household during the nineteenth century. *Accounting, Organizations and Society* 23(6): 485–514.
Walker, S.P. (2003) Professionalisation or incarceration? Household engineering, accounting and the domestic ideal. *Accounting, Organizations and Society* 28(8): 743–772.
Yin, R.K. (2014) Case study research: Design and methods (Applied Social Research Methods). London: Sage.

4 Exploring Sustainability Practices and Reporting in the Brewery Industry

The Case of Birrificio Angelo Poretti—Carlsberg Italia (1877–1980)

Federica Doni, Alberto Frausin and Andrea Gasperini

INTRODUCTION

This study assessed the following research topic: "Accounting, Business and Financial History of Food producers," focussed on the production of the beer in Italy over the period 1877–1980.[1]

The historical study has been carried out in the genetic and evolutionary analysis of the company Birrificio Angelo Poretti—Carlsberg Italia. The company, founded in 1877 and formalized 3 years later with the creation of Angelo Poretti & C., started from Angelo Poretti's idea focussed on the introduction of a new kind of beer, the Bohemian Pilsner, in Italy. Compared to kinds that had been sold in Italy up until that time (named "Vienna" and "Chiavenna"), Bohemian Pilsner was lighter and more delicate and was produced using first-class ingredients. Poretti's lengthy experience in central Europe had convinced him of the feasibility of his initiative. The popularity of the brewery Angelo Poretti is also due to the fact that the first factory was located near the caves of Valganna, where there was a spring known as the *fontana degli ammalati* (Fountain of the Sick), which was famous for its miraculous effects locally, and even as far off as Milan. Angelo Poretti purchased both properties, which provided for an immediate advertising effect: the water from the *fontana degli ammalati* became the foundation of his beer (Zanzi, 1879; Macchione, 1992). The company developed dramatically popular only a few years later (1881) with the World's Fair held in Milan (http://www.museoweb.it/imprese/carlsberg-italia/).

This research analyzes the evolutionary process of the major organizational changes (DiMaggio and Powell, 1983) from the company's inception until the second half of the 1890s through the analysis of internal company's materials and a variety of secondary sources, preserved in the company's archive in the major factory of Induno Olona, in the province of Varese.

We adopted a longitudinal thematic analysis with the aim of understanding how the content of the documents changes according to the different institutional settings experienced by the company (Adams and McNicholas, 2007; Moreno and Càmara, 2014). After an in-depth analysis of the historical background of the company (1877–1980), this chapter uses the institutional theory framework to emphasize the different institutional pressures and the major organizational changes that influenced management behavior in response to environmental opportunities and threats (DiMaggio and Powell, 1983; Powell, 1991, 1997; Scott, 2001, 2008). The primary topic focussed on the development of corporate reporting in relation to a company's growing commitment to sustainability and its corporate business strategy and policies. In this analysis, the chapter also shows the entrepreneurial qualities of the company's founder and his innovative role in adopting organizational practices, which does not support the major criticism of the institutional theory that ignores the role of individuals in the institutionalization process (DiMaggio, 1988; Powell, 1991; Dacin, 1997; Sargiacomo, 2008).

This study may offer a contribution to the existing literature because studies on the brewery industry are scarce (Gourvish and Wilson, 1985; Mager, 2008), in particular studies focussed on a historical analysis in terms of both business history and accounting history. In addition, the brewery industry has different critical elements during production both for environmental impact and for water consumption. Best practices in the area of sustainability thus become essential to the competitive advantage of companies operating in this industry (Cormier et al., 2005; Hopwood et al., 2010).

The remainder of the chapter is organized as follows: the next section explains the methodology and the primary/secondary sources analyzed. Next, the main features of the brewery sector are assessed and a brief historical background of the company is provided. The following section describes the main tenets of the institutional and legitimacy theories, and through these perspectives it discusses the results of the historical analysis of Angelo Poretti & C. The next section focusses on the institutionalization of the sustainability field, and the final section gives concluding remarks.

METHODOLOGY

This research is positioned in the core of historical research called the "history of companies and enterprises" (Amaduzzi, 2004), where the national and international literature highlights some critical issues in the relationship between accounting history and business history (Marriner, 1980; Licini 2012). Business history has been the subject of studies in the field of economic history, and the individual business cases analyzed serve only as examples of the general trends of industrial development in order to identify their contribution in terms of economic progress (Franceschi, 1998). In particular, the theme that has been the subject of most debate concerns the role played by accounting reports as an indispensable support for the understanding of the history of the company (Johnson, 1975; Lister, 1981; Mason, 1982; Parker, 1991; Boyns, 1993; Arnold, 1995; Friedenson, 2007).

The study aims to use primary and secondary sources (Amaduzzi, 2004). The documents analyzed from the archive of the company are letters, reports, budgets and other administrative and accounting documents and bibliographic material authors of the period analyzed (books, magazine articles, national and international papers).

The material from the archive of the company covers the period 1868–2002 and contains not only financial and nonfinancial reports of company but also lists of products and advertising corporate image brochures (http://www.museoweb.it/imprese/carlsberg-Italy/). Regarding secondary sources, a recognition of bibliographic material processed at later dates to the period analyzed assessed issues related to the production and marketing of beer and documentation collected and reworked in commemorative volumes written by the same company at the company anniversaries.

The framing of the research from the point of view of the historical reference period (periodization according to the chronology and importance of the studies) is placed in the "Period of general accounting and technology Administration in the period 1870–1920"; in the "Period of training and first assertion business economics and classification of its branches of study in the period 1920–1950"; and finally in the "Period of affirmation and consolidation of business economics, its evolution and development since 1950 on." The historical study is performed according to the synchronic conception (Amaduzzi, 2004) because the historical analysis is aimed at studying the evolutionary process of the company and business reporting perspective of awareness of the significant commitment of Carlsberg Italia towards sustainability.

THE BEVERAGE INDUSTRY

The brewery segment belongs to the beverage industry, which consists of the total revenues generated through the sale of soft drinks, beers, ciders, flavoured alcoholic beverages (FABs), spirits and wines, valued at retailing selling price (inclusive of all applicable sale taxes). The global[2] beverages market has experienced moderate growth in recent years and this is forecast to continue at an accelerated rate towards 2018 . It grew by 3.4% in 2013 to reach a value of $1,836.1 billion, and the compound annual growth rate of the industry in the period 2009–2013 was 3.3%. In 2013 it reached a volume of 794.3 billion liters. Regarding category segmentation, soft drinks is the largest segment of the global beverages industry, accounting for 34.4% of the industry's total value. Beer, cider and FABs account for 31.6% of the industry; this segment ranks in the second position.

Regarding geographical segmentation, Europe accounts for 39.2% of the global beverages industry value; the Coca-Cola Company and Anheuser Busch InBev are the leading players of this sector. The beverage market is highly fragmented, although there is some concentration within various segments in certain countries. Typical buyers within this sector are large retailers with a great amount of financial muscle, although beverage manufacturers produce differentiated products in order to reduce their reliance on revenues from one single product. Especially in the case of the beer segment, some brewers have integrated forwards by operating chains of pubs or other outlets, hence this fact reduces buyer power as brewers can sell directly to consumers.

The production of beverages requires different raw materials and processes that depend on the type of beverage. Beer production needs malted grain and hops, which are highly specific materials, and this fact makes beverage manufacturers reliant on suppliers.

The beverage market is characterized by significant brand loyalty, which can therefore provide increased competition. Some beverage manufacturers adopt innovative packaging and design in order to differentiate the products, with value-added functional features that are used to attract more consumers. Most countries apply stringent requirements on beverage production, in particular that of alcoholic beverages, which coupled with only moderate market growth over recent years could prove off-putting to new entrants. There is a moderate degree of rivalry: the market is fragmented between the four leading players, Coca-Cola, PepsiCo, Anheuser Busch InBev and Nestlè; therefore the large number of market players' increases rivalry. There is a large number of brands and beverages, which are easily differentiated and can be chosen by retailers straightforwardly.

The situation of the beer market in Italy shows the presence of seven breweries with industrial production: Heineken Italy, Peroni, Carlsberg Italy, Birra Castello, Forst, Menabrea and Theresianer; together they manage a total of 13 factories in the Italian territory. Market leaders are subsidiaries of the largest international multinationals, Heineken, SABMiller, AB-Indev and Carlsberg. In addition to industrial production, craftsmanship units are added such as microbreweries and brewpubs. According to data compiled by Beverfood and Assobirra, the Italian subsidiary of Carlsberg is ranked in fourth place for sales of beer in the period 2009–2013 (AssoBirra, 2013). The company produces and distributes the beer of the brewery Angelo Poretti, the group's primary brands Carlsberg and Tuborg, Devil's beers and France's Kronenbourg.

In Italy and across the world the present scenario is the result of an evolutionary process that began in ancient times with the production of beer, one of the first foods processed by man along with bread and wine. In Italy beer was already known at the time of the Etruscans and then entered into ancient Rome where it spread into poor neighborhoods. Beer is, therefore, a drink linked to Italian historical tradition in the same way as wine, even though the low temperatures typical of Northern Europe, being better suited to the needs of yeast has, in fact, meant a progressive specialization in the South (for wine) and Northern Europe (for beer) (AssoBirra, 2014). The Italian tradition of brewing is, thus, millennial, although the first factories only date back to the late nineteenth century, when they were designed on the basis of the technology of artificial cold and the new technology of the production of bottom-fermented lagers. The first breweries started thanks to the will of certain entrepreneurs in Northern Europe (Dreher, Von Wunster, etc.), and in some cases Italian ice traders used the sale of beer as an ancillary activity to the main one. In the last few years we have seen the entrance of foreign capital from large multinational companies that have bought a majority or substantial shareholdings of Italian companies (Heineken, SAB-Miller, Carlsberg, Anheuser Busch InBev).

HISTORICAL BACKGROUND OF ANGELO PORETTI & C.

Beginning of the Company under the Leadership of Its Founder Angelo Poretti

The history of Poretti beer is strongly linked to its founder Angelo Poretti (1829–1901). He spent time in Austria, Germany and Bohemia, and then during the mid-1870s returned to Italy with his Bohemian wife to dedicate himself to the production of that beer, which was so appreciated and famous in the North of Europe. The entrepreneurial idea of Angelo Poretti stemmed from the will to introduce into Italy a new type of beer, the Bohemian Pilsner, through the creation of a large factory in Induno Olona, near Varese, thanks to the work of 40 workers coordinated by a German "skilled brewer" (*Varesina Chronicle*, 5 August 1877, written by Gian Pietro Porro).

The choice of the area was not accidental: Bohemian Pilsner beer required greater lightness and delicacy than other beers sold in the same period (i.e., Vienna and Chiavenna), and thus arose the need to use first-class ingredients. The choice of the place of establishment of the plant was related to the use of the water that came from a source well known at the time, known as the Fountain of the Sick, situated near the caves of Valganna (Macchione, 1991). The official announcement of the foundation of the company was given in 1878 and was published in the *Varesina Chronicle* where the following aspects were emphasized:

1. "Novelty" due to the characteristics of the beer production (i.e., Pilsen method, Bohemia);
2. Attribution of primacy as a type of industrial plant in the Italian territory;
3. Indication of the Fountain of the Sick, and thus the use of the water as a source for the production of beer;
4. Description of the characteristics of the beer, made with raw materials and innovative production methods unknown in Italy at that time.

In view of the competitive scenario in which the Poretti brewery was operating, it is possible to identify some factors (i.e., technical and quality parameters, objective and subjective factors) (Bertini, 1990, 2013) that can be considered the drivers of the company's success:

1. Use of the miraculous water of the Fountain of the Sick;
2. Wide availability of Angelo Poretti's financial resources, resulting from his previous business activity developed in Bohemia, resources earned through contracts for the construction of railway systems;
3. Implementation of specific skills for the production of beer characterized by uniqueness of the technical know-how learned abroad using highly qualified technical staff, with expertise and specific skills[3] able to assure the right technical implementation of the Pilsner method;
4. The strong personal will of Poretti to create a beer with distinctive features compared to beers of Varese (i.e., Chiavenna and Vienna beers) and in general of the national territory;[4]
5. The adoption of sophisticated machinery and raw materials such as malt and yeast from Vienna and special aromatic hops from Czechoslovakia.

The will of Poretti was therefore to establish a genuine national industry, but it should be characterized by specific peculiarities compared to competitors operating in the rest of Italy. Luigi Zanzi, editor of the *Varesina Chronicle*and secretary of the chamber of commerce, authoritative witness of the time, highlights the entrepreneurial skills of Poretti, emphasizing the leadership role of his company in the field of breweries:

> thanks to courage and the intelligent initiative of Mr. Angelo Poretti and of our other neighbors, here, not far from Varese, near the Fountain of the Sick a brewery arose and it is growing, which, I am certain, in a short time will beat the foreign competition, and thus will develop a powerful new national industry.
>
> (Macchione, 2013, pp. 35–37)

The action of strong growth and forward thinking of Poretti are demonstrated by the proposal to build a large ice chest in 1879 at the train station of Varese (never actually completed), with the purpose of storing barrels and bottles for retail sale of beer and the construction of an elegant kiosk for the Angelo Poretti Company for the sale of beer (1895).

Another distinctive aspect of the personality of Poretti was the constant attention to the needs of consumers: even though his priority remained the Pilsner brewing method, he remained aware of the wide range of tastes possible and continued to suggest various types of traditional beers, in particular the type named Vienna. As of February 1877 the first batches of beer were ready to be marketed and Poretti established a first point of sale at his home in Piazza Beccaria, a local garden that he had renovated and beautified in 1874. This was a real opening with a select group of people who were invited for a visit to the factory so that they could make a judgement on the beer produced by the Pilsner method. The *Varesina Chronicle* gave wide publicity to the event by qualifying the company as the Poretti "new domestic factory" and "the first in Italy" (*Varesina Chronicle*, 1878). Starting with this event the company began a custom that at the time seemed very innovative: periodically the company "opened the gates to all kinds of curious people who were able to check out the processes and sample the different kinds of beer" (Macchione, 2013, p. 43). This business strategy allowed a wide advertising of the company and, at the same time, the visitors themselves promoted the beer produced by Angelo Poretti.

The official recognition of the national importance of Poretti occurred in 1881 at the Industrial Exhibition in Milan,[5] which took place 5–10 November (AA.VV., 1881). Angelo Poretti & C. obtained permission to erect a Swiss-style chalet in the enclosure of the Expo designed by a famous architect of the time, G. Ferrari, where visitors could sample the company's products but also observe drawings of the factory, descriptions of the machinery and production methods used.

Poretti was awarded the silver medal by the jury and a special mention was published in the Official Acts of the Expo, although a more important recognition was represented by the great success in terms of the number of visitors to the pavilion. This confirmed the high capacity for market penetration and consumer satisfaction. As a result of this event Poretti decided to strengthen the company's distribution channels by opening a number of outlets in various locations in Lombardy: in the end, this policy proved to be a mistake because operating costs proved to be excessive. The exhibition also became the occasion for more awards for Poretti; at the Congress of Italian brewers in Milan in October, he was appointed vice president and became part of a committee of government that was responsible for this sector, which actually covered a secondary role in the national economy compared to viticulture. At other exhibitions (Torino, Varese, etc.), the company of Angelo Poretti received various awards, and Poretti himself was elected to various important positions (such as the chairmanship of the Standing Committee of the Association of Brewers, headquartered in Milan).

A few years after Poretti's death a testimony by Ambrogio Codara (Codara, 1901) that describes the state of the company's plants can be considered in all respects a remarkable synthesis of the work of Angelo Poretti, from both an entrepreneurial and technological point of view. The author attributes to the company a supremacy in Italy. Another unique aspect of company strategy undertaken by Poretti was the work of industrial architecture that Poretti commissioned to a well-known firm of architects, Alfred Bihl Woltz of Stuttgart, for the building of a new brewhouse (1898). The skills in industrial construction required by the need to achieve a high level of professionalism meant that, thanks to the vision of Angelo Poretti, sophisticated and advanced models of industrial architecture were imported into Italy. This aspect of industrial architecture was embodied in the construction of the facades of the new brewhouse that reproduce the style known as Liberty (1908), where we find a perfect blend of the functional requirements related to the production process (technology) combined with the desire to preserve the outward appearance[6] (aesthetics) and to combine art with industrial technology.

Poretti Angelo & C.: Corporate Strategies and Generational Succession

Although the key reference figure was always Angelo Poretti, an entrepreneur with undisputed leadership, the corporate structure of the company upon incorporation on 23 November 1880, consisted of three partners, Angelo Poretti, Angelo Nicora and Romeo Lanfranconi. Under the provisions of the articles of association, the share capital amounted to 1,200,000 Italian Lire: three-sixths belonged to Poretti, two-sixths to Nicora and one-sixth to Lanfranconi. Share capital actually paid up was 600,000 Italian Lire, and the company was expected to last for a period of 25 years (until 30 April 1902). Operational headquarters for the manufacture of beer were at the Fountain of the Sick, while the head office was established in Varese. The act also provided for a project to start the cultivation of crops of barley and hops.

With regard to corporate functions: Poretti was in charge of the administration of the company with powers of representation, while Lanfranconi was to deal with the management of the company, both in terms of the organization of industrial processes and the administration of funds held for social purposes. Nicora was in charge of the control of brewing processes and related industrial equipment. As for the issues of succession, the Statute stated that in the case of the death of a partner, his heirs had to be paid in cash the share capital corresponding to the last financial statements, within 3 years and with related interests.

Relationships among the three partners, issues related to the company's profitability and the standards established by the Statute quickly led to control of the company by a single shareholder, Angelo Poretti. Following significant losses due to investments made for the expansion of the plant and for the acquisition of machinery, as well as higher marketing costs, in 1884 losses had already caused the loss of more than two-thirds of the equity. As required by Article 19 of the Statute one of the partners, Lanfranconi decided to retire from the company and asked for the liquidation of the share capital, which was taken up by Poretti who thus came to hold five-sixths of the share capital. A final step came with the death of Nicora in 1893, when, after the liquidation of the share to Nicora's widow, Angelo Poretti became the only shareholder, holding the full share capital.

An Overview of Angelo Poretti & C.'s Financial Reporting

When the company was established, the share capital amounted to 90,000 Italian Lire, of which Angelo Poretti contributed 60,000 Italian Lire and Angelo Nicora 30,000 Italian Lire. An analysis of primary sources, that is, accounting records (double entry books, ledgers, account books and in particular the double entry journal for the period from 12 October 1889 to 28 December 1890) shows that:

1. The financial year ended on 30 November (see Figure 4.1 and Figure 4.2):[7] the reason of this choice was the seasonality of the beer market, for which the fiscal year-end at the beginning (or end) of the autumn was certainly more appropriate than the general criterion of the calendar year (Andreolotti, 1993a, 1993b);
2. The balance sheet as of 30 November 1890 shows cash and cash equivalents and other accounts receivable; in particular, the item "Receivables" from customers is recorded as "Beer receivables";
3. The item "Inventories" shows end-of-year inventories, that is, the amount of beer remaining in stock and the value of raw and ancillary materials, also reported in the profit and loss account;
4. The account "Fixed assets" shows the value of the company's land and buildings; some records indicate the construction of cellars and the purchase of land and buildings;
5. The account "General material" includes both the value of fixed assets net of depreciation, such as machinery, plant and equipment and the value of "Nonfixed material" for the sale of beer such as drums, crates and bottles.

A particular account in Poretti's balance sheet is the "Self-propelled" item, which shows the inventory value of oxen and steers that were used in the department for loading and unloading goods for transport inside the factory. The operation of this account provides for the recording of costs and revenues, respectively, when buying "oxen for work" and at the time of sale of "oxen for slaughtering" valuated at a certain price. This account also includes the records of other costs relating to hay for the animals or the costs of cattle shed workers, as well as revenues from the sale of materials obtained from the land and buildings owned by Poretti (hay and manure).

It is also interesting to note how the total cost attributed to the "Self-propelled" account (which is indicated in the class of fixed assets in the balance sheet) was proportionally allocated among the various cost centers showing the different items of expenditure (barley, coal, ice, hops, etc.).

The analysis of accounting records also provides a picture of the relationships between the company and certain groups of stakeholders, especially customers, suppliers and employees. In the double entry book of 1890 we find the presence of an extensive network of customers (6,342 delivery notes in the years 1890–1891), widespread especially in Lombardy but also in areas across the Po river as far as Parma, Modena and into the Piedmontese side of Lake Maggiore, up to Novara and Vercelli. Revenues for the same period, amounting to 254,308 Italian Lire were generated by the production of beer, totalling 655,000 liters.

As for suppliers, expense entries disclose high costs related in particular to the raw materials that were imported, such as barley, malt and hops, impacted by transport costs and customs duties. Among the costs related to ancillary materials, it is important to highlight the annual cost related to 89.6 metric tons of ice for 2,800 Italian Lire; the ice was mined during the winter and stored for long periods in the colder areas of the cellars. Beer production is also characterized by the presence of the manufacturing tax

CONTO PROFITTI E PERDITE AL 30.11.1890

Ricavi datle vendite:				
Ricavo birra 1890	(per ricavalo nell'anno)		£. 254.308,92	
Cascami d'orzo	II II		II 892.40	
			£. 255.201,32	
– Rimanenze iniziali	(residao birra '89)	£. 12.900		
+ Rimanenze finali	(residao birra '90)	II 11.100		
Variazione nelle rimanen ae di birru			– II 1.800, II	
Valore detla produzione nell'anno				£. 253.401,32
Costi di produzione:				
Orzo	nelle lavorazioui	£. 73.030,13		
Luppalo	II	II 11.917,67		
Lievito	II	II 633,43		
Pece	II	II 1.955,30		
Ghiaccio	II	II 2.296,16		
Carbone	II	II 4.672,21		
Legna d'ardere	II	II 2.428,24		
Torba	II	II 3.038,48		
Olio e petrolio	II	II 263,- -		
Candele	II	II 490,50		
Costi delle malerie prime e sussidiarie			£. 101.225,12	
Tassa di fabbricazione			II 44.895,46	
Onorari e Stipendi			II 18.230,70	
Speše generali			II 35.401,10	
Totale dei cosli di produzione				£. 199.752,38
Utile netto sulla fabbricazione				£. 53.648,94
Ammortamenti e svalutazioni				
Deperimento calcolato sul materiale generale			£. 8.417,75	
Perdite e svalutazioni sui crediti			II 7.124,52	II 15.542,27
Risultato operativo netio				£. 38.106,67
Oneri e proventi diversi				
Svalutazione immobilizazioni finanziarie			– £. 7.500, - -	
Ricavi netti da "Editier della fabbrica"			+ II 1.961, - -	
Proventi vari			+ II 307,39	II 5.231,61
Oneri finanziari				£. 32.875,06
Interessi su conti liberi, c/c e mutui passivi			£. 14.484,49	
Interessi sul capitale iniziate della gestione			II 15.905,74	II 30.390,23
Utile nelto della gestione				£. 2.484,83

Figure 4.1 Profit and loss statement at 30 November 1890

Datia
A. PORETTI & C.
Varese

SITUAZIONE PATRIMONIALE AL 30.11.1890

per le sequenti ATTIVITA':				
Attivita disponitbili:				
Cassa contanti	£.	12.366, - -		
Cauzioni ed Effeciti	ll	1.479,66		
Debitori al c/ Birru (crediti verso clienit)	ll	72.194,83		
Crediti verso Soci (A. Nicora)	ll	28.917,34		
Altri crediti	ll	29,65	£.	114.987,48
Giacenze di magazzino:				
Residuo birra 1890 (per rimaste in contina)		11.100, - -		
Materia prime, sussidiarie ed accessorie	ll	35.848,53	ll	46.948,53
Immobilizzazioni tecniche:				
Edifici della fabbrica	£.	273.386,27		
Materiate generale (per valore attribuito)	ll	110.000, - -		
Materiate pr. depositi e birrerie esterne	ll	9.371,50		
Semoventi (esistenza d'inventario)	ll	7.360, - -	ll	400.119,77
Immobilizz, finanziarie:				
Crediti residui da ammomizare (conjugi Veronesi)			ll	2.500, - -
Totale delle attivita			£.	564.555,78
per le sequenti PASSIVITA'				
Passivita a breve termine:				
Banca di Varese (c/c bancario)	£.	83.225,64		
Fornitori e creditori diversi	ll	46.855,53	£.	130.081,17
Passivita a media e a Jungo termine:				
Finanziamenti da soci (cav. A. Poretti)	£.	116.043,13		
Mutuo de Cassa di Risparmio di Milano	ll	50.851, - -	ll	166.894,13
Totale delle passivita			£.	296.975,30
Patrimonia neuo				
Stalo Capitale alla chiusura dell'esercizio		265.095,65		
Utile nello di gestione	ll	2.484,83	ll	267.580,48
Totale a pareggio			£.	564.555,78

Figure 4.2 Financial statement at 30 November 1890 (cont'd)

that was paid on the basis of quantities produced; in the year under review the company paid a sum of 44,895 Italian Lire or 17.6% of sales of the current fiscal year.

With regard to personnel costs, compensation paid to the two shareholders was quite high (1,800 talian Lire per year), while compensation for the administrative and operational management amounted to 100 and 200 Italian Lire per month. The staff included brewers and coopers from Bohemia with a monthly salary of 120–140 Italian Lire.

Poretti's Death and the Succession to the Grandchildren

For 8 years the company led by Poretti obtained remarkable results with further growth of the industrial plants. After his death in October 1901, the situation of the company was destined to undergo profound changes. Subsequent events led to the ownership of the company, as well as the inheritance of Poretti's personal wealth, passing to the four grandchildren in different proportions. In fact, the management of the company passed to Edoardo Chiesa and Angelo Magnani, both of whom had already gained professional experience under the guidance of their uncle in the brewery.

The succession took place in the manner prescribed in the will by Poretti since he required that:

1. The company's activities continued with the same company name, A. Poretti & C.;
2. The company shares of the grandchildren could not be sold to outsiders;
3. In order to maintain continuity in the company's top management heirs were required to confirm the function of "advice and administrative supervision" of a trusted person of Poretti, Silvio Macchi, who was paid a monthly salary and a share in company profits equal to 10% of net.

These conditions were accepted by the heirs, who took on specific business functions (AA.VV., 1901). Chiesa took care of the administrative and marketing areas while Magnani was in charge of the purchase of raw materials and the technical direction of the factory. In the first decade of the twentieth century the Poretti company was characterized by a remarkable development thanks to the careful direction of Michele Diermeyer (1901–1915), who created a brewhouse with a capacity of 150,000 hectoliters, and then Alfredo Spath (1915 to 1959) and finally his son Luigi Riccardo Spath.

The Twentieth Century and the Transformation of Poretti's Company into a Limited Company

From 1900 the company went through a positive phase, albeit also characterized by moments of crisis. The production at the end of the first decade had increased to values close to 60,000 hectoliters of beer produced. Over the next decade this reached 100,000 hectoliters and 120,000 in 1922. Another important step was the transformation of the company Angelo Poretti & C. into a limited company on 22 December 1922 (AA.VV., 1927). The legal transformation happened thanks to the unanimous vote of the three cousins and Credito Varesino: the company's name was changed to "Birra Poretti—stock company" whose corporate structure was composed of Edoardo Chiesa, Angelo Magnani, Tranquillo Magnani and Credito

Varesino. The share capital consisted of 5 million Italian Lire, which was made up of 1 million paid by the bank and the remaining from the valuation of assets and the group's share of the historical shares (Sanvito, 1931). The presidency of the company was entrusted to Edoardo Chiesa, while Angelo Magnani became vice president. After the latter's death and also his brother's, the direction of the company remained with Chiesa, who also held the role of chief executive officer. This position was confirmed until the general meeting (company assembly) of 1938.

After the departure of Chiesa in 1939, the situation changed radically. During the fascist period the newspapers often named Poretti beer as one of the top products in Italy. This seems to invalidate the widespread belief that the primacy of Italian beers compared to those produced in Germany had been facilitated by the closed economy (autarky), which was characteristic of the fascist period. The success of Poretti beer should therefore be attributed to the entrepreneurial skills of Poretti, Magnani and Chiesa, the features of the plants, their production organization, as well as the prestige of the brand and the product, divided into two branches, "Pilsen-type" and "Munich-type," which had long been appreciated by consumers.

The turning point in terms of getting over the crisis came with the arrival of the Bassetti family on the company's board of directors (1939). They were entrepreneurs from Gallarate who had already bought the beer Spluga. The share capital was held by the majority of Ermete, Felice and Giovanni Bassetti, who took the role of president. After World War II the company undertook several actions in terms of growth, including the acquisition of modern equipment and technologies, the expansion of the fermentation cellar and storage characterized by high capacity of approximately 50,000 hectoliters of beer. In particular, some actions were particularly conservative, such as the cessation of production of Spluga beer for logistical and financial reasons; this led to a large enhancement of the production at the Poretti company, thus making it the fifth largest Italian beer factory, with 700,000 hectoliters produced.

From the promotional point of view the company also used its great resources in order to promote the consumption of beer, especially among young people, while also trying to emphasize the health benefits (for example, a slogan of the 1930s was revived: "Drink beer and you'll live to a hundred"). Another objective was also to combine the consumption of beer with good food, and in 1964 a booklet was published, "Why Splugen Brau, 32 Recipes with Beer on the Table" (Benzoni, 1964), which had the ambitious goal of competing with the traditional Italian food culture linked to the consumption of wine.

Other important steps taken by Poretti S.p.A.—the name taken in the 1960s—were certain strategic decisions made by the company in the 1970s (Consolini, 1977; Gallerani, 1981):

1. The acquisition of the Hemed brewery in Ceccano based in the province of Frosinone (1974), which aimed to give the commercial

penetration in the southern regions, where it was expected State policies would favour certain production industries;

2. Production agreement with the Danish company United Breweries (1975) with the goal of producing and marketing Tuborg and Carlsberg beer.

The two joint actions constitute the premise of a new scenario emerging during the 1980s through the sale of increasing amounts of share capital from Poretti S.p.A. to Carlsberg Italy, with headquarters in Milan and the factory in Induno Olona (Castelli, 1989). In 2002, the process ended with the takeover by the Italian subsidiary of Carlsberg Breweries, which now owned 100% of the shares. This evolutionary process testifies to the close union between tradition and modernity: the need for innovation and adoption of the internationalization process does not deny but confirms the respect for tradition and the historical origin of the company. Thereafter Poretti and Carlsberg have two different built-in realities, aimed at the enhancement of a quality beer, characterized by a prestigious brand that has its origins in Italy but has Central European characteristics.

A HISTORICAL ANALYSIS OF ANGELO PORETTI & C. THROUGH THE INSTITUTIONAL THEORY FRAMEWORK

This historical analysis uses institutionalism to explain the evolution of the present case study, analyzed with a particular focus on sustainability disclosures and practices. In addition, the development of the sustainability field in Angelo Poretti & C. is discussed from the perspective of the legitimacy theory. Organizational fields follow an evolutionary path from diversity to a homogenizing process that has been conceptualized as isomorphism. It has been defined as "a constraining process that forces one unit in a population to resemble other units that face the same set of environmental conditions" (DiMaggio and Powell, 1983, p. 149).

DiMaggio and Powell distinguished two different kinds of isomorphism: competitive and institutional. The first is associated with competitive markets where the primary performance criterion is economic fitness (Tuttle and Dillard, 2007); the second is not influenced by competitive forces but is characterized by processes and procedures that become routine, providing stability. The institutionalization process strongly influences the tendency to adopt behaviors similar to those of successful entities. Thus, institutionalization was defined in terms of the processes by which sequences of activities achieve normative and cognitive fixity and become taken for granted (Meyer et al., 1987). The primary evaluation criterion is institutional legitimacy. The issue of organizational change and adaptation is a key milestone for assessing the complexity of political, regulatory and technological changes in several organizations. A few decades ago, some scholars (Meyer and Rowan, 1977; Zucker, 1977; Meyer and Scott, 1983) formulated *neo-institutionalism*, suggesting a new orientation by which the formal organization structure reflected not only technical demands and resource dependencies, but was also shaped by institutional forces, including rational myths, knowledge legitimated through the educational system and by professions, public opinion, and the law. As a result, the organizational practices and structures are often either reflections or responses to rules, beliefs and conventions built into the wider environment (Powell, 1991, 2007).

Institutionalization starts with internal and/or external pressure for a shift in institutionalized forms. DiMaggio and Powell (1983) identified coercive, normative and mimetic factors of reproduction. Coercive factors can be identified as political pressures and the force of the state, providing regulatory oversight and control (DiMaggio and Powell, 1983; Carmona et al., 1998; Carmona and Macias, 2001; Carpenter and Feroz, 2001). International legislations and bodies exert strong pressure on the need to have the same reporting systems with respect to accounting practices and information disclosures (Arnold, 2005). Normative factors refer to the potent influence of the professions and the role of education. According to DiMaggio and Powell, "the professions are subject to the same coercive and mimetic pressure as are organizations" (1983, p. 152). The major force is the professionalization of the workforce, which is essentially determined by the growth of educational and training courses as well as the activities and the initiatives promoted by professional bodies (DiMaggio and Powell, 1983). This factor influenced important organizational changes such as the adoption of innovative management systems such as total quality management, which was adopted by managers in many companies.

Finally, mimetic factors are the habitual, taken-for-granted responses to circumstances of uncertainty. The existence of ambiguous goals and a high level of uncertainty push companies to copy the same practices that are perceived as legitimate and successful (Carmona et al., 1998). Scott (2001) developed three pillars of the institutional order: regulative, normative and cultural/cognitive. Regulative factors involve rule-setting and sanctioning; normative aspects refer to an evaluative and compulsory dimension; and cultural/cognitive factors highlight shared conceptions and frames that give an added meaning. Scott's pillars show three different rationales for legitimacy, either by virtue of being legally sanctioned, morally authorized or culturally supported (Powell, 2007). Given these premises, different combinations of the three elements shape organizations and organizational fields. Consequently, the institutional analysis can serve to identify the relevant factors in particular contexts and to understand the extent to which the mechanisms are able to reinforce the prevailing social order or undercut one another. The level of analysis in institutional research is the organizational field or societal sector. Much of the initial research on institutional effects showed that organizations are obliged to conform to the expectations of the fields of which they are members (Clemens and Cook, 1999).

From a historical perspective, researchers have begun to explore several case studies in order to ascertain changes in meaning and the transformation of organizational practices and identities (Ventresca and Mohr, 2002). Institutional theory frames our investigation. This theory has been developed within and outside of accounting, and it offers a valid support for exploring the forces that influence individuals within social organization (Lemke et al., 2001; Dillard et al., 2004). We use the framework built by DiMaggio and Powell (1983) and DiMaggio (1988), who amplify and develop the work of Meyer and Rowan (1977). It allows us to go beyond the mere consideration of economic pressures and to get an in-depth understanding of the evolution of systems and the constraining factors that have influenced the actors within these systems.

The First Phase: Mimetic Isomorphism

The first phase is characterized by the high level of uncertainty consequent on open and competitive fields, where perceptions are becoming more important in order to establish legitimation, and where, in fact, the primary aim is to improve performance by copying behaviours of successful entities. Mimetic pressures include benchmarking and identifying of best practices and leading players in the field (Tuttle and Dillard, 2007). The first step of Angelo Poretti's development was characterized by a mimetic process because beer production in a country like Italy was unknown and the founder of the company enlisted the advice of a Pilsen master brewer, Emanuele Anger, who evaluated the place near the Valganna caves as an excellent one for building the factory and installation of equipment. The presence of water that flowed from the sources and the natural reservoir's production of ice—needed to cool the fermentation containers and to mature the beer during the summer—were highly appreciated.

Localization near the Fountain of the Sick

We can identify some *economic pressures* in relation to the localization of the company. The choice of first ingredients for the production of the beer represents a competitive advantage and thus the use of the water was perceived as crucial in realizing the company's success. The choice of this area was not accidental: Bohemian Pilsner beer required greater lightness and delicacy than other beers sold in the same period (i.e., Vienna and Chiavenna), and thus arose the need to use first-class ingredients. The choice of the locality for establishment of the plant was related to the use of one of the main ingredients in beer: the water that came from a source well known at the time, the Fountain of the Sick, situated near the caves of Valganna. This name is due to the effects of the water, locally considered miraculous, whose fame reached as far off as Milan. The particular name given to the water indicated its "effectiveness in helping those who have lost their health to find it again" (*l'efficacia di essa a richiamar la salute in chi l'ha perduta*), The source is located in a place "most agreeable and charming in the summer" and is considered so "fresh, clear, crystalline and light" that a doctor from the Hospital Fate-Bene Fratelli of Milan in 1867 advocated its "industrial use."[8] Even though no confirmation of the excellent quality of the water coming from the Fountain of the Sick has ever been corroborated by chemical analysis, the popular belief in the miraculous effects of the water persisted to such an extent that the area became a popular tourist attraction.

There are also *coercive pressures* connected to the localization. In addition to the specific features of the water of the Fountain of the Sick, the decision about the company's localization had been influenced by another aspect. The need for road links connecting the valley of the Fountain of the Sick and Induno Olona and then later the city of Varese was urged, not only in the interests of nature tourism but also because of requirements related to the industrial development of the area and in particular the emergence and consolidation of the Poretti Brewery. The area of the Fountain of the Sick and the Valganna was, therefore, the result of a mixture of nature, health and business interests.

Technology, Raw Materials and Know-How Importation

In the first phase of the company's development the entrepreneurial idea of Angelo Poretti was to implement specific skills for the production of a beer characterized by uniqueness of the technical know-how learned abroad. The high quality of production required importing the plants from Vienna as well as raw materials such as hops and malt. The mimetic process implies that the primary motivation is associated to copying similar successful organizations to legitimate its own activity and to improve performance.

Many coopers and brewers came from Pilsen, and they started to work in the company because they had specific skills in setting fermenters and tanks. The company used highly qualified technical staff, with expertise and specific skills[9] able to assure the right technical implementation of the Pilsner method.

Sales Management

Another interesting event was a change in the marketing policy adopted by the company, which was one of the drivers of the success of the product. To allow the purchase of beer by families in small quantities through bottles, retailers had transferred the beer in small quantities into barrels with a capacity of 25 to50 liters, with a clear deterioration of the product during the summer months. Starting from 1883 Poretti decided to sell the beer not only in traditional barrels but also in bottles of various sizes that were initially sealed with a cork and then with metal clasps. The policy of expansion of the Poretti brewery led, in 1880, to the creation of a department with special machinery for the "barley tollitura," and this desire for growth on the part of the Poretti company produced, in fact, a strong change in the area of the Fountain of the Sick, even to the point of channeling the waters directly to the brewery for the production of beer.

The Second Phase: Coercive Isomorphism

In this phase, organizational change is the result of dependence on other entities. The major factor is transactions with State-like bureaucratic agencies (i.e., university administrations). Coercive isomorphism usually "stems from political influence and the problems of legitimacy (DiMaggio and Powell, 1983, p. 150). In the case of Angelo Poretti & C., coercive pressures were exerted by the State during the fascist period.

Coercive Pressures: Autharky

The characteristics of beer production that required the importation of raw materials, machinery and know-how from abroad, as intended from the beginning by the founder of Poretti, made it difficult to coexist with the historical, economic and sociocultural context of the fascist period.

Economic Pressures: The Postwar Period

The economic situation of the postwar period stimulated many Italian companies to transform themselves into joint stock companies, in what was perceived as the most suitable instrument to qualify business management and redesign the decision-making structure. In particular, company management sought to attract new capital on the basis of an appropriate assessment of the management activities promoted by the shareholders. The industrial and commercial growth of Poretti suffered a setback following the Great Crisis of 1929, which drastically reduced the consumption of beer. Beer production dropped to around 14,344 hectoliters, with serious reflections in terms of profitability. The deep crisis in consumption led the board to consider whether to seek new markets, which was given concrete form in a proposal made by Costanzo Emolli, main dealer of Poretti, on the feasibility of launching the product on the African market, particularly in Tripoli and in Libya in general, which was at the time an Italian colony. After obtaining the approval of the president, this proposal then led to the company creating retail outlets in Tripoli (the Giacciaie of Tropolitana).

Coercive Pressures: The Company's Colonial Policy

The perspective of exporting Poretti beer abroad, particularly to Africa, reflects a typical attitude of the period with its colonial policy aiming to encourage agricultural and industrial activities in Libya. However, some external factors, such as the Ethiopian colonial policy and inadequate management of Libyan resources by the Italian government led to the failure of the initiative. In addition, factors related to specific religious traditions were not considered, but these imposed a ban on drinking alcohol. Besides that, there was also the lack of knowledge of beer, not only among the local population but also in the Italian settlers, who largely came from the southern regions of Italy. After about a year this initiative was completely rejected; the company's inventory was sold off and the employees returned to Italy.

The Third Phase: Normative Isomorphism

Normative pressures determine established norms and values, entrance requirements and socialization mechanisms. The organizations have a primary motivation, which is conformity with expectations as required by established norms and values (Tuttle and Dillard, 2007). In the case of Angelo Poretti & C., professionalization of the workforce and its structuration are the major aspects. In the early 1970s, the management of Poretti launched an interesting initiative, which can be included in the process of professionalization of the workers. However, what the accounting records do not reveal is the company's focus on human resources—noticeable, in particular, in Lettera Poretti of 25 January 1961, Year III No. 1 Special Issue;, which started an interesting practice that is still followed by the company. The letter announced that a questionnaire would be sent to all employees by registered mail, and invited everyone "to complete in total freedom and under the guarantee of anonymity." It was a questionnaire by which management sought to ascertain the major issues at the plant and start a dialogue with employees, of which this survey is but the first step (see Figures 4.3 and 4.4).

The aim was thus the improvement of relations between the company and its employees in pursuit of greater freedom of communication and possibilities of mutual information. In fact, the document ends with the announcement that "the next issue of Lettera Poretti will report extensively and in detail the results of the survey which, we believe, will lay the foundations for fruitful and concrete work."

Information concerning human resources, analyzed through a total of 20 questions are as follows:

1. The work and its conditions
2. The work environment
3. Company and staff relations
4. Communication and information.

A question at the end of the survey, asking to rate the level of interest in completing the questionnaire, shows a rating of 76.8%, indicating high employee satisfaction with the initiative. The response rate is also high: 94.1% of the questionnaires were completed.

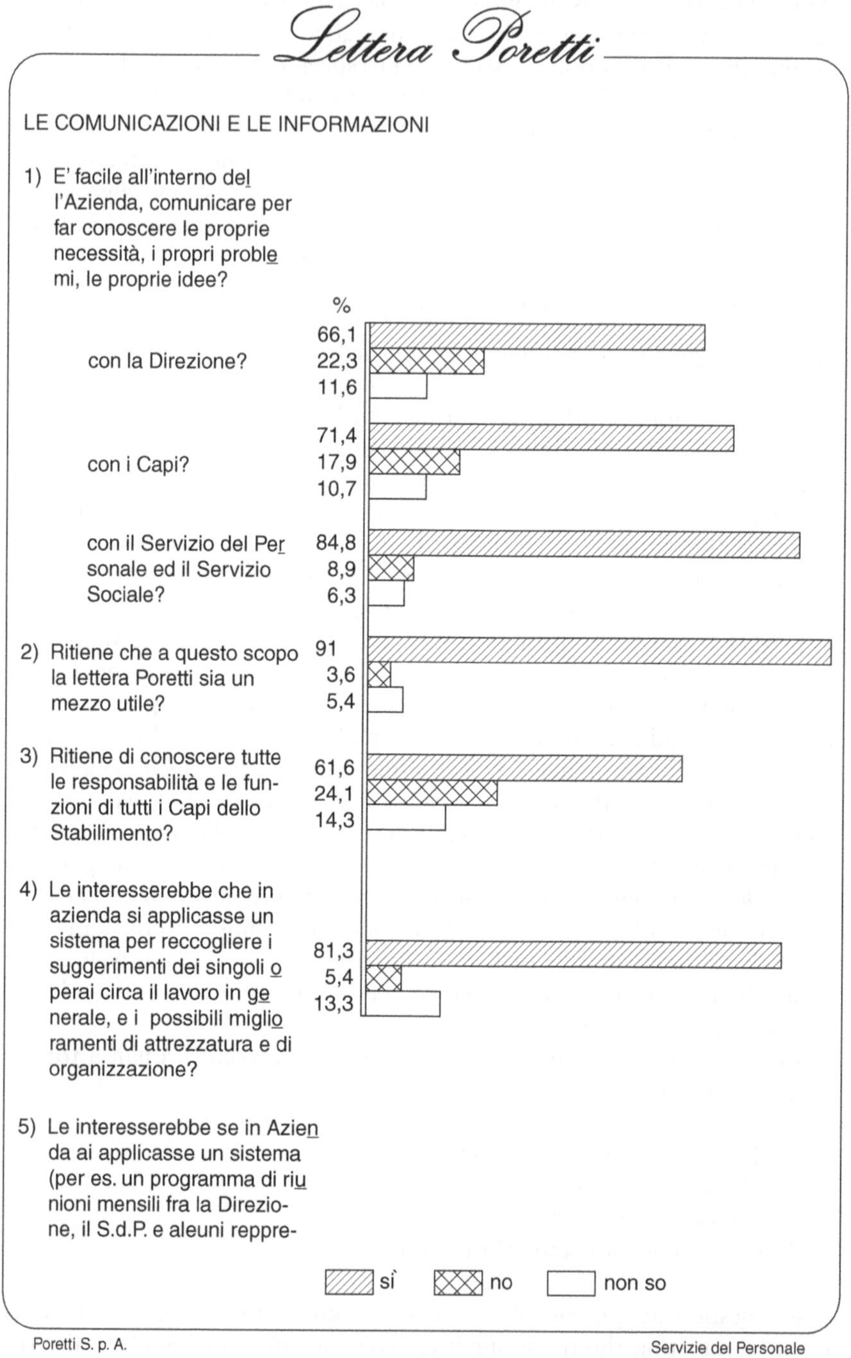

Figure 4.3 Poretti letter: questionnaire survey on "disclosure and information"

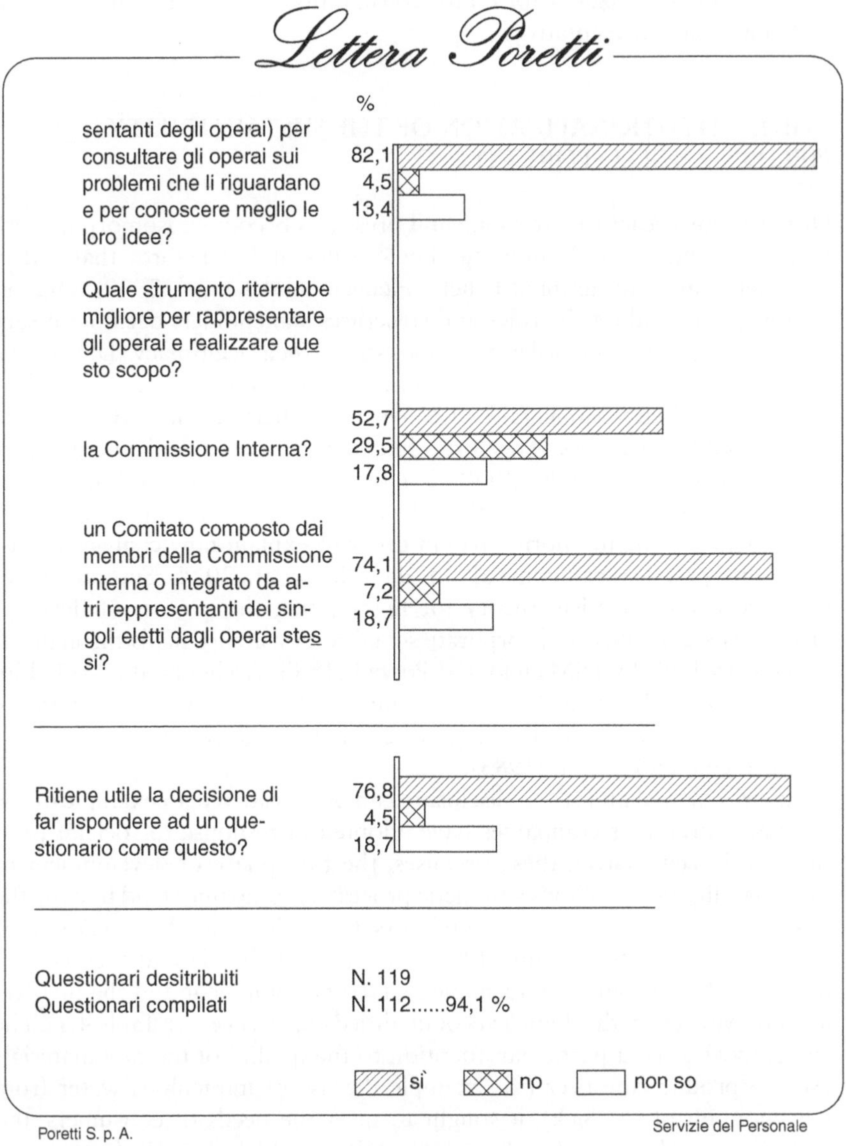

Figure 4.4 Poretti letter: questionnaire survey on "disclosure and information" (cont'd)

An analysis of the questionnaire answers shows that the judgement on the working conditions and remuneration, also in comparison with other companies, is positive, although workers deem it useful to improve the exchange of information within the company. The judgement on the questionnaire is favorable for the 76.8% of respondents, and an interesting finding is the need to appoint a regular forum for consultation between the management and employee representatives.

THE INSTITUTIONALIZATION OF THE SUSTAINABILITY FIELD IN ANGELO PORETTI & C.

Organizations react to environmental pressures becoming isomorphic with their environment and adopting similar rules and structures that reflect managers' taken-for-granted beliefs (Heugens and Lander, 2009). Organizations tend to adopt the rules and structures stakeholders deem necessary (Deephouse, 1996) in order to demonstrate their legitimacy. During the 1960s and 1970s new societal expectations required companies to disclose the social and environmental consequences of their activities (Gray et al., 1996), facilitating access to resources like finance, custom and labour (Scott, 2008; Heugens and Lander, 2009). The field of sustainability follows a process of development and it can also advocate the three types of isomorphism (mimetic, coercive and normative) in order to explain how changes in sustainability practices can come about (de Villier et al., 2014). Several studies used the institutionalism theory for highlighting the process of development of sustainability and corporate social responsibility fields through the framework built by DiMaggio and Powell (1983; Archel et al., 2011; Lim and Tsutsui, 2012) and the implementation of environmental accounting (Larrinaga-Gonzalez and Bebbington, 2001) through the framework built by DiMaggio and Powell (1983).

Environmental and social disclosure can be considered an example of the rules and structures companies have adopted in response to societal pressures and needs. Given these premises, the first phase of development of sustainability fields follows a mimetic process as companies tend to copy the business models of successful competitors. In the first stage Angelo Poretti & C. mimic the practices adopted by breweries in Bohemia and Vienna with respect to beer production technology, factory equipment and the involvement of workers with a high level of qualified experience (see Table 4.1). The company showed a particular attention to the quality of the raw materials used to produce the beer (for example the use of miraculous water from the Fountain of the Sick), it sought to meet the needs of consumers and had an unusual respect for the environment in which Poretti's factory was established.

The second and third phases involved regulators, national and international legislation and stakeholders, all of which led to the maturity phase of the sustainability field. Since 1970 the company has started to adopt sustainability practices and disclosures. Recently there were coercive and normative pressures exerted by national and international frameworks (compulsory requirements about energy and water consumption, rules for responsible consumption of beer, guidelines on environmental and social reporting, etc.).

Table 4.1 Institutionalization of Angelo Poretti's development process

	Mimetic isomorphism	Coercive isomorphism	Normative isomorphism
Description	Early stages characterized by uncertainty around the response to pressures	Early stages, but pressures are starting to formalize around new regulations and demands from influential stakeholders	Towards maturity through professionalization driven by similar training and social interactions between professionals
Dominant logic processes	Copy successful competitors Benchmark and identify best practices	Conform to demands Formal and informal influence	Conform to taken-for-granted norms Internalization of new norms
Applied to Angelo Poretti & C.	The company imports raw materials, equipment and know-how from Bohemia (brewers and coopers) for the production of Pilsner beer. Given the high uncertainty of the target market, the will to realize a brewery imitating the model of those of Bohemia and Bavaria starts to take shape. Use of the water from the Fountain of the Sick. Attention to the quality of the characteristics of the raw materials and environmental protection.	Strong pressure from stakeholders' needs, particularly in the postwar period; consequences of the sharp drop in the consumption of beer; demand for a product with certain quality characteristics, strong pressure of the government towards self-sufficiency. Compliance with rules laid down by the political power of the time and the consequent adoption of policies aimed at reducing imports of raw materials.	Rationalization of production processes; development of employees through a careful program of staff training. Achieving a high degree of attention to the stakeholders and sharing on the part of managers and consultants of rules for the respect of human resources, the environment and the community. The entry into Poretti's company of the Carlsberg Group highlights the fact that the process of professionalization has reached a mature stage.

Source: Adapted from DiMaggio and Powell (1983); Tuttle and Dillard (2007); de Villiers et al. (2014).

Whereas normative isomorphism involves the internalization of norms and practices that derive from professionalization, the historical analysis of Angelo Poretti & C. is highlighted as one of the most important organizational changes within the sustainability field the moment Lettera Poretti was published (1961). It undoubtedly represents the first step of the company's significant and continuous commitment to sustainability best practices, with a particular focus on human capital by promoting several initiatives such as the rotation of tasks that allowed for the enrichment of team work, or, in the early 1970s, the creation of quality teams ("Circoli di Qualità").

CONCLUSIONS

The historical investigation of corporate business practices and reporting during a time span of a decade or so is aimed at a correct interpretation of the genesis and subsequent development of the major business idea of Angelo Poretti, the founder of the company. In particular, corporate reporting and the practices adopted were evaluated as a result of some moments of change that have influenced corporate life and business decisions (Meyer, 1986; Moreno and Càmara, 2014).

The case study analyzed involved the assessment of a variety of primary and secondary sources and the key aim was to identify and have an in-depth look at the major organizational changes that have characterized the process of development of the company during the period 1877–1980. Different kinds of pressures influenced the behaviour and the choices made by Angelo Poretti & C.'s management, which have been assessed through the institutional theory framework built by DiMaggio and Powell (1983). Two main factors emerge from the historical analysis: the will to assert the primacy of a company founded and developed on Italian territory and, at the same time, the path towards internationalization, based from the beginning on the importation of raw materials, equipment and personnel from abroad. The influence exerted by environmental pressures determined a process of imitation conforming to the best business practices adopted by successful competitors, but the company was able to "institutionalize" the sustainability practices that Angelo Poretti & C. managed to create right from the beginning, particularly in specific areas, such as environmental protection, customer satisfaction and human resources development.

The historical analysis highlighted the key role of Angelo Poretti and Edoardo Chiesa, according to the need of evaluating individual behaviours through an analysis of the cultural, political and social setting and the historical period within which they operate (Powell, 1991; Sargiacomo, 2008).

Further development of this research may lead to an in-depth analysis of the main competitors within the beverage industry in Italy, in order to compare the different strategic decisions responding to several economic, mimetic, coercive and normative pressures.

NOTES

1. The previous version of this chapter was presented at the conference Accounting and Food Milano for EXPO 2015, Milano-Bicocca University, 13 June 2015, Milan, Italy. The authors would like to acknowledge the conference chairs Prof. Roberto Di Pietra, Prof. Luciano D'Amico and Prof. Massimo Sargiacomo, and all participants for their useful comments and suggestions. Although this chapter is the result of a conjoint analysis, Sections 1, 3 and Subsection 2 of Section 4 have been written by Andrea Gasperini; Subsections 1 and 5 of Section 4 have been written by Alberto Frausin, while Section 2, Subsections 3 and 4 of Section 4, Sections 5, 6 and 7 have been written by Federica Doni.
2. The global market consists of North America, South America, Western Europe, Eastern Europe, Middle East Africa and Asia-Pacific (MarketLine, 2014).
3. They were experienced brewers who came from Austria and Bohemia, who had a qualified professional experience and were recognized internationally. Some names are found in the journal of the company (1889–1890): Vincenzo Minowsky, Franz Adamek, Giuseppe Domenik, Franz Petráček and Antonio Kranz (Macchione, 2013, p. 33). In particular, some of them received high wages for their work performance.
4. The beer at the time, the "Beer of March," was usually made in Italy during the winter season with raw materials (barley and hops). It was not of the highest quality and was not highly refined, so as not to require the use of expensive machinery for processing and cooling (Macchione, 2013, p. 30). The qualitative characteristic was the high alcohol content, which also allowed consumption in the summer months, until about October.
5. The Brewery Poretti had already participated in similar events such as the Regional Exhibition of 1879 in Monza where the entrepreneur received the gold medal (Macchione, 2013, p. 45).
6. The architects also received the task to restructure the brewery, with works that continued until 1921, with interruptions due to the Great War (1915–1918).
7. Carlsberg Italy currently closes its financial statements on 30 September.
8. This news was published in the magazine *Varesina Chronicle* in June 1867 by the Honorary Dr. Giuseppe Papis (Macchione, 2013, p. 8).
9. See note n. 4.

REFERENCES

Primary Sources

Archivio Cancelleria Tribunale di Varese (Archive Chancery Court of Varese).
Archivio di Stato Como (State Archives Como).
Archivio di Stato Varese (State Archives Varese).
Archivio Notarile di Como (Notarial Archives Como).
Archivio Notarile Milano (Notarial Archives Milan).
Archivio Storico Camera di Commercio Varese (Historical Archives of the Chamber of Commerce Varese).
Archivio Storico Comune di Induno Olona (Historical Archive Induno Olona).
Archivio Storico Comune di Varese (Historical Archives of the City of Varese).

Secondary Sources

AA. VV. (1881) *L'Esposizione Industriale di Milano del 1881* (The industrial exhibition in Milan 1881), Milan: Sonzogno.

AA. VV. (1879) *Le nostre industrie Cronaca Varesina*, 30 novembre (Our factories. *Varesina Chronicle*, 30th November).
AA. VV. (1901) I funerali del Cav. Poretti, *Cronaca Prealpina*, 23 ottobre (The funeral of Cav. Poretti, Chronicle Prealpina, 23th October).
AA. VV. (1927) Birra Poretti—Società Anonima—Varese, L'Illustrazione Italiana, anno LIV, n. 28, 17 luglio 1927. (Poretti Beer—Limited Company—Varese, The Italian Illustration, year LIV, No. 28, July 17, 1927.
Adams, C.A. and McNicholas, P. (2007) Making a difference: Sustainability reporting, accountability and organizational change. *Accounting, Auditing & Accountability Journal* 20(3): 382–402.
Amaduzzi, A. (2004) *Percorsi di ricerca fra Storia della ragioneria, aziende e contabilità, dottrine e professioni* (Search paths between History of accounting, business and accounting, doctrines and professions). Milan: Giuffrè.
Andreolotti, L. (1993a) Bilanci di un secolo fa alla Birra Poretti, Lombardia Nord-Ovest, n.2 (Balance Sheets of a century ago at Birra Poretti, Lombardy East, No. 2).
Andreolotti, L. (1993b) Una passeggiata nella storia della vecchia Poretti. Dal libro giornale Ottobre '89/Dicembre '90, Poretti News del 1890 (A walk in the history of the old Poretti. From the journal October '89/December 90, 1890 News Poretti), pp. 8–13.
Archel, P., Husillos, J. and Spense, C. (2011) The institutionalisation of unaccountability: Loading the dice of Corporate Social Responsibility discourse. *Accounting Organizations and Society* 36: 327–343.
Arnold, A.J. (1995) Should historians trust late 19th century company financial statements? *Business History* 38(2): 40–50.
AssoBirra, Associazione degli Industriali della Birra e del Malto (Industrial Association of Beer and Malt), Annual Report 2013. Available at: www.assobirra.it
Bertini, U. (1990) *Il sistema d'azienda. Schema di analisi* (The business system. Analysis scheme). Turin: Giappichelli.
Bertini, U. (2013) *Scritti di politica aziendale* (Writings of business policy). Turin: Giappichelli.
Boyns, T. (1993) Editorial comment: Business history through accounting records. *Accounting Business Financial History* 3: 249–253.
Carlsberg Italia. Available at: http://www.museoweb.it/imprese/carlsberg-italia/ [Accessed: 30th January 2015].
Carmona, S., Ezzamel, M. and Gutierrez, F. (1998) Towards an institutional analysis of accounting change in the Royal Tobacco Factory of Seville. *The Accounting Historians Journal* 25(1): 129–157.
Carmona, S. and Macias, M. (2001) Institutional pressures, monopolistic conditions and the implementation of early cost management practices: The case of Royal Tobacco Factory of Seville (1820–1877). *Abacus* 37(2): 139–165.
Carpenter, V.R. and Feroz, E.H. (2001) Institutional theory and accounting rule choice: An analysis of four US state government's decisions to adopt generally accepted accounting principles. *Accounting, Organizations and Society* 26(7): 565–596.
Castelli, R. (1989) La Birreria Poretti di Varese. In: Barbieri, F. and Negri, A. (eds.), *Archeologia Industriale. Indagini sul territorio in Lombardia e Veneto*. Milan: Editions Unicopli, pp. 123–147.
Clemens, E.S. and Cook, J.M. (1999) Politics and institutionalism: Explaining durability and change. *Annual Review of Sociology* 25: 441–466.
Codara, A. (1901) *Varese nel 1901: guida ufficiale dell'esposizione: città e dintorni, cenni storici, arti, industrie, commerci, ecc.* Varese: Typografia Cronaca Prealpina.
Cormier, D., Magnan, M. and Van Velthoven, B. (2005) Environmental disclosure quality in large German companies: Economic incentives, public pressures or institutional conditions? *European Accounting Review* 14(1): 3–39.

Corsolini, G. (1977) La Poretti S.p.A. di Induno Olona. In: Colombo, S. (ed.), *Varese Vicende e Protagonisti* (Poretti S.p.A. Induno Olona, Varese events and leading actors). Bologna: Edizioni Edison, pp. 54–76.

Dacin, M.T. (1997) Isomorphism in context: The power and prescription of institutional norms. *Academy of Management Journal* 40(1): 46–81.

Deephouse, D.L. (1996) Does isomorphism legitimate? *Academy of Management Journal* 39(4): 1024–1039.

de Villiers, C., Low, M. and Samkin, G. (2014) The institutionalisation of mining company sustainability disclosures. *Journal of Cleaner Production* 84: 51–58.

Dillard, J., Rigsby, J. and Goodman, C.C. (2004) The making and remaking of organization context: Duality and the institutionalization process. *Accounting, Auditing and Accountability Journal* 17(4): 506–542.

DiMaggio, P.J. (1988) Interest and agency in institutional theory. In: Zucker, L.G. (ed.), *The new institutionalism in organizational analysis*. Chicago: University of Chicago Press, pp. 3–22.

DiMaggio, P.J. and Powell, W.W. (1983) The iron cage revisited: Institutional isomorphism and collective rationality in organizational fields. *American Sociological Review* 48: 147–160.

Franceschi Ferraris, R. (1998) *Storia delle imprese, storia dell'azienda: scopi e metodi d'indagine*, in Atti del IV Convegno Nazionale di Storia della Ragioneria. Storia di imprese tra il XVI ed il XIX secolo, Perugia, 2–3 Ottobre 1997, (*Business history, history: aims and methods of investigation*, in Proceedings of the IV National Conference of Accounting History. History of businesses between the sixteenth and nineteenth centuries, Perugia, 2–3 October, 1997) Roma: Rirea, pp. 7–15.

Friedenson, P. (2007) The bilateral relationships between accounting history and business history: A French perspective. *Accounting Business and Financial History* 17(3): 375–80.

Gallerani, G. (1981) Poretti S.p.A., Oltre cento anni di vita—una tradizione che si rinnova (Poretti S.p.A., Over one hundred years of life—a tradition that is renewed). In: Gallerani, G. (ed.), *Varese e Provincia*. Milan: Edizione Evoluzione del Lavoro, pp. 46–75.

Gourvish, T.R. and Wilson, R.G. (1985) Profitability in the brewery industry, 1885–1914. *Business History* 27: 146–165.

Gray, R., Owen, D. and Adams, C.A. (1996) *Accounting and accountability: Changes and challenges in corporate social and environmental reporting*. London: Prentice-Hall.

Heugens, P. and Lander, M. (2009) Structure! Agency! (and other quarrels): A meta-analysis of institutional theories of organization. *Academy of Management Journal* 52(1): 61–85.

Hopwood, A., Unerman, J. and Fries, J. (eds.) (2010) *Accounting for sustainability: Practical insight*. London: Earthscan.

Johnson, T. (1975) The role of accounting history in the study of modern business enterprise. *The Accounting Review* 50(3, July): 444–450.

Larrinaga-Gonzalez, C. and Bebbington, J. (2001) Accounting change or institutional appropriation?—A case study of the implementation of environmental accounting. *Critical Perspective on Accounting* 12: 269–292.

Lemke, D., Schminke, M., and Donaldson, L. (2001) *Wither goest thou? Seeking trends in organization theory research in the 1990s*. Working paper. Revision of D. Lemke, M. Schminke, N. Clark, and P. Muir, 1999, Best Papers: Proceedings of the Academy of Management.

Licini, S. (2012) Scritture contabili e storia d'impresa: un caso di studio (1838–1882). In: Rossi, C., Rusconi, G. and Servalli, S. (eds.), *Saggi di storia delle discipline aziendali e delle dottrine economiche. Scritti in onore di Antonio Amaduzzi Professore Emerito* (Accounting records and business history: A case study (1838–1882),

Essays on the history of the business disciplines and economic doctrines. Essays in honor of Professor Emeritus Antonio Amaduzzi). Rome: Rirea, pp. 127–179.

Lim, A. and Tsutsui, K. (2012) Globalization and commitment in corporate social responsibility: Cross-national analyses of institutional and political-economy effects. *American Sociological Review* 77(1): 69–98.

Lister, R. (1981) Comment: Company financial statements as source material for business historians: Observations on the underlying conceptual framework. *Business History* 23: 233–239.

Macchione, P. (1991) *Una provincia industriale. Miti e storia dello sviluppo economico tra Varesotto e Alto Milanese, Vol. I Dal XVIII secolo alla Prima Guerra Mondiale; Vol. II Ventesimo secolo* (*An industrial province. Myths and history of economic development between Varese and Alto Milanese, Vol. From the eighteenth century to the First World War, Vol. II Twentieth Century*) Varese: Edizioni Latina, 1989–1991.

Macchione, P. (1992) Dalla "Fontana degli Ammalati" la premiata birra di Angelo Poretti e Compagni, Lombardia Nord-Ovest (From the "Fountain of the Sick" the award-winning beer Angelo Poretti and Companions, Lombardy East) n.1/1992.

Macchione, P. (2013) Angelo Poretti & C., Storia, immagini e protagonisti della birra nata in Valganna. (Angelo Poretti & C., History, images and actors of the beer born in Valganna). I diamanti, Pietro Macchione Editore.

Mager, A.K. (2008) Apartheid and business: Competition, monopoly and the growth of the malted beer industry in South Africa. *Business History* 50(3): 272–290.

MarketLine Industry Profile. (2014) Global Beverages. July 2014. Available at: www.marketline.com

Marriner, S. (1980) Company financial statements as source material for business historians. *Business History* 22: 203–235.

Meyer, J.W. (1986) Social environments and organizational accounting. *Accounting, Organizations and Society* 11(4/5): 345–356.

Meyer, J.W., Boli, J. and Thomas, G. (1987) Ontology and rationalization in the Western cultural account. In: Thomas G., Meyer J., Ramirez J.W. and Boli J. (eds.), *Institutional structure*. Beverly Hills, CA: Sage, pp. 104–123.

Meyer, J.W. and Rowan, B. (1977) Institutionalized organizations: Formal structure as myth and ceremony. *American Journal of Sociology* 83: 340–363.

Meyer, J.W. and Scott, R. (1983) *Organizational environments: Ritual and rationality*. Beverly Hills, CA: Sage.

Moreno, A. and Càmara, M. (2014) Evolution of information content from an institutional perspective: *El Alcàzar* brewery (1928–1993). *Accounting History* 19(3): 369–398.

Papis, G. (1867) La Fontana degli Ammalati. *La Cronaca Varesina*, 9 giugno 1867.

Parker, R.H. (1991) Misleading accounts? Pitfalls for historians. *Business History* 33: 1–18.

Powell, W.W. (1991) Expanding the scope of institutional analysis. In: Powell, W.W. and DiMaggio, P.J. (eds.), *New institutionalism in organizational analysis*. Chicago: University of Chicago Press, pp. 183–203.

Powell, W.W. (2007) The new institutionalism. In: Clegg, S. and Baily, J.A. (eds.), *The international encyclopedia of organization studies*. London: Sage Publisher, pp. 58–75.

Sanvito, M. (1931) La Birra Poretti. Uno stabilimento modello, *La Provincia di Varese*, 7 luglio 1931.

Sargiacomo, M. (2008) Institutional pressures and isomorphic change in a high-fashion company: The case of Brioni Roman style, 1945–89. *Accounting, Business & Financial History* 18(2): 215–241.

Scott, W.R. (2001) *Institutions and organizations*, Thousand Oaks, CA: Sage Publications.

Scott, W.R. (2008) *Institutions and organizations: Ideas and interests*, third edition. Thousand Oaks, CA: Sage Publications.

Tuttle, B. and Dillard, J. (2007) Beyond competition: Institutional isomorphism in U.S. accounting research. *Accounting Horizons* 21(4): 288–309.

Ventresca, M.J. and Mohr, J.W. (2002) Archival research methods. In: Baum Joel, A.C. (ed.), *The Blackwell companion to organizations*. Oxford: Blackwell Publishers, pp. 2–44.

Zanzi, L. (1879) Le nostre industrie. La fabbrica di birra alla Fontana degli ammalati, *Cronaca Varesina*, 23 Marzo 1879 (Our industries. The brewery at the Fountain of the sick, *Varesina Chronicle*, March 23, 1879).

Zucker, L.G. (1977) The role of institutionalization in cultural persistence. *American Journal of Sociology* 42: 726–743.

Websites

http://www.assobirra.it
http://www.beverfood.com
http://www.carlsbergitalia.it
http://www.beviresponsabile.it

5 Context-Specific and Firm-Specific Factors and Their Effect on the Amarelli Bookkeeping System between 1874 and 1920

Franco Rubino, Romilda Mazzotta and Stefania Veltri

INTRODUCTION

This chapter presents a case study based on the bookkeeping system of an established southern Italian family firm, Amarelli, still operating in the liquorice industry[1].

The choice of Amarelli is not casual. Amarelli is one of the longstanding Italian firms and it could be seen as a successful firm in the Calabrian context: the only surviving firm of the proto-industrial district of Calabrian firms producing liquorice juice. Amarelli runs an industrial activity in a rural territory, as highlighted by the bookkeeping documents filed since 1874.

The chapter addresses the call for an interdisciplinary approach, using the Bourdieu framework to analyze the Amarelli accounting practices. Giving importance to the logic of the practice, we adapted Bourdieu's framework investigating which contextual and firm-specific factors most affected the way in which Amarelli held its accounts (the research question).

Document analysis and semi-structured interviews were used as a means of investigation. In detail, old books, journals and ledgers were analyzed in order to address the research question, and the CEO and family owner, Fortunato Amarelli, was interviewed in Rossano, where Amarelli is located. A qualitative data analysis was applied to the interview data, using an interpretative approach.

The chapter contributes to enlarging the knowledge of the functioning of the bookkeeping system in practice within the Italian context; Italy is a country that strongly contributes to the development of accounting practices.

The originality of the chapter lies in the use of an interdisciplinary approach, specifically a Bourdieusian framework, to analyze the accounting practices of a firm.

THE THEORETICAL FRAMEWORK

In his recent article, Carnegie (2014) encourages present and future accounting historians to conduct critical and interpretive histories of the nature, role, uses and effects of accounting within its organizational and social contexts across all organizational forms. This exhortation draws inspiration from the well-known article by Hopwood (1983), which affirms that accounting is not an "independent art"; rather, it "can shape, mould and even play a role in constructing the setting in which it forms a part" (Hopwood, 1983, p. 288). In other words, accounting is enacted to serve specific purposes; therefore, rather than "detaching accounting from its organizational setting" (Hopwood, 1983, p. 288), researchers should treat it as a context-specific and firm-specific discipline.

Investigating the story behind the accounts within the contexts in which these account books were prepared gives potentially more interest and significance to the accounting historical studies from the point of view of accounting as social practice (Carnegie, 2014).

Following this approach, historical analysis on accounting practices should be conducted by taking into consideration national, local and juridical frameworks surrounding the organization chosen as the object of study. In fact, accounting may have followed different development paths in different countries, resulting from different processes that reflect the socio-economic contexts prevailing in each country (Boyns and Edwards, 1996; Sargiacomo, 2008).

Moreover, the reflection that accounting should be seen as a social practice, with consequences for human behaviour, rather than merely technical practice (Hopwood, 1983; Napier, 1989; Hopwood and Miller, 1994; Miller, 1994; Gomes, 2008), implies that accounting research could become the subject of new theories and methods, drawn from other relevant disciplines such as sociology, political and organizational theory instead of referring back just to economics, as did accounting research up to the 1980s (Carnegie and Napier, 2012).

Doing a research in accounting history from this new perspective means carrying out an interdisciplinary accounting research, which implies a switch from accounting history as a niche research area to a research area open to multiple contributions (Bertalan and Napier, 2013). This "new accounting history" (Miller et al., 1991) has the merit of widening the working area of accounting research, which moves from a specialist research area in itself to a discipline that permeates other specializations, allowing both to favour the "growth in historical accounting research" (Carnegie and Napier, 2012, p. 330) and a deeper understanding of the past, potentially providing further insights into both the present and the future.

Addressing the call for an interdisciplinary approach, both in accounting history (Carnegie, 2014) and in accounting research (Parker and Guthrie, 2014), we decided to complement the contextual approach (Hopwood, 1983) with an approach derived from Bourdieu (1972, 1980, 1984), a sociologist who emphasizes the role played by the actors, together with the context and the resources owned, in deploying social practices.[2]

Briefly speaking, Bourdieu's theory of practice derives from the interaction of three key concepts: capital, habitus and field (Bourdieu, 1984). By capital Bourdieu means the useful resources that could be used by social actors to distinguish and compete with each other. In the social space, capital includes economic, cultural, social and symbolic capital. By habitus he means an actor's cultural dispositions (Bourdieu, 1972, 1980). Habitus can be both conscious and unconscious to the actor who possesses it, but it is the factor that determines the actor's strategy. The concept of habitus applies not only to each individual actor, but also to a group, an organization or a society (Baskerville et al., 2014). Finally, the field is where habitus and capital are conditioned and meaningful. Practice is where capital, habitus (which we can consider as internal or firm-specific factors) and field (which we can consider as external or context-specific factors) interrelate, and where they are manifested (Everett, 2002). In this sense, to enact Bourdieu's practical theory in a social study, practice has to be studied. Bourdieu's theory of practice has such universal dimensions that it can be used to explore any field in social theory, including accounting history (Hopwood, 1983). As Bourdieu did not provide clear instruction to the researcher using his theory, we refer to a recent article (Baskerville et al., 2014) that identifies four approaches to using the Bourdieu framework, of which we use the focus on the social actors' practice.

We believe that practices such as accounting are a product of both context-specific (external) and firm-specific (internal) factors and that here is a need to investigate, together with the contextual factors, the accounting practices of the actors in the field and how the actors (here, the Amarelli firm), through the use of the resources, deploy the accounting national recommendations and local uses.

In the chapter we aim to offer a more holistic theoretical framework, derived from Bourdieu, to take into consideration both contextual and internal factors whereas, generally speaking, the main concern of historical researchers has been to investigate the existence of a link between the theories of accounts and the accounting practices within a firm (Mussolino et al., 2005).

Although we believe that accounting practices are the product of both external and internal issues, in the chapter we would like to analyze the role played by the two categories of drivers in explaining the firm's bookkeeping system.

Bearing in mind that, in the Bourdieu framework, the analysis of the firm's practices derives from both field and internal factors, we adapt his framework to our research approach. In our Bourdieu-like approach, we consider the field as the context-specific (external) factors, while the habitus and capital are included in the firm-specific (internal) factors.

To pursue the main research objective, we posit the following research question:

> *RQ: Were accounting choices in Amarelli affected mostly by external (context-specific) factors or instead by internal (firm-specific) factors?*

THE METHODOLOGY

To address the chapter's research question, a case study methodology has been used. A case study approach is appropriate when a researcher needs to conduct a holistic and in-depth analysis of a complex phenomenon in its real-life context (Yin, 2003; Berry and Otley, 2004). Moreover, the case study methodology offers the possibility of investigating accounts from a practical rather than from a theoretical perspective, through the exploration of a phenomena in a specific context. The use of a case study also allows researchers to use different methods of collecting data, thereby giving them a rich source of data from real settings, with the aim to deepen the understanding of the investigated phenomenon (Yin, 2003).

As such, this method is particularly suitable for exploring accounting practices, which are by nature complex, context dependent and firm dependent (Parker, 2012). Therefore, the case study research method fits very well with the purpose of this chapter. For these reasons, the article analyzes a single in-depth case study of a private Italian organization that has been doing accounting bookkeeping since the late nineteenth century. Using a longitudinal case study to address the research questions is considered appropriate since accounting is a social subject and, in order to be understood, it has to be contextualized—that is, put into the specific time, space and minds in which it develops (Jørgensen, 2006).

The selected firm, Amarelli, presented (and still does present) many features we judge interesting as a case history. Amarelli started an extremely diversified, mainly agricultural family holding, and afterwards it introduced an industrial firm, liquorice juice production, which became its core activity. The research was carried out using a qualitative approach (Parker, 2012), and two qualitative tools, document analysis and semi-structured interviews, have been employed to address the triangulation issue (Moll et al., 2006).

Owing to the nature of the chapter, document analysis (Bowen, 2009) was the main tool to collect the accounting data (primary sources) needed to provide evidence of the research question. The collection and storage of the accounting data was at Amarelli's museum, where the archival accounting documents from 1874 to 1920 are stored.

The other tool used to collect qualitative data, to solve accounting doubts that emerged from the analysis of the accounting documents, were the semi-structured interviews with the CEO of the firm, Dr. Fortunato Amarelli. We chose to use the semi-structured interview because of its high degree of flexibility and because it offers the opportunity to address themes that may come to light during the semi-structured interviews (Qu and Dumay, 2011).

Our recognition process can be articulated in five phases. In a first phase, we had a look at all Amarelli's documents, including journals, ledgers and account books such as bill notes, payables and receivables; then we decided to exclude bill notes, commercial letters and credit letters and focus only on the strictly accounting documents (journals, ledgers, cash records and family wealth). In the second phase we examined the functioning of the Amarelli bookkeeping system. Our comprehension of the functioning of Amarelli's bookkeeping system was also helped by the qualitative semi-structured interviews conducted with the Fortunato Amarelli (third phase), to make sense of some puzzling accounts and to gain knowledge of some events that could justify the existence of certain accounts rather than others. A qualitative data analysis was applied to the interview data. This allowed researchers to focus on the answers delivered by the respondent in terms of their meaning, while also maintaining sensitivity to the context (Denzin and Lincoln, 2000). In the fourth phase we studied the external and internal factors, while in the fifth phase we analyzed the Amarelli accounting practices in the light of our Bourdieu-like framework. In doing so we followed an interpretive approach. In the light of interpretivism, sociological phenomena cannot simply be observed but must also be interpreted by the researcher. This means that there is no one absolute reality, but rather different possibilities are generated by the perspective adopted to interpret the facts (Ryan et al., 2002).

ANALYZING AMARELLI'S CONTEXT-SPECIFIC FACTORS

There are several external factors hypothesized to affect a firm's bookkeeping system. Among external factors that could have affected Amarelli's bookkeeping system we can include juridical context, the economic context and the evolution of the accounting theories.

The *juridical context* is relevant as it influences directly the way in which the firm's accounts were held. As Amarelli was a diversified firm, operating both in the industrial (liquorice juice production) and in the agricultural field (small production of olives and corn) it was, at least potentially, affected by two different juridical norms: those valid for industrial and trade firms and those valid for agricultural firms. In Italy, the reference framework for industrial and trade firms was the Commercial Code of 1882, which provided a distinction between "limited companies" and "individual firms." The legislation was not restrictive: the Code stated which documents were compulsory, but it also allowed firms to choose the bookkeeping system to adopt. As regards the individual company, as Amarelli was, the Commercial Code of 1882 stated that the entrepreneur was obliged to hold accountancy books for the firm's operations, a statement of earnings and a statement reporting the family wealth. The reference framework for agricultural firms was the Civil Code of 1865, which regulated the sharecropper contract.

As regards the *economic context*, the Italian economic scenario was dominated by domestic farms, farms run by noble families and religious institutions (Mussari and Magliacani, 2007). These farms dominated the Italian economic scene until the 1920s, when profound changes took place in the socioeconomic context, as it underwent transformation from a predominantly agricultural to an industrial context accompanied by intense urban development.

As regards the Calabrian territory, we can, as well as articulating our analysis, distinguish between the economic context surrounding the agricultural activity (agricultural context) and the business context surrounding the production activity of liquorice juice, which was the main business activity of Amarelli (business context).

As regarding the *agricultural context*, it should be underlined that in the period investigated, the farm was of the most widespread type of firm in the Calabrian economy (Merzario, 1975), although the Calabrian territory can be identified as an underdeveloped territory, as the presence of agricultural farms was 2% with respect to total Italian agricultural farms (Argenziano, 1914). As regards the typology of agricultural farm, the census of 1881 shows that the owner-run farms were the most widespread type of farm in the Calabrian economy between the nineteenth and early twentieth centuries (owner-run farms, 69%; lease-run farms, 18%; and sharecropper farms, 13%; Argenziano, 1914). As regards the *business context*, the Southern Italian area where the production of liquorice juice has been historically most successful is Northern Ionian Calabria, the territory to which Amarelli belonged. Calabrian firms produced the largest quantity per year, and always the best sorts, of Italian liquorice juice, the best paid juice on the world market (Piccioni, 2009). Regarding the business aspects, for more than two centuries Calabria experienced a peculiar mix of small and medium firms, often with very short life spans, and big firms embedded in the aristocratic *latifundia*. For the owners of these *latifundia*, the production of liquorice juice was usually the most profitable among their many activities, and it was carefully pursued to improve the global economic balance of the estate. Moreover, the large amount of land owned by these families allowed them to obtain the root more easily, it being often scarce and subject to strong commercial competition, by cultivating it. This kind of business structure allowed the formation, during the eighteenth and nineteenth centuries, of a solid network of great Northern Ionian enterprises—very long-lived—whose trademarks soon became famous all over the world (Piccioni, 2010).

The analysis of the *evolution of the accounting theories* has been carried out at national level, mainly referred to scholars who have mainly trade (and industrial) firms as their examples and also referring to the writings of scholars focussed on agricultural firms. Briefly, this is considered an important factor as Italy is well known as the country of origin of double entry bookkeeping (Antonelli et al., 2006); from an evolutionary point of view, changes in theory are expected to affect a bookkeeping system of a firm belonging to a context in which theory evolves. Moreover, it has to be underlined that, generally, accounting theories require a time lapse to be put in practice. For this reason, despite the period examined being between the last decades of the nineteenth up to the second decade of twentieth century, we focussed just on the nineteenth century because these are the theories more likely to have affected Amarelli's bookkeeping system.

As regards the *evolution of the accounting theories* in the area of trade activities, we divide the nineteenth century into two main periods. In the first half of the nineteenth century, Italian studies overcome a period of stagnancy and decline and suffered the influence of foreign accounting thinkers, specifically French scholars and their "personalistic accounting theory," devised by the French scholar Degranges. His theory, which focussed on small and medium enterprises in trade business, simplified the accounting systems to include just five accounts (goods, cash statement, receivables, payables and profits and losses), all related to the owner (merchant) (Degrange, 1795). In this first period, the accounting scholars belonged to the Degrangian Italian school (Doni, 2007). Two main scholars of this period are Crippa and Villa. Crippa (1838) introduced two different series of accounts, objects and subjects, and both referred to the owner. Villa (1840, 1841), following Crippa's teachings, proposed two series of accounts, "conti di deposito," embracing all patrimonial activities except credits and "conti individuali," involving debits and credits of third parties towards the owner of the firm (Doni, 2007). In the second period, accounting theories reached a higher degree of maturity, enough to identify the Italian personalistic theory of accounts. The two main representative scholars of this period are Marchi and Cerbioni. Marchi (1873), made a strong critique of De Granges personalistic theory, issuing his own personalistic theory based on four logismologic personalities (*proprietario* [owner], *gerente* [manager], *corrispondenti* [correspondents] and *consegnatari* [stakeholders]) and two series of accounts: external and internal. The personalistic theory of accounts of Cerboni (1886) with respect to Marchi's idea recognizes just two general personalistic accounts, one entitled to the owner and the other to the agents and correspondents. Moreover, he substitutes the relationships between owner, agents and correspondents and manager, who personifies the firm, the juridical principle of juxtaposing between duties and rights of the owner towards duties and rights of agents and correspondents.

As regards the *evolution of the accounting theories* in the agricultural sector, it is particularly important to remember the contribution of Degranges De Rancy, who devoted a book to agricultural accounting, *Traité de comptabilité agricole* (1857), in which he expounded the "personalistic accounting theory" and the idea of a specific type of Ledger ("Grand-Livre"). There ideas are echoed in Italian accounting regulations regarding agricultural farms. A few years later, he wrote the *Petite Traité de comptabilité agricole en partie simple* (1860), in which he gives to the small agricultural farms the possibilities of accounting in a simple bookkeeping system.

ANALYZING AMARELLI'S FIRM-SPECIFIC FACTORS

Among the internal factors that could have affected Amarelli's bookkeeping system, we can cite the type of firm, the ownership structure, the size, the diversification, the high technical standards of production and the interior characteristics of the managers.

As regards the *type*, Amarelli was a family firm, and this is likely to have had an effect on Amarelli's bookkeeping system, owing to the overlap between family and firm. In fact, for all kinds of family firms, the main aim was not the wealth of the business, but family wealth.

As regards the *ownership structure*, Amarelli, as with the majority of family firms, had a strong ownership concentration. For this reason, in Amarelli there was no separation between ownership and control, as the owners were also the managers, meaning that all the business units of Amarelli were run by the family members, except for the business unit of olives, which was entrusted to an external subject, the sharecropper Gennaro Fusaro.

As regards the *size*, an increase in this feature is supposed to effect the number of the accounts, for example, for the growth of transactions both with suppliers and with customers.

As regards *diversification*, Amarelli was a diversified family holding. In the first phase Amarelli's owners focussed on land management and agriculture, but suddenly they diversified their business. Amarelli, in fact, has a farm activity in Sibari (in the Northern Ionian Calabrian territory) where it has a small production of olives and corn; it worked on the business of liquorice juice production, which suddenly became the core business of Amarelli; and it also managed residual activities, such as real estate management.

As regards the *high technical standards of production*, it was based on two main factors: the existence of a traditional nucleus of well-skilled workers (Piccioni, 2009), and the trend towards improvements in technical innovation, which led to the installation of a new steam boiler in 1907. With the term skilled workers we mean not manual workers but technical workers who, owing to their competence, became masters in the production of liquorice juice (*mastro liquiriziaio*).

As regards the *interior characteristics of the managers*, this is a multifaceted factor, including attitude towards risk, innovation propensity, managerial ability, technical competencies, accounting knowledge, relational ability and so forth. This is one of the key factors in the perspective adopted in the article and it is relevant, as the accounting choices are supposed to be, as with other typologies of strategic choices, the result of the decisions of the key actors.

AMARELLI'S BOOKKEEPING SYSTEM

The Italian Commercial Code of 1882 obliged individual firms to hold books related to the firm's operations, to the family wealth and to a statement of earnings, without forcing firms to follow a well-defined representational system.

Figure 5.1 The central role of the cash account
Source: Our elaboration

As family firm, Amarelli hold both accounting books at company level and accounting books at family level. All accounts are contained in a general book, named *Libro de' Conti*. The main book that underlines the overlap between company and family level is the cash statement, which acted as *trait-de-union* among Amarelli's different accounts (Figure 5.1)

The bookkeeping system is based on two kind of accounts, with a different role and a different way of being credited/debited. One type is named to each person (suppliers, customers, sharecropper, etc.) who has a stable relation with the firm (*conto al soggetto*). These accounts are balanced at the end of the year and express debt and credit positions of the subject versus the firm into two opposite sections: *dare* (to be given by) and *avere* (to give to). The other type of accounts are entitled to a general object (i.e., "cash") in order to measure increases and decreases in the amount. The two opposite sections are named *introito* (entry/increase) and *esito* (exit/decrease); they never balanced (Mussolino et al., 2005). Table 5.1 summarizes the different account books related to Amarelli's activities.

The *Concio book* is the accounting document related to the company industrial activity of liquorice juice production. The *Concio book* had its own index, listing many accounts: the suppliers, the *conti diversi concio*; the root, the *concio esito generale*.

Table 5.1 Amarelli's accounts

Name of the general account book/ aggregate	Name of the documents included in the general book	Content	Activities	Level	Area
Concio book	*Concio esito generale*	All the expenses from the plant for licorice production	Liquorice juice production	Company	Industrial
	Conti ai fornitori	Accounts named to relevant customers			
	Conti diversi concio	All the small purchases of liquorice roots with less relevant suppliers			
	Radice (root)	An account that recorded quantities acquired of liquorice roots			
Farm activity	*Sylva*	All the introits and expenses related to the farm activity	Farm activity (olive and corn)	Company	Agricultural
	Gennaro Fusaro	For the activities carried out with the mediation of the sharecropper Fusaro			
	Barone Nicola Amarelli	For the activities related to the corn trade			

(*Continued*)

Table 5.1 (Continued)

Name of the general account book/ aggregate	Name of the documents included in the general book	Content	Activities	Level	Area
Financial transactions	Borrowings and loans	All the inflows and outflows of financial resources with third parties	Financial transactions	Company	Financial
	Discounts	Interests allowed on borrowings			
Administration (of other activities)		All the introits and expenses related to residual activities	Other activities	Company	Administration
Other accounts		Accounts named to relevant customers	Liquorice sales	Company	Relations with customers and suppliers
Family report		All the ordinary entries and expense referred to the family members' activities	Family entries and expenses	Family	Ordinary entries/expenses
Gain and losses		All the extraordinary expenses and entries of family members	Family entries and expenses	Family	Extraordinary entries/expenses
Cash statement		All the transactions related to Amarelli (family and company)	Cash	Company/ family	Financial

Source: Amarelli's archival accounting documents.

The main account, *concio esito generale*, summarized all the expenses afforded to maintain the plant, such as liquorice roots, maintenance works, woods and so on. There was not an ending balance (Figure 5.2).

Two different series of accounts were devoted to the suppliers: suppliers, which summarized all the accounts named to the single relevant suppliers; and the *conti diversi concio*, which included the small purchases of liquorice roots with less relevant suppliers. Accounts to the suppliers are balanced only at the end of the liquorice harvest (from October to April); the *avere* section recorded the quantity of roots traded with a single supplier, while the *dare* section recorded the amount paid in advance to the supplier by the firm. Root, instead, recording the quantity and the price of the liquorice roots, was a memory account, as on one side it contains the quantities of the root purchased, and on the other side the total amount paid for the root. Each transaction was recorded three times: for instance the same amount was recorded in the account named to a supplier, then it was summarized in the general account *concio esito generale* and in the cash account, all in the same left section (*Esito*).

As regards the "Farm activity," Amarelli employed a person to manage the farm, a sharecropper named Gennaro Fusaro, for the olive cultivation and sales. For this reason, we found two types of accounts: those entitled directly to Amarelli and others entitled to Gennaro Fusaro when he mediated the transactions between third parties and Amarelli. If an operation was paid by Gennaro Fusaro, the amount was signed in the left section of the account titled to Gennaro Fusaro (*avere*), as Amarelli had a debt with him and in the right section (*Esito*) of the general account *Sylva*, which summarized all the transactions related to the farm activity. At the end of the year, the Sylva account has neither a balance nor a final amount. When Gennaro Fusaro was repaid, the amount was signed in the right hand of the account titled to

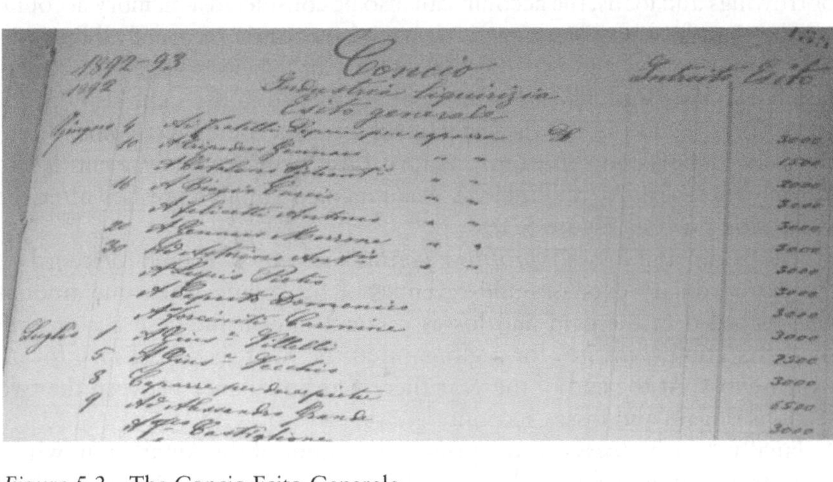

Figure 5.2 The Concio Esito Generale

Source: Amarelli's archival accounting documents

him (*dare* section), as Amarelli had repaid its debt, and in the right side of the cash account (*Esito*). In case of a sale, the accounts worked in a symmetrical manner. The activity related to the corn production and selling, for the years 1892–1893, was committed to the son of the Barone Fortunato, Nicola, to whom was entitled an account, *Nicola Amarelli*, in which debts and credits versus the family were recorded as he was a mediator. As for the *Gennaro Fusaro* account, the two sections were balanced at the end of the year.

All the revenues and expenses coming from residual activities (i.e., real estate management) were recognized in a specific account, named "Administration" (of other activities) account, then in the same section of the cash account. At the end of the year, as for the Sylva account, there is neither a balance nor a final amount highlighting the contribution of administration to the final cash flow.

The "Other accounts" heading includes accounts entitled to important customers (i.e., *Aselmeyer* and *Loquis)* and worked every time the liquorice was sold; more specifically, when goods were delivered, the credit towards the customer was written in the left section, named *dare* for the customers' account; when the credit was paid, the customer's account were charged in the right (*avere*) section and simultaneously written in the left section (*introito*) of the cash account. The two sections of the statement were balanced at the end of the year.

The "Borrowings and loans" (*movimento di capitali*) account records all the inflows and outflows of financial resources. In the case of an inflow, the left section (*introito*) of both borrowings and loans accounts and cash account was moved; when the loan was repaid, the right section (*exit*) of both borrowings and loans accounts and cash account was moved. Interests to be paid are written in an account called *sconto*, moved just on the right section (*exit*) when the loan was repaid. As the final sum was not reported the borrowings and loans, the account can also be considered a memory account.

The "Family report" (*conteggio di famiglia*) account recorded all the ordinary family entries and expenses; in the case of expenses the two accounts family expenses and the cash statement are moved in the same section, the left section (*Esito*); in the case of gains the two accounts were moved into the same right section (*Introito*). Before 1902, the account was entitled to Barone Fortunato Amarelli, but it was renamed Family expenses after the succession process (Figure 5.3).

The "Gain and losses" (*profitti e perdite*) account was used to record all the extraordinary expenses and revenues of the family. The same amount was recorded in the gain and losses account and in the cash account, in the left section (*Introito*) for a gift/gain, in the right section (*Esito*) for an expense/loss. At the end of the year there was no balance between the two sections of gain and losses account.

Finally, "Cash" (*cassa*) is the principal account of the Amarelli, in which every transaction was recorded regardless of the areas or subjects involved (Figure 5.4). The two sections of the statement were balanced at the end of the year.

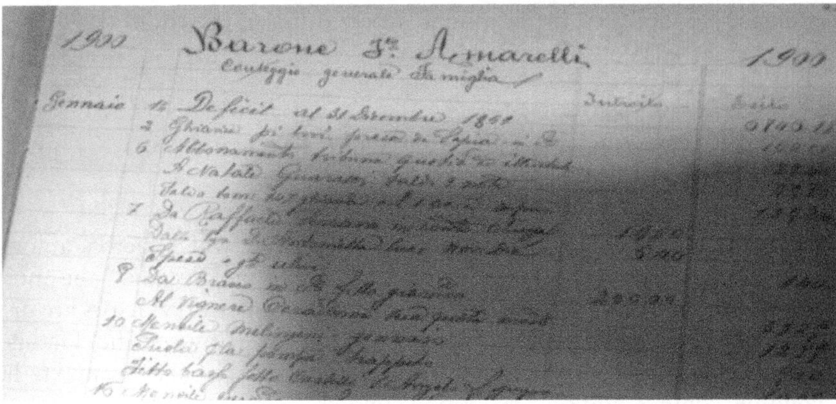
1900 Barone F.lli Amarelli 1900

Conteggio generale di famiglia

Figure 5.3 The family report

Source: Amarelli's archival accounting documents

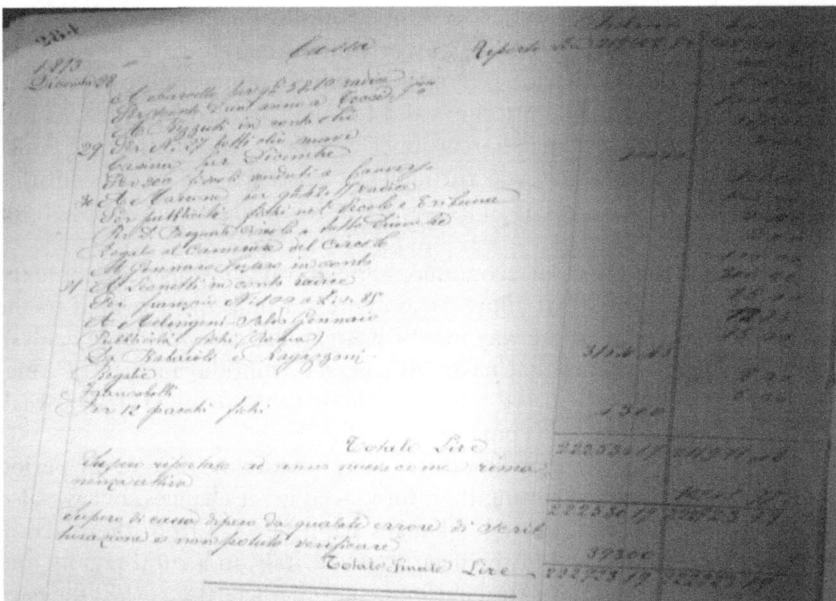

Figure 5.4 The cash statement

Source: Amarelli's archival accounting documents

Summarizing, even though each transaction is recorded twice (or three times as for the *Concio* book), in our opinion Amarelli's accountants did not follow a "pure" double entry system; in fact, when debts or credits had to be extinguished (i.e., the financial aspect of the transaction) the double entry system is applied, while when recording deals with increases or decreases in an object amount (i.e., the economic aspect of the transaction) the double entry system was not followed.

CONTEXT-SPECIFIC AND FIRM-SPECIFIC FACTORS AND THEIR EFFECT ON AMARELLI'S ACCOUNTS

The research question of the chapter was to analyze which factors among the overall factors considered to affect the firm's practices had the most effect, bearing in mind that, in our Bourdieu-like framework, factors are distinguished in external (context-specific) and internal (firm-specific) factors.

Among the context-specific factors, we analyzed the juridical context, the economic context, and the accounting context.

As regards the juridical aspect, the Commercial Code of 1882 required the individual firm, as Amarelli was, to hold accountancy books that record the firm's operation, the statement of the earnings and a family report, but it did not provide any rule about the representational systems. From the analysis of Amarelli's accounts, a weak effect emerges as to how the juridical system affected the way in which Amarelli kept its accounting book, owing to lack of reference to which representational system to use. The same consideration is valid for the Civil Code, as it was just relevant for regulating the sharecropper contract, whose effect on Amarelli's bookkeeping system was through the existence of accounts entitled to the sharecropper Gennaro Fusaro, when he mediates the transactions for Amarelli.[3]

As regards the effect of economic, agricultural and business contexts, there are no elements that allow us to express a judgement related to the effect of this context on the way in which Amarelli's accounts were held. In the absence of outcomes that have not emerged from the analysis of Amarelli's bookkeeping system, we can conclude that these contexts had a weak effect on Amarelli's bookkeeping system.

As regards the accounting literature, we can underline that, in the period under examination, accounting literature faced great changes, but we also have to underline that all these changes happened far from the place in which Amarelli operated, in the deep south of Italy, in a rural region, and this must be kept in mind as the environmental characteristics affect the pace with which changes spread in a territory. Moreover, at the time considered, accounting was considered neither a science nor a teaching subject at universities; it was taught just at high schools and it was focussed on practical rules mainly related to trading firms. From the analysis of the thought of the more relevant accounting scholars operating in the period considered, we can conclude that Amarelli's bookkeeping system did not match exactly with any of them. Considering that accounting scholars focussed on the field of agriculture, we can say that Amarelli's bookkeeping system did not match exactly with any of the accounting systems proposed by these authors. For instance, Amarelli's financial accounts follow a double entry approach. Instead Amarelli's cost accounts follow a simple-entry approach, as allowed in the *Petite Traité*, 1860.

All considered, contextual factors, in our opinion, weakly affected Amarelli's bookkeeping system.

Among the internal factors, we considered the type of firm, ownership structure, size, diversification, high technical standards of production and interior characteristics of the managers.

As regards the *type* of firm, Amarelli was a family firm and this had obviously an effect on its bookkeeping system; family accounts were recorded separately. In fact, from the analysis of Amarelli's accounts, it emerges that family expenses were distinguished into ordinary and extraordinary and recorded into two separate accounts (family report and profit and gains). Moreover, this characteristic makes the family's wealth a central feature, emerging as the increase/decrease of the cash statement, which included both family and firm entries and exits. The character of family firm had an effect both on the management, as the aim was both the firm's wealth and the family's wealth, and on the control, as managers should control both the firm's expenses and the family owners' expenses.

As regards the *ownership structure*, in Amarelli there was an overlap between managers and owners; managers did not have to report their activities to (different) owners; in other words there were no agency problems. This, in our opinion, makes managers accountable just to themselves (as they were the owners) without taking into account other issues of different stakeholders. This of course affected the way in that Amarelli's managers held the firm's accounts.

As regards the *size* of Amarelli and its *diversification*, we can definitely say that the firm's growth caused an increase in the number of subjects with whom Amarelli had dealings, as Fortunato Amarelli confirms in the semi-structured interviews, while diversification increased the complexity of the system, as Amarelli had as many accounts as there were activities.

As regards the *high technical standards of production*, the decision to buy and put in use a new steam boiler had great importance to the way in which Amarelli held its accounts, identifying a sort of proto-cost-accounting approach. This led to the issue of a specific book account, the *Concio book*.

Finally, as regards the *interior characteristics of the Amarelli's managers*, of course we believe that managerial decisions such as increasing production, selling lands, focusing on production instead of on trade activities and so forth had an effect on the way in which Amarelli held its accounts, nevertheless the effects of managerial decisions cannot be traced back, since we know neither the technical abilities nor the cultural background of the managers appointed to hold Amarelli's accounts. Nevertheless, we can say that this is a key factor in explaining the Amarelli bookkeeping system, as the articulation of accounts is likely to reflect the information needs of the managers/owners.

Summarizing, the internal factors seem to have had a stronger effect (with respect to the external factors) in affecting Amarelli's bookkeeping system.

CONCLUSIONS

The research aims to analyze the bookkeeping system of a company situated in Calabria (south of Italy) during the nineteenth and early twentieth centuries, addressing the recent calls for a contextualized and interdisciplinary accounting history research. The analysis was carried out in Amarelli, a family firm operating mainly in the area of liquorice juice production within the Northern Ionian Coast territory of Calabria, Italy.

In order to examine the accounting practices, we adapted the Bourdieu-like framework, which allows us to take into consideration also internal factors together with external factors. In fact, the majority of historical accounting research considers mainly the contextual factors in investigating the firms' bookkeeping accounting system.

In the chapter, starting from the consideration that both factors are relevant in affecting the firm's bookkeeping system, we investigated which factors most affected the way in which Amarelli holds its accounting books.

In our Bourdieu-like framework, we proxied the field factor with the following external factors: juridical context; accounting literature and economic context. Similarly we proxied the habitus and capital with the following internal factors: type of the firm, ownership structure, size, diversification and interior characteristics of the managers.

From our analysis it emerges that external factors had a weak influence on Amarelli's accounts, whereas the factors that most affected the accounting system are internal ones. Specifically, from the diversification, it emerges that each area in which Amarelli did business (liquorice production, farm activity, other activity) had its own accounts, and because it is a family firm, family expenses (ordinary and extraordinary) are recorded in specific accounts. In addition, to account for the complexity of Amarelli's bookkeeping system, important customers and suppliers have dedicated accounts and Amarelli's borrowings and loans are recorded in separate accounts. Moreover, the interior characteristics of the Amarelli managers played a relevant role in the holding of Amarelli's accounts, as these had to answer to precise information needs, specifically financial ones, so the main aim was the increase/decrease of the cash, which functions as *trait-de-union* between the different accounts and the approach was more towards a simple than a double approach.

Since this is a single case study, it is clearly not possible to generalize on the basis of Amarelli's experience, therefore more cases are needed of other companies operating in the South of Italy to ascertain how typical the Amarelli bookkeeping system was of the family sector in the nineteenth century in the Southern Italian area.

Future research directions could investigate the existence, in Amarelli, of a proto-industrial approach in the practice, which could have led to the development of an effective cost accounting system.

NOTES

1. We would like to thank Fortunato Amarelli, CEO and family owner of Amarelli, for his helpful support. Although this work is the fruit of joint reflection and collaboration, for academic reasons the introduction and the conclusions are to be attributed to Franco Rubino. The analysis of Amarelli's firm-specific factors and bookkeeping system and of the effect on Amarelli's accounts of the context-specific and firm-specific factors are to be attributed to Romilda Mazzotta. The theoretical framework and methodology and the analysis of the Amarelli's context-specific factors are to be attributed to Stefania Veltri. Corresponding author: romilda.mazzotta@unical.it.
2. A recent article (Malsch et al., 2011) examined the influence of Pierre Bourdieu's work on accounting research, analyzing 18 articles published in Accounting, Auditing & Accountability Journal , Critical Perspectives on Accounting and Accounting Organizations and Society in the period 1999–2008, but his influence on critical accounting research is far from exhaustive as proved by recent accounting articles and papers based on Bourdieu's framework, such as Spence and Brivot (2011), Ikin et al. (2012), Lodhia and Jacobs (2013), Baker (2014) and Khadaroo (2014).
3. The analysis of the sharecropper contract between Amarelli and the sharecropper Gennaro Fusaro is outside the scope of the chapter.

REFERENCES

Antonelli, V., Boyns, T. and Cerbioni, F. (2006) Multiple origins of accounting? An early Italian example of the development of accounting for managerial purpose. *European Accounting Review* 15(3): 367–401.

Baker, C.R. (2014) *A critical analysis of internal control in bank trading information systems in relation to Bourdieu's concept of habitus*. Paper presented at the Critical Perspectives on Accounting Conference, Toronto, July 7–9.

Baskerville, R., Fowler, C. and Huang, G. G. (2014) *The (Mis)uses of Pierre Bourdieu's practical epistemology in accounting-related social research*. Paper presented at the Critical Perspectives on Accounting Conference, Toronto, July 7–9.

Berry, A.J. and Otley, D.T. (2004) Case-based research in accounting. In: Humphrey, C. and Lee, B. (eds.), *The real life guide to accounting research, a behind-the-scenes view of using qualitative research methods*. Oxford: Elsevier, pp. 231–255.

Bertalan, N. and Napier, C.J. (2013) *The emergence of the 'new accounting history*. Working paper, School of Management, Royal Holloway University of London, July.

Bourdieu, P. (1972) *Outline of a theory of practice*. Cambridge: Cambridge University Press.

Bourdieu, P. (1980) *The logic of practice*. Stanford, CA: Stanford University Press.

Bourdieu, P. (1984) *Distinction*. Cambridge: Harvard University Press.

Bowen, G.A. (2009) Document analysis as a qualitative research method. *Qualitative Research Journal* 9(2): 27–40.

Boyns, T. and Edwards, J.R. (1996) The development of accounting in mid-nineteenth century Britain: A non-disciplinary view. *Accounting, Auditing and Accountability Journal* 9(3): 40–60.

Carnegie, G. (2014) The present and future of accounting history. *Accounting, Auditing & Accountability Journal* 27(8): 1241–1249.
Carnegie, G.D. and Napier, C.J. (2012) Accounting's past, present and future: The unifying power of history. *Accounting, Auditing & Accountability Journal* 25(2): 328–369.
Cerboni, G. (1873) *Primi saggi di logismografia*. Florence: La Minerva.
Crippa, L.G. (1838) *La scienza dei conti*. Milan: G.B Bianchi e Comp.
Degrange, E. (1795) *La tenue des livres rendue facile* (Book-keeping made easy). Paris.
De Granges Rancy, E.D. (1860) *Petite Traité de comptabilité agricole en partie simple*. Paris: Lacroix et Baudry.
Degranges de Rancy, E.D. (1857) *Traité de comptabilité agricole*. Paris: Librairie agricole.
Denzin, N.K. and Lincoln, Y.S. (2000) Introduction: The discipline and practice of qualitative research. In: Denzin, N.K. and Lincoln, Y.S. (eds.), *Handbook of qualitative research*, second edition. Thousand Oaks, CA: Sage Publications, pp. 1–28.
Doni, F. (2007) *La teoria personalistica del conto. Aspetti evolutivi ed approfondimenti critici*, Milan: Giuffrè editore.
Everett, J. (2002) Organizational research and the praxeology of Pierre Bourdieum. *Organizational Research Methods* 5: 56–80.
Gomes, D. (2008) The interplay of conceptions of accounting and schools of thought in accounting history. *Accounting History* 13(4): 479–509.
Gualerni, G. (1982) *Lo stato industriale in Italia: 1890–1940*. Milan: Etas Libri.
Hopwood, A.G. (1983) On trying to study accounting in the contexts in which it operates. *Accounting, Organizations and Society* 8(2/3): 287–305.
Hopwood, A.G. and Miller, P. (eds.) (1994) *Accounting as social and institutional practice*. Cambridge: Cambridge University Press.
Ikin, C., Johns, L. and Hayes, C. (2012) Field, capital and habitus: An oral history of women in accounting in Australia during World War II. *Accounting History* 17(2): 175–192.
Khadaroo, I. (2014) *Interests in the field of public private partnership: A Bourdieusian perspective*. Paper presented at the Critical Perspectives on Accounting Conference, Toronto, July 7–9.
Lodhia, S. and Jacobs, K. (2013) The practice turn in environmental reporting. *Accounting, Auditing & Accountability Journal* 26(4): 595–614.
Malsch, B., Gendron, Y. and Grazzini, F. (2011) Investigating interdisciplinary translations: The influence of Pierre Bourdieu on accounting literature. *Accounting, Auditing & Accountability* 24(2): 194–228.
Marchi, F. (1867) *I Cinquecontisti, ovvero la ingannevole teorica che viene insegnata negli Istituti Tecnici del Regno e fuori del Regno, intorno al sistema della scrittura a partita doppia, e nuovo saggio per la facile intelligenza e applicazione di quel sistema*. Prato: Giachetti.
Merzario, R. (1975) *Signori e contadini di Calabria. Corigliano Calabro dal XVI al XIX secolo*. Milan: Giuffrè.
Miller, P. (1994) Accounting as social and institutional practice: An introduction. In: Hopwood, A.G. and Miller, P. (eds.), *Accounting as social and institutional practice*. Cambridge: Cambridge University Press, pp. 1–39.
Miller, P., Hopper, T. and Laughlin, R. (1991) The new accounting history: An introduction. *Accounting, Organizations and Society* 16(5/6): 395–403.
Moll, J., Major, M. and Hoque, Z. (2006) The qualitative research tradition. In: Hoque, Z. (ed.), *Methodological issues in accounting research, theories and methods*. London: Spiramus, pp. 375–398.
Mussolino D., Pugliese, A. and Viganò, R. (2005) *Evolution in book-keeping in the Amarelli company between 1880 and 1920*. Proceedings of the International

workshop on Accounting History in Italy. Pisa, 27–28 January 2005. *Rivista italiana di ragioneria e di economia aziendale*. pp. 499–522.

Mussari, R. and Magliacani, M. (2007) Agricultural accounting in the nineteenth and early twentieth centuries: The case of the noble Rucellai family farm in Campi. *Accounting History Review* 17(1): 87–103.

Napier, C. J. (1989) Research directions in accounting history. *British Accounting Review* 21(3): 237–254.

Parker, L.D. (2012) Qualitative management accounting research, assessing deliverables and relevance. *Critical Perspectives on Accounting* 23: 54–70.

Parker, L. and Guthrie, J. (2014) Addressing directions in interdisciplinary accounting research. *Accounting Auditing & Accountability Journal* 27(8): 1218–1226.

Piccioni, L. (2009) Liquorice juice production in Calabria XVIII-XX centuries. *Daedalus* 2: 1–15.

Piccioni, L. (2010) Le manifatture locali: uno sguardo al lungo periodo. In: Branda, R. and Cersosimo, D. (eds.), *Il Cosentino. Cento pagine di storia, imprese e territorio*. Rome: Sipi, pp. 59–70.

Qu, S.Q. and Dumay, J. (2011) The qualitative research interview. *Qualitative Research in Accounting & Management* 8(3): 238–264.

Rabbeno, A. (1895) *Manuale pratico della Mezzeria e dei vari sistemi della colonia parziaria in Italia*. Milan: Ulrico Hoepli Editore.

Ryan, B., Scapens, R. and Theobald, M. (2002) *Research method and methodology in finance and accounting*. London: Thomson.

Sargiacomo, M. (2008) Institutional pressures and isomorphic change in a high-fashion company: The case of Brioni Roman Style, 1945–89. *Accounting, Business & Financial History* 18(2): 215–241.

Spence, C. and Brivot, M. (2011) No French, no more: Language-based exclusion in North America's first professional accounting order, 1879–1927. *Accounting, Business and Financial History* 22: 163–184.

Villa, F. (1840) *La contabilità applicata alle amministrazioni private e pubbliche*. I. Milan: Angelo Monti Press.

Villa, F. (1841) *La contabilità applicata alle amministrazioni private e pubbliche*. II. Milan: Angelo Monti Press.

Yin, R.K. (2003) *Case study research, design and methods*, third edition. Thousand Oaks, CA: Sage.

6 Piemonte, the Most Famous Italian Chocolate 'District'

Accounting and Business History of Caffarel, 1900–1979

Francesca Magli and Alberto Nobolo

INTRODUCTION

The history of chocolate in Europe began with its import from the Americas by the Spanish, its religious spread through the Catholic world, and its geographical spread in southern Europe, particularly in Spain and Italy. Arriving in Spain in 1527, chocolate became an essential food, authorized by the Vatican at convents and monasteries during long periods of fasting. Its nutritional value was quickly recognized, but only liquid chocolate was initially produced and marketed (Schivelbusch, 1999, p. 93).

In sixteenth-century Europe, the use of cocoa and chocolate spread widely, with the latter becoming a common drink of the ancien régime. In the same period, cocoa was imported into Piemonte, Italy, by Catherine Michelle, the daughter of Philip II of Spain, who in 1585 married Carlo Emanuele I, Duke of Savoy. By the end of the seventeenth century, the number of chocolate factories increased steadily, particularly in Europe, and these had acquired the art of making a higher-quality product. It seems that in Piemonte, and especially in Turin, during the eighteenth century, a method to make solid chocolate was discovered. Until that point, chocolate in Italy was consumed in liquid form, as a beverage. In Turin, the art of making chocolate has deep roots: the corporation of confectioners and liqueur makers dates back to 1739.

During the nineteenth and twentieth centuries, industrialization, reduced taxes, and the development of transport contributed to the increase in the production and trade of chocolate. After World War II, chocolate arrived in liberated Italian cities with the Americans, and its consumption increased greatly. Up to that point, chocolate was considered a luxury item, but from then onward, it became accessible to everyone.

THEORETICAL FRAMEWORK AND METHODOLOGY

Thanks to the Milan EXPO 2015, our interest is now on the food sector. In particular, we wanted to select companies that produce and commercialize an atypical Italian product and to observe the development of industries in

Italy that already exist in other nations. For this reason, and the aforementioned historical and economic reasons, we focus on analyzing the chocolate industry.

In our analysis, we note that there are few studies on the business history of the chocolate industry (Bachstadt-Malan, 2002; Chiapparino and Romano, 2007), particularly studies into the history of the financial and accounting systems of such industries. This work is developed by analyzing chocolate enterprises, their ability to capture innovations in processes and products, competitive strategies and internationalization, and history in the Italian confectionery sector, as well as their economic and financial performance over time.

This chapter focusses on an analysis of the various features in the organizational models and management, administration, and accounting systems at Caffarel, a chocolate company from Piemonte. Through an analysis of the innovations and changes in the habits and customs over time, we offer some reflections on this company's ability to excel in this industry.

Given that chocolate, at the beginning of the period under analysis, was not a particularly developed industry in Italy, we observe that Caffarel copied models from other companies in other sectors already established in Italy. Therefore, our study will explore if and how economic, mimetic, and legislative pressures (DiMaggio and Powell, 1983, p. 150) influenced Caffarel's behaviour. By the early 1900s, the chocolate sector was successful and it developed further in Italy. 'Once a field becomes well established, there is an inexorable push towards homogenization' (DiMaggio and Powell, 1983, p. 148).

'The concept that best captures the process of homogenization is isomorphism' (DiMaggio and Powell, 1983, p. 149). There are two types of isomorphism: competitive and institutional. Competitive isomorphism emphasizes market competition, niche change, and fitness measures, while institutional isomorphism is much more important for understanding the politics that pervades much modern organizational life.

Institutional isomorphism contains three types of isomorphism: coercive, mimetic, and normative (DiMaggio and Powell, 1983, p. 150). Coercive isomorphism relates to the formal or informal influence that certain organizations have on other organizations working in the same field, or cultural expectations emerging from the environment in which the organization works. Mimetic isomorphism becomes important in dealing with the uncertainties that affect organizations. When the environment is very uncertain, companies follow examples provided by more legitimate organizations or organizations that are recognized as the most successful. Normative isomorphism concerns professionalism, understood as the discussions that members of a category hold related to working conditions and methods.

Although most of the studies into isomorphic pressure are in the public sector, more attention should be directed to the core sectors of the economy, such as manufacturing and finance (Sargiacomo, 2008, p. 216).

The application of institutional isomorphism as part of our case study (Yin, 2014) will demonstrate the existence of isomorphic changes (DiMaggio and Powell, 1983). Based on the premise presented earlier, we study in particular mimetic isomorphism. Many other scholars probed this theory in other national contexts and business sectors (Slack and Hinings, 1994; Greenwood and Hinings, 1996; Roberts and Greenwood, 1997; Carolan, 2008), although there are no studies in the chocolate industry.

To pursue a rigorous research methodology and to have an exhaustive historical accounting overview, our study thoroughly reviews the literature (Yin, 2013, p. 3). The research method adopted provides for the analysis of different sources. To analyze the chocolate industry, our main secondary sources are the companies' own corporate histories and the histories of chocolate and chocolate industries, which we use to frame the issues related to the product and, consequently, to the businesses. To analyze the accounting, we use accounting manuals related to scholars of the time, particularly the writings of Zappa, such as *Reddito d'impresa* (*Business Income*) of 1929 and 1950 and *Produzioni nell'economia delle imprese* (*Productions in Enterprises*) of 1957, and the common accounting rules of the time. Then, we review specific scientific works on Caffarel, the company under analysis, and as one of the primary sources, some original management and accounting documents and Statistics Annuals. In particular, we analyze the board of directors reports, the supervisory board reports, and the company's financial statements between 1936 and 1979.

The research methodology pursued is based also on a case study (Yin, 2013, p. 3) of Caffarel. We chose this case study because of Caffarel's enormous success in the field of chocolate and the availability of data, particularly accounting data. The Chamber of Commerce of Turin holds financial statements and the previously mentioned documents from 1936 to 1979. Statements of the prior period, detainees from the Turin archives, unfortunately, did not survive the flood of 1994.

In order to pursue the research objective, this chapter is organized as follows. The first section analyzes the chocolate industry globally from both a social and economic perspective. The second section provides an additional analysis of the main peculiarities of the chocolate industry in Italy, and then in Piemonte, the most famous Italian chocolate 'district'. The following section presents Caffarel, one of the most important companies in the chocolate sector created in Piemonte, followed by an analysis of the company's historical background, focusing on its administration, strategy, accounting, ownership structure, and corporate governance in the period between 1900 and 1979. In the last section, we analyze the relations between institutional changes and Caffarel's administration, in which we observe the important role of the entrepreneur and of environmental and social changes occurring in Italy and in the chocolate sector.

THE CHOCOLATE INDUSTRY: SOCIAL AND ECONOMIC CHANGES

At the end of the seventeenth century in Europe, countries with greater capacity to apply technological innovations to the production process (France, the Netherlands, and Great Britain) saw growth in the number of chocolate factories.

French chefs acquired the art of creating a quality chocolate, and the exceptional dynamics of the Dutch navigation companies ended Spanish domination of the cocoa trade. Amsterdam, in fact, quickly became the main European port for the import of chocolate, and in 1828, Van Houten introduced the modern process for manufacturing cocoa powder. This process ended the Spanish tradition of chocolate that was replaced by cocoa powder, which was easier to prepare and more digestible.

This invention led to various developments. First, it increased the large-scale production of cheap chocolate for the people, but, from a social perspective, it created the basis for inventing a new kind of breakfast based on instant products (Nesquik, Ovomaltina) or chocolate substitute products, making it faster for mothers to prepare breakfast and easier to guarantee children a nutritious meal.

Further innovation in the chocolate industry became evident in 1847 with the Fry company, which found a way to mix cocoa powder with sugar and cocoa butter, creating a soft and easy-to-shape paste: solid chocolate. Chocolate bars were introduced officially in 1849.

The development of the chocolate industry, which began gradually in the first half of the nineteenth century, accelerated in the second half of the century, reaching its peak in the decades before World War I (Chiapparino, 1997, p. 273). This process contributed to the increase in international trade and in demand, reflecting higher incomes thanks to the intensified economic development of some Western countries. During the nineteenth and twentieth centuries, industrialization, tax cuts, and transport development all led to an increase in chocolate consumption.

The picture that emerges is one of growth in chocolate production and consumption that is fairly differentiated in various Western countries in the nineteenth century. The country where it was most widespread was France, which saw imports of cocoa quadruple by mid-century. The sector was also growing in Britain, albeit in a more moderate way. In the last three decades of the century, the chocolate industry developed in the United States and in Germany, which became, as far as the volume of raw material is concerned, the two biggest producers in the world (Chiapparino, 1997, p. 42).

In Italy, the chocolate sector development was delayed. Neighbouring countries, such as Germany and Switzerland, held leading positions. The former had a high production volume and the latter a high level of exports, especially at the beginning of the twentieth century.

Until the world wars, chocolate consumption in Italy remained too low to support an internal manufacturing industry, and demand was satisfied by imports. At the end of the nineteenth century, according to the number of employees in the Italian chocolate sector, we observe 136 people in chocolate manufacturing and 1,031 in facilities producing 'chocolate and jam' (Ministero dell'Agricoltura, Industria e Commercio [Agriculture, Industry and Commerce Ministry], 1885–1903).

In early twentieth-century Italy, we observe a high number of production units with small dimensions and the low use of motive power (Chiapparino, 1997, p. 225). In Europe we notice, around 1900, how far behind the Italian chocolate industry lags. In this period, we can see the emergence of net exporting countries, such as Holland and Switzerland; the former specialized in the production of powder, and the latter in dark and milk chocolate.

The situation changed between the two world wars. We see a remarkable improvement in the Italian situation, which increased per capita consumption (from 0.03% to 0.19%) but also domestic production so much that it became an exporter, and the Swiss situation, in which consumption increased so much that it found itself becoming an importer of chocolate.

However, it was during World War II that this consumption intensified. American chocolate, especially milk chocolate in bars, arrived in Italian cities liberated by the Americans, and helped to feed the children and the rest of the population, who had been deprived of nutritious foods for a long time.

After World War II, due to the changing economic and social environment, there was an explosion in the consumption of chocolate, which had finally become accessible to the whole population. Subsequently, chocolate makers were primarily concerned with varying the supply of chocolate products, creating filled chocolates, chocolate bars, chocolate pralines, ganaches, and so forth.

World War II rationing imposed many restrictions. Confectionery products, stimulants, and products considered unsuitable in wartime were banned. From June 1940, supplies were minimal and it was increasingly difficult to produce chocolate products. Not only did the raw materials become scarce, but staff also decreased, as thousands of men went to war. There were also problems shipping goods by rail because in many areas the service ceased to exist.

In the postwar economic boom period (1958–1962) and the subsequent economic recovery (1966–1969), the confectionery industry also grew and developed, although less so than other sectors, exceeding the threshold of a cottage industry. However, the increase in the consumption of confectionery—and in particular of chocolate—remained below what was practically possible, because of the very high price of sugar and cocoa. Sugar prices were high because of policies implemented by the sugar industry, which was traditionally favoured by tariff protection. The high price of cocoa was due to heavy taxation on imports. This encouraged the industry to replace cocoa with a surrogate, obtaining a less expensive product but also one of lower quality.

However, this move led to an increase in the consumption of chocolate, still at very low levels in Italy, where it was considered a luxury item and not a foodstuff, as in other countries.

The most plausible reason for the lack of large companies in Italy dedicated to the production of chocolate appears to be the low consumption of luxury foods, but also the failure to modernize the industry. Additional variables that influenced the lack of progress in the chocolate market were insufficient growth in national income, the burdensome tax and customs arrangements, and low private consumption. The private consumption preferred, still, the domestic production of confectionery products instead of resorting to the international market.

The main Italian cities where the artisanal production of chocolate is rooted are Turin, Naples, and Rome—where there are large numbers of French and Spanish nationals plus members of the clergy—but also Milan, Bologna, and Venice. Milan had 22 chocolatiers in 1901; Naples had 12 in 1891; and Turin had 29 in 1909 (Chiapparino, 1997, p. 229).

The Italian chocolate industry was made up of many small handicraft businesses and a few more advanced enterprises. Milan and Turin, in particular, became the home of major confectionery companies such as Talmone, Moriondo & Gariglio, Lombardi & Macchi, Novi, Venchi, and Gallettine Biscuits (Chiapparino, 1997, p. 246).

THE CHOCOLATE INDUSTRY IN PIEMONTE

In the twentieth century, Piemonte became famous for chocolate processing. Here, chocolatiers created the first chocolates and many products made from cocoa (*gianduiotti*, chocolate creams, pralines, Easter eggs, cream, and ice cream). Some towns in Piemonte are famous for particular types of chocolates. For example, in Cherasco, the Barbero company introduced its *Baci di Cherasco* chocolate confectionery in 1881; in Vicoforte, Silvio Bessone produced the *Fuego*, aphrodisiac chocolates made with cocoa beans; and the historic pâtisserie, Giordanino of Asti, produced *Alfierini*, pralines with a portrait of poet and dramatist Vittorio Alfieri.

The only city for which the Annals of Statistics (1889) refer to a complex of specialized activities in cocoa processing, in the second part of the nineteenth century, is Turin (Ministero dell'Agricoltura, Industria e Commercio, 1889, p. 72). In this city, in 1852, *gianduiotti* were first produced, and eventually became one of the symbols of Turin, the first sweet wrapped in an atypical golden paper wrapper.

At the end of 1880 in Turin, there were already four large chocolate companies, Talmone, Moriondo & Gariglio, Caffarel, and Gaj & Revel (Chiapparino, 1997, p. 249). In the early twentieth century, the small pâtisserie underwent a process of industrialization, and many businesses moved out of the centre of Turin in order to have more space. Other centres of chocolate production were created in Novi Ligure (the birthplace of Novi, an important chocolate industry, now a part of Elah Dufour Group), in the provinces of Alessandria and Alba (the birthplace of Ferrero) and in the province of Cuneo.

The artisans of Piemonte, always looking for recipes and variations, laid the foundations for a national confectionery industry.

In the first half of the nineteenth century in Turin, chocolate was produced in two ways: by hand or through industrial processing.

In Turin, chocolate is an institution. It is served in a cup, with or without cream, in the best historic cafés of the city, between the mirrors of Baratti & Milano, the stucco of Platti, the marbles of Mulassano, in the retro atmosphere of Bicerin. It was worked and kneaded in craft workshops such as Candifrutto, Stratta, Odilla, and Avidano.

During the nineteenth century, many artisanal producers were active in the citycentre. Among these, the most notable were the Ema, the Giambone, the Giroldi, and the brothers Bianchini.

In 1819, Giovanni Martino Bianchini conceived and built a *macchina pel tritolamento del caccao, zuccaro e droghe, e per tutte le operazioni ad un tempo della fabbricazione del cioccolato* (a machine for the crushing of cocoa, sugar and drugs, and for all the operations of the manufacture of chocolate). A similar machine was also used by Pier Paul Caffarel, heir to the factory that would subsequently be called Casa Caffarel (Caffarel house). In the late nineteenth century, specialties appeared in the form of products such as the *gianduja* and 'Turin candy', and a number of companies, such as Caffarel, became better known.

In the following years, the interest in chocolate products, in Turin and elsewhere in Italy, encouraged many industrialists to turn their cotton mills and mechanical industries into chocolate factories. Numerous companies in Turin were founded for the production of chocolate. Besides the ones previously mentioned, there were also Prochet, Gay, Risso, Beata & Perrone and, at the end of the century, the Querio & Leone company.

In Italy, on the eve of World War I, there were only two Italian companies comparable to the Swiss and German high-skilled factories: Talmone and Moriondo & Gariglio, both based in Turin (Chiapparino, 1997, p. 250). These companies, founded in 1850 and 1868, respectively, were the two major Italian chocolate companies for their ability to market their advertising image and enlarge their facilities and production capacity in the period before World War I.

HISTORY OF ONE IMPORTANT COMPANY IN THE CHOCOLATE SECTOR: CAFFAREL SpA

In order to analyze the region's ability to create one of the most famous Italian chocolate districts, we focussed on Caffarel, one especially noteworthy company with an interesting history in terms of innovation and value creation, particularly in the period 1900–1979. Caffarel is the oldest firm still in existence in the Italian chocolate industry.

Caffarel SpA is an Italian company that specializes in the production and sale of confectionery products and in the production of chocolate. The company now belongs to the Lindt & Sprüngli Group, a Swiss multinational. Caffarel was founded in 1826 by Pier Paul Caffarel in the San Donato quarter of Turin. Caffarel was the first to invent *gianduiotti*, during the carnival of Turin, named in honour of Gianduia, a carnival character that Caffarel used to distribute the new chocolates, which soon became famous among the carnival crowds.

Pier Paul Caffarel took over a small tannery located in San Donato in 1826 and turned it into a laboratory for the production of chocolate. He went on to buy machines suitable for chocolate production, including an industrial machine capable of producing more than 320 kg per day (a substantial amount for the time), a water wheel for grinding cocoa beans, and a hydraulic machine able to refine cocoa powder and mix it with sugar and vanilla.

In 1828, Caffarel bought the Landò chocolate factory, running one of the first machines for chocolate production invented a few years earlier by Bianchini, a master chocolatier. In 1837, after Bianchini's death, Paul Caffarel replaced him permanently, creating Caffarel Padre e Figlio (Caffarel & Son). Caffarel decided to invest in the project and was able to obtain a reduction in the fee to use the motive force of the Turin water channel from the public administration.

Administration and Strategy at Caffarel

In the period of Italian unification, Caffarel expanded and became well known at the national and international levels, thanks to its participation in fairs and exhibitions.

In 1847, the brothers Isidore and Paul (Pier Paul's sons) expanded the Caffarel plant in San Donato of Turin. In 1852, Prochet, Caffarel's partner, carefully mixed cocoa and sugar with hazelnuts, creating a new kind of chocolate mixture. In 1865, Caffarel began to market one of the most famous and best-loved chocolates in the world: the *gianduiotto*, a boat-shaped chocolate created with a soft paste of cocoa and hazelnut, wrapped in a gold wrapper, which takes the name from Gianduja,[1] the main character in the Turin carnival. In 1869, *gianduiotto* marketing intensified, and in the 1870s and 1880s, some changes in the corporate structure and disagreements on accounting issues created a difficult situation for the company.

In 1897, there was a change in the company's management. Caffarel Prochet, submerged in debt, was dissolved, and Successori Caffarel Prochet was founded. Following a number of business changes and some corporate management difficulties, the company was liquidated in 1931.

After liquidation, a new company called Successori Caffarel Prochet & C.ia SA Fabbrica di cioccolato, caramelle e confetti was founded. The entrepreneurial action of new members dedicated to rebuilding and consolidating Caffarel's prestige, focussed on product quality and the originality of the packaging, and targeted the medium-high market customers who were able to buy more expensive items. During a period of falling prices, Caffarel had to reduce costs, including through improvements in its facilities. Between 1932 and 1935, the company reported a loss, despite an increase in sales. The negative effects in terms of costs and raw material procurement persisted in the years 1939 and 1940, as Italy became involved in World War II.

In the period between 1943 and 1945, Caffarel reduced its capital and sales, these last related only to products not destroyed during the war. The company produced only for third parties and in small quantities, without being able to define any industrial and commercial program of work.

In the years of reconstruction, Caffarel produced high-quality finished products and focussed on packaging and advertising expenses. At the end of the 1940s, the company had not reached the level of technical and commercial organization necessary to maintain market share as they lacked financial resources. The necessary financial resources were made available only in 1950, with capital increasing up to 50 million Italian Lire (from 10,000 Italian Lire prewar), rising to 240 million Italian Lire in 1953 and 360 million in 1955; through bond issues, significant investments in mechanization became possible.

Between 1950 and 1965, Caffarel increased production and sales. However, due to protective duties and increased taxation on cocoa imports, the industry focussed on cocoa substitutes, and the company had trouble in recovering. In order to increase its status in the confectionery industry, in 1958 Caffarel established a company in Switzerland, Helca SpA, which, with Saida, a company formed in the 1950s, is the future of the company.

By the late 1960s, Caffarel's profile had changed in terms of both business and production. In 1967, a new plant in Luserna San Giovanni (Turin) came into operation, and after 140 years Caffarel's original factory closed. Caffarel Prochet SpA stopped production activity, and manufacturing and sales were transferred to Helca SpA.

The effects of starting the new plants, in addition to generating significant productivity gains, included changes in the product's sales, which rose from 900 to 1,399 tons between 1966 and 1970, with an increase in French and German markets.

While in the 1950s and 1960s Caffarel grew with difficulty, in the difficult 1970s, by contrast, the company entered a phase of great expansion (see Table 6.1). In fact, during the 1950s and 1960s, the company still had an artisanal production and organizational structure. In the 1970s, however, the company crossed the threshold of artisanal structures and became an industrial enterprise with new, modern, and efficient facilities, located in a new production facility, maintaining the product quality.

We can see the positive aspects of this new structure in the company accounts from the decade, as it was always profitable, with constantly

Table 6.1 Caffarel joint stock evolution in the period 1922–1979

1922	1936	1940	1944	At the end of 1944	1945	1946	1950	1953	1955	1969	After 1979
300,000 Lire	850,000 Lire	800,000 Lire	1 million Lire	10,000 Lire	100,000 Lire	2.5 million Lire	50 million Lire	240 million Lire	360 million Lire	600 million Lire	2 billion Lire

increasing sales and capital increases to over 2 billion Italian Lire, in regular expansion.

In 1978, Helca incorporated Caffarel Prochet and created a new group with Ghirlanda SpA, a trading company recently acquired for diversification in Milan.

Accounting and Financial Reporting in Caffarel

The first available financial statement in the archive of the chamber of commerce of Turin is the balance sheet of 31 December 1935 (Figure 6.1).

BALANCE SHEET	BILANCIO AL 31 DICEMBRE 1935		
ASSETS	ATTIVO		
Credits	Crediti	L.	497.420.96
Inventories	Materie prime –prodotti finiti-materiale di confezionamento e scorte varie		488.027.45
Tangible assets	Impianti e macchinari		480.374.15
Loss previous year	Perdite da ammortizzare		29.555.00
		Totale Lire	1.496.377.56
Securities	Cauzione Amministratori		36.00.000
LIABILITIES	PASSIVO		
Share capital	Capitale sociale		600.000.00
Debts	Debiti		881.405.16
Profit	Utile dell'esercizio		14.972.40
		Totale:	1.496.377.56
Securities	Amministratori per cauzione		36.00.000

Figure 6.1 Financial statement of 1935

In analyzing the financial statement of the reporting period, the main differences are:

- In 1942, 'Property' contained unrecorded property that is not mentioned again in the financial statement of 1936.
- In the same year, accountants introduced the 'inventory' of stock in the assets that remained until 1947, but returned to the financial statements from 1956 to 1960.
- On the liabilities side, in 1942, reserves appear (before there was only capital), particularly the extraordinary reserve of 183,735 Italian Lire, and accumulated depreciation appears.
- In 1942, the income statement ('Profitti e Perdite') remains essentially divided into 'leaks' and 'profits' with some detail of the leak: amortization and general expenses. General expenses are described in more detail in 1945 with the addition of industrial and labour expenses.
- In 1947 there is greater detail in the financial statement. The asset items increase, liabilities: reserves increase, and the funds originate. The items in the 'profit and loss' are not detailed.
- In 1948, liabilities show some funds as a result of war losses and in particular a 'deteriorations fund' and 'dissolution fund'.

The item 'Finanza—danni di Guerra' (Finance—war damage), appears for the first time in financial statement of 1944, and includes the amount of compensation for war damage (World War II) due to bombings, damage, roundups, requisitions, and other damage to property, persons, and legal entities.

This account is established in 1940 with the law passed on 26 October 1940, n. 1543 (which was followed by the Viceregal Decree of 31 August 1945, n. 532, the DL 19 April 1948, n. 517, and the final L. 27 December 1953, n. 968) and represented contributions to 'loss, destruction, or damage occurred of movable or immovable property in the Kingdom, as a consequence of any fact of this war'. Applications had to be submitted to 'Intendenza di Finanza' (commissariat of finance). Most of compensation practices are dealt with by the end of the 1960s; however, there are numerous cases where the discussion goes beyond the early 1980s. In the Caffarel financial statement the war damage item ranges from 1,724,637 Italian Lire in 1944 to 75,725,547 Italian Lire in 1950.

Caffarel's accounts increase in their analytical suitability after Italian accounting legislation passed in 1942, with the enactment of the Royal Decree of 16 March 1942, n. 262 (in particular, in the Caffarel financial statement we see the introduction in 1942 of reserves and accumulated depreciation, and in 1947, funds). We find more detail only in the balance sheet (in the Italian legislation of that time, it was considered the entire financial statement) as suggested by that law. In 1942, in fact, it was not obligatory to prepare and file the income statement.

In the 1950s, we look at the financial statement of 1956, which further details assets and liabilities and shows the current division between 'fixed assets', 'inventory (stock)' and 'working capital'. In passing, however, we have 'equity' with the division between capital, reserves, and previous profits, 'medium term debts', 'long-term debts' (bonds), 'funds', and 'amortization funds'. Memorandum accounts appear at the bottom of the financial statement until 1959.

The innovations introduced by the Caffarel accounting seem more the result of accounting books of the time rather than a result of the legislation.

The division between fixed capital and working capital already exists with Pantaleoni in 1901, and later with Zappa in 1950 (Pantaleoni, 1901, p. 53; Zappa, 1950; Baldassarri, 1997). The equity is, however, mentioned by Zappa in business income

> in the balance sheet are inscribed synthetic classes for both positive and negative elements of the assets, i.e. assets and liabilities as well as their sum, i.e. the equity and its abstract parts. The voice capital is often used to designate only the equity. The structure of the share classes in its opposing elements is usually known as business assets; the assets and liabilities, constituting a given capital are known as assets.
>
> (Zappa, 1950, p. 457)

The indications of Gino Zappa, one of the leading scholars of this period, on the financial statements already appear in the financial statements of Caffarel and will intensify in the next decade.

In the 1960s, the changes include:

- In 1962, an accurate classification of items appears in assets. In particular, we find 'fixed assets', 'loans and long-term availability' (titles and advances of suppliers), and 'loans and short term availability' (cash, bank, and customers). In passing, there is no previous division, but there is only capital and reserves, amortization funds, and debts.
- In 1965, the item *rimanenze d'esercizio* (inventories of exercise) appears for the first time rather than *inventario* (inventory); memorandum accounts return; and the items' details increase, also in terms of 'profit and loss'.
- In 1968, the item 'availability' is introduced, placed between inventory of exercise and short-term credits.

The 1960s appear important for the Caffarel's accounts. In fact, we can observe an increase complexity both in balance sheet items from the income statement and new divisions in macro-items to clarify and make more transparent the financial statement to an outside party. In these areas, it appears most influenced by Gino Zappa's thinking.

In addition to introducing the concept of business administration and *Azienda*, he introduced the system of income and faced a thorough analysis of the financial statements and assessments (Poddighe et al., 2005, p. 268). The commitment to the definition of income items can be seen in the clarity and completeness of Caffarel's statements of income. The type of income statement prepared by Caffarel is the account 'Profits and losses' in pretax results, one of three types of profits and losses Zappa described in *Reddito d'impresa* (*Business Income*), one of the author's most famous books (Zappa, 1950, p. 609).

In the 1970s, we note that in 1971, taxes appear in the 'loss' part of income statement; and that in 1978, the financial statements of 'Caffarel Prochet SpA' consist of the essential items of assets and liabilities that will be merged within Helca.

Law 216 of 1974 introduces Article 2425 bis, which establishes the contents of the 'profit and loss' account, a financial statement scheme with guidelines rather than rigid contents.

In our analysis, we already observe in 1965 an improvement in the detail of items in the income statement. We look at the losses: credit losses, various, rental expenses, administrative expenses, depreciation, and profit for the year. Profit contains gross profit for the year, discounts and allowance income, miscellaneous income, recurring income, dividends, and interest income.

We observe in Figure 6.2 that in 1962, the statements were much less detailed, in particular in the income statement.

The analysis of operating profit and loss during the study period shows that in the period 1932–1935, the company reported a loss, despite an increase in sales. In 1936 and 1937, the company achieved an operating profit, but because of a new import quota (important for a firm that imports cocoa beans), the company went back into the red in 1938. The negative effects in terms of cost and procurement of raw materials persisted into 1939 and 1940, as Italy became involved in World War II.

The later situation is illustrated in Table 6.2.

While the company's economic performance marked a downward trend in the 1950s, from 1962 onward the company was profitable, and then experienced losses between 1968 and 1971, as shown in Table 6.2.

Ownership Structure and Governance

The ownership structure of Caffarel faithfully represents a classic family business. In 1837, father and son created Caffarel Padre e Figlio, and the business remained in the hands of the Caffarel family until 1897, after three generations (In 1837 Pier Paul Caffarel; in 1846 Isidore, Pier Paul's son; and in 1877 Ernesto, Pier Paul's nephew).

On 20 August 1897, liquidators dissolved Caffarel Prochet, which had become submerged in debt. The liquidators were Ernesto Malan and

PROFIT ANS LOSS ACCOUNT	CONTO ECONOMICO		
Losses	Perdite		
Administrative expenses	Spese amministrative	£	103.618,631
Depreciation	Ammortamenti	£	63.220.653
		£	167.039.284
Net profit	UTILE NETTO	£	29.710.814
Profits	Profitti		
	c/Gestione		
Gross profit (sales)	Utile lordo d'esercizio	£	177.702.376
Extraordinary income	Sopravvenienze attive	£	15.047.722
	Utile dell'esercizio		14.972.40
		£	192.750.098

Figure 6.2 Income statement in 1962

Table 6.2 Financial results in the period 1936–1979

Year	Operation profit/loss	Amount (Italian Lire)
1941	Operation profit	147,512
1942	Operation profit	2,546,918
1947	Operating profit	1,308,168
1948	Operation profit	3,214,021
1950	Operation profit	8,064,961
1959	Loss	26,918,936
1962	Operation profit	25,710,814
1965	Operation profit	1,117,028
1968	Loss	22,233,203
1969	Loss	9,297,217
1970	Loss	4,002,855
1971	Loss	45,651,784
1978	Operation profit	411,676

Michele Prochet (a prior partner of Caffarel family) who came back into the company.

In 1897, new members took over anew Caffarel Prochet & C.ia, which became Successori Caffarel Prochet & C.ia. It is a first important step in the company's history. In fact, the Caffarel family maintained only their ownership of the buildings and the name of the new partnership, formed in July 1897 by Malan and Prochet. After Prochet's death, Ernesto Malan remained alone at the head of the enterprise, and the company grew during the expansion phase of the industrial boom in the Giolitti era.

In the years leading up to the economic crisis of 1929, the company underwent a number of changes and corporate management difficulties. Ernesto Malan died in 1916, in the middle of World War I, and his wife, Noelie Charbonnier, became the owner of the company by acquiring the entire share capital and the plant. She did not take the lead in the business and management, but entrusted it to technical managers. This situation thus remained for a few years. In 1922, Charbonnier sold the company, but by 31 January 1931, Successori Caffarel Prochet was once more in liquidation.

In 1931, a new pair of partners, Walter Bächstädt-Malan[2] and Paolo Audiberti,[3] took over the company and, within a few years, managed to revive it. A few months after the takeover, on 11 May, a new company was formed: Successori Caffarel Prochet & C.ia SA, Fabbrica di cioccolato, caramelle e confetti (chocolate and candy factory). Walter Bächstädt-Malan was appointed president of the company's board in 1931 and Audiberti became vice president in 1933 (Bächstädt-Malan, 2002). In 1946, upon Audiberti's death, the other partner continued alone, in an establishment badly damaged by bombing.

In 1956 and 1957, two young people joined the company: Calisto Audiberti, son of Paolo, and Hans Bächstädt, son of Walter, representing the second generation after the founders of 1931. Calisto managed the administration and Hans managed the production. In 1966 they joined the board of directors, the first as CEO and the second as vice chairperson.

In 1968, the production plant was transferred from Turin to Luserna San Giovanni, the birthplace of the founder, and in 1969, Carlo, brother of Hans Bächstädt, active in retail and sales, joined the company. In 1978, Carlo and Hans Bächstädt and Calisto Audiberti become administrators of Helca, the company merging with Caffarel Prochet, and in 1980, Carlo Bächstädt-Malan and Calisto Audiberti were appointed CEOs of Caffarel SpA. In 1997, the company was sold to Lindt & Sprüngli, of which it is still a part.

INSTITUTIONAL CHANGES AND CAFFAREL ADMINISTRATION

The events at Caffarel and major changes in the company governance had a significant effect on the progress of the administration and management of Caffarel. Most of the changes appear as a result of the policy undertaken by the families to head the company. This situation is due mainly, in our view, to the adaptation to the surrounding environment and the historical events that Caffarel faced, especially the two world wars.

In Table 6.3, we can see, in parallel, the main economic and social change in Italy and in Caffarel.

The company Caffarel, as previously indicated, is a family business, initially owned by the Caffarel family (1828–1897) and then the Bächstädt-Malan and Audiberti families.

In management and administration, the greatest difficulties for the company lie in the period between 1897 and 1931, where the firm suffers two

Table 6.3 Main events at Caffarel in the period 1900–1979

Period	Industrial and business history (in particular, the chocolate industry trend)	Caffarel (S. Donato di Torino)
Before 1900	• Increase in industrialization • Decrease in taxes • 1849: Introduction of chocolate bar production	1837: Establishment New products 1865– Gianduiotto—marketing and sales
1900–1920	• Further industrial development • Particularly in Italy, low chocolate consumption • No internal market	
1920–1930	• Chocolate is a luxury food in Italy, so there is low consumption	Alternations in corporate governance and management difficulties
1930–1934	• Higher domestic production of confectionery, cakes, and biscuits instead of industrial production	• New partners • Increased quality • Reduced costs, plant improvements
1935–1945	• Failure to modernize the sector	• Decrease in social capital and sales • Production only for third parties
1946–1955	• Explosion of chocolate consumption • Increase in chocolate products	Increase in: • products and packaging quality • marketing costs • investments in production processes
1956–1970	Economic boom: • increases in taxation on imports • high prices of cocoa and sugar • chocolate goes from luxury product to common food	Internalization Helca plant Openness to French and German markets New plant in Switzerland and in Luserna S. Giovanni
1970–1979		1978: Helca incorporates Caffarel

liquidations and remains in the hands of people (the wife of Ernesto Malan, and from 1922, new entrepreneurs) with little interest in Caffarel's survival.

Apart from these difficulties, and more connected to the ownership structure, we find that the difficult times in Caffarel are similar to those detected in the environment, which according to the period analyzed, related to difficulties in the economy and politics, and difficulties related to the managing the two world wars.

The main environmental and social changes in the period 1900–1979, the period analyzed, are as follows:

- The Giolitti period;
- The period of the two world wars;
- The period of reconstruction;
- The period of the economic boom;
- The 1970s.

The Giolitti period saw the development of industrialization and the birth of the industrial triangle: Turin-Milan-Genoa. In Italy, primarily engineering, automotive, and chemical companies grew, but also the food industry, thanks to lower prices and the development of new processing equipment. In this period, we have little information about Caffarel and the internal difficulties that it had to solve and more related to the ownership structure and governance. Additionally, there was a radical change in the family heading the firm, but the firm was then liquidated and subsequently revived. Also, at this time the consumption of chocolate is still unable to interest Italian society.

The most difficult period was during the two world wars. The First World War brought many hardships. Chocolate continued to be a luxury item, and consumption was so low that it made no sense for businesses to have large industrial structures. Caffarel survived but was sold in 1922 and subsequently put into liquidation in 1931. In this period, Caffarel experienced several alternations in corporate governance and management difficulties.

In 1931, a new company was founded by the son of the previous owner Ernesto Malan and that of this latter's companion and friend. New members, full of good intentions, invested on several fronts: increasing the quality of products, replacing and improving the plants and equipment, and trying to reduce costs.

After an initial period of improvement due to the profits in 1936 and 1937, the devastation of World War II had serious repercussions for Caffarel in both sales and production, which stopped in 1945. In this period, we see that different accounts were used to quantify deteriorations and destruction caused by the war (FINANCE–war damage, reconstruction fund, burned finished products, emergency fund). The reconstruction period was the best time for Caffarel, in which it changed from an artisanal structure to an industrial structure and managed to succeed. One of the main reasons that

Caffarel could position itself well in the market—which is very important up to the present day—was the ability of governance members to address the needs of consumers and to develop and innovate in the surrounding environment. In this period, Caffarel took care to increase product and packaging quality and marketing costs, and invest in production processes.

In 1956 and 1957, new members joined the company, the sons of Walter Bächstädt-Malan and Paolo Audiberti, with the ability and willingness to adapt to the needs of the markets and strategic policies adopted by other successful businesses.

In the postwar economic boom period (1958–1962) and the subsequent recovery (1966–1969), the confectionery industry, like other businesses, grew and developed. Caffarel management understood the need to innovate, thanks to new entrepreneurs and to its ability to adapt to the environment. In particular, the company created new, larger plants, in Luserna, which increased production; and in order to increase sales, adopted new policies to develop advertising and internationalization (Caffarel entered the French and German markets). We will see that these decisions determined the future of Caffarel. On examining other companies that had developed in the same period, we can see that some companies (such as Ferrero) that followed the same trend of Caffarel have managed to become leaders in the field, and others that did not pursue internationalization and the use of appropriate policies in marketing (such as Novi), have been acquired by other companies to survive, at least as a trademark. An important decision was the deliberate choice not to produce and market product surrogates alongside pure chocolate during this period. In fact, the ability to increase the product quality offered, the reduction in the prices of these products, and the different views people held about chocolate helped Caffarel remain a leading company during these years. Caffarel, in fact, targeted the middle-high market and worked with the new idea of chocolate as good food and not a luxury.

The following period (1970–1979) showed further improvements and refinements in the policies adopted in the previous decade, with operating profit until 1978, the year in which the company was sold to Helca, the family's holding company.

DISCUSSION AND CONCLUSION

The chocolate sector in Italy has attracted limited attention because of some issues arising during the reporting period:

- Economic: high taxes and duties on imports of raw materials, such as cocoa and sugar, and the two world wars;
- Social: consumers' inability to perceive chocolate as a food and not just as a good stimulant, and the continuing tradition of Italians to make cakes at home;

- Industrial: failure to modernize the sector, while the sector remained artisanal and failed to expand; the struggle to become an industry;
- Commercial: there are few needs that can be satisfied, even by goods sold by foreign manufacturers who only market in Italy.

The market in Italy did not grow for all of these reasons. The company analyzed is one of the few that managed to establish itself nationally and internationally. Caffarel, thanks to its adaptation to environmental and social changes, has been able to survive and become more attractive to the international market.

The process of institutional change in Caffarel was born when it emulated the chemical industry. The development of this sector and the search for new chemical processes and new combinations of ingredients is copied (mimetic isomorphism) by the confectionery industry, in particular by the chocolate industry, through the creation and use of new machinery and new production processes (machinery and processes to produce cocoa first and then chocolate bars).

Technological innovations are an important general guideline of institutional change. This is the idea of Veblen's 'cumulative change', where the process begins with discoveries and technological innovations that alter the habits and behaviours of a community, such as the changing laws and regulations, in turn causing the subsequent technological changes and increased susceptibility to subsequent innovations (Veblen, 1919).

In Caffarel, we also observe the creation of a new product, the *gianduiotto*, which will subsequently be copied by all other chocolate manufacturers. This innovation (1865) could not, however, change the values and social expectations at this time due to other historical and social changes that had more depth and impact at the national level, such as the creation of a new state (Italy) and then two world wars.

Only after these important events did Caffarel, which resisted, manage to change permanently from a craft business to an enterprise. Thanks to the managerial skills of its entrepreneurs and its ability to adopt subsequent innovations (for 'cumulative change'), Caffarel was able to pursue strategic policies that in the 1950s and 1960s, proved successful for other companies, such as marketing and internationalization policies.

From our study, it therefore appears that to remain a successful business in a little-considered market in Italy, such as chocolate, the way forward is through an ability to adapt to the changing needs of consumers and society.

NOTES

1. Gianduja (Giand'laduja, or John with the Mug) was a principal character in the Turin carnival. He wore a typical Piemontese tricorn hat, which was a symbol of the struggle for independence that was fought in Piemonte in 1799.

During the 1865 carnival, Caffarel dressed in this character's mask to offer the crowd assembled under his carnival wagon his company's new chocolates.
2. Walter Bächstädt, a 27-year-old German, was the grandson of Noelie Charbonnier, owner of the company. He worked as a sales consultant for a German tire manufacturer.
3. Paolo Audiberti, a friend of Bächstädt and administrative worker at the same company in Germany.

REFERENCES

Bächstädt-Malan, C. (2002) *Per una storia dell'Industria dolciaria torinese: il caso Caffarel* (*For a history of confectionery industry in Turin: The case of Caffarel*). Doctoral Thesis, Università degli studi di Torino, Turin.

Baldassarri, M. (1997) *Maffeo Pantaleoni, At the origin of the Italian School of Economics and Finance*. London: MacMillan.

Carolan, B.V. (2008) Institutional pressures and isomorphic change: The case of New York City's Department of Education. *Education and Urban Society* 40: 428–451.

Chiapparino, F. (1997) *L'industria del cioccolato in Italia, Germania e Svizzera. Consumi, mercati e imprese tra '800 e la prima guerra mondiale* (Chocolate industry in Italy, Germany and Switzerland. Consumption, markets and enterprises between '800 and the World War I). Bologna: Il Mulino.

Chiapparino, F. and Romano, R. (eds.) (2007) *Il cioccolato: Industria, mercato e società in Italia e Svizzera (XVII–XX sec.)* (Chocolate: Industry, market and society in Italy and Switzerland (XVII–XX century)). Milan: FrancoAngeli.

DiMaggio, P.J. and Powell, W. (1983) The iron cage revisited: Institutional isomorphism and collective rationality in organizational fields. *American Sociological Review* 48(2): 147–160.

Greenwood, R. and Hinings, C.R. (1996) Understanding radical organizational change: Bringing together the old and the new institutionalism. *Academy of Management Review* 21: 1022–1054.

Ministero dell'Agricoltura, Industria e Commercio. (1885–1903) Notizie sulle condizioni industriali. . . . *Annali di Statistica (Statistics Annals)*, IV.

Ministero dell'Agricoltura, Industria e Commercio. (1889) Notizie sulle condizioni industriali della provincia di Torino (News about the conditions of the industrial province of Turin). *Annali di Statistica (Statistics Annals)*, IV: 32.

Poddighe, F., Coronella, S., Madonna, S., and Deidda Gagliardo, E. (2005) *Il contributo di Gino Zappa e di Alberto Ceccherelliallosviluppo dell'informativa contabile*, in Atti VII Convegno Società Italiana Storia della Ragioneria, *Riferimenti storici e processi evolutivi dell'informativa di bilancio tra dottrina e prassi*, Atri—Silvi Marina, 22–23 settembre 2005, 2° tomo.

Roberts, P.W. and Greenwood, R. (1997) Integrating transaction cost and institutional theories: Toward a constrained-efficiency framework for understanding organizational design adoption. *Academy of Management Review* 22: 346–373.

Rugafiori, P. (2012) *Caffarel: il cioccolato (e non solo) traindustria e artigianato* (*Caffarel: Chocolate (and others) between industry and handicrafts*). Available at: http://www.impreseneltempo-torino.it/

Sargiacomo, M. (2008) Institutional pressures and isomorphic change in a high-fashion company: The case of Brioni Roman style, 1945–89. *Accounting, Business & Financial History* 18(2): 215–241.

Schiaffino, M. (2006) *Dolce Italia: Storia, immagini, protagonist dell'industria dolciaria italiana* (Sweet Italy: History, images, players in the Italian confectionery). Florence: Fratelli Alinari.

Schivelbusch, W. (1999) *Storia dei generi voluttuari: Spezie, caffè, cioccolato, tabacco, alcol ed altre droghe* (History of stimulants: Spices, coffee, chocolate, tobacco, alcohol and otherdrugs). Milan: Mondadori.
Slack, T. and Hinings, B. (1994) Institutional pressures and isomorphic change: An empirical test. *Organizations studies* 15(6): 803–827.
Veblen, T. (1919) *The place of science in modern civilization and other essays*, reprint edition of 1961. New York: Russell & Russell.
Yin, R.K. (2014) *Case Study research. design and methods*, fifth edition.Thousand Oaks, CA: Sage Publications.
Zappa, G. (1950) *Reddito d'impresa* (Business income). Milan: Giuffrè editore.
Zappa, G. (1957) *Le Produzioni nell'economia delle imprese* (Productions in enterprises), I, II, III tomo. Milan: Giuffrè editore.

Websites

http://www.caffarel.com/
http://www.dallasfood.org
http://www.ilcinzanino.org/2010/12/novi-industria-piemontese-leader-del.html
http://www.ilmondodegliarchivi.org
http://www.impreseneltempo-torino.it/
http://www.oltre.it/sestri/sestrini.htm
http://www.piemonteitalia.eu/
http://www.unioncamere.gov.it/

7 The Parma Ham Consortium (Consorzio del Prosciutto di Parma)

Some Insights from a Historical Perspective

Paolo Andrei, Federica Balluchi, Katia Furlotti, Pier Luigi Marchini and Veronica Tibiletti

INTRODUCTION

This chapter relates to the Parma Ham Consortium because of the importance of the manufacture of this typical product in Parma, and that of the role played by the Consortium with regard both to the activities of promotion and protection of the ham and to its sale[1]. The aim of this study is to highlight the history of the Consortium, making reference to the changes made to the functions carried out and the corporate governance structure. The chapter, drawing on the financial statements and other documents disclosing accounting and governance matters, highlights the main elements that have characterized the evolution of the role played by the Consortium and the impact it has had on the production and sale of Parma Ham.

There are four main motivations that lead to study the evolution of the Parma Ham Consortium:

1. Parma Ham is one of the most popular foods in the world, and a symbol of the Italian agro-food production of higher quality.
2. For a "typical product" of the agribusiness sector, the birth and development of the Consortium testify to the need for forms of cooperation between producers that aim to protect the quality of products, to promote sales and, jointly, to protect the mark that qualifies and summarizes the distinctive features.
3. The case of Parma Ham Consortium, although newly established, is an important example of how, since the 1960s, forms of cooperation between small and medium producers are developed in Italy for the protection of local products.
4. The issue of development and consolidation of forms of collaboration in the agro-food industry has not yet been treated by accounting history literature and, in particular, with reference to associations for the protection of "typical products."

Since its establishment (18 April 1963) some events have made a significant impact on the history of the Consortium and its role; 1970 in particular marked a very important moment in the development of the industry with the enactment of Law n. 506 of 4 July 1970, which contained the "Regulations relating to the protection of the designation of origin of Parma Ham." This law was a fundamental tool with which to prosecute and limit fraud and unfair competition. Then in 1978, the DM (Ministerial Decree) of 3 July entrusted the Consortium with the task of supervising the compliance of the regulations concerning the protection of the product. Within this context, the Consortium took on a public function under the direct control of the central government.

Over the years, the evolution in terms of membership of companies within the Consortium has also been significant: the initial 23 companies that founded the Consortium were soon followed by an increasing number of other members, which today stands at a total of 150 companies united under the Parma Ham Consortium. Their overall production totals about 9 million euro of units and revenues of 740 million euro, and 237 million euro in sales and exports.

Considering those premises and referring to the objectives of the work, this chapter aims to analyze the following aspects:

1. The origins of the Parma Ham Consortium and the main characteristics that have marked its development (main motivations, purposes and functions of the Parma Ham Consortium; main stages that have characterized its evolution with particular attention to changes in terms of functions performed; dimensional development of the Consortium, in terms of the evolution of the number and characteristics of the member companies; changes in production volumes in the Parma Ham industry).
2. The corporate governance structure of the Consortium, with particular reference to the changes over time, also reflecting the regulatory, environmental and functional changes that have characterized the history of the Consortium previously described.
3. The financial reports, with particular attention to characteristics of the financial statement of the Consortium over time, as well as the evolution of costs and, linked to this, to the directions of development of the Consortium's activities.

In accordance with the methods used for historical research, the first part of the study defines the historical referring framework and aims to outline the main elements that directly and indirectly influenced the establishment and development of the Consortium; we have outlined the research hypotheses at this stage. Subsequently, the study analyzes the evolution that has characterized the role and activities of the Consortium with reference both to the functions performed and corporate governance structures. In this sense, the chapter analyzes the corporate governance structure adopted by the Consortium, mainly by the study of direct sources as well as the main activities, again using the information provided by the financial reports.

The descriptive and interpretive analysis of the main direct sources investigated is the basis for the elaboration of the considerations set out in the latter part of the work.

The research will mainly use direct sources (accounting documents, financial reports, Statute of the Consortium) made available by the Parma Ham Consortium. The analysis of the documents will be further enriched by information from direct interviews of the Consortium employees.

LITERATURE REVIEWS

To date, Italian and international business and management literature have not paid much attention, if at all, to the business realities operating in meat processing. Not suprisingly, and despite few notable exceptions, there are very few studies on the business history of Italian companies (e.g., Sargiacomo, 2008), especially with particular regard to accounting history.

Nevertheless, several Italian contributions deal with the food industry in general. Indeed, some authors take a historical perspective on large Italian companies, focusing on corporate governance and financial reporting. For more on the former, see Cavazzoni (1998) on Buitoni-Perugina; for the accounting dimension, see Mari et al. (2008) on Perugina.

Focusing on the meat industry, Esteban Hernàndez-Esteve (1995) addresses meat supplying within accounting history. More specifically, he deals with meat supplying in Burgos in the years 1536–1537 by concentrating on the Libro Caxa, or the Ledger of Burgos's Meat Purveyor, who serviced the town's meat supply during that period.

Food has received extensive attention first and foremost by Anglo-Saxon researchers, who have focussed on management accounting but not in the historical dimension. To name a few, take Abdel-Kader and Luther (2006) on management accounting practices in the British food and drinks industry, or Groot (1997), Adejuyigbe et al. (2013), Bogdanoiu (2012) and Ernst and Young LLP (1995).

Works on general issues in business management are Riley (2005), Mann and Adebanjo (1997) and Mann et al. (1999a, 1999b). For research into supply chain or market access, see Wright and Lund (2003) and Henchion and McIntyre (2005).

Back to research on ham and to Parma Ham in particular, several studies focus on agribusiness (Arfini, 2000; Dentoni et al., 2000; O'Reilly et al., 2002, 2003; Donati et al., 2012; Mancini, 2012; Giacomini et al., 2010, 2013). While not investigating the issue from the point of view of business management, however, they serve as a good starting point for our work, especially as regards corporate governance dimension.

Finally, as noted in the introduction, with specific reference to the form of aggregation such as the consortium, no relevant contributions are found in the accounting history literature. In this sense, as is clear from this brief literature review, we think that the issue of the consortium for the protection of local products represents an interesting research topic and an issue that calls for extensive investigation.

PARMA HAM

Parma Ham is registered, with the Parma Ducal Crow, as a Protected Designation of Origin product (PDO) and forms part of a regional area of production that is key to the food and agricultural sector in Italy: the Emilia Romagna region. This geographical territory in fact produces the largest number of cured meat products certified as PDO and PGI (Protected Geographical Indication) in Italy,[2] and several of these products are made in specific regions (Lombardia, Piemonte, Emilia Romagna). With regard to the Province of Parma, the manufacture of typical cured meats is significant; Parma Ham stands out among these.[3]

In 2014 the number of branded hams totalled 8,800,000 units, down by 3.1% compared to 2013 (Figure 7.1 underlines the impact the crisis that started aroud 2008 has also had on the Parma Ham industry, where production has shown a generally negative trend since 2009), and the number of producers stood at 150.

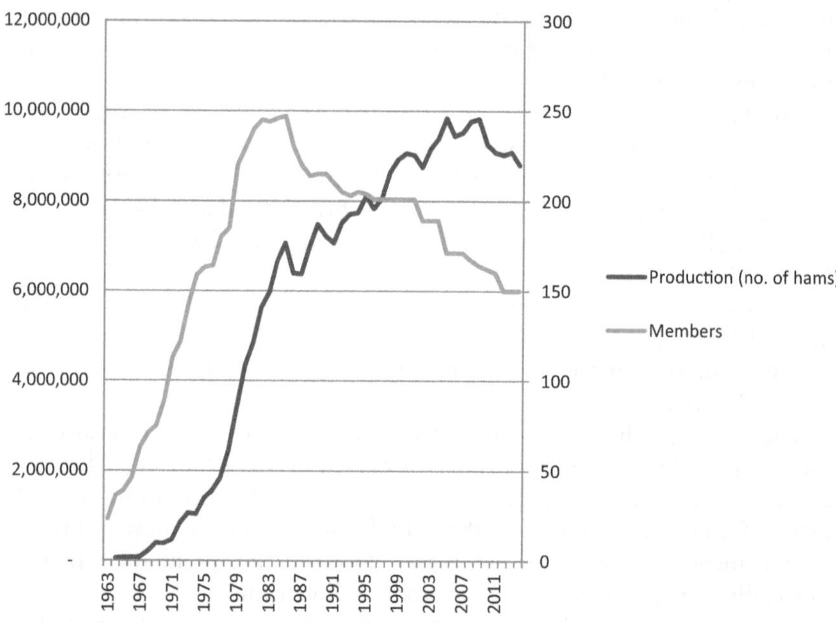

Figure 7.1 Production of Parma Ham and trend in number of Consortium members
Source: Processed by the author with data supplied by the Parma Ham Consortium

Consumption has registered a drop of 6.1%, although this is lower than that of the product's main competitors, and there has consequently been an increase of 32.8% in market share (San Daniele Ham 11.8%; other hams 55.4%).[4]

The domestic market accounts for 70% of Parma Ham sales. Conversely, the share of branded products exported abroad has gone up, generating a long-term positive trend for an overall increase of almost one million units over the past decade.[5]

This limited yet significant data highlights the way in which Parma Ham has represented and continues to represent one of Italy's most important products, not only at the national but also at the international level. It was therefore essential to set up the Parma Ham Consortium, the official body that safeguards the product, the role it has played since 1963, the year of its constitution.

The time span analyzed in this study (1963 to the 1980s) corresponds to a period of significant development for the Consortium, both in terms of production volumes and the increase in number of members. It is therefore interesting to examine the characteristics of the governance processes and accounting instruments adopted in these years. However, because of the importance assumed by certain events in the following years, the chapter briefly traces the most important events on corporate governance.

THE CONSORTIUM: CONSTITUTION AND DEVELOPMENT, ACTIVITIES

The Consortium was created as a "Voluntary Consortium for Producers of Ham Typical of Parma" in April 1963. In 1970 the Consortium became the "Parma Ham Consortium" and acquired by law the power to regulate the production of Parma Ham in a specific geographical area. In 2014 (the latest available data from the *Management Report 2014*), the number of members of the Consortium totalled 150 compared to 247, the highest number, which was reached in 1985 (see Figure 7.1).

Over the years, the way in which the Consortium has evolved from an organizational, managerial and governance point of view has been influenced by the regulatory changes introduced both at the national and community levels and by fluctuating local, national and international economic conditions.[6] It is therefore possible to identify the following three main phases of development:[7]

- Establishment and development: 1963–1985
- Consolidation and reorganization: 1986–2000
- Last 15 years.

In this section we focus in more detail on the period analyzed in this work; however, we believe should be drawn, albeit briefly, the main events that characterized the life of the Consortium in the following years too, in the light of the influence that they have had especially on the dynamics of corporate governance.

From Its Establishment to Its Development (1963–1985)

The main reason for founding the Consortium was the sharp increase in demand for ham characterizing the market at that time and the subsequent need to raise production levels. The intention of a group of small producers (23 companies) was therefore to join forces to draw up a common code of conduct and introduce a designation of origin that would distinguish Parma Ham. In this way they would promote a collective brand to protect at both national and international level. On 18 April 1963 the "Voluntary Consortium for Producers of Ham Typical of Parma"[8] was founded.

Over the next few years, the members of the Consortium operated within the scope of Italy's tutelage legislation, identifying the production processes and the name of the product with their related geographical area. The high level of protection offered by the Consortium to its members in the earliest years of its establishment pushed numerous producers to join; at the end of 1970 the number of members had reached 89 companies, reaching 247 companies in 1985 (in the following year the trend reverses, and the number of producers decreases until 2011 (Figure 7.1). The production of hams also increased rapidly: from 379,000 product units (branded hams) in 1970 to 7,000,000 in 1985 (see Figure 7.1).

The Consortium's members in this period possessed different characteristics and can therefore be subdivided into three main categories:[9]

1. Parma Ham producers, frequently small- or medium-sized businesses that usually sell via wholesalers and that sometimes outsource production or buy from the wholesale market themselves;
2. Contract producers, usually small in size, which produce on behalf of other companies or for investors speculating on price fluctuation (e.g., slaughterhouses);
3. Large multiproduct companies, predominantly Italian cured meat factories, which include Parma Ham in their product portfolio and which sometimes process the hams on the basis of subcontracts.

The main reasons behind producers gradually joining the Consortium lay in the possibility of small companies achieving economies of scale in the procurement phase of production means and of limiting the negative effects generated by uncertain market conditions. Empirical research (2002)[10] has also highlighted the fact that the most important factors influencing members to join the network were related to small and medium-sized enterprises capacity, such as product differentiation (86%), promotion (86%) and "to increase consumer demand" (82%). Furthermore, these activities all promote a collective brand name. However, market access and market information were also important (82% and 64% of companies interviewed, respectively) as was the flow of information from the trade (71%).

The very essence of this collective brand required autonomous companies to join forces and work together. Therefore, the proposition that small food companies establish/join networks to improve access to resources is supported, in that they found it necessary to pool resources in order to build and promote a brand. Yet this collective effort is reinforced within a legislative framework that provides "tutelage" or protected denomination of origin.

On 4 July 1970, Italian legislators intervened to protect consortiums with Law n. 506, which essentially granted the Consortium the authority to prosecute fraud and unfair competition. In 1978 this legislation came into effect with Regulation n. 83 (3 July), which officially assigned the Consortium the task of ensuring that the regulations were observed (further legislative updates were made in the nineties, also following European Community intervention)

Consolidation and Reorganization (1986–2000)

The positive trend of the number of Parma Ham producers affiliated with the Consortium was interrupted in 1986. As highlighted in Figure 7.1, from then on there is a drop in the number of producers, which today (data from 2014) stands at 150. Furthermore, the increase in production in this period led to a drop in prices and the risk that the ham was of a lower quality. In order to limit the effects of the difficult climate on the supply chain (from the breeders to the slaughterhouses and producers), an interprofessional body was set up in 1990 so that an agreement could be reached between the three categories; regrettably, the founding of this body did not generate common grounds for discussion.[11]

In 1993, the consortium membership agreed to impose production quotas to tackle the issue of pressure on prices and the risk of a reduction in the quality of the ham. Quotas were first approved at the Annual General Meeting on 26 June and were based on the production of the previous year. There was also provision for some increase in production depending on circumstances. The Consortium legislation (article 30, 1993) empowered the consortium to impose such production quotas.[12] These production quotas annoyed farmers and slaughterhouses since they capped the number of pigs entering the Parma Ham supply chain. In 1996 the Italian Competition Authority ruled against the Consortium, although it allowed a transition period up to 1998 after which no production quotas could be used.[13] In this period, legislative intervention from the European Community and national intervention (Tutelage Law no. 26/90; DM n. 25 15 February 1993, assignment of the task of vigilance to the Consortium, August 1994) played a key role.

In 1996 the Parma Ham PDO came under the protection of the European Community. Initially with EEC Regulation n. 2081 of 1992 and subsequently with Law n. 526 of 1999, the role and the function of consortiums were redefined on the basis of the tutelage, promotion and enhancement of geographical indications. In particular, Law n. 2081/92 (subsequently replaced by Council Regulation [EC] n. 510/2006 and lastly by Regulation [EU] n. 1151/2012 of the European Parliament and Council) provided for the creation of a system of checks carried out by an external or independent figure aimed at ensuring that consortium producers respect the rules concerning PDO and PGI products and contained in the production regulations. As the control function is carried out by an external figure, it is therefore distinct from the task of vigilance assigned to the protection consortiums.[14]

In order to comply with the new legislation and strengthen relations between all of the companies within the entire supply chain for the production of Parma Ham with certification procedures, the Consortium set up in 1997 as a "second level Consortium," (as of January 1998, Istituto Parma Qualità, or IPQ), with the function of verifying documentation and carrying out inspections and analyses at companies and certifying Parma Ham breeders, slaughterhouses and producers. In 1998, with a decree from the Ministry of Agriculture and Forestry, the Institute was recognized and authorized to register on the list of private vigilance bodies for PDO and PGI products set up by the Ministry itself.[15] Thus, with the creation of the IPQ and the abolition of market quotas and, as already mentioned, Law n. 526 of 1999, the role and functions of consortia with reference to the tutelage, promotion and enhancement of geographical indications were redefined.

In this period, therefore, the Consortium began a series of legal proceedings against imitations and abuse of the brand (tutelage) and committed itself to enhancing and promoting the product in particular in foreign markets, in light of the difficulties in the domestic market.[16]

Recent History (2000–2014)

The introduction of the euro marked the beginning of the twenty-first century, resulted in reduced purchasing power and a decrease in consumption, and ultimately led to the economic and financial crisis beginning in 2008 and an unfavourable economic situation at both national and international level. This situation that made it increasingly difficult for Parma Ham to be assimilated by the market, in particular in Italy, and created a subsequent drop in prices. In order to cope with this situation, the Consortium implemented a project strategic for the relaunch of the sector by:

- Intensifying communication activities to inform national consumers about the product's qualities;
- Introducing activities aimed at opening up new foreign markets and developing programmes to enhance the image of the product and

promote it abroad, in particular in the emerging countries (export has become an indispensable outlet for the product);
- Introducing measures designed to limit the possibility of imitation products;
- Implementing actions to protect the designation of origin and the brand in international markets;
- Urging the competent authorities to create an agri-food district for ham as soon as possible.

From a regulatory point of view, both European and Italian legislators have made key changes in this period (e.g., Decree Law n. 297/04 "Sanction Decree" for the PDO and PGI product sectors, applying EEC Reg. n. 2081/92; EU Reg. n. 1169/11 covers provisions concerning the labelling and quality of food products; Reg. E 1151/12 concerns quality systems for agri-food products; this is also the period (2003) when the European Council assigned the headquarters of the European Food Safety Agency to Parma). Yet the most important development for the Consortium and its members was the acceptance in 2013 on the part of the European Commission (with Regulation n. 1308/2013) of the Italian government's request regarding the management of production volumes for PDO hams. The Brussels Agreement laid the foundation for a provision that will permit the regulation of the production of PDO hams on the basis of market trends. In fact, the possibility of managing production volumes represents a means of support for the prevention of market crises and constitutes a fundamental prerequisite to ensure the balanced development of the market in question. Throughout 2014 and the first few months of 2015, the competent Consortium organs focussed on the implementation of the new community provisions. In 2014 the Assembly approved the Regulation Plan for the supply of Parma Ham 2015–2017.[17]

It should also be noted that the period from 2000 onwards has been characterized by key statutory amendments, following the process of harmonization with community legislation. These changes have made a significant impact on the governance aspect of the Consortium, which are dealt with in this chapter in greater detail in previous paragraphs

The Consortium's Main Activities

The activities of protection, enhancement and promotion that the Consortium carries out for Parma Ham are based on the production regulations stipulated by the Consortium itself and approved by the European Union and, as it concerns regulations for all of the stages of the supply chain, also by the breeders for the production of Parma Ham. In particular, the objective was to regulate access to the use of the geographical name and protect production in accordance with defined standards.[18] The production regulations geographically define the boundaries of the typical production area, requiring all the phases of raw material processing to be carried out there.[19]

It is clear that these "rules" contribute to establishing a strong connection between product and territory, and make an significant impact in terms of employment and local income, not only affecting the ham processing sector but also that relating to the services provided for producers and the tourism sector.

Thus, the aims of the Consortium's activities in this area are to protect, enhance and provide information for the consumer, and can be summarized in three categories:

- Application of the regulations
- Research and development
- Promotion and advertising (marketing).

More specifically, the Consortium helps companies to improve production and commercialization processes in Italy and abroad, for example by activities related to technical production consultancy, and assistance for business, health, insurance and financial aspects. It also supports producers by continuously supplying information with domestic and foreign market analyses, and research and development activities. The Consortium deals with the task of enhancing the value of Parma Ham in Italy and abroad by creating joint advertising campaigns and promotional initiatives both with traditional retail outlets and major names in large-scale distribution.[20]

THE CONSORTIUM: CORPORATE GOVERNANCE SYSTEM

The main governance issues concerning the Parma Ham Consortium can be found in its Charter (with which it was established in 1963 by 23 curing firms as the "Voluntary Consortium for Producers of Ham Typical of Parma") and in its Statute. These documents provide useful information regarding both the characteristics of the ownership (members of the Consortium) and the management, and the relationship between the two.

Since its establishment, the Consortium has grown considerably: the number of member companies has increased from the 23 original firms to stand at 150 (2014 data), and over the years the characteristics of its members and the way they interrelate have also significantly evolved, as have the ways they manage the Consortium. Regulatory evolution is therefore also important, as it has characterized the legislative environment in which the Body operates. The various responsibilities of the Consortium have in fact been accompanied both by changes to the characteristics and qualifications of the members and to the governance bodies of the Consortium itself. In fact, as far as the latter are concerned, the regulations modify various aspects, operating both with regard to the organs to be set up and the appointment of several of their components. Of particular note, although the composition of the organs of the Consortium and its policies are subject to intervention on the part of its members alone, DM 253, 15 February 1993 (Art. 31) also refers to the Consortium's organs.

The governance of the Consortium, as with the governance of any company, can be analyzed by looking at the characteristics of the ownership (in this case, the companies belonging to the Consortium), the governing organs (Shareholders' Meeting, Board of Directors, Board of Auditors and other executive or control organs) and the relations and powers of intervention between the two—characteristics partly dictated by the regulations and partly self-determined by the members in the Statute.

This chapter has examined the Consortium's Charter and Statutes, as well as the Management Reports, which have been modified over time, to analyze the actions that have generated modifications either in the governing organs or the membership base, that is, in the Consortium's members. These actions have also been interpreted in light of regulatory changes or those within the sector and studied with particular reference to any other impact they may have had on the Consortium's own management. As already mentioned, this research focusses on the period in which the Consortium had the largest membership (the 1980s), although in the governance area it would also seem appropriate to analyze the subsequent years owing to the significant changes to the ownership and governance structures resulting from national and community regulatory intervention.

1963–1985: Characteristics of the Consortium's Members and Organs

The original Charter stipulated (Art. VI) that the members could only be producers of the Ham typical of Parma, defining producer as a "ham curer who professionally provides for both the salting and curing operations, on his own behalf or that of a third party." Furthermore, "in order to join and gain admission to the Consortium, the producer's factory in which the combined processes of salting and curing take place must be in the Province of Parma, to the south of a line parallel to the via Emilia not above an altitude of 900m." Producers could not be members of the Consortium if they only cured hams from pigs bred and slaughtered outside Emilia Romagna, Lombardy, Veneto and Piedmont.

Thus, the Consortium was initially only constituted by producers resident in the municipality of Langhirano, yet the immediate interest also shown by producers belonging to other municipalities pushed for the membership base to be extended. Subsequent to the legal protection afforded by the designation of origin to Parma Ham and the authority granted to the Consortium to prosecute fraud and unfair competition, the number of applications for membership continued to rise until the peak was reached in 1985 (247 members).[21]

With respect to the *organs within the consortium*, Art. XI of the Charter provided for the General Members' Meeting, the Board of Directors, the Board of Auditors and the Board of Arbitrators.

With respect to the General Meeting, each member had the right to a certain number of votes relating to the number of branded hams produced in the previous year (one vote for up to 5,000 units; two votes for 5,000–10,000units; three votes for over 10,000 units).

Regarding the validity of General Meeting resolutions, quorums were only required for the first convocation (a favourable vote from the majority of members enrolled for the Ordinary Meeting and from two-thirds of the members for the Extraordinary Meeting) At the second convocation, however, whether ordinary or extraordinary, the Meeting ruled on the basis of majority irrespective of the number present. There are no further details specified in the document as to how these meetings functioned.

With respect to management, according to the original Charter and the first Statute this was entrusted to the Board of Directors; this was granted more extensive powers of management and can organize itself internally by nominating a Chairman, Vice Chairman and an Executive Committee (Art. XIII, XIII bis and XIV).

The Board of Directors is composed of elected members and appointed members. There are 11 elected members and they are nominated by the General Meeting, which for each election can stipulate their number between five and 11 (Art. XIII).[22] There are two appointed members and they are nominated, among the members of the Consortium, by the Chamber of Commerce, Industry and Agriculture in Parma.

In the articles that follow, the Charter outlines the tasks and characteristics of the control organ (Board of Auditors) and the Board of Arbitrators, the organ in charge of resolving disputes arising between the Consortium's members; problems concerning admission, forfeiture, exclusion or any disagreement regarding relations between the Consortium and its members.

The Subsequent Period: Characteristics of the Consortium's Members and Organs

The Statute was modified a number of times to accommodate the changing needs arising from the increase in size of the Consortium, the new tasks it undertook to carry out and legislative intervention, which in some cases brought about significant changes to the group of members, making a radical impact on the ways the Consortium is managed and the role of its members.[23]

In respect of the *members' characteristics*, the first amendment to the 1988 Statute sets out in greater detail the prerequisites for admission to the Consortium, stipulating that those eligible to join are

> all Parma Ham producers whose production in the previous financial year on their premises in the typical area consisted of: 1) a minimum of 70% thighs destined for the protected production of Parma Ham on the date the new tutelage law for the nomination of origin "Parma Ham"

> comes into effect [. . .]; 2) a minimum of 80% thighs destined for the protected production of Parma Ham by December 31st 1990.
>
> (Statute, 1988, art.3)

Furthermore, the 1988 Statute expressly states (Art. 9) that Consortium members can make use of the active and passive electorate for the formation of the Consortium's organs.

Yet it is the 2004 amendment to the Statute that significantly changes the characteristics of the members for admission to the Consortium (Art. 12), as it includes the regulatory reference to the Ministry of Agriculture, Food and Forestry Policies Decree dated 12 April 2000[24] and therefore extends the range of subjects admitted to the Consortium; in addition to Parma Ham producers, also breeders, slaughterhouses, portioners and packagers can join the Consortium, provided they are recognised businesses operating within the supply chain for the production of PDO "Parma Ham."[25] Following the implementation of the 1999 Community Law, the Statute offers all those forming part of the production chain the possibility of joining the Consortium, ensuring they are represented in the social organs, although as will shortly be explained, the votes of the various categories are of different weight. At the same time, a minimum production quota is no longer required, thus allowing all companies to join the Consortium irrespective of the percentage of their Parma Ham production in relation to their total production.

With respect to the *rights of the electorate*, Article 17 of this version of the Statute specifies that members of the Consortium only have the right to passive electorate if at least two thirds of the total raw ham they process is intended for the production of PDO "Parma Ham."[26] This specification aims to continue to reserve, in spite of the extended group of members, greater power in defining the Consortium's management policies for the firms whose production of Parma Ham is the principle focus of their business. The subsequent amendments made in 2007, 2009 and 2012 do not substantially change the aspects influencing the characteristics of the members and the rights of electorate, despite modifying the articles relating to these areas so as to further simplify the text.[27]

With respect to the *Consortium's organs and boards*, the provisions of the original Charter were modified in subsequent versions of the Statute. In 1988, the Statute listed the Consortium's organs as the General Meeting, the Board of Directors, the Executive Committee, the Chairman, the Board of Auditors and the Board of Arbitrators. However, the 2004 amendment specifies that the Consortium's organs are the General Meeting, the Board of Directors and the Board of Auditors, and that the Board of Directors is organized internally by the appointment of a Chairman, two Vice Chairmen and an Executive Committee.[28] Again, in 2004 the interprofessional Commission was introduced, which is constituted by representatives from the processing companies, breeders, slaughterhouses and portioners-packagers, whose function is to provide guidance and expertise to ensure the correct application of current legislation, production procedure guidelines and the regulations and directives adopted by the Consortium. Subsequent amendments made to the Statute do not significantly affect this issue.

Regarding the General Meeting, a number of statutory amendments are made in particular on the subject of the assignment of the rights to vote, also in relation to the changes already mentioned and the expansion of the membership base. The 1988 Statute modifies the rights to vote, attributing one vote to members who have on average in the past three financial years branded up to 10,000 hams with the Consortium's seal, and two votes for over 10,000 hams.

Yet it is with the 2004 statutory amendment, also in relation to the substantial change in the Consortium's admission criteria introduced in this period and illustrated earlier, that there is a significant distinction made between the assignment of votes to the various Consortium member categories. Article 32 of the 2004 Statute, in fact, stipulates that the category of processing companies is entitled to a percentage representation of 66%, the pig breeders category is entitled to a percentage of 11.33%, the slaughterhouse category a percentage of 11.33% and the category of portioners-packagers a percentage representation of 11.33%. In the event that the category does not represent 100% of the quantity produced for the purposes of PDO "Parma Ham" by its own category, the representation is reduced to a quantity proportional to the production quota introduced in the PDO circuit by the operators in the same category who do not form part of the Consortium.[29] So the representation percentages of the General Meeting is divided among the four member categories.

Then, Article 35 stipulates the number of votes for each member, which is determined on the basis of the production class they belong to.[30] These classes are created by setting minimum and maximum production limits so that the number of members in each class is about 20% of the total number of Consortium members from the corresponding production category. This subdivision is carried out separately for each category of Consortium members. All the members within the same class have the right to the same number of votes; those belonging to the first class have one vote, those in the second have three votes, those in the third class have six votes, the members of the fourth have nine votes, and those in the fifth class are divided into two groups each with 50% representation: the companies in the first group are allocated 13 votes, whereas those in the second group have 18 votes. Furthermore, the number of votes is increased by 30% for the processing companies that exclusively produce PDO "Parma Ham." Therefore, to adopt the decisions, each category makes its own vote separately; a record is drawn up of the voting session indicating the number of votes that are in favour, against, abstentions and void. For each category's voting session, the percentage value of votes in favour and against are worked out, and the sum of the percentage values expressed by the individual categories is then calculated according to the percentages indicated earlier, in order to verify whether the majority required for the various resolutions has been reached.

In respect of the attendance and resolution quorums, the first amendments made in 1988 and 2004 do not significantly modify the Statute; for example, at the second convocation both were considered valid however many members participated and decided by simple majority—as specified earlier—or, for the matters pertaining to amendments of the statute, production regulations, production programme, stipulation of technical regulations and interprofessional agreements, by a qualified majority of 75% of the votes made.[31] An attendance quorum was only provided by the amendment made in 2009 for the validity of the Extraordinary Meeting also in second convocation, requiring at least a third of the overall available votes to be present. The same Statute reduces the qualified majority required to amend the Statute, production regulations and production programme from 75% to 66%.[32] In the subsequent amendments to the Statute there are no particularly important developments concerning the way Ordinary and Extraordinary General Meetings functioned.[33] It is clear that the amendments made, both to the way votes are distributed and that of the implementation of decisions, respond to the need to regulate the decision-making powers concerning the Consortium following the expansion and diversification of the membership base. The amendments made to the sections concerning the composition of the administrative board, covered by the articles subsequent to those already illustrated, also move in this direction.

The original Board of Directors (named in the Charter "*Consiglio direttivo*" and renamed "Consiglio di Amministrazione"[34] with the first amendment in 1988), was composed of 15 components in 1988 and of between 10 and 27 components in the 2004 version and those that followed. However, while the 1988 Statute stipulates that the small producers must be represented on the Board, in the 2004 version and those that followed, emphasis is placed on representation for the various categories on the Board owing to the changes in the characteristics of the Consortium members. In the case of the Board of Directors, which is composed of 27 members, up to a maximum of 18 must represent the processing companies, up to a maximum of three of the breeders, three of the slaughterhouses and three of the portioners-packagers.[35]

The election of the members of the Board of Directors takes place separately for each category and is based on the principle of open opposing lists. Each Consortium member votes on a specific list composed of a predetermined number of candidates and selects a maximum of five preferences. The list that wins is the one achieving an absolute majority of the votes from the Consortium members belonging to the reference category at the General Meetings, and the candidates on the list that wins and those from the list that loses who obtain the highest number of preferences in accordance with the provisions stipulated in the Statute's articles are elected members of the Board of Directors .[36] The articles dedicated to the composition, election, powers, functioning, resolutions, Executive Committee, Chairman and Vice Chairmen establish the main ways in which the management organs function, with a view to guaranteeing the participation of all the member categories and protecting those that are mainly involved in the production of ham. The contents of the various versions of the Statute (2004, 2007, 2009 and 2012) do not differ widely from one another, and restrict themselves to clarifying or specifying some aspects or quantifying differently the quorums required for the adoptions of decisions or the size restrictions of the Board of Directors and the Executive Committee, in particular relating to the variations in size of the Consortium introduced over the years.

With respect to the Board of Auditors and the other technical and control organs there are no particular characteristics making an unusual or characteristic impact on the way the Consortium is managed.

Summary Observations

An analysis of the documents examined has made it possible to make several summary observations regarding the governance of the Consortium. The most significant impact was made by the earliest amendments to the Statute and those made in 2004 in particular. These amendments resulted from the need to adapt the management of the Consortium to its changing characteristics, partly due to the increasing membership and the precise definition of the roles of the Consortium, and partly due to legislative intervention. The fact that the latter has opened up membership to different figures operating within the PDO Parma Ham production chain has radically transformed the characteristics of both the Consortium's members and the Consortium itself.

In light of these different member categories, it is therefore necessary to ensure that they all have the opportunity to express their own opinion, yet at the same time allow those whose main business focus is the production of Parma Ham greater influence. In fact, very different entities coexist within the Consortium, including both producers (often small—or medium sized businesses) that exclusively produce Parma Ham and large groups for which the product only represents a limited part of their production; this diversity is reflected by differences in strategy and in the participation of the Consortium's various categories. The statutory amendments introduced were aimed at successfully managing the heterogeneity of the members, providing for different means of expression in the General Meetings and precisely regulating the possibility of taking on operative roles within the management organs.

THE CONSORTIUM OF PARMA HAM: ACCOUNTING INFORMATION

The historical documents stored at the headquarters of the Consortium in Parma and in the Chamber of Commerce, Industry and Agriculture in Parma include a range of materials relating to the accounting information, with particular reference to the Annual Reports (*Rendiconti Annuali*) and to the Reports of the Executive Board (*Relazioni del Consiglio Direttivo*) related to the early life of the Consortium, and the Financial Statements (*Bilanci di Esercizio*) and Reports of the Board of Directors (*Relazioni del Consiglio di Amministrazione*) for the most recent years.

Since 1991, the financial data are audited by an independent auditor, and since 1993 the financial statement has been prepared as required by the Civil Code, and so with a separate balance sheet and notes.

It is important, before going through the detail of the composition of the reporting package and the evolution of the most significant items, to analyze the characteristics of the constituent Annual Reports, which can be represented with reference to the three periods through which the phases of development of the Consortium were analyzed.

Establishment and Development: 1963–1985

The first Annual Report that is quoted in the acts of the consortium (in the Reports of the Executive Board to the meeting of the associated member) is the one of the year of the establishment, that is at the end of the financial year 1963 (31 December 1963).[37]

The Annual Report on the original copy consists of the following documents:

- Report of the Executive Board (Relazione del Consiglio Direttivo);
- Financial Account (Conto Finanziario) as of 31 December 1969;
- Report of the Statutory Auditors (Relazione del Collegio Sindacale).

The structure of the "Financial Account" is composed as follows:

- "Cash flow statement," consists of "Assets" ("in terms of cash") and "Liabilities," represented according to a cash accounting representation, and with evidence of positives and negatives surpluses, as well as allocation of separate "Accounting of Memory" related to tangible and intangible assets and accumulated depreciation;
- "Profit and Loss," with indicated summary of income and expenditures for the financial year;
- "Expenditure Analysis," which provides a breakdown of the expenditure on the basis of the following macro-categories:
    - institutional costs;
    - surveillance and brand protection;
    - other institutional costs;
    - functional costs;
    - other functional costs;
    - overhead costs.

- "Financial sheet," containing the balances of banking relationships, financial investments and guarantee deposits recorded at the end of the financial year;
- Details of positive and negative surpluses.

At the end of the aforementioned statements, in the reporting package are disclosed some additional information related to the managerial activity developed during the financial year:

- Detail of the veterinary compensations;
- Bank conditions in force at the end of the financial year;
- Amount overdue receivables towards associated at the end of the financial year not yet received;
- Costs incurred during the year for investing abroad;
- Ratios of the cash flow statement;
- Synthesis of the supervision and judicial activity.

Consolidation and Reorganization: 1986–2000

In this period, we can find an evolution in the contents of the Annual Reports of the Consortium. The first substantial change was recorded in 1988, with the entry into force of the Income Tax Code (the Italian TUIR); from that year, as costs, is also included the depreciation of tangible assets.

We can subdivide into two periods. The first, from 1988 to 1993, was characterized by an increased information determined by a wider detail in the items represented in Financial Account; in particular, it is represented the detail of the marketing expenses split by country of business (France, Germany, the United States, United Kingdom, Belgium, Italy). The second one, from 1994 to 2000, was characterized by the adoption of the structure of the Financial Statement required by the European Rule 127/1991, that completely change the way to represent the values of the Consortium.

Recent History: 2001–2014

In these years, the increase in the disclosure of the notes of comment are noticed, in which the information about the most important item was expanded.

As we can summarize after analyzing the documents carried out, the financial statements of the Consortium were from early on accompanied by a series of management information aimed to give the representation of the activities it performs through the proposition of summary tables and economic data, in order to synthesize to the associates all the major aspects of management, including the supervision and protection of trademarks activities of the associated companies.

Considering a more qualitative analysis on the items that composed in particular the "profit and loss statement" of the consortium, the main items (suitable for quantitative importance) are the following:

Revenues

Consortium membership fee
Consortium annual fee
Production grant
Interest receiveable

Costs

Advertising/marketing costs
Marking costs
Supervision and brand protection
Employee costs

In terms of revenues, the most consistent part are the contributions paid by members of the Consortium, while in terms of costs the most significant items are related to advertising and marketing costs and those incurred for brand protection, consistent with the nature of the Consortium.

From 1963 to 1987, the structure of the financial statements reporting package doesn't change significantly. And it is particularly interesting to analyze the evolution of some items in that period, first of all because the oldest period is the most meaningful for a study in the field of accounting history, and also because it could be find a representation of those items that doesn't change over time, while in the further financial statements there was an extension of the disclosure that doesn't allow a perfect comparison over time.

Considering this, it is interesting to make some concerns related of the values represented in the financial statements of the Consortium.

In particular, it is meaningful to analyze the main items in terms of revenues and costs (as shown in Figure 7.2), considering their evolution over time.

The difference found in the values of 1973 and 1974 was determined by a very crucial moment in the life of the Consortium, in which it was perceived a shift from the producers of ham in Parma and the producers of ham in Langhirano, and this determined for the year 1974 a new evaluation of the membership and annual fees. The litigation was immediately recomposed.

The great increase in the value of the marking costs for the year 1982 was determined by a redefinition of the "chart of accounts" that allow a better reallocation of each cost to the items that is by nature better linked to it.

The main items of revenues are membership fees and annual fees, together with marking contribution. In the early years of the Consortium, the relative weight of the membership fees compared to the marking contributions is on

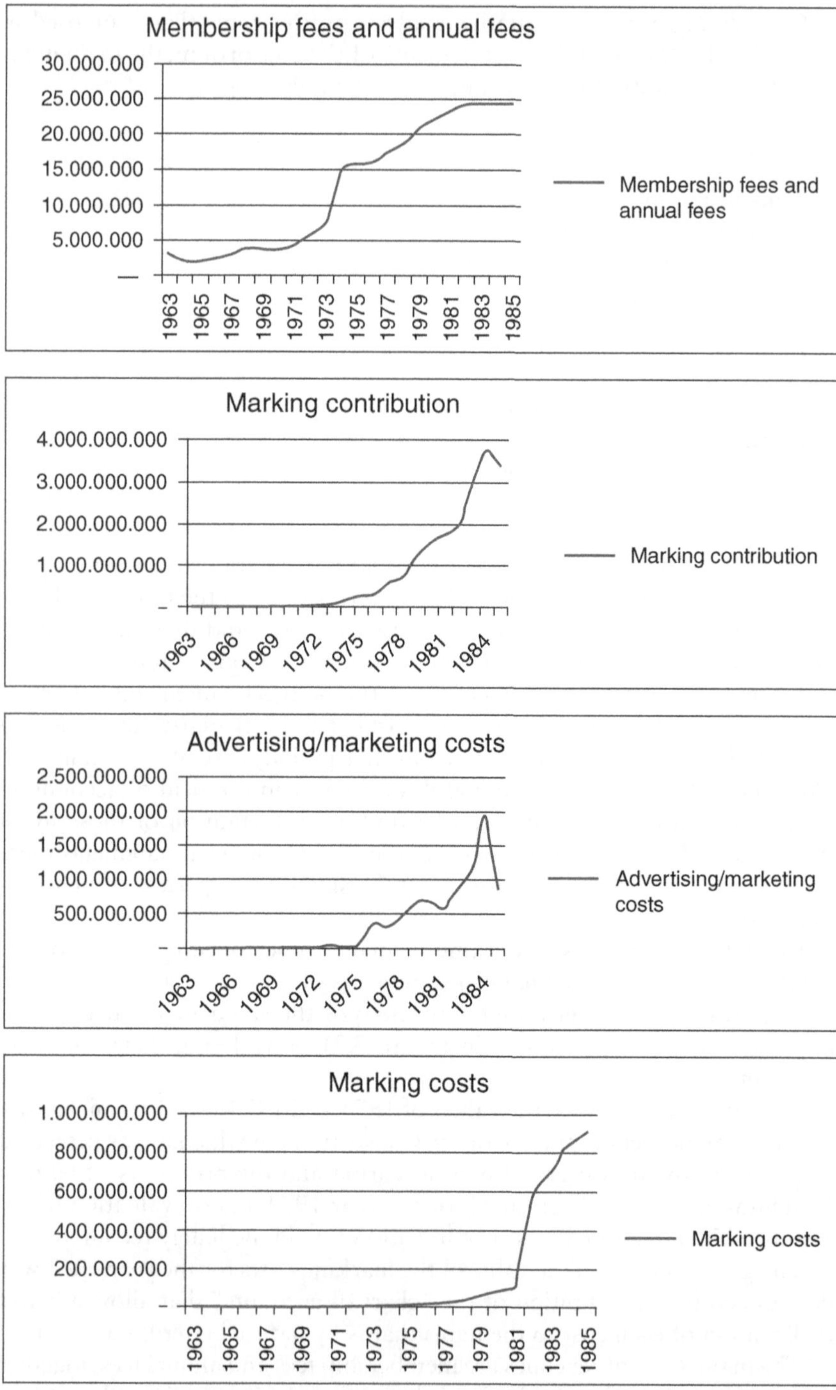

Figure 7.2 Trends in membership fees and annual fees, marking contributions, advertising/marketing costs, advertising/marketing expenses

the order of a ratio of 1 to 7. As shown in Tables 7.1 and 7.2, in time the ratio grows exponentially in favor of the marking contributions, that appear to be quantitatively the most significant value in terms of revenues (see Figure 7.3, Part 1). The figures represented show the values at the early life of the Consortium, from the year in relation to which we are able to recover the book value (1969).

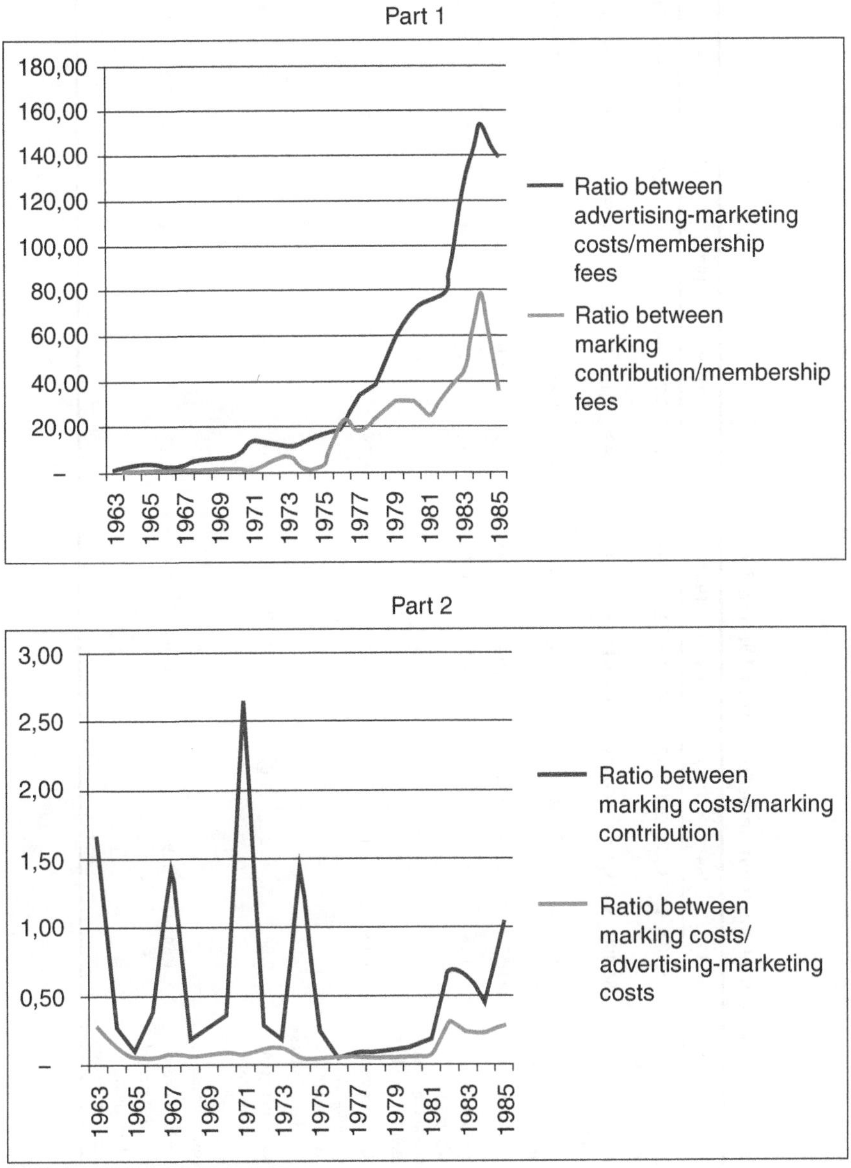

Figure 7.3 Trends in financial statement ratio

Table 7.1 Financial statement indicators from 1963 to 1974

Years	1963	1964	1965	1966	1967	1968	1969	1970	1971	1972	1973	1974
Membership fees and annual fees	2,805,000	1,853,850	2,053,650	2,472,319	2,902,001	4,016,300	3,757,000	3,700,000	4,350,000	5,600,000	7,250,000	15,100,000
Marking contributions	3,186,400	5,945,355	7,952,331	5,444,640	9,443,233	23,196,843	23,183,734	26,265,890	60,335,730	70,691,880	77,811,930	205,480,170
Advertising/ marketing costs	514,635	2,791,445	3,883,069	621,878	494,860	7,594,000	5,881,328	6,140,140	1,464,977	27,672,959	54,041,355	5,356,038
Marking costs	841,577	720,835	352,210	243,800	721,498	1,282,795	1,639,145	2,209,243	3,901,260	7,647,874	9,303,532	7,991,386
Ratio between advertising-marketing costs / membership fees	0.18	1.51	1.89	0.25	0.17	1.89	1.57	1.66	0.34	4.94	7.45	0.35
Ratio between marking contribution/ membership fees	1.14	3.21	3.87	2.20	3.25	5.78	6.17	7.10	13.87	12.62	10.73	13.61
Ratio between marking costs/ marking contribution	0.26	0.12	0.04	0.04	0.08	0.06	0.07	0.08	0.06	0.11	0.12	0.04
Ratio between marking costs / advertising-marketing costs	1.64	0.26	0.09	0.39	1.46	0.17	0.28	0.36	2.66	0.28	0.17	1.49

Table 7.2 Financial statement indicators from 1975 to 1985

Years	1975	1976	1977	1978	1979	1980	1981	1982	1983	1984	1985
Membership fees and annual fees	15,800,000	16,000,000	17,700,000	18,500,000	21,100,000	22,300,000	23,400,000	24,300,000	24,300,000	24,500,000	24,600,000
Marking contributions	267,610,980	296,803,640	601,713,800	714,279,200	1,243,434,000	1,591,302,600	1,783,667,400	1,925,471,700	3,128,816,500	3,787,599,000	3,424,709,500
Advertising/ marketing costs	45,564,671	372,299,156	326,475,384	434,393,148	668,500,585	698,778,714	571,409,738	865,429,111	1,071,597,193	1,963,846,586	888,857,312
Marking costs	10,768,510	12,136,366	28,382,420	36,707,661	64,742,776	82,858,137	102,116,053	595,000,638	707,747,491	853,666,581	907,981,277
Ratio between advertising-marketing costs/ membership fees	2.88	23.27	18.44	23.48	31.68	31.34	24.42	35.61	44.10	80.16	36.13
Ratio between marking contribution/ membership fees	16.94	18.55	34.00	38.61	58.93	71.36	76.23	79.24	128.76	154.60	139.22
Ratio between marking costs/ marking contribution	0.04	0.04	0.05	0.05	0.05	0.05	0.06	0.31	0.23	0.23	0.27
Ratio between marking costs/ advertising-marketing costs	0.24	0.03	0.09	0.08	0.10	0.12	0.18	0.69	0.66	0.43	1.02

From the point of view of costs, it is noted that the two main cost items are the advertising/marketing costs and the marking costs (see Figure 7.3, Part 2). The evolution of relations between the two accounting items is quite unusual; the incidence of advertising/marketing costs is higher, but in some years, probably as a result of specific management decisions, the marking costs are higher than the advertising/marketing ones, or very closed to them.

It is also interesting to analyze the relationship between marking costs and marking contributions (see Figure 7.3, Part 2). In the early years of the Consortium, it moves to a much larger gap in the following years, perhaps as a symptom of the need by the Consortium to increase this difference in order to ensure the coverage of the incremental overhead costs.

Finally, it is interesting to analyze the relationship between advertising/marketing costs and membership fees (see Figure 7.3, Part 1); we could appreciate how, over time, expenditure on promotions aimed at protecting the brand of Parma Ham have increased exponentially over time than the contributions required by the associates. This could be explained by the increased needs of promotion, at international level and not only nationally, that require to spend more and more in time; probably, the Consortium did not intend to cover in direct proportion those increasing needs, and consequently costs, with the membership fees, but with other sources of revenues.

The analysis carried out on the carrying values of the Consortium, with particular reference to the period 1969–1985 (for the complete database see Table 7.1 and Table 7.2), explain that there has been an increasing trend in revenue and costs book value as a consequence of the growth of structure and size of the Consortium. It must not clearly seen specified increments related to increases in book value during years and periods in which there has been changes in the composition and in the corporate governance structure of the Consortium.

CONCLUSIONS

In the analysis carried out can be underlined the following elements:

- The development of the Consortium over time shows that, on the basis, on the one hand, of the number of members and of the production of hams and, second, of the regulatory changes in the national and international context, it is possible to identify three main phases: the first relating to its establishment and development (1963–1985); the second relative to consolidation and reorganization (1986–2000) and last one concerning last 15 years.
- The corporate governance structure of the Consortium over the years, with particular attention to the years of the constitution of it and the most significant changes that have occurred from 2004 onwards.

- The evolution of the representation inside the financial reports, with particular attention to their characteristics over time, as well as the evolution of costs.

From the analysis defined, it is possible to synthesize the findings based on the following considerations:

- The Consortium has become an operational institution for the protection of the typical Parma Ham, with a significant development from the 1970s since the mid-1980s, where there are the major increases in the activity of the Consortium.
- According to the increasing complexity of the economic environment in the food industry, organizational structure of governance have been adopted that could meet the changing needs of the market, both domestically and internationally.
- In this context, marketing/advertising investments to strengthen the image of the product have recorded an upward trend.
- The contributions of the members, in addition to the fixed annual fee, have increased exponentially mainly with reference to the marking contributions. This could be explained according to the fact that the function of the Consortium of Parma Ham exerts its effects not just in increasing promotional activities, but in creating a distinctive brand to protect the local products.

NOTES

1. The chapter is the result of the joint contribution of the authors; However Paolo Andrei is the author of "Introduction" and "Conclusions"; Federica Balluchi of "Literature Reviews," "Parma Ham," "The Consortium: Constitution and Development, Activities"; Katia Furlotti of "The Consortium: Corporate Governance System"; and Pier Luigi Marchini and Veronica Tibiletti of "The Consortium of Parma Ham: Accounting Information."
2. See data processing provided by the Ministry of Agricultural, Alimentary and Forestry Policies (MIFAAP) at http://www.politicheagricole.it.
3. Giacomini et al. (2003, p. 14). See also Mancini (2003, p. 86). With regard to the importance of typical product, see Agri2000 (2000), Arfini (2000), Barjolle and Sylvander (2000) and Belletti (2002).
4. Parma Ham Consortium, *Management Report 2014*.
5. Ibid.
6. Giacomini, Arfini and Menozzi (2010, p. 59).
7. See also O'Reilly et al. (2003) and Mancini (2003).
8. Regarding this, see the first Annual Report 2013, p. 5:

   > the Board once again hopes that all the operators within the branch realise that their membership, whilst strengthening the Consortium, is as much to their own advantage as that of others: to remain objective, however, the Board does not create false illusions and is, in all honesty, fearful of seeing wasted the most favourable opportunity for the coalition of the interests of

everyone, for the creation of the conditions for the category to make itself heard, for a discipline which, within the scope of absolute company individuality and freedom, have to strengthen the major axes of the purchase and sale of the product in a shared sector and in safeguarding the tutelage of the product at commodity, industrial and commercial level. [. . .] Producers [. . .] cannot ignore the fact that all over the world only organized producers are able to make themselves heard both by the government and the market: to remove themselves from the changing times would mean day by day losing ground which could no longer be recovered.

9. O'Reilly et al. (2003) and Mancini (2003, p. 89). The heterogeneity of the member undertakings significant influence on the processes of governance of the Consortium.
10. O'Reilly et al. (2002, p. 772).
11. Mancini (2003, p. 90).
12. O'Reilly et al. (2002, p. 772).
13. Ibid., p. 773.
14. For an analysis of aims, characteristics and management aspects of protection consortiums see Mancini (2003, p. 61–80).
15. See http://www.parmaqualita.it.
16. Mancini (2003, p. 91).
17. For more detail on the technical aspects of the Regulation plan see *2014 Management Reports*.
18. Arfini et al. (2010, p. 60).
19. There are different restrictions relating to the geographical breeding area of the pigs, which extends across 11 Italian regions, from north to south as far as the Lazio Region.
20. O'Reilly et al. (2002, pp. 774–775); Mancini (2003, pp. 101–103); Arfini et al. (2010, p. 69).
21. Law 506/1970 granted the Consortium sanctioning powers for fraud and unfair competition; the legislation was then modified in the years that followed. EEC Regulation 2081/92 and the subsequent Community Law 526 of 1999 later introduced a division between the duties of control assigned to an independent third party (for Parma Ham, the Parma Quality Institute, or Ipq) and the vigilance function carried out by the tutelage consortia, which can only be exercised once the control activity has been completed by the authorized third party. (Giacomini et al. 2010, p. 59).
22. The indication of the numbers is the result of the amendment introduced by the extraordinary meeting held on 15 April 1969. The Charter indicates the first elective members, which appear to be five in number.
23. In particular, the amendments were made in 1988, 2004, 2007, 2009 and 2012.
24. See Decree Law n. 61413 and n. 61414 of 12 April 2000.
25. In particular, Art. 12 provides that:

    Those admitted singularly include:

    a. all Parma Ham producers (defined as processing companies), provided they are recognised businesses, whether they are companies, individual firms, or other kinds of body, which produce on premises—that are available to them—whose suitability for the production of PDO "Parma Ham" has been certified; for the purposes of admission to Consortium, every processing enterprise must be admitted and specifically identified in the "Parma Ham" certification system by the authorised controlling organ;
    b. the breeders, slaughterhouses, portioners-packagers, provided they are recognised businesses operating in the production chain for PDO "Parma Ham," whether they are companies, individual firms, or other kinds of

> body; for the purposes of admission to the Consortium, every subject belonging to the aforementioned categories must be admitted and specifically identified in the "Parma Ham" certification system by the authorised controlling organ.

Furthermore, those "admitted as members are subjects complying with the abovementioned sections 1 and 2 who have granted collective mandate with representation for all the activities pertaining to the running of the Consortium to an agent, forming part of the same production category".

26. In particular Art. 17 (sections c. and d.) stipulates that members have the right

> c. to active electorate, on condition that, at the moment the application for admission to the Consortium is submitted, they are carrying out activities for the production of Parma Ham, or breeding and slaughtering activities associated with the production of Parma Ham, or slicing and packaging activities of the same; d. to passive electorate with the following restrictions exclusively pertaining to production companies: only representatives of companies in which a share of 2/3 (two thirds) of the total raw ham processed is designated for the production of PDO "Parma Ham" in the last 3 years (3 consecutive financial years) or should the company have operated for a shorter period of activity, at its own premises situated in a typical area of production and certified as complying with current regulations and this Statute can make use of the passive electorate.

27. In the management reports for the years in question, commenting on the statutory amendments, reference is made to the amendments which have affected the technical-formal aspects, specifying the intended purpose as being that of simplifying the formulation of the articles, reducing content to the essentials.
28. The Charter also provided for the board of directors to elect a chairman and a vice chairman and the appointment of an executive committee composed of a chairman and vice chairman and a maximum of three other members. The specific functions and powers granted to the executive organ were not however indicated, as is later specified in subsequent versions. Further details can be found in later sections of this chapter and those concerning the board of directors.
29. Art. 32, section 4. To work out the division of costs and define the right to vote at the general meeting, the board of directors establishes the actual representative percentages within the general meeting relating to each member category of the Consortium (Art. 32, section 5) at the beginning of each financial year.
30. The classes are listed in sections 3 and 4 of Art. 34 of the Statute in accordance with the principles of DM 12 April 2000.
31. For statutory amendments pertaining to the contribution of categories other than processing companies, the resolutions have been adopted with a qualified majority of 75% of the votes made, representing the relevant categories (Art. 36, section 7–2004).
32. Amendment introduced following the evident operative difficulties relating to the strict application of this qualification for resolutions. Management Report 2008.
33. The general meeting is presided over by the chairman or the person acting in his stead. The ordinary general meeting is convened by the board as often as it is considered necessary and, in any case, at least once a year, in accordance with the legal conditions for the approval of the Consortium's final balance. Furthermore, it must be convened when requested by the board of auditors or one-fifth of the members. The extraordinary general meeting is convened by the board on its own initiative or following a justified request from the board of auditors. The voting sessions, whether ordinary or extraordinary, usually

take place as an open vote whereas they are carried out by secret ballot when they concern the appointment of the Consortium's organs or measures pertaining to individual people, or at the majority's request. The administrators must abstain from voting on resolutions concerning their work. The general meeting resolutions are binding on all Consortium members, even if they are not present or dissent.

34. Note that in 1978 management reporting began making reference to Consiglio di Amministrazione instead of Consiglio Direttivo, whereas it is in 1979 that the new name appears in the titles of the balance sheets.
35. The numbers indicated are valid when the category has full representation in the general meeting and are progressively reduced when the level of representation is lower, on the basis of the abovementioned rules for Consortium member representation. The Statute (2004) establishes the minimum threshold for the various categories, indicated under Art. 39, section 3.
36. Reference is made to the articles concerning the composition of the board of directors; Statute 2004, Art. 39, section 5 and thereafter. The numbering is slightly different in the subsequent versions (2007, 2009, 2012) concerning the different numbering of the articles. In the regard, it should also be noted that in the subsequent versions the procedure and ratio behind the appointment process is not modified even if the quorums are modified at certain points; for example the list of processing companies must contain a minimum of 20 names in the 2004 and 2007 versions, 15 names in the 2009 version and 13 in the 2012 version.
37. The Annual Reports from the financial year 1963 to 1968 were found in the in the Chamber of Commerce, Industry and Agriculture in Parma. Since the financial year 1969, the Annual Reports were found in the headquarters of the Consortium in Parma.

REFERENCES

Abdel-Kader, M. and Luther, R. (2006) Management accounting practices in the British food and drinks industry. *British Food Journal* 108: 336–357.

Adejuyigbe, S.B., Mogaji, P.B. and Adesida, V.K. (2013) Effective management accounting system in food and drinks industries in Lagos State, Nigeria. *Journal of Emerging Trends in Economics and Management Sciences (JETEMS)* 4(6): 501–511.

Agri 2000 (2000) *Consorzi di valorizzazione dei prodotti agroalimentari tipici: ruolo e funzioni in relazione al rinnovato quadro legislativo*, in Atti del Convegno "Sana Edizione 2000".

Arfini, F. (2000) The value of typical products: The case of "Prosciutto di Parma" and "Parmigiano Reggiano Cheese". In: Sylvander B., Barjolle D. and Arfini, F. (eds.), *The socio-economics of origin labelled products in agro-food supply chains: Spatial, institutional and co-ordination aspect*,Versailles: INRA, pp. 10–45.

Barjolle, D. and Sylvander, B. (2000) *Some factors of success for origin labelled products in agro-food supply chains in Europe: Market, internal resources and institution*, in Atti del 67° Convegno EAAE, INRA.

Bogdanoiu, C. (2012) Critical analysis of management accounting and cost calculation system from the food industry of manufacturing dairy products and ways of improving it. *Journal of Academic Research in Economics* 4(2, July): 180–193.

Cavazzoni, G. (1998) *La Buitoni-Perugina*, in Atti del IV Convegno Nazionale di Storia della Ragioneria: *Storia di imprese tra il XVI ed il XIX secolo*. Perugia, 2–3 ottobre 1997, Roma: Rirea, pp. 121–128.

Dentoni, D., Menozzi, D. and Capelli, M.G. (2000) Heterogeneity of members' characteristics and cooperation within producer groups regulating geographical indications: The case of the "Prosciutto di Parma" consortium. 116th EAAE seminar:

Spatial dynamics in agri-food systems: Implications for sustainability and consumer welfare. Parma (Italy) October 27th–30th, 2010.

Donati, M., Mancini, M.C. and Menozzi, D. (2012) Il distretto del Prosciutto di Parma tra tipicità e sostenibilità. *Economia & Diritto Agroalimentare* XVII: 133–159.

Ernst & Young LLP (1995) *Activity-based costing: Usage and trends in the food industry.* Ernst & Young Document, USA.

Giacomini, C., Arfini, F. and Menozzi, D. (2010) Processi di qualificazione e *spillovers*: il caso del Prosciutto di Parma DOP, QA—Rivista dell'Associazione Rossi-Doria, n. 3, pp. 55–80.

Giacomini, C., Arfini, F. and Menozzi, D. (2013) Qualification and spillover effects for geographical indications: The case of *Prosciutto di Parma* PDO. *Revista de la Facultad de Agronomia*, La Plata 112(3): 11–22.

Groot, T. (1997) Activity based costing in the food industry. *Research Memorandum no. 46*, Vrije Universiteit, Amsterdam.

Henchion, M. and McIntyre, B. (2005) Market access and competitiveness issues for food SMEs in Europe's lagging rural regions (LRRs). *British Food Journal* 107(6): 404–422.

Hernàndez-Esteve, E. (1995) Notice on the meat supply in Burgos, 1536–1537: Ledger of the Town Meat Purveyor. In: Tsuji, A. and Garner, P. (eds.), *Studies in accounting history: Tradition and innovation for the twenty-first century*. Westport, CT: Greenwood Publishing Group, pp. 207–234.

Mancini, M.C. (2012) La Denominazione di Origine Protetta: uno strumento di tutela del consumatore? Il caso del Prosciutto di Parma. *Progress in Nutrion* 14(3): 161–176.

Mann, R. and Adebanjo, O. (1997) *Business excellence in the food and drinks industry: Practical ways to improve performance*. London: FT Retail & Consumer Publishing.

Mann, R., Adebanjo, O. and Kehoe, D. (1999a) An assessment of management system and business performance in the UK food and drinks industry. *British Food Journal* 101(1): 5–21.

Mann, R., Adebanjo, O. and Kehoe, D. (1999b) Best practices in the UK food and drinks industry. *British Food Journal* 101(3): 184–199.

Mari, L.M., Cavazzoni, C., Bellucci, A. and Cardoni, A. (2008) *La storia della Perugina (1907–1985). La vicenda imprenditoriale attraverso l'analisi dei bilanci societari*, Paper presented at the IX Convegno Nazionale Società Italiana di Storia della Ragioneria: *Dalla rilevazione contabile all'economia aziendale*, Perugia, 27–28 settembre 2007 (.pdf version on CD-ROM).

O' Reilly, S., Haines, M. and Arfini, F. (2002) Small and medium sized food enterprise networks in supply chains: The case of Parma Ham. In: Trienekens, J.H. and Omta, S.W.F. (eds.), *Paradoxes in food chains and networks: Proceedings of the fifth international conference on chain and network management in agribusiness and the food industry*, Noordwijk, Netherlands, 6–8 June 2002, Wageningen Academic Pub, pp. 768–779.

O' Reilly, S., Haines, M. and Arfini, F. (2003) Food SME networks: Process and governance—the case of Parma Ham. *Journal of Chain and Network Science* 3(1): 21–32.

Parma Ham Consortium, *Management Report*, years 1963–2014.

Riley, M. (2005) Food and beverage management—A review of change. *International Journal of Contemporary Hospitality* 17(1): 88–93.

Sargiacomo, M. (2008) Institutional pressures and isomorphic change in a high-fashion company: The case of Brioni Roman style, 1945–89. *Accounting, Business & Financial History* 18(2): 215–241.

Wright, C. and Lund, J. (2003) Supply chain rationalization: Retailer dominance and labour flexibility in the Australian food and grocery industry. *Work, Employment and Society* 17(1): 137–157.

8 The *Her*story of the Società Anonima Per Azioni Perugina

The Role of Luisa Spagnoli in the Development of the Italian Chocolate Industry in the First 30 Years of the Twentieth Century

Andrea Bellucci, Libero Mario Mari, Francesca Picciaia and Simone Terzani

INTRODUCTION

This chapter introduces Luisa Spagnoli (1877–1935), a famous Italian businesswoman, co-owner of Perugina, the Italian chocolate company, and creator of *Baci* (kisses) chocolates, among other world-famous products. She is also known as the founder of the Luisa Spagnoli clothing company, another successful family business, which still operates in Perugia, with a global distribution chain.

This study focuses on the role played by Luisa Spagnoli in the development of the Perugina company, with particular attention to the period 1924–1935, one of the most interesting time frames in Perugina's history, from its transformation into a public company until the year of Spagnoli's death.

While studies exist on women and accounting (Lehman, 1992; Loft, 1992; Kirkham and Loft, 1993; Annisette, 2007) and business history (Kwolek-Folland, 1994; Gamber, 1997; Peiss, 1998; Beachy et al., 2006), there is a lack of literature on the role of women in the history of food companies. For this reason it was decided to focus this chapter on the achievements of an exemplary Italian businesswoman, Luisa Spagnoli. The period under investigation (1924–1935) is of particular interest if one considers that she died in 1935, the same year, as Peiss (1998) observes, that Fortune magazine published a series of articles on "Women in Business," which focused on the dearth of female entrepreneurs. This account reveals an extraordinary female figure working for the success of a major Italian food company, in the context of the male-dominated business world of the time.

There is also a gap in the literature with regard to the historical analysis of food companies, especially in the chocolate sector (Szogyi, 1997). Italy was one of the first European countries to see the distribution of this imported product: at the end of the sixteenth century, Catherine (a daughter of Philip II of Spain) introduced chocolate in Piedmont, which became one of the most important chocolate districts in the world (Chiapparino, 1997; Ciuffoletti, 2003). Another important city in the history of Italian chocolate is Modica (in Sicily), which under the Spanish protectorate saw the introduction of the first raw cocoa processing, which remains a popular local product. Nonetheless it took until the beginning of the twentieth century for Umbria to witness the first industrial project in the chocolate sector, with the birth of Perugina. Perugia, the regional capital, is now famous for Eurochocolate, a 10-day international chocolate festival that has been held every October since 1994 (Chirieleison et al., 2013).

Through biographical and narrative research, an archival method (Bal, 1999; Holstein and Gubrium, 2000; Fillis, 2006), and the adoption of a synchronic approach (Amaduzzi, 1997; Servalli, 2007), this chapter aims to examine the extent to which the presence of Luisa Spagnoli influenced the strategic choices, policies, and activities of the company. The primary sources consist of documents conserved in the company archive at the Perugia headquarters of the company, which is currently owned by the Nestlè Corporation.

First, this chapter seeks to contribute to research on business and gender by widening the understanding of the position of women at the beginning of the twentieth century, and their role in business (Peiss, 1998; Cooper, 2010). It explores Luisa Spagnoli's life in order to mirror and rationalize her role as a woman and entrepreneur in the Italy of that time. Second, the article shines a light on the almost unexplored relationship between accounting, business, and the chocolate industry.

The remainder of the chapter is structured as follows. After providing an overview of the existing literature on women and business, the methodological approach and study material is presented. A brief outline of Spagnoli's life and the history of the Perugina company is then presented, while the following sections aim to describe Luisa Spagnoli as a businesswoman, a creative talent and philanthropist, in order to verify how and why she became an iconic figure at a famous food company, despite the adverse social context and dominant culture.

PREVIOUS LITERATURE

Gender and race are not traditional accounting and business history research topics (Cameron, 1985; Loft, 1992). It was only in the early 1990s that gender and race dimensions become accepted as relevant issues among academics (Butler, 1990; Loft, 1992; Butler, 1993; Kirkham and Loft, 1993; Annisette, 2003, 2006, 2007). At that time Lehman (1992) identified the analysis of the roles and functions played over time by professional women with the term "herstory."

If issues related to women in management positions were rarely investigated, this is due, in large part, to the position of women, in particular at the beginning of the last century, which effectively prevented them from being independent of male figures. Accounting and business has long appeared to be a male practice in Western culture, constructed around a male conception of the economy (Shearer and Arrington, 1993; Cooper, 2001; Virtanen, 2009). The presumption at the time was that upper level positions are more complex, and therefore only suitable for men (Welsh, 1992; Spruill and Wootton, 1995). Of course this approach reduced women's role in business, and consequently the related literature. As Peiss observed,

> until recently, business history left undisturbed such assertions about the nature of business and the nature of women. Historical analyses of the corporation, mass-production industry, technological innovation, and business strategy typically examined the actions of men without rendering masculinity a problematic category.
>
> (Peiss, 1998, p. 219)

It can also be said that the general development of studies on female entrepreneurs increased significantly with the development of small business studies. Indeed, if women were generally excluded by large corporations—which were the main subject of business history studies for a long time—they were often involved in small and family businesses, or self-employed (Gamber, 1998). The widening academic attention paid towards this company model has revealed a large number of women that were involved in business affairs as shareholders and managers. In any case, in the last 20 years publications that focus on women and accounting, finance, and business history have started to appear.

In terms of accounting history, the new approach has opened unexplored research fields, and some academics have taken up gender issues in recent years (Napier, 2006). Most papers on the relationship between women and accounting history focus primarily on the development of the accounting profession (Kirkham and Loft, 1993; Wootton and Spruill, 1994; Spruill and Wootton, 1995; Hammond, 2003; Ikin et al., 2012) and on the role of the accounting profession in enhancing women's position in the job market, and the conquest of economic independence and political power (Komori, 2007). Other scholars have focused on the effect of institutional contexts in developing a role for women in accounting (Emery et al., 2002) or on the use of accounting in women's private lives (Walker, 1998; Virtanen, 2009).

The role of women in business has also been studied in other fields, not strictly related to accounting. In financial terms, some authors studied the financial acumen of women and their behaviour with regard to investments (Rutterford and Maltby, 2007) and stock transactions (Carlos et al., 2006). Johns (2006) and Newton and Cottrell (2006) focused on the role of women as bank shareholders, Wiskin (2006) investigated how women managed financial aspects of their enterprises in the eighteenth century in the United

Kingdom, and Sparks (2004) studied informal borrowing networks among businesswomen in northern California between 1870 and 1920.

Recent publications also exist on the role of women in business in general (Hisrich and Brush, 1984, 1985; Carter and Allen, 1996; Kwolek-Folland, 1998; Beachy et al., 2006) and in different business activities. If women were mainly found to be involved in service industries (Kwolek-Folland, 1998; Honeyman, 2007; Muoz and Prez, 2007), the literature also provides examples of women working in different sectors, such as agriculture (Effland et al., 1993), clothing manufacturing (Gamber, 1997), and the beauty industry (Plitt, 2000). Other researchers focused on the role of women as shareholders (Freeman et al., 2006; Laurence, 2006) or on the behaviour of businesswomen during specific historical periods, in particular during wartime (Mundy, 1998).

A NEW APPROACH TO ENTREPRENEURSHIP

In order to gain a deeper understanding of the entrepreneurial characteristics of Luisa Spagnoli, it might be useful to go beyond the classic perspective that places entrepreneurship in a symbolic male universe (Ahl, 2006). Entrepreneurial action generally only sustains and places value on a form of masculinity, and sees entrepreneurship as a set of norms and values based on hegemonic masculinity, which raises a cultural barrier against femaleness and alternative forms of gender. This concept of entrepreneurship, while it may appear neutral, comprises a gender subtext that renders maleness invisible, and sustains the uncritical reproduction of hegemonic masculinity, which involves a process of "othering" women entrepreneurs.

As well as being an economic phenomenon, entrepreneurship also has a cultural sphere (Bruni et al., 2004). Entrepreneurial action could therefore be seen as an archetype of social action, and it can be related to gender for a cross-reading of how gender and entrepreneurship are culturally produced and reproduced in social practices. These discourses can be applied to business as to gender, but common sense attributes gender to the corporeality of a person, and therefore to their "being," rather than their "doing." Entrepreneurial figures are traditionally associated with masculine roles such as conquerors, lonely heroes and patriarchs (Mulholland, 1996; Reed, 1996). In particular, two dimensions of patriarchy are presented: the private and public (Hearn, 1992), in which the latter is an extension of the former, and each reinforces the other, exerting a control over sexuality and female work. Although masculinity does not constitute a homogeneous class, men have a "class interest" to maintain power over women. The entrepreneurial literature has never concerned itself with the exploration of the power relations inherent in economic structures, in its place establishing an automatic relation between the qualities of an entrepreneur (leadership, risk-taking, rational planning) and a model of male rationality (Mulholland, 1996).

The patriarchy is not just a system of domination; it is also a cultural framework, which celebrates femaleness (Goffman, 1977) yet ratifies its subordinate role. This patriarchal structure is developed in the family, which is important as a reality, structure, and metaphor (Gagliardi and Turner, 1993). It manifests itself as a reality in the law, in habitative patterns, and in socialization processes; as a structure it is reproduced mimetically in the ramifications of industrial development; and as a metaphor it extends the expectations and obligations of the domestic sphere to the productive one, to the point that those who are not part of the family group are treated with suspicion. So, at a cultural level, the family is a metaphor for enterprise, while the enterprise is also a metaphor for the social relations of the family. The relation between how gender is "done" in the family and how it is done in entrepreneurial activity is a complex one, because the family acts as an intermediary for it (Bruni et al., 2005). From this perspective, sex differences have large and important effects with regard to power relations between men and women, which can also be reflected in work relationships.

The entrepreneurial literature has never concerned itself with an exploration of the power relations comprised in economic structures, instead establishing an automatic relation between the qualities of an entrepreneur and a model of male rationality (Mulholland, 1996).

This approach can be useful in describing the role of business women at the beginning of the previous century, when there were many barriers to the affirmation of women in the workplace, and it was very difficult to balance a career with family commitments; indeed, some studies have shown that in Europe the amount of time spent caring for children has a negative correlation with professional success (Stoner, Hartman, and Arora, 1990; Williams, 2004).

LUISA SPAGNOLI: WOMAN AND ENTREPRENEUR

Luisa Sargentini Spagnoli was a respected woman and entrepreneur, characterized by her great humanity and personal values, and the ability to influence the destiny of a company of the level of Perugina, at a time when the role of women in business was marginalized or associated with low-level functions. Luisa was also a modern woman; some scholars described her as a mix of

> very different characters that make her capable of being deeply nonconformist, without forcing the form of a company, Perugina in the early twentieth century. She became one of the most important female entrepreneurs that Italy has produced in an underdeveloped region.
>
> (Mecucci, 2003, p. 176, our translation)

Luisa Spagnoli was born in Perugia, in modest circumstances, on 30 October 1877. As soon as she came of age she was married to Annibale Spagnoli, from Assisi, and together they opened a small workshop in Perugia for the production of dragées (Corvisieri, 2001). It was their experience and success in this initiative and, most importantly, their capacity as entrepreneurs, that led them to establish, with three other business partners, the historic Perugina company. Francesco Buitoni wanted to create a structured company for the production of chocolates and confectionary, and decided to involve the Spagnolis in the project. While Buitoni did not want initial financial capital from them, he did require their knowledge and workshop.

In these early years the role of Luisa Spagnoli, her decision-making skills, and her influence in the running of the small shop began to emerge. These were difficult times for women with an interest in business in Italy: in this period the Civil Code of 1865 was in force, which imposed the institution of "marital authorization." This obligation effectively precluded any married woman from running commercial and entrepreneurial activities without the permission of her husband, as "a way to emphasize the image of the female entrepreneur as a social anomaly, an exception to the rule of the immaturity and inability of women to be full citizens" (Curli, 2005, p. 27, our translation). In other words, Italian society of the time saw economic activities carried out by women as a real threat, which could undermine the stability of the family and, more generally, of society itself.

The situation at Perugina was very different, however: Luisa, while she had no official role in the organizational structure of the company, undertook a number of initiatives aimed, first, at expanding the production of confectionary and chocolates, and second, at making the workplace a familiar environment where employees could be monitored and protected.

It was during the period of the First World War that the entrepreneurship of Luisa Spagnoli truly became evident. When the men at the company were enlisted, Luisa, together with her sons Aldo and Mario, took control of Perugina and, thanks to her decision making (including some painful choices, such as the suspension of confectionary production), she managed to expand the company in terms of turnover and employee numbers (Corvisieri, 2001).

Between 1922 and 1923, two significant events took place: the first related to the creation of "Baci" (kisses) chocolates—in order to make use of waste materials left over during other production processes (Boneschi, 2001)—although at the beginning Luisa called them "Cazzotti" (punches) because of their particular shape. "Baci" remain among the most famous chocolates in the world.

The second event concerns her separation from her husband Annibale, who would leave Perugina and return to Assisi. Luisa became a board member, and her role was officially recognized when she was appointed as director of the luxury packaging division (Corvisieri, 2001). This latter opportunity was also favoured by the repeal, in 1919, of "marital authorization," the recognition of the legal capacity of women, and the resulting possibility for them to find employment.

In this period, Luisa became close with Giovanni Buitoni, 14 years her junior. They soon became romantically involved, even if, in the name of discretion and confidentiality, no official information or documents exist regarding their relationship.

Luisa's initiative was not limited to the Perugina company: in the second decade of the twentieth century she founded Luisa Spagnoli, which remains a global Italian fashion company. She was unable to follow the development of her new company, however, as she died of cancer on 21 September 1935. She had moved to Paris in order to receive the best treatment, accompanied as always by Giovanni Buitoni.

PERUGINA: FROM ITS FOUNDATION TO THE END OF THE 1930S

Perugina was established by four men and a woman who lived in Perugia at the beginning of the twentieth century. On 30 November 1907 Leone Ascoli, Annibale Spagnoli, and the entrepreneur Francesco Buitoni established the "Società perugina per la fabbricazione dei confetti" (Confectionary Production Company of Perugia) (Ceserani and Covino, 1997).

It should be noted that the name Luisa Spagnoli does not appear, for obvious reasons, related to the marginalization and subordination of women's role in business, even if the active role she played in the foundation of Perugina was recognized. Indeed, the new company absorbed a previous business initiative that had been launched by Annibale and Luisa in 1901. They decided to join the new Perugina together, pooling their assets in order to overcome a financial crisis that had affected their business.

The initial capital of Perugina was just 100,000 Italian Lire, mostly raised through money transfers (60,000 Italian Lire at its foundation and 30,000 Italian Lire before 1911), while the balance was covered by the value of Annibale and Luisa Spagnoli's workshop.

The first 15 years of company history, in the lead-up to becoming a limited company in 1923, are characterized by a lack of official accounting documents, apart from a register, starting from 1911, which briefly outlines all assets and liabilities. The available historic references, therefore, are mostly limited to the various Buitoni family publications.

These early years were certainly not straightforward. Perugina seemed set to suffer the same destiny as a number of other regional business ventures, namely to have a very short life, ending in bankruptcy, mainly due to large debts (Ceserani and Covino, 1997, p. 13).

Business began in January 1908, in a building in the centre of the city. Francesco Buitoni was the manager and the administrative director, while Annibale Spagnoli assumed the role of technical director, due to his previous experience, assisted by his wife Luisa. Production grew, almost exclusively thanks to the initiative of Luisa, who also introduced the production of confectionary and chocolates.

Perugina grew fast, but in a completely inadequate business context: a patent lack of capital that led to uncontrolled dependence on bank loans; an absence of any planning, or any internal control structure; a lack of adequate accounting procedures; headquarters and a production plant that were inappropriate for new processes and new products; highly expensive and unprofitable business strategies; and expansion into the wealthy but more competitive market in northern Italy (Masia, 2007, p. 100).

This difficult situation was well understood by the owners, who attempted to resolve the problems without success. In this context, characterized by losses and an excessive dependency on bank loans, Francesco Buitoni sought the help and intervention of his 18-year-old son Giovanni (Buitoni, 1972, p. 30).

Giovanni had no experience in management and administration, but after a series of meetings with the other owners, he recognized the aspects that he believed had led to the difficult situation. First, he identified the absolute lack of any accounting system that would make it possible to know not only the financial and economic situation of the company, but also the cost and the price of each product. He also argued that expansion into other markets would be a real risk, without adequate financial resources. Finally, he considered it a strategic error to focus on the northern Italy sales territory, due to the presence of far more experienced competitors.

In this sense, he changed the company's business strategy, switching the focus to the local market, and expanding activities in the south of Italy, through the use of a strong advertising campaign, involving the introduction of trading cards in the packaging of their products. In addition, he chose new and more adequate funding, taking out medium-term loans. The results were immediate: by 1911, Perugina was already making a profit, which was not distributed to the owners.

However, the old stable still remained totally inadequate for the development of business activities, so in 1913 the company acquired an area of over 4,000 square meters near Fontivegge, site of the central train station, where the new factory was built in 1915.

The First World War, however, changed these strategic plans. Some production, such as confectionary and dragées, was suspended, because of difficulties in the sourcing of the necessary raw materials, while other new products were introduced, among them a range based on cocoa powder. This latter decision was "also motivated by public procurement aimed at supplying food to troops, in which Perugina participated, albeit intermittently and in a limited fashion" (Ceserani and Covino, 1997, p.98). This period, also thanks to the wise leadership of Luisa Spagnoli, represented a phase of expansion and development. The number of employees reached 150, and turnover also increased significantly. In short, the war was not all a bad period in the development of Perugina. In the years after World War I the aim, in addition to structural and productive renewal, was to focus on new commercial activities, with the opening of a chain of retail outlets in a number of Italian cities, for the sale of own-brand products (Chiapparino and

Covino, 2008, p. 29). Between 1919 and 1925, 13 stores were inaugurated, "six located in central Italy and three in the south (two in Naples), which indicates how the company would continue to concentrate attention in these areas" (Chiapparino and Covino, 2008, p. 243, our translation).

Marketing was another important element in the company's competitive advantage. Each new product was accompanied by a specific attractive advertising campaign: "the poster campaign to promote Tripolitalia candies, the marketing of the Luisa chocolate bar in 1919, the nutritional quality of which was emphasized; the invention of Baci in 1922" (Chiapparino and Covino, 2008, p. 27, our translation). In particular, the success of "Baci," which still symbolizes Perugina, was due not only to product quality, but also the creativity of one of the great designers of the time, Federico Seneca.

The return of Giovanni Buitoni coincided with a period of crisis, which affected the entire Italian confectionery industry. At the time there was a growth in the consumption of chocolate, driven by both the low cost of raw materials and an increase in the lowest salaries. This situation saw the leading Italian confectionery companies make significant new investments, involving high levels of debt, which led to the crisis years of 1921–1925, and the collapse of many national companies, such as Moriondo & Gariglio, Talmone, and Monatti, which were all absorbed and incorporated into the Unica company owned by Riccardo Gualino in 1924. Perugina managed to stay afloat due to a less ambitious investment policy, and was thus able to withstand this critical moment and avoid the risk of incorporation into Unica. In 1920 Perugina changed its name to La Perugina—Cioccolato e confetture (Perugina—Chocolate and Confectionary); despite financial difficulties, which were complicated by external events, such as the collapse of the Banca di Sconto and the bankruptcy of Ascoli, a partner in Perugina, the company continued its growth and, at the beginning of 1922, employed about 400 workers, 300 of them women (Chiapparino and Covino, 2008, p. 245).

In that year, Giovanni Buitoni decided to radically change the strategy of the company, leading to its transformation into a limited company and the attempt to liquidate the interest of those partners that he believed had not participated in any way, even financially, over the years, as they were only interested in receiving adequate dividends (Buitoni, 1972, p. 41).

Thus, after a period characterized by meetings, protests and accusations, there followed the exit of three historical owners of Perugina. In his report of 20 November 1922 Giovanni proclaimed the merits of the Buitoni family in the management of the company, proposing a capital increase that would, on the one hand, improve the company's financial resources, and on the other, allow the Buitoni family to attain, in legal terms, the majority of capital; otherwise, the Buitoni family would abandon the company. This company crisis ended in August 1923 with the "liquidation of the interest of the old partners, and the transformation into a limited company, in which the controlling share of 73.1% was acquired by the Buitoni family of Perugia, a share of 8.3% went to the Buitoni family of Sansepolcro, and 18.6%

was acquired by the Spagnoli family" (Chiapparino and Covino, 2008, p. 34, our translation).

The board of the revamped company consisted of Francesco Buitoni, who remained in the role of president; Giovanni Buitoni, the chief executive officer; Bruno Buitoni, who was appointed general manager; Mario Spagnoli (Luisa's son), who had the role of technical director; and Federico Seneca, who was responsible for the highly successful advertising campaigns. Despite the absence of Annibale as a member of the company, Luisa Spagnoli became part of the board, having decided to continue her activities with her son. At the same time Luisa began to introduce a range of important social initiatives that presented Perugina as a modern enterprise that paid particular attention to its employees.

These developments led to an extraordinary period of growth; the company invested heavily to strengthen trade policy and automate industrial plants. Promotional activities increased Perugina's reputation; Mario Spagnoli was awarded prizes for his scientific organization of work as a technical director; and consumers appreciated the quality of the Perugina product range.

The beginning of the 1930s saw a significant decline in confectionary and chocolate consumption, as a result of the decreased spending power of the majority of Italians, and the categorization of chocolate as a luxury good. The company survived, despite lower prices, export difficulties, and production and exchange problems due to the fascist policy of autarky. During this period the company increased its sales network by opening additional stores, confirming its position in the Italian confectionery market.

The success of Perugina in these years was also due to its successful advertising campaigns: the popularity of the company grew enormously, with an immediate effect on the company's profitability.

In this period Perugina also structured various business activities in order to penetrate foreign markets with new internationalization strategies. The Societé Francaise des Produits Buitoni was founded in 1934, marking an important first step towards the relocation of food production.

With the death of Luisa in 1935, an important period in the history of Perugina came to an end. During this period the company consolidated a strategy of high product quality and brand recognition, with diversified sales and an international presence, and reached satisfactory standards of sales organization and production. The main advantages of these changes were reflected in terms of growth, profitability, and cash flows over the subsequent decades.

KEYS TO THE SUCCESS OF LUISA SPAGNOLI'S GENDER ENTREPRENEURSHIP FROM ARCHIVAL SOURCES

While archival sources offer limited information, in terms of annual report documentation and, in particular, company decision-making processes, they do offer evidence of the key steps in the development of Luisa Spagnoli's success.

Spagnoli's first initiatives in attempting to create a close link between private life and the company environment were the steps taken to improve the welfare of employees. A wide range of measures to help employees can be seen in a company report published the year after her death (ASBP, General Manager-CEO Fund, b. 24, chart 12): from public assistance in the factory during the working day, to a company mutual health fund, an integrated pensions system, a company kindergarten and nursing mothers' rooms, company restaurant, education, company sports activities, and company savings schemes. These documents detail the health and social care provided by the company for the year, and the extent of the systematic approach to meeting employees' needs is evidence of the importance of Luisa Spagnoli's welfare policies. In addition to these initiatives, other acts of generosity to individual employees and their families have been recorded. Thus a rhetoric of her personality spread among employees, company executives and directors. It is interesting to read Giuseppe Alberti's letter of condolence on Luisa Spagnoli's death (ASBP, General Manager-CEO Fund, b. 24, chart 193–194), in which he described her care and attention towards employees and their families, and proposed that Giovanni Buitoni name the company kindergarten after Luisa Spagnoli in recognition of her commitment to its creation and development.

One of the most important documents that attests to Luisa Spagnoli's benevolence and diligence was the letter sent to employees by the CEO Giovanni Buitoni in her memory (ASBP, General Manager-CEO Fund, b. 24, chart 196), in which he evoked and emphasized the managerial, entrepreneurial and human qualities of Luisa, and spoke about "Her exceptional intelligence . . . her unusual intuition" (our translation) with regard to packaging and innovation and the "precious contribution" (our translation) of her experience on the board of directors and in the general management of the company.

Luisa Spagnoli's role grew most during the First World War, especially in the years 1917–1918, when

> the great war came and the young Buitoni family members Bruno, Luigi, Marco and Giuseppe left in grey-green. Mrs. Luisa Spagnoli remained alone with her young sons, Mario and Aldo, to run the company. It was at this time that she revealed the skills which made her the most visionary entrepreneur Perugia had seen.
>
> (Ranieri di Sorbello, 1969, p. 513, our translation)

The years after the First World War were crucial in the development of Perugina and Luisa Spagnoli's consistency. Giovanni Buitoni's decision to remove the other shareholders Ascoli and Andreani and transform Perugina into a limited company provided the means and the opportunity to give the company the desired structure.

Company documentation presents the definition of the share value for the settlement of outgoing shareholders and the change of management from Luisa Spagnoli's husband Annibale to Luisa herself, who definitively became part of the board of directors of Perugina (ASBP, General Manager-CEO Fund, b. 1, chart 1). She worked to ensure a relevant position and a share in the company for her sons.

What emerged in the minutes of shareholders' meetings was the epilogue of a long history of disputes and conflicts between Luisa Spagnoli and her husband. In that sense it is highly significant to read of Luisa's strategy to present a legal warning to the other shareholders, in order to liquidate Annibale's share interest, claiming a sum of money for his work in the company (ASBP, General Manager-CEO Fund, b. 1, chart 5). The legal warning submitted to the other shareholders by the bailiff was based on the fact that

> Luisa Spagnoli dedicated all her activities and efforts to her entrepreneurial activity in the confectionary industry with her husband, and the results achieved were mostly due to her . . . both spouses, even if under the name of the husband, contributed to the constitution of Perugina, to whose shareholders, thanks to Luisa's efforts, her husband Annibale is now creditor of a large sum of money for the liquidation of his share and much of it is due to her.
>
> (our translation)

The precise description of her professional duties, her increasingly important role in the company, and her showdown with her husband on his departure from Perugina, were the final affirmation of Luisa Spagnoli and her role within the company.

In this sense, it is clear that, through her behaviour, and with the support of Giovanni Buitoni, Luisa Spagnoli broke the conditioning of the patriarchy, establishing herself, her affective relationships, and her sons within the company.

After 1923 the composition of the shareholders in Perugina remained unchanged, until the company was sold in the 1980s, and the bond, and indeed dualism, between the Buitoni and Spagnoli families that characterized the history of the company continued through the years. It can be said that, thanks to Luisa Spagnoli, the elements of unity and synergy continued to prevail up to her death.

Part of the mythology surrounding the figure of Luisa Spagnoli is the belief that she was not able to write: the long search for a trace of her writing has only produced a signed transfer of shares between herself and her sons in 1926, which has been analyzed in the company archive (ASBP, General Manager-CEO Fund, b. 1, chart 5).

THE ENTREPRENEURSHIP OF LUISA SPAGNOLI

The previous sections not only outline the picture of "Signora Luisa" as a strong, resolute, and unconventional woman at the beginning of the twentieth century, but also highlight her fundamental role in the development of Perugina during the most important period of its growth, when it became one of the leading Italian chocolate production companies. Perugina's expansion coincided with the evolution of the habits of the Italian middle class, which, after the First World War, began to purchase chocolates for self-consumption (not only as a gift) (Curli, 2005, p. 202), and also due to the autarky of the fascist regime, which promoted Italian products over imported ones. This context led to a new concept of entrepreneurship, involving the contribution of Luisa Spagnoli, founded on product innovation and new promotion and distribution techniques. As a matter of fact, she was the main protagonist, along with Giovanni Buitoni, in the success of Perugina in the second decade of the twentieth century.

In particular, it is possible to identify the contribution made by Luisa Spagnoli in two aspects:

- Her operational creativity, which led to the introduction of several new products (many of which are still on the market today) and new forms of market penetration (such as Perugina shops);
- Her commitment to the improvement of working conditions, through which she offered workplace kindergartens, summer camps, and other activities open to all employees (who were mostly women) of the enterprise (a form of company welfare system).

Both aspects could be analyzed in the light of wider studies on women's entrepreneurship, and might introduce new elements for the analysis of female figures and their role in Italian enterprises.

Luisa, "the maker of confectionaries and chocolates" (Buitoni, 1972, p. 3, our translation) was continuously on the lookout for new recipes and new mixtures of ingredients for chocolate products, such as the famous "Baci," and "Luisa," a dark chocolate bar, which are both still popular today. Her creativity, however, was not limited to the production process, but also regarded product distribution. It appears that, along with Giovanni Buitoni, she was the creator of the "negozi Perugina," a chain of retail outlets directly managed by the company, similar to those operated by British retail chains at the end of the eighteenth century (Chiapparino, 1997, p. 29). These shops were created and designed (also in aesthetic terms) in order to be immediately recognizable, and they were located, as previously noted, in the centre of the most important Italian cities, thus also promoting the corporate image of Perugina through a direct relationship with customers (Curli, 2005, p. 202).

Mrs. Spagnoli, defined by "her great and creative imagination" (Buitoni, 1992, p. 52, our translation), did not own these property assets, but she made full use of them, and was free to make decisions and move freely around the company, managing and combining company resources to the best of her ability, thus becoming the motor of the company.

As initially argued by Brush (1992), and then developed by Brush et al. (2009), an integrated and holistic approach to women's entrepreneurship can be useful, in order to analyze these figures with multilevel tools. In particular, moving beyond from the well-known "3M" (market, money and management) framework, Brush et al. focused on the necessity to introduce external factors to enhance the quality of the discussion about the role of females in business. These elements are tied to the cultural, social, and historical background in which women's businesses develop. In this sense, the authors expanded the 3M framework to also include motherhood and macro/meso environment, in order to evaluate more completely the impact of women's entrepreneurship and to highlight the possible barriers to the normal and linear growth of female business. Motherhood is, specifically, "a metaphor representing the household/family context, thus drawing attention to the fact that family/household contexts might have a larger impact on women than men" (p. 9), while the macro/meso environment "captures considerations beyond the market, including factor such as expectations of society and cultural norms, for example reflected in media representations of female entrepreneurs" (Brush et al., 2009, p. 9). Indeed, these two elements appear to crucially affect women's personal perceptions, which "may restrict their possibility to recognize (the whole range of) business opportunities" (de Bruin et al., 2007, p. 330), and, despite the presence of "technical and operational factors" (market, money, and management), they could introduce gender asymmetries in the development of female businesses.

Starting from these considerations, and what was underlined in the previous section about a new approach to entrepreneurship, the entrepreneurial role of Luisa Spagnoli assumes some interesting nuances. She lived in a social and cultural context in which, as highlighted, women were excluded from a public and active life outside the household, and, even when employed, they were mostly marginal figures. Spagnoli's macro/meso environment, therefore, appears to have been completely against the development of her entrepreneurial role within Perugina, and, some years later, the foundation of the Luisa Spagnoli angora wool factory. It is noteworthy, however, that this social conditioning was overcome through Luisa's self-perception, and her household situation, where she played the dominant role, both with her husband (to whom she did not feel any affective bond, preferring the young Buitoni) and with her sons (who actively supported their mother in her business decisions). In particular, we can see that she used the complementary social resources of her relationships to her advantage (Greve and Salaf, 2003, p. 2), confirming the approach through which women's entrepreneurship is more integrated in female lives than the male equivalent (Brush, 1992, p. 6).

Another interesting aspect of Spagnoli's entrepreneurship was her commitment to the improvement of working conditions. In 1922, Perugina employed almost 400 workers, 300 of whom were women, thus it was a female-centred factory with an unusual internal welfare and business philanthropy structure.

Many initiatives were developed and organized in this period, largely due to the efforts of Luisa Spagnoli, in order to give workers better conditions: she introduced a company kindergarten and nursing mothers' rooms to allow mothers to return to work as soon as possible; summer camps from which 30–40 female workers with poor health would come back "stronger and more peaceful" and "more industrious" (Curli, 2005, p. 205, our translation); and a number of leisure initiatives (such as trips and after work activities), representing a sort of "revised" corporate paternalism (also due to the subjects involved).

Corporate (industrial) paternalism as a concept developed in the nineteenth century to describe all activities undertaken by entrepreneurs in favour of their workers (especially women and children) within the factory, as defined by the Italian politician Buttè as the "voluntary initiatives and donations on behalf of entrepreneurs without however legal or contractual obligations" (House of Deputies, Senate of the Republic, 1959, p. 228, our translation). In other words, while it is mostly considered negatively (for a brief overview, see Benenati, 1993), paternalism consists of a series of activities in order to "attract, maintain, and train the workforce [. . .]. Also the presence of care and recreational services, the construction of a pleasant working environment, or initiatives regarding the personalisation of working relationships can have the same function" (Benenati, 1993, p. 52, our translation).

The "Perugina welfare system" had unusual characteristics, due to the presence of women in the roles of both entrepreneur and worker, indicating an innovative relationship that was apparently closer and more sensitive to the needs of the recipients.

Moreover, such activities represented a new approach with which to manage human resources, to control the workforce and improve productivity, to justify lower salaries in comparison with the national average, and more generally, to strengthen the relationship between the workers and the interests, values and aims of the company. In this sense, this case supports the argument of those who consider paternalism—and all activities related to it—to be "not just a set of institutions that employers offer to workers to supplement wages" (Reid, 1985, p. 580), but a managerial strategy.

In this manner, this aspect can be considered as another component of the entrepreneurial role of Luisa Spagnoli, a type of key strategy for the management of human resources, an element that can be included in the wider managerial approach of this incredible and unusual woman.

CONCLUDING REMARKS

The chapter discusses the role of Luisa Spagnoli (1877–1935), a famous Italian businesswoman, in the development of the Perugina company, with particular attention to the period between 1924 and 1935. This was one of the most interesting time frames in Perugina's history, from its transformation into a public company until 1935, the year of Luisa Spagnoli's death. Using an archival approach this chapter has aimed to examine the role of this woman in the development of Perugina in the first 30 years of the twentieth century, her entrepreneurial characteristics, and how and why these characteristics developed, despite the adverse social context and dominant culture. Her role was—and still remains—an anomaly in the traditional (and not only in Italy) business world. She was not only a leading figure in the management structure of the company, and the creator of a range of famous products, and an innovative welfare system within the organization, but also the archetype of a new woman, with the courage of her convictions, which led her to leave her husband and enjoy an open relationship with another man.

The analysis of the primary sources presents an outline of the figure of an entrepreneur who broke the cultural and social barriers against female management, also thanks to her family situation, and the complementary social resources of her relationships. The closer link between a woman's life and work also allowed, in the case of Luisa Spagnoli, for the introduction of an innovative form of company welfare system, in order to enhance the working conditions of her employees. These initiatives represented not only a different manner in which to manage human resources, and control the workforce in order to improve productivity, but also, primarily, a new strategic and managerial approach to company organization.

In this sense, Luisa Spagnoli can be considered not only an interesting historical figure, and an appropriate case study for a gender approach to business, but also a model for a new approach to entrepreneurship.

Future strands of research into the life and activities of Luisa Spagnoli might consider a variety of subject areas. For example, there is still much to learn about the ways in which she improved working conditions in her factory, at the same time improving both company welfare and production management. In a related fashion, comparative studies with other chocolate producers led by male entrepreneurs would enhance an understanding of their similarities and differences. Moreover, as stated at the introduction, Luisa Spagnoli also launched a namesake company, which still operates in the fashion industry, a relatively ignored field of research (Sargiacomo, 2008), which deserves attention from the accounting community in the near future.

This chapter also represents one of the first attempts to analyze the history of a chocolate company from an entrepreneurial and managerial perspective: in this sense, future research could compare the development of Perugina with other Italian chocolate factories, and similar international companies, in order to highlight their similarities and differences.

REFERENCES

Primary Sources

Archivio Storico Buitoni Perugina (ASBP)

ASBP, General Manager-CEO Fund, b. 1, chart 5.
ASBP, General Manager-CEO Fund, b. 24, chart 12.

ASBP, General Manager-CEO Fund, b. 24, chart 193–194.
ASBP, General Manager-CEO Fund, b. 24, chart 196.
SBP, General Manager-CEO Fund, b. 1, chart 1.

Secondary Sources

Ahl, H. (2006) Why research on women entrepreneurs needs new direction. *Entrepreneurship Theory and Practice* 30(5): 595–621.

Amaduzzi, A. (1997) *La storia della ragioneria nell'insegnamento universitario*, in Atti del III Convegno Nazionale di Storia della Ragioneria. Pisa: Pacini, 215–218.

Annisette, M. (2003) The colour of accountancy: Examining the salience of race in a professionalisation project. *Accounting, Organization and Society* 28(7): 639–674.

Annisette, M. (2006) People and periods untouched by accounting history: An ancient Yoruba practice. *Accounting History* 11(4): 399–416.

Annisette, M. (2007) Editorial: International perspectives on race and gender in accounting's past: An introduction. *Accounting History* 12(3): 245–251.

Bal, M. (1999) *Narratology: Introduction to the theory of narrative*. Ontario: University of Toronto.

Beachy, R., Craig, B. and Owens, A. (2006) *Women, business and finance in nineteenth-century Europe: Rethinking separate spheres*. London and New York: Berg Publishers.

Benenati, E. (1999) Cento anni di paternalismo aziendale. In: Musso, S. (ed.), *Tra fabbrica e società. Mondi operai nell'Italia del Novecento*, Vol. 33. Milan: Feltrinelli, 43–81.

Boneschi, M. (2001) *Di testa loro. Dieci italiane che hanno fatto il Novecento*. Milan: Mondatori Editore.

Bruni, A., Gherardi, S. and Poggio, B. (2005) *Gender and entrepreneurship. An ethnographic approach*. New York: Routledge.

Brush, C.G. (1992) Research on women business owners: Past trends, a new perspective and future directions. *Entrepreneurship Theory and Practice* 16(4): 5–30.

Brush, C.G., De Bruin, A. and Welter, F. (2009) A gender aware framework for women's entrepreneurship. *International Journal of Gender and Entrepreneurship* 1(1): 8–24.

Buitoni, G. (1972) *Storia di un imprenditore*. Milan: Longanesi.

Butler, J. (1990) *Gender trouble: Feminism and the subversion of identity*. Routledge: London.

Butler, J. (1993) *Bodies that matter*. Routledge: New York.

Camera dei Deputati, Senato della Repubblica. (1959) Relazione della Commissione Parlamentare di inchiesta sulle condizioni dei lavoratori in Italia, Vol. XIV, Roma.

Cameron, D. (1985) *Feminism and linguistic theory*. Hong Kong: Macmillan Press.

Carlos, A.M., Maguire, K. and Neal, L. (2006) Financial acumen, women speculators, and the royal African company during the South Sea Bubble. *Accounting, Business and Financial History* 16(2): 219–243.

Carter, N.M. and Allen, K.R. (1997) Size-determinants of women-owned business: Choice or barriers to resource. *Entrepreneurship and Regional Development* 9(3): 211–220.

Ceserani, G. and Covino, R. (1997) *Perugina. Una storia d'azienda, ingegno e passione*. Cinisello Balsamo: Silvana Editore.

Chiapparino, F. (1997) *L'industria del cioccolato in Italia, Germania e Svizzera: consumi, mercati e imprese tra '800 e prima guerra mondiale*. Bologna: Il Mulino.

Chiapparino, F. and Covino, R. (2008) *La fabbrica di Perugia*, ICSIM.

Chirieleison, C., Montrone, A. and Scrucca, L. (2013) Measuring the impact of a profit-oriented event on tourism: The Eurochocolate Festival in Perugia, Italy. *Tourism Economics* 19(6): 1411–1428.

Ciuffoletti, Z. (ed.) (2003) *Dolceamaro. Storia e storie di cioccolato*. Florence: Alinari.

Cooper, C. (2001) From women's liberation to feminism: Reflections in accounting academia. *Accounting Forum* 25(3): 214–245.

Cooper, K. (2010) Accounting by women: Fear, favour and the path to professional recognition for Australian women accountants. *Accounting History* 15(3): 309–336.

Corvisieri, V. (2001) *Una famiglia di imprenditori del novecento. Gli Spagnoli da Assisi a Perugia (1900–1970)*. Perugia: Grafica Di Salvi e C.

Curli, B. (2005) *Donne imprenditrici nella storia dell'Umbria. Ipotesi e percorsi di ricerca*. Milan: Franco Angeli.

De Bruin, A., Brush, C.G. and Welter, F. (2007) Advancing a framework for coherent research on women's entrepreneurship. *Entrepreneurship Theory and Practice* 31(3): 323–339.

Effland, A.B.W., Rogers, D.M. and Grim, V. (1993) Women as agricultural landowners: What do we know about them? *Agricultural History* 67(2): 235–261.

Emery, M., Hooks, J. and Steward, R. (2002) Born at the wrong time? An oral history of women professional accountants in New Zealand. *Accounting History* 7(2): 7–34.

Fillis, I. (2006) A biographical approach to researching entrepreneurship in the smaller firm. *Management Decision* 44(2): 198–212.

Foucault, M. (1972) The discourse on language. In: *The archeology of knowledge & the discourse of language*. New York: Pantheon Books, 215–237.

Freeman, M., Pearson, R. and Taylor, J. (2006) "A doe in the city": Women shareholders in eighteenth-and early nineteenth-century Britain. *Accounting, Business & Financial History* 16(2): 265–291.

Gagliardi, P. and Turner, B. (1993) Aspects of Italian management. In: Hickson, D. (ed.), *Management in Western Europe*. Berlin: de Gruyter, 149.

Gamber, W. (1997) *The female economy: The millinery and dressmaking trades, 1860–1930*. Urbana: University of Illinois Press.

Gamber, W. (1998) A gendered enterprise: Placing nineteenth-century businesswomen in history. *The Business History Review* 72(2): 188–217.

Goffman, E. (1977) The arrangement between the sexes. *Theory and Society* 4: 301–331.

Good, B. (1994) *Medicine, rationality and experience: An anthropological perspective*. Cambridge: Cambridge University Press.

Greve, A. and Salaf, J.W. (2003) Social networks and entrepreneurship. *Entrepreneurship Theory and Practice* 28(1): 1–22.

Hammond, T. (2003) History from accounting's margin: International research on race and gender. *Accounting History* 8(1): 9–24.

Hearn, J. (1992) *Men in the public eye*. London: Routledge.

Hisrich, R.D. and Brush, C. (1984) The woman entrepreneur: Management skills and business problems. *Journal of Small Business Management* 22(1): 30–37.

Hisrich, R.D. and Brush, C. (1985) Women and minority entrepreneurs: A comparative analysis. In: Hornaday, J.A., Shils, E.B., Timmons, J.A. and Vesper, K.H. (eds.), *Frontiers of entrepreneurial research*. Boston: Babson College,. 566–586.

Holstein, J.A. and Gubrium, J.F. (2000) *The self we live by: Narrative identity in a postmodern world*. New York: Oxford University Press.

Honeyman, K. (2007) Doing business with gender: Service industries and British business history. *Business History Review* 81(3): 471–493.

Ikin, C., Johns, L. and Hayes, C. (2012) Field, capital and habitus: An oral history of women in accounting in Australia during World War II. *Accounting History* 17(2): 175–192.

Johns, L. (2006) The first female shareholders of the bank of New South Wales: Examination of shareholdings in Australia's first bank, 1817–1824. *Accounting, Business and Financial History* 16(2): 293–314.

Kirkham, L.M. and Loft, A. (1993) Gender and the construction of the professional accountant. *Accounting, Organizations and Society* 18(6): 507–558.

Komori, N. (2007) The "hidden" history of accounting in Japan: A historical examination of the relationship between Japanese women and accounting. *Accounting History* 12(3): 329–358.

Kwolek-Folland, A. (1994) *Engendering business: Men and women in the corporate office, 1870–1930.* Baltimore: Johns Hopkins University Press.

Kwolek-Folland, A. (1998) *Incorporating women: A history of women and business in the United States.* New York: Twayne Publishers.

Laurence, A. (2006) Women investors, 'that nasty south sea affair' and the rage to speculate in early eighteenth-century England. *Accounting, Business & Financial History* 16(2): 245–264.

Lehman, C.R. (1992) 'Herstory' in accounting: The first eighty years. *Accounting, Organizations and Society* 17(3/4): 261–285.

Loft, A. (1992) Accountancy and the gendered division of labour: A review essay. *Accounting, Organizations and Society* 17(3/4): 367–378.

Masia, L. (2007) *Buitoni. La famiglia, gli uomini, le imprese.* Perugia: Silvana Editoriale e Volumnia.

Mecucci, G. (2003) *Luisa Spagnoli.* In: Roccella, E. and Scaraffia, L. (eds.), Italiane, Volume II, Rome: Presidenza del Consiglio dei Ministri, 41–52.

Mulholland, K. (1996) Entrepreneurialism, masculinities and the self-made man. In: Collinson, D. and Hearn, J. (eds.), *Men as managers, managers as men.* London: Sage, 123–132.

Mundy, R. (1998) Norfolk businesswomen during the Civil War Era. *International Social Science Review* 73(3/4): 75–90.

Muoz, L.G. and Prez, P.F. (2007) Female entrepreneurship in Spain during the nineteenth and twentieth centuries. *Business History Review* 81(3): 495–515.

Napier, C.J. (2006) Accounts of change: 30 years of historical account research. *Accounting, Organizations and Society* 31(4/5): 445–507.

Newton, L. and Cottrell, P.L. (2006) Female investors in the first English Joint-Stock Banks. *Accounting, Business and Financial History* 16(2): 315–340.

Peiss, K. (1998) "Vital industry" and women's ventures: Conceptualizing gender in Twentieth Century business history. *The Business History Review* 72(2): 218–241.

Plitt, J.R. (2000) *Martha Matilda Harper and the American dream: How one woman changed the face of modern business.* Syracuse, NY: Syracuse University Press.

Ranieri di Sorbello, U. (1969) *Perugia della Bell'Epoca.* Perugia: Volumnia Editrice.

Reed, R. (1996) Entrepreneurialism and paternalism in Australian management: A gender critique of the "self-made" man. In: Collinson, D. and Hearn, J. (eds.), *Men as managers, managers as men.* London: Sage, 99–122.

Reid, D. (1985) Industrial paternalism: Discourse and practice in Nineteenth-century French mining and metallurgy. *Comparative studies in society and history* 3: 579–607.

Rosen, M. (1984) Myth and reproduction: The contextualization of management theory, method, and practice. *Journal of Management Studies* 21: 303–322.

Rutterford, J. and Maltby, J. (2007) The nesting instinct: Women and investment risk in a historical context. *Accounting History* 12(3): 305–327.

Sargiacomo, M. (2008) Institutional pressures and isomorphic change in a high-fashion company: The case of Brioni Roman Style, 1945–89. *Accounting, Business & Financial History* 18(2): 215–241.

Servalli, S. (2007) Il metodo e l'analisi sistemica nelle ricerche di Storia della Ragioneria. *Contabilità e cultura aziendale* 7(2): 59–78.
Shearer, T.L. and Arrington, C. E. (1993) Accounting in other wor(l)ds: A feminism without reserve. *Accounting, Organizations and Society* 18(2/3): 253–272.
Sparks, E. (2004) Terms of endearment: Informal borrowing networks among Northern California businesswomen, 1870–1920. *Business and Economics History On Line* 2: 1–12.
Spruill, W.G. and Wootton, C. W. (1995) The struggle of women in accounting: The case of Jenny Palen, pioneer accountant, historian and poet. *Critical Perspectives on Accounting* 6(4): 371–389.
Stoner, C.R., Hartman, R.I. and Arora, R. (1990) Work-home role conflict in female owners of small business: An exploratory study. *Journal of Small Business Management* 28(1): 30–38.
Szogyi, A. (ed.) (1997) *Chocolate: Food of the gods*. Westport: Hofstra University.
Virtanen, A. (2009) Accounting, gender and history: The life of Minna Canth. *Accounting History* 14(1/2): 79–100.
Walker, S.P. (1998) How to secure your husband's esteem: Accounting and private patriarchy in the British middle class household during the Nineteenth Century. *Accounting, Organizations and Society* 23(5/6): 485–514.
Welsh, M.J. (1992) The construction of gender: Some insights from feminist psychology. *Accounting, Auditing & Accountability Journal* 5(3): 120–132.
Williams, D.R. (2004) Effects of child-care activities on the duration of self-employment in Europe. *Entrepreneurship. Theory and Practice* 28(5): 467–485.
Wiskin, C. (2006) Businesswomen and financial management: Three Eighteenth-Century case studies. *Accounting, Business and Financial History* 16(2): 143–161.
Wootton, C.W. and Spruill, W.G. (1994) The role of women in major public accounting firms in the United States during World War II. *Business and Economic History* 23(1): 241–252.

9 Food, Health and Isomorphism in the Accounting System of the Storehouse of the Society of Pinerolo Workers (1864–1906)

Tiziana Di Cimbrini

INTRODUCTION

Today, it is all too obvious that the quality and quantity of nutrition are key components to the health of body and mind; therefore, food producers and traders must consider the logical food-health association in their policies. However, the effect of such a combination on the accounting systems of these types of organizations remains unexplored.

This study explores the power of the logical food-health combination to affect the accounting system of an organization, focusing on two competitive isomorphic pressures. Isomorphic pressure is one of the most debated issues within the framework of institutional theory.

Considering the recent study by Souritaris et al. (2012), who introduced new concepts of isomorphism that apply to subunits in dual uncoordinated environments, this study investigates the accounting system adopted in the late nineteenth century by a subunit in dual environments: the storehouse of the society of workers of the town of Pinerolo, an example of a consumer cooperative formed within a mutual aid society and inspired by the logical food-health association. Through their storehouses, mutual aid societies sought to give their associates the opportunity to buy groceries at the lowest prices in the market as a form of assistance, which was in addition to their institutional purpose of providing subsidies for sickness and health care services. Consequently, because these storehouses had to manage two environments—their parent organization pursuing a welfare purpose and the consumer cooperatives industry—they were exposed to two different sources of isomorphic pressures.

This study assumes that the accounting system adopted by the Pinerolo storehouse in the late nineteenth century conformed to the model adopted by its parent organization—the mutual aid society of the workers of Pinerolo (MASWP)—in the same period, instead of that of the Italian consumer cooperatives industry of the time. This hypothesis is compatible with the results of Souritaris et al. (2012) on organizational structure, namely that in the presence of institutional pressures from two different environments, the subunit tends to focus its isomorphism on the environment with which it seeks legitimacy and on the professionalization of their top management teams. In the case investigated, the two determinants of isomorphism favored the MASWP. In fact, first, the storehouses established within mutual aid societies were legally obliged to sell only to the society's associates. Second, the top management of Pinerolo's storehouse was selected from among the members of the MASWP's executive board. Consequently, the parent organization was also the only source for both legitimacy and accounting professionalization of its subunit.

To verify the hypothesis, this study compares the storehouse's accounting system with that of the MASWP and with the model generally in use at Italian consumer cooperatives in the late nineteenth century. Regarding the MASWP and its storehouse, this study is based on primary sources, such as statutes, regulations, minutes, accounting records, and reports, kept in the Pinerolo Mutual Aid Society Historical Archive. In contrast, the reconstruction of the accounting system generally adopted by the Italian consumer cooperatives of the time is based on a secondary source.

This study contributes to the literature in several aspects. First, this study allows to observe whether the combination of the subunit's marketing of food and the parent organization's general purpose of health protection was able to affect the storehouse's accounting system and significantly condition the impact of competitive isomorphic pressures.

Second, this study allows to verify whether the results from Souritaris et al. (2012) can be confirmed in a scenario different from that in which they conducted their investigation. In this study, the two environments are not uncoordinated but share a common core of norms and values concerning the principle of self-help of the working class to ensure that they, despite being different, do not represent separate "worlds." Moreover, this study focuses on accounting systems instead of organizational structure and considers nonprofit organizations instead of corporate venture capital programs.

Third, this study describes the entire architecture of the accounting systems in use in three different settings to provide an overview of some integration modes between the management accounting system (MAS) and the financial accounting system (FAS). Recent literature on accounting history expressed a clear need for further research that addresses the integration of MAS and FAS, particularly in the form of integration of financial and cost accounting (Levant and Nikitin, 2012). To meet this need, a description of each accounting system will distinguish between the internal architecture of the MAS, the accounting statements constituting the FAS, and the conversion mechanism of the partial pictures of the former into the big picture of the latter.

Finally, this study responds to the general need for further studies on the issues of charitable and social institutions and emancipation of the poor, as noted by the literature on accounting history (Walker, 2004, 2008; Hollister and Schultz, 2010; Sargiacomo and Gomes, 2011; Ó hÓgartaigh et al., 2012).

The remainder of this chapter is organized as follows. The next section is devoted to deepening the concept of isomorphism and its latest developments, related to institutional theory, as used in this study. Then the chapter describes the accounting systems of Italian consumer cooperatives, the MASWP, and Pinerolo's storehouse, respectively. The three systems are then compared, and finally some concluding comments are presented.

THEORETICAL OVERVIEW

To orient readers, this section briefly overviews the concepts and literatures used to inform the study.

This study applies the concept of institutional isomorphism to a historical case study concerning the Italian scenario in the late nineteenth century. Although several accounting history studies have adopted the institutional theory framework (Carmona et al., 1998; Carmona and Macias, 2001; Baker and Rennie, 2013; Moreno and Càmara, 2014; Caria and Lima Rodrigues, 2014), only Sargiacomo (2008) has applied the concept of isomorphic pressure to an Italian case study and explored the different sources of institutional pressures, highlighting the major isomorphic changes that shaped managerial behavior at a high-fashion company.

DiMaggio and Powell defined isomorphism as a "constraining process that forces one unit in a population to resemble other units that face the same set of environmental conditions" (1983, p. 149). They proposed three "mechanisms" of isomorphism. Coercive isomorphism occurs when organizations are motivated to avoid sanctions from parties on which they depend (Greenwood et al., 2008, p. 7). Mimetic isomorphism occurs under uncertainty, when organizations model themselves after other organizations in their field that are perceived to be legitimate or successful. Finally, normative isomorphism refers to conformity pressures arising from professionalization. The literature suggested that isomorphism provides legitimacy (Deephouse, 1996; Deephouse and Suchman, 2008), which is a general perception that the actions of an entity are desirable (Suchman, 1995).

A criticism of the concept of isomorphism is that it precludes institutional theory from explaining variations in practice (Greenwood et al., 2008; Thornton and Ocasio, 2008). Several recent management studies have tackled the inability of isomorphism as a concept to explain heterogeneity in institutional environments by examining competing logics that simultaneously exist in one institutional environment (Lounsbury, 2001, 2007; Thornton, 2002; Durand et al., 2007; Marquis and Lounsbury, 2007; Reay and Hinings, 2009; Pache and Santos, 2010). These scholars have argued that competing logics cause contestation in an environment and variations in the adoption of a practice until a new dominant logic emerges. Souitaris et al. (2012) addressed the topic of competing logics coming from different institutional environments. They argued that it is a common phenomenon for organizational subunits to be simultaneously part of two worlds—alternative institutional environments with different norms. Organizational subunits are problematic because they frequently must resolve competing institutional forces from their parent and their industry or market of entry. Because the two environments are uncoordinated and will not converge naturally to a single logic, such subunits often face permanent contestation that does not move toward resolution. They contributed to institutional theory to explain how organizations address this problem by showing that the cases they analyzed did not converge to a noncoherent mix of practices acceptable to both worlds (as also suggested by D'Aunno et al., 1991) and by identifying new forms of isomorphism, endoisomorphism (alignment with an internal environment), and exoisomorphism (alignment with an external environment). They also developed the concept of "focus of isomorphism," which enables institutional theory to incorporate multiple environments by theorizing that subunits choose to align with one of their two environments. In particular, their study on corporate venture capital programs showed that these subunits became isomorphic with one of their two environments. They finally found that the focus of isomorphism (endo vs. exo) depends on two factors: prioritization of the constituencies with which the new subunits seek legitimacy and professionalization of the team members of a subunit's top management. Specifically, endoisomorphism is more likely to be observed when a new subunit prioritizes legitimacy with the parent in a quest to sustain its support and resources (demonstrating the coercive mechanism of isomorphism). Endoisomorphism is also more likely to be evident when top management team members are professionalized as corporate managers and follow familiar corporate norms (where a normative mechanism of isomorphism is the driver). In contrast, exoisomorphism is more likely to be observed when the new subunit prioritizes legitimacy with its new market and/or industry (where a mimetic mechanism of isomorphism is the determinant). Exoisomorphism is more likely to occur when top management team members are professionalized in the new industry and follow familiar industry norms (demonstrating the normative mechanism of isomorphism).

In addition to shifting the focus of the analysis to nonprofit organizations, this study differs from that of Souitaris et al. (2012) for two reasons. First, this study focuses on the accounting system structure instead of the organizational structure, as a suitable conceptualization of systems of practices. An analogy between the two studies is possible because of the identification of accounting as a social and institutional practice realized by the literature on new accounting history (Burchell et al., 1980; Napier, 1989, 2006; Miller et al., 1991; Miller and Napier, 1993; Hopwood and Miller, 1994; Carnegie and Napier, 1996; Potter, 2005). The view of the new accounting history allows as deep as possible an identification of the effects of accounting on organizational and social functioning to appreciate how accounting practices come to be embedded in organizational action to shape and construct the perceptions of problems, priorities, and solutions, defining possibilities and scope for action, forging patterns of human and organizational interdependencies, and rendering calculable and visible activities.

Second, the two institutional environments involved in this study are not uncoordinated because the worlds of Italian consumer cooperatives and mutual aid societies of the late nineteenth-century shared basic norms. Consistent with the principles of Rochdale Equitable Pioneers, the recurring theme in Italian consumer cooperatives of the late nineteenth century was the union of the poor to have access to goods of quality, mostly food, at lower prices than in the market. The market supply did not meet the demand for healthy foods because retailers selling basic necessities agreed to keep prices high and adulterated food to increase profits. Therefore, groups of ordinary citizens, mostly workers, created a storehouse at their own expense to market healthy products without any speculative purpose. Then, the phenomenon spread to other economic sectors.

Additionally, the Italian mutual aid societies developed in the late nineteenth century were based on the union of poor people—mostly workers—with the purpose of operating a fund, formed from the contributions of its members, that was intended to pay subsidies and/or pay for medical care in the event of disease affecting the latter (Di Cimbrini, 2015). They were also engaged in prevention activities aimed at educating members to live healthier lives and, in particular, at combating the scourge of alcoholism, which was widespread among the working class at the time.

Although the two types of organizations engaged in different activities, they shared the principle of self-help of the poorer classes with the aim of improving their living conditions.

THE ACCOUNTING SYSTEM IN THE INDUSTRY

This reconstruction of the accounting system in use in Italian consumer cooperatives of the late nineteenth century is based on the contents of a secondary source representing, during that time, a landmark for their bookkeeping activity: the handbook "Ragioneria delle Cooperative di Consumo" published in 1896 by Giovanni Rota. This volume reports accounting instructions for this type of organization and represents evidence of their accounting systems.

In fact, to develop his instructions, Rota—the chief accountant of a major Italian consumer cooperative—adopted an inductive method based on the widespread practice in use. Moreover, his volume presents many case studies on the accounting practice of several Italian consumer cooperatives operating in the late nineteenth century to demonstrate that his accounting instructions conformed to the state of the art in the industry.

Rota describes the accounting system of consumer cooperatives as follows (1896, p. 32):

> Every service, every office, every part of the administrative body, is subject to accounting recognition and the accounting includes a number

> of sections corresponding to that of the services that are done. While for each of these sections there is a special, analytical, elementary accounting collecting and classifying little events and numbers, a part of the accounting is devoted to summarize these separate elements, order them and represent their effects on the assets, by comparing and connecting them in a body of complex and general accounting records.

The traits of the accounting system are subsequently described.

Internal Architecture of the MAS

Consumer cooperatives' MAS were structured in analytical accounts classified on a functional basis. According to Rota, they typically adopted the following model:

1. Accounting of share capital concerning the recognition of shares subscribed to and paid for by the members;
2. Accounting of goods concerning the recognition of the cost and quantity of goods purchased;
3. Accounting of warehouses and sales concerning the recognition of revenues and quantities of goods leaving the warehouses;
4. Accounting of suppliers concerning the recognition of purchase contracts;
5. Accounting of general and personnel expenses concerning the recognition of expenses other than those for the purchase of goods.

These separate accounts are completely independent from each other. The account books shown by Rota contain examples of each of them and no trace exists of connections among them concerning the transfer of money or goods from one function to another.

Accounting Statements Constituting the FAS

Rota (1896, p. 315) noted that consumer cooperatives' accounting statements tend to be similar to those of commercial companies with minor modifications. The statements consist of a statement of assets and liabilities and a demonstration of the losses and profits, in which the latter separately reports assets, liabilities, social capital, and profits and losses of the period. The balance of the demonstration of profits and losses does not coincide with a cash surplus or deficit but has economic substance because it also includes costs that did not generate outputs of money. Moreover, Rota reported that in some cases, these two statements were not sufficient to provide members with all of the information they desired on the progress of the cooperative; therefore, other statements were added.

These additional documents were usually one or more of the following types:

1. Statistical annex reporting monthly sales;
2. Statistical annex reporting sales for each product category;
3. Annex reporting information on members and their shares;
4. Annex reporting the composition of inventories valued at cost price;
5. Annex reporting the amount of the last financial year's expenses compared with those of previous years;
6. Annex reporting the cooperative's progressive development since its establishment through comparisons of sales, or other results, of different years;
7. Annex reporting the distribution of profits;
8. Annex reporting expenses other than purchase goods.

Conversion Mechanism

Rota (1896) noted that, in addition to the analytical accountings, general or complex accounting was devoted to summarizing, arranging, comparing, and connecting these to show their effects on assets and liabilities. In fact, each department produces individual results but is connected to the functioning of the entire organization so that the individual results must contribute in a clear and manifest manner toward the purpose of each accounting system: knowledge of the economic outcome of the entire management. Therefore, the analytical accountings converge into a single body of accounting records representing the cooperative's assets and liabilities as a whole and in their transformations.

Consequently, the conversion mechanism appears to be an additional system of accounting records devoted to the integration of the single analytical accountings. Rota (1896) argued that the conversion mechanism is generally present in all consumer cooperatives even if the bookkeeping method may differ. In particular, he found different types of double entry bookkeeping: the simple double entry and that based on the *giornal-mastro*; the simple, the ordinary, or the complete *logismografia*; and the *statmografia*.

The accounting records converge in a trial balance whose results are used to prepare the statements constituting the FAS. Once the trial balance was drafted, managers only had to group and transfer its results into the two financial statements on the basis of their needs.

As a first step, the conversion mechanism implements a systematic integration of the analytical results. As a second step, the mechanism aggregates them in a synthesis of results to be displayed in the financial statements.

The entire architecture of the accounting system is shown in Figure 9.1.

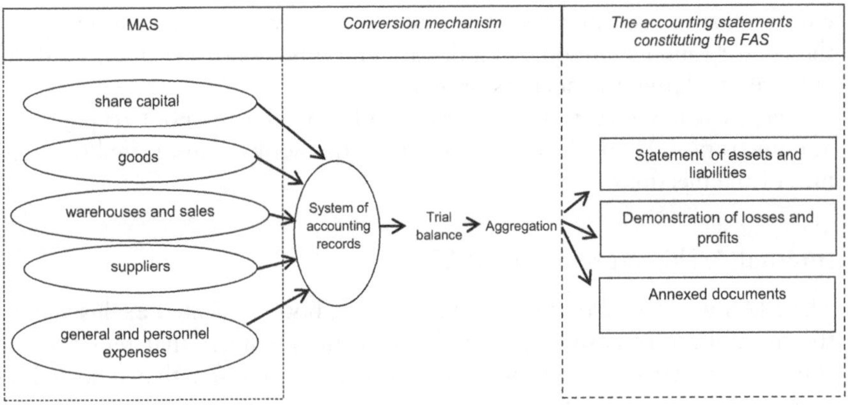

Figure 9.1 The accounting system in use in the Italian consumer cooperatives in the late nineteenth century

ACCOUNTING SYSTEM OF THE PARENT ORGANIZATION

The mutual aid society established in Pinerolo in 1848, whose number of members varied between 200 and 500 over the years, is known for being the first general society gathering of all workers of the territory, independent of their jobs. In legal terms, the association's target for distribution of a subsidy was the welfare-dependent associate—or more precisely, the needy associate—who, for a while, could not perform his job and thus could not support his family and himself. In administration terms, that activity was characterized as a payment of a contribution by each associate and, as a reward, the distribution of a subsidy by the society during times of need.

As was generally the case for all Italian mutual aid societies, the purpose of the Pinerolo society was not limited to financial aid, but included, according to Article 1 of its Statute, the general welfare of the working class (PMASHA, Regolamento della Società degli operai stabilita nella città di Pinerolo, 1848). In view of the general improvements in the living conditions of its members, the MASWP also managed several business functions: a bakery, a storehouse, and *Cassa di Riserva* (reserve cash) to obtain funds to enable subsidies to be given to chronically ill associates in a more punctual manner.

The MASWP had an administrative committee (or directive council) comprised of a president, a vice president, a treasurer secretary, and 14 councilmen from the 14 classes that identified every job done by the associates.

The most important function of MASWP was controlling the state of illness of the ill-declared associates. The control, which was given to a couple of councilmen, changed every week and the councilmen were obliged to make at least two visits to the ill associates. The controlling councilmen were compensated for this task and were paid every 3 months. At first the *society* allowed every associate to have his own doctor, but since 1850 took on a paid doctor to visit all associates. The aid subsidy was provided only after the doctor found symptoms of a disease and if no controller discovered the associate violating the doctor's orders.

The treasurer secretary was responsible for general bookkeeping and administration. He dealt with money, kept the books, and drafted the minutes of the meetings.

Internal Architecture of the MAS

The MAS was based on two account books, both dedicated exclusively to the recognition of cash flows: the book of the members that reported the state of payments for each of them, and the cash register that reported all cash inflows and outflows of the society except for those of the storehouse because it was managed separately. In addition to the account books, the MAS included a system of budgets and periodic reports structured in different sections devoted to the general mutual aid cash, the reserve cash, and the storehouse.

The treasurer secretary had to prepare weekly cash reports that distinguished cash flows related to subsidies' management from other cash movements. In the early years of the society, the weekly cash report was also presented at the weekly general meeting of members, in addition to being presented to the directive council. However, from 1869, the report was intended solely for the directive council (PMASHA, Regolamento della Società degli operai di Pinerolo, 1869). The treasurer secretary also had to submit a monthly cash report to the directive council that indicated cash inflows (loading) classified by nature and cash outflows (unloading) classified by destination. The Statute of 1869 also introduced a half-yearly report, later replaced by a quarterly report, which was to be formally approved by the president. This half-yearly report classified cash inflows from the members on the basis of the class identifying their job, and cash outflows depending on who received the cash (e.g., associate, supplier) and the payment's aspect (subsidies, different expenses, and money paid to the savings and loan company).

Since its establishment, the MASWP prepared annual budgets whose content was much more detailed than the reports. The MASWP distinguished cash inflows and outflows according to a detailed scheme of categories and items defined by the Statute. The level of detail was attributable to the fact that this budget, in addition to being used as a tool to authorize expenditures, was a guarantee of compliance with the principle of fund allocation stated by the MASWP's Statute. According to this principle, which a number of mutual aid societies used, a specific type of expense could only be covered by a specific type of revenue. Therefore, any changes in the criteria defined by the Statute required specific authorization by the directive council. Although a copy of this budget was also annexed to the annual report, the possibility of checking deviations was limited because the structure of the budget was only partly comparable with the cash flow movements in the annual report.

In summary, the architecture of the MAS only concerned cash movements monitored through an integrated system of budgets, cash books, and interim reports.

Accounting Statements Constituting the FAS

In the early years of the MASWP, the accounting statements constituting the FAS also included the weekly cash report. However, when this cash report started to be addressed only to the directive council, members' external information needs were met only by the annual report presented at their general meeting. The annual report was composed of the following documents (PMASHA, Rendiconti dal 1892 al 1900, SOMSP 178).

1. "Cash movements" reported the initial availability of cash, cash inflows, and cash outflows of the year, classified by nature and destination respectively, and the final result. This document was structured in several sections corresponding to different management areas:
    a. the mutual aid general fund, concerning temporary subsidies for diseases;
    b. the chronically ill fund, concerning subsidies for permanent incapacity for work;
    c. the widows' and orphans' fund, concerning subsidies for families of deceased members;
    d. the storehouse, which reported the final outcome of this subunit.
2. "Economic management" expressed costs, revenues, and profits calculated by adding costs and revenues without cash movements (e.g., for deterioration or donation of goods) to the cash flows. This document was structured in sections in the same manner as the "Cash movements" document.
3. A statement of assets and liabilities that classified them according to their belonging to the society or to the storehouse.
4. The budget approved by the directive council at the beginning of the year, divided into assets and liabilities. Its structure was only partially similar to that of the "Cash movements" document. In particular, unlike the latter, subsidies were classified on the basis of recipients' names; the aid to widows and orphans was not included because of its exceptional nature compared with the activities of the society.

Conversion Mechanism

The conversion mechanism adopted by MASWP did not transform the results of the MAS but provided an additional recording process.

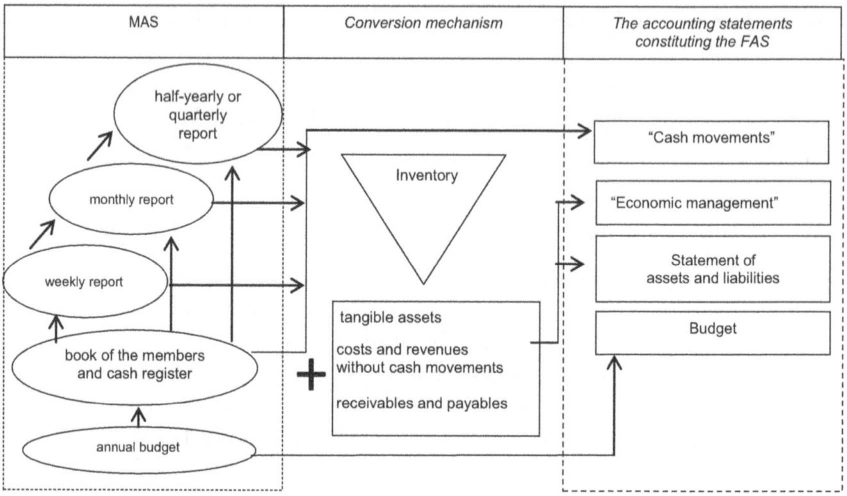

Figure 9.2 The accounting system in use in the mutual aid society of Pinerolo in the late nineteenth century

The presence of a MAS based on integrated cash accounting enabled the immediate transfer of the results of the first into the various statements constituting the FAS. However, the need to also include nonfinancial values in the FAS imposed a further recording process during the preparation of the annual report. For this purpose, as the Statute of 1887 also required, the treasurer secretary prepared an inventory at the end of the year from which all remaining components (e.g., the tangible assets owned by the society) emerged (PMASHA, Associazione generale degli operai di Pinerolo, Statuto organico, Tipografia sociale, Pinerolo, 1887). In other words, the conversion mechanism consisted of a recording process that simply added other results to those of the MAS.

The entire architecture of the accounting system is shown in Figure 9.2.

THE STOREHOUSE OF THE SOCIETY OF PINEROLO WORKERS AND ITS ACCOUNTING SYSTEM

The MASWP established the storehouse in 1864 and ensured that access to it was reserved for only the society's members who had purchased a share of the fund needed for its functioning, and only for their families' daily or weekly needs. In 1906, the storehouse, which had reached 400 members, became completely autonomous from the MASWP and acquired the legal status of an ordinary consumer cooperative. The storehouse continued to operate until the First World War when it was forced to cease trading because of severe economic crisis and the absence of top administrators.

Until 1906, the storehouse was chaired by a committee of 17 members appointed by the society's directive council. The committee elected among its members a president, a vice president, a secretary, a treasurer, and a caterer (PMASHA, Regolamento del comitato di Previdenza della società degli operai di Pinerolo, 1864). The storehouse's management was completely independent from that of the society because the society wanted no responsibility for the debt from the sale of food. The caterer was responsible for bulk purchases and had to deliver the goods to the storekeeper, who dealt with retail sales. Originally, the storehouse sold higher consumption food, such as bread, rice, wine, and flour. Later, additional foods, such as pasta, beans, chickpeas, chestnuts, sugar, semolina, and other foods were added.

The parent organization's focus on health protection inevitably oriented the storehouse's policies toward the logical food-health association, whose priority was publicly declared by the MASWP. The MASWP wrote the following text in a local newspaper:

> above all, the workers could have good stuff, first quality food, and protect their health, whereas before they were forced to gobble the rejection of others; all the small retailers' spoiled, subpar, rotten foodstuffs went to the poorest workers' homes.
>
> ("La Lanterna Pinerolese," n. 9, 3 marzo" ["1883 The Pinerolo's Lantern," n. 9, 3 March 1883])

This priority resulted in policies regarding the assortment and markups applied, which were oriented toward the promotion of healthy eating habits primarily consisting at the time of limited use of alcohol. The MASWP showed strong sensitivity to the scourge of alcoholism in the working classes, and its Statutes stipulated that disease from abuse of wine and spirits was ineligible for aid (Art. 35 of the Statute in 1869) or only provided the right to a lower amount of subsidies than the ordinary ones (Art. 67 of the Statute in 1887). The storehouse's policies were oriented to the purpose of deterring the abuse of alcohol and stipulated that the caterer had to focus on purchases of basic necessities rather than alcohol and that the storekeeper had to apply the highest markups on wines and liquors. The caterer's selection criterion was guided by the statutes and regulations that attributed to the storehouse the mission of first selling necessary goods, and by the committee, which periodically met to deliberate over the appropriate assortment in terms of quantity and quality of goods. In its meetings, the committee also deliberated about the markups that, on the one hand, in their total had to cover the storehouse's administrative expenses and the acquisition cost of groceries, and on the other hand, had to be internally differentiated as follows: "no less than one cent per kilogram for bread, two cents for other foodstuffs, three cents for alcoholic beverages" (Art. 145 of the Statute in 1887).

Internal Architecture of the MAS

The storehouse's MAS was structured according to its functions, each of which was assigned to a different subject.

The bulk purchases function was entrusted to the caterer, who negotiated with suppliers, kept notes in the register of contracts concluded, and gave payment orders to the cashier. Then, he delivered the goods to the storekeeper who dealt with retail sales. The caterer also kept a product index that reported the typology and cumulated quantities of each foodstuff purchased (PMASHA, Indice dei generi che si smerciano nel magazzino, SOMSP 486).

The storekeeper recorded the taking care of goods in a book called *parallelo di compra-vendita*. This book was divided into parts, each devoted to a specific food item (PMASHA, Parallelo di compra-vendita 1892–1903). For each food item, the left side, "buying," reported the stocks at the beginning of the year, the quantities purchased during the year, the purchase price per unit, and the total price of the single batch of goods. The right side, "selling," indicated the revenue expected from the sale of the entire batch calculated on the basis of the established markup and, by difference, the net income expected from the entire batch. These records were made at the moment when the food came into stock, indicating that this book, in addition to reporting the purchase prices, presented the budget for the sales of each batch and at year end, by addition, the budget for sales relative to all batches of a single food item that entered the storehouse that year. At year-end, for each food item, the records on the left side showed the total amount purchased against the purchase price and, on the right side, against the expected sale price and the net income derived from the sale of the entire quantity purchased. On both the "buying" and "selling" sides, the amounts unsold were then subtracted at the end of the year to highlight only the amounts actually sold. All parts of the equation "purchased quantity—unsold quantity = sold quantity" were then valued using actual purchase prices on the "buying" side and actual selling prices on the "selling" side to highlight the portions of the net income that were actually realized and unrealized, allowing for an analysis of deviations. The value of unsold stocks was based on the latest purchase price per unit on the "buying" side and the latest unit sales price on the "selling" side, resulting in a FIFO (first in, first out) method.

Finally, cash management was entrusted to the storehouse's treasurer, who made payments for goods ordered by the caterer and for other expenses ordered by the committee. The treasurer received daily payments of the sale proceeds made by the storekeeper and payments from members for the purchase of the storehouse's shares, and deposited the cash surplus in the bank. These cash flows were recorded on the cash register, which detailed the expenses for purchasing goods on the basis of vendor name and the payment order number (PMASHA, Registri di cassa, SOMSP 508). Sales were synthetically recorded as monthly total amounts without classification by product category.

A monthly report based on these three analytical accountings was presented to the committee.

Accounting Statements Constituting the FAS

The storehouse's FAS was aimed at making the committee accountable to the parent organization. The accounting statements constituting the FAS were as follows:

1. A statement of "Cash movements," which reported cash inflows and outflows of the year, classified by nature and destination respectively, and the final result;
2. A statement of "Economic management," which expressed the costs, revenues, and profits calculated by adding costs and revenues without cash movements (e.g., for deterioration or donation of goods) to the cash flows and also showed profit allocations;
3. A statement of assets and liabilities whose balance represented the storehouse's capital assets;
4. A detailed picture of buying and selling activity, reporting—for each type of food and the quantity marketed during the year—purchase costs, selling prices, and net earnings, and also the totals for these items and the total net earnings from the marketing of all foodstuffs;
5. A list of administrative expenses other than those for the purchase of food.

Conversion Mechanism

The conversion mechanism did not include any further accounting recording process because the MAS produced all balances needed to compile the documents constituting the FAS. The conversion was carried out by the committee's secretary who, as required by Article 28 of the Regulation, compiled the statements using the partial accounts presented by the storehouse's treasurer, storekeeper, and caterer. These partial accounts already reported all of the balances that he needed. The treasurer's cash register already provided all of the information concerning the "Cash movements," the list of administrative expenses, and the entries for the statement of assets and liabilities related to cash. The *parallelo di compra-vendita* kept by the storekeeper represented the information base of the summary table of the storehouse's management and of the entries for the statement of assets and liabilities concerning food inventories.

Finally, the caterer's accounts provided data on debts to suppliers. No receivables from customers existed because the Regulation required the storehouse to sell only in cash. Therefore, the conversion mechanism consisted of a redistribution process of the balances coming from partial accounts, which were assigned to the different documents constituting the

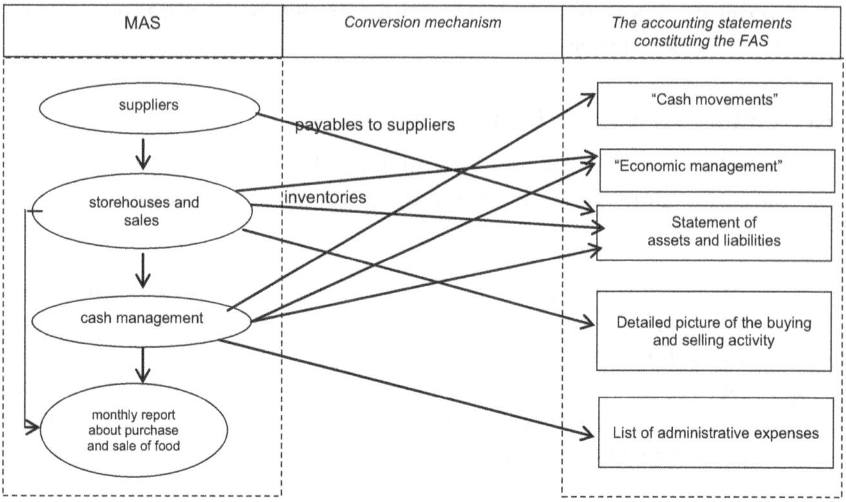

Figure 9.3 The accounting system in use in the storehouse of Pinerolo in the late nineteenth century

FAS. Neither integrative nor additional accounting recording processes were required.

The entire architecture of the accounting system is shown in Figure 9.3.

COMPARISON OF THE THREE ACCOUNTING SYSTEMS: RESULTS

In this section, the comparison among the three accounting systems is organized on the basis of the components investigated: the internal architecture of the MAS, the documents constituting the FAS, and the conversion mechanism.

Following Gordon and Miller (1976) and others (Chenhall and Morris, 1986; Mia and Goyal, 1991; Bouwens and Abernethy, 2000), four dimensions of MAS are examined: scope, integration, aggregation, and timeliness. The scope dimension has three subdimensions: focus (internal or external), quantification (financial or nonfinancial), and time horizon (historically based or future oriented) (Gorry and Scott-Morton, 1971; Gordon and Miller, 1976; Larcker, 1981; Gordon and Narayanan, 1984; Chenhall and Morris, 1986).

The integration dimension consists of information on the activities of other departments within the organization and information on how the decisions made in one department may influence the performance of other departments. This information could relate to the inputs, outputs, operating processes, and technology employed by other departments. For example, integrated information could include reports that provide information on the type and volume of output produced by other departments and information on the costs, revenues, and prices associated with that output.

Both the MAS of the MASWP and of its storehouse indicated significant integration. In fact, the society articulated the overall cash management into subsections—each dedicated to a different type of aid—to grasp the links between the management of the different funds. The storehouse with the *parallelo di compra-vendita* integrated information on the purchasing function (i.e., quantity and purchase prices), the planning function (i.e., expected outcomes), and the sales and inventory management function (sold and unsold quantities and their prices). In contrast, the MAS described by Rota showed minimal integration because each analytical accounting only reported the results of the function to which it was devoted and the integration of partial information only occurred in the following steps of the conversion mechanism.

The aggregated dimension concerns summary information by functional area (i.e., summary reports on activities of other business units or other functions of the organization). Information aggregated at the functional level provides managers with information on the outcomes or results of the decisions made in other departments. For example, aggregation by period enables managers to assess the results of their decisions over time. This dimension, which is therefore linked to the preparation of periodic reports, is present in both the MASWP and its storehouse, whereas it was not in use in consumer cooperatives.

Timeliness is conceptualized in a previous study (Bouwens and Abernethy, 2000) as having two subdimensions: frequency of reporting and speed of reporting. Frequency refers to how often information is provided to managers, whereas speed pertains to the time lag between when a manager requests information and when it is made available.

In the systems investigated, the dimensions concerning the focus and speed of reporting have no discriminant power because all three models adopted an internal focus and were designed to allow an immediate view of all accounting records on demand.

In contrast, even if the prevailing organizational criterion of the documents constituting the MAS was not considered by the literature previously cited, it is added to the comparison given its high discriminant power. In fact, the consumer cooperatives and Pinerolo's storehouse adopted a functional criterion, whereas the MASWP adopted a time criterion that marked the preparation of the reports.

The comparison among the three MAS is shown in Table 9.1.

Regarding the documents constituting the FAS, the comparison is shown in Table 9.2, which verifies the presence or absence of each document considered in its information purposes.

Finally, the storehouse's conversion mechanism converged toward neither of the two institutional environments. In fact, both the consumer cooperatives

Table 9.1 The comparison among the three MAS

	Scope					Timeliness		
	Focus	quantification	time horizon	Integration	Aggregation	frequency of reporting	speed of reporting	Organizational criterion
consumer cooperatives	internal	financial and nonfinancial	historically based	low	not present	annual report	high	functional
mutual aid society of the workers of Pinerolo	internal	financial	historical based and future orientated	high	present	interim report	high	time
storehouse of the workers of Pinerolo	internal	financial and nonfinancial	historical based and future orientated	high	present	interim report	high	functional
prevailing model in the storehouse	**nondiscriminating factor**	**industry**	**parent organization**	**parent organization**	**parent organization**	**parent organization**	**nondiscriminating factor**	**industry**

Table 9.2 The comparison among the documents constituting the FAS

	"Cash movements"	"Economic management" (demonstration of losses and profits)	Statements of assets and liabilities	Budget	detailed picture of the activities afforded to members	List of administrative expences
consumer cooperatives	not present	present	present	not present	optional	optional
mutual aid society of the workers of Pinerolo	present	present	present	present	not present	not present
storehouse of the workers of Pinerolo	present	present	present	not present	present	present
prevailing model in the storehouse	parent organization	nondiscriminating factor	nondiscriminating factor	industry	industry	industry

and the MASWP adopted further processes for accounting recognition, albeit of a different nature, to obtain the documents constituting the FAS, whereas the storehouse implemented a simple direct distribution of balances.

In other words, given the functional organizational criterion, the inclusion of financial and nonfinancial values, and the high level of internal integration, the MAS of the storehouse was self-sufficient in producing accounting values to be allocated into the documents constituting the FAS.

CONCLUSIONS

Similar to Sargiacomo (2008), this chapter adopts the concept of isomorphism to inform a historical case study in the Italian context. Otherwise, this study differs from his study because, instead of exploring isomorphic pressures over the managerial behavior in a company managing a single institutional environment, it investigates the ability of the food-health combination to condition isomorphic pressure over the accounting system of a nonprofit subunit in dual environments.

Unexpectedly, the analysis highlighted that the storehouse's accounting system converged to neither the typical model of its industry nor the one adopted by its parent organization. Instead, the system chose a customized model. Regarding the MAS and the accounting statements constituting the FAS, the accounting system adopted a perfect compromise solution (five dimensions shared with each environment) with the parent organization's prevailing influence in the MAS and the industry's influence in the FAS. Moreover, the conversion mechanism was completely different from that used in both the consumer cooperatives and the MASWP. The subunit's accounting system became isomorphic with neither of the two institutional environments, and a third solution was selected on the basis of hybridization of the reference models.

The reason for this hybridization is primarily found in the influence of the food-health combination on the storehouse's policies and in how they affected its accounting system. Concerning the MAS's dimensions, the storehouse differed from its parent organization in the inclusion of nonfinancial quantifications and in the functional criterion. This first dimension was probably inevitable given the storehouse's nature but was also functional to verify the caterer's compliance with the storehouse's mission. In particular, the presence of a product index expressed the need for keeping under control the fact that storehouse investments were primarily oriented toward healthy foods. In contrast, the functional criterion was certainly the result of a division of management tasks that, in turn, highlighted the fact that the policies concerning assortments and markups were of such importance that they were attributed to different individuals in specific positions. These individuals had to be expressly accountable to the committee for the policies. In addition to control over the caterer through the product index, this criterion allowed the committee to verify that the storekeeper properly applied the markups thanks to the *parallelo di compra-vendita*, which realized feedforward, concurrent, and feedback controls on the markup policies. In fact, the book guided the storekeeper in the sale conditions to be applied and, finally, monitored the markups actually applied by reporting the established markups from the moment of supply. Regarding the documents constituting the FAS, the storehouse differed from its parent organization in terms of replacing the budget with a picture of buying and selling activities and a list of administrative expenses. This substitution occurred among documents intended to prove compliance with the fundamental principles of the respective organizations to stakeholders. Thus, the MASWP's budget that aimed to demonstrate respect for the principle of allocation of funds was replaced by documents useful to justifying the composition of the storehouse's investments and the total amount and internal differentiation of the markups applied. In fact, the picture of the buying and selling activity reported quantity and markup for each category of food, whereas the list of administrative expenses demonstrated the existence of management costs to be covered by the total amount of the markup. The configuration of the storehouse's conversion mechanism appears simply as a consequence of the other accounting choices that induced the MAS to be autonomous in producing results for the documents constituting the FAS.

Reaching the conclusion that the diversion of the focus of the storehouse's isomorphism from the parent organization to the industry is primarily attributed to the influence of the logical food-health association is possible, even if the difference between a product trader and a service provider in terms of information needs played some role in the final result. The strength of this logical association originated from the particular interweaving of values that inspired the two environments and that was absorbed by the subunit's accounting system precisely to find full legitimacy with the parent organization.

This finding questions the concept of endoisomorphism and exoisomorphism when the institutional environments are not coordinated and allows the perception that the degree of coordination between the two institutional environments is not neutral in the definition of the focus of a subunit's isomorphism.

This study suggests the need for further research to understand the link between the focus of subunits' isomorphism in dual environments and the degree of the divergence of the rules governing the two types of environments.

ACKNOWLEDGEMENTS

The author would like to thank the board of directors of the Società Mutua—Associazione Generale Operaia Arti e Mestieri di Pinerolo, its president, Dr. Ermanno Sacchetto, and Simona Chiosso for her precious support.

REFERENCES

Primary Sources

Associazione generale degli operai di Pinerolo, *Statuto organico*, Tipografia sociale, Pinerolo, 1887.
"La Lanterna Pinerolese," n. 9, 3 marzo, 1883.
Pinerolo Mutual Aid Society Historical Archive (PMASHA)
PMASHA, Regolamento del comitato di Previdenza della società degli operai di Pinerolo, 1864.
PMASHA, Regolamento della Società degli operai stabilita nella città di Pinerolo, Tipografia di G. Chiantore, Pinerolo, 1848.
PMASHA, Regolamento della Società degli operai di Pinerolo, Tipografia G. Loretti-Bodoni, Pinerolo, 1869.
PMASHA, Rendiconti dal 1892 al 1900, SOMSP 178.
PMASHA, Indice dei generi che si smerciano del magazzino, SOMSP 486.
PMASHA, Parallelo di compra-vendita 1892–1903, SOMSP 469.
PMASHA, Registri di cassa, SOMSP 508.

Secondary Sources

Baker, R. and Rennie, M.D. (2013) An institutional perspective on the development of Canada's first public accounts. *Accounting History* 18(1): 31–50.
Bouwens, J. and Abernethy, M.A. (2000) The consequences of customization on management accounting system design. *Accounting, Organizations and Society* 25: 221–241.
Burchell, S., Clubb, C., Hopwood, A., Hughes, J. and Nahaphiet, J. (1980) The roles of accounting in organizations and society. *Accounting, Organizations and Society* 5(1): 5–27.
Caria, A.A. and Lima Rodrigues, L. (2014) The evolution of financial accounting in Portugal since the 1960s: A new institutional economics perspective. *Accounting History* 19(1–2): 227–254.
Carmona, S., Ezzamel, M. and Gutierrez, F. (1998) Towards an institutional analysis of accounting change in the Royal Tobacco Factory of Seville. *The Accounting Historians Journal* 25(1): 115–147.
Carmona, S. and Macias, M. (2001) Institutional pressures, monopolistic conditions and the implementation of early cost management practices: The case of the Royal Tobacco Factory of Seville (1820–1887). *Abacus* 37(2): 139–165.
Carnegie, G.D. and Napier, C.J. (1996) Critical and interpretive histories: Insights into accounting's present and future through its past. *Accounting, Auditing and Accountability Journal* 9(3): 7–39.
Chenhall, R.H. and Morris, D. (1986) The impact of structure, environment, and interdependence on the perceived usefulness of management accounting systems. *The Accounting Review* 61: 16–35.
D'Aunno, T., Sutton, R.I. and Price, R.H. (1991) Isomorphism and external support in conflicting institutional environments: A study of drug abuse treatment units. *Academy of Management Journal* 34: 636–666.
Deephouse, D.L. (1996) Does legitimacy legitimate? *Academy of Management Journal* 39: 1024–1039.
Deephouse, D.L. and Suchman, M. (2008) Legitimacy in organizational institutionalism. In: Greenwood, R., Oliver, C., Sahlin, K. and Suddaby, R. (eds.), *The Sage handbook of organizational institutionalism*. Thousand Oaks, CA: Sage, pp. 49–77.

Di Cimbrini, T. (2015) Welfare or politics? The identity of Italian mutual aid societies revealed by a latent class cluster analysis of their annual reports. *Accounting History* 20(3): 310–341.

DiMaggio, P.J. and Powell, W.W. (1983) The iron cage revisited: Institutional isomorphism and collective rationality in organizational fields. *American Sociological Review* 48: 147–160.

Durand, R., Rao, H. and Monin, P. (2007) Code and conduct in French cuisine: Impact of code changes on external evaluations. *Strategic Management Journal* 28: 455–472.

Gordon, L.A. and Narayanan, V.K. (1984) Management accounting systems, perceived environmental uncertainty and organization structure: An empirical analysis. *Accounting, Organizations and Society* 9: 33–47.

Gordon, L.A. and Miller, D. (1976) A contingency framework for the design of accounting information systems. *Accounting, Organizations and Society* 1: 59–69.

Gorry, G. and Scott-Morton, M.A. (1971) A framework for management information systems. *Sloan Management Review* 13: 55–70.

Greenwood, R., Oliver, C., Sahlin, K. and Suddaby, R. (2008) Introduction. In: Greenwood, R., Oliver, C., Sahlin, K. and Suddaby, R. (eds.), *The Sage handbook of organizational institutionalism*. London: Sage, pp. 1–46.

Hollister, J. and Schultz, S. (2010) Slavery and emancipation in rural New York: Evidence from nineteenth-century accounting records. *Accounting History* 15(3): 371–405.

Hopwood, A.G. and Miller, P. (1994) *Accounting as social and institutional practice*. Cambridge: Cambridge University Press.

Larcker, D.F. (1981) The perceived importance of selected information characteristics for strategic capital budgeting decisions. *The Accounting Review* 56(3): 519–538.

Levant, Y. and Nikitin, M. (2012) Can cost and financial accounting be fully re-integrated? The role of the French state in the separation of accounting systems and the failed attempt of the système croisé to re-integrate them. *Accounting History* 17(3–4): 437–461.

Lounsbury, M. (2001) Institutional sources of practice variation: Staffing college and university recycling programs. *Administrative Science Quarterly* 46: 29–56.

Lounsbury, M. (2007) A tale of two cities: Competing logics and practice variation in the professionalizing of mutual funds. *Academy of Management Journal* 50: 289–307.

Marquis, C. and Lounsbury, M. (2007) Vive la resistance: Competing logics and the consolidation of U.S. community banking. *Academy of Management Journal* 50: 799–820.

Mia, L. and Goyal, M. (1991) Span of control, task inter- dependence and usefulness of MAS information in not-for-profit government organizations. *Financial Accountability and Management* 7: 249–266.

Miller, P., Hopper, T. and Laughlin, R. (1991) The new accounting history: An introduction. *Accounting, Organizations and Society* 16(5–6): 395–403.

Miller, P. and Napier, C. (1993) Genealogies of calculation. *Accounting, Organizations and Society* 18(7–8): 631–647.

Moreno, A. and Càmara, M. (2014) Evolution of information content from an institutional perspective: *El Alcázar* brewery (1928–1993). *Accounting History* 19(3): 369–398.

Napier, C. (1989) Research directions in accounting history. *British Accounting Review* 21(3): 237–54.

Napier, C. (2006) Accounts of change: 30 years of historical accounting research. *Accounting, Organizations and Society* 31(4–5): 445–507.

Ó hÓgartaigh, C., Ó hÓgartaigh, M. and Tyson, T. (2012) Irish property should pay for Irish poverty: Accounting for the poor in pre-famine Ireland. *Accounting History Review* 22(3): 227–248.

Pache, A.C. and Santos, F.S. (2010) When worlds collide: The internal dynamics of organizational responses to conflicting institutional demands. *Academy of Management Review* 35: 455–476.

Potter, B.N. (2005) Accounting as a social and institutional practice: Perspectives to enrich our understanding of accounting change. *Abacus* 41(3): 265–89.

Reay, T., Hinings, C.R. (2009) Managing the rivalry of competing institutional logics. *Organization Studies* 30: 629–652.

Rota, G. (1896) *Ragioneria delle cooperative di consumo*. Milan: Hoepli.

Sargiacomo, M. (2008) Institutional pressures and isomorphic change in a high-fashion company: The case of Brioni Roman style, 1945–89. *Accounting, Business & Financial History* 18(2): 215–241.

Sargiacomo, M. and Gomez, D. (2011) Accounting and accountability in local government: Contributions from accounting history research. *Accounting History* 16(3): 253–290.

Souitaris, V., Zerbinati, S. and Liu, G. (2012) Which iron cage? Endo- and exoisomorphism in corporate venture capital programs. *Academy of Management Journal* 55(2): 477–505.

Suchman, M.C. (1995) Managing legitimacy: Strategic and institutional approaches. *Academy of Management Review* 20: 571–611.

Thornton, P.H. (2002) The rise of the corporation in a craft industry: Conflict and conformity in institutional logics. *Academy of Management Journal* 45: 81–101.

Thornton, P.H. and Ocasio, W. (2008) Institutional logics. In: Greenwood, R., Oliver, C., Sahlin, K. and Suddaby, R. (eds.), *The Sage handbook of organizational institutionalism*. London: Sage, pp. 99–129.

Walker, S.P. (2004) Expense, social and moral control. Accounting and the administration of the old poor law in England and Wales. *Journal of Accounting and Public Policy* 23: 85–127.

Walker, S.P. (2008) Accounting, paper shadows and the stigmatised poor. *Accounting, Organizations and Society* 33(4–5): 453–487.

10 Exporting Marsala Wine and Importing Accounting Practices

The Business Relationship between Benjamin Ingham and Vincenzo Florio

Roberto Di Pietra[1]

INTRODUCTION[2]

The business transactions and correspondence examined in this chapter are set against the backdrop of the particular geopolitical situation that characterized the European continent during the second half of the eighteenth century, of the military conflict between the United Kingdom and France, and of the "discovery" of Marsala wine as a perfect substitute for similar wines (Portuguese Porto and Madeira and Spanish Jerez or Sherry).

In an "accident of history" (Nobes, 1998; Nobes and Parker, 2008), the English merchant John Woodhouse happened upon a new and undiscovered wine production area in Sicily in 1773. Subsequently, several other English merchants began to operate from this area in the centre of the Mediterranean Sea, setting up important industries and trading Marsala wine throughout the world. Among the most successful were first Benjamin Ingham and later Joseph Whitaker, who managed to establish an international company. This company, based mainly on the production and trading of Marsala wine, gradually became a sort of conglomerate, producing and trading in several different business areas.

The aforementioned English merchants/entrepreneurs played a fundamental role in the depressed and emerging economics of the area, establishing a sort of preindustrialization in Sicily prior to the unification of Italy. On the one hand these Englishmen, and above all Benjamin Ingham, exported Marsala wine throughout the world, and on the other hand they imported their knowledge, including accounting practices.

Many studies referring to different periods have investigated how accounting technology was disseminated between countries (Bedford, 1966; Parker, 1979, 1989; Carnegie and Parker, 1996) or between industries (Boyns and Edwards, 1996) and in many other directions: (1) including the double entry bookkeeping as a factor of critical importance in the development of capitalism in Europe (Bryer, 2000; Toms, 2010; Robertson and Funnell, 2012); (2) examining the relationship between accounting theory and accounting practices (Yamey, 1981; Jones, 1985; Fleischman and Parker, 1990, 1991, 1992; Boyns and Edwards, 1995); (3) observing the establishment of the accounting profession and its institutions (Carnegie and Varker, 1995); and (4) supporting the development of new and required accounting area (Boyns and Edwards, 1996).

The dissemination of accounting technology implies the identification of the change agents (or factors) fostering this process (Parker, 1979; Yamey, 1981). Among the change agents supporting the accounting developments between countries we could include the role played by people such as owners, merchants, and entrepreneurs.

The dissemination of the accounting knowledge helped fertilize the entrepreneurial environment in Sicily during the second half of the nineteenth century (Gray, 1988). Clear evidence of this learning process could be provided by the business relationship between Benjamin Ingham and Vincenzo Florio (see Figure 10.1), which illustrates how Ingham imported knowledge

Figure 10.1 Portraits of Benjamin Ingham and Vincenzo Florio

adopted in his business, including accounting practices, from the United Kingdom.

The possibility to consult and examine documents in the Ingham-Whitaker archive constituted a particularly important and scientifically interesting opportunity. The documents conserved in the archive give access to information normally far beyond the knowledge of individual management operations.[3]

The aim of this chapter is twofold. The first objective is to offer evidence of the business relationship between the well-reputed English businessman Benjamin Ingham and the young Sicilian entrepreneur Vincenzo Florio (Brancato, 1991). The second objective is to examine the characteristics of the Ingham business accounting system and practices, seeking to ascertain whether and how it was influenced by the British accounting environment, following the argument proposed in Parker (1979, 1989).

Through the first objective we wish to emphasize how Benjamin Ingham represented a sort of "entrepreneurial" model to be imitated and adopted: as he did for Vincenzo Florio. Ingham imported his entrepreneurial culture into Sicily, and Florio learned the main characteristics of this culture. This process emerges from the relationship between the two entrepreneurs and the kind of business they conducted in a period covering more than 30 years.

As for the second objective, we aim to emphasize how accounting practices tend to circulate, following the migration of economic actors and the paths along which their businesses move and settle. The movement of merchants, entrepreneurs, accountants, and auditors were accompanied by the movement of notions, theories, institutions, and practices. Hence the exportation of a new wine from Sicily to the United Kingdom led to a transfer of accounting knowledge in the opposite direction.

In this study we examine the commercial relations, business affairs, and entrepreneurial actions that emerge from the accounting books or can be gathered from the commercial correspondence sent by the Ingham firm to that of Ignazio & Vincenzo Florio. This allows us to underline the importance that the two entrepreneurs had in common in early nineteenth-century Sicily, as well as the affinity that renders the Florio family worthy continuers of Benjamin Ingham's work in the second half of that century (Giuffrida and Lentini, 1985; Candela, 1986; Lentini, 1993). Examination of the most important business conducted between Ingham and the Florio family is intended to furnish a series of observations of use to clarify and reinforce understanding of the characteristics of the two entrepreneurs, the factors of success of their entrepreneurial initiatives, and the causes that led to the decline of businesses that had developed so quickly.

We support the idea that the approach adopted should be based on the evolution of economic and business scenarios alongside the use of bookkeeping. In other words, we intend to highlight the existence of elements of both continuity and evolution deriving from the presence of the British in Sicily, by comparing the accounting systems proposed and adopted in Britain at the end of the eighteenth century and the beginning of the nineteenth century with what we could glean from the account books of the Ingham-Whitaker firm. More specifically, we compared the account books of the Ingham firm in the period 1863–1867 and the manual of Benjamin Booth published in London in 1789, the latter being one of the most widely known treatises on bookkeeping at the time when Benjamin Ingham was training.

With reference to the aforementioned account books and the volumes of correspondence, it should be clarified that in our consultation of the letter books conserved in the Ingham-Whitaker archive we found a series of 34 commercial letters sent by Ingham's firm to that of Florio in the period 1828–1862, and a series of 33 accounting records for the period 1863–1867.

To understand the relative importance of the correspondence between the two entrepreneurs, consider that 34 letters spread over the period between 12 February 1828 and 5 December 1862 is a very small number in the vastness of the 23 volumes of Italian letter books. The Ingham-Florio business relationship would appear marginal if compared to the abundant correspondence between the English entrepreneur and his agents in Sicily and/or nephews dispersed in the firm's most important centres of activity. What renders reading of the few letters sent by Benjamin Ingham to Vincenzo Florio interesting is the nature of the business relationship between the two entrepreneurs, due to the importance of both in the economic and business scenario of nineteenth-century Sicily (on this topic see also Lentini, 1993, and Pulejo, 1993). Both entrepreneurs and particularly Florio are considered the specimens of the so-called Sicilian golden age in the nineteenth century.

It is worth to remark that the study of the Ingham-Florio business relationship could constitute a signal aiming to highlight a broad phenomenon with which English merchants played a role of change agents importing the accounting technology in Sicily and fostering the industrialization process in that island (Parker, 1979; Boyns and Edwards, 1996).

Thus, consultation of the correspondence and examination of the account books allowed us to check and add elements to further comprehension of these illustrious entrepreneurs' work, as well as adding interesting information about the role of the English operating in Sicily in the mid-nineteenth century. Before proceeding with an examination of the transactions recorded in the Ingham account books, we will look at the correspondence between the English entrepreneur and Florio.

IMPORTING AND EXPORTING WINE AND ACCOUNTING PRACTICES

As cited in Carnegie and Parker (1996, p. 24) according to the Dewey classification accounting is categorized as a technology assuming that a technology is a body of "skills, knowledge and procedures for making, using and doing useful things" (Merrill, 1968). This is perfectly consistent with the aims of the accounting domain that includes the skills of writing materials, calculating machines and account books (Parker, 1989).

The accounting technology doesn't belong to the proprietary technologies and couldn't be considered as a marketable capital good. At the same time this technology has the characteristic to be transferred from one country to another (Carnegie and Parker, 1996, p. 25). Even if it is not possible to capture the capacity to disseminate accounting technology in a specific formula and/or model we could identify in some change agents the vehicles to which this was possible in particular cases in the history.

Change agents (or factors or recipients) could provide an explanation of differences within accounting practices and between countries (Parker, 1979, p. 125). The focus on these factors should allow to identify "the methods of communication used, the kind of participation obtained from the recipients, the manner in which the innovation is used and adapted to the existing cultural patterns" (Boyns and Edwards, 1996, p. 12). The reference to the change agents could constitute a sort of framework that can be used to examine accounting developments within a single country or between countries. Among the various kinds of change agents and their role in generating accounting developments we could include the individuals such as firm owners, merchants, entrepreneurs, bookkeepers, managers, and employees. Even if it is not so simple to detect the role played by individual in contributing to disseminate and transfer accounting knowledge, we agree that this is relevant and worthy (Yamey, 1981, p. 131).

In this respect Carnegie and Parker (1996) have examined the impact of a single individual, William Butler Yaldwyn, in the process of disseminate accounting technology throughout the British colonies in the Southern Hemisphere during the nineteenth century. As both authors affirm, it would be wrong to support the idea that a specific transfer of accounting technology couldn't happen without a single individual, but its identification could represent a signal and a track confirming such a process.

As clearly stated in Parker (1989), the transfer of capitals from one country to another is not a sufficient condition to determine the transfer of accounting techniques, institutions, and concepts. This dissemination is possible on the basis of movements of people and their cultural values and despite the existence of a process of heavy investments in the same place.

Our study is based on the Parker (1979, 1989) approach and it follows the idea of the importing and exporting of accounting practices and the change agents' perspective (Parker, 1979; Boyns and Edwards, 1996). According to Parker (1989, p.7), "accounting techniques, institutions and concepts are all capable of being imported and exported from one country to another." The identification of this kind of phenomenon was based on a literature survey and was the specific case of Benjamin Ingham's entrepreneurial activity, his business relationship with Vincenzo Florio, and the accounting practices observed in his business.

On the basis of this framework the main research questions of our study are the following:

1. Did Benjamin Ingham and Vincenzo Florio develop a business relationship?
2. Can a learning process be discerned from this relationship?
3. Did Benjamin Ingham import British accounting practices to manage the production of and trade Marsala wine?

It has been highlighted on many occasions and in numerous studies that commercial traffic follows international routes, and that the initial spread of accounting techniques can be observed in the wake of merchants, goods, and transactions. Traders learned the double entry method by reading texts that illustrated how it worked (in their own language or in another language; first in the Italian vernacular), by learning from a local teacher, a foreign teacher or merchant, or even by travelling abroad (Parker, 1989, p. 9). As we mentioned before numerous studies have clarified how this type of "technology" transfer took place, in all the aforementioned forms, over a period spanning at least five centuries (from the fourteenth to the nineteenth) (Melis, 1962; Nobes, 1982; Catturi, 1988; Perrone, 1995; Di Pietra, 1996; Catturi and Di Pietra, 2001; Robertson and Funnell, 2012).

The importation of accounting technology from certain countries to others was followed by the exportation of institutions linked to the organization and functioning of the accounting profession, that is, concepts related to the drafting and contents of financial statements and other financial reporting documents (Carnegie and Parker, 1996). This expanded the initial spread of accounting techniques to a global level.

These remarks are certainly related to Parker's considerations in his original contributions (Parker, 1979, 1989), and Catturi similarly identifies a process of dissemination of "waves of knowledge" between different countries (Catturi, 1997, pp. 75–76).

Catturi describes the propagation of accounting culture using the metaphor of "refracted waves" generated by a stone thrown onto the surface of a pond. Through this analogy, he intends to express the behaviour of culture and knowledge as they spread from a starting point to other places in a series of waves of different amplitudes and varying speed (Catturi, 1997, pp. 77–78).

The transfer of knowledge does not follow a regular pattern. The extent to and the intensity with which concepts, techniques, data, and technologies affect environments other than their source one depend on many variables. First, the strength with which the information signal is launched from its point of origin and the means of communication used both play a fundamental role. Second, they depend on the response and the reactivity to stimuli of the environment in which the new information seeks to insert itself.

The successful importation of new knowledge also depends largely on the active or passive attitude of the parties involved. Obviously, the presence of countries exporting a given theory or technique on the one hand, and countries importing the same concept on the other hand, will increase the likelihood of the process being completed quickly and efficiently (Parker, 1989, p. 25).

Accounting practices are susceptible to an almost "natural" dissemination at an international level, following the ancient paths of merchants and commercial trade and, after the industrial revolution, the operations of big companies, multinationals, accounting professions, and the relative firms and institutions. While the first wave initially involved the dissemination of an accounting technique and practice (systematized and transmitted in the seminal work of Luca Pacioli) from Italy to the rest of Europe, its subsequent propagation has affected a wider context (i.e., the whole world) and the institutional profile of both concepts and theories (Nobes and Parker, 2008).

> Accounting concepts, techniques and institutions have been diffused through both space and time. Accounting historians whose interest has extended beyond a single person or organization have, however, typically concentrated on studying development in specific countries or regions of a country. . . .We suggest [. . .] that a synthesis across both dimensions will enrich the perspectives not only of students of the contemporary scene but also of historians.
>
> (Carnegie and Napier, 2002, pp. 689–690)

With regard to the transfer of knowledge, Catturi returns to the metaphor of "waves" (Catturi, 1997, pp. 75–99). Seeking to emphasize the varying intensity and amplitude of the signals transmitted, Catturi likens the flow that characterizes the transfer of knowledge to the backwash that occurs after waves have crashed onto the beach. As well as meeting with other environments, the culture/knowledge transmitted may return, changed and enhanced by the nuances it has acquired through contact with a culture other than its own. What hence originates is a process that sees the same concept subjected to countless cultural transfers, which enrich it and change it each time, so that identifying its true origins can become difficult.

Any environment that is affected by a flow of knowledge receives and assimilates it differently from another, reacting to background changes and to cultural contaminations of its own values in a unique way, like the living beings it is composed of. Even if the destination does not seem responsive and positively inclined to accept changes from the outside, the flow will nonetheless create consequences and the environment it impacts will undergo transformations that will mark the evolutionary path of the original culture. The assimilation and the process of decoding the new item transmitted, which take place in line with the values of the place of destination, will in turn modify the message, so that when it returns to the original context it will never be the same as it was on departure.

We believe the Parker (1979, 1989) approach can be adopted in examining the business relationship between Benjamin Ingham and Vincenzo Florio during the nineteenth century. This framework, jointly considered together with the change agents perspective, could contribute to understanding of the commercial development of a business based on the exportation of Marsala wine throughout the world. The development of this relationship not only generated new kinds of business, but also favoured the corresponding importation of accounting practices to Sicily (Parker, 1979; Carnegie and Parker, 1996).

The Ingham-Whitaker archive is a rich source of historical information through which the aforementioned business relationship can be studied. This archive includes 75 letter books covering a period 35 years, as well as a large series of accounting books. Within the 80 years of existence of the Ingham-Whitaker business we focused our analysis on the periods in which we detected a business relationship with the Florio firm, from 1828 to 1862 (see the archive catalogue in Aa, Vv. 1990).

As for our analysis of the Ingham-Whitaker accounting system, we chose to examine the period 1862–1867. By referring to these 6 years we were able to observe the most complete group of accounting books in the Ingham-Whitaker business archive. In order to highlight the adoption of British accounting practices in Sicily through the Ingham-Whitaker business, we compared the characteristics of its accounting system with those described in one of the most popular accounting books printed and reprinted in the United Kingdom.

THE BUSINESS RELATIONSHIP BETWEEN INGHAM AND FLORIO REFLECTED IN THEIR COMMERCIAL CORRESPONDENCE (1828–1862)

Above all it is interesting to note that the letters sent by Benjamin Ingham were copied following a series of rules that facilitate the reconstruction of the related business activities.[4]

These solutions are very effective, considering the quantity of letters copied, the length of trade operations in the nineteenth century and the enormous amount of business transactions that a merchant such as Benjamin Ingham was involved in at any one time.

A chronological reconstruction of the 34 letters examined—bearing in mind the date and place of posting, the recipient, the date of any letter being replied to, and the Ingham-Whitaker archive number—reveals some of the characteristics of the business relationship between Benjamin Ingham and Vincenzo Florio. We first noted that all the correspondence was sent from and received in Palermo. Indeed, the original offices of the two entrepreneurs were located in the centre of the Sicilian capital and the respective headquarters of the two companies remained in the same place, despite their subsequent growth and diversification (Candela, 1986; D'Aleo and Girgenti, 1992; Pulejo, 1993). Second, a higher concentration of letters was observed around two particular periods in time, pinpointing corresponding phases in the evolution of the business relationship: a first set in 1828–1834 and a second set in 1843–1862.

The letters in the first set correspond to a phase of "getting to know each other." In this sense the initial frequency of the letters, especially in the years 1832–1834, stands out; this indicates a preliminary type of business centred, as we shall see, on trade-related activities. All the letters sent by Benjamin Ingham respond, within the space of a few days, to letters received from Vincenzo Florio, almost as if the stimulus to do business together flowed solely in the direction Florio-Ingham. The fact that the letters are addressed to "Sig.ri I. & V. Florio" and are written in a very clear but formal style confirm that this was the initial phase in the business relationship between the two entrepreneurs, and probably hints at a certain sense of superiority on the part of the already established Benjamin Ingham.

The second set of letters, on the other hand, illustrates the shift towards a subsequent phase of development. These letters cover a longer period of time, characterized by more frequent exchanges. Some letters sent by Ingham do not explicitly respond to previous letters from Vincenzo Florio, and the business relationship seems to be on more equal terms and mutually engaging. Moreover, the form of address used varies and the style, while remaining within the canon of precision typical of business correspondence, is less detached.

Therefore, after the initial contact between the two entrepreneurs the business has evolved in a way that is consistent with the change agents approach proposed initially by Parker (1979) and subsequently by Carnegie and Parker (1996). From one side Benjamin Ingham, in developing his businesses in and from Sicily, has contributed to transmit accounting practices to the rising entrepreneurial class. From the other side Vincenzo Florio has greatly learned from the English merchants operating in Sicily, becoming after three decades an entrepreneur able to set and propose complex business with them. This is evident from the evolution of the kind of businesses emerging from the Ingham correspondence.

The observations made while examining this correspondence can be summarized in the following double entry tables. Table 10.1 highlights

Table 10.1 Frequency of letters in the Ingham-Florio business relationship

	1828–1843	1843–1862	1828–1862
Years	15	19	34
Number of letters	11	23	34
Average per year	1.36	0.82	1

the separation between the two phases in relation to the frequency of the correspondence.[5]

The distinction between the two phases emerges more clearly if we examine the evolving contents of the letters. The following reflections constitute an attempt to reorganize the letters sent by Ingham to Florio in relation to the type of activity they deal with. Therefore we have classified the 34 letters into the following areas of business: (1) commercial; (2) financial; (3) financial investment in the tuna fisheries (*Tonnare*); and (4) financial investment in Vincenzo Florio's shipping company.[6]

Commercial

We collected and classified in chronological order the series of letters sent from Ingham to Florio regarding transactions of a commercial nature. The time sequence of this type of business further confirms the distinction proposed. In fact, the correspondence illustrates how the relationship between the two entrepreneurs is based on the most classical foundations of reciprocal trade. However, it should be pointed out that the purchase of consignments of sugar, rum, and other end products is made with reference to an international trade organization that, at the time, only merchants such as Benjamin Ingham could sustain.[7]

From 1844 the business relationship continues—no longer concerning finished products to be marketed, but the purchase or sale of raw materials directly connected to industrial activities. The two entrepreneurs established their respective business networks in this period and broke away from each other from the point of view of ordinary commercial operations, having consolidated their work in the wine industry by pursuing specific market sectors and having launched steam shipping in Sicily. The reciprocal business relationships thus shifted towards the purchase and sale of raw materials (such as coal and sulphur) or use of each other's business network in particular situations (specific contingencies in the sale of Marsala wine).

Financial

The series of letters regarding financial activities related to business transactions further confirms the distinction between the two phases of the Ingham-Florio business relationship. One of the first outcomes of a reciprocal and frequent business relationship between two or more entrepreneurs is the activation of a series of agreements, with the aim of regulating and simplifying the financial aspect of their operations. This leads to the birth of the main instruments of payment, starting with the use of the current account and credit instruments. The business relationship between Benjamin Ingham and Vincenzo Florio, which from a financial viewpoint involved other subjects, also featured the use of instruments for the settlement of reciprocal debit/credit positions in the form of payment methods such as customers' notes and/or bills of exchange.

Ingham and Florio systematically settle their business transactions through remittance on current accounts, as well as using bills for the transfer of credit. Precisely because they deal with the financial activities typically connected to ordinary trade, almost all such letters belong to the first set, prior to 1840.

Financial Investment in Tuna Fisheries

Transactions related to financial investment in tuna fishing on the Egadi Islands further corroborate the distinction between the types of business conducted in the different phases of the evolving business relationship. Vincenzo Florio began to manage (*in gabella*) the tuna fisheries of Favignana and Formica in 1841 and, except for a brief period, continued until his son Ignazio bought the Egadi Islands from the Marchese Pallavicini in 1873. From the early years of Florio's management, Benjamin Ingham held a partnership share (*carato*) and hence was allocated a share of profits from the sale of tuna and all derived products.[8]

It should be pointed out that the manager (*gabelloto*) was required to account for his administration and submit a proposal to the shareholders for the allocation of any profits or losses realized, beyond the share capital subscribed and paid up. We found many significant letters in the archive in which Benjamin Ingham granted his approval to the distribution of profits proposed in a previous letter received from Vincenzo Florio. In this case the two entrepreneurs' business relationship can only concern the development phase, and ends up becoming a relationship on equal terms, based on mutual respect. Indeed, Florio proposes to Ingham an investment that, due to the nature of the activity, has a highly uncertain outcome, to be realized only several years later. Interestingly, even after Benjamin Ingham's death, Vincenzo Florio submits his proposal for the distribution of profits made on the sale of leftover stock of salted tuna fished in previous financial years to the approval of Ingham's nephew and heir, William Whitaker.

Financial Investment in Vincenzo Florio's Shipping Company

The financial investment in Vincenzo Florio's shipping company, set up on 25 August 1861, signals a point in which Benjamin Ingham's heir recognizes the now greater importance of the Sicilian entrepreneur and appreciates the courtesy of being invited to join this new company. In this sense, the related letters are extremely significant as they concern approval of the offer to join the business, confirming Vincenzo Florio's role as the leading Sicilian businessman in the postunification period.

The whole correspondence between Ingham and Florio is summarized in Table 10.2:

Table 10.2 Phases in the Ingham-Florio business relationship, based on the contents of their letters*

Period / Activity	1828–1843	1843–1862	Total by activity
Commercial	Sugar: 3. Rum: 1	Sulphur: 2. Sugar and cigars: 1. Coal: 1. Wine: 2	10
Financial	Sugar storage: 6. Payment on current account: 3	Customers' note: 3	12
Financial investment in tuna fisheries		Payment of profits: 3. Approval of allocation proposal: 8. Subscription of partnership shares: 2	13
Financial investment in Vincenzo Florio's shipping company		Approval of offer: 1. Subscription of shares in Postal Steamship Company (*Società dei Piroscafi Postali*): 1	2
Total in the period	13	24	37

*Content of letters sent by Ingham's firm to that of Florio (1828–1862).

PRACTICES IN INGHAM'S ACCOUNTING SYSTEM BASED ON IMPORTED KNOWLEDGE

In the correspondence examined the development phase in Benjamin Ingham and Vincenzo Florio's business relationship emerges through a radical shift in the contents of the letters, towards different types of activities from the initial trade management. This could be interpreted in the wrong way if we fail to consider accounting information.

In effect, while there is no longer any trace of the business transactions between the two entrepreneurs in the copied letters, such transactions continue even after Benjamin Ingham's death. In fact, from an organizational viewpoint, the process of diversification of their activities meant that business was recorded directly in the accounts, at least in relation to transactions conducted most frequently and their more consolidated business relations, thus avoiding letters being sent from the headquarters in Palermo. In this context, examination of the accounts kept in the archive helps complete the picture we are seeking to paint.

The decision to examine the Ingham company accounts for the period 1863–1867 was made with the aim of acquiring as much information as possible about the business it conducted with the Florio firm. Although the period in question follows the demise of Benjamin Ingham, it furnishes us with an overview of the administration-related accounting records in a fairly coordinated set of accounting books. The Ingham-Whitaker archive includes the following account books and records:

1. Two series of *Registri di Cassa* (Cash Books):
   a. three volumes of the first series regarding the period September 1860 to December 1882.
   b. three volumes of the second series regarding the period July 1866 to 31 March 1891.
2. Six volumes of the *Libro Giornale* (Daybook) referring to six nonconsecutive periods;
3. One volume of the *Libro Mastro* (General Ledger) regarding the period 1923–1925;
4. One volume of the *Squarcio* (Waste Book) referring to the period from 10 April 1863 to 17 October 1867;
5. One volume called an Invoice Book regarding the period 1810–1813;
6. One volume called a Sales Book for the period 1815–1823;
7. Three volumes of records of foreign financial investments, including two Books of American Investment (1861 and 1866) and a Sundry Investments Book (1888).

It is clear from the list above that the only period of time common to a coordinated set of records and account books is from April 1863 to October 1867, including a phase in which transactions are visible in the *Registri di Cassa* and *Squarcio*, and a phase beginning on 2 July 1866 in which the accounting information also covers the entries in the *Libro Giornale*.

Before conducting a systematic analysis of the information gleaned from the abovementioned account books, some remarks should be made about the characteristics of the accounting method adopted by Ingham & Co. in that period. Benjamin Ingham was educated in a Methodist family, where the lifestyle was rigorous and essential. The father of Benjamin, William Ingham, was himself the founder of a cult called Inghamites based on similar rules of the John Wesley's organization . During his adolescence, Benjamin had learned, among other topics, bookkeeping within the family firm in Leeds, and this was based on the knowledge of accounting manuals that were commonly used in late eighteenth-century England.

English merchants who went to Sicily with the occupying forces remained on the island even after the restoration of the monarchy, bringing a common cultural background and widespread knowledge of the double entry bookkeeping method, known at the time as "Italian bookkeeping."[9] Among them, Benjamin Ingham adopted the double entry bookkeeping method to record all the business he conducted, transmitting its use to his nephews, employees, and agents throughout Sicily and beyond. Considering the enormous number of business relationships Ingham entered into, we can understand to what extent he was able to contribute to the use and spread of this instrument within the nascent Sicilian merchant middle class. This was also the case of Vincenzo Florio who learned how to use the double entry bookkeeping method from English merchants.

The coordinated set of account books for the period 1863–1867 conserved in the Ingham-Whitaker archive is therefore of great importance as it permits comparison with the most widely used bookkeeping systems in late eighteenth-century England.[10]

In this sense, the identification of any elements of continuity and/or affinity constitutes an interesting hint of how the Sicilian economic and business scene evolved under the influence of British culture in the first half of the nineteenth century. Thus the idea of a "circular" evolution of bookkeeping emerges: from the first version used by Italian merchants in the late Middle Ages, which spread to Europe; via refinement of the method in line with the demands of eighteenth-century European merchants; to the new Italian bookkeeping method, which spread to markets all around the world, including Italy and Sicily. Within this circular process, it is clear that bookkeeping evolved in relation to the demands and management goals of businesses and, in turn, their goals were connected to contemporary business, economic and anthropological culture.

This economic scenario was so different if compared with the rural economy hypothesized in one of the most diffused accounting treaty published in Palermo two centuries before: Lodovico Flori (1636). This was a dramatic change towards the industrial revolution and the introduction of capitalism in Sicily. The English merchants, such as Benjamin Ingham, were the agents of this change (Carnegie and Edwards, 1996; Robertson and Funnell, 2012).

The birth of the Sicilian merchant middle class was prompted by the active presence of the English, and their cultural background provided elements that steered the evolution of the economic and business scenario in the nineteenth century. The management goals of Sicilian merchants became connected to the adoption of the bookkeeping tool as used by English merchants, the latter acting as vehicles for the transmission of economic and business culture.

Comparison between the Ingham & Co. account books and accounting manuals commonly used in England in the second half of the eighteenth century allowed us to test this hypothesis. Among others we chose the treatise of Benjamin Booth (see Figure 10.2), first because it was published in 1789 and widely used in the following years, and therefore could corresponds to Benjamin Ingham's period of training, and second because the very heading of the manual has a series of characteristics that render it particularly suited to the needs of a merchant such as Ingham.[11] In this context, the image of the opening page of Booth's work prompts the following remarks:

1. The book is eminently practical, as it offers numerous examples, especially of the trade conducted within the vast British colonial empire.

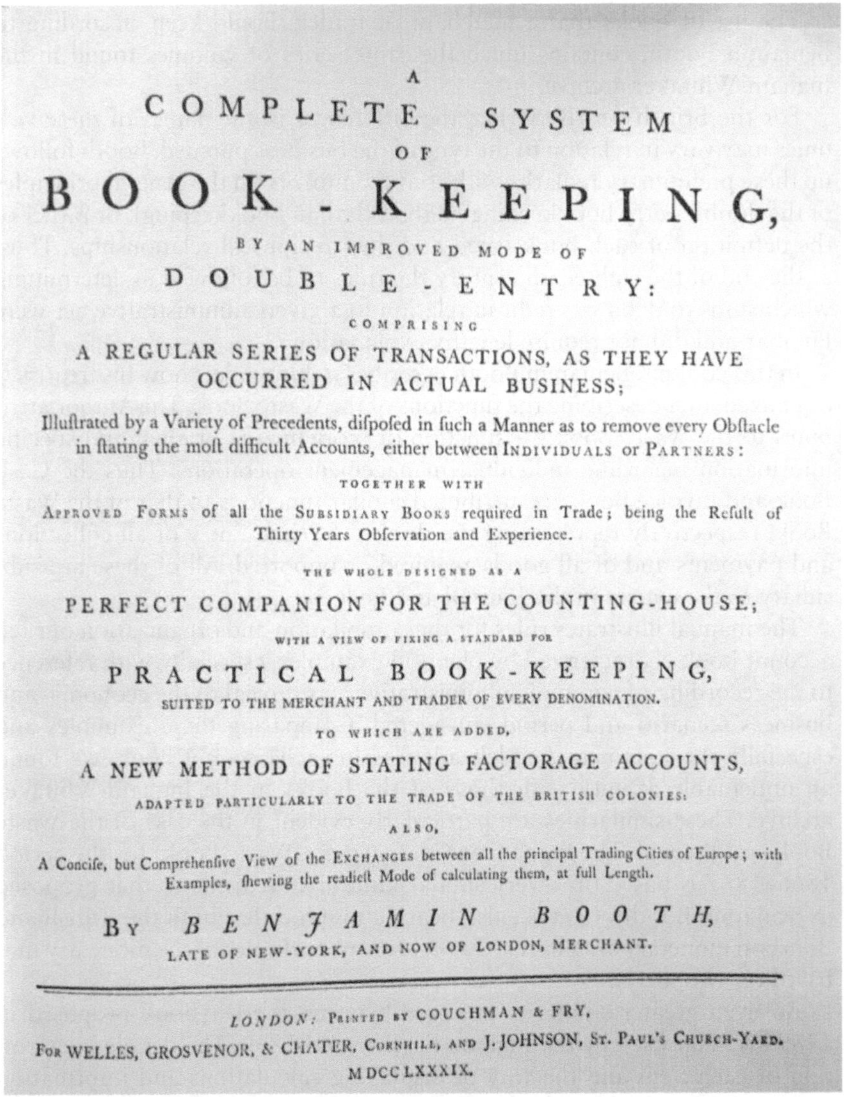

A
COMPLETE SYSTEM
OF
BOOK-KEEPING,
BY AN IMPROVED MODE OF
DOUBLE-ENTRY:
COMPRISING
A REGULAR SERIES OF TRANSACTIONS, AS THEY HAVE OCCURRED IN ACTUAL BUSINESS;
Illuftrated by a Variety of Precedents, difpofed in fuch a Manner as to remove every Obftacle in ftating the moft difficult Accounts, either between INDIVIDUALS or PARTNERS:
TOGETHER WITH
APPROVED FORMS of all the SUBSIDIARY BOOKS required in Trade; being the Refult of Thirty Years Obfervation and Experience.
THE WHOLE DESIGNED AS A
PERFECT COMPANION FOR THE COUNTING-HOUSE;
WITH A VIEW OF FIXING A STANDARD FOR
PRACTICAL BOOK-KEEPING,
SUITED TO THE MERCHANT AND TRADER OF EVERY DENOMINATION.
TO WHICH ARE ADDED,
A NEW METHOD OF STATING FACTORAGE ACCOUNTS,
ADAPTED PARTICULARLY TO THE TRADE OF THE BRITISH COLONIES:
ALSO,
A Concife, but Comprehenfive View of the EXCHANGES between all the principal Trading Cities of Europe; with Examples, fhewing the readieft Mode of calculating them, at full Length.
BY *BENJAMIN BOOTH*,
LATE OF NEW-YORK, AND NOW OF LONDON, MERCHANT.

LONDON: PRINTED BY COUCHMAN & FRY,
FOR WELLES, GROSVENOR, & CHATER, CORNHILL, AND J. JOHNSON, ST. PAUL'S CHURCH-YARD.
MDCCLXXXIX.

Figure 10.2 Front cover of the Benjamin Booth bookkeeping treatise (1789)

2. Thanks to his own experience as a merchant, the author is aware of the economic and business scenario in which English merchants operate and therefore provides plenty of useful information, for example regarding exchange practices between the main European cities.
3. The accounts are based on the debtor-creditor method, in line with previous treatises published in England.

The list of books that a merchant or trader should keep, according to Benjamin Booth, contains much the same series of volumes found in the Ingham-Whitaker archive.[12]

For the British treatise writer, the differences in the names of these volumes may vary in relation to the type of the business pursued. Booth follows up these preliminary remarks with some comments on the general principles of the double entry bookkeeping method (Italian bookkeeping), or rather of the definition of each book listed and their reciprocal relationships. Thus, at the end of the eighteenth century the rules to be followed in determining which sums to debit or credit in relation to a given administrative act were familiar and did not require lengthy explanation.[13]

In this context, Benjamin Booth describes to his readers how his treatise is organized, first describing the functions of the Waste Book. The Author attributes to the Waste Book the function of reorganizing original and specific information regarding individual management operations. Thus the Cash Book and Invoice Book are attributed similar functions to that of the Waste Book, respectively representing the Books of Prime Entry of all collections and payments and of all goods acquired or imported. All of these are subsidiary to the entries in the Journal and Ledger.

The manual illustrates rules for the compilation and organization of each account book characterized by plentiful examples, especially with reference to the recording of common administrative acts typical to the economic and business scenario and period considered. Comparing these examples and especially the statements/models adopted in each account book, we found an undeniable affinity with those of the books in the Ingham-Whitaker archive. These similarities are particularly evident in the case of the Waste Book and Journal. The Ingham & Co. *Squarcio* (Waste Book) for the period 1866–1867 is based on a very similar kind of statements to that proposed in Benjamin Booth's treatise, also bearing in mind that both the British and Bourbon monetary systems used a scale of submultiples of the monetary unit based on two levels.

An even greater similarity emerged between the Daybook proposed in 1789 and that used by the Ingham firm around 1860. The detailed description of each item and the way of displaying calculations and information seem to justify the hypothesis of a lasting connection between the Ingham company accounts and late eighteenth-century British accounting practices.

The greatest differences are observed between the Cash Book of Benjamin Booth's treatise and the Ingham company's *Registri di Cassa*, where the latter does not use separate debit-credit columns for "At the Bank," "At the Banker," and "At Home."

The lack of specification of the subjects involved in Ingham's accounts is probably due to the particular Sicilian environment. Ingham did not need to distinguish between the debit and/or credit positions set up by financial agents for the simple reason that no such system existed in Sicily and it was the entrepreneur himself who improvised as a banker.

Further differences are revealed by comparison between the Invoice Books and Sales Books proposed by the English author and the same account books kept by Benjamin Ingham. While the subsidiary books are initially written in English, the structure of the statements differs according to the specific operations of purchase and sale or loading and unloading of ships. In this sense, the symbols, initials, and abbreviations used in the Ingham company's Sales Book are of particular interest, as their meaning may be related to a specific ship, the portion occupied by loads, the initials of the buyer or seller, the different units of weight, capacity, or currencies.[14]

Finally, it is interesting to note the importance of the *Registri di Cassa* (Cash Books) within an accounting system, as they are used to demonstrate the existence of credits and/or debts between two merchants. In other words, we intend to underline the fact that the system described by Benjamin Booth and that adopted by the Ingham company have a largely financial basis: the complex/general subject of the accounts is determined only by the financial portion of the capital, and the financial aspect of management makes it possible to determine the financial income as, from a financial viewpoint, the costs are given by immediate or deferred income and expenditure.

The merchant middle class wanted to know the positive or negative outcome of its numerous and often unrelated initiatives, in other words the financial surplus or deficit at the end of each financial year. Thus profit derives from a greater amount of collections in relation to payments made in a given year, and loss derives from the opposite situation.

Although the nineteenth century saw many changes take place, the characteristics of the Ingham company accounts remained strongly influenced by its founder's cultural and educational roots. In this sense, the introduction of the Lira to substitute the Onze following the unification of Italy led, in July 1866, to:

1. The introduction of a second series of *Registri di Cassa*, for many years followed by the parallel and preexisting first series;
2. Changes to the notes in the *Squarcio* to adapt to the monetary standard of the Lira;
3. The recording of administrative facts in the *Libro Giornale* in Lira from 2 July 1866.[15]

Joint examination of the *Registri di Cassa*, *Squarcio*, and *Libro Giornale* for the period 1863–1867 revealed a series of transactions between Ingham & Co. and Ignazio & Vincenzo Florio (see Table 10.3) that provide important information for evaluation and comparison with Benjamin Booth's treatise and regarding the contemporary evolution of bookkeeping in relation to the economic and business culture. The overall picture that emerges from the 33 records identified in the accounts confirms first the importance of the *Squarcio* (Waste Book), as the record dates in this book

Table 10.3 Business transactions between the companies Ingham and Florio in the period 1863–1867

Type of business Cash	Commercial	Financial	Financial investment	Total
Debits	Sulphur: 1	Acceptance: 1. Bills: 3	Shares: 2	7
Credits	Sulphur: 4. Merchandise costs for freight (various): 6. Merchandise costs for freight (wine): 15	Bills: 1		26
Total	26	5	2	33

all precede those in the *Libro Giornale* and the *Registri di Cassa* had the function of Books of Prime Entry for collections and payments made.[16]

Second, they confirm the existence and continuation of a commercial relationship that would seem from the correspondence to have come to an end or at least dwindled. In this context, we present in the table below the 33 administrative acts that took place between the two companies considered in the period 1863–1867, distinguishing between the type of business mentioned and in relation to their presence in the *Registri di Cassa*.

The picture that emerges allows us to propose the following observations with reference, above all, to the clear prevalence of accounting entries regarding commercial transactions, especially in relation to the sale of Ingham Marsala wine via the steamships of the Ignazio & Vincenzo Florio Postal Steamship Company (*Società dei Piroscafi Postali*). It should be added that there was a clear preponderance, in terms of both the number and size of the sums involved, of cash-based transactions. In other words, while no longer visible in correspondence, the commercial activity between the two companies continues and is characterized by the Ingham heirs' use of services provided by Vincenzo Florio's steamship company. Lastly, a common fact leads us to one of the conclusions of this study: a few years after Benjamin Ingham's death, his followers not only acknowledged the leading role taken on by Vincenzo Florio but also, in their running of the company, set out on the path that would lead to the company's inescapable decline within the space of a few decades.

CONCLUDING REMARKS

Reconstructing the life and times of an entrepreneur is without doubt a far more complex task in relation to the narrow focus of this contribution. The observation of the documents in the Ingham-Whitaker archive has allowed us to identify many similarities between Benjamin Ingham and Vincenzo

Florio. The latter saw the English entrepreneur as a model, followed his development and was able to take over from him as the leading Sicilian businessman thanks to a characteristic that Benjamin Ingham lacked and could not hope to acquire: a sense of belonging to the Sicilian cultural environment. More than for his business acumen, the Sicilian entrepreneur should be recognized for his ability to take part in and define the evolution of the contemporary social, economic and political scene, as he consciously played a role in nineteenth-century Sicilian culture. This significant aspect prompts the need to identify two phases in the development of the business relationship between Ingham and Florio, which we can define "getting to know each other" and "development."

The first refers to the period in which Vincenzo Florio contacted the English entrepreneur about launching and expanding his own business, due to the Ingham company's sound and large organization. During the development phase, on the basis of a relationship that was then on equal terms, the two entrepreneurs launched a series of undertakings that were not only economically significant, but also important from the point of view of their personal success.[17]

The identification of these two phases in the Ingham-Florio business relationship is confirmed on several occasions by analysis both of the series of letters sent by the English entrepreneur to Florio in the period 1828–1862 and the sequence of accounting records found in the Ingham company account books regarding the period 1863–1867.

The observations concerning the account books, made thanks to the joint examination of the *Registri di Cassa*, *Squarcio* and *Libro Giornale*, ultimately allowed us to identify a remarkable affinity between the system adopted by Ingham & Co. and comparable bookkeeping systems used in late eighteenth-century Britain.

The Ingham company account books have been compared with what was one of the most popular treatises in Britain when the English entrepreneur was training: that of Booth, published in London in 1789. The similarities detected support the hypothesis that Benjamin Ingham managed to transmit to the Sicilian economic and business scene the accounting knowledge he learned from precisely that treatise, which curiously, like many others, was conceived in England with the aim of perfecting the Italian method of accounting. In this sense, we can conclude that the presence of English merchants in nineteenth-century Sicily represents one of the factors that influenced the birth of the Sicilian merchant middle class, through the diffusion of a successful business model. This highlights the role played by British economic and business culture, and by bookkeeping as a vehicle to disseminate that culture and to transfer that accounting technology as argued in Parker (1979, 1989), Boyns and Edwards (1996), Carnegie and Parker (1996), Catturi (1997) and Robertson and Funnell (2012).

Moreover, the difficulties of understanding the many-faceted profile of any businessman, also taking into account the changing economic, social, and political scenario in which he worked, become even greater when the documentary sources available are incomplete, indirect, and imprecise. In this sense, we have sought to provide a small contribution to more in-depth knowledge of the business relationship between Ingham and Florio, with the aim of fostering greater understanding of these two entrepreneurs, operating in Sicily in the first half of the nineteenth century. We believe that reconstruction of the Ingham-Florio business relationship through the Ingham-Whitaker archive is relevant. First, it provides a clear support to the framework proposed by Parker (1979, 1989) stating that some actors could play a positive role as change agents, as certainly did Benjamin Ingham importing in Sicily its business knowledge included the accounting technology adopted in Britain. Second, it is worth noting that the examined business relationship could contribute to better understand the entrepreneurial figure of Vincenzo Florio, despite the loss of part of the Florio archive.[18]

On the one hand, the study of documents conserved in the Ingham-Whitaker archive has confirmed information already presented in other research fields regarding the two illustrious businessmen; on the other hand it has allowed us to investigate further sources of information from the point of view of the history of accounting. Moreover, we believe that the stories of two entrepreneurs like Ingham and Florio, set in the context of the tumultuous changes of the nineteenth century, can be better understood when many different interpretations are used.

The approach of accounting historians therefore offers an analytical viewpoint that complements and enriches previous studies, with the aim of gleaning from the past interpretative models of use in the present. In this context, the opportunity to consult an archive like that of the Ingham-Whitaker company, characterized by documents dating back to the early nineteenth century and comprising an extremely significant and complete set of account books, constitutes an unusual and particularly fruitful opportunity.

The reflections that emerged from our reconstruction of the business relationship, through examination of the commercial correspondence and account books, have allowed us to confirm the role of change agents played by the two entrepreneurs. In the specific case of Benjamin Ingham and Vincenzo Florio we could affirm that both have managed to understand their times and contribute to their evolution. Their actions as all-round businessmen perfectly fitted the contemporary economic and business scenario, and the strategy of pursuing all possible opportunities for profit through the investment of their own resources and energy proved to be a winning one at least until 1870.

This was coherent with the first steps moving the rural and feudal Sicilian economy towards capitalism. The dissemination of the accounting technology imported from the English merchants has contributed in this process (Robertson and Funnell, 2012). Unfortunately the political change related to the Italian unification has modified (or maybe stopped) the development of this process.

In this respect, we believe that the death of Vincenzo Florio in 1868 can probably be seen as a turning point, after which the long process that led to the affirmation of the capitalist firm in the twentieth century began. The Ingham and Florio heirs failed to comprehend this evolution and continued to follow a business model that was progressively further removed from the nascent reality.[19]

Vincenzo Florio's success and the epilogue of his company unfortunately demonstrate how economic and business scenarios can only be changed on the basis of a solid, widespread, and common cultural basis. And this wasn't the case of the transition to capitalism in Sicily after the unification in Italy. Many where the changes in that society but not so many where real and grounded in that society. The febrile economic, political, and social changes that took place in Sicily in the first half of the nineteenth century were destined to have little impact if their boost to business initiatives ultimately affected only one, unfortunately isolated, company: that of Ignazio & Vincenzo Florio. The menacing echo of one of the most bitter paradoxes in the Sicilian writer Tomasi di Lampedusa's *The Leopard* (*Il Gattopardo*) comes to mind: the discovery that "if we want things to stay as they are, things will have to change."

NOTES

1. Roberto Di Pietra is a Full Professor of Accounting and Business Administration at the Department of Business and Law, University of Siena, and President pro tempore of the Italian Society of Accounting History.
2. The first version of this study dates back to the proceedings of the second SISR National Conference held in Messina in 1993 (16–17 December). As a coincidence, in this small world where we live, I had the chance to meet a nephew of a daughter of Joseph Whitaker, in Sydney in March 2012. From the lucky chance to meet Patrick O'Neill I have been stimulated to work on this chapter in order to emphasize the role played by English merchants and entrepreneurs in developing a fortunate economic season in Sicily just before the political unification of Italy.
3. In the archive we found volumes only of the letters sent by Ingham to other counterparts, in contrast to other archives which contain copies (or originals) of the letters received as well as letters sent.
4. We refer to the system by which, to aid the entrepreneur's comprehension, each letter in the volumes of letter books was identified by a number in the margin. This number indicated the page in the volume that held the previous letter sent to the same recipient, thus permitting the reconstruction and recognition of the key features of a given transaction. At the end of each volume was an alphabetical list of letters classified by recipient and destination, with the relative sequence of page numbers in the volume in question.
5. The distinction, among the set of 34, of a series of letters sent by Ingham in response to Vincenzo Florio confirms the existence of the two phases and is further confirmed by the observation that Ingham took a total of 182 days to reply to letters in the first period, and only 82 days in the second period.
6. As the contents of each letter differ and regard various types of business, the number of letters classified in the tables is greater than the total of 34.

7. Concerning the contents of the correspondence, it is interesting to note the language used in the letters written by a British merchant working in Sicily and writing in Italian, transcribed on his behalf. The mixture of three languages is frequently evident, such as in the transformation of English terms into Sicilian, especially names (the American ship *Laurence*) or use of the Sicilian word for goods (*Zuccaro*, *Sigarri* and *Summaccu*). Thus the evolution of the language is favoured by the activation of international trade relations and encounters an important means of communication in bookkeeping.
8. The term *carato* corresponds to a partnership share, generally a 25th or 24th part of the financial investment related to the management *in gabella* of a tuna fishery. For more about the economic and risk-related characteristics of investment in tuna fishing, as well as the role of the *gabelloto*, meaning he who was called upon to manage relations between the fishery workers (*tonnaroti*), the other partners (*caratari*) and the owner (Sarà, 1983; Lentini, 1986).
9. The British cultural environment brought to light the need to intensify and improve the use of bookkeeping in trade, with the aim of keeping precise records of business conducted and profits earned. Accounting history studies have revealed the significant spread of the double entry method in Britain. To understand how widespread the Italian double entry method was and indirectly to what extent the British Protestant culture indirectly influenced the adoption of this method for use in trade (Catturi, 1988; Mussari, 1988). In the early years of the eighteenth century the British had such a clear idea of the importance, effectiveness and spread of the double entry bookkeeping method that they organized many specific training events and printed related information, publicized through frequent advertisements in newspapers on the courses held in London academies at the time (Catturi, 1988, pp. 353, 358). The British began to elaborate upon the Italian method as early as 1543, with the work of Hugh Oldcastle from London, who was directly inspired by Paciolo. In the seventeenth century the method was further refined, with numerous treatises starting to "bend" the tool to the specific needs of commerce (Mussari, 1988, p. 458).
10. According to Catturi (1992) the double entry bookkeeping method followed a circular path over the centuries. From the first formulations and layouts used by late Middle Ages merchants in Italy to its spread throughout Europe; and from the refinements in line with the demands of eighteenth-century European merchants to its new and broader diffusion in markets around the world, including Italy and Sicily.
11. In addition to the work of Benjamin Booth, other English texts published in the second half of the eighteenth century can be mentioned by way of example. See, in this sense, the works of James Dodson (1750), John Williamson Fulton (1800) and Patrick Kelly (1801).
12. Booth's proposed list (1789, p. 7) comprises the following volumes: (1) Cash Book; (2) Bill Book; (3) Invoice Book inward, Bought Book or Book of Imports; (4) Invoice Book outward, Day Book, or Book of Exports; (5) Waste Book; (6) Journal; (7) Ledger; (8) Account of Sales Book; (9) Account Current Book. Booth specifies that a merchant should also keep other books, including the Order Book, Letter Book, Petty Cash Book, Debenture Book and Diary.
13. In contrast, those who sought to illustrate and clarify the problems related to bookkeeping using the Italian method in the first half of the same century focused at length on the "debtor and creditor method" (Mussari, 1988).
14. It should be pointed out that particular systems of measurement were used in Sicily at the time. The unit of currency was the *Onze* (*Oz*). One *Onza* corresponded to 3 *Ducati* and to 30 *Tarì* (*t*). In some of his letters Benjamin Ingham provides information about the exchange rate between the *Oz*. and the pound

or dollar. For example, in his letters of 15 February 1834 and 19 February 1839 a pound sterling is worth 54 t, while a dollar is worth 12 t.

15. The company Ingham & Co. used an administrative period that did not correspond to a calendar year, but started on 1 July and ended on 30 June with the calculation of the results of business conducted. This obviously reflects British accounting practice, as, to the present day, the financial year begins on 1 July. In the Ingham accounts the annual financial statement was accompanied by 6-month accounts on 31 December. In this context see the *Registri di Cassa*, *Squarcio* and *Libro Giornale* for the period July 1866–July 1867. Lastly, it should be pointed out that from March 1867 the habit was adopted of noting the accounts affected by each specific operation in the margin of the sums collected and/or paid column in the *Registri di Cassa*.
16. It should be pointed out that for the first eight transactions considered we do not have information from the *Libro Giornale*, as the volumes conserved in the archive at Marsala skip a period. Moreover note that, as in the descriptions of the transactions recorded (especially in the *Squarcio*) there is an original mixture of English and Italian, such as in the frequent use of the preposition "of" ("Zolfo of Licata" or *spese di mercanzie per nolo* of *diversi*).
17. The establishment of the first Sicilian steamship company in 1840 represents the apex of Benjamin Ingham's affirmation; while the establishment of the Società dei Piroscafi Postali in 1861, a few months after the death of the English entrepreneur, and the accompanying personal success of Vincenzo Florio represent the point in which the latter became the leading Sicilian businessman.
18. On the 150 years of Florio existence we could find documents in the archive not earlier than 1929. The Florio archive (conserved at the Legler Foundation in Bergamo) before this year a total loss.
19. The work of William Whitaker and especially Ignazio Florio Jr. was marked by a dedication to seeking the most diverse profit-making opportunities, probably greater than that of their predecessors, in an economic and business scenario that was beginning to demand the specialization of individual companies in response to more competitive markets.

REFERENCES

AA. VV. (1990) *L'archivio Ingham-Whitaker di Marsala*. Trapani: Libera Università del Mediterraneo.

Bedford, N.M. (1966) The international flow of accounting thought. *International Journal of Accounting* 1(2): 1–7.

Booth, B. (1979) *A complete system of book-keeping*, 1789. In: Bywater, M.F. (ed.), Historic accounting literature), Vol. 19. London: Scholar Press and TokyoYushodo Press.

Boyns, T. and Edwards, J.R. (1995) Accounting systems and decision-making in the Mid-Victorian period: The case of the Consett Iron Company. *Business History* 37(3): 28–51.

Boyns, T. and Edwards, J.R. (1996) Change agents and the dissemination of accounting technology: Wales' basic industries, c.1750–c.1870. *Accounting History* 1(1): 9–34.

Brancato, F. (1991) I "mercanti" inglesi nell'Ottocento in Sicilia: Vincenzo Florio nei rapporti con Ingham. In: AA. VV (ed.), *L'Economia dei Florio. Una famiglia di imprenditori borghesi dell'800*. Palermo: Sellerio Editore, pp. 21–34.

Candela, S. (1986) *I Florio*. Palermo: Sellerio Editore.

Carnegie, G.D. and Napier, C.J. (2002) Exploring comparative international accounting history. *Accounting, Auditing & Accountability Journal* 15(5): 689–718.

Carnegie, G.D. and Parker, R.H. (1996) The transfer of accounting technology to the southern hemisphere: The case of William Butler Yaldwyn. *Accounting, Business and Financial History* 6(1): 23–49.

Carnegie, G.D. and Varker, S.A. (1995) Edward Wild: Advocate of simplification and an organised profession in colonial Australia. *The Accountig Historians Journal* 22(2): 131–149.

Cassandro, P.E. (1975) *Le rilevazioni aziendali.* Bari: Cacucci Editore.

Catturi, G. (1987) *La scrittura in partita doppia come mezzo di comunicazione tra operatori economici di differenti aree territoriali*, Saggi di Economia Aziendale per Lino Azzini. Milan: Giuffré.

Catturi, G. (1988) *La diffusione in Inghilterra del metodo italiano di contabilità documentata dalle inserzioni pubblicitarie: 1700–1720*, Scritti di Economia Aziendale per Egidio Giannessi. Pisa: Pacini.

Catturi, G. (1989) *Teorie contabili e scenari economico-aziendali.* Padua: Cedam.

Catturi, G. (1992) Cultura aziendale e strumenti per il controllo della gestione. *Studi & Informazioni*, no. 4.

Catturi G. (1992) *Le "onde della conoscenza" degli strumenti di controllo gestionale ed i "nuovi eremiti"*, in Intervento al IV Convegno Nazionale della SISR, Perugia 2–3 ottobre 1997.

Catturi, G. (1997) *Le "onde della conoscenza" degli strumenti di controllo gestionale ed i nuovi eremiti*, in Atti del IV convegno nazionale di storia della Ragioneria, Perugia, pp. 75–101.

Catturi, G. and Di Pietra, R. (2001) I valori toscani si diffondono nell'ambiente londinese, Storia di traffici mercantili via mare e di flussi finanziari agli inizi del XVIII secolo. *Quaderni Senesi di Economia Aziendale e di Ragioneria, Serie interventi n. 66*, Siena.

D'Aleo, C. and Girgenti, S. (1992) *I Whitaker e il capitale inglese tra l'Ottocento e il Novecento in Sicilia*, Trapani: Libera Università del Mediterraneo.

Di Pietra, R. (1996) *Il "Rapporto d'affari" fra Benjamin Ingham e Vincenzo Florio, Cultura economico—aziendale e rilevazioni contabili nella Sicily del XIX secolo.* Padua: Cedam.

Dodson, J. (1979) The accountant, or, the method of book-keeping deduced from clear principles, and illustrated by a variety of examples, London 1750. In: Bywater, M. F. (ed.), *Historic accounting literature*, Vol. 19. London: Scholar Press and Tokyo: Yushodo Press.

Fleischman, R.K. and Parker, L.D. (1990) Managerial accounting early in the British industrial revolution: The Carron Company, a case study. *Accounting and Business Research* 20(79): 211–221.

Fleischman, R.K. and Parker, L.D. (1991) British entrepreneurs and pre-industrial revolution evidence of cost management. *The Accounting Review* 66(2): 361–375.

Fleischman, R.K. and Parker, L.D. (1992) The cost accounting environment in the British industrial revolution iron industry. *Accounting, Business and Financial History* 2(2): 141–160.

Giuffrida, R. and Lentini, R. (1985) *L'età dei Florio.* Palermo: Sellerio Editore.

Gray, S.J. (1988) Towards a theory of cultural influence on the development of accounting systems internationally. *Abacus* 24(1): 1–15.

Kelly, P. (1980) The elements of book-keeping both by single and double entry: Comprising a system of merchants accounts, founded on real business, arranged according to modern practice, and adapted to the use of schools, London, 180. In: Bywater, M. F. (ed.), *Historic accounting literature*, Vol. 19. London: Scholar Press and Tokyo: Yushodo Press.

Jones, H. (1985) *Accounting, costing and cost estimation.* Cardiff: University of Wales Press.

Lentini, R. (1986) Economia e storia delle tonnare in Sicily. In: Consolo, V. (ed.), *La pesca del tonno in Sicilia*. Palermo: Sellerio, pp. 14–37.

Lentini, R. (1993) *Modelli di imprenditorialità nell'800 siciliano: i Florio e gli Ingham-Whitaker*, in Atti del Secondo Convegno Nazionale di Storia della Ragioneria, Roma: Rirea, pp. 129–140.

Merrill, R.S. (1968) The study of technology. In: Sills, D.L. (ed.), *International encyclopedia of the social sciences*, Vol. 15. London and New York: Macmillan, pp.576–589.

Mussari, R. (1988) La base teorico-pratica del metodo partiduplistico nella Gran Bretagna del XVIII secolo. *RIREA*, n° 9/10.

Nobes, C. and Parker, R.H. (2008) *Comparative international accounting*, tenth edition. Harlow, Essex, UK: Pearson Education Limited.

Parker, R.H. (1976) Explaining national differences in consolidated accounts. In: Lee, T.A. and Parker, R.H. (eds.), *The evolution of corporate reporting*. Sunbury-on-Thames: Nelson.

Parker, R.H. (1989) Importing and exporting accounting: An introduction. In: Hopwood, A.G. (ed.). *International pressures for accounting change*. London: Prentice Hall International, pp. 7–29.

Perrone, E. (1995) *Il giovane ragioniere dei Fugger e la divulgazione "post-pacioliana" della partita doppia nel Cinquecento*, in Atti del Convegno internazionale Straordinario per celebrare frà Luca Pacioli, Venezia, 9–12 aprile 1994, Milano: IPSOA.

Pulejo, L. (1993) *La diversificazione dell'attività economica degli Ingham-Whitaker*, in Atti del Secondo Convegno nazionale di Storia della Ragioneria, Roma: Rirea, pp. 177–190.

Robertson, J. and Funnell, W. (2012) The Dutch East-India Company and accounting for social capital at the dawn of modern capitalism 1602–1623. *Accounting, Organizations and Society* 37: 342–360.

Sarà, R. (1983) *Tonni e tonnare, Una civiltà una cultura*. Trapani: Libera Università di Trapani.

Williamson Fulton, J. (1980) British-Indian book-keeping. A new system of double entry and progressive adjustment; exemplified in a variety of compendious methods, for the practical purposes as well of the private gentleman as of the merchant, London, 1800. In: Bywater, M.F. (ed.), *Historic accounting literature*, Vol. 19. London: Scholar Press and Tokyo: Yushodo Press.

Yamey, B.S. (1981) Some reflections on the writing of a general history of accounting. *Accounting and Business Research* 11(42): 127–135.

11 Faith, Food and Benevolentia in the Sarzana Cathedral Chapter

Evidences from the Eighteenth Century

Arianna Lazzini and Simone Lazzini

INTRODUCTION

This study is the result of a renewed interest by researchers in the study of the clergy and religious orders from an accounting history perspective (Laughlin, 1988; Booth, 1993; Quattrone, 2004; Di Pietra and Landi, 2007; Baldarelli, 2013; Bigoni et al., 2013; Bigoni and Funnell, 2014; Madonna et al., 2014; Poli and Gatti, 2014; Dobie, 2015). The economic role played by the clergy, both in the mediaeval and in the modern era, is well known. Churches, monasteries and convents were not only mere places of worship or caskets of precious art treasures but also the pillars of the entire economic and social system. They were the repositories of culture and education, the places where intellectuals were trained to maintain, enhance and transmit knowledge. The clergy played a primary role throughout the history of accounting (Carmona and Ezzamel, 2006); notable bookkeepers and accountants such as Fra Luca Pacioli, Angelo Pietra and his disciple Lodovico Florio belonged to religious orders (Antoni, 1983; Antonelli and D'Alessio, 2011; Gallizzi, 2012).

In addition, the church possessed, and accumulated over the centuries, large patrimonial estates, buildings, financial resources, and the rights and privileges on property and persons as a result of the endowment of emperors, nobles or, more simply, the legacy of the faithful (Landi, 2005).

Starting from these premises, the chapter aims to study how a specific subsystem of the secular clergy, the Chapter of the Cathedral of Sarzana, managed its properties and privileges in the eighteenth century. The period analyzed is particularly important for the history of the Chapter because it represents the passage from its full flowering to decadence.

The breadth and complexity of this research subject has required the main objective to be broken down into subobjectives in order to analyze one section of the topic at a time. First of all, the following aspects had to be clarified: the organizational and governance structure and the methodologies and tools of control and accountability related to both the management of property and privileges and the work of the Chapter's members.

The town of Sarzana is a particularly interesting case because, for several centuries, it was the territory of the ancient Diocese of Luni, therefore a unified centre of ecclesiastical tradition. This ecclesiastical district was identified, beyond political and feudal divisions, with that common geographical, linguistic and civil region recognized as *lunensis provincia*. Agriculture was the primary industry in the economic system of the town. The most common crops were wheat, rye, grapes and, in the hills, olive trees. Although wheat, rye and olive oil were sold in the local market of Sarzana, wine was exported in large quantities, even to foreign countries.

We used the Chapter's archival documents stored in the Niccolò V library of Sarzana as the primary source for our research. The analysis is mainly based on the archival records concerning the relationships between the Chapter and agriculture/food in the eighteenth century.

The chapter is so structured: the next section defines the theoretical framework of the analysis of the national and international literature; then the historical social and economic context is analyzed. In the history of accounting research, several have recommended a contextual approach (Hopwood, 1983; Loft, 1986) to liberate the study from the constraints of the present time and set the subject in its context. According to Laughlin (1988), accounting systems are not context-free technical phenomena; rather, they find their scope in the social and historical context that is implicit in any organization. Focusing on the history and characteristics of the Sarzana Cathedral Chapter is therefore of paramount importance to facilitate the understanding of the heterogeneous framework of its development.

Next, the chapter analyzes and discusses the documents related to the relationships between the Chapter and the rural world. Finally, conclusions and implications for further research are explored.

LITERATURE REVIEW

This chapter has been developed around the basic idea that governance, if referred to as "the systems by which organizations are directed, controlled and made accountable" (Cornforth, 2003), is a central topic in all times and in every kind of organization (Paisey and Paisey, 2011; Jones, 2008).

Governance issues arise in every context in which responsibilities and powers are assigned to different actors. Consequently, the requirement arises for the use of adequate accounting and control tools (Fleischman and Parker, 1991).

When governance, accounting and control issues are studied from a historical perspective and in specific contexts, such as religious institutions, they take on peculiar features that require adapting the typical perspective of analysis to their definition (Hopwood, 1978; Burchell et al., 1980; Berry et al., 1985).

In accounting history literature, accounting is defined in several ways. Adopting a broad definition to emphasize the aspects related to quantification and calculation accounting can be referred to as the "genealogies of calculation" (Miller and Napier, 1993), or differently as the attribution of financial values to a wide range of social practices to make them visible and calculable (Miller, 1990). According to previous studies (Paisey and Paisey, 2011) and consistently with the main purpose of this chapter, Miller's approach is considered to be more useful for the study of religious institutions.

Likewise, the perspective selected for the study of governance issues has to be used consistently with the main purpose of the research and the social and historical context. In accordance with current studies and researches, the perspective adopted in this chapter is based on the concept of governmentality proposed by Foucault (1980), which is considered by the literature to be a useful representation of the rational connotations that characterize modern states (Lai et al., 2012). The concept of governmentality has been promoted to an influential position, thus becoming one of the most frequently quoted notions (Carter et al., 2002), even in the field of accounting (Sargiacomo, 2008, 2009; Lai et al., 2012; Bigoni et al., 2013; Bigoni and Funnell, 2014; Madonna et al., 2014).

The idea of governmentality can be defined as "the set of methods and procedures used to direct human behaviour," "the conduct of conduct"—a term that ranges from "governing the self" to "governing others" (Foucault, 1977, 1980).

The governmentality approach appears to be mostly suitable in the analysis and study of accounting practices in religious institutions (Laughlin, 1988; Quattrone, 2004; Nahar and Yaacob, 2011), and can be used to understand and explain the mechanisms of millenarian clerical power when the church was the dominant social institution and owned and managed huge material resources (Landi, 2005; Di Pietra and Landi, 2007). In Foucault's perspective, the basic idea of human government arises within the Christian church, where it actually became a power, the pastoral power conceived as an art to govern separately from the political power (Bigoni and Funnell, 2014). Pastoral power is therefore considered the embryonic seed of government power (Foucault, 1981).

A new way to exercise power arose from the seventeenth and eighteenth centuries. Governments were faced with significant increases in the population and consequently in the level of expenditure; the population became a new subject for government, in addition to territories (Foucault, 1991). New social and cultural models arose. The Enlightenment vision began to emerge and evolve. The ideals of cosmopolitanism and individualism determined the need for guiding behaviour in a renewed and completely new way.

In the history of the Roman Church, the requirement of managing things and people constantly existed. An interesting perspective on this dichotomy was proposed by Laughlin (1984), who made a distinction between the "sacred" and the "profane"; the former was related to the "management of souls" and the latter to the "management of duties." In his studies based on the Church of England, Laughlin (1984, 1988) argued that the significance of accounting was connected with the relationship between the sacred and the profane. While the sacred is associated with the religious ends of the church, the profane is linked to its administrative functions, which also support the sacred. The profane could not be allowed to compete with the sacred (Laughlin, 1984). Following this direction, Booth (1992) considered that the sacred and the secular divide separates the "legitimate" part of a church from profane support activities. As accounting is a support activity, it is only tolerated and regarded as irrelevant for the life of the church. Such an approach has been strongly criticized by other scholars not only for the intrinsic limits of its assumptions (Hardy and Ballis, 2005; Jacobs, 2005), but also for its overall inability to interpret a context characterized by different ranges of religious institutions and beliefs (Bigoni et al., 2013).

A few considerations arise when trying to see the Roman Church within this context. Until the mid-nineteenth century, the Roman Church exercised temporal power explicitly and the Papal State was its highest expression. Temporal power certainly requires accounting systems and control mechanisms to manage duties, people and territories. Therefore, the profane side of the problem played a crucial role.

In the literature, there is a widespread opinion that the system of internal auditing is one of the most important mechanisms of delivering accountability and supports organizations in the monitoring and control of their operations. According to Anderson (1977, p. 72), mistakes may be made even "with the best of intentions." He defined mistakes as possible "errors in the end results of their work, needless inefficiencies in achieving those end results, or both." Any organization, to conduct its business efficiently and effectively, has to produce accounting information and needs auditing systems to minimize the effects of "endemic human failings" (Anderson, 1977). Accounting is therefore the basic element for the performance of any sort of control, even in religious organizations.

Considering the particular historical and social context analyzed and consistent with the main purpose of the chapter, we will investigate the role of accounting in the management of the relationship between the secular clergy and the rural world. Since the system of privileges enjoyed by clergy until the nineteenth century was of feudal origin, it seems particularly interesting to adopt the perspective of manorial accounting. There are many studies in the literature on manorial accounting, which is analyzed from different points of view (Stone, 1962; Chatfield, 1977; Postles, 1981; Noke, 1994; Harvey, 1999; Dodds, 2002). Harvey adopted a historical perspective in his analysis of the written form of manorial accounts and identified three main development stages: an early stage from 1200 to 1270, a second stage from 1270 to 1380 and a third stage from 1380 to 1530. While the first period was characterized by an embryonic form of accounting, with a large variety of forms produced mainly by religious entities, in the second period accounting became more standardized and detailed, to subsequently lose part of this detail in the third stage, when a greater percentage of demesnes were leased out (Harvey, 1999, pp. 25–40). Chatfield adopted an agency perspective in analyzing manorial and government accounting, while Dodds (2002) focused on the tithe and agrarian output. Postles (1981) and Noke (1991) conducted studies that focused more on the technical features of accounting and the legal aspect of the "excessus" balance; Stone (1962) and Postles (1994) investigated profit and loss accounting.

This chapter explores the topic of accounting with particular attention to two strictly related aspects: the financial control systems and accountability practices.

Consistent with an institutional perspective, the control and coordination mechanisms selected by an organization are affected by environmental rules and the social influence, such that they are forced by social rules to follow generally accepted conventions in shaping their forms and practices (Ingram and Simons 1995; Hung, 1998). Control practices are relatively formalized by organizations and used only for symbolic purposes (Meyer and Rowan 1977), while control over members is exercised by means of social and idiosyncratic measures.

Starting from these premises, this chapter will develop the theoretical framework described (Figure 11.1) in a subsystem of the secular clergy: the Chapter of a cathedral.

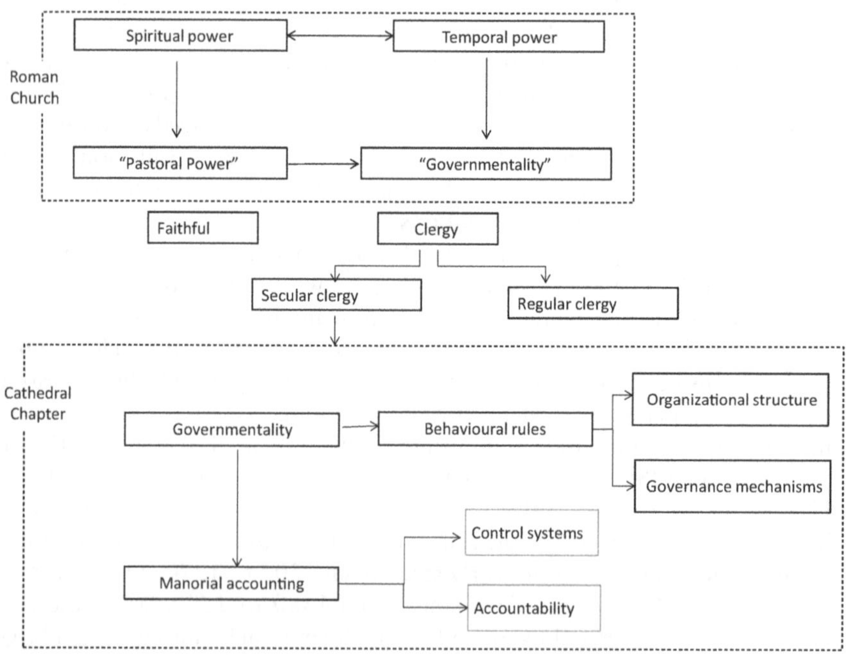

Figure 11.1 The theoretical framework

Source: Our processing

THE SOCIAL AND ECONOMIC CONTEXT

The seventeenth century was characterized by the rise of new social classes to guide states and the emergence of new movements of thought. Such new aspirations of the bourgeoisie are fully reflected in the Enlightenment, the new philosophical movement that harshly criticized metaphysics; in fact, all the knowledge was critically reviewed by the Enlightenment. Diderot's work entitled "Encyclopedia or Reasoned Dictionaries of Sciences, Arts and Crafts", published in 28 volumes between 1751 and 1772, is very important in this context. During that age, religion was also challenged with the intention to prune all superstitions from it. In the name of reason, not only intolerance, superstition and religious fanaticism were condemned, but also the legal status, the divine right of kings, the laws, the judicial systems, the privileges of the nobility and the clergy—in other words, all the residues of the Middle Ages. From a historical point of view, the sixteenth and seventeenth centuries were characterized by a depressive economic cycle. One of the possible causes highlighted by historians was the significant demographic decrease caused by the huge damages of wars, plague epidemics, famines and natural catastrophes (Cipolla, 1974).

In fact, the period was dramatically marked by the terrible plague epidemics of the 1630s, which spread in the northern and central parts of the Italian peninsula. The subsequent demographic decrease produced severe economic consequences in a system that based its wealth on agriculture. The reduction in the population caused a decrease in the demand for agricultural commodities, and the price of wheat and cereals was reduced in most of Western Europe (Cipolla, 1974). The value of land decreased, as did the related annuities.

During the period of the sixteenth and seventeenth centuries, the extension of the clergy's property was huge and included wealth and estates of inestimable value. Over that period, it was impossible to travel a road for more than a few miles or enter a town without finding a sacred or profane building that proved the presence of religion (Landi, 2005).

At that time, the papacy still aspired to the same power it had had during the Middle Ages and tried to defend its traditional spaces that were being undermined by the modern states with their redefinitions of borders.

Regarding landed property, feudal privileges such as grants, the perpetual lease system and the tithe were still widespread among both the secular and regular clergy (Landi, 2005). The tithe was a tax levied on property, based on the obligation to pay a percentage on the land's produce either in nature or in cash. It was collected by the church under its authority and used for purposes of general interest. The tithe was generally determined as one-tenth of the net produce of the land and had to be paid by all farmers. The tithe system mainly concerned cereals, vegetables, wine, fruits and livestock.

The perpetual lease system was another legacy of the feudal system and a typical feature of the clerical and secular manorial capitalism. Analyzed from a clerical point of view, the levels can be related to three main categories: enfranchised, perpetual lease and with obligation of Saint Mass.

The category on which we will focus our study is that of "perpetual lease levels," a sort of farming contract by which the owner (lessor) provided a plot of land to a second actor, the leaseholder (*livellario*), for a given amount of time in exchange for an annual fee or lease (*livello*). This relationship implied the subordination of the leaseholder to the lessor, who was the one who fixed terms and dictated the basic rules for the management of land.

With the introduction of the Siccardi laws (9 April 1850, n. 1013; 5 June, n. 1037), initially in force only in the Reign of Sardinia and then extended to the whole Reign of Italy, these manorial privileges were abolished (Anselmi, 1993). Consequently, the temporal power of the highest religious institutions, including the Chapters, started to decrease rapidly.

ORGANIZATION AND GOVERNANCE OF THE SARZANA CATHEDRAL CHAPTER

Cathedral Chapters constitute a first example of collective political and religious organizations established in the barbarian age and then developed during the Carolingian era (Rotelli, 2005). The Canons of the Cathedral Chapters were initially institutions responsible for leading a life in common and assisting the bishop in the care of the *animarum* and in the administration of the local church. With the passage of time, the Chapters became privileged organs both for the functions they were charged to carry out and for the privileges granted to them, which transformed them into true centres of power of the city. The Canons were often appointed from among the members of the upper classes, the elite of the town, so that they could play a major role in the local church.

Although the origins of the Sarzana Cathedral Chapter cannot be defined with accuracy, it can be assumed that it already existed at the end of the tenth century. In an early period, the seat of the Chapter was Luni. The transfer of the office to Sarzana was implemented only around 1201 after an agreement between the bishop and the Chapter, and with the consent of Rome (Gentile, 1912).

From an organizational point of view, the number of Canons in the Sarzana Cathedral varied over the centuries. The maximum number of Canons was determined following the provisions of the Council of Aachen (816 B.C.). The maximum number was determined in relation to the profitability of the Chapter (Polonio, 1990).

The number of members ranged from a minimum of 12 to a maximum of 16 (in 1206) with the possibility, sometimes, to deviate from that limit by admitting supernumerary members. To supernumerary members were paid half the ordinary prebend. Most of the Canons came from the noblest and most prestigious families of the city, and some of them even had academic qualifications.

The Statute of 1228 contemplated that the members of the Chapter had to be at most 14, including six priests (including the Dean), four deacons (including the archdeacon) and four subdeacons. With the introduction, in 1368, of a new Statute, the number of the members was reduced to 12, of whom six were to be priests, three deacons and three subdeacons. At the outset of his mandate, each new member had to pay a certain sum to the farmer. This amount was used to increase daily distributions and, after the death of the cleric, for the votes of his soul.

The organization of the Chapter was rigidly hierarchical, reflecting the graduation income level, which consisted of a fixed income (stipends) and personal emoluments (choir distributions—*distribuzioni corali*).

Based on the provisions set forth in the 1368 Statute, being entitled to receive the prebend was conditional to being a resident of Sarzana for at least 8 months per year, a period that was reduced to 6 months after 1389. However, the residence obligation was not personal, as a Canon could be replaced by another member of the clergy, provided that he was of the same order and enjoyed no other benefit in the same area. The residence obligation did not apply to those who were authorized to follow a course of studies as commuting students or those who conducted any institutional activity on behalf of the bishop or the Chapter itself. A peculiar provision was the one with which the Sarzana chapter justified the distance from the sear even for reasons of "personal security" (Polonio, 1990).

The 1368 Statute also said:

> *item statuterun quod si dividentur praebendae qua ad praesens sunt communes, non residentes nihil percepiant de praebenda sua ultra staria decem frumentis et tunc procurator generalis dicti capituli sive massarius exigat fructus et redditus praebendae distincte illius canonici absenti non residentis, et convertantur in commune utilitatem canonicoum residentium.*

This meant that those who had lost their title to the prebend still retained all the related economic benefits, as they could rely on the distribution of 10 bushels of wheat per year.

Conversely, choir distributions were determined as a function of the daily and monthly presence of the person in the life of the community. A register was kept for this purpose called *puntationes* where the numbers of presences in the community and religious life (Masses, vespers, etc.) were daily annotated for each cleric. If the funds available for the Chapter were not sufficient for the disbursement of daily distributions, each Canon was required to use a portion of his prebend to cover the need, with the risk of a negative balance between the "daily token" and the personal disbursement. This mechanism implied that a given number of absences by certain members was positive for others, with a greater rooting in the territory.

The system of rules, statutory and not, established by the Chapter was necessary to achieve the life and behaviours of its members. This system was consistent with the governmentality idea perceived as the "conduct" of the "conduct," as a set of rules and technics with the aim to direct human behaviours.

From this perspective, the same mechanism to record the presence in the register of *puntationes* to tie the value of the choral distributions to participation in the collective life can be considered a clear example of an instrument to direct the conduct. More specifically, a monetary incentive was used to motivate the members to take part in the community life.

The governmentality paradigm was also carried out by the construction of an organizational structure of hierarchic type (see Figure 11.2) and by the governance mechanisms based on the proxy of power and responsibilities among the members.

The first authority of the Chapter was the archdeacon, who replaced the bishop in religious, liturgical and pastoral tasks. The archdeacon had the highest authority in the field of penance. In the community life of the clerics, the provost carried out a number of important functions; he administered the temporal affairs of the Chapter under the Statute's regulatory framework, as *maior circa ea que temporalia sunt* (Polonio, 1990). The provost assigned new Canons seats in the choir, in the Capitular Hall, in the refectory and in a room for living. It was his task to support those who made mistakes in the performance of any duty, and, in some cases, he could suspend them from their duties for a certain amount of time. However, the removal from the post of member of the Chapter could only be the result of a collegial decision by the Chapter. For the peculiar responsibility of the provost and the role of the archdeacon, a special remuneration was determined

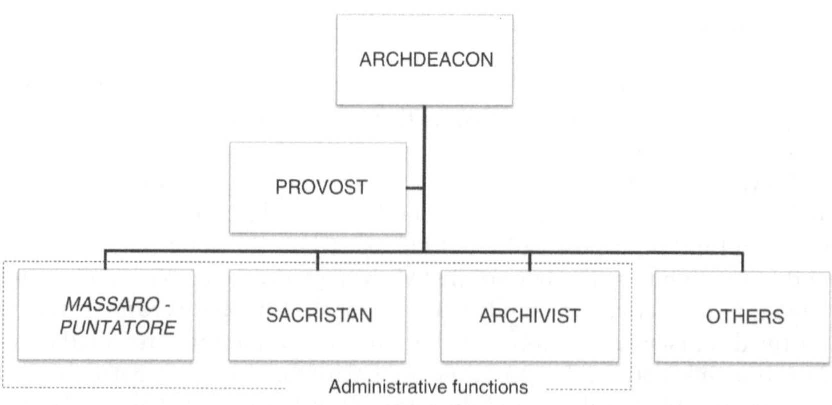

Figure 11.2 The hierarchical organization of the Chapter

consisting of 10 bushels of wheat (corresponding to a container of about 20 liters), plus those to which each Canon was entitled. If the archdeacon or the provost were not permanently resident in Sarzana for the minimum period established of eight months, they received only 50% of their annuity (five bushels of wheat).

The provost or, in his place, the *massaro*, annotated the resident canons, the period of their residence and their canonical hours, and then distributed the daily fee, thus playing the role of *puntatore*.

Unlike the archdeacon and the provost, the *massaro* had no permanent rank but performed his tasks on a temporary basis. Both the Canons and the chaplains of the Chapter could be appointed as *massaro* with an annual election that took place on the day of the feast of the Most Precious Blood. The task of the *massaro* consisted in dividing and distributing income, revenues, alms and all the other assets for the Luni Chapter and canons according to the accurate instructions set forth in the Statutes. The *massaro* was the person who administered ordinary things. In addition to filling the Chapter's income register and another record of leftovers, he had to give due remuneration to the chaplain and his assistant clerics, hand out charity on behalf of the Chapter and pay the expenses incurred for feasts and other celebrations.

The sacristan's task was to manage all the monetary and nonmonetary resources of the sacristy, the lighting of the church, the purchase and maintenance of sacred vestments, and the conservation of furnishings, ornaments and books. In particular, this task included the storage of the capitular seal.

The archivist was charged with archiving and preserving the main documents of the Chapter.

The Sarzana Chapter, with its common funds, sustained a chaplain and two clerics whose task was to accompany the Chapter's canons during their journeys and assist priests during celebrations. Although they did not belong to the Chapter, they were required to attend religious functions, could take care of the souls (*cura animorum*), had to swear faith to the Statutes and were obliged to give the alms received to the *massaro*.

As regards the governance of the Chapter, in spite of the accurate assignment of tasks, every general decision had to be made by the entire Chapter with a general assembly. Based on the indications of the Statute, the Chapter met the first Friday of each month upon call by the archdeacon or deacon. The quorum for the meeting was one third of the entitled members. Resolutions were made with the majority of attendees.

DISCUSSION: FAITH, FOOD ACCOUNTING AND ACCOUNTABILITY

The analysis of the documents stored in the archive of the Sarzana Cathedral Chapter in the Niccolò V library of the Sarzana seminar and kept in the building of the historical archive of the Diocese of La Spezia, Sarzana and

Brugnato allowed us to trace the accounting methods used to manage the accounts of the Chapter's assets over the period being examined.

The main purpose of the analysis is to understand the operation of the accountability system and the related mechanisms of control practiced by the Chapter by adopting a manorial accounting perspective. In order to investigate the adopted accounting methodologies accurately, the research focuses on the books from the year 1779. The year was chosen on the basis of the state of preservation of the documents and their legibility.

The bookkeeping activity was the task of one of the clerics of the Chapter, the *massaro*, who recorded the harvest, revenues "in money for leases and other," and cash flows each year in a special register.

The logic scheme of the annual reporting is represented in Figure 11.3.

For each year, the *massaro* had to indicate on a form the amounts produced of each of the following products of the land under the authority of the Chapter: wheat, corn, broad beans, beans, lupin beans, switchgrass and panic grass, scandella, rye and mixture, olive oil and wine. The information was then accounted for in a section called *introito*—harvest or revenue—which was counterbalanced by a second section recorded on the opposite mirror page of the register called *esito*—outcome.

The method used was obviously balancing, as the *introito* section contained the values regarding the amounts of the fruits obtained, while the *esito* section reported their allocation (sale, remuneration of the clerics, remuneration of farmers). The measurement unit for the accounts in the first sections of the register was the amount of foodstuff expressed in different measures depending on the specific product.

The measurement unit used to record solid products was the bushel, whose multiples were the large *mina* for wheat and the small *mina* for the other cereals. Submultiples were the *secchia* (bucket) and the *quartaro* (quarter). Fluids were mainly measured in barrels, which were divided into *sogi*, flasks, *mezzette* and *boccali* (mugs) for wine, in ounces and pounds for oil. The value attributed to each of said measures and their ratio varied between markets, which made exchanges rather difficult and required the use of conversion tables.

A special care was devoted to the accounting of wheat, which comprised the largest revenue share of the Chapter by virtue of the associated agrarian contracts (tithes, leases or levels, rents) (see Figure 11.4). The amount of the harvest was subdivided based on the quantities due to the Chapter depending on the applicable agrarian contract. The following contracts existed: wheat levels, wheat tithes and wheat rents.

Although levels and tithes required payment in kind, rents were paid with mixed methods; a portion of the tax due was paid in nature (wheat) and another portion in money.

The rent portion paid in cash was recorded in a special section of the register called "List of collections, rents and other in cash" ("*riscossi, affitti e altro a contanti*"). For each contract owner, this section contained annotations of the person's name, date of payment and amount paid.

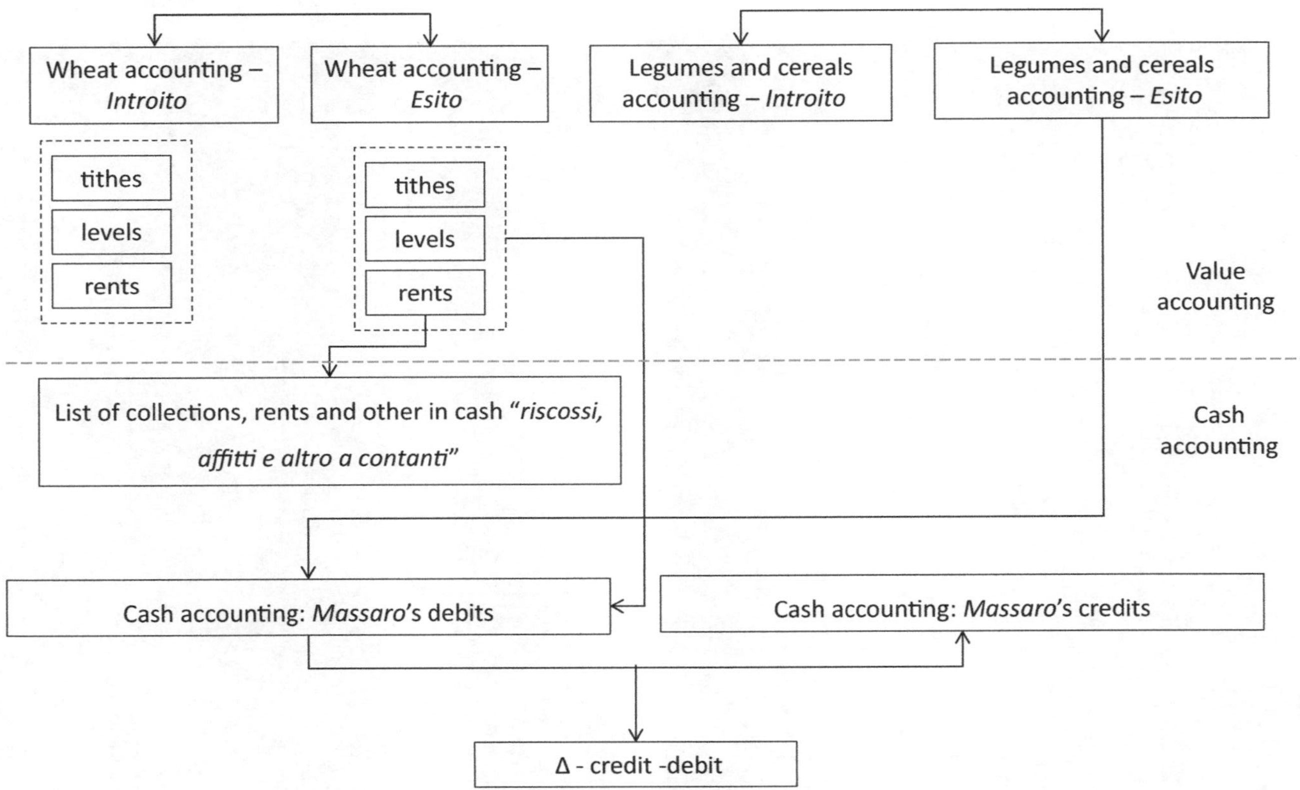

Figure 11.3 The system of reporting: scheme

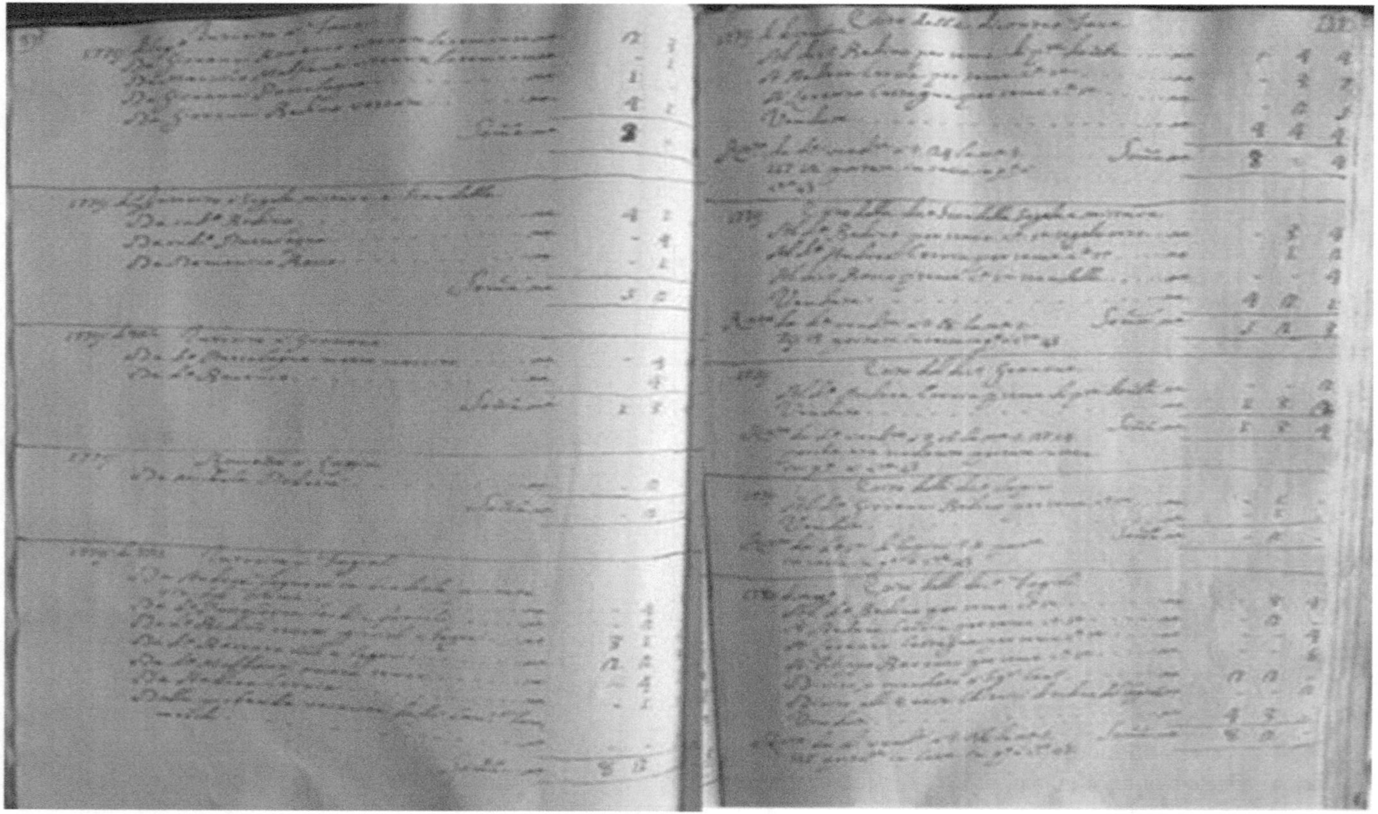

Figure 11.4 The accounting of foodstuffs

The accounting unit used was money, with its multiples; the *soldo* corresponded to 12 *denari* and the *lira* to 20 *soldi*. Unlike *denaro*, *soldo* and *lira* were exclusively accounting units because they never had a metal equivalent.

The analysis of these registers shows how, in addition to wheat, the following other products were grown in the Chapter's crops: broad beans, rye, mixture, scandella, corn, lupin beans, beans, millet, panic grass, olives and grapes. Evidence of the amounts contributed by each sharecropper (revenues) was systematically kept for each of these foodstuffs—*Introito*. The opposite section, called *Esito* (Outcome) contained annotations of the amounts sold, transferred for seeds or allocated to clerics or other third parties.

The Chapter's bookkeeping continued with a section devoted to cash flows. The cash account was also divided into two sections, one called "Debit cash of the canon Martinelli, *massaro* for the year 1779," and the other called "Credit cash of the canon Martinelli, *massaro* for the year 1779."

The credit cash account contained all the amounts due by the Chapter to third parties, and the debit cash account contained all the receipts in cash from collections and sales.

The breakeven amount after debit and credit was annotated below the account and then repeated in the records of the subsequent year in the debit cash account.

The rights and duties of the *massaro*, who played the role of administrator, refer to the Chapter; the *massaro*'s debit amounts must therefore be intended as credits of the Chapter and, vice versa, for debit amounts (Marchi, 1867).

The Chapter required periodic and systematic checks of these books. Two clerics, in the role of auditors, periodically audited the books kept by the *massaro*. This form of control can be considered as an embryonic form of internal auditing practice (Figure 11.5).

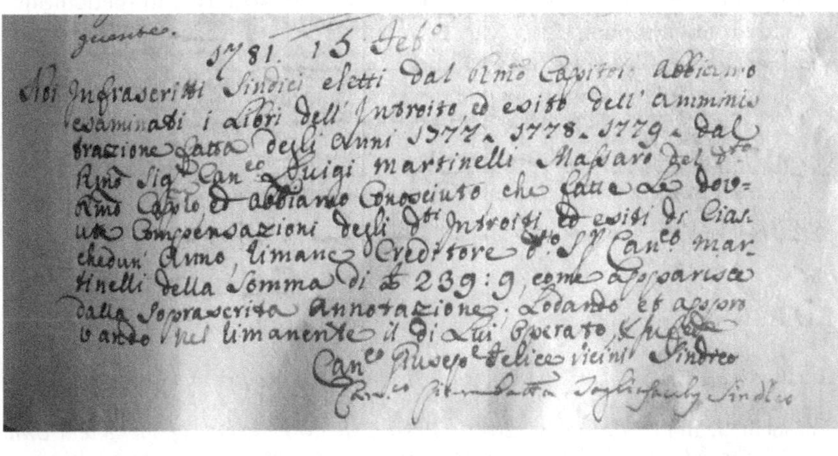

1781. 15 Feb.°
Noi Infrascritti Sindici eletti dal R.mo Capitolo abbiamo
esaminati i libri dell'Introito ed esito dell'amminis-
trazione fatta degli anni 1777. 1778. 1779. dal
R.mo Sig.r Can.co Luigi Martinelli Massaro del d.to
R.mo Capitolo ed abbiamo conosciuto che fatte le dov-
ute compensazioni degli d.ti Introiti ed esiti di cias-
chedun anno, rimane Creditore d.o S.r Can.co Mar-
tinelli della somma di £ 239:9, come apparisce
dalla soprascritta annotazione. Lodando et appro-
vando nel rimanente il di lui operato
Can.co Giuseppe Felice Vicini Sindico

Figure 11.5 The auditing report

CONCLUSIONS AND IMPLICATIONS FOR FURTHER RESEARCH

Most of the previous studies concerning the clerical institutions have been focused mainly on the features of the regular clergy. More limited attention has been given, instead, to the study of the secular clergy as well as to those concerning Chapters, although in terms of social and political impact, these institutions played a central role in the life of the Church for many centuries.

The study has highlighted how strong the governance mechanisms were and the tools of accountability and control systems set up by the Chapter to guide the behaviour of its members in order to avoid or limit opportunistic behaviour.

The management of landed property and its foodstuffs constitute the primary source of livelihood for the chapter, which used them for purposes of consumption and for sale. From the accounting evidence seems to emerge a dual need for control: control over the amount and control over the value. This duality reflects the object and the typical features of the manorial accounting approach to which is necessary to add control of the cash.

The same need for accountability is demonstrated by a systematic record-keeping accounting system organized in sections, operating with a balancing logic and characterized by mutual ties. The setting of the accounting system was based on the theories specific to their context.

The system developed by the Chapter of the Cathedral of Sarzana to control the behaviour of its members is therefore characterized by a double soul: a first component is directed to the control and management of its members' behaviour, a second to the control of the performance of subjects with administrative proxies.

The first perspective is related to governance problems. From this perspective emerges a rigid hierarchical connotation that permeates the entire organization. The number of members, their roles in the daily life of the chapter and the rules of estate management were strictly and meticulously regulated. Such a perspective can be related to the governmentality framework elaborated by Foucault (1980).

The second perspective is related to the accounting controls. Periodically, the accounting records were subjected to verification by persons appointed by the chapter's members in order to check the good and proper keeping of records.

In conclusion, a strong requirement for instruments of accountability and control seems to emerge.

REFERENCES

Amaduzzi, A. (1957) *L'azienda nel suo sistema e nell'ordine delle sue rilevazioni*. Turin: Utet.

Antonelli, V. and D'Alessio, R. (2011) *Gli studi di Storia della Ragioneria dall'Unita d' Italia ad oggi. Evidenze, interpretazioni e comparazioni in tema di autori, opera, oggetto e metodo*. Milan: Franco Angeli.

Antoni, T. (1983) Due religiosi nella storia della Ragioneria: Angelo Pietra, benedettino (XVI section) e Lodovico Flori, gesuita (XVII section). *Rivista Italiana di Ragioneria ed economia aziendale*, November.

Anselmi, L. (1993) *Percorsi economico aziendali per le pubbliche amministrazioni*. Turin: Giappichelli.

Berry, A., Capps, T., Cooper, D., Ferguson, P., Hopper, T. and Lowe, E. (1985) Management control in an area of the NCB: Rationales of accounting practices in a public enterprise. *Accounting, Organizations and Society* 10(1): 3–28.

Bigoni, M., Deidda Gagliardo, E. and Funnell, W. (2013) Rethinking the sacred and secular divide. *Accounting, Auditing & Accountability Journal* 26(4): 567–594.

Bigoni, M., Deidda Gagliardo, E. and Funnel, W. (2014) Contabilità e potere pastorale. Il contributo delle tecniche contabili al rafforzamento del potere della Chiesa nel XV secolo. *Contabilità e Cultura Aziendale* 2: 55–83.

Bigoni M. and Funnell W. (2014). Ancestors of governmentality: Accounting and pastoral power in the 15th century. *Critical Perspectives on Accounting* 27: 160–176.

Booth, P. (1993) Accounting in Churches: A research framework and an agenda. *Accounting, Auditing and Accountability Journal* 5(4): 37–67.

Burchell, S., Clubb, C., Hopwood, A., Hughes, J. and Nahapiet, J. (1980) The roles of accounting in organizations and society. *Accounting, Organizations and Society* 5(1): 5–27.

Carmona, S. (2004) Accounting history research and its diffusion in an international context. *Account History* 9(3): 389–402.

Carmona, S. and Ezzamel, M. (2006) Accounting and religion: A historical perspective. *Accounting History* 11(2):117–127.

Carnegie, G.D. and Napier, C.J. (1996) Critical and interpretive histories: Insights into accounting's present and future through its past. *Accounting, Auditing and Accountability Journal* 3(9): 7–39.

Carter, C., McKinlay, A. and Rowlinson, M. (2002) Governmentality, power and organization. *Management & Organizational History* 7(1): 1–13.

Chatfield, M. (1977) *A history of accounting thought*. New York: Robert E. Krieger.

Cipolla, C.M. (1974) *Storia economica dell'Europa pre-industriale*. Bologna: Il Mulino.

Cornforth, C. (2003) *The governance of public and non-profit organizations*. London: Routledge.

Di Pietra, R. and Landi, F., (2007) *Clero, economia e contabilità in Europa: tra Medioevo ed età contemporanea*. Rome: Carocci.

Dobie, A. (2015) The role of the general and provincial chapters in improving and enforcing accounting, financial and management controls in Benedictine monasteries in England 1215–1444. *The British Accounting Review* 47(2): 142–158.

Dodds, B. (2002) *Tithe and agrarian output between the Tyne and Tees, 350–1450*. Unpublished Ph.D. Thesis, University of Durham.

Duncan, J., Flesher, D. and Stocks, M. (1999) Internal control systems in US churches: An examination of the effects of church size and denomination on systems of internal control. *Accounting, Auditing and Accountability Journal* 12(2): 142–163.

Foucault, M. (1972) *Archaeology of knowledge*. London: Routledge.

Foucault, M. (1975) *Birth of the clinic: An archaeology of medical perception*. New York: Vintage Books.

Foucault, M. (1980) *Power/knowledge: Selected interviews and other writings 1972–1977*. Sussex: Harvester Press.

Foucault, M. (1991) Governmentality. In: Burchell, G., Gordon, C. and Miller, P. (eds.), *The Foucault effect: Studies in governmentality*. Chicago: University of Chicago Press, pp. 87–104.

Foucault, M. (2008) *The birth of biopolitics: Lectures at the college de France, 1978–79*. London: Palgrave.

Gentile, M.L. (1912) *Il regesto del Codice Pelavicino, (a cura di)*, in Atti della Società Ligure di storia patria, XLIV.

Hardy, L. and Ballis, H. (2005) Does one size fit all? The sacred and secular divide revisited with insights from Niebuhr's typology of social action. *Accounting, Accountability & Auditing Journal* 18(2): 238–254.

Harvey, P.D.A. (1999). *Manorial records*. London: British Records Association.

Hopwood, A.G. (1987) The archaeology of accounting systems. *Accounting, Organizations and Society* 12(3): 207–234.

Hung, H. (1998) A typology of the theories of the roles of governing boards. *Corporate Governance* 6(2): 101–111.

Ingram, P. and Simons, T. (1995) Institutional and resource dependence determinants of responsiveness to work-family issue. *Academy of Management Journal* 38: 1466–1482.

Jacobs, K. (2005) The sacred and the secular: Examining the role of accounting in the religious context. *Accounting, Accountability & Auditing Journal* 18(2): 189–210.

Jones, M.J. (2008) Internal control, accountability and corporate governance: Medieval and modern Britain compared. *Accounting, Auditing, Accountability Journal* 21(7): 1052–1075.

Landi, F. (2004) *Confische e sviluppo capitalistico. I grandi patrimoni del clero regolare in età moderna in Europa e nel Continente Americano*. Milan: Franco Angeli.

Landi, F. (2005) *Storia economica del clero in Europa, secoli XV-XIX*. Rome: Carocci Editore.

Laughlin, R.C. (1988) Accounting in its social context: An analysis of the accounting systems of the Church of England. *Accounting, Auditing and Accountability Journal* 1(2): 19–42.

Loft, A. (1986) Towards a critical understanding of accounting: The case of cost accounting in the U.K., 1914–1925. *Accounting Organizations and Society* 11(2): 137–169.

Madonna, S., Maran, L. and Cestari, G. (2014) The 1771 and 1824 reforms of the University of Ferrara: A Foucauldian analysis of papal interests. *Accounting History* 19(4): 507–532.

Marchi, F., (1867) *I cinquecontisti ovvero la ingannevole teorica che viene insegnata negli istituti tecnici del regno e fuori del regno intorno il sistema di scrittura a partita doppia, e nuovo saggio per la facile intelligenza ed applicazione di quel sistema*. Prato: Tipografia F. Giachetti.

Nahar, H.S. and Yaacob, H. (2011) *Accounting and accountability in the sacred context: The case of a Malaysian Cash Awqaf Institution*, Proceedings of the 9th Annual International Conference on Business, Accounting, Finance, Management, Marketing.

Noke, C. (1994) Agency and the excessus balance in manorial accounts. In: Parker, R.H. and Yamey, B.S. (eds.), *Accounting History: Some British Contributions*. Oxford: Clarendon Press, pp. 74–96.

Paisey, C. and Paisey, N.J. (2011) Visibility, governance and social context. *Accounting, Auditing & Accountability Journal* 24(5): 587–621.

Poli, S. and Gatti, M. (2014) Accounting and the Papal States: The influence of the Pro commissa Bull (1592) on the rise of an early modern state. *Accounting History* 19(4): 475–506.

Polonio, V. (1990) *Vescovi e capitoli cattedrali in Liguria: Albenga, Genova, Luni-Sarzana*. Rome: Herder.

Postles, D. (1981) The 'Execessus' balance in manorial accounts. *Bulletin of the Institute of Historical Research* 54: 105–110.

Quattrone, P. (2004) Accounting for God: Accounting and accountability practices in the Society of Jesus (Italy, XVI–XVII centuries). *Accounting, Organizations and Society* 29(7): 647–683.

Rotelli, E. (2005) *Il capitolo della cattedrale di Firenze dalle origini al XV secolo.* Florence: Florence University Press

Sargiacomo, M. (2006) Using accounting records to enhance an understanding of a seventeenth-century Italian feudal community: The case of the Commune of Penne (1664–90). *Accounting History* 11(4): 475–502.

Sargiacomo, M. (2008) Accounting and the art of government: Margaret of Austria in Abruzzo (1539–1586). *European Accounting Review* 17(4): 667–695.

Sargiacomo, M. (2009) Accounting for the "good administration of justice": The Farnese State of Abruzzo in sixteenth century. *Accounting History* 14(3): 235–237.

Stone, E. (1962) Profit-and-loss accountancy al Norwich Cathedral Priory. *Transactions of the Royal Historical Society*, 5lh Series, 12: 25–48.

Ughelli, F., Italia Sacra sive De Episcopis Italiae, et insularum adjacentium, rebusque ab iis praeclare gestis, deducta serie ad nostram usque aetatem. Opus singular provinciis 20 distinctum, I-XX, Venetiis, 1717–1722.

12 The Case of Giuseppe D'Agata & Figli, Avola, Sicily from 1937 to 1956

Luisa Pulejo and Giovanna Centorrino

Le sue dita parevano zampe di ragno, tanto erano magre e indaffarate a raccogliere mandorle, come se tessessero una rete sulla terra. Fu allora che le affibbiarono il nomignolo "la Mennulara," che le rimase.
—La Mennulara, Simonetta Agnello Hornby, 2002

INTRODUCTION

Talking about food from a historical point of view means examining every single dimension of human history. From an ethno-anthropological perspective, there may be interesting insights on food as a marker of ethnic, cultural and social identity, and changes in the various historical periods, in tastes, flavours, customs, knowledge and cultural traditions. From a business viewpoint, however, the history of food relates to new techniques and processes of production, conservation and distribution of food and agricultural produce, and the development of entrepreneurial activities that, over time, have contributed to changes in consumer habits, changing, in some cases, the relationship between man, food and nature.

Although approaches to analysis and research in this area may be different, the link between food and territory is always strong; a place of production and/or consumption, which can be interpreted today in a new, more modern way, also looking at sustainable development.

In this context, Sicily has always been characterized by elements of biodiversity and specialization from which important elements of development have often derived, mainly in the past. Each of these elements has become a centre of historical interest that has brought specific features and different growth patterns to the various areas. Among the most common plant species in Sicily, dried fruit has always represented a very important sector. Throughout the centuries, the production of carob, pistachio, almonds, walnuts and hazelnuts has consolidated the continuation of traditions and culture and, in some cases, encouraged the development of the local economy.

This chapter concerns a business enterprise, which originated in Catania in the first half of the nineteenth century, and developed in the last century in

Avola (Siracusa), becoming one of the leading companies in the manufacture of almonds. Until its closure, which occurred in the late 1950s, it was a supplier of major agribusiness companies and had established business relations all over the world (from Europe to Hong Kong, from Latin America to the Middle East).

The strong connotation of a globalized company was also acquired thanks to a profoundly innovative entrepreneurial choice in those early years, related to the purchase of technologically advanced systems and equipment in foreign markets (England and Germany).

In the following sections, the growth and decline of the firm are seen to have derived from both endogenous and exogenous variables. In particular, we have tried to highlight the role that personal attitudes and sociocultural priorities had on bookkeeping. The analysis also takes into account that the firm was deeply embedded in Sicilian society during the first half of the twentieth century, a time of great changes.

CONCEPTUAL FRAMEWORK AND RESEARCH DESIGN

> *Capire il presente, indirizzare il futuro e non isolare il passato nel passato.*
>
> *Understand the present, direct the future and not to isolate the past in the past*
>
> (Amaduzzi, 1996, p. 26)

In accordance with Amaduzzi, the main reason of this study is to remember and valorize a business venture that, in the twentieth century, contributed to the evolution of Sicilian entrepreneurship, as well as to analyze all the documents concerning company accounting and management.

With this idea in mind, our analysis followed the approach used by new accounting historians that considers accounting "more as a cultural phenomenon than simply as a technical practice" (Gomes, 2008, p. 492). From this point of view, accounting is mainly an "instrument of power and domination" and not a "value-free body of ideas and techniques for putting into effect and monitoring contracts freely entered into between equals" (Gomes, 2008, p. 492; see also Carnegie and Napier, 1996, p. 8). From this perspective, "accounting needs to be understood in the contexts in which it operates, as a phenomenon local in both space and time" (Gomes, 2008, p. 492). For this reason, our level of analysis is the firm and its history, examined through both the lens of Italian accounting rules and the evolution of the environment where the firm was embedded. In order to develop this idea, the present study will analyze the G. D'Agata & figli company, trying to highlight different perspectives of its history and of the way this firm grew, together with the history of the family, and of Sicilian society.

We conducted a case study analysis in order to answer these two main questions:

- Q1: How did this firm work from 1939 to 1956?
- Q2: Why, notwithstanding its positive results, did this firm suddenly decline?

The case study approach was adopted as it is in line with our research questions and, in addition, because it best explains both the story of this company and the evolution of its environment, allowing us to emphasize "how" the phenomena were generated, how they were addressed by the actors and what meaning was given to them (Yin, 2003).

Referencing multiple sources of information, the life of the firm from 1939 to 1956 was chronologically analyzed. The prevalent techniques were: analysis of documents collected from outside (i.e., local business records and newspaper archives) and from within (among these, historical accounts, institutional mission statements, annual reports, institutional minutes of meetings, internal memoranda, client information cards) (Guba and Lincoln, 1981; Lincoln, 2002); direct (of what remains of the company) and indirect (through the examination of written and video) observation a posteriori; and interviews, unstructured and vis-à-vis, with the last descendant of the family, Prof. Lidia Toscano—the last heir of the firm who, with utmost care, preserves the factory building and some of the equipment used for production. The several interviews enabled us to deepen our understanding of certain documents, but also allowed us to carry out important checks on the correct interpretation of information.

The first step of this research starts with the analysis of company archives at G. D'Agata & figli still kept in the original building located in via Napoli in Avola (Siracusa) where, in the last century, production took place. In the factory, still full of charm, many components of the almond processing plant are still to be found; it was the most modern factory of the sector for several years at the beginning of the twentieth century.

It is necessary to point out that there are many documents available that testify to the strong connections between company files and family files. Financial reports and advertising material written in various languages have been found, together with magazines and private correspondence. This was characteristic of the agro-food companies of the time, with family size of the company or ownership having a strong influence. Size, in turn, affected the functional roles of company organization, but also the relationship of the company with the surrounding society.

Due to age and storage conditions, paper documents have been damaged. It should be mentioned that the conservation of documents did not depend on regulatory constraints, but is the result of the interest of one person whose free choice of how to preserve the documents was determined only by an emotional bond towards a family activity and the interest to keep the memory of her roots. It should also be noted that it is the archive of a company that has been closed for over half a century and that events have meanwhile occurred that have led to changes in structure and organization of the documentation. Thus, the analysis of the documents was initially addressed to understanding the original organization and the role of financial reports in fulfilling the legal requirements in force at that time. Furthermore, we tried to understand the "value" that the archive once held in the pursuit of corporate objectives.

Despite the limitations associated with conservative choices, and the still not full recognition of the documents found, we believe that, at present, the archive of the G. D'Agata & figli company represents a tool to protect its reference value and "give continuity" and "cultural depth" to its activity (Valacchi, 2007, p. 74).

Considering the vast quantity available and the poor organization of these documents, analysis of the documents was limited to the period September 1937—February 1956. The shareholder's meeting minutes, the board of directors' minutes and annual financial statements referring to this period have been collected and classified. With no intent of imposing the historiography of business management, these documents have been studied in order to investigate company events through its economic and financial behaviour.[1] In order to interpret the events, the company thinking of that period, the accounting tools used—which can be considered a vehicle of transmission of the times (Di Pietra, 1993, p. 241)—and the events that characterized the social and economic context where the company was active were all taken into consideration.

THE CASE GIUSEPPE D'AGATA & FIGLI COMPANY

Historical Background

The Giuseppe D'Agata & figli anonymous cooperative company was established at the end of 1935, with a registered capital of 2,000 Italian Lire. On 1 October 1936, it began activity in the trading and manufacturing of agricultural products.

The activities of the company, in truth, had an older origin, dating back to 1820, when Giuseppe D'Agata established the Giuseppe D'Agata & figli company, with registered office in Catania. During those years, Sicily was in a state of total backwardness and a situation of obvious disequilibrium compared to the rest of the country. The main infrastructures such as roads, railways and aqueducts were lacking, illiteracy was widespread and social and economic development was hindered by problems of a different order. Nevertheless the business was continued by Gaetano (Giuseppe's son) and, later, by his grandson Antonino who—when his father died in 1901—abandoned his studies to manage his father's company. From 1912, the company operated under the name Marzipan in the territory of Avola (Siracusa), a region characterized by certain climatic and soil conditions, and consumption patterns of the population that led to the spread of almond tree cultivation.

In those years, almond tree cultivation, together with olive trees, was considered of great value in the field of agriculture, because of the positive economic results that derived from the commercialization of the product. Until the 1950s, the production, processing and marketing of almonds from Avola brought high levels of employment to the surrounding area, becoming a leading sector of the local economy. It should be remembered that Sicily—the first region in Europe where the Greeks introduced the almond tree in the fifth century B.C.—has always been the leading region in Italy for almond production.

Marzipan, from its foundation, aroused so much interest that its establishment was announced in the *Almanacco Italiano* of 1913, which reported the main events of 1912. It was presented—in a special section of the news magazine entitled "Our Industries"—together with the industrial giants of the time. The company earned "unanimous praise and unlimited encouragement." Indeed, it stood out in both size and capacity to trade among the many companies operating in the almond sector in Sicily. With this initiative, moreover, the Italian origin of the industry for processing almonds was reclaimed. Until then, production had developed mainly in northern Europe (Germany, France and England).

Expectations of development connected to the modern processing equipment were high, along with manufacturing precision, location of the factory in the centre of the almond growing area, and the opportunity to buy the best quality almonds without transport costs or duties. These expectations were not disappointed; the company, indeed, soon became a leader in the processing and marketing of almonds and derived products in Italy and abroad. Its international activity is well documented by thousands of information cards, stored alphabetically and by location in the archive, of the companies with whom they carried on business relationships. Most of these countries were geographically close, but some were on other continents. In addition, also the promotional material found in the archives testify to widespread public relations abroad.

The history of the G. D'Agata & figli company has always been strongly permeated by the history of the family that created it and determined the success of the activity. The D'Agata family were entrepreneurs in Sicily in a time when those with large amounts of capital, bourgeois or rentiers and local landowners were not always willing to take the risk of running an enterprise. Antonino D'Agata, called *U Cavaleri*, in particular was an entrepreneur who, thanks also to his political commitment, took steps to deal with the effects of underdevelopment and lack of infrastructure in southern Italy. With the construction in 1912 of the Marzipan factory, Antonino D'Agata promoted the idea of exploiting locally produced almonds on an industrial scale. He brought back into Italy a business that had become the prerogative of foreign countries. Its active contribution in alleviating the misery prevailing on the territory of Avola, generated the utmost respect. He is remembered today as a person more interested in feelings than in profit. Because of his left-wing politics, however, he was the subject of numerous acts of intimidation by the fascist regime. During this regime, as is well known, every aspect of social life was strictly delimited in party organizations; every information source was controlled by the government through a sophisticated system of propaganda aimed at the dissemination and glorification of the ideas and work of Mussolini. Anyone promoting ideas that were contrary to the ideology and behaviour of the regime was marginalized or even sentenced to physical or psychological violence.

The D'Agata company history—from its beginning on 1 October 1936 until activity ceased on 29 February 1956—has been "reconstructed" by means of analysis of part of the documents available in the company's archive and by the information collected from other primary and secondary sources. Many aspects of the management, financial issues, results obtained, accounting techniques used and the values that inspired the business decisions would have been possible to analyze. However, after a preliminary survey of the available sources in this first phase of the research, it was decided to report on only a few considerations, which mainly arose from the analysis of financial statements and the reading of the shareholder's meeting minutes and of the board of directors' minutes. They can be considered the first results of a study that requires further in-depth analysis.

Preliminary Remarks

It is necessary to start by saying that with regard to form and content of the company's financial statements, in the first period, there would appear to be, albeit not so directly, reference to the provisions of the Commercial Code of 1882. The few and generic provisions contained therein specified that the financial statements must indicate the capital actually existing and must demonstrate "the earnings actually achieved in the year, and the losses suffered with evidence and truth."[2] They referred back to the deed of incorporation or the articles of association regarding the rules to be observed to draw up financial statements and to calculation and allocation of net income.[3] It was also indicated that the auditors must "establish the type of financial statements and the condition of shares in agreement with the directors of the company."[4]

Therefore, there were many gaps regarding the contents and the form that the financial statements should take. Wide discretion originated from the lack of specific references to objective criteria of measurement of items, with a resulting limited transparency of the financial statements drawn up in the early years of the company. It must be considered, moreover, that, in the early 1900s,—despite the contribution of accountancy in the definition of accounting rules, which could aid the directors in drawing up the financial statements—the lack of specific rules to be observed altered the veracity of information provided, in some cases.

The provisions of the Commercial Code remained in force for 60 years, although there were numerous proposals to change, suggested by scholars and various ministerial committees established ad hoc (Codice di Commercio Pel Regno D'Italia, 1882). In 1942, new rules were introduced by the Civil Code that had thoroughly reformed the discipline of joint stock companies (Codice Civile, 1943).

After 1942, until the closure of the company, from reading the financial statements of the D'Agata company a gradual transition to the provisions of the Civil Code emerges. It acted as a first step in limiting the wide powers of discretion that, as mentioned earlier, were left to the directors and auditors. The criteria were rigorous, yet not rigid. In the case of special and contingent circumstances, in fact, the directors were given the opportunity to depart from these criteria with the obligation, however, to give notice and justification to the shareholders.

The analysis showed also that the patrimonial system in use at the time in Italy was referred to for the accounting.[5] This system was well suited to interpret and express the situation of new industrial and commercial companies—also family businesses—in which the assets and any increase were considered to measure the achievement of business objectives. The financial position, the only guarantee of the creditors, had to be represented and made clear in its actual consistency from the balance sheet, which had, in turn, to accurately and clearly reflect the objective truth (Broglia, 1922, p. 521).

Accounting referred to the patrimonial system also when the new doctrinal orientations began to appear.[6] They responded to the accounting needs of the new industrial companies that, in the early decades of the twentieth century, were operating in a rapidly changing economic environment. In those years, compared to the past, production units in Italy underwent profound changes in the legal status they adopted and in the way they operated. There were increasing investments in plant and equipment, and many were the sources from which to draw the huge monetary resources necessary. In this context, also new information needs on the activities performed by the companies and results achieved arose (Coronella, 2014, p. 380).

In order to facilitate the reading of what has emerged, it was considered appropriate to divide the presentation of the results into two periods: the first concerns the time from the establishment of the company until the 1945–1946 accounting period; the second concerns the time from the 1946–1947 accounting period until the closure of the company. For the choice of the two periods, some events that were considered significant for identifying a line of demarcation in the evolution of the company's history were taken into account; these were events that influenced management decisions taken. Above all, they refer to changes in the governance and in the transformation of the corporate form.

In the first period, the company, had been managed by Antonino D'Agata, who was appointed chief executive and served until his death on 26 February 1947. Rather than personal profit, his business decisions were always inspired by moral values and by his constant commitment to defend the dignity of workers and solve the problems of the territory. In the early 1940s, moreover, he had to contain the war repercussions. By adoption of a set of measures, he was able to mitigate the disastrous effects of the war and prepare the groundwork for the future development of the business. From the 1946–1947 accounting period until the closure of the company, Antonino D'Agata was replaced by his widow Mrs. Pennella and, in 1951, by Mr. Vincenzo Toscano—partner of the society—who administered the company until liquidation.

Furthermore, in the first period, the company had operated as a limited cooperative company first, and then as an ordinary limited company. In the second period, it took the form of a joint-stock company. This transformation also resulted in the increase of the share capital to 1 million Italian Lire. This was realized through the issuance of 990 shares of 1,000 Italian Lire each, offering in option these shares to existing shareholders and, accordingly, making appropriate amendments to the articles of association. After transformation into a joint-stock company, amounts of money were invested in new areas of business, which consolidated the company's success.

For each period, some financial and nonfinancial events will be outlined, which contributed to the company's administration and which are considered important for understanding the evolution of the history of the D'Agata company.

From the Foundation of the Company to the Accounting Period 1945–1946

As mentioned, the company D'Agata began operating on 1 October 1936. At the end of the first financial cycle—which, according to the provisions of the Articles of Association (Statute), was closed on 30 June—despite the limited resources available, a net income of 10,302.25 Italian Lire was obtained. With the consent of the auditors, it was assigned to the extent of 10% to the "Ordinary reserve fund" and the remainder to the "Extraordinary reserve fund". The conservative choice, by the board of directors, concerning the sharing arrangements of net income, was justified by the need to increase the limited resources available to the company for future activities.[7] This approach took into account the criterion of "prudence" that had inspired the legislator, whereby, as indicated in the Commercial Code, the payment of dividends to shareholders should be limited only to the actual profits (Art. 180), and that at least one-twentieth of net income should be put aside in reserve, with the aim to safeguard social obligations for third parties, until the reserve reached one-fifth of the share capital (Art. 181).

From the analysis of the first financial statement (30 June 1937), the emphasis attributed—as already mentioned—to the financial position by the accounting system used during that period has come to light: only the balance sheet was considered as the financial statement as such, different and separate from the income statement. The structure of the balance sheet has a very simple structure; it remained almost unchanged for many years. In the absence of clear regulations on the balance sheet's content, the two sections contain a limited number of items (seven in both assets and liabilities). The accounts "Banks," "Customer" and "Suppliers" showed the debit balance in Assets and the credit balance in Liabilities. Also part of assets were "Promissory active," "Goods" and, as the only fixed assets, "Office furniture." On the other hand, as part of liabilities, in addition to "Promissory passive" and "Invoices to pay" accounts, there was "Equity," equal to 2,000 Italian Lire, and "Net income" (Figure 12.1).

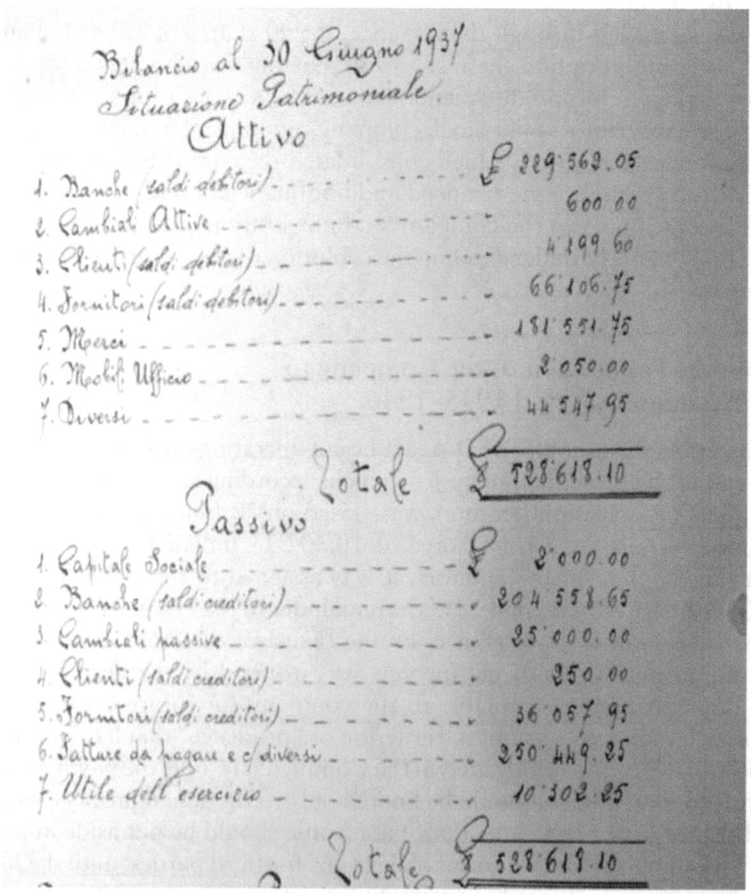
Bilancio al 30 Giugno 1937
Situazione Patrimoniale
Attivo

1. Banche (saldi debitori)	£ 229.563.05
2. Cambiali Attive	600.00
3. Clienti (saldi debitori)	4.199.60
4. Fornitori (saldi debitori)	66.106.75
5. Merci	181.551.75
6. Mobili Ufficio	2.050.00
7. Diversi	44.547.95
Totale	£ 528.618.10

Passivo

1. Capitale Sociale	£ 2.000.00
2. Banche (saldi creditori)	204.558.65
3. Cambiali passive	25.000.00
4. Clienti (saldi creditori)	250.00
5. Fornitori (saldi creditori)	36.057.95
6. Fatture da pagare e c/diversi	250.449.25
7. Utile dell'esercizio	10.302.25
Totale	£ 528.618.10

Figure 12.1 Financial statements of 30 June 1937

This was in line with the operating practices of the time that, in many ways, tended to group together balances of the ledger accounts in a single account, which should have been clearly marked in the financial statement. The exhibition of "enormous" items—in the case of the D'Agata company, for example, the "Banks (debit balances)" or "Goods" accounts—according to the doctrine of the time, would seem indicative of the aim "to hide something" from those who were to examine the financial statement (Vianello, 1930, p. 488).

It should be considered that the Commercial Code made reference to the need to seek the "truth" of financial statements (Art. 175). However, the "accounting truth" of the results of the accounts—which formed the basis of documentation produced at the end of any accounting period—could hardly be considered relevant to the "real" amount of the financial position (Broglia, 1923, p. 34). For some fundamental parts that were subject to usage, deterioration or depreciation, indeed, it was necessary to use evaluation processes that largely determined net income. In the absence of specific laws on the criteria to be observed, they depended only on the general guidelines contained in the articles of the association concerning the financial statement and distribution of net income.

The net income was the result of two distinct areas of business: the first concerned business in dried fruits and its derivatives—which we can consider as the core business of the company—and the second concerned the activity of citrus fruit processing.

The origin of net income is shown by two prospectuses named "Example of Profit and Loss accounts" and "Example of Profit and Loss accounts of a citrus fruit processing factory." It was like a segmentation to analytically determine how to reach results that came from different activities. The prospectuses were made up of two sections that were separate and opposed. The configuration would seem to recall gross results that—among the forms used—permitted administrators not to give details on cost and income. The account called "Gross income of production" (or industrial) indicated the algebraic result between costs and income "directly" attributable to the industrial manufacturing process. In those two prospectuses, reference is made to other costs (on the debit side) and income (credit side) that were not considered related in a strict sense to the production process. Thus, for example, in the right-hand section (credit side) of the first account "Example of Profit and Loss accounts" there is the account "Gross income," whose value represents almost all of the income. This account is believed to be related to the sale of products that were the result of the processing of almonds. The accounts "Profit account hazelnuts" and "Profit account pistachio," however, stemmed from the sale of other types of dried fruit that had not undergone any process (Figure 12.2).

The registration of the sale of goods (or products) resulted in the allocation of a negative change on the original patrimonial account "Goods" (or "Products"); this account showed their purchase cost. Since the income

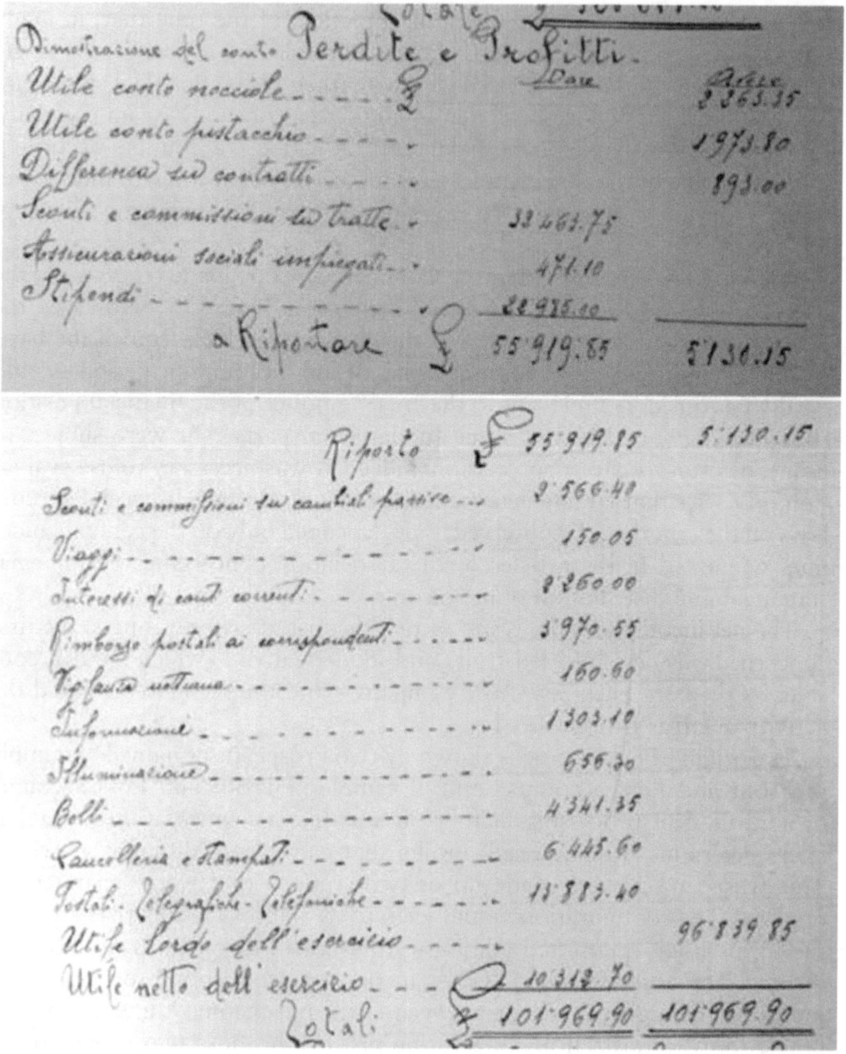

Dimostrazione del conto Perdite e Profitti.

		Dare	Avere
Utile conto nocciole	£		2 363.35
Utile conto pistacchio			1 973.80
Differenza su contratti			793.00
Sconti e commissioni su tratte		33 463.75	
Assicurazioni sociali impiegati		471.10	
Stipendi		21 985.00	
a Riportare	£	55 919.85	5 130.15
Riporto	£	55 919.85	5 130.15
Sconti e commissioni su cambiali passive		9 566.40	
Viaggi		150.05	
Interessi di conti correnti		8 260.00	
Rimborso postali ai corrispondenti		3 970.55	
Vigilanza notturna		160.60	
Informazioni		1 303.10	
Illuminazione		656.30	
Bolli		4 341.35	
Cancelleria e stampati		6 445.60	
Postali - Telegrafiche - Telefoniche		11 883.40	
Utile lordo dell'esercizio			96 839.85
Utile netto dell'esercizio		10 318.70	
Totali	£	101 969.90	101 969.90

Figure 12.2 Financial statements of 30 June 1937: example of Profit and Loss accounts

derived from sales was normally different from the cost of goods sold, the difference was charged to a derived account called "Profit (or loss) goods." It should be remembered, however, that in the balance sheet of the D'Agata company there is a single account, "Goods", without any distinction of different types of products (hazelnuts, pistachios, almonds). This, in our opinion, confirms the hypothesis of the specific intention of the directors who, because of general obligations regarding content of the balance sheet, preferred to limit the disclosure of information provided in the financial statement.

Costs that were not strictly related to production were reported in the left-hand side (Debit) of the prospectus. They concerned, mainly, financial charges and staff costs and other costs, some of which were related to marketing and exports in foreign countries. The "Information" account, for example, is related to costs incurred in gathering information on the "reliability" of potential customers.[8] It refers to business skills, punctuality in meeting commitments and the moral profile of the owner of the company. This information is reported in the "information cards" of customers, which are still placed alphabetically in the card index cabinet kept in the company premises.

The second statement, called "Example of Profit and Loss Accounts of a citrus fruit processing factory" concerns an area of specific business. In the right-hand section (credit side), it contains a single account called "Gross yearly profit" that, according to what was previously mentioned, should represent the balance of costs and income directly attributable to the industrial manufacturing process. In the left-hand section (debit side), however, all costs that were not considered directly attributable to the production process of citrus fruits were shown (Figure 12.3).

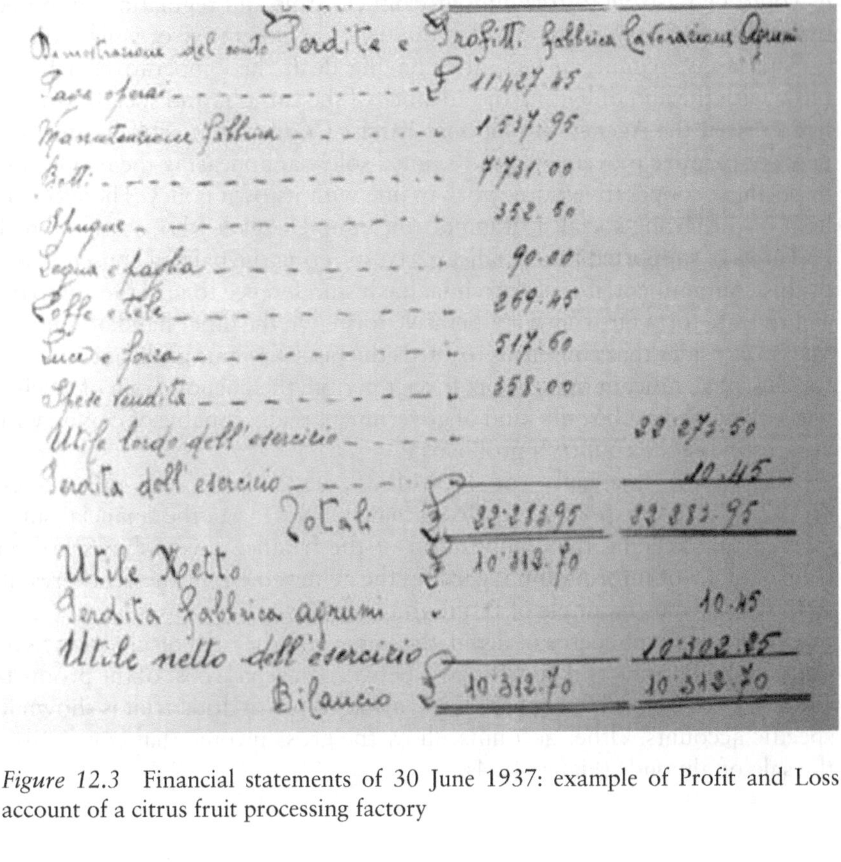

Dimostrazione del conto Perdite e Profitti Fabbrica Lavorazione Agrumi

Paga operai	£ 11'427.45	
Manutenzione fabbrica	1'517.95	
Botti	7'731.00	
Spugne	352.50	
Legna e paglia	90.00	
Coffe e tele	269.45	
Luce e forza	517.60	
Spese vendita	358.00	
Utile lordo dell'esercizio		22'273.50
Perdita dell'esercizio		10.45
Totali	£ 22'283.95	22'283.95
Utile Netto	£ 10'312.70	
Perdita fabbrica agrumi		10.45
Utile netto dell'esercizio		10'302.25
Bilancio	£ 10'312.70	10'312.70

Figure 12.3 Financial statements of 30 June 1937: example of Profit and Loss account of a citrus fruit processing factory

This area of business incurred a very modest loss, that was carried forward, decreasing the net income of the core business of the company. Starting from the following year, in the financial statements, there is no reference to processing of citrus fruits. The unsatisfactory result achieved in the first financial cycle was probably the reason for not continuing in this specific area of business.

In the second financial cycle, ending 30 June 1938, net income was still limited (1,046.15 Italian Lire). It derived mainly from "Gross income," which, as mentioned, should have come from the sale of almonds and derived products.[9] Net income was distributed in the same manner as the previous year. Interestingly, in the report of the board of auditors included in the shareholder's meeting minutes—on the occasion of approval of the financial statement—agreement on the prudential approach contained in the proposal of the director is explicitly underlined (Board of Director's Minutes, (October 1, 1936 – February 29, 1956)).[10]

In the same meeting, as extraordinary item, the transformation of the company from anonymous cooperative to ordinary anonymous company was proposed and subsequently approved, together with some changes to the Articles of Association that would regulate the company. Welcoming the form of ordinary anonymous company, the director probably thought it would be possible to free himself from controls and regulations imposed by the Fascist Party, particularly in the field of cooperative organizations.

The fascist regime, in fact, after having dealt the cooperatives a heavy blow with the aim of halting the advance of the catholic and socialist forces, had created the Agency of National Fascist Cooperation as promoter of a new cooperative movement, really aimed solely at appeasing the people and imposing a cooperative framework in line with its own policy. Therefore, in light of the strong socialist origin of Antonino D'Agata who, as mentioned, had always supported the socialist party, suffering the painful consequences of this commitment, it is easy to imagine his preference to give the company a corporate form far from a cooperative form. On the other hand, it is necessary to consider that consensus towards the fascist regime grew quickly, also for lack of significant opposition. In that period, the phenomenon of fascism was considered as the only kind of government really capable of coping with and resolving the country's problems.

Also in the financial year 1938–1939, net income was still modest (2,137.55 Italian Lire). Starting from that financial year, the financial statement, while keeping the composition of the balance sheet, shows greater transparency of information regarding the achievement of the yearly result. In the prospectus Example of Profit and Loss, indeed, it is possible to recognize, with a greater degree of detail, the impact on the final results of the sale of individual products. The difference between purchase cost of the products and revenues derived from the sale of various types of dried fruit is shown in specific accounts. Other accounts, show the gross income that comes from the sale of almonds (Figure 12.4).

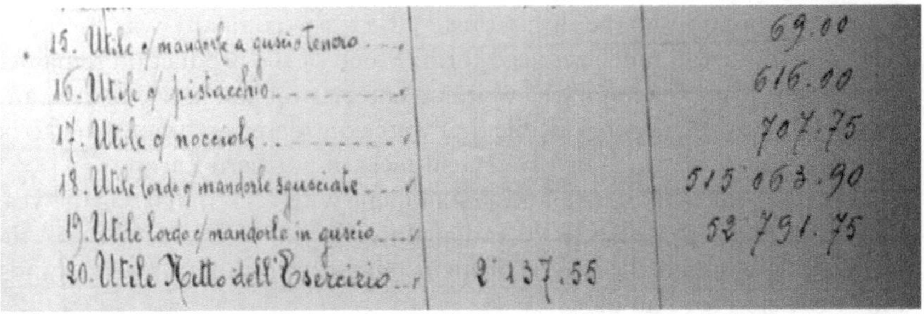

15. Utile c/ mandorle a guscio tenero		69.00
16. Utile c/ pistacchio		616.00
17. Utile c/ nocciole		707.75
18. Utile lordo c/ mandorle sgusciate		515 063.90
19. Utile lordo c/ mandorle in guscio		52 791.75
20. Utile Netto dell'Esercizio	2 137.55	

Figure 12.4 Financial statements of 30 June 1939: example of Profit and Loss account

Net income, as in previous years, was entirely allocated to ordinary reserve and extraordinary reserve. Indications on the reasons for this allocation—noted on the shareholder's meeting minutes—is evidence of the need felt by the chief executive in those years to increase the financial resources on which the company could count (Company, Shareholder's Meeting Minutes (October 1, 1936–February 29, 1956). Therefore it was necessary to hold back net income rather than distribute it. In this first period of activity, capital share owner's equity was quite modest, and indebtedness appeared high. In the financial statements of 1939 and 1940 the capital share owner's equity was still equal to that of the initial contribution (2,000 Italian Lire) and the net income continued to be held back. The subsequent periods, despite the continuing conflict, were characterized by a positive trend. Starting from 1941, net income (21,088.12 Italian Lire) was distributed not only to ordinary reserve and extraordinary reserve, but in part was also allocated to the staff severance fund and to the provision for bad and doubtful debts.

Only from the following year (1942) was a portion of the net income distributed to shareholders, while the same rules from previous year were observed for distribution of other portions.

The later years were characterized by historical changes of the most significant ever recorded, in addition to the change in currency value. Suffice to mention the war repercussions, which the D'Agata company had to contain with. The financial year 1942–1943, although closing with a net income (10,413.40 Italian Lire), was characterized by a series of measures to mitigate the disastrous effects of the war. In the director's report, the air strikes of the enemy, suspension of trade with the continent, monetary inflation and the complex military-political situation are all given as causes of significant write-downs or removal of receivables and of approximation in calculation of interest allowed on current accounts of some banks. Inevitably, therefore, the results of the financial statements in those years were subject to estimates and conjectures that were heavily affected by the climate of uncertainty and unpredictability related to the possible socioeconomic evolution of the future. In 1944, however, due to the transport crisis linked to the continuation of the disastrous conflict, the company was forced to carry out activity in much reduced form. Much of the production remained unsold, and it was necessary to write inventories for the previous year and remove numerous notes receivable that were considered as "impossible to be collected," most of which involved customers in northern Europe.

This produced the first financial statement with a loss, that for the year 1944 was equal to 188,532.90 Italian Lire; it was resolved to cover the entire value through the use of ordinary and extraordinary reserve funds, and "Provision for bad debts."

Starting from the subsequent financial year, the first signs of recovery in business were observed and the results of the business decisions of diversification undertaken in previous years began to consolidate (Figure 12.5).

From the Financial Year 1946–1947 to Closure of Business on 29 February 1956

In the last years of the company, a tragic event that struck the D'Agata family had repercussions on corporate governance.[11] On 26 February 1947 Antonino D'Agata—newly elected member of the Constituent Assembly—died suddenly. He had been Chief Executive of the G. D'Agata & figli company from the first year of operation. Mrs. Benedetta Pennella, D'Agata's widow, took over. This decision was approved in the extraordinary shareholders' meeting on 12 April 1947. Subsequently, Mrs. Pennella—forced to resign for health reasons—was replaced in 1951 by Mr. Vincenzo Toscano, who administered the company until liquidation.

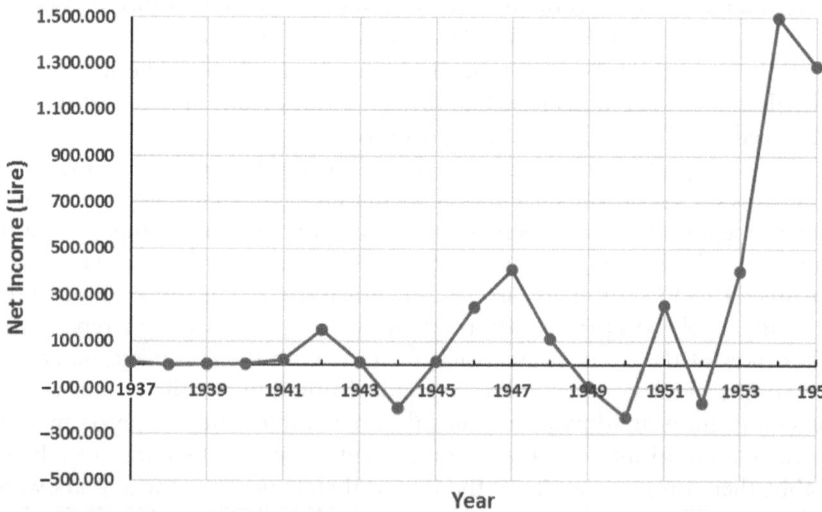

Figure 12.5 Trend of the company's net income 1937–1955 (annual financial statements, October 1, 1936–February 29, 1956)

During the extraordinary shareholders' meeting on 12 April 1947, in the presence of all shareholders[12] and of members of the Board of auditors, as already mentioned, it was also resolved to transform the G. D'Agata & figli ordinary anonymous company into a joint-stock company.

At that time, the share capital of 2,000 Italian Lire—which had remained unchanged since its establishment—was increased to 1 million Italian Lire. This responded to the new rules introduced by the 1942 Civil Code that had thoroughly reformed the discipline of joint stock companies. The intention of the legislature to impose a minimum capital of 1 million Italian Lire (Art. 2327) was aimed, on the one hand, to "ensure greater strength to the institution," and on the other, to "guarantee the savings of investors in the company, creditors and, above all, the higher interest of the national economy."[13]

The assumption of this new legal form was justified by significant changes in the size and nature of company business that had been diversified. Besides the processing of almonds and marketing of its derivatives and other types of dried fruits, in 1941 the company resumed the production of citrus fruit derivatives to a significant extent. In 1943, moreover, given the numerous requests of herbal products from Italy and from other foreign countries, the company decided to entrust the management of a new business unit to a specialized professional, where the cultivation and sale of aromatic and medicinal plants would be implemented. It was, in other words, a form of outsourcing of processes. These needed specific knowledge with regard to the conservation of spices and medicinal herbs, and the most effective type of packaging in order to keep their active ingredients unaltered during shipment. For this purpose, it was deliberated to entrust the direction of the specific department to the pharmacist Antonino Caldarella, who would be responsible for the conservation, packaging and everything concerning research and development of the sector. According to the agreement between the parties, Mr. Caldarella and the D'Agata company were, in equal parts, to participate financially in the acquisition, processing and marketing of products. In addition, the company was to provide the logistics structure with the fixed assets and facilities required for marketing, both in Italy and in foreign countries.[14]

With the transformation of the legal form of the company, also, the beginning of a new positive phase in the life of the company can be seen. Albeit with alternating phases, significant positive results were obtained until shareholder approval of the liquidation of the company (Figure 12.5).

From 1947, the recovery that had occurred as early as 1945 was consolidated, although there were still certain phenomena present in Sicily, which had developed under the fascist regime (the welfare state, for example, or the management of patronage of political consensus), which created many difficulties in the revival of the economy in the territory. The financial statement at 30 June 1947 closed with a significant net income (409,569.20 Italian Lire) compared to previous periods.

Although in some subsequent periods (1948–1949, 1949–1950, 1951–1952) negative results were recorded, they were due to situations where it was difficult to intervene. In those years, stagnation in business was due, for example, to an overall decline in prices and increasing difficulties in exports.[15]

The years to come however, were characterized by a growth of results with sometimes considerable increases, linked to business decisions and investments that, in some cases, led to a saving of production costs. Reference is made, for example, to the purchase and installation of the boiler and oven for drying almonds: an innovative system exploited the energy produced by the combustion also of waste (almond shells) processing. Initially, it had been placed in some rooms rented by the company. Later it was necessary to remove it and install it at the site of the company placing the boiler on the ground floor and the dryer on the first floor of the factory. In view of such a move, the Council on 30 June 1954 decided to amortize the total amount of expenditure for its purchase and implementation in a lump sum, rather than the usual rate of 20% yearly. The investment was a strong point that contributed to the consolidation of the company's success.

The use of a plant—which was fuelled from a saving of energy costs—meant, at the same time, a limited environmental impact. This seems to meet, in advance, the specific needs of our time related to environmental protection. It is a fine example of "technological assets" and can still be seen in its original location.

Analyzing the financial statements, the shareholder's meeting minutes and the board of directors' minutes that relate to this period of the life the company, it has not been possible to understand the precursors of a situation that was soon to come about and that would determine the liquidation of the business.

Despite the positive results that emerged from last financial statements, on 29 February 1956, the director, Mr. Vincenzo Toscano, summoned an extraordinary meeting to communicate their will to liquidate the company, and report on the origin of the problems arising in the last year that forced him to come to this decision. They were related to the imposition by the tax authorities of a "lump sum" tax of 12,165,462 Italian Lire. On that occasion, after recalling the milestones of the company's history, the director pointed out that, from the first year of business, the financial statements of the company had been subject to tax audits. The tax authorities had always challenged their veracity on the basis of their "own motivations."[16] The company had always rejected this, based on terms and conditions provided for by law. He was confident that they had always acted in accordance with the provisions of the law—which required that taxation be carried out based on the results of the financial statement—which were regularly presented, starting from the first year, with an income tax return, including a copy of the financial statement. That certainty had led the company, in 1955, to send the tax authorities a copy of the financial statements from 1937 to 1954, so that it could definitively resolve the situation of "controversial income."[17]

The tax authority, after an audit limited to the years 1952–1954, found nothing to justify discontinuance of accounting results for determining the annual net income of the company. Despite this, the tax authorities—based on an inductive investigation extended over the entire period—did not intend to derogate from their arguments.[18] They did not take the actual costs incurred by the company into account, which—on the basis of what was claimed by the director—were regularly reported in every income statement. The director informed the meeting that, given the onerous taxation imposed, an irreversible state had emerged where the debt situation with the tax authorities would have definitely produced a significant corporate crisis. To pay the debt, indeed, in the following years it would have been necessary to achieve a net income for the sale of almonds that, taking into account the total expenditure to be incurred, would not allow the company to compete in the market.

Therefore, despite the positive trend in financial performance throughout the life of the company and the potentiality in the sector in which it operated, the history of the D'Agata company ended on 29 February 1956, with its termination and liquidation.[19]

Discussion

Through this case study analysis, we intended to answer two main questions:

- Q1: How did this firm work from 1939 to 1956?
- Q2: Why, notwithstanding its positive results, did this firm suddenly decline?

The entrepreneurial story of the D'Agata family has been reconstructed by trying to interpret the information that emerged from the analysis of the available documentation, taking into account the historical, political, cultural and legislative environment. This was the system of constraints and opportunities in which the activity of the company developed.

Q1. How did this firm work from 1939 to 1956?

During its life, the G. D'Agata & figli company—despite being located in a very small town in a Sicilian province—operated successfully in various business areas, ranging from the processing and marketing of dried fruit (carob, pistachio, almonds, walnuts and hazelnuts) to the activity of citrus fruit, and production and marketing of aromatic and medicinal plants. The company, however, owes its success to the processing and marketing of almonds and derived products, which were mainly supplied directly on site. The Avola *terroir*, in fact, was characterized by singular climatic and soil conditions, by consumer's needs and by the desire of the population. All these variables contributed to the spread of the cultivation of the almond tree.

Despite the inherent constraints of the scarcity of economic and structural resources that affected the Sicilian territory in the early twentieth century, and despite the problems connected to the war events, the company became the leader in the processing and commercialization of almonds and obtained significant financial results, thanks to its innovative approach both in production and customer and supplier management.

Q2. Why, notwithstanding its positive results, did this firm suddenly decline?

From the analysis of available sources, it emerged that the liquidation of the D'Agata company was determined not by issues related to operations or to financial requirements, but from the troubled relationship with the tax authorities. It is founded on the rigorous attitude held by the tax legislator in tax investigations, and in uncompromising interpretations made by the authority responsible for them. Even from the early years of the twentieth century, the conflict that was emerging between the perspective of those who "want to strike at everything" and the perspective of those who "try to hide," hindered and compromised the sincerity of the accounting and financial statements (Broglia, 1923, p. 31). On the other hand, according to the practice of the time, the criteria used to draw up the financial statement to be attached to the tax return, were intended to strengthen the company's assets and to defend its integrity against potential losses not admitted by the tax authorities. This practice was not dictated by any desire to avoid taxpayer's tax obligations, but by the need to take into account the real conditions of the course of business. Conversely, the tax authorities tended to limit deductible costs and to multiply the nondeductible ones that, in consequence, were subjected to taxation.

It must be considered that, from the analysis of the shareholder's meeting minutes, the board of directors' minutes and annual financial statements, it was not possible to perceive the signs of the troubled relationship between the company and the tax authorities. The financial statements of D'Agata company seem to be configured only for internal use.

There are no references to costs relating to taxation, nor is the increase of the debt with the tax authorities ever indicated among the liabilities. On the other hand, the legal directions of the legislation relating to the financial statement (Commercial Code of 1882 and Civil Code of 1942) had not always been rigorously enforced. This, unfortunately, has compromised the clarity of the financial statements and transparency of the information contained in it.

Therefore, we believe that—if we consider the positive economic results achieved, specific skills (know-how) developed, as well as trade relationships activated with Italian and foreign clients—the reasons given by the administrator are not sufficient to justify the decision not to continue the business and to liquidate the company. Thus, we ask ourselves, why was a more rigorous approach not adopted, and the indebtedness that was emerging with the tax authorities not considered? Why did nearly 20 years pass from the beginning of the activity to settle the dispute related to taxation?

It was not possible to find a certain answer to these questions. The only fact we know is that, after the winding up of the company, the activity was resumed again in the form of an individual company. It finally closed at the end of the 1970s, once again for exogenous variables.

CONCLUSION

Reconstructing the history of the D'Agata company from an economic point of view has allowed us to follow the path through time and space of the almond, a product of the land, which unites so many different peoples. Almonds, thanks to their shelf life, have always been used worldwide, in places far from those of production. Their use is quite versatile: from the food sector, where almonds are mainly used for the preparation of confectionery products, to that of cosmetics. In ancient times, even the wood from the pruning was used to feed the ovens for bread baking; from the outer husk, first dried in the sun and then burned (*scebba*), an alkaline fertilizer rich in potassium and phosphorous was obtained, and almond shells were used for burning in fireplaces. Also in cultural terms, the almond crop has played a leading role with the almond representing a symbol of hope or expectation, of wisdom, of love. The flowering of the almond trees, in addition to being celebrated through stories, legends and old traditions—also in distant lands—has inspired the paintings of famous artists such as Vincent van Gogh and Edward Coley Burne-Jones.

In the twentieth century, the industrial perspective of Sicily was linked to processing and marketing of the most valuable agricultural products. Until the 1950s almond growing, in particular, was one of the leading sectors of the economy. It was a production that was soundly linked to the values and traditions of the island and, at the same time, the subject of an excellent entrepreneurship open to innovation.

Antonino D'Agata, chief executive of the G. D'Agata & figli company, played a leading role in the socioeconomic events of Sicily. Politically active, opposed to the fascist regime of those years, he managed to develop a project of capitalism that gave prosperity and fame to the territory of Avola. He constantly worked with the aim of pursuing paths of growth and innovation, rather than keep to maintaining conditions of mere survival. Thus, with commitment and determination, he was able to realize a fair distribution of wealth in the territory and to develop the activity of the company, at an international level. Moreover, he produced fair profits in return for the efforts made. The *Cavaleri*, in fact, with great clarity and foresight was the undisputed author of winning business decisions, ferrying the company during a period characterized by major social and political changes, that deeply affected the economic development of the country.

Through the analysis of D'Agata company history, we have described the "how" and "why" of a phenomenon that occurred in a specified period (time) and in a specific context (place).

Accounting has been considered as the central idea of the investigation. The financial statements from 1937 to 1955 allowed us to interpret the events and values of the company's choices. Through the accounts found in the vast archive of the company, it was possible to carry out a sort of swing of the historical narrative on the arrow of time. In other words, the freedom, characteristic of historical research, to move in both directions of time—forward and backward—has been used, not only as a reporter, but in the perspective of understanding the events (Topolski, 1997). In this way, it was possible to give an interpretation of the company's history, which is a typical aspect of historical narrative.

To reach this aim, the contribution of oral testimony was crucial, but also places, machinery and other objects were fundamental that, together with the business archive, were, until now, jealously preserved by the heir of the family. They represent a heritage to be protected and to made accessible to the community, as evidence of a significant business reality that—despite the backwardness of the area and the lack of infrastructure in the territory at that time—was able to stand out, even in the international market.

Our work is based on a single case study and, as such, cannot be generalized. Moreover, the analyzed documentation is only a part of the whole archive that needs to be examined to fully understand the history and organizational behaviour.

Notwithstanding these limits, G. D'Agata & figli can be considered one of many cases of companies characterized by decisional processes strictly linked to entrepreneurial will (Sargiacomo, 2008); for this reason it can be said that private vicissitudes and exogenous variables influence activities and performances in meaningful ways.

Finally, this analysis highlights the importance of optimizing management and accountability systems of the firms as a *condicio sine qua non* to preserve and develop the distinctive characteristics of the *terroir*.

Further steps may complete the investigation with a rigorous systematization and cataloguing of existing and available documentation. Only in this way can the archive—originally produced to serve a practical managerial or administrative function—become a cultural and historical value to be passed on to future generations.

NOTES

1. As was authoritatively asserted,

   > *Agli occhi di un'aziendalista appare quanto mai singolare—anche accettando l'ipotesi preliminare di limitare l'oggetto di studio all'impresa—che si possa pensare di penetrare in profondità nelle vicende economiche di una unità di produzione economica curando molteplici aspetti della vita di questa senza tuttavia toccare il nucleo centrale della sua matrice economica e finanziaria che risiede nella documentazione quantitativa.*
   >
   > Ferraris Franceschi (1997, p. 21).

2. Commercial Code of 1882, art. 175, c. 2.
3. Ibid., art. 88, c. 1, n. 6.

4. Ibid., art. 183, c. 1, n. 1.
5. According to the Bestana system, as is known, the financial statement was designed to

    mostrare quali sono i reali elementi patrimoniali che riuniti insieme costituiscono il patrimonio dell'impresa (capitale sociale e fondi di riserva, se ve n'hanno) in quella misura a cui esso deve ascendere.
    It was also designed to show "*il montante del dividendo che spetta agli azionisti o ai soci*".

    (Besta, 1922, p. 607)

6. A key role was played by Gino Zappa in this evolutionary process. As we know, the transition from patrimonial system to income system is attributable to his school of thought. With his keynote speech on "New Trends in studies of Accounting," the birth of "Economia Aziendale" as an independent scientific discipline, is also attributable to Zappa.
7. Shareholder's meeting minutes, p. 3.
8. Due to limitations of the systems of communication and of the flow of information, the company would contact a company specializing in the production of information. This practice was maintained over time, with the exception of the years 1944 and 1945.
9. However, the value of the sale of other dried fruits is very limited, nor is reference made to the processing of citrus fruits.
10. "*Pel riparto degli utili ci associamo al criterio prudenziale dell'Amministratore per potere sempre più consolidare la vita della Cooperativa.*" Shareholder's meeting minutes of 4 September 1938, p. 8.
11. The company had a series of financial and control organs. In particular, the financial management was entrusted to a chief executive; control was exercised by a board of auditors who had the task of ensuring proper accounting regularity, accuracy and compliance of accounting records with applicable laws, and how they corresponded to the data of the balance sheet and the profit and loss account. From the second year, the board of auditors was chaired by a president appointed by the shareholders. (Under Article 4 of the Royal Decree-Law 24 July 1936, n. 1548 Provisions relating to the auditors of commercial companies. [036U1548] [GU 197 of 26 August 1936] came into force on 10 September 1936 [see http://www.normattiva.it/]).
12. They represented the total share capital consisting of 20 shares of 1,000 lire each.
13. *Relazione alla Maestà del Re Imperatore del Ministro Guardasigilli (Grandi) presentata nell'udienza del 16 Marzo 1942-XX per l'approvazione del "Codice Civile"*, in Ministero di Grazia e Giustizia, *Codice Civile. Testo e Relazione Ministeriale*, Istituto Poligrafico dello Stato, Roma 1943—Anno XXI, p. 213.
14. In 1945, the management of citrus processing was entrusted to Mr. Paolo Nunzio who took charge of shipments of citrus fruits abroad on behalf of the D'Agata company, as well as on behalf of his own company. The agreement provided for an allocation of 50% of the results produced. The initial financial commitment and logistics were the responsibility of the D'Agata company, and control of the manufacturing process and packaging of Mr. Nunzio.
15. For example, in 1952 the French government banned the import of shelled almonds in their territory. Therefore, it was impossible to handle a request for the supply of 530 tonnes of almonds made previously by some customers from across the Alps, and the company was forced to sell the merchandise remaining in Italy. This episode generated, on the one hand, a decrease of "gross profit," due to the lower price that Italian customers were willing to pay, and, second, an increase of costs associated with the long storage in stock. Moreover, in the same year, an unfortunate event, along with the one just described, was the cause

of a loss in the financial year: a dishonest employee, taking advantage of the family atmosphere which was always characteristic of the management of the company, misled the cashier and obtained money for old bills previously paid.
16. Board of director's minutes, p. 137.
17. Ibid., p. 45.
18. Ibid., p. 138.
19. Administrator Toscano, who assumed the office of liquidator, was given the task to implement the procedure according to the requirements of Art. 2277 of the C.C. 1942.

REFERENCES

Primary Sources

Archivio della Società "G. D'Agata & figli", Avola (Siracusa):

Board of Director's Minutes (October 1, 1936—February 29, 1956);
Company, Shareholder's Meeting Minutes (October 1, 1936—February 29, 1956);
Annual Financial Statements (October 1, 1936—February 29, 1956);
Statute;
Client information cards.

Assemblea Costituente, *Verbale della seduta di giovedì 27 febbraio 1947*. [Online] Available at: http://www.camera.it [Accessed: 24th February 2015].
A Capa xvid [Online] Available at: https://www.youtube.com/watch?v=dGGlKXlFxqo&feature=youtu.be [Accessed: 12th January 2015].
Codice Civile. Testo e Relazione Ministeriale, Istituto Poligrafico dello Stato, Roma 1943—Anno XXI. [Online] Available at: http://www.consiglionazionaleforense.it/site/home/pubblicazioni/collana-studi-storici-e-giuridici/articolo6388.html [Accessed: 24th February 2015].
Codice di Commercio Pel Regno D'Italia. Gazzetta Ufficiale del Regno d'Italia Supplemento al numero 86–11 aprile 1882. [Online] Available at: augusto.digitpa.gov.it/gazzette/index [Accessed: 24th February 2015].
La Fabbrica Marzipan di Avola.mp4 [Online] Available at: https://www.youtube.com/watch?v=BdG3dKvasAM&feature=youtu.be [Accessed: 12th January 2015].

Secondary Sources

AA. VV. (1996) *L'evoluzione degli studi di ragioneria dalla fine del XVIII secolo. Storie di imprese siciliane*. Pisa: Pacini Editore.
AA. VV. (2005) *Cultura Aziendale e Professionale tra passato e futuro*. Tomo A—F., Rome: Rirea.
AA. VV. (2006) Sulle Orme del Mandorlo (Amygdalus communis L.). In: Avanzato, D. and Vassallo, I. (eds.), *Coltura e cultura, folclore e storia, tradizioni e usi*, CRA-ISF. Scripta Horticulturae, Numer 4, Published by ISHS, [Online] Available at: http://www.actahort.org/chronica/pdf/sh_4.pdf [Accessed: 27th January 2015].
Almanacco Italiano. (1913) *Piccola Enciclopedia popolare della vita pratica e Annuario diplomatico amministrativo e statistico. Anno XVIII. 1913*. Florence: R. Bemporad & Figlio Editori. [Online] Available at: https://archive.org/details/almanaccoitalian1913floruoft [Accessed: 16th February 2015].
Amaduzzi, A. (1996) Storia della Ragioneria, Uomini e opere, (Abbozzo di un'idea). In: AA. VV. (ed.), *L'Evoluzione degli Studi di Ragioneria dalla fine del XVIII Secolo. Storie di imprese siciliane*. Pisa: Pacini Editore, pp. 21–41.

Antinori, C. (2001) Introduzione allo studio della Storia della Ragioneria. *Contabilità e Cultura Aziendale* I(1): 10–13.
Antonelli, V. and D'Alessio, R. (2011) *Gli studi di storia della ragioneria dall'unità d'Italia ad oggi: Evidenze, interpretazioni e comparazioni in tema di autori, opere, oggetto e metodo*. Milan: Franco Angeli.
Apolloni, C. (2002) L'onorevole Antonino D'Agata "U Cavaleri". *Gli Avolesi nel mondo, Associazione Culturale* 3(1): 4–9.
Apolloni, C. (2004) L'occupazione delle terre in provincia di Siracusa nel 1920. I Parte. *I Siracusani* 52: 51–55.
Apolloni, C. (2005) L'occupazione delle terre in provincia di Siracusa nel 1920. II Parte. *I Siracusani* 53: 46–50.
Besta, F. (1922) *La Ragioneria*, Vol. III, second edition. Milan: Vallardi.
Bhimani, A. (1994) Accounting enlightenment in the age of reason. *The European Accounting Review* 3(3): 399–442.
Bianca, G. (1983) *Manuale della coltivazione del mandorlo in Sicilia*, rist. an. dell'edizione del 1872. Avola: Libreria Editrice Urso.
Bonfiglio-Dosio, G. (2003) *Archivi d'impresa. Studi e proposte*. Padua: Cleup.
Broglia, G. (1922) Verità, sincerità e chiarezza delle scritture contabili e dei bilanci delle società anonime. *Rivista Italiana di Ragioneria* 12: 519–523.
Broglia, G. (1923) Verità, sincerità e chiarezza delle scritture contabili e dei bilanci delle società anonime. *Rivista Italiana di Ragioneria* 1: 30–38.
Calabrese, G. (ed.) (2007) *Gli archivi d'impresa in Sicilia*. Milan: Franco Angeli.
Cancilia, O. (1995) *Storia dell'industria in Sicilia*. Rome: Editori Laterza.
Canziani, A. (1997) Evoluzione e rivoluzione della Ragioneria Italiana tra le due guerre mondiali. *Storia della Ragioneria* 1(0): 74–89, Rome: Rirea.
Ceriani, G. and Fraza, B. (2007) *Metodi, sistemi contabili e connesse strutture di conto economico nelle imprese*. Padua: Cedam.
Consorzio di tutela della mandorla Avola. Available at: http://www.consorziomandorlaavola.it/ [Accessed: 12th January 2015].
Coronella, S. (2014) *Storia della Ragioneria Italiana Epoche, Uomini e Idee*. Milan: Franco Angeli.
Croce, B. (1989) *Teoria e storia della storiografia*. Milan: Adelphi.
Di Pietra, R. (1993) Corrispondenza e libri contabili inerenti il rapporto di affari Ingham-Florio nella prima metà del XIX secolo. In: AA. VV. (ed.), *L'evoluzione degli studi di ragioneria dalla fine del XVIII secolo*, Pisa: Pacini Editore, pp. 217–247.
Ferraris Franceschi, R. (1978) *L'indagine metodologica in Economia Aziendale*, Milan: Giuffrè editore.
Ferraris Franceschi, R. (1997) Storia della ragioneria, storia dell'impresa, storia dell'azienda e della pubblica amministrazione. *Storia della Ragioneria* I(0): 16–26. Rome: Rirea.
Fleischman, R.K. and Radcliffe, V.S. (2005) The roaring nineties: Accounting history comes of age. *Accounting Historians Journal* 32(1): 61–110.
Gomes, D. (2008) The interplay of conceptions of accounting and schools of thought in accounting history. *Accounting History* 13(4): 479–509.
Gomes, D., Carnegie, G.D., Napier, C.J., Parker, L.D. and West, B. (2011) Does accounting history matter? *Accounting History* 16(4): 389–402.
Guba, E.G. and Lincoln, Y.S. (1981) *Effective evaluation: Improving the usefulness of evaluation results through responsive and naturalistic approaches*. San Francisco: Jossey-Bass.
Hobsbawm, E.J. (1995) *Il secolo breve*, trad. di Brunello Lotti. Milan: Rizzoli.
Lincoln, Y.S. (2002) *On the nature of qualitative evidence*. Annual Meeting of the Association for the study of Higher Education, Sacramento, California, 21–24 November 2002.

Melis, F. (1950) *Storia della ragioneria*. Bologna: Zuffi.
Michael, G. (2011) What is (accounting) history? *Accounting History* 16(3): 235–251.
Muscato Daidone, C. (2011) *Avola. Storia della città. Dalle origini ai nostri giorni*. Siracusa: CMD Edizioni.
Nobolo, A., Guarini, E. and Magli, F. (2013) Il processo di unificazione del Regno d'Italia e l'armonizzazione dei preesistenti sistemi contabili (*The unification of Italy and its accounting harmonization*). *Contabilità e Cultura Aziendale* 1: 63–90.
Onida, P. (1949) Bilanci economici e bilanci fiscali delle imprese. *Moneta e Credito* 2(5): 42–50.
Parker, R.H. and Yamey, B.S. (eds.) (1994) *Accounting history: Some British contributions*, Oxford: Clarendon Press.
Regione Siciliana, Assessorato Agricoltura e Foreste, Unità Operativa 50 S.O.A.T. Siracusa. *Appunti per una storia della mandorla di Avola*. [Online] Available at: www.consorziomandorlaavola.it [Accessed: 11th February 2015].
Renda, F. (1984) *Storia della Sicilia dal 1860 al 1970*, Vol. 1. Palermo: Sellerio.
Sargiacomo, M. (2008) Institutional pressures and isomorphic change in a high-fashion company: The case of Brioni Roman Style, 1945–89. *Accounting, Business & Financial History* 18(2): 215–241.
Servalli, S. (2007) Il metodo e l'analisi sistemica nelle ricerche di Storia della Ragioneria. *Contabilità e cultura aziendale* 3(2): 59–78.
Topolski, J. (1997) *Narrare la Storia. Nuovi principi di metodologia storica*. Milan: Bruno Mondadori Editore.
Valacchi, F. (2007) Informazione e memoria: risorse per l'impresa. Elementi per la valutazione dell'efficienza di un sistema documentario aziendale. In: Calabrese, G. (ed.), *Gli archivi d'impresa in Sicilia*. Milan: Franco Angeli, pp. 65–72.
Vallone, C. (2011) *L'evoluzione del capitalismo familiare al mutare del sistema legislativo e finanziario italiano dall'Italia pre-unitaria ad oggi*, in Atti del XI Convegno Nazionale di Storia della Ragioneria su *Finalismo e ruolo delle aziende nel processo di costruzione dello Stato Unitario. Modelli aziendali e sistemi di produzione in Italia dal XIX al XX secolo*, Roma, 2–3 Dicembre 2011.
Vianello, V. (1930) *Istituzioni di Ragioneria Generale*, Sesta edizione. Milan-Genoa-Rome-Naples: Società Anonima Editrice Dante Alighieri.
Yin, R.K. (2003) *Case study research: Design and methods*. Thousand. Oaks, CA: Sage Publications.
Zappa, G. (1927) *Tendenze nuove negli studi di ragioneria*. Milan: Istituto Editoriale Scientifico.

13 Accounting in International Grain Trade

The Case of Nicolò Di Negro of Genoa, 1580s–1600s

Francesco Avallone, Andrea Zanini, Paola Ramassa and Alberto Quagli

INTRODUCTION

Our work stems from the analysis of the original accounting records of Nicolò Di Negro, a Genoese grain trader operating in the second half of the sixteenth century, when the Republic of Genoa reached the top of its celebrity. The analysis of Nicolò Di Negro's commercial activity and accounting techniques is possible thanks to the survival of a rich collection of manuscript records of the Di Negro family, which are now part of a larger family archive, that of the Doria di Montaldeo, preserved in the Centro di Studi e Documentazione di Storia Economica "Archivio Doria" of the University of Genoa. These primary sources include above all several kinds of accounting records, especially double entry ledgers and journals, cash books, waste books and related accompanying materials, like drafts of preliminary accounts, notes and trial balances (Saginati, 2004).[1]

Admittedly, several Italian organizations and societies of the sixteenth and early seventeenth centuries have already been investigated by accounting historians. Nevertheless, while prior literature has been inclined to analyze either religious societies (e.g., Quattrone, 2004) or State government (e.g., Sargiacomo, 2008, 2009; Sargiacomo et al., 2012), as well as proto-industrial settings (e.g., Zambon and Zan, 2007), it seems that there is still much to appreciate about the role played by accounting in international grain trade. In a related manner, while there already exist prior investigations on the role of merchants, which have built up drawing on evidences emerged in Italian archives (i.e., Heers, 1959 on Giovanni Piccamiglio; Peragallo, 1977 and 1981 on Jachomo Badoer, both operating in the fifteenth century), there is still space for investigations of the activities of leading Italian merchants at the turn of the sixteenth century.

With the above premises, our study could be of interest as it shows two main original findings. Since Nicolò Di Negro was a trade agent working on behalf of other principals, his records show how an ancient "agency relationship" was translated into accounting terms. This case helps modern scholars to understand the relevance of verifiability as the main principle for accounting and, more generally, the stewardship function of accounting records.

Second, it demonstrates how accounting records do not automatically flow in a financial statement. Nicolò's accounting records do not include any capital or income accounts related to his business. This point relates to the previous one, taking into account the nature of Nicolò's business. Due to his job as a trade agent, he did not operate with his capital, eliminating the need to follow the evolution of the capital with accounting records.

Another interesting finding of our analysis is the combined nature of the accounting approach used by Nicolò, as a mix of cash and accrual accounting. We try to demonstrate that this approach was functional to Nicolò's objective to prove his honesty and trading capacity to his principal.

This chapter is structured as follows. In the first section we describe the main features of the Nicolò's life, his work and the economic and historical context where he ran his business. The second section analyzes his accounting records, dealing with both formal characteristics and substantial objectives. Finally we compare the Nicolò's accounting technique with the existing practices of his time.

Nicolò's records demonstrate the tight link of accounting with the food business, the most ancient economic industry. The evolution of that business, as in our case an agent relationship, influenced the evolution of accounting, giving rise to very distinctive features.

NICOLÒ DI NEGRO: A LATE SIXTEENTH-CENTURY'S COMMISSION AGENT AND HIS BUSINESS RECORDS

Nicolò Di Negro was born in Genoa on 17 February 1565, the second-born son of Francesco and Battina Spinola (ADG, DM, 166, fo. 1; 168, fo. 1). Both his parents belonged to old and prominent families of the Genoese patriciate, whose members often played important roles in the political and economic scene (Doria, 1991; Saginati, 2004).

Since the 1560s, his father Francesco was an active businessman engaged in long-distance trade—especially wool, silk, spices, grain and coral—as well as in several financial operations (Saginati, 2004; Piccinno, 2006). It should be pointed out that in sixteenth-century Genoa there was not a merchants' guild, so citizens of every social class could be involved in wholesaling and long-distance trade, without belonging to any formal association (Massa, 2004).

Differently from his elder brother Bonifacio, who took up the ecclesiastical career, Nicolò followed his father's steps, and thus was quickly involved in the family business (Saginati, 2004). After a period of apprenticeship, in 1588, he began his mercantile career at the age of 23. In this early phase, he acted essentially as a commission agent in long-distance grain trade. This choice was not uncommon. Commission business represented an ideal nursery of young merchants: on the one hand, it was less risky than trade for their own account, as it was the principal who bore the entrepreneurial risk; on the other hand, it allowed them to acquire experience and reputation while requiring small investments (Kohn, 2003).

In the following years, Nicolò's activity gradually enlarged and he entered a partnership with his younger brother Gio Geronimo (1571–1628). Like many Genoeses of the time, Gio Geronimo was already involved in important financial operations in Spain together with other relatives: the brothers Lazzaro and Benedetto Pichenotti (Felloni, 1978; Drelichman and Voth, 2014). Although this change contributed to a progressive shift toward finance, Nicolò and Gio Geronimo Di Negro continued to deal in cereals, up to Nicolò's death, on 9 February 1605, just a few days before his fortieth birthday (ADG, DM, 198, annex n. 1). This continuity was due to the characteristics of the demand and the supply in the international grain market of the time and to high potential profit connected to the buying and selling of this specific commodity (Aymard, 1966; Mercier, 1999).

Nicolò's business records make it possible to delve into his business, with a particular focus on his role in international grain trade. In this respect, his activity as a commission agent can contribute to improve our knowledge concerning important aspects of early modern long-distance trade. Although merchant houses and their foreign agents have long attracted scholars' attention, they have been studied mainly from the point of view of the principal, while several aspects of commission agents' activity remain neglected. This is particularly true when considering the way in which commission agents operated, especially as regards the accounting techniques they used to manage their everyday business, as most of these essays focused on commercial letters rather than on accounting records (Edler, 1938; Kohn, 2003; Greif, 2006; Fiorentino, 2007; Trivellato, 2009).

At the beginning of his entrepreneurial career, the core business of Nicolò Di Negro was the selling of grain in Genoa *al meglio* (to the best of his ability) for the account of foreign merchants, in return for a commission. His activity is well documented by two double entry accounting records: a ledger entitled Libro propprio di Nicolò Di Negro [Nicolò Di Negro's own book] (ADG, DM, 181) and its corresponding journal (ADG, DM, 158), covering the period 1588–1592, together with several annexes. Both of these books are in quarto and have vellum covers.

It should be pointed out that Nicolò's choice to focus on grain is due to the high demand of this product in the Genoese market. Since the Middle Ages, Genoa had become one of the most active Mediterranean ports and a hub of international trade for primary goods, such as raw materials and foodstuffs (Grendi, 1987; Piccinno, 2000; Felloni, 2003). Differently from other commodities, the grain was mainly sold in Genoa itself or within the State boundaries. In fact, the scarcity of the domestic cereal production had always forced the Republic of Genoa to import large quantities of wheat (Grendi, 1970; Calcagno, 2012).

After the 1580–1581 plague, when Genoa's population fell to 48,000, the city population quickly start to increase again, reaching 62,000 in 1597 and 68,000 in 1608 (Felloni, 1952). As a consequence, from the 1580s to the 1600s, the demand for foodstuffs rose considerably, stimulating the growth of grain trade. Moreover, in 1590 the government declared Genoa a free port for grain. The aim of this decision, adopted after several years of lean harvests, was to attract an increasing volume of wheat in order to meet the population needs and to keep prices low (Giacchero, 1972; Kirk, 2005). This measure was connected to the state intervention in the domain of cereal provision started in 1564 with the foundation of the Magistrato dell'Abbondanza, a public body aimed to prevent famine and to organize the making and selling of bread (Massa, 1998; Calcagno, 2012).

Nicolò received essentially several consignment of *roccella*, a variety of soft grain also called Majorca, and some hard grain—both coming from Sicily, which, during that period, was an important trader in cereals and one of Genoa's leading grain suppliers (Grendi, 1970; Davies, 1983; Epstein, 1992; Cancila, 1999). This was due to the fact that, since the late Middle Ages, Genoese businessmen were present on a large scale in the Sicilian economy, mainly involved in foodstuffs (especially cereals and sugar) and the silk trade (Doria, 1986; Epstein, 1992).

Differently from other commission agents of the time who usually served many principals, during these 5 years Nicolò worked almost entirely on behalf of a Genoese firm based in Palermo (the capital of Sicily), Pasquale Di Negro & Antonio Spinola (ADG, DM, 181, fos. 2, 4, 9). The surname of the partners suggests the existence of family ties with Nicolò (directly and through his mother), although Pasquale and Nicolò belonged to different branches of the family, one can surely state that the presence of blood bonds explains the existence of such an exclusive and trustworthy business relationship. Of course, this is not a coincidence: in fact, family links, together with self-enforcement contracts, are two key elements to overcome information asymmetries in long-distance trade and to prevent the well-known principal-agent problem (Greif, 2006; Fusaro, 2012).

It should be pointed out that Nicolò was not involved in the Di Negro & Spinola partnership in any way, neither was he one of their employees. Rather he was a commission agent. His accounting records clearly prove that he sold the grain on behalf of Di Negro & Spinola but in his own name, acting totally independently from his principal. Moreover he did not receive a regular wage or a share of profit, but he was rewarded with a percentage of the value of the gross proceed once each cargo of cereals was sold (ADG, DM, 181, fos. 2, 9).

Normally the grain was shipped from Castellamare del Golfo, along the northwestern coast of the island, which was one of the so-called *caricatori*, or small ports, closed to the areas of production, where cereals converged in order to be shipped, both inside and outside the Kingdom of Sicily (Davies, 1983; Epstein, 1992). When the ship arrived in Genoa, Nicolò had to manage the unloading of the grain and its storage, facing occasional problems occurred during transport, such as storms, shipwrecks, fires, pirates or privateers, which might determine damages or shortfalls of the grain. In the meantime he had to pay freight and taxes (custom duties and other indirect taxes) for the account of Di Negro & Spinola, while the principal directly paid the insurance premium before shipping. At the end of this phase, he started to sell the grain as best as he could. Selling operations required specific professional skills and market knowledge: he had to choose the best moment to sell and to identify the most reliable customers, especially if they agreed on special conditions, in particular in case of payment extension (ADG, DM, 181, fos. 7–8).

Once the whole cargo of grain was sold, Nicolò had to draw up the statement of account, to be sent to the principal. The aim of this document—based on information from his accounting books—is to inform Di Negro & Spinola about their credit, that is to say the net proceed of the selling activity. On this occasion, he showed them each phase of the whole procedure: the gross proceeds and all the deductions, such as freight, storage and porterage charges, sales expenses, taxes and, of course, his fee, which was usually 2% of the gross proceeds. Once Di Negro & Spinola approved the statement of account, Nicolò had to agree with them for money transfer, in order to conclude the commercial transaction (ADG, DM, 181, fos. 4; annex n. 2).

THE ACCOUNTING PROCEDURES ADOPTED BY DI NEGRO

The Essence of the Bookkeeping System

In this section we provide insights into the accounting techniques used by Nicolò Di Negro to record his business as a commission agent in the grain trade, especially referred to the relationship with principals, sub-agent, customers and suppliers of services (e.g., shipping and storing).

As already explained in previous paragraphs, Di Negro essentially acted as a commission agent in grain trade shipped from Castellamare del Golfo, in the northwestern coast of Sicily. He mainly sold grain in Genoa *al meglio* (to the best of his ability), almost entirely on behalf of a Genoese firm based in Palermo (Pasquale Di Negro & Antonio Spinola). Hence Di Negro, who acted through a sub-agent (Benedetto Ottone), sold the grain in return for a commission, thus reducing the capital invested in the business and leaving to the principal both the cost of grain and the resulting entrepreneurial risk. Also, the principal directly paid the insurance premium before shipping. When the whole cargo was sold, Di Negro drew up the net sales account to be sent to the principal in order to retain his profit.

The evidence as to the accounting techniques adopted by Di Negro is provided by both the double entry ledger and the bookkeeping entries in the journal, that cover Nicolò's activity over the period 1588–1592.

As suggested by coeval bookkeeping manuals (Peri, 1638; Lerici, 2003), all bookkeeping entries specifically related to accounts identified on the left side of the journal by a fraction where numerator recognized the number of the account recorded on the debit side, and denominator showed the number of the account recorded on the credit side. Additionally, according to the T-account ruling of dividing the debit side (left) from the credit side (right), each account (identified by a specific number) was recorded in two separate and opposite pages of ledger, identified with the same number, unless the need to fill in the page (to avoid empty blank space) required recording more than one account in the same sheet. Specifically, if the space in a page was filled before the conclusion of the operations, the account was closed and transferred in a new page of the ledger.

Thus, even if throughout the various books the use of the terms debit (*dare*) and credit (*avere*) was missing, the aforementioned accounting techniques clearly imply that the system was a double entry one. The entries were periodically recorded in the journal, usually on a monthly basis instead of a daily one, and they included meticulous descriptions. The language used was Italian and figures were in Arabic numerals, although several Genoese account books of the time were still in Latin with Roman numerals (ADG, DM, 158 and 181).[2]

In order to easily appreciate the use of accounts by Di Negro in his everyday business, we focus on a specific order of grain ("Conto di 580 grani di Rucchelle del Regno di Sicilia caricati nel porto de Castellamare del Golfo"), from its shipment (from Sicily island) until the whole cargo was sold.

To better understand the adopted accounting procedures, especially the interlocking between accounts, we isolate the following five accounts of the general ledger:

- The account (identified by the number 2, hereinafter fo. 2) recording the net profit from sales (net of the operating costs and Nicolò's percentage fee on the gross proceeds) and its link with receivables arising from sales on credit ("vendita a respiro").
- The account (identified by number 6, hereinafter fo. 6) recording the detail of grain sold at a lower price or on credit because of the damages or shortfalls received during transportation.
- The account (identified by the number 1, hereinafter fo. 1) recording the net position (in terms of net receivables) between Nicolò Di Negro and his sub-agent (Benedetto Ottone).
- The account (identified by number 4, hereinafter fo. 4) recording the net position (in terms of net debt) with the principal.
- The account (identified by number 15, hereinafter fo. 15) recording the freights to be paid to shipmaster, after any savings in freight due to damages or shortfalls occurred during shipments.

Certainly, of these accounts the central one is the net profit account (fo. 2). It collects together all sales and expenses related to a specific order of grain. Particularly, the account is credited with all trades, both sales on credit and those that are paid for in cash, together with sales of damaged grain. On the left-hand side, the account is debited with all the operating expenses that the sell-agent had to pay at the arrival of the cargo (grain handling, rent for warehouse, measure of grain at the arrival in the port), and the net freight, that is the transportation costs on the grain to sell less the discount granted by the shipmaster in case of damages or shortfalls. As already explained, the account was not debited with the insurance premium since the principal already paid it. Nicolò's fee, estimated as a percentage on the gross proceeds, and the total amount of sales on credit are debited as well. The latter record enables the account to deal with the need to draw up the statement of the account to be sent to the principal, after the whole cargo of grain was sold, to conclude the commercial transaction through a money transfer. Actually, the account is balanced, and the balance is the "cash" net profit, a profit already gained without any sales on credit (see Figure 13.1). So, this is the amount the agent had to pay to the principal when the whole order of grain was sold, together with any cash inflows received but referred to previous cargos of grain sold on credit. Thus, the account seems to record both sales and expenses in the principal's perspective, even if it obviously does not consider any costs already covered by the principal.

Operating expenses...(detail).....£	62. 5	Cash sale (detail) ....£	4773.15
Operating expenses...(detail).....£	577.19.8	Cash sale (detail) ....£	1357. 3.4
Operating expenses...(detail).....£	64. 4.5	Sales on damaged grain (both on credit and cash) ....£	8094.14
Operating expenses...(detail).....£	28.17.9	Discount granted by the shipmaster for damages or shortfalls..........£	150
Operating expenses...(detail).....£	157. 4.8	Discount granted by the shipmaster for damages or shortfalls..........£	702
Operating expenses...(detail).....£	29. 2.3	£	15077.12.4
Sales on credit..........£	7892.10		
Freight (on the grain to sell) ......£	1187. 3.4		
Di Negro's fee (on total amount credited)..........£	301.11		
Net profit (base of money transfer with principal)..........£	***4776. 14.3***		
£	15077.12.4		

Figure 13.1 Net profit account (580 grain picked up in Castellamare del Golfo by Pietro Remezzano)

Source: ADG, DM, 181(19), fo. 2

Note: Monetary figures are expressed in Italian Lire (£), soldi and denari (there were 12 denari in each soldo, and 20 soldi in each lira).

The account identified in the Nicolò's bookkeeping with number 6 (fo. 6) allows an in-depth analysis of interesting accounting features: the sales on damaged grains and the sales on credit.

The account depicts a detail of the sell of damaged grain, by crediting the account with quantity, price and amount of every trade. The account easily distinguishes between cash sales and sales on credit as well. Each cash sale transaction (achieved by the sub-agent) recorded in the specific account of damaged grain had an effect in the net financial position toward the sub-agent (fo. 1), with an increase in receivables (debit side). On the contrary, the record of sales on credit for damaged grain increased receivables in specific accounts for each debtor. Thus, personal accounts existed for people who owed money. The periodical balance of these personal accounts was determined by debiting the net profit account (fo. 2) with sales on credit, thus showing in the net profit account the previously described "cash" net profit (Figure 13.2).

The account referred to the total amount of damaged grain sold was periodically balanced, giving rise to an entry on the right-hand side of the net profit account (fo. 2).

Three other (financial) accounts provide interesting insight into Nicolò's accounting procedures: the net financial position with the sub-agent (fo. 1), the net financial position with the principal (fo. 4) and the net financial position with the shipmaster (fo. 15), respectively.

The account identified by number 1 (fo. 1) was a financial account providing the net receivable between Nicolò Di Negro and his sub-agent (Benedetto Ottone). In other words, the balance of the account showed the money that Di Negro had to collect from his agent when a specific order of grain was sold.

Specifically, the account was credited with all the payment Di Negro made on behalf of the principal (even if not referred to the specific order of grain) through the medium of Benedetto Ottone, and with all the operating cost paid by Benedetto Ottone at the arrival of the cargo (e.g., grain handling, rent for warehouse, measure of grain at the arrival in the port). The Ottone's fee (a percentage on the grain sold) credited the account as well.

Cash sales by Benedetto Ottone, together with the detail of damaged goods (due to bad transportation) sold in cash, and all the payments Benedetto Ottone should have received, were recorded by debiting the account. Figure 13.3 aggregates and summarizes the previously described records.

Nicolò's net financial position with the principal was summarized in fo. 4. The specific account was recorded by the balance of fo. 2 (net "cash" profit for a specific order of grain) in the credit side, together with the cash inflows referred to previous sales on credit received by the agent (or by his sub-agent). Any receivable with principal was stored in the left side of the "net financial position with principal" account, especially due to cash outflows made by the agent (or by his sub-agent) on behalf of the principal.

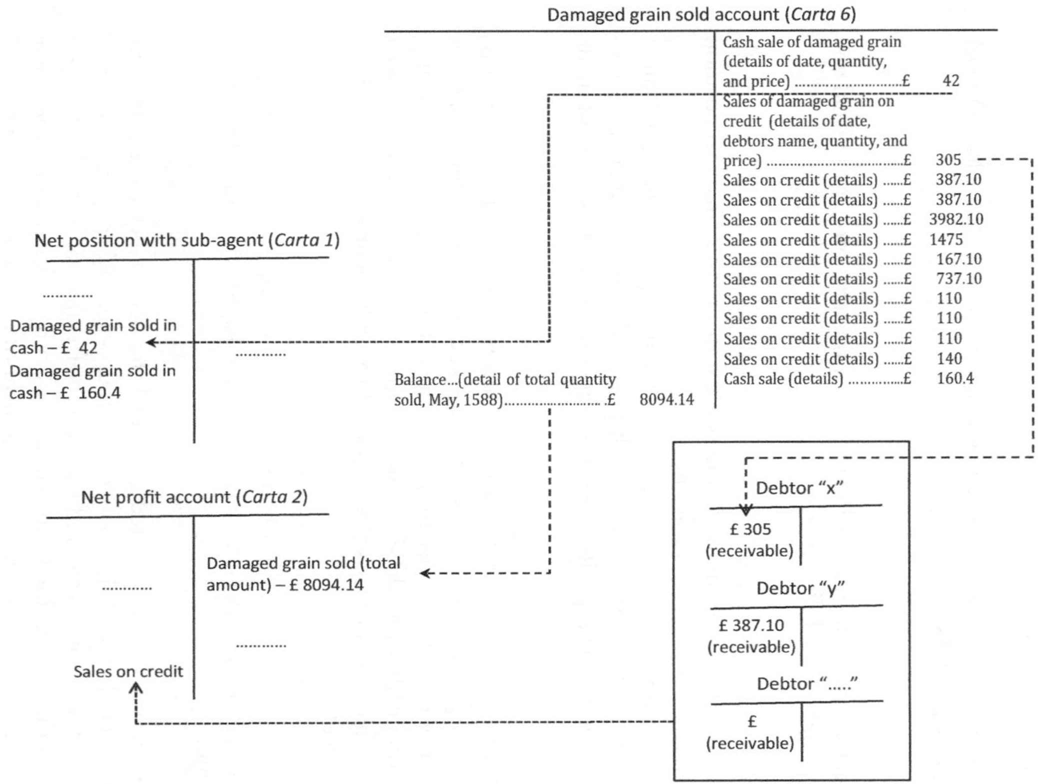

Figure 13.2 Detail of "damaged grain sold account"

Source: Fo. 6, March–May 1588

Note: monetary figures are expressed in Italian Lire (£), soldi and denari (there were 12 denari in each soldo, and 20 soldi in each lira).

Freights (received by sub-agent)..£	....	Payment on behalf of the principal.......................................£	....
Cash sales ....£	....	Operating cost paid (e.g. grain handling, rent for warehouse, measure of grain at the arrival in the port).......................................£	....
Cash sales of damaged grain (detail)..£	....	Sub-agent fee (on total sales)......£	....

Figure 13.3 Summary of net financial position with sub-agent (Benedetto Ottone)
Source: Fo. 1, January 1588

With reference to the interlocking between the accounts, the journal and the ledger suggest the following:

1. Cash sales were recorded in the right-hand side of the "net profit account" (revenues in fo. 2) and debited in the "net financial position with sub-agent" (receivables in fo. 1).
2. Cash outflows made by sub-agent on behalf of principals were debited in the "net financial position with principal" (fo. 4) and credited into the "net financial position with sub-agent," since the sub-agent made payments (fo. 1).
3. Cash sales of damaged goods gave rise to an entry on the left-hand side of the "net financial position with sub-agent" (fo. 1), and a record on the right-hand side of the "damaged grain sold account" (fo. 6). In other words, an increase in this revenues (the specific nature of transaction justify more detailed information in the account) was followed by an increase in receivables (toward the sub-agent who received the payment).
4. Sales of damaged goods on credit gave rise to an entry in the credit side of the "damaged grain sold account" (fo. 6), followed by an increase in receivables in personal accounts existing for everyone who owed money.

Finally, a specific account existed to record the net financial position with the shipmaster that was the basis of the following cash payment (fo. 15). Particularly, the account was credited with the freight that was split into two records: (1) the freight due to the shipment of the order of grain the agent had to sell; (2) the freight due to the shipment of other goods the ship could take on, paid by the agent who managed the main part of the cargo and refunded by persons in charge of that part of the shipment.

Thus, the record of the former part of the freight (1) was followed by an entry on the left-hand side of the net profit (expenditure in fo. 2), while the record of the latter part of the freight (2) gave rise to a record on the left-hand side of the net financial position with sub-agent, since the sub-agent received the cash inflows from persons in charge of the other part of the cargo. If any damages on the stocks of wheat (or part of them) occurred during the shipment, the compensation from shipmaster was debited in the account (fo. 15), and it gave rise to an entry on the right-hand side of the net profit account (fo. 2). Therefore, a net freight was recorded into the net profit account, reducing the revenues from sales together with the other operating expenses.

Overall, the essence of accounting procedures adopted by Nicolò Di Negro is summarized in Figure 13.4.

Some Insight into the Accounting System Adopted

The above-described accounting system adopted by Nicolò Di Negro provides us with original insights into the use of accounting as an instrument to support the grain business from an agent's point of view.

The net profit account (fo. 2) is an interesting example illustrating the use of a statement of account between an agent (Nicolò Di Negro) and his principal (Pasquale Di Negro & Antonio Spinola) in the grain trade.

First, Nicolò's fee recorded on the debit side shows that he worked as a commission agent and not as an employee, even if in the 5-year period of analysis he almost entirely worked on behalf of the Pasquale Di Negro & Antonio Spinola. Furthermore, Nicolò's reward (301.11 Italian Lire) was a 2% fee on the total amount credited in the account, including both sales on credit and discounts granted by the shipmaster for damages or shortfalls, hence revealing that the principal bore entirely the entrepreneurial risk (both credit and profit risk).

Additionally, the debit side of the account was recorded by the total expenses the agent bore in order to sell the goods, and by the amount of sales on credit. Thus, since the account had to support the conclusion of a specific commercial transaction between principal and agent, expenses and revenues were based on the cash paid or received (cash basis accounting) rather than on the accrual basis accounting. The net "cash" profit was required to isolate the amount due to the principal, thus justifying the exclusion of sales on credit from total sales.

With reference to the account n. 6 (fo. 6), this accounting procedure based on the split between cash sales and sales on credit reveals that "standard" sales were usually made in cash, with the exception of sales of damaged grain that could be completed at better condition for customers (on credit and at a lower price).

Additionally, it is interesting noting that within payments received by Nicolò Di Negro's sub agent (Benedetto Ottone), debited in the account n. 1 (fo. 1) together with the freights on the grain to sell, there were also some freights paid by other users of the ship (merchants or agents). That provides evidence that only one person (probably people managing the main part of

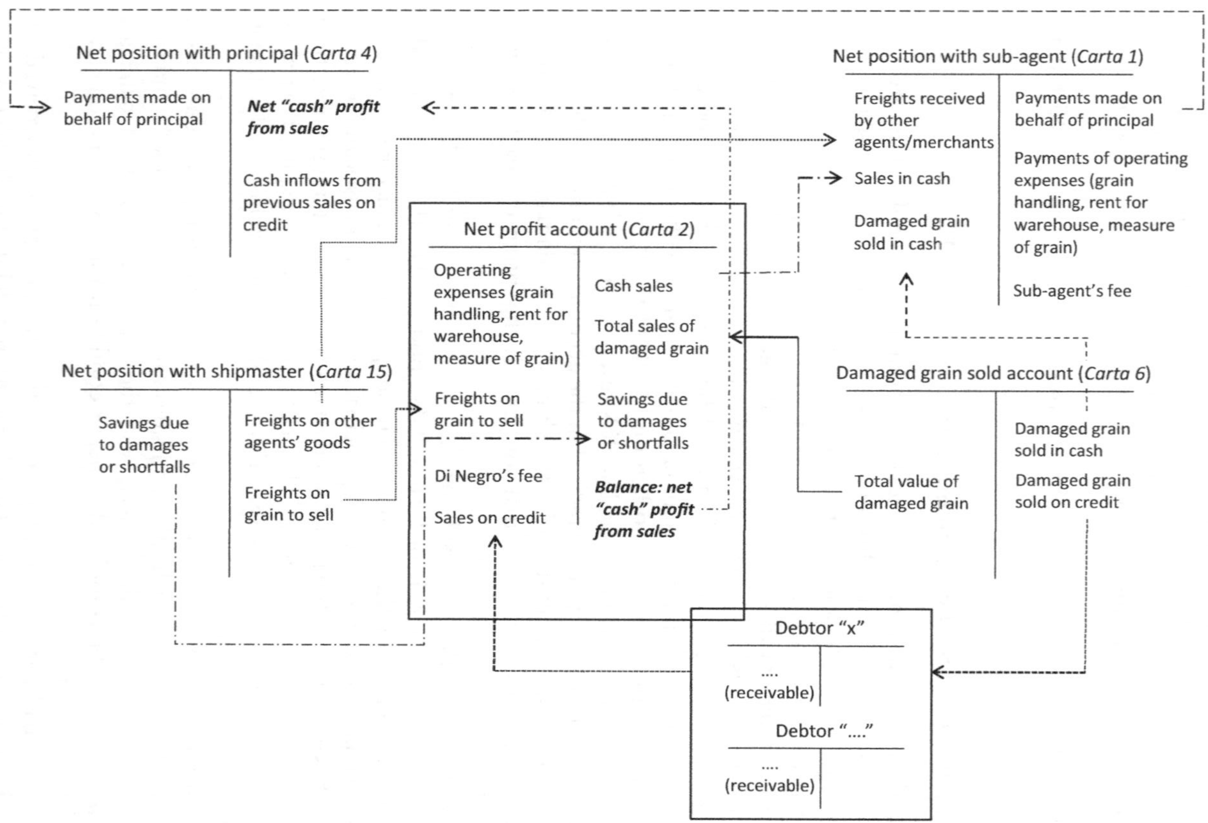

Figure 13.4 Accounting procedures adopted by Nicolò Di Negro (1588)

the cargo) entered into contract with the shipmaster, paying the freight of the full cargo. Consequently, it seems that the cargo was entirely received by one person who gradually released part of the cargo as soon as the payment of its portion of freight was received from the person in charge.

Overall, the accounting procedures seem to be based on the Nicolò's need to know the net value of cash sales (net of his commission and any expenditures the agent supported to sell the order or grain) since the balance of that account deals with the need to draw up the statement of the account to be sent to the principal (after the whole cargo of grain was sold) to conclude the commercial transaction through the final money transfer. Actually, the balance of the account is the "cash" net profit (without any sales on credit) the agent had to pay to the principal when the whole order of grain was sold, together with any cash inflows received but referred to previous transactions on credit.

Hence, since the net profit account had to support the partial conclusion of commercial transaction between principal and agent, expenses and revenues were based on the cash paid or received (cash basis accounting) rather than on the accrual basis accounting. However, it is useful to point out that the perishable nature of the grain sold required fast business transaction, thus reducing the differences between the periods to which the expenses/revenues related and the periods in which cash was paid/received.

Strictly linked with the net profit account are both the net financial position with principal account, credited with the net "cash" profit on sales (the balance of the net profit account), and the net financial position with the sub-agent account, recorded on the left-hand side with the amount of cash sales made by sub-agent. These two accounts enabled the agent to know the cash payment to make and the cash inflows to receive, respectively.

Thus, the accounting procedures seem to be influenced by the need to reduce cash money transfer, and to easily settle financial positions with both principal and sub-agent. The estimate of Nicolò's fee was significant as well. The fee, computed on the total amount credited in the net profit account, included both sales on credit and discounts granted by the shipmaster for damages or shortfalls, and reveals that the principal bore entirely the entrepreneurial risk (both credit and profit risk).

SOME REFLECTIONS ON NICOLÒ DI NEGRO'S ACCOUNTING PRACTICE INTO ITS HISTORICAL PERSPECTIVE

The distinctive features of this case in terms of geographical context (the Genoese Republic), business (international grain trade) and perspective (the commission agent's one) can be of interest to accounting historians to improve our understanding of Italian accounting between the sixteenth and seventeenth centuries. Indeed, accounting practices of that period so far have been studied mainly with regard to religious and public institutions (Di

Pietra, 1999, 2003; Mussari and Mussari, 2006; Sargiacomo, 2006; Zambon and Zan, 2007; Bracci et al., 2010; Lai et al., 2012; Servalli, 2013).

In pursuit of this main objective, we build on our analysis of Nicolò's activity and accounting records putting his accounting practice into its historical perspective. In particular, we base our analysis on accounting treatises written in the sixteenth and seventeenth centuries by Italian authors. We consider the former in order to analyze his accounts in the light of provisions included in coeval works. Additionally, we take into account the fact that at that time accounting treatises often described what was already happening in practice (Melis, 1950), especially as regards Genoa and Venice. In such a perspective, Nicolò Di Negro' s accounting practices could follow prescriptions included in books published in the sixteenth century or precede the content of treatises to be authored in the following decades.

Despite a scarce number of works covering accounting techniques, during the sixteenth century accounting made remarkable advances in the Italian area. Double entry bookkeeping turned out to be much more complex, both as a technical and cultural phenomenon, than was previously believed (Goldthwaite, 2015). It was in the first decades of the sixteenth century that were published the first books aimed at giving merchants a basic understanding of double entry booking (Coronella, 2014). Indeed, they could not base their knowledge on the long and difficult *Summa* by Luca Pacioli (Serra, 1999). During the following century, Italian accountants authored many accounting treatises producing some high-quality essays and a few works aimed at educational purposes (Coronella, 2014).

The most relevant accounting treatises of the two centuries were the ones authored respectively by Pietra (1586) and Flori (1636), both focused on religious institutions (Melis, 1950; Coronella, 2014). Among their distinctive features, it is worth recalling the introduction of concepts aimed at the adoption of an accrual-based accounting. In particular, Pietra used a sort of profit and loss account ("Entrata e spesa generale") and its balance was then recorded as a component of equity in a specific account named "Monastero nostro". His treatise introduces the idea that the statement of accounts were prepared not only to check the correctness of accounting records, but also to serve a stewardship function.

Due to the commercial activity of Nicolò Di Negro as a commission agent, the work by Casanova (1558)—who deeply influenced also Grisogono (1609) and Moschetti (1610)—is of interest to our study with reference to examples of accounting records for sales through commission agents (Coronella, 2014). In particular, the Venetian accountant illustrated how to account for a purchase of different kinds of merchandise to be sent and sold abroad through commission agents.

Other accounting treatises by Genoese authors witness the advances in accounting practice in the area where Nicolò Di Negro operated. In particular it is worth recalling the works by Ambrogio Lerici (2003) and Giovanni Domenico Peri (1638).

The treatise by Antonio Lerici is a relatively recent discovery for Italian accounting history scholars attributable to Carlo Antinori (2000), who found the second volume of this work written in German and published in Danzig by the Genoese businessmen. The place of publication itself shows the considerable interest expressed abroad in advanced Italian accounting techniques and practices. Indeed, Lerici grew up and studied in Genoa, starting his career as an accountant for several merchants. When he was 32, he moved to Danzig where he taught accounting and worked as an accountant for over 30 years, contributing to the diffusion of double entry bookkeeping in Northern European countries. His treatise is of particular interest not only for its clarity, but also for being the first work with a specific focus on international trade.

The work by the Genoese Peri was printed in Genoa in 1638 as regards its first part and then extended until the final version divided into four parts published in 1673. Its contents are not always linked together, but offer a wide range of information within a scope not strictly limited to accounting considering many areas related to business administration. Notwithstanding its limited originality compared to other coeval treatises, it is a valuable source about common accounting practices adopted in Genoa at the time. Additionally, some of his examples were referred to grain trade and to sales through commission agents (see for example the *Manuale del libro di me Pietro Ventura cominciato in Genova à 2. di Genaro dell'anno 1637* in the first part of the treatise).

When putting Nicolò Di Negro's practice into its historical perspective, a first significant aspect to examine refers to some formal and methodological features of his bookkeeping activity. This can be regarded as a first important indicator for understanding how advanced his practice was. Additionally, it is to note that at the time order in bookkeeping was not only aimed at clarity, but had relevant practical—and eventually legal—implications. There was not an obligation to show accounting books in trial, but if they were regularly kept they could be exhibited and parties had to accept them as a proof (Peri, 1673, fourth part: 6).

Overall, the variety of our primary sources and the techniques used suggest a quite advanced accounting practice in terms of double entry bookkeeping.

All the accounting records were expressed in Arabic numerals, in line with directions provided by major coeval treatises (Pietra, 1586) and works by Genoese authors (Peri, 1638; Lerici, 2003). This practice became common among Genoese businessmen during the second half of the sixteenth century to speed and make easier accounting entries compared to records expressed in Roman numerals. However, some treatises printed in that period and in the following century still suggested the use of Roman numerals to reduce forgery risk. It is the case of Manzoni (1540), who uses only Roman numerals for records, and of Venturoli (1666), who proposes to debit and credit accounts using Roman numerals and Arabic numerals respectively. Also coeval accounting books referred to the activity of Nicolò's father Francesco and his brother Giacomo had entries in Roman numerals, thus demonstrating the coexistence of records in Arabic and Roman numerals in Genoa in that period.

The journal entries had a unique money of account (the Genoese lira), an ideal money used by Genoese businessmen for accounting purposes and as a measure for salaries and tariffs (Fantacci, 2008). Commercial transactions within the same business were settled with real money in different currencies, and the journal entry specified the real money originating the transaction in the operation description. This practice is consistent with treatises of that period, even if some authors accepted multiple moneys of accounts as well (Coronella, 2014). Ledger entries were recorded using both the Genoese lira and the real money in two separate columns only to account for highly complex operations, such as the ones taking place during trade fairs (as in fo. 3).

The journal records are in line with the models used at the time in the Genoese context. Each entry could be connected to accounts in the ledger thanks to a sort of fraction written on the left, showing the page number of the account debited (as numerator) and of the one credited (as denominator). This scheme is consistent with examples provided by treatises of the sixteenth and seventeenth centuries (Casanova, 1558; Pietra, 1586; Grisogono, 1609; Peri, 1638). Peri (1673) also illustrated that this model contained relevant information in terms of entry timing. According to his work, the line between the numerator and the denominator had to be written after debiting the corresponding account in the ledger and the long line below the entire journal entry had to be drawn after crediting the account shown in the denominator.

In the operation description in the journal, the account debited and the one credited are separated with the expression *vanno per*, in line with the Peri treatise (1638). This practice was common for all entries that did not show the term *a* that became widespread afterwards and at that time was adopted by authors from Venice (Casanova, 1558; Grisogono, 1609). It is interesting noting that journal records already used the term *partimenti* in entries requiring to debit (or credit) more than one account, as illustrated for the first time in 1586 Pietra's treatise (Yamey, 1981; Coronella, 2014).

As regards the more substantial aspects of Nicolò's accounting practice, his fee debited in the net profit account—clearly showing the role of commission agent of Di Negro—is consistent with theoretical rules proposed by Peri (1673) in the third part of his treatise. In particular, he distinguishes the principal's own accounts and accounts of others in a case of wool sale from Genoa to Milan through a commission agent.

Additionally, debits and credits recorded in the net profit account conformed to an example provided by Peri in the third part of his treatise, where a Genoese commission agent (Giovanni Battista di Genova) sold grain for the account of a principal (Francesco di Messina). In this example the net profit account (reproduced in Figure 13.5) was debited for freight, other

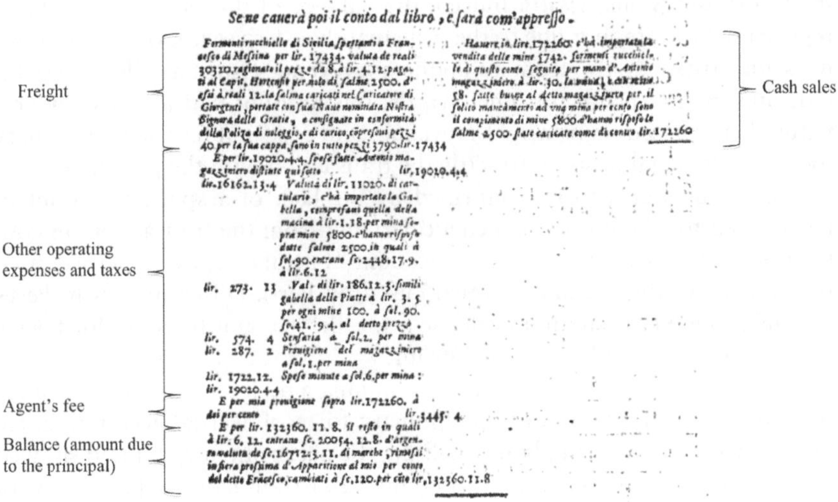

Figure 13.5 Example of net profit account in Peri (1673)

operating expenses, taxes and Giovanni Battista's fee, and credited for cash sales. As in Nicolò's case, the commission agent's fee was 2% of sales and the balance of the account represented the amount due to the principal to conclude their commercial transaction.

The approach adopted by Nicolò Di Negro as regards sales on credit—described in the previous paragraph—was not recalled by Peri, but seems to be in line with the cash-based accounting that was common at that time. It should be interpreted taking into consideration the main purpose of merchants' accounts that consisted in understanding the benefit or the damage deriving from each initiative (Catturi, 1997). That result could be measured as the net financial value of sales when determining the balance of the accounts at the end of the commercial transaction.

Cash inflows deriving from sales on credit after the end of the transaction were to be recorded only in accounts referred to net positions without any impact on the net profit of the following transaction. As a consequence, the balance of net position accounts did not always derive from a single sale. It could be influenced by other transactions and also by payments done by other individuals on behalf of Di Negro, as it was common at the time in order to reduce the number of cash payments.

The net profit account included revenues and costs recorded in the principal's perspective, but cannot be interpreted as a statement of accounts showing the final results and profitability of the single business as illustrated in coeval and following treatises (Pietra, 1586; Flori, 1636; Peri, 1638). This supports the idea that accounting records did not automatically flow in a financial statement and that double entry bookkeeping has not always aimed at this final purpose (Melis, 1950). Indeed, the balance of this account essentially represented the amount due to the principal that derives not only from revenues and costs, but also from nonmonetary revenues (such as sales on credit) reducing the net profit. In other words, this account had a sort of hybrid nature being based on principal's revenues and costs but having as a primary focus the financial position to settle the transaction with the principal.

This focus seems to be confirmed by the lack of a specific account to be credited for the economic benefit deriving from the transaction, in contrast with coeval treatises (i.e., the account "Entrata e spesa generale" used by Pietra, and the account "Avanzi" used by Peri). Differently from Peri's examples, Di Negro did not even use a specific account to credit for his fee in order to represent his personal profit.

Nicolò's practice did not aim at determining a periodic result for his or his principal's activity based on a preliminary form of accrual accounting. He determined his profit simply by crediting the net profit account and showed his principal the outcome of each commercial transaction separately with the balance of the same account.

The commission agent and principal information needs were significantly influenced by the nature of the good traded. Indeed, the perishable nature of cereals led to a quick commercial transaction: the first debit in the net profit account (referred to freight payment) was dated 6 February 1588 and the last credit (referred to the payment to the principal) was about 6 months later on 19 August. In this perspective, it is clear that the very short term characterizing the nature of the business reduced the need for accrual accounting and for an overall firm periodic result.

Information about investments and equity were not recorded either in Nicolò's accounts. With respect to coeval and following accounting treatises, this is another distinctive feature that should be considered in the light of his activity. Trading grain for the account of other merchants did not request considerable investment (Kohn, 2003) and at that time it was an ideal career for young businessmen who generally did not have a considerable capital as they had rarely come into their inheritance. As a result, Di Negro had not a considerable need to follow the evolution of capital with accounting records.

In the light of these considerations, the statement of account representing net profit seems to be strictly linked to Nicolò's and his principal's information needs. Essentially, it served a stewardship function and might be seen as a *redde rationem* in the relationship between the principal and the agent. This is particularly clear considering that it was included in Nicolò's correspondence with the Pasquale Di Negro e Antonio Spinola to report the amount due to the principal and to justify his fee. These objectives were pursued by means of regular and verifiable accounting records. So, the use of a mix of cash and accrual accounting can be interpreted a useful and rational approach considering his interest in showing his honesty and trading capacity to the principal.

In summary, the objective of highlighting business strengths with clarity and display weaknesses with timeliness seems to be met by following an adequately accurate and reliable procedure. Nicolò's procedures supports the idea that accounting practice should avoid additional—and time-consuming—operations not relevant to that purpose, provided that accounting books could represent an accurate picture of the business (Melis, 1950).

CONCLUSIONS

Logically, the study of the accounting practices adopted in the past requires a sequential process that begins with the analysis of the adopted practical procedures and ends with the derivation of the main features of the coeval accounting theory that have been used as a guide. Thus, our study has presented some important facets of the accounting procedures adopted by Nicolò Di Negro in the grain trade in the second half of the sixteenth century, comparing them with the coeval accounting background.

It aims to contribute to the rich literature on this period (e.g., Quattrone, 2004; Sargiacomo, 2008, 2009; Sargiacomo et al., 2012 for the Italian context, and Yamey, 2000; Edwards et al., 2009 for other geographical contexts) by focusing on international grain trade from a commission agent's perspective. Particularly, Nicolò's accounting practices, in line with the models used at the time in the Genoese context, show some interesting aspects. First, selling grain on the account of a principal, Di Negro was interested in showing the result of his activity to the principal, thus pointed out the relevance of verifiability as the main principle for accounting and, more generally, the stewardship function of accounting records.

Additionally, since the accounts had to support the conclusion of a specific commercial transaction between principal and agent, expenses and revenues were based on the cash paid or received (cash basis accounting) rather than on the accrual basis accounting.

The fact that the accounting records did not automatically flow in a statement of account is interesting as well, showing that agents, due to their limited capital, were not interested in monitoring capital through accounting records.

The use of accounting by agents in the late sixteenth century leaves us with the fact that accounting was a discipline with practical rules and supporting theories. The accounting discipline emerging from this case was practical but also rather complex and supported by theory, definitely a discipline aspiring to be at the core of the trade-business economy.

NOTES

1. When referring to primary sources we indicate the abbreviation of the name of the archive, the section (ADG, DM) and the record number.
2. Differently from other cases, Nicolò's ledger has not an alphabetical index of the accounts.

REFERENCES

Primary Sources

ADG, DM (Centro di Studi e Documentazione di Storia Economica "Archivio Doria", of the University of Genoa, Fondo Doria di Montaldeo [Doria of Montaledeo section]), records nos. 158, 166, 168, 181, 198.

Secondary Sources

Antinori, C. (2000) Ambrogio Lerici, ragioniere Genovese attivo a Danzica nella seconda metà del secolo XVI, in *La Ragioneria verso il terzo millennio tra continuità e rinnovamento*. V Convegno naizonale della Società Italiana di Storia della Ragioneria. Bergamo, 8–9 ottobre 1999, Padua: Cedam, pp. 65–72.

Aymard, M. (1966) *Venise, Raguse et le commerce du blé pendant la seconde moitié du XVIe siècle*. Paris: SEVPEN.

Bracci, E., Maran, L. and Vagnoni, E. (2010) Saint Anna's Hospital in Ferrara, Italy: Accounting and organizational change during the Devolution. *Accounting History* 15(4): 463–504.

Calcagno, P. (2012) Il Dominio genovese e il grano in Antico regime: un sistema federale sotto la sorveglianza dello Stato. *Storia Urbana* 35(1): 75–94.

Cancila, O. (1999) *Baroni e popolo nella Sicilia del grano*. Palermo: Palumbo.

Casanova, A. (1558) *Specchio lucidissimo, nel quale si vedeno essere diffinito tutti i modi, & ordini de scrittura, che si deve menare nelli negotiamenti della mercantia, cambii, recambii, con li loro corrispondentie, disgarbugliando, & illuminando l'intelletto a negotianti*. Venice: Comin da Trino di Monferrato.

Catturi, G. (1997) *Teorie contabili e scenari economico aziendali*, seconda edizione. Padua: Cedam.

Coronella, S. (2014) *Storia della ragioneria italiana. Epoche, uomini e idee*. Milan: FrancoAngeli.

Davies, T. (1983) Changes in the structure of the wheat trade in seventeenth-century Sicily and the building of new villages. *Journal of European Economic History* 12(2): 371–405.

Di Pietra, R. (2005) *L'Archivio del Seminario Arcivescovile di Siena nella seconda metà del XVII secolo, Storici della Ragioneria ed Archivisti: risultati di una proficua collaborazione multidisciplinare*, in Atti del VII Convegno Nazionale della Società Italiana di Storia della Ragioneria, Roma: Casa Editrice Rirea, pp. 365–401.

Di Pietra, R. and Di Toro, P. (1999) *Amministrazione e contabilità nel XV e XVI secolo, Lo Spedale senese del Santa Maria della Scala attraverso i libri contabili*. Padua: CEDAM.

Doria, G. (1986) Conoscenza del mercato e sistema informativo: il know-how dei mercanti-finanzieri genovesi nei secoli XVI e XVII. In: De Maddalena, A. and Kellenbenz, H. (eds.), *La repubblica internazionale del denaro tra XV e XVII secolo*. Bologna: Il Mulino, pp. 91–155.

Doria, G. (1991) Un banchiere e la costruzione di un palazzo. In: Doria, G., Gavazza, E. and Pellegrino, G. (eds.), *Palazzo Di Negro in Banchi*. Genoa: Costa & Nolan, pp. 7–22.

Drelichman, M. and Voth, H.-J. (2014) *Lending to the borrower from hell: Debt, taxes, and default in the age of Philip II*. Princeton: Princeton University Press.

Edler, F. (1938) The Van der Molen, commission merchants of Antwerp: Trade with Italy, 1538–44. In: Cate, J.L. and Anderson, E.N. (eds.), *Medieval and historiographical essays in honor of James Westfall Thompson*. Chicago: University of Chicago Press, pp. 78–145.

Edwards, J.R., Dean, G. and Clarke, F. (2009) Merchants' accounts, performance assessment and decision making in mercantilist Britain. *Accounting, Organizations and Society* 34(5): 551–570.

Epstein, S.R. (1992) *An island for itself: Economic development and social change in late medieval Sicily*. Cambridge: Cambridge University Press.

Fantacci, L. (2008) The dual currency system of Renaissance Europe. *Financial History Review* 15(1): 55–72.

Felloni, G. (1952) Per la storia della popolazione di Genova nei secoli XVI e XVII. *Archivio Storico Italiano* 110(2): 236–254.

Felloni, G. (1978) *Asientos, juros y ferias de cambio desde el observatorio genovés (1541–1675)*. In: Otazu, A. (ed.), *Dinero y Credito (Siglos XVII al XIX)*. Madrid: Benzal, pp. 335–359.

Felloni, G. (2003) Organización portuaria, navegación y tráfico en Génova: un sondeo entre las fuentes de la Edad Moderna. In: Ribot García, L.A. and De Rosa, L. (eds.), *Naves, puertos e itinerarios marítimos en la Época Moderna*. Madrid: Actas, pp. 237–267.

Fiorentino, A. (2007) *Il ruolo del commercio di commissione nel Basso Medioevo. Il caso delle pelli e delle cuoia*. Turin: Giappichelli.

Flori, L. (1636) *Trattato del modo di tenere il libro doppio domestico col suo esemplare*. Palermo: per Decio Cirillo.

Fusaro, M. (2012) Cooperating mercantile networks in the early modern Mediterranean. *The Economic History Review* 65(2): 701–718.

Giacchero, G. (1972) *Origini e sviluppi del portofranco genovese, 11 agosto 1590–9 ottobre 1778*. Genoa: Sage.

Goldthwaite, R. (2015) The practice and culture of accounting in renaissance Florence. *Enterprise & Society* 16(3): 611–647.

Greif, A. (2006) *Institutions and the path to the modern economy: Lessons from medieval trade*. Cambridge and New York: Cambridge University Press.

Grendi, E. (1970) Genova alla metà del Cinquecento: una politica del grano? *Quaderni storici* 5(1): 106–160.

Grendi, E. (1987) *La Repubblica aristocratica dei Genovesi. Politica, carità e commercio tra Cinque e Seicento*. Bologna: Il Mulino.

Grisogono, S. (1609) *Il mercante arricchito. Del perfetto quaderniere: overo, specchio lucidissimo, nel quale si scopre ogni questione, che desideare si possa per imparare perfettamente a tenere libro doppio*. Venice: Alessandro Vecchi.

Heers, J. (1959) *Le livre de comptes de Giovanni Piccamiglio, homme d'affaires Génois*, 1456–1459. Paris: SEVPEN.

Kirk, T.A. (2005) *Genoa and the sea: Policy and power in an early modern maritime republic, 1559–1684*. Baltimore and London: The Johns Hopkins University Press.

Kohn, M. (2003) *Business Organization in Pre-industrial Europe*, Working Paper 03–09, Department of Economics, Dartmouth College, Hanover, NH 03755, July 2003. Available at: http://dx.doi.org/10.2139/ssrn.427744

Lai, A., Leoni, G. and Stacchezzini, R. (2012) Governmentality rationales and calculative devices: The rejection of a seventeenth-century territorial barter proposed by the King of Spain. *Accounting History* 17(3–4): 369–392.

Lerici, A. (2003) *Una bella forma della contabilità secondo la vera e propria maniera italiana, redatta a regola d'arte e adattata al commercio prussiano, Impresso a Danzica da Wilhelm Willemoth nell'anno 1606*. Parma: Grafiche Step, (Original work published 1606).

Manzoni, D. (1540) *Quaderno doppio col suo giornale, novamente compost, e diligentemente ordinate, secondo il costume di Venezia. Opera a ogni persona illustrissima, & molto necessaria*. Venice: Comin da Trino di Monferrato.

Massa, P. (1998) The Genoese Guilds (XVI-XVII Centuries). The food administration offices and the food sector Guilds in Genoa: organisation and conflict. In:

Guenzi, A., Massa, P. and Piola Caselli, F. (eds.), *Guilds, markets and work regulation in Italy, 16th-19th centuries*. Aldershot: Ashgate, pp. 246–265.

Massa, P. (2004) Una città di mercanti e di banchieri (secoli XV-XVIII). In: Massa, P. (ed.), *Attori e strumenti del credito in Liguria. Dal mercante banchiere alla banca universale*. Genoa: Fondazione Carige, pp. 15–41.

Melis, F. (1950) *Storia della Ragioneria*. Bologna: Cesare Zuffi Editore.

Mercier, S. (1999) The evolution of world grain trade. *Review of Agricultural Economics* 21(1): 225–236.

Moschetti, G.A. (1610) *Dell'Universal trattato ai libri dopii, ne' quali con regole universali & esempi particolari ampiamente s'insegna il modo di girar in scrittura doppia qual si voglia negotio mercantile*. Venice: Luca Valentini.

Mussari, R. and Mussari, B. (2006) Bookkeeping in the sixteenth-century building yard of the Castello of Crotone: An accountancy and architectural analysis. *Accounting History* 11(3): 319–355.

Peragallo, E. (1977) The ledger of Jachomo Badoer: Constantinople September 2, 1436 to February 26, 1440. *The Accounting Review* 52(4): 881–92.

Peragallo, E. (1981) Closing procedures in the 15th century ledger of Jachomo Badoer, a Venetian merchant. *The Accounting Review* 56(3): 587–95.

Peri, G.D. (1638) *Il negotiante*. Genoa: Pier Giovanni Calenzano.

Peri, G.D. (1673) *Il negotiante, diviso in quattro parti*. Venice: Gio.Giacomo Hertz.

Piccinno, L. (2000) *Economia marittima e operatività portuale. Genova, secc. XVII-XIX*. Genoa: Società Ligure di Storia Patria.

Piccinno, L. (2006) Le popolazioni liguri e la pesca del corallo nel Mediterraneo. L'impresa di Francesco Di Negro e soci. In: Ravazza, N. (ed.), *Un fiore degli abissi. Il corallo: pesca, storia, economia, leggenda, arte*. Trapani: Associazione turistica pro loco, pp. 117–134.

Pietra, A. (1586) *Indirizzo degli Economi, o sia ordinatissima Instruttione da regolatamente formare qualunque Scrittura in un Libro doppio*. Mantua: Francesco Osanna.

Quattrone, P. (2004) Accounting for god: Accounting and accountability practices in the Society of Jesus (Italy, XVI-XVII Centuries). *Accounting, Organizations and Society* 29(9): 647–683.

Saginati, L. (ed.) (2004) *L'Archivio dei Doria di Montaldeo. Registri contabili, manoscritti genealogici e pergamene*. Genoa: Brigati.

Sargiacomo, M. (2006) Using accounting records to enhance an understanding of a seventeenth-century Italian feudal community: The case of the Commune of Penne (1664–90). *Accounting History* 11(4): 475–502.

Sargiacomo, M. (2008) Accounting and the 'art of government': Margaret of Austria in Abruzzo (1539–1586). *European Accounting Review* 17(4): 667–695.

Sargiacomo, M. (2009) Accounting for the "good administration of justice": The Farnese state of Abruzzo in the sixteenth century. *Accounting History* 14(3): 235–267.

Sargiacomo, M., Servalli, S., Carnegie, G.D. (2012) Accounting for killing: Accountability for sheath. *Accounting History* 17(3–4): 393–413.

Serra, L. (ed.) (1999) *Storia della Ragioneria Italiana*. Milan: Giuffrè.

Servalli, S. (2013) The interface of power and charity in the government of poor: A case from the Italian context in the sixteenth-seventeenth centuries. *Accounting, Auditing & Accountability Journal* 26(8): 1306–1341.

Trivellato, F. (2009) *The familiarity of strangers. The sephardic diaspora, livorno, and cross-cultural trade in early modern period*. New Haven and London: Yale University Press.

Venturoli, G. (1666) *Scorta di economia o sia dialogo di scrittura famigliare, opera non solo necessaria a' computisti tutelary, e famigliari, mà ancora à qualsivoglia amministratore di università, e collegi*. Bologna: heredi di Evangelista Dozza.

Yamey, B.S. (1981) The 'partimenti' account: A discarded practice. *Abacus* 17(1): 3–7.
Yamey, B.S. (2000) The 'particular gain and loss upon each article we deal in': An aspect of mercantile accounting, 1300–1800. *Accounting, Business & Financial History* 10(1): 1–12.
Zambon, S. and Zan, L. (2007) Controlling expenditure, or the slow emergence of costing at the Venice Arsenal, 1586–1633. *Accounting, Business & Financial History* 17(1): 105–128.

14 Accounting and Food Trade in Sixteenth-Century Ragusa

The Diffusion of Early Double Entry Bookkeeping: An Institutional Perspective

Dario Dell'Osa and Stella Lippolis

INTRODUCTION

Throughout the sixteenth century, the city-state of Ragusa, today Dubrovnik in Croatia, went through a phase of strong economic growth, helped by the expansion of maritime trade and the intensification of exchanges with the Balkan hinterland (Di Vittorio, 2001; Moroni, 2011). Characterized by a restricted territory and poorly productive agriculture, the Republic of Ragusa had built its economic fortune on trade and in particular on maritime traffic. Many of the most important and influential families of the nobility and the bourgeoisie in fact held shares in the ownership of ships, which were used for navigation in the Mediterranean.

In those years, the discovery of new ocean routes to the Indies had not weakened the Mediterranean commerce that absorbed much of the investments involved in international trade. In this context, the transport of foodstuffs, such as wheat, spices and salt assumed great importance for the supply of major European cities. Each of these three types of products generated traffics characterized by extremely complex dynamics. In particular, the grain trade, and cereals in general, was a very important lever of power and, above all, a political and international tool, linked to the chronic difficulties in the international food supply the great cities of the modern age were suffering from (Aymard, 1966; Braudel, 1986, p. 361).

There was a high demand of spices in the European market. Spices were in fact considered an essential product for the families belonging to the upper classes and were a true symbol of wealth and prosperity. Finally, irreplaceable and essential, salt was important for food preservation. For this reason it was in great demand in Ragusa, where maritime trade also demanded an adequate supply of vessels with food that could be kept for long periods. In this study we will examine in particular the case of one of the largest and most efficient mercantile companies in Ragusa, active in the second half of the sixteenth century, that of merchant ship owner Vincenzo Stefani.

While different sixteenth-century Mediterranean scenarios have been already investigated by accounting historians, especially referring to the

Italian states (e.g., Sargiacomo, 2008a, 2009; Zambon and Zan, 2007; Sargiacomo et al., 2012), there is still much to learn about the role played by merchants and companies in foodstuffs trade. This chapter[1] seeks to address all these lacunas, highlighting, through the study of accounting records concerning foodstuff, the issue of the spread of accounting techniques (Boyns and Edwards, 1996; Carnegie and Parker, 1996) via the channels of international trade, with particular reference to the role played by merchants and companies of merchants as first forms of collective enterprises (Catturi, 2009).

The accounting books kept in Ragusa and, in particular, the study of the books belonging to the merchant and held according to the rules of double entry bookkeeping between 1555 and 1588, very clearly show Stefani's remarkable mastery of the most advanced accounting techniques, which was also due to his many opportunities for contact with the merchants of the Italian peninsula. New institutional sociology offers the theoretical framework for an investigation that is centered on the early double entry bookkeeping as an institutionally determined practice (Meyer and Rowan, 1977; DiMaggio and Powell, 1983).

The level of analysis is twofold. First, we will investigate the main environmental and social pressures that influenced the operations of the merchant companies of the Republic in the period under review, taking as an example, to this end, the case of the Stefani company, and highlighting the role the merchant played in the international trade of food products. Second, through the analysis of the accounting books of the Stefani company, attention will be paid to the importance of the diffusion of the double entry technique in the Balkans, and to the fact that the accounting technique—extremely advanced and sophisticated in the context of the Italian Renaissance—had induced a spontaneous process of imitation among merchant companies in Ragusa. Through the observation of the accounting system suitable for the detection of very complex operations involving multiple operators and consequently entailing an extremely advanced accounting technique, this work shows how early double entry bookkeeping can be considered as institutionalized insofar as it was embedded in a complex network of practices, and was already invested with widely recognized cultural meanings (Scott, 1987; Strang, 1994). Special emphasis is given to the process of diffusion of accounting techniques from an institutional perspective (Strang and Tuma, 1993; Seo and Creed, 2002), in order to understand the ways in which this innovation spread across the network of the international trade of food, showing the role of individual traders and of companies as actors and agents of the changes underway in the Renaissance.[2]

INSTITUTIONAL PERSPECTIVE

The new institutional theory of sociological matrix attributes the spread of new forms of organization to their adaptation to institutional pressures

(Meyer and Rowan, 1977); it is based on the cardinal principle that organizational contexts are characterized by the development of rules and requirements to which organizations must comply if they want to receive support and legitimacy (Scott and Meyer, 1983). Rules and requirements are commonly known as institutions, which can be considered as "cultural-cognitive, normative, and regulative elements that, together with associated activities and resources, provide stability and meaning to social life" (Scott, 1995). According to a broader definition that allows one to analyze change and to reproduce institutions as a general and historically embedded process, which is useful for the purpose of this study, institutions are interpreted as "shared rules and typification that identify categories of social actors and their appropriate activities or relationships" (Barley and Tolbert, 1997). Such definition makes no assumption about the nature of the "relevant social actors" so that one can refer to individuals, groups, organizations and large communities.

Although variously defined, the concept of institution involves essentially two modes. First, a social practice is institutionalized if it is deeply embedded in a complex network of other practices or obligations that give them strength. At the same time, it is such if it is socially invested with deep and widely accepted cultural significance (Strang, 1994). From this perspective, the process of institutionalization may be considered as the process of connection—through which a social practice is linked to another—as well as of generation and legitimization of its cultural interpretation.

The principle of legitimacy that is based on the adaptation and organizational compliance to institutional pressures, turns out to be, on the one hand, the trusted servant of the so-called survival strategy, and, on the other, is connected to the phenomenon identified as isomorphism, which is connoted as a process whereby an organization tends to look like others in the same context. In Hawley's description, it turns out to be "a constraint process that forces one unit in a population to resemble other units that face the same set of environmental conditions" (Hawley, 1968).

The theory on the subject identifies three types of institutional isomorphism (DiMaggio and Powell, 1983). *Coercive* isomorphism refers to the pressure exerted by the formal and informal organizations on which it depends, for example, by the action of the State and by international law; usually, it stems from political influence and problems of legitimacy. *Normative* isomorphism is related to the pressure exerted by the action of professions, for example when professional associations identify rules and regulations that have a significant impact on administrative procedures. The related theory identifies an important aspect of professionalization that represents a source of isomorphism: the growth and development of professional networks that connect organizations and through which new models are spreading rapidly. Universities and training centers become important agents of normative isomorphism, as do professional associations (Carpenter and Feroz, 2001).

Finally, *mimetic* isomorphism refers to the pressure deriving from the imitation of successful organizations of the same type: such mimetic process is developed in case the objectives are not clearly defined or there is high environmental uncertainty.

> The advantages of the mimetic behavior in the economy of human action are considerable: when an organization faces a problem with ambiguous causes or unclear solutions problemistic search may yield a viable solution with little expense. Modeling, as we use the term, is a response to uncertainty.
>
> (DiMaggio and Powell, 1983, p. 152)

Through imitation, past choices are legitimized among those generally accepted practices, which, since they are used by organizations working in the same field and that enjoy greater legitimacy and success, appear to be culturally supported and conceptually correct (Carmona et al., 1998; Sargiacomo, 2008b).

Referring to accounting practices, scholars consider accounting as a key element in the mythological structure of rationalized societies. As Miller states, organizations, incorporating accounting practices and procedures, increase their legitimacy and their survival prospects (Hopwood, 1983; Miller, 1994). Viewed in institutional terms, accounting is a social and institutional practice on which the environment exerts strong pressures, and the studies on the subject have as their main purpose to analyze the nature and direction of that causal process connecting accounting and institutional context.[3] As we shall see, the analysis of the emergence of double entry bookkeeping in the sixteenth century will be carried out from the perspective of the relation between accounting and institutional environment.

The use of institutional theories is not without criticism, including the consideration that the process of isomorphism is far from being linear and unidirectional or that the same theories focus their attention on the dissemination of existing institutions, but little space is left for the survey on the processes of institutionalization and on the neglected role of individuals in these processes (Powell, 1991; Dacin, 1997; Sargiacomo, 2008). However, the reference to the dialectic between embeddedness and change has produced in some studies the identification of a model of institutionalization within which specific mechanisms outlining the modes of formation of contradictions are identified, that is:

> how institutional arrangements create various inconsistencies and tensions within and between social systems (contradictions), how those contradictions transform the embedded social actors into the change agents of the very institutional arrangements and how those contradictions further enable and foster the subsequent change processes.
>
> (Seo and Creed, 2002, p.223)

Institutions are constantly produced and reproduced through social interaction; this ongoing and multilevel process produces, in turn, a complex array of interrelated but often incompatible institutional arrangements, a source of contradictions within institutions and between institutions themselves. These contradictions reshape the consciousness of individuals, who in some circumstances act, transforming institutions and themselves. The contradictions resulting from internal and external tensions—such as nonadaptability to external factors, the multiplicity and complexity of institutions at various levels, the nonalignment between the institution and the divergent interests of the embedded subjects—are crucial for the transformation of socially embedded actors into agents of change of those institutional systems that they themselves had to preserve and, therefore, represent the seed of institutional change.

Another important concept related to the dialectic underlying the theoretical stance itself is the concept of Praxis, that is, the essential mechanism of relationship connecting seemingly conflicting entities such as institutional embeddedness, contradictions and change. Where contradictions create potential openings to institutional changes, it is practice that constitutes the "doing" of change and provides for the reconciliation of the two seemingly contradictory principles mentioned earlier, namely institutional embeddedness and transformational agency. For Praxis is meant a particular type of human action set in a specific social and historical context, and driven by the inevitable consequences of the social contradictions of the social context itself (Benson, 1977). From such a perspective, the concept assumes a double meaning: it is reflexive insofar as it implies a search for alternatives to existing social patterns; it is active as it implies an action intended to modify the existing order perceived as not in accordance with the needs and interests of the actors involved. From a dialectic standpoint, the ways in which contradictions facilitate a change in the consciousness of the actors and therefore give rise to the reflexive level of human action, are of two types: we speak of "gradual reshaping of consciousness from within the institutional context" and of "revolutionary disruption from outside" (Oliver, 1991, p. 151).

In the first case there is a process of "de-institutionalization," that is, a process in which the legitimacy of an institutionalized practice gradually erodes (Oliver, 1991). Generally, this happens because there was an "efficiency gap," as shown by Oliver, in the case where a current practice is considered not consistent with the criteria of efficacy and efficiency; in this case alternative practices are consciously searched for. In the second case, however, the reflexive level of human action is stimulated by a shock, by an institutional crisis that breaks institutional embeddedness, rendering the system highly unstable and enabling a dramatic shift in the collective consciousness of the actors. The active significance of the concept of Praxis implies then that individuals, the agents of change, do not adopt new models created by themselves, but use models or practices already established and accepted as part of the institutional context. This interpretation by Seo and

Creed highlights the role of individuals as agents of change,[4] and it points out how institutional change is born where and when institutional norms and practices with day-to-day functional/efficiency needs, become incompatible with and unresponsive to changing economic and institutional environments, and/or no longer serve the interests and ideas of participants who enacts those norms and practices.

THE MERCHANT COMPANIES OF THE RAGUSA REPUBLIC AND RAGUSAN ACCOUNTING SOURCES

In order to understand the role and function of Ragusan merchants in the trade of food, it is important to remember that, in those years, the Mediterranean was affected by the conflict between the Christian West and the Ottoman East. In this context, Ragusa had maintained a state of neutrality, which allowed the small Adriatic republic to maintain good business relations—on the one hand with the states of the Italian peninsula and Spain, and, the other, with the Ottoman Empire, which controlled the coasts of North Africa and the eastern Mediterranean. The neutrality of Ragusan foreign policy protected both the merchants of the Republic who worked abroad, and the boats of the local fleet that could, therefore, land freely in the territories under Ottoman control. Therefore, the merchants of Ragusa were free to trade in Ottoman ports as well as the ports of Western Europe, playing an important role as intermediaries for all exchanges between East and West that could not take place directly. For this reason, the most important or valuable goods that had to be transported by ship were often entrusted to vessels from Ragusa that, because of their neutrality, were normally not subject to the danger of attacks by the Ottoman corsairs (Fenicia, 2010). Among these goods there were naturally many foodstuffs of great importance for the southern European markets, such as wheat, barley and legumes, spices and salt, but also salted meat, wine and oil.

Since the Middle Ages, in order to have adequate knowledge of the business affairs they had carried out, the merchants of Ragusa had adopted a complex and advanced accounting system, described succinctly by Cotrugli in his work *Della mercatura e del mercante perfetto*. Although Cotrugli's writings were published in 1458, in principle the structure of Ragusan company accounting remained virtually the same for the entire following century.[5] In particular, according to the author, the merchant had to keep three books: a Great Book (or Ledger), including a "Rubrica," a Journal and a Book of Recollections (Cotrugli, 1990). The accounting ledgers of the Stefani company are conserved in the Ragusa archive, they date to the second half of the sixteenth century, and they are kept in accordance with the correct rules of double entry. There is a Great Book, which contains data gathered from 1555 to 1572, and then a Journal that contains data gathered by the merchant between 1585 and 1588.[6]

The central element of the accounting of the Ragusan merchants was the Ledger, which contained all the data collected during the multifarious economic activities undertaken by the company owner. It was vital that this book of accounts be kept in an orderly manner and in full respect of the rules of double entry since it acquired an official character even in civil cases in which the company could be involved.[7] For this reason, even after all accounts had been settled the book was not destroyed, but carefully stored and conserved as evidence of the economic activity carried out over a certain number of years by the merchant who had supervised its compilation. The importance of the Ledger and the fact that it was conserved by the merchant for a very long period of time, often until his death, meant that the latter also contained information that had little or nothing to do with the accounts of the company, such as the registration of the dates of signing more important notary deeds or the dates of birth and death of people close to him.[8] Given the exclusively private nature of accounting ledgers, it can be assumed that the books of accounts were deposited at the Ragusan Chancellery after the death of the merchants who had drafted them. These documents were considered to be a sort of addition to the testament and were explicitly cited in the wishes of the testator. Therefore, they provided testimony that took on an official nature and that was used by the executors to reconstruct the patrimonial affairs of the deceased, making it possible to collect any outstanding receivables and to pay any debts he had contracted during the course of his life.[9]

Of course, depending on the main type of trade handled by each of these merchants, certain types of accounts appear more frequently and are used more often than others. From the consideration of this last aspect of the private bookkeeping of the merchants of Ragusa, it can be seen that some of them dedicated themselves more to sea trade and shipping; others cultivated commerce with the Balkan hinterland; and still others, retired from business activity, devoted themselves mainly to the administration of their accumulated wealth through safer property and financial investments.[10] The common denominator for all of them was the need to arrange for payments and collections on markets distant from Ragusa, and from this need arose the necessity to make use of appropriate accounting tools, reliable and suitable to meet the needs of international markets.

THE STEFANI COMPANY

In this section we will investigate the main environmental and social pressures that influenced the operations of the merchant companies of the Republic in the period under review, taking as an example the case of the Stefani company and describing the role it played in the international trade of food products. It should be specified, in this regard, that the merchant companies of the time will be considered, in the analysis, the organizational units subject to institutional pressures, with the aim of identifying the role of individuals in the process of institutionalization.

The Stefani family company was formed by its progenitor, Thomas, in the early decades of the sixteenth century; its activity was mainly based on the maritime trade that was conducted with boats built in a private shipyard situated on the island of Šipan, a short distance from Ragusa. It was here, in 1534, that Vincenzo Stefani was born,[11] son of Thomas and main architect of the commercial successes achieved by the family business in the second half of the sixteenth century. After a short time spent at sea, the merchant settled in Ragusa and joined his father in the practice of shipping and mercantile activities, going numerous times to the Italian peninsula for business matters. Upon the death of Thomas, in 1559, Vincenzo inherited a considerable estate with his brother. In 1561, following the untimely death of his brother, he became the sole heir to the family company that he managed in a wise and prudent manner, so much so as to double, in about 20 years, the inheritance received from his father. He died in Ragusa in December 1588.

Much evidence of Vincenzo Stefani's activity remains, providing an idea of the great wealth of this Renaissance merchant. Among the buildings he owned in Ragusa and the nearby islands, still standing are his city residence, the villa with a garden in the town Tre Chiese, and the fortified residence of Suđurađ on the island of Šipan. But the most valuable testimony that Stefani left of his work are the two accounting books that belonged to him, which are now conserved in the State Archives of Ragusa. These are, of course, a small part of the accounting records that the merchant needed for the management of his assets, nevertheless these books are a valuable source for the study of the economic situation of sixteenth-century Ragusa. Starting with these documents it is possible to make a detailed reconstruction of the characteristics of the merchant's activity and the business decisions that he made and that made the company's fortune, increasing it to the point where it excelled in the sphere of the Ragusan merchant and shipping class.

If, to quote Braudel, in the modern age "the best way to earn money in big business [. . .] is to already have money" (Braudel, 1979, p. 386), then we can say that Vincenzo Stefani had an advantage in conducting his business in comparison with many of his contemporaries who, like him, were high-level traders. He could rely on the legacy obtained from his father that, in October 1559, stood at 37,001 Ragusan ducats.[12] On 2 January 1585, the date the accounts were opened in a new ledger, Vincenzo Stefani's capital amounted to 73,924 Ragusan ducats, about twice the face value of the assets inherited from his father 25 years earlier.[13]

If we focus on the experience of the merchant Vincenzo Stefani, it can be seen how his professional training played a key role in the success he achieved in the practice of his business activity. His training was initially based on the teachings that the merchant had received in the family business and, later, was perfected over long periods in Italy, especially in Naples and Florence, before his definitive return to Ragusa because of the sudden death of his father. In the large Italian cities the merchant had the opportunity to improve his accounting technique and, at the same time, to enter into trade agreements that greatly favored his work in markets distant from Ragusa. Indeed, during this period he formed a company that was based in Florence[14] and that was responsible, among other things, for the sale of the grain unloaded from Stefani ships on the Tuscan coast. Stefani company business was not limited, however, only to trade with Florence, but also involved other areas of the Italian peninsula and, in particular, the Kingdom of Naples and the coasts of the Papal States. Here actual companies were not formed, but, more generally, there were long-term trade agreements with local merchants who worked as agents. There were numerous links with the traders of the Kingdom of Naples, to whom the merchant turned for the purchase of cereals on the Abruzzo and Apulia coasts, and for the subsequent resale of the same in the port of Naples.[15] Other important business connections were established with merchants in Genoa, Messina, Ancona and Venice.

In the contribution of Stefani's vocational training to the entrepreneurial success of his company, it is possible to trace *in nuce* the nature of so-called normative isomorphism (DiMaggio and Powell, 1983; Carpenter and Feroz, 2001). In the absence of an institutional educational system, the younger members of the families of Ragusan nobility and bourgeoisie were welcomed and housed in the workshops of the merchants of Genoa, Florence, Naples, Messina and Venice, and there they learned the rudiments of technical accounting and so-called trade practices (Catturi, 2009). The workshops of the Italian merchants (or of the Ragusan agents that operated in Italy), and the first schools, transmitted theoretical and operational knowledge, performing the vocational and professional training that universities and institutes of higher education would take on many centuries later. The numerous and frequent contacts with Italian enterprises also stimulated, in the activity of the Stefani company, a process of emulation and adaptation to local business customs that was caused by the need to adapt to a much more complex and detailed milieu than that of the Balkans. The high level of uncertainty in the environment in which the Stefani company operated led to a process of mimetic isomorphism, the imitation of the organization of Italian merchants who were more advanced in business, finance, and in accounting and mercantile techniques. In this case, the contradictions arising from external inconsistencies—the difficulty of adapting to a changing and complex environment—led Stefani to take note of the need to resort to models and practices already established in the institutional context.[16]

The influences and forms of pressure that affected companies from Ragusa did not come, however, only from the sphere of international trade, but also from a more strictly local milieu. In a limited area such as the Republic of Ragusa it was extremely simple for merchants to learn from the commercial successes achieved by their countrymen. Therefore, local operators were encouraged to invest in new lines of business that, at that time, were more profitable. In this context, merchant companies played an extremely important role (Catturi, 2009); through the sharing of business risk, they favored investments in commercial lines characterized by a higher level of risk.[17] In this way, companies were created with the aim of carrying out a particular type of business, such as the purchase of a batch of wheat in the Ottoman Levant, the purchase of animals destined for slaughter, or food supply for boats that operated in the service of the great European Courts.

As we will explain, the clearest example of the process of the merchant's training and the emulation of Italian models can be seen in his accounting. The Stefani company ledgers, compared to other contemporary accounting books belonging to other companies from Ragusa, show a significantly higher degree of accuracy both in what was recorded and in command of accounting technique. Stefani's frequent contact with the Italian milieu was also important for cultivating the information circuit that the company needed to guide its choices in an uncertain and complex market like that of the Mediterranean maritime trade in the sixteenth century. As evidence of the contribution of the Italian information network in the decision-making process implemented by the merchant, there are major expenses for couriers, who were needed to maintain trade relations with the most important commercial markets of the Balkan Peninsula and the Italian territory.

Another factor of great importance to the activities of the merchant is the social legitimacy that his company and he, personally, had obtained in Ragusan society and that was a direct consequence of the process of isomorphism.[18] It should be specified, in this regard, that achieving positive economic results and an increase in wealth could not be certified through information tools that would make public the financial results achieved by the individual merchant companies, because in the society of sixteenth-century Ragusa, there were no disclosure obligations that companies had to obey. The social validation of the work of the merchants was thus obtained by giving clear and obvious proof of the results achieved and the volume of revenues, and this process was very often carried out through large donations to ecclesiastical institutions or with the purchase or construction of particularly valuable properties. Stefani was famous in Ragusa for his generosity, for the large donations he had made to the churches and convents of the city, but also for having used his extensive network of Italian contacts to the benefit of the foreign policy of the Republic of Ragusa. The last point also gave the merchant the possibility to elevate his rank, moving from the middle class to which he belonged by birth, to the nobility of the city, who were the only ones to wield political power within the Republic. According to Serafino Razzi, an Italian Dominican friar who lived for some years in Ragusa and who met Vincenzo Stefani personally, it seems that the Ragusa Senate expressed its intention to accept the latter among the ranks of the nobility in exchange for a large payment of money to the Republic. However, the elevation of Vincenzo to the rank of Ragusan nobleman was to be considered as an *ad personam* privilege that he could not, in any way, convey to his descendants (Razzi, 1595, p. 163); Stefani did not like the imposition of this condition and did not want to continue the negotiations with the Senate, so he chose to remain in the middle class.

In addition to the successes that the merchant had in his activities in trade, ship ownership and finance, and the generosity that always characterized his work, it should be remembered that Stefani distinguished himself in the Ragusan milieu for being a man of culture, a lover of comfort and convenience, open to innovations and Renaissance fashions that came, in large part, from Italy (Tadić, 1948, p. 215). The most obvious result of this process of social legitimacy was the accreditation of the merchant as trustee and executor of a number of significant assets left by other merchants of the city.

THE DIFFUSION OF EARLY DOUBLE ENTRY BOOKKEEPING: THE FOOD TRADE IN STEFANI'S COMPANY

In the perspective adopted in this study, the analysis of the institutional pressures that influenced the operations of the merchant companies of the Republic of Ragusa in the period under scrutiny results functional to the survey on the dissemination process of early double entry bookkeeping, in order to understand the ways in which this innovation spread through the network of international trade, with particular reference to the trade of food.[19] As widely shown by authoritative doctrine (Catturi, 1993, 2009), foreign merchants who were in business relationships with the Italians could not but appreciate the operational validity of double entry bookkeeping, indeed a language effective and easy to understand, which they adopted and adapted to their aims. Taking into consideration the case of merchant Stefani, it should be noted how in terms of accounting and organization, the company showed itself extremely advanced, closer to innovations in business and accounting techniques carried out by commercial companies of major Italian cities than to the general backwardness characterizing instead most of the Balkan peninsula.

The accounting books of Stefani company, compared to other contemporary records belonging to other companies from Ragusa, are of a higher degree of accuracy in measurements and mastery of accounting technique. The particular complexity of the accounting records emerges from the ability to record even extremely complex operations, such as those related to investments in exchange fairs in which each consignment was packed with data and information. These allowed the merchant to understand the context in which the investment developed as well as to promptly quantify the profit or loss that each transaction had generated, on time. More specifically, as will be seen with reference to the trade of food and foodstuffs, great importance assumed the correct recording not only of acquisition costs but also all the charges related to the transport of these goods, in order to establish the precise overall cost of each consignment of goods. These measurements were possible also thanks to the use of elaborate techniques, such as the one that led to the use of compound entries according to the double entry bookkeeping.

This work shows how Stefani's adoption of records in articulated double entry, especially in relation to trade of food, was determined by the need to resort to effective and efficient means of information and control that would suit the changing needs of an increasingly complex socioeconomic environment. In fact, with the growth of the territorial limits for the activity of the merchant, which had become much more complex and articulated, the contradictions emerged between the increasingly advanced needs of management and control and the extant information tools. This aspect provides the seed of institutional change: institutionalized practices were no longer consistent with the criteria of effectiveness and efficiency, and thus the need emerged to take action in search of alternative practices. In such a case the two already highlighted aspects of the concept of Praxis are observed, the reflexive and the active, in order to amend the existent, seeking alternative practices, which were already established and accepted. In the case of Stefani's mercantile company, numerous and frequent contacts with Italian commercial reality led, as was said, to the use of double entry accounting techniques, the so-called Italian method, by activating a kind of mimetic isomorphism, the imitation of an effective and flexible tool that could adapt to the needs of companies operating in any geographical area.

From the observation of the reality of the Ragusa merchants and in the case of merchant Stefani, in particular, it is possible to infer how early double entry bookkeeping can be actually considered a practice institutionalized and legitimized in the context under examination, insofar as it was rooted in a complex network of other practices, and had a widely accepted cultural significance (Strang, 1994). Indeed, along with the technical procedures with which economic and financial operations were realized, known as mercantile practices, it was one of the organizational variables that presided over the functioning of small businesses. Through the use of account—a process tool that allowed the merchants to cumulate events translated into quantitative and monetary terms—and of double entry bookkeeping, not only was the memory of mercantile facts kept, but also the economic and financial results achieved with those facts could be synthetically expressed. The cultural significance of the Italian method is also evident; the introduction of early double entry bookkeeping in the economic area considered had clearly changed the attitudes of operators, creating new needs and stimulating a process of socioeconomic unification and dissemination of culture. In turn, if corporate culture appeared to have changed, so did the needs and objectives of the company bodies, requiring the adaptation of tools from which to draw information in order to decide and control the effects. Thus a process of circular dependency between corporate culture, objectives of management and accounting tools was activated. All the experiences acquired with the use of accounting technique became heritage of the people who used it, changing the dominant culture and thus perfecting the process of institutionalization of accounting practices. In this way the organization incorporating the conventions of early double entry bookkeeping increased its legitimacy and its prospects of survival and development (Hopwood, 1983; Miller, 1994). As has been said, the complexity of the accounting procedures of trade of foods in merchant Stefani's company is considered in this study as symptomatic of how the Italian method represented in fact a practice embedded and legitimized in the context analyzed.

Wheat

The Stefani company's business in the food trade was linked in particular to the trade of cereals, spices from the islands of the Indian Ocean, and salt that was imported to Ragusa from Spain, Sicily or the coasts of Puglia. Every purchase of this type of asset required the merchant to keep a series of accounting records that enabled him to keep under control those costs that had to be allocated to orders of goods purchased. This recordkeeping was made even more complex by the fact that sometimes the high cost of purchasing these goods required the establishment of special purpose companies specifically for the purchase of goods in the markets of origin, their transport and, finally, their sale on the markets. To do this, as well as taking into account the capital shares granted by each of the participants, the merchant had to impute properly pro rata costs incurred during the journey and, at the end of the latter, distribute profits among all entitled parties.[20]

Materially, business operations were carried out by a trustee of the merchant who, more often than not, was also the captain of the vessel. These trustees received the money from the merchant at the time of departure, bought the grain in the supplying markets and then took care of the sale of the same on the sales market, organizing transportation down to the smallest detail. After making the sale, the trustee also took care of sending the proceeds to the mother country by bills of exchange, retaining a small percentage for himself as a commission. His task would then conclude with sending the merchant client a statement of accounts related to the expenditures incurred during the voyage and, finally, with the approval of the accounts by the merchant.

Wheat was one of the most important types of goods that were transported by Ragusan boats in the sixteenth century, and from the accounting records of Stefani it can be seen how the cereal trade required a great deal of attention and extreme caution on the part of the merchants. First of all, grain, as well as barley or other types of cereals, was a very heavy commodity, but also very precious and its importance was even greater in periods of agrarian crisis or actual famine. In fact, transporting grain attracted the attention of the rulers and the naval fleets and for this reason, although the Ragusan ships enjoyed neutrality in the conflict between East and West. In any case, the merchants of the republic had to take all precautions possible to avoid running into ships, or actual fleets, with hostile intentions. This problem prolonged the duration of the voyages well beyond the time frame required for the navigation, increased costs for marine insurance and, despite the care and precautions of the captains of the ships and the merchants, there were often seizures that occurred for the sole purpose of supplying nations, or individual cities that faced the Mediterranean, with wheat.

Sometimes business operations that concerned the sale of grain were the cause of diplomatic crises, even very serious ones, as in the case where a boat belonging to the Stefani family, carrying a load of wheat from Puglia to Naples on behalf of Spanish and Neapolitan merchants, was hijacked by the crew and taken to Ragusa to increase the grain supply of the republic. The reaction of the Viceroyalty of Naples was extremely harsh and went so far as to seize the payment of the annuity on Neapolitan government debt that was owed to the merchants of Ragusa, as compensation for the damage caused.[21] The seizure of the annuities then sparked a lively protest by the Ragusans against their government, which took it upon itself to repay some of the money lost. Apart from the specific case described above, sometimes losses were recorded in the trade of the grain itself because of the confiscation of vessels that were boarded and seized as they passed by cities and peoples who were struggling for their food supply. In the best cases, the rightful owners were even paid for the grain, but obviously the price paid for the cargo seized was much lower than the price that could be asked for when selling grain on the free market.[22]

From the point of view of quality, the grains traded in the Mediterranean of the sixteenth century could be divided into three main types: strong grains, medium grains and weak grains. The strong grains were of better quality: they were the most sought after and corresponded roughly to what today we call durum wheat. The purchase of strong grains by Stefani took place mainly in Sicily:[23] at Sciacca, Messina or Termini (today called Termini Imerese). It was to these ports that the merchant sent his boats for the supply of the best grains that were then sent to Tuscany or Liguria, but also to Spain. The distances did not affect the price of the wheat on the markets as much as the difficulties encountered along the route and the greater or lesser probability that the convoys would encounter hostile vessels. While the stronger and more robust grains came from Sicily, the weak grains, which were instead more similar to today's common wheat, often came from the Ottoman East and, more rarely, from Abruzzo and the Adriatic territories of the Papal State.

The quality of these cereals was not very well appreciated on the Mediterranean markets; this was linked to the fact that they were produced in territories in which the correct crop rotations were not observed and so the land, which was exploited intensively, did not give a satisfactory yield. Instead, the medium grains were an intermediate quality between the two extremes just described, and were usually bought in the markets for strong grains, but were, in this context, the lower quality product and, therefore, were less valuable. Of course, the price of wheat on the markets had to take into account all the factors just mentioned, and in particular, the quality of the goods handled, their origin and also the costs of transport and the objective difficulties faced by the crew during the voyage, insurance costs and expenditures in ammunition and gunpowder necessary for the defense of the boats.

The role of accounting and the system of accounting records of the merchants of Ragusa was of fundamental importance in an area of trade as difficult and complex as that of wheat. The first problem that arose for the merchant was to properly record the purchase price. The problem was not easy to solve because the grain was often purchased abroad in foreign currency, and this made it necessary to convert the price into the currency in which the reference account was held. Even the weight of the grain purchased was difficult to determine because it was expressed in the units of measurement used in the markets of purchase, which, of course, were different from those used in Ragusa, and also different from those used in the sales markets. For this reason, the entry that was recorded by the merchant included all available information in order to reconstruct exactly the fundamental characteristics of the acquisition.

In addition to the purchase cost of the cereals, it was then necessary to record the additional costs that were primarily related to the payment of customs duties, both in procurement markets and in sales markets. In addition to the duty officers, it was necessary for the workers who loaded the grain not to be hindered in their work, and for this to happen they had to bribe customs officials and, at the same time, pay armed watchmen to guard against theft.[24] It was also necessary to bear high costs for the transport of the grain from the docks to the ships, and this transportation sometimes had to be done by recruiting porters and using barges or small boats, especially in places where the big cargo ships from Ragusa were not able to enter the ports to load directly from the mainland.

Once the transport was concluded, the operations previously described were repeated in reverse for the unloading of the cereals and their sale. The money was not brought back on the ship, but for safety reasons it was preferable that it be sent to Ragusa in bills of exchange. When the sale took place in a financial center of extreme importance such as Genoa, it was even more desirable that the money from the sale of the grain be used in investments in international exchange fairs. In this regard, it is possible to cite an example that illustrates the dynamics of the financial flows headed to Ragusa. During July and August of 1555, the merchant Vincenzo Stefani imported to Genoa about 7,000 *chilò* of grain, as per the measurements of Constantinople.[25] After clearing it through customs, the sale of the cereal was entrusted to Genoese merchants Lazzaro Vivaldi, Agostino Biscotto and Isnardo Cattaneo. From the sale of the Levantine grain Stefani obtained 18,263 Italian Lire in the coin of Genoa, which was entirely entrusted to Cattaneo, together with proceeds from the sale of another lot of wheat. In total, the latter received 18,871 Genoese Italian Lire that were invested in the exchange fairs of Besançon until April 1559. This is a clear example of the interaction between trade and finance, and, in this case, the accounting source shows very clearly and with great effectiveness the reuse of the sums arising from commercial activity, but also the subsequent process of investments and disinvestments that each sum of money went through in the exchange fairs.

The amount of money earned from the sale of the grain cargo transported by vessels of the republic was truly large and was a vital element in the growth strategy of Ragusan merchant companies. Conversely, buyers of these huge quantities of grain would not be private clients or small merchants, but particular customers who purchased large quantities. They were, for example, public welfare agencies or the Renaissance courts. The agencies and institutions that purchased wheat and barley from Stefani included the Court of Sicily, the Spanish Armada, the Genoa Offizio delle Vettovaglie,[26] and the Lucca Offizio dell'Abbondanza.[27] In particular, the latter, on one occasion, not having cash available to immediately pay for the purchase, obtained a deferral of payment from the merchant, paying one-third of the sum in cash immediately, one-third in cash after 4 months and the final third in cash after 8 months.[28] The buyers of large quantities of cereals also included the Spanish court, directly or through the Viceroys of Naples and Sicily. In these cases, however, the payment for the grain purchased was frequently made late, or there were losses because of sums that were unpaid and considered no longer collectable.[29]

Pepper and Spices

The Stefani company also used many of its resources in the purchase of spices, although in this case the volume of trade was far lower, both in quantity and value, in comparison with the trade in grain. The supply market was located in particular in Alexandria, Egypt, and therefore was in Turkish hands, but the neutrality of the Ragusan merchants and boats made it possible for them to trade even in these places without particular problems. Spices arrived in Alexandria after travelling up long caravan routes that branched off from the Red Sea, and were supplied by Asian merchants. The discovery, in the early sixteenth century, of the sea route to reach the Indies by rounding the Cape of Good Hope had greatly eased the transit of spices to the Egyptian market. Most goods arriving from the islands of the Indian Ocean were, in fact, purchased by the Portuguese and carried by sea to the coasts of the Atlantic. Nevertheless, the traffic of spices in the Mediterranean continued erratically throughout the sixteenth century, and involved the Ragusans, but also the Venetian and French merchants (Lane, 1933). In particular, in the period 1550–1570, the pepper trade in the Mediterranean seemed to have regained importance, even though, starting in 1580, there had been a new pepper supply crisis that greatly reduced the commercial trade of this product (Braudel, 1986, p. 607).

The dynamics of the operations that were conducted for the purchase of pepper was similar to those implemented in the trade of cereals, with a few minor differences in relation to the supply market that, in the case of pepper, was exclusively that of Alexandria in Egypt, and regarding the purchasers of the product on the sales markets who were not big institutions, but small retailers or private buyers.[30] This differentiation depended in large part on the small amount of spices transported by the Ragusans. Spices, especially pepper, were transported in bales of variable weight and dimension to be marketed either directly in the homeland or in major Italian cities. Pepper, and spices in general, were used almost everywhere for food directly on the table, or for long-term storage of food, and sometimes just as sheer ostentation of wealth. Because of the limited amount traded, the retail price of spices was very high, but despite this they were also commonly used by the lower classes.

From the point of view of accounting, the entries related to the recording of the cost of pepper showed all the elements necessary to remind the merchant of the circumstances in which the purchase transaction had taken place. The price of the spices, the weight and the quantity of goods purchased, as well as the number of bales loaded on the ships, were pieces of information easily found in every entry. The purchase transaction was, also in this case, carried out materially by a trustee of the merchant who earned a commission on the purchase cost. The various records for orders of pepper include the imputation of ancillary costs, such as those related to costs for the customs tax, for porters and guards, as well as for sea freight and insurance.

Salt

Among the products intended for human consumption carried by Stefani vessels was also salt. It was a poor commodity, with a high weight and low cost per unit; nevertheless it was vital for the nutrition of the people of Europe, and was also used for some manufacturing related processes such as the processing of hides and skins. Markets for the procurement of salt were located in Corfu, but also in Sicily, particularly in Trapani, and especially in the Spanish territories of Alicante and Ibiza.[31] For this reason, the salt trade was tied to that of wheat, because the boats on their way to the coasts of the Iberian Peninsula to deliver loads of cereal would often pick up salt to bring back to the big Italian cities or even to Ragusa. The markets for the sale of the salt carried by Stefani ships included the city of Genoa and Livorno, but also Menton in Provence,[32] Gaeta, Naples, Ancona and Venice. Given the heavy weight of the goods carried, the captain of the ship was often forced to forbid the sailors to take on other goods, as it was their ancient custom to buy and negotiate independently on the basis of Ragusan maritime traditions. However, in this case, the commander was required to repay the sailors for the income that they had not been able to earn.[33] These repayments were recorded as ancillary costs of transportation and noted in the record of the product transported. Finally, Stefani's records show that the transport of salt was not associated with higher insurance costs. The transport of this commodity was, in fact, much safer than the transport of grain and pepper as the low per-unit value of salt did not make it particularly attractive to pirates and corsairs.

CONCLUSIONS

This study has developed along two main tracks. First, using the institutional perspective of sociological matrix, the main environmental and social pressures have been identified, that influenced the activity of the commercial companies of the Republic of Ragusa in the period under scrutiny, using for this purpose the case of Stefani's merchant company. Second, through the study of the advanced accounting technique used by Stefani for accounting related to trade in foodstuffs, evidence has been given of the importance of the spread of double entry bookkeeping in the Balkans in order to understand the ways in which this innovation spread through the network of international trade, becoming cultural heritage of the community. Through the acceptance of the method of double entry bookkeeping—which was an effective language, understandable and adaptable to different realities—markets expanded and experiences were communicated, disseminating corporate culture.

In the case of the Stefani company, the complexity of the accounting records of trade of foods is considered as symptomatic of how double entry bookkeeping represented a practice embedded in the context. Every purchase of food required the merchant to keep accounting records that enabled him to keep under control those costs that had to be allocated to orders of goods purchased. This recordkeeping was made even more complex by the fact that sometimes the high cost of purchasing these goods required the establishment of special purpose companies and then the merchant had to impute properly pro rata costs incurred during the journey and, at the end of the latter, distribute profits among all entitled parties. Referring to the trade of wheat, the entries were recorded by the merchant including all available information in order to reconstruct exactly the fundamental characteristics of the acquisition. Indeed, the proper recording of the additional costs, which were primarily related to the payment of customs duties, was necessary.

It has been highlighted how the adoption by Stefani of such surveys in articulated double entry was determined by the need to use efficient and effective information tools suited to the changing needs of a more complex economic environment.

In particular, referring to Stefani's significant case and applying to his work the concept of Praxis—that is, a type of human action placed in a specific social and historical context but driven by the inevitable consequences of the contradictions of that social context—the key role of individuals has been highlighted, as agents of the diffusion of early double entry bookkeeping and, more generally, as actors of change in Renaissance economy. In this sense this study constitutes a relevant example of investigation of the behavior of individuals and the choices they make as part of the process of institutionalization. A further extension of this research is implied in the double perspective here offered, the economical and the historical, and in their interaction in a specific historical period. The present investigation has meant to illustrate the possibility for an analysis of the spread of double entry bookkeeping, not dependent on abstract rules but observed in its making and in its potential development. It also aims to show how historical analysis can fruitfully give insight into accounting dynamics.

NOTES

1. While this contribution is the result of the integrated collaboration of the two researchers, Dario Dell'Osa has written parts 3, 4, 5.1, 5.2, 5.3 and Stella Lippolis is author of parts 2, 5, 6. They have jointly written part 1.
2. "A history of accounting . . . without some knowledge of the actors—those for whom as well as those by whom the records were kept—must be rather anaemic and thin" (Yamey, 1981, p. 131).
3. "We can distinguish three kinds of relations in the study of accounting, the organization and the environment: (i) the influence of the environment on the accounting systems of the organization; (ii) the influence of the accounting on the environment and (iii) the influence of accounting on other aspects of organizational life." Núnez (2002, p. 301).
4. According to Parker, it is only by studying the role played by "change agents" and "recipients" that it is possible to understand the way in which accounting thought and practice is developed and transferred (Parker, 1979, quoted in Boyns and Edwards, 1996).
5. For a more in-depth examination of the work by Cotrugli see Melis (1950, pp. 604–608).
6. The documents are Državni Arhiv, Dubrovnik (D.A.D.), XIX, *Privata*, 7/a, and D.A.D., XIX, *Privata*, 32.
7. In the words of Melis, in fact, the bookkeeping of Ragusan merchants was not only necessary for recording company affairs, but it was also used as a means to prove them (Melis, 1950, p. 605).
8. Cf. D.A.D., XIX, *Privata*, 7/a, cc. 384 and 385. Note that in a society where there was no registrar service, and in which even the parish registers were updated on an irregular and discontinuous basis, there was no other way to establish with absolute certainty what the date of birth or death was for a particular person.
9. Another merchant, Stefano di Polo Radognich, wrote in his will and testament on 10 July 1585:

   e tra le altre cose li prego [i curatori testamentari] che vogliano aver cura del mio libro segnato "L," acciò che quando si trovassero [. . .] conti et partite che non fussero sottoscritte a dette cautele [riportate nel testamento] si abbia a dare credere al detto mio libro però in conto di dare e avere, come si trovarà a esso libro et non altrimenti, per l'aver tenuto li detti crediti tanto del dare quanto dell'avere con ciascuno e così ad iscarico di mia coscientia et per giustizia.

D.A.D., X.1, *Testamenta Notariae*, n. 47, c. 273v/274r.

10. According to the teachings of the Ragusan Benedetto Cotrugli, the perfect merchant should, in fact, retire from business at the age of about 50, elect to reside in one of his villas outside the city and live by investing the money accumulated in the course of his life in safe assets (Cotrugli, 1990, p. 253).
11. The year of birth was derived from the statements of Serafino Razzi, according to which Vincenzo Stefani died in December 1588 at age 54 (Razzi, 1595, p. 163).
12. D.A.D., *Privata*, 7/a, c. 385.
13. The increase in capital must be adjusted up, taking into account the *revolution in prices* which affected Europe in the second half of the sixteenth century and did not leave Ragusa unscathed. On the revolution in prices in Spain and the rest of Europe see Luzzatto (1955, p. 199). To have an idea of the general increase of prices we can refer to Tadić, who said that the cost per tonne of ships built in Ragusa hovered around 10 Ragusan ducats at the beginning of the sixteenth century, while it increased to 30 Ragusan ducats at the end of the century due to the increase in the prices of materials. (Tadić, 1962, p. 105).
14. D.A.D., XIX, *Privata*, 7/a, cc. 124 e 315.
15. Ibid., c. 58.
16. See, in this regard, the model of institutionalization previously recalled , where it is evident that the contradictions give way to institutional change and the concept of Praxis represents the role of human action in the implementation of change.
17. As of the fourteenth century the term "company" was used for associations of merchants and bankers who joined their economic forces for the management and further development of trade. These companies are the first examples and the first forms of collective companies, and the origin of modern trading companies. Definition by Alberto Seccherelli (1924), quoted in Catturi (2009).
18. An organization derives its legitimacy and social consensus when its values and behaviors are consistent with the values and expectations of the social actors (Deephouse, 1996).
19. Although this chapter focuses attention on international trade, we are aware that this is not the only means by which the knowledge of the Italian method of double entry bookkeeping was spread. As highlighted by scholars, in fact, it should be remembered that there are other types of media, including the establishment of *fondachi* (warehouses) of Italian merchant companies in foreign markets, the activities of religious congregations, public and private schools, the partial or total reprint of the Treaty of Pacioli (Thompson, 1994).
20. D.A.D., XIX, *Privata*, 7/a, c. 13 e c. 14.
21. D.A.D., XIX, *Privata*, 32, c. 154.
22. D.A.D., XIX, *Privata*, 7/a, c. 10.
23. Ibid., 7/a, c. 103.
24. Ibid., 7/a, c. 1.
25. Ibid., 7/a, c. 18 and c. 64. The *chilò* was a measure of capacity used to Constantinople to the grain, and corresponded approximately to a volume of 33 liters. The wheat was sold for the most part to the Genoa Offizio delle Vettovaglie.
26. Ibid., 7/a, c. 24.
27. Ibid., 7/a, c. 98.
28. Ibid., 7/a, c. 25.
29. Ibid., 7/a, c. 117 e 236.

30. Ibid., 7/a, c. 177, 193, 245, 295.
31. D.A.D., XIX, *Privata*, 32, c. 44.
32. Ibid., 32, c. 153.
33. Ibid., 32, c. 174.

REFERENCES

Primary Sources

Državni Arhiv u Dubrovniku (Dubrovnik Historical Archive), XIX—Privata, 7/a, Libro Mastro di Vincenzo di Tommaso Stefani (1555–1572).

Državni Arhiv u Dubrovniku (Dubrovnik Historical Archive), XIX—Privata, 32, Libro di Negozio segnato "C" di Vincenzo di Tommaso Stefani (1585–1588).

Secondary Sources

Aymard, M. (1966) *Venice, Raguse et le commerce du blè pendant la seconde moitiè du XVI siècle*. Paris: SEVPEN.

Barley, S.R. and Tolbert, P.S. (1997) Institutionalization and structuration: Studying the link between action and institution. *Organization Studies* 18(1): 93–117.

Benson, J.K. (1977) Organizations: A dialectic view. *Administrative Science Quarterly* 22: 1–21.

Boyns, T. and Edwards, J.R. (1996) Change agents and the dissemination of accounting technology: Wales' basic industries, c.175.1870. *Accounting History* 1(1): 9–34.

Braudel, F. (1986) (first edition 1949) *Civiltà e imperi del Mediterraneo nell'età di Filippo II*. Turin: Einaudi.

Braudel, F. (1979) *I giochi dello scambio*. Turin: Einaudi.

Carmona, S., Ezzamel, M. and Gutierrez, F. (1998) Towards an institutional analysis of accounting change in the Royal Tobacco Factory of Seville. *The Accounting Historians Journal* 25(1): 115–147.

Carnegie, G.D. and Parker, R.H. (1996) The transfer of accounting technology to the southern hemisphere: The case of William Butler Yaldwyn. *Accounting, Business and Financial History* 6(1): 23–49.

Carpenter, V.L. and Feroz, E.H. (2001) Institutional theory and accounting rule choice: An analysis of four US state government's decisions to adopt generally accepted accounting principle. *Accounting, Organization and Society* 26(7/8): 565–596.

Catturi, G. (1993) *Evoluzione storica del conto come fonte di informazioni per le decisioni aziendali*, in Atti del Primo Convegno nazionale di Storia della Ragioneria, Siena, 20–21 Dicembre 1991, SISR, pp. 1–11.

Catturi, G. (2009) *Gestazione, "nascita" e diffusione in Europa del Metodo italiano di contabilità scuole e libri d'abaco dal XIV al XVII secolo*, in VI Encuentro de trabajo sobre Historia de la Contabilidad. Ponencias y comunicaciones. Valladolid, 5 a 7 de noviembre de 2008. Asociación Española de Contabilidad y Administración de Empresas, AECA, 1–25.

Cotrugli, B. (1990) *Il libro dell'arte di Mercatura*. (c. 1456, first edition 1573). Venice: Arsenale Editrice.

Dacin, M.T. (1997) Isomorphism in context, the power and prescription of institutional norms. *Academy of Management Journal* 40(1): 46–81.

Deephouse, D.L. (1996) Does isomorphism legitimate? *Academy of Management Journal* 39(4): 1024–1039.

Dimaggio, P.J. and Powell, W.W. (1983) The iron cage revisited: Institutional isomorphism and collective rationality in organizational fields. *American Sociological Review* 48: 147–160.
Di Vittorio, A. (2001) Tendenze ed orientamenti della storiografia marittima ragusea. In: Di Vittorio A. (ed.), *Tra mare e terra*. Bari: Cacucci, pp. 177–221.
Fenicia, G. (2010) Il commercio dei cereali nel Mediterraneo del XVI secolo. *Nuova rivista storica* XCIV/2: 625–638.
Hawley, A. (1968) Human ecology. In: Sills, D. (ed.), *International encyclopedia of the social sciences*. NewYork: MacMillan, pp. 328–337.
Hopwood, A.G. (1983) On trying to study accounting in the contexts in which it operates. *Accounting, Organizations and Society* 8(2/3): 287–305.
Lane, F.C. (1933) Venetian shipping during the commercial revolution. *The American Historical Review* 38(2): 219–239.
Luzzatto, G. (1955) *Storia Economica dell'età moderna e contemporanea*. Padua: Cedam.
Meyer, J.W. and Rowan, B. (1977) Institutionalized organizations: Formal structure as myth and ceremony. *American Journal of Sociology* 83(2): 310–363.
Melis, F. (1950) *Storia della Ragioneria*. Bologna: Zuffi.
Miller, P. (1994) Introduction. In: Hopwood, A.G. and P. Miller (eds.), *Accounting as social and institutional practice*. Cambridge: Cambridge University Press, pp. 1–39.
Moroni, M. (2011) *L'impero di San Biagio. Ragusa e i commerci balcanici dopo la conquista turca (1521–1620)*. Bologna: Il Mulino.
Núnez, M. (2002) Organizational change and accounting: The gunpowder monopoly in New Spain, 1757–87. *Accounting, Business & Financial History* 12(2): 275–315.
Oliver, C. (1991) Strategic responses to institutional processes. *Academy of Management Review* 16(1): 145–179.
Parker, R.H. (1979) Explaining national differences in consolidated accounts. In: Lee, T.A. and Parker, R.H. (eds.), *The evolution of corporate reporting*. Sunbury-on-Thames: Nelson, pp. 3–48.
Powell, W.W. (1991) Expanding the scope of institutional analysis. In: Powell, W.W. and DiMaggio, P.J. (eds.), *The new institutionalism in organizational analysis*. Chicago: The University of Chicago Press, pp. 183–203.
Razzi, S. (1595) *La Storia di Raugia*. Lucca: Busdraghi.
Sargiacomo, M. (2008a) Accounting and the 'art of government': Margaret of Austria in Abruzzo (1539–1586). *European Accounting Review* 17(4): 667–695.
Sargiacomo, M. (2008b) Institutional pressures and isomorphic change in a high-fashion company: The case of Brioni Roman style, 1945–89. *Accounting, Business & Financial History* 18(2): 215–241.
Sargiacomo, M. (2009) Accounting for the 'good administration of justice': The Farnese state of Abruzzo in the sixteenth century. *Accounting History* 14(3): 235–267.
Sargiacomo, M., Servalli, S., Carnegie, G.D. (2012) Accounting for killing: Accountability for death. *Accounting History* 17(3/4): 393–413.
Scott, W.R. (1987) The adolescence of institutional theory. *Administrative Science Quarterly* 32: 493–511.
Scott, W.R. (1995) *Institutions and organizations*. Beverly Hills: Sage Publications.
Scott, W.R. and Meyer, J.W. (1983) The organization of societal sectors. In: Meyer, J.W. and Scott, W.R. (eds.), *Organizational environments: Ritual and rationality*. Beverly Hills: Sage Publications, pp. 129–153.
Seccherelli, A. (1924) *Enciclopedia di Amministrazione, Ragioneria, Commercio, Banca, Borsa* (ed. U. Monetti). Milan: Vallardi.
Seo, M.G. and Creed, W.E.D. (2002) Institutional contradictions, praxis and institutional change: A dialectical perspective. *Academy of Management Review* 2: 222–247.

Strang, D. (1994) Institutional accounts of organizations as a form of structural analysis. *Current Perspective in Social Theory* Supplement 1: 151–174.
Strang, D. and Tuma, N. B. (1993) Spatial and temporal heterogeneity in diffusion. *American Journal of Sociology* 99: 614–639.Tadić, J. (1948) *Dubrovacki portreti.* Belgrade: Srpska Književna Zadruga.
Tadić, J. (1962) Ragusa e il suo porto nel Cinquecento. *Quaderni dell'archivio storico pugliese* 7: 99–109.
Thompson, G. (1994) Early double-entry bookkeeping and the rhetoric of accounting calculation. In: Hopwood, A. G. and Miller, P. (eds.), *Accounting as social and institutional practice, Cambridge studies in management*, Cambridge: Cambridge University Press, pp. 40–66.
Yamey, B. S. (1981) Some reflections on the writing of a general history of accounting. *Accounting and Business Research* 11(42): 127–135.
Zambon, S. and Zan, L. (2007) Controlling expenditure, or the slow emergence of costing at the Venice Arsenal,1586–1633. *Accounting, Business & Financial History* 17(1): 105–128.

15 Accounting and Food Provisioning for Public Interest

The Case of the Azienda Annonaria Di Vigevano (1915–1920)

Michela Magliacani and Francesca Pepe

INTRODUCTION

Food policy is at the centre of the ongoing political debate on sustainable development. The direct evidence of this claim is "The Charter of Milan: Commitment to Healthy, Safe and Nutritious Food for All." This is a protocol, focused on the big global issues on food, that is going to be signed by citizens, institutions, companies, associations, academia and international organizations. The Charter of Milan is an act of commitment delivered to UN Secretary General Ban Ki-Moon at the end of the Universal Exposition hosted in Milan in 2015 (http://carta.milano.it/en/).

A further evidence on the relevance of food policy, also at local context, is the "Urban Food Policy Pact," an international protocol for the development of a city food systems, based on the principles of sustainability and social justice. The Urban Food Policy Pact will be subscribed among the mayors of several cities around the world and it comes together with the theme of the Universal Exposition 2015: "Feeding the Planet, Energy for Life." Both the Charter of Milan and the Urban Food Policy Pact aim to discuss about the existing imbalance between the availability and the consumption of resources and to make the decision makers aware about this issue. In addition, in the Urban Food Policy Pact much attention has been focused on the relation between food and city, because the rural population is being reduced, as a consequence of half of the world's population living in cities (United Nations, 2014).

Food procurement deeply affects citizens' well-being and the way in which public services should be managed and delivered. Food procurement and provisioning have ever been considered as a theme of public interest, both at the central and local government levels. The international debate on this theme shows a gap related to the speculations on "food accounting" as a political-economy practice both in historical and contemporary accounting studies. Nonetheless, the accounting research on agro-food calls for more investigations (Jack, 2007).

The notion of accounting as a mean for understanding the past or the contemporary organizations is based on the "symbolic nature" that has been acknowledged to the accounting records (Catturi, 2005). Indeed, the accounting is able to highlight the organization's culture or, in other words, the values that characterize the way of working within and outside the organizational borders (Hopwood, 1976, 1977).

Furthermore, Cooper and Sherer (1984, p. 208) argue that "accounting contains a representation of a specific social and political context." It depends on the use of language in accounting, considering that the political economy of a community shapes any social practice, such as accounting language, and the background contexts shape how people make decisions (Lehman, 2006).

Acknowledging the call for more accounting research in the field of food production and trade, this study aims at filling this gap under a historical perspective by considering the food provisioning system during the First World War in Italy.

More specifically, the research objectives are twofold:

- To augment the understanding of the interrelations among accounting food provisioning for public interest and the Italian local authority at that time (Sargiacomo and Gomes, 2013).
- To demonstrate how the accounting language of the provisioning system portrays the socioeconomic and political environment of that war context (Antonelli et al., 2014).

In order to achieve these research objectives, the study introduces the theme of food procurement and provisioning as a public interest. Then, a critical literature review on the use of accounting language for knowing the past has been carried out. Adopting an interpretative research methodology, the case of the "Azienda Annonaria di Vigevano" has been explored. It represented a local public entity, set up by the Municipality of Vigevano in Lombardy (Northern Italy) for developing the provisioning system during the First World War. The case study has been carried out by gathering information from the historical archive of the Municipality of Vigevano. More specifically, these primary sources are represented by two data sets:

1. The correspondence among the AAV, the other local authorities operating in the surrounding area of Vigevano, the local delegate of central government ("Prefetto"), various consortium of food distribution in that territory, the food producers, the food traders and the food retailers.
2. The accounting records of the AAV, the financial statements, the invoices relating to the distribution of foods and the receipts and payment records.

The discussion of the findings and the final remarks are presented in the concluding section.

FOOD PROCUREMENT AND PROVISIONING AS PUBLIC INTEREST

As the economic literature on food system stressed (Morgan and Sonnino, 2007; Forson and Counihan, 2012; Goodman et al., 2012; Marsden and Morley, 2014; Nagothu, 2015), we should rethink the relations between: public sector and the chain of food provision, local governments and civil society, public choice and private matters. In fact, Renting et al. (2012) paid attention to the "governance triangle" structure, which put in relation the state, market and civil society. According to them, the governance bias is to consider food like other products in the market and to address the price mechanism. In addition, the agricultural policies, the rural development policies and the food safety and security policies legitimate the state intervention in the food governance system (Morgan, 2011). As Morgan and Sonnino (2008, p. 65) highlighted about the Italian school food system, "the public sector has been actively fighting against the generalized deterioration in the population's nutritional habits." Moreover, the "Green State" is responsible in promoting the "economic development, democracy, and environmental integration" (Morgan and Sonnino, 2008, p. 18).

From this standpoint, the basic role of the market as well as the state intervention have been assured in the food governance system. However, the civil society has not been sufficiently engaged yet, albeit the role of "citizens-producers" within food system is being strengthened (Renting et al., 2012).

Even if the debate about the balancing among market, state and civil society in food governance is still open, it is common statement that the public sector plays a central role in "taking food public" (Forson and Counihan, 2012) and to deliver "the public plate" mainly to the "vulnerable consumers" (Morgan, 2014). But this isn't new in the history. In the present public food institutions operate (i.e., schools, hospitals, care homes and prisons), but also in the past the state intervention in food procurement and provisioning was considered as a public interest. In the early United States, for example, the availability and the consumption of food resources were public policy issues. As Baics (2013) pointed out, the first stage of New York city urbanization (1790–1820) caused a strong urban population concentration, based on a nonagricultural economy. The need of fresh food for the residents required that the local government should become owner, manager and controller of the urban provisioning system. As a consequence, a monopolistic municipal market system for provisioning fresh food was created to ensure food quality and to promote equal access to food. In this case, it is interesting to highlight that food provisioning was not only an economic policy matter, but it also called a direct engagement of local government for its management.

The public policy to fulfil the citizens' food needs is relevant not only in strong periods of urbanization, but also in temporary urban food shortages, such as in time of crises or war. Hence, during the First World War the food shortage required local government to take ownership of and manage the food procurement and provisioning system. However, how local authority food management and accounting had been developed during the First World War has not been fully investigated yet. On this basis, Jack (2007, p. 907) called more research on agri-food accounting; Walker (2008, p. 297) underlines the increasing research interest on accounting in social institutions. Furthermore, in order to provide a deep understanding on the role of accounting in organizations and society and consistently to the first research objective, Sargiacomo and Gomes (2011, 2013) called more accounting history investigation on the exercise of power by and within local government. Moreover, relating to the second research objective, Antonelli et al. (2014) called further investigations on state accounting in Italy during wartime.

Following these claims, this study attempts to research local government food accounting during the First World War, and to extend knowledge on the role of accounting as a socioeconomic and political practice. Additionally, the relation between accounting and accountability for food is explored.

THE USES OF ACCOUNTING LANGUAGE FOR KNOWING THE PAST: A LITERATURE REVIEW

Accounting as a human practice represents a rationale in the academic studies, since Hopwood (1976) introduced the research call to extend the understanding of the place and the meaning of accounting in the society. This accounting research stream has overcome the practice-oriented approach on accounting as a mere technical phenomenon (Bower, 1970; Burchell et al., 1980). More specifically, Hopwood (1977, p. 277) argues that:

> Rather than being static and purely technocratic accounting has had, and hopefully still has, the potential of being responsive and adaptive calculative technology that can relate to and facilitate broader processes of enterprise and social development.

Going further in this reasoning, accounting as a human practice is based on human interaction (Carnegie and Napier, 2011). The latter is developed through a language that is itself "a social institution" (Burke, 1987). According to the sociolinguistic studies, words have powerful role in the society, because they can be used by individuals for controlling behavior as well as justifying, legitimizing and defending deeds (Handlin, 1979; Pfeffer, 1981). Linguistic frameworks have been adopting in an array of accounting studies (Belkaoui, 1989; Potter, 1999; Lehman, 2006), in order to improve the knowledge of accounting in its relation with the society. From this research stream, the definition of "accounting as a language" comes out. It encompasses the double functions of accounting language as "mediator and shaper of the environment" (Belkaoui, 1978, p. 97). This argument has been developed in the philosophical debate about the ability of accounting language to reveal things as they are (Solomons, 1978, 1991; Davidson, 1997). The objectivity of accounting has been analyzed within the relation between language and reality. The previous literature explains why language in general and accounting as a language, in communicating reality, constructs reality (Hines, 1988).

In addition, language, as a human practice, changes because "while communicating, we reify what is in our mind and thereby reinvent language every time we speak" (Blank, 1999, p. 61). Thus, change is inherent to the language: it is caused by "the man's mind and human social interaction" (Blank, 1999, p. 63).

The theory of language change has been applied to accounting language. How accounting is relative and progressive, by responding to the environmental change, was before underlined by Littetton (1933, p. 361), who states that "the phenomena which form its subject matter are constantly changing."

Furthermore, accounting language is made up of words used by social groups for identifying themselves in the name of the stake they claim (Thornborrow, 1999). On this basis, accounts and their registers serve to demarcate group identity and to take apart other individuals (Crystal, 2003; Neu, 2006; Evans, 2010). In an attempt to extending knowledge of the ability of accounting to construct reality, the process of socialization has been referred to. In fact, that process implies the transmission of cultural knowledge as well as social skills, so it allows to learn how to speak and behave within a specific society (Johnson, 2006). According to Taylor's viewpoint the language structure is shaped by culture and the background nuances shape people's being-in-the-world (Lehman, 2006, p. 763).

That accounting is not a passive effect of its environment but that it shapes this environment is recently acknowledged as rationale in the accounting research stream (Hopwood, 1992; Carmona, 2004). Regarding the reflective and constitutive facets of accounting, Napier (2006, p. 456) remarks:

> The constitutive power of accounting arises not just in the context of the individual organization, but also in a wider social context. In the organization, accounting makes possible particular modes of action, such as budgeting, but also shapes the organization itself, for example as a hierarchy of cost centres. More particularly, accounting helps to make things visible within an organization, not in a neutral sense of enabling more precise and detailed management in rational pursuit of unproblematic economic goals but rather to make possible the pursuit of economic goals in the first place.

From the previous standpoint, the motivations and the mechanisms of accounting language change has been explored in order to achieve an in-depth knowledge of the societal and cultural environment (Evans, 2010).

In fact, accounting uses words that make up a "language for specific purposes" (Mills, 1989). However, the specialized terminology used in the registers represents the accounting culture spreading at a referring time (Goldberg, 1956). From this reasoning, the research calls for exploring the meaning of accounting words in their historical context. In that perspective, Mills (1989) suggests accounting historians understand the sense of the words in which they are used. What matters is not the origin of the word, but the development and the application of the words concerned over time (Potter, 1999). Indeed, as Cahen (1921, p. 1) states, "the facts of the vocabulary are intimately tied to facts of civilization." According to this quotation, the relation between discourse and practice should be explored. As the discourse represents the use of language as a form of social practice, discourse analysis explores how text works within the sociocultural environment (Fairclough, 1995).

These theoretical hints are aligned to the "critical" perspective in accounting history research (Carnegie and Napier, 2012). The *New Accounting History* is the consequence of the emergence of the interdisciplinary of accounting introduced by Hopwood (1976, 1977). It has been also emphasized in numerous contributions developed outside of the econometric accounting research approach (Hoskin and Macve, 1986; Tinker et al., 1988; Miller and Napier, 1993; Laughlin, 1999; Milne et al., 2007; Baker, 2011). The *New Accounting History* analyzes the past, combining an anthropological perspective with geographic, demographic, economic and sociologic ones (Napier, 2006, p. 455).

Within the *New Accounting History*, the political economy of accounting has been developed (Burchell et al., 1980; Tinker, 1980). Although Cooper's bias on the use of the historical approach in social science, his contribution has boosted the critical research perspective to accounting, stressing how different economics, as political economy, requires different accounting. According to this critical research stream:

> Accounting contains a representation of a specific social and political context. Not only is accounting policy essentially political in that it derives from the political struggle in a society as a whole but also the outcomes of accounting policy are essentially political in that they operate for the benefit of some groups in society and to the detriment of others.
>
> (Cooper and Sherer, 1984, p. 208)

That narrow accounting research stream has been overcome by further critical accounting studies through which the historical approach back to recover a proper space within the political economy of accounting perspective (Miller and Napier, 1993; Napier, 2006). The emphasis on the historical approach into critical accounting has been boosted by the adoption of Foucault's philosophy on knowledge (1972). According to the latter, because of the closely connection between power and knowledge, the genealogical approach sounds suitable for analyzing the cultural and social practice of accounting in which power and knowledge are tied (Hoskin and Macve, 1986; Miller and O'Leary, 1987, 1993; Stewart, 1992; Neu et al., 2001). In this light, the Foucauldian-inspired accounting histories have shown how accounting is not a practice in itself, but a part of an "accounting constellation" including "networks of people, principles and practices" (Miller and Napier, 1993). The results of these researches are consistent with the constitutive nature of accounting. As Stewart (1992, p. 65) emphasized, accounting, in a web of power/knowledge structures, creates an "architecture of power."

This analysis seems to be particularly suitable in the historical research, focusing on accounting and the state (Carnegie and Napier, 2012). Coming back to Foucault, though, the close relation between language and politics has to be stressed. The French philosopher introduces the notion of governmentality as an "ensemble formed by the institutions, procedures, analyses and reflections, the calculations and tactics, that allow the exercise of this very specific albeit complex form of power" (Foucault, 1979, p. 20). Within this framework, discourse—such as accounting—represents a technology of government (Miller and Rose, 1990, p. 8). As Miller and Rose (1990, p. 6) underline:

> All government depends on a particular mode of "representation": the elaboration of a language for depicting the domain in question that claims both to grasp the nature of that reality represented, and literally to represent it in a form amenable to political deliberation, argument and scheming. This gives us a clue to a further way in which language is significant for government.

From this reasoning, accounting does not have a neutral recording function, but it is in itself a way of acting political programs. The previous literature review represents the theoretical background of this study.

RESEARCH METHODS

In order to fulfil the research objectives of this chapter, this study will be carried out by adopting an interpretative research methodology (Ryan et al., 2002), based on an "explanatory" case study (Yin, 1984). The choice of case study is connected, in relation to the first research objective, to the relevance of public policy to fulfil citizens' food needs; regarding the second research objective, the accounting language of food provisioning system can provide the picture of the socioeconomic and political environment of a local community.

The case study is about the history of the Azienda Annonaria di Vigevano during the First World War. At that period of time, food provisioning was managed in different ways by local authorities. One of this managerial solution was the public entity in the legal form regulated by the Law n. 103/1903. The Azienda Annonaria di Vigevano (hereinafter AAV) has been chosen because of the richness of sources included in the historical archive of the Municipality of Vigevano. In fact, that archive encompasses the entire administrative and accounting documents of the AAV (1915–1921): 163 files gathered in 20 folders (primary sources).

In order to depict the food provisioning context in Italy during the First World War, secondary sources have been analyzed. They refer to the book on the failures of procurement and provisioning policy (Ricci, 1921), and to three reports on the food provisioning system in the Brescia, Mondovì and San Secondo Parmense Municipalities (Città di Mondovì, 1917; Cavalleri, 1918; Comune di San Secondo Parmense, 1919).

THE CASE STUDY: THE AZIENDA ANNONARIA OF VIGEVANO (AAV)

Food Provisioning System

In wartime, food policy aims to guarantee primary goods for the whole population. An interesting overview of food policy in Italy during the First World War (May 1915—November 1918) is showed by a historical source, the book on the failures of procurement and provisioning policy written by Ricci (1921).[1] The following quotation remarks the Ricci's (1921, p. vii) point of view about the public policy in wartime:

> If the people with great voice claim requisitions, ration cards and price control, the public authority has to fix prices and rations, because through aware destruction of wealth the policy-makers buy social peace.
>
> Likewise, if one day Italians, gathered in assemblies, proclaim the need for a train directed to the moon, governors should establish a direct train to the moon; and print out the itinerary with all intermediate stations. This is! But then such politicians should applaud and not sneer, when economists attempt to make it clear that the trains are not able to go to the moon. After years of recriminations and protests, the promises of free trade began to hear in early 1921; they seem to be honest.
>
> (translation from Italian)

It will easily be grasped how this quotation is not in favour of Italian food policy during the First World War because its effect was an increase in food prices. This food policy was different from the one in Belgium, which was based on free trade, and caused a decrease in food prices (Ricci, 1921, pp. 461–462). Far from the judgement about the food political choice, the present section of the study focuses on the main features of the Italian food provisioning system in the First World War.

At that period of time, the agricultural production declined dramatically, albeit the food consumption, especially from the military community, increased. The Italian lira decreased in value and food prices increased. Besides, there were difficulties in obtaining food, and there was no way to find it abroad because imports from other countries were restricted. Also the national market was limited; indeed exportation among Italian territories (provinces) was forbidden even at the end of the war.[2] This caused competition among territories with different level of economic prosperity, raised the smuggled goods, and modified the food needs. The bans and the illegal practices also increased the cases of food deterioration, albeit the majority of people felt this need.

The commodity prices were monitored so that the sellers' opportunistic behaviour occurred, determining social inequalities and inducing to buy substitute foods. In addition, the control of prices implied food rationing system to satisfy population primary needs, but it also necessitated the same quality and quantity of food for each social group (i.e., male, female, children, the elderly, the sick). Another consequence of food rationing was also the problems of smuggling and cronyism.

Furthermore, consumers created cooperatives for buying directly food from producers without the presence of authorized intermediaries sellers, which in consumers' opinions had speculative behaviours on food prices. In order to avoid scalping, it local government intervention was instituted. As Ricci (1921, p. 156) highlighted:

> The market is a public place where the right to sell is precious and thus can be regulated by the Municipality according to the rules it has to be applied. It's not wrong that the Municipality in its markets imposes rules for the sale and gives the right to sell only to those who agree not exceed a percentage of the purchase price. It's not wrong, or rather it's very good, if the ration commissioner ensures directly, or better by municipal experts, that the negotiations take place from retailer to consumer expelling scalpers, preventing the proliferation of unnecessary wheels. It's a job that is successful only if it is carried out consistently, competently, with obstinacy.
>
> (translation from Italian)

The intervention of local government was legitimated also when, in 1917, the "Commissario Generale degli Approvigionamenti" (General Commissioner for Provisioning) proposed to create a state authority of consumption ("Ente centrale dei consumi"). This authority was supposed to encompass the Italian consumer cooperatives, and to be in charge of food procurement and provisioning system at the central government level (Ricci, 1921; Cavalleri, 1918). However, this proposal was disapproved, because it would have reduced the municipalities power of monitoring and managing food rationing. In fact, the Operating Report of procurement and provisioning system of Municipality of Brescia in 1918 (Cavalleri, 1918, p. 3) stated:

> The proposal, albeit, laudable in its aims, was to hurt the efforts of municipalities and local authorities [. . .] But, denying the power from the municipalities, it pushes them to bind to the central government entity so that they get caught in bureaucratic net.
>
> (translation from Italian)

That, briefly, is the socioeconomic and political scenario in which local authorities became directly responsible in food procurement and provisioning. The governance systems adopted by municipalities were slightly different among themselves.

The Municipality of San Secondo Parmense (1919), in Emilia Romagna Region, outsourced the food procurement and provisioning to private agents during the Great War.

In the Municipality of Mondovì (1917), in Piedmont Region, the mayor was in charge of food procurement and provisioning, in collaboration with a special commission. The latter, appointed by the local delegate of central government (Prefetto), represented every social group of the local community. The commission played an advisory role in relation to the mayor and a representative role in relation to the community. In addition, there was a supervisory commission, appointed by the mayor, that supported and monitored the population about the application of the provisioning regulation.

In order to manage the food provisioning, the Municipality of Brescia (Cavalleri, 1918), in Lombardy Region, set up a municipal entity in 1915. Until the end of the war, that municipal entity was in charge of the management of municipal food shops (increased by 26 in 1918), food trade operations, ration cards and the food quota system. The municipal entity was headed by the mayor or by its delegate, elected within the municipality executive board.

The Municipality of Vigevano, explored in this study, is not so different from the Brescia's case in term of governance system. Nonetheless, the wide variety and the large quantity of primary sources, founded from the historical archive of the city, allow more in-depth research on the relation between accounting and food. Vigevano is a city located in the territorial area called Lomellina in Lombardy Region (Northern Italy). The local economy of the city is mainly based on the secondary sector, even if the primary one has a long tradition. Rice production, indeed, was started in 1470 by the Duke of Milan, Galeazzo Maria Sforza.

At the end of the nineteenth century, there was an intensive production of silk, which was exported to the national market and abroad. Nevertheless, before the outbreak of the war, this production declined, due to a lower emphasis on agriculture and to the increasing competition from Asian markets. The manufacturing and cotton-ginning sectors, instead, survived to the industrialization and gained from innovation. But the main sector has ever since been shoe production, which increased during and after the First World War.

As the AAV Archive shows, the outbreak of the First World War called the municipality to be responsible for ensuring the survival of the population. Hence, it managed the food provisioning system through its public office ("Ufficio degli approvigionamenti") until 1917. Thereafter, when procurement and provisioning activities increased, the Municipality of Vigevano opened an account at a local bank ("Banca Popolare di Vigevano") in order to set up an entity, the "Azienda Annonaria Municipale" for managing the local food procurement and provisioning.

The City Council Act, regarding the bank account opening, stated the mission of the food provisioning entity: "for purchasing the primary goods, not only flour, so that the community doesn't feel the need of bread and other goods" (Folder 13, File 4, AAV Archive).

The AAV used its own human resources, that were seconded from the Municipality and the director was the Mayor or his delegate (Folder 9, File 1, AAV Archive). Moreover, the AAV managed also the municipal mill (Folder 7, File 1, AAV Archive).

The Title 1 (named "Provisioning" and including 99 files gathered in 9 folders) of AAV Archive allows to describe how the entity operated in provisioning foods such as butter, coffee, meat, bran, dry fruits, cheese, wheat, bacon, milk, olive oil, pasta, potatoes, fish, rice, eggs, sugar and so forth.

The food producers had to report the entire amount collected or produced. The state allowed producers to keep a part of food for new production, for their family feeding and for their employees. The remaining part of the production was requisitioned by the central government ("Ministero per gli approvvigionamenti e consumi", or the Ministry for Provisioning and Consumption) and redistributed, first to the military, and then to the municipalities with a supplement of imported food. Regarding to the latter, the food imports were allowed only to the central government (Folder 2, AAV Archive).

The redistribution of food was done through the provincial procurement consortia ("Consorzi di approvvigionamento"). The central government provisioning plan was annual, but it was monthly reviewed. The allocation of food to each province and municipality was based on a fixed quota in relation to the amount of their population, and also to the consumption habits. The food prices, also, were decided by the central government or its delegate (Prefetto) (Folder 6, File 4, AAV Archive).

At the local government level, the AAV distributed food rations to local producers (such as wheat for mills and flour for bakeries), cooperatives and retailers.

The AAV gave ration cards or coupon cards to each family, temporarily allowing them to purchase food. The food provisioning system also included another kind of rationing for some items of food. The retailers were obliged to deliver not more than a certain amount to each beneficiary. A ration book was compiled by the AAV to record this information.

The consumers were able to choose the food store, but not the food quantity and quality, and its price. The producers, for example of wheat, sometimes had the chance to deposit food in the own repository and could obtain flour and make bread for their consumption.

The Title 1 of the AAV Archive includes also the correspondence among the entity, the Vigevano Municipality, and other local public authorities (i.e., Provincial Consortium of Wheat, Municipality of Mortara, Chamber of Commerce, Manufacturing and Industry, Provincial Consortium for Provisioning, Mandatory Consortium for the Butter Regulation, Prisons), the central government (i.e., Railways Department, Ministry for Provisioning and Consumption, General Commissionaire for Provisioning, Ministry of Treasury, Ministry of Munitions), suppliers, producers, trade agents and banks.

The previous source highlights how food procurement and provisioning system was at the centre of public and private relations, both at the local and national levels. At wartime, food was considered as a public interest. Hence, how was the food provisioning system depicted by the AAV accounting language?

The Reflective and Constitutive Facets of Food Accounting Language

The analysis of the accounting documents of AAV has been carried out by adopting the "contextualizing accounting" approach (Napier, 1989). This approach implies the consideration of accounting in its double facets: reflective and constitutive. In fact, accounting as a language reflects the socioeconomic and political environment in which it is used. The Foucauldian framework on governmentality provides an interpretative scheme in which the constitutive facet of accounting comes out. As a technology of government, accounting language is able to develop government programs, and in doing so it creates the socioeconomic and political environment. Moreover, the notion of accounting as a "language for specific purpose" provides a framework for an in-depth understanding of the phenomena occurring through accounting.

According to Evans (2010), accounting historians can benefit not only from knowing the earlier meaning of the words, but also the origin of words and the conditions and motivations surrounding changes in meaning.

From these theoretical hints, this study focuses on accounting language used in the accounting documents of the food provisioning system of the Vigevano Municipality in the First World War.

The accounting sources on food provisioning are included in 64 files gathered in 11 folders available in the AAV Archive. They are listed in the Archive's Inventory, starting with number 100: "Allegati di bilancio, 1917" ("Notes to the Financial Statement, 1917").

This analysis has adopted the taxonomy between "main accounting documents" (which follow a method of accounting record) and "auxiliary accounting documents" (which support to compile the main documents), introduced by Fabio Besta (1932).

First of all, it is interesting that the first financial statement of the AAV dates back to 1917, in compliance with the Law n. 103/1903. The latter allowed Municipality to set up a public entity (named Azienda municipalizzata), for providing primary goods and services (setup of pharmacy, refuse collection management, setup and management of mills, corn production and provision of corn, etc.) for the local community.

Moreover, the net profit was found to be part of the regular budget of the municipality and any losses were covered with the extraordinary part of the expense of the municipal budget (with the reference to the Art. 2, Law n. 103/1903). The financial statements of the municipal entities had to be approved by the City Council and by the provincial government. In fact, they were subject to the control of the local delegate of the central government (Prefetto) (with the reference to the Art. 2, Law n. 103/1903).

The term *Azienda* for identifying the organization that was in charge of the food provisioning in the Municipality of Vigevano was consistent with the aforementioned law. It was also consistent with the notion of the firm, spreading in the Italian accounting literature at that time. Adopting the French accounting theory—the logismography—Giuseppe Cerboni defined the term Azienda twofold: from an objective perspective, it is identified by the administrative matter (assets) and the managerial action; from a subjective perspective, by the owner, the manager, the agents and the stakeholders (Doni, 2008; Antonelli et al., 2014). This definition reflects the public environment where the author was engaged as paymaster general of the Kingdom of Italy (1876–1891), included the notion of municipal entity spreading in the past. In other words, the term Azienda for the AAV was properly used considering the accounting culture of that period of time.

Consistently with the state accounting and reporting system regulated by the Law n. 1455/1883 (the "Legge Magliani"), the financial statement of the AAV was based on cash accounting. The term "Bilancio" (financial statement) included the Statements of Financial Position and the Cash Flow Statement. Nonetheless, the first financial statement of the AAV included only the latter and a detailed Current Account (Folder 15, File 1, AAV Archive), which allowed the AAV to be accountable for the financial fund (200,000 Italian Lire) used for purchasing wheat, flour and other items of foods. That financial fund (200,000 Italian Lire) represents the first account reported on the revenue part (Entrata) and on the expense part ("Spesa") as a fund flow ("Movimento di capitali"). In the account named "Partite di giro", the revenue and the expense about food provisioning of that year were reported. Moreover, each part of the Cash Flow Statement was articulated in seven columns. The first pair regarded the number of the records; the third column reported the name of the accounts; the following ones related to the single phases that the financial cycle of revenue and expense were, respectively, composed of. They were concerning the forecast ("Stanziamenti") of revenue and expense, the receipted revenue ("Riscosse") and the paid expense ("Pagamenti"); the last two columns of both parts are related to the revenue to be receipted ("Da riscuotere") and total revenue ("Totale accertamenti") and to the expense to be paid ("Da pagare") and total expense ("Totale accertamenti").

According to the public accounting regulation, the Cash Flow Statement allowed public authorities and their entities to be accountable about the public financial fund used in providing public services. In fact, this statement assured that the AAV had used financial resource, in compliance with the budget approved by the City Council. In the Foucauldian perspective, the public accounting system enabled the Municipality of Vigevano to control how the financial resources had managed by the "Azienda annonaria".

According to the public service law (Art. 2, Law n. 103/1903), the Municipality of Vigevano executive board ("Giunta") introduced to the City Council the financial statement through a note attached to the document (Folder 10, AAV Archive). The executive board discourse stressed the going concern of the AAV and the comprehensive of its management ("because the management goes on and forms an unity until its end"; translation from Italian).

The Financial Statement of the year 1918 included not only the Cash Flow Statement, but also the Statement of Financial Position. The former had the same structure of the Cash Flow Statement of the previous financial year. The only difference regarded the credits ("Residui attivi") and debits ("Residui passivi") that allowed the AAV to be accountable towards the local authority for the food provisioning relations with the retailers and the suppliers. The following pages of the Cash Flow Statement provided details, respectively, on the number of the receipt and of the payment orders.

Focusing on the Statement of Financial Position, its structure was articulated in two sections: Assets on the left side and Liabilities on the right side (Figure 15.1).

The Assets ("Attività") were made up of Inventories ("Merci"), Trade Receivables ("Crediti") and Credits from the Municipality of Vigevano ("Residui attivi") and Cash and the balanced total ("Denaro in cassa e pareggio"). The Liabilities ("Passività") were composed of Trade Payables ("Debiti"), Debts to the Vigevano Municipality ("Residui attivi"), and Debts to the local bank ("Debito verso Banca Popolare di Vigevano"). The lack of equity among the Liabilities confirms that the AAV operated as a public entity instead of a firm. What also matters is the transparency of the Statement of Financial Position: relating to the Inventories, each food account reported the market price, the quantity and the total value. Moreover, the Trade Receivables are composed of advances to food suppliers or trade receivables to beneficiaries of the food provisioning. These accounts, reported in the each Statement of Financial Position of AAV, identified the group or the individuals (stakeholders) that the Azienda had trade relations with during wartime (Table 15.1).

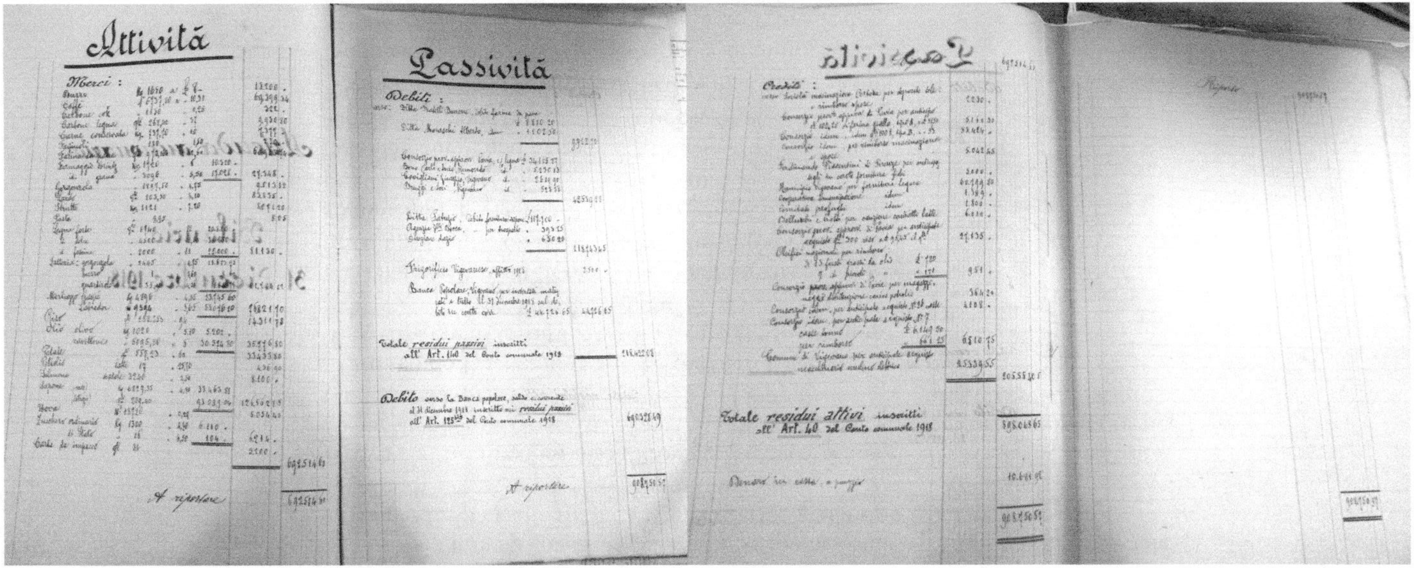

Figure 15.1 The statement of financial position of AAV (1918)

Source: Folder 15, File 2, AAV Archive

Table 15.1 The food provisioning stakeholders identified in the AAV main accounting documents (1917–1921)

	1917	1918	1919	1920	1921
Food suppliers		"Società macinazione Certosa" (Millstone Company of Certosa) "Consorzio Provinciale di Pavia per farina gialla tipo A e tipo B" (Provincial Consortium of Pavia, supplier of Flour, type A and type B) "Ferdinando Piacentini di Firenze conto fornitura fichi" (Ferdinando Piacentini of dried figs from Florence) "Municipio di Vigevano per legna" (Municipality Food Shop, supplier of wood) "Belluschi contratto latte" (Supplier of milk) "Consorzio Provinciale di Pavia per fornitura di riso" (Provincial Consortium of Pavia, supplier of rice) "Oleifici nazionali"	"Società macinazione Certosa" (Millstone Company of Certosa) "Consorzio Provinciale di Pavia per farina gialla tipo A e tipo B" (Provincial Consortium of Pavia, supplier of Flour, type A and type B) "Ferdinando Piacentini di Firenze conto fornitura fichi" (Ferdinando Piacentini of dried figs from Florence) "Municipio di Vigevano per legna" (Municipality Food Shop, supplier of wood) "Belluschi contratto latte" (Supplier of milk) "Consorzio Provinciale di Pavia per fornitura di riso" (Provincial Consortium of Pavia, supplier of rice)	"Società macinazione Certosa" (Millstone Company of Certosa) "Consorzio Provinciale di Pavia per riso e formaggio" (Provincial Consortium of Pavia, supplier of rice and cheese)	

		(National olive oil mills) "Consorzio Provinciale di Pavia per petrolio" (Provincial Consortium of Pavia, supplier of olive oil) "Consorzio Provinciale di Pavia per casse di burro" (Provincial Consortium of Pavia, supplier of butter)	"Oleifici nazionali" (National olive oil mills) "Consorzio Provinciale di Pavia per petrolio" (Provincial Consortium of Pavia, supplier of olive oil) "Consorzio Provinciale di Pavia per casse di burro" (Provincial Consortium of Pavia, supplier of butter)		
Food beneficiaries	Spaccio comunale (Municipality Food Shop)	"Cooperativa Emancipazione" (Emancipazione cooperative society) "Comitato profughi" (Refugee Committee)	"Comune di Casselnuvo" (Casselnuovo Municipality) "Cooperativa Emancipazione" (Emancipazione cooperative society) "Comitato profughi" (Refugee Committee)	"Cooperativa Emancipazione" (Emancipazione cooperative society) "Orfanotrofio" (Orphanage) "Pio Istituto dei poveri" (Pius Poorer Institution) "Istituto Roncalli" (Roncalli School) "Spaccio comunale" (Municipality Food Shop)	"Cooperativa Emancipazione" (Emancipazione cooperative society) "Pio Istituto dei poveri" (Pius Poorer Institution) "Istituto Roncalli" (Roncalli School) "Ospedale civile" (Civil Hospital) "Spaccio latte" (Municipality Milk Food Shop)

Source: AAV Archive, Folder 15

Table 15.2 The impact of food inventories on total assets of the AAV (1917–1921)

	1918	1919	1920	1921
Inventories*	692,514,60	810,252,99	30,863,95	1,581
Total assets*	908,750,57	1,162,451,68	229,671,14	163,976,99
%	76%	69%	13%	0,9%

*The values are expressed in "Italian Lire," the Italian currency.

Source: Statement of financial position of AAV, 1918–1921

The analysis of the Trade Receivable taken from the Statement of Financial Position of AAV (1917–1921) shows how the Azienda core activity was intensively developed during wartime, and how it decreased after the end of the war. In fact, the current assets were mostly composed by the credits to the food beneficiaries (Table 15.1), and the percentage of the food inventories dropped by almost 1% on the total assets in 1921 (Table 15.2). The previous evidences show how the accounting language is able to reflect the managerial condition of the entity and its relations with the socioeconomic and political environment. Indeed, the AAV was closed down in 1920, but it continued in food provisioning until 1921. The relations between that provisioning entity and its food suppliers were decreasing from 1917 to 1920, because after the end of the war the public interest on food provisioning was reduced.

The "Bilancio" of the AAV, from that of 1917, included—in attachment—the "Balance of Food Accounts". Hence, the food accounting system recorded the purchase value ("Spesa") and the market value ("Entrata") of each food item (Figure 15.2). The balance of each food account was reported in the Balance of Food Accounts (Figure 15.3) and in the Statement of Financial Position recorded as the first asset named "Merci" (Figure 15.1).

Differently to the public sector accounting practice based on the logismography, the accounting system aligned to the food provisioning entitled accounts to food value, rather than to individual. It also has been shown by the Annual Report of the Municipality food shop (Folder 15, File 1, AAV Archive). Moreover, the food accounting and reporting were not compulsory. These practices were consistent with the Besta's accounting theory (which was against the logismography) and with the public accounting reform proposal, designed by the Besta-D'Alvise Committee (Andrei, 2010; Sargiacomo et al., 2012; Frugatti et al., 2014).

The AAV food accounts were crafted by public accountants, in order to allow the entity to be accountable for the food provisioning toward the local authority. Hence, this food accounting practice was consistent with the Vigevano governmentality.

FINAL REMARKS

Food procurement and provisioning has ever been a public interest especially during wartime. During the First World War the local authority intervention

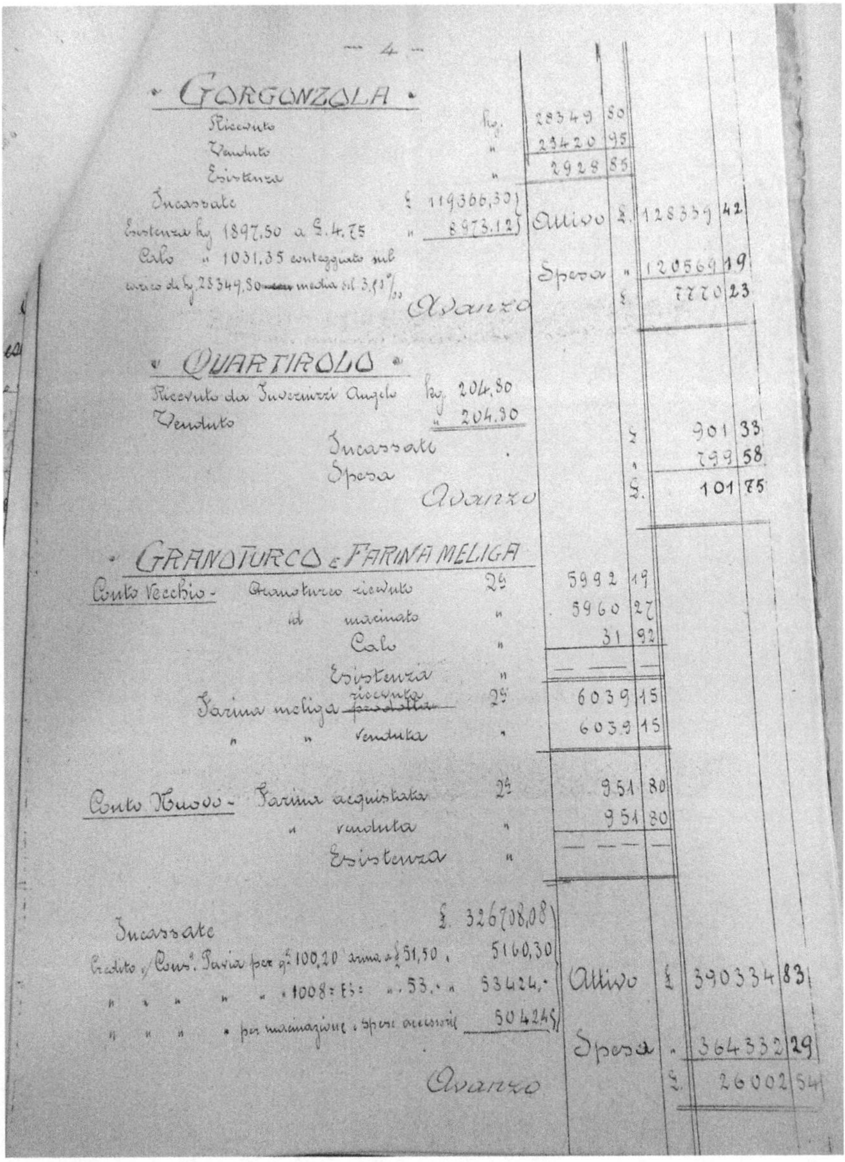

— 4 —

• GORGONZOLA •

Ricevuto kg. 28349 | 80
Venduto " 25420 | 95
Esistenza " 2928 | 85
Incassate £ 119366,30
Esistenza kg 1897,50 a £. 4,75 " 8973,12 Attivo £. 128339 | 42
Calo " 1031,35 conteggiato sul carico di kg 28349,80 media del 3,63 % Spesa " 120569 | 19
Avanzo £. 7770 | 23

• QUARTIROLO •

Ricevuto da Invernizzi Angelo kg. 204,80
Venduto " 204,80
Incassate £ 901 | 33
Spesa " 799 | 58
Avanzo £. 101 | 75

• GRANOTURCO E FARINA MELIGA

Conto Vecchio - Granoturco ricevuto q.li 5992 | 19
id macinato " 5960 | 27
Calo " 31 | 92
Esistenza " — — —
Farina meliga ricevuta q.li 6039 | 15
" " venduta " 6039 | 15

Conto Nuovo - Farina acquistata q.li 951 | 80
" venduta " 951 | 80
Esistenza " — — —

Incassate £. 326708,08
Credito v/Cons. Pavia per q.li 100,20 farina a £ 51,50 . 5160,30
" " " " " 1008 : … " 53 . " 53424,- Attivo £ 390334 | 83
" " " per macinazione e spese accessorie 5042,45 Spesa " 364332 | 29
Avanzo £. 26002 | 54

Figure 15.2 Food accounts

Source: AAV Archive, Folder 15

in food provisioning was so relevant that it set up public entity to fulfil primary needs.

In order to extend the understanding on the relation between accounting and the state during that period of time, this study investigated local government accounting of food provisioning. This is a new accounting research field focused on "food accounting."

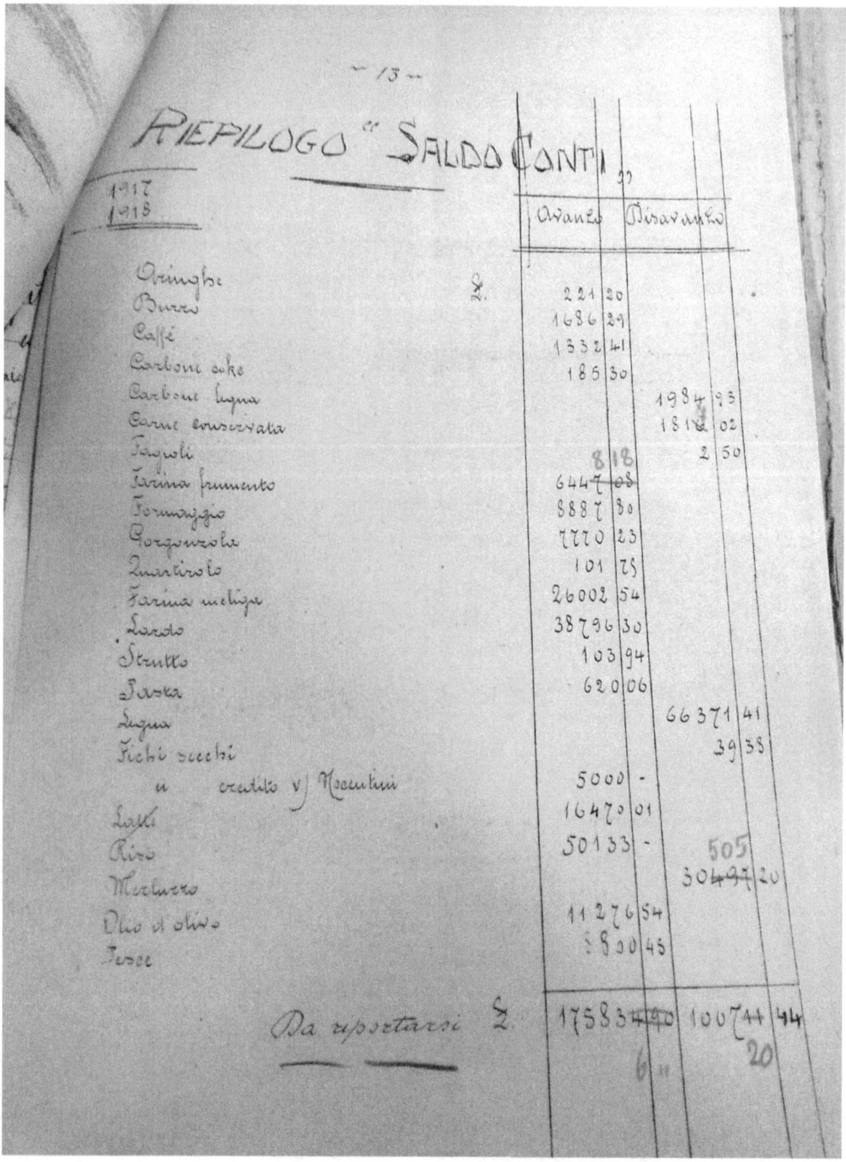

– 13 –

Riepilogo "Saldo Conti"

1917
1918

		Avanzo	Disavanzo
Aringhe	L.	221 20	
Burro		1686 29	
Caffè		1332 41	
Carbone coke		185 30	
Carbone legna			1984 93
Carne conservata			1812 02
Fagioli			2 50
Farina frumento		6447 03 (818)	
Formaggio		8887 80	
Gorgonzola		7770 23	
Quartirolo		101 75	
Farina meliga		26002 54	
Lardo		38796 30	
Strutto		103 94	
Pasta		620 06	
Legna			66371 41
Fichi secchi			39 38
" credito v/ Nosentini		5000 -	
Latte		16470 01	
Riso		50133 -	
Merluzzo			30497 20 (505)
Olio d'olivo		11276 54	
Pesce		3800 45	
Da riportarsi	L.	175834 90 (6)	100744 44 (20)

Figure 15.3 Balance of Food Accounts

Source: AAV Archive, Folder 15

The interpretative analysis of AAV accounting documents has extended the knowledge about the role of accounting as a socioeconomic and political practice. In fact, according to the *New Accounting History*, the financial statement of that municipal entity was able to reflect its relations with the socioeconomic and political environment during the First World War. The AAV accounting system encompasses not only the compulsory accounting documents, such as the Statement of Financial Position and the Cash Flow Statement, but also the Balance of Food Accounts. Indeed, the latter reflects the citizens' primary needs and makes AVV accountable for their fulfilment. Moreover, the accounting was the basis of the food provisioning decision making, such as food rationing. In addition, from the AAV Statement of Financial Position the relations with the socioeconomic environment came out. For instance, the Trade Receivables and Payments identified the food suppliers and beneficiaries of the AAV food provisioning. Furthermore, both the AAV Statement of Financial Position and the Cash Flow Statement highlighted the financial relation with the local bank ("Banca popolare di Vigevano").

Regarding the political environment, the AAV Statement of Financial Position also demarcated the institutional groups engaged in food procurement and provisioning at the local authority level (Provincial Consortium of Pavia).

The AAV financial statement encompassed a noncompulsory accounting document such as the Balance of food accounts. It was a crafted accounting document that allowed the municipal entity to be accountable toward the central and local authorities for food provisioning, respectively, in relation to the food price and to its quantity and quality.

According to Miller and Napier (1993), the accounting system of AAV represents an example of accounting constellation considering the aforementioned networks of people, principles and practices. In particular these accounting constellations show the constitutive facet of accounting, by creating an "architecture of power" (Stewart, 1992).

These evidences, extending the knowledge on food accounting in the First World War, demonstrate how the accounting language of the food provisioning system depicted the socioeconomic and political environment of Vigevano community. Moreover, the critical accounting perspective has demonstrated its usefulness in accounting history research, enforcing the constitutive facet of accounting as a public interest (Neu and Graham, 2005).

The previous findings open to historical researches on food accounting in different socioeconomic and political context. To overcome the limitation of this study, further investigations on food provisioning system in other national and international local authorities during wartime will be carried out.

ACKNOWLEDGEMENTS

The authors would like to thank Dr. Pier Luigi Muggiati and Paola Rossi, the Director of the Historical Archive of Vigevano Municipality and its Library Assistant, respectively, for providing precious support in developing the case study.

NOTES

1. In 1921 Umberto Ricci was dean of the statistics department at the International Institute of Agriculture and taught, as professor of economics and statistics, at Macerata, Parma and Pisa Universities.
2. For instance, the Decree of 11 March 1916 (Art. 3) enabled the local delegate of central government (Prefetto) to ban the export of wheat from the provinces.

REFERENCES

Primary Sources

Municipality of Vigevano. Historical Archive, Azienda Annonaria Municipale di Vigevano (1915–1921)

Inventory of the AAV Archive's Title 1: Provisioning Documents

- Folder 1, files 1–4: Approvvigionamento di burro. Corrispondenza (1918, 1919, 1920) ["Butter provisioning. Correspondence, 1918, 1919, 1920"].
- Folder 1, files 5–7: Approvvigionamento di caffè. Corrispondenza (1918, 1919, 1920) ["Coffee provisioning. Correspondence, 1918, 1919, 1920"].
- Folder 1, file 8: Approvvigionamento di calzature. Corrispondenza (1920) ["Shoes provisioning". Correspondence, 1920"].
- Folder 1, files 9–11: Approvvigionamento di carbone. Corrispondenza (1918, 1919) ["Coal provisioning. Correspondence, 1918, 1919"].
- Folder 1, files 12–16: Approvvigionamento di carne (bovina, suina e congelata). Corrispondenza (1918, 1919, 1920) ["Meat provisioning (beef, pork and frozen). Correspondence, 1918, 1919, 1920"].
- Folder 1, files 8 and 17: Approvvigionamento di carta. Corrispondenza (1920 e 1918) ["Paper provisioning. Correspondence, 1920 and 1918"].
- Folder 1, file 18: Approvvigionamento di fagioli. Corrispondenza (1917) ["Beans provisioning. Correspondence, 1917"].
- Folder 1, file 19; Folder 7, file 2: Approvvigionamento di farina per pane. Corrispondenza con i mulini (1918 e 1919) ["Flour for bread provisioning. Correspondence with mills, 1918 and 1919"].
- Folder 1, files 21 and 22: Approvvigionamento di farina per pane. Elenchi nominativi degli esercenti per la distribuzione (1918 e 1919) ["Flour for bread provisioning. Retailers list for bread distribution, 1918 and 1919"].
- Folder 2, file 1: Approvvigionamento di farina per pane. Corrispondenza (1920) ["Flour for bread provisioning. Correspondence, 1920"].
- Folder 2, files 2 and 3: Approvvigionamento di fichi secchi. Corrispondenza (1918 e 1919) ["Dry figs provisioning. Correspondence, 1918 and 1919"].
- Folder 2, files 4–6: Approvvigionamento di formaggio. Corrispondenza (1918, 1919, 1920) ["Cheese provisioning. Correspondence, 1918, 1919, 1920"].
- Folder 2, files 7 and 8: Approvvigionamento di gorgonzola. Corrispondenza (1918 e 1920) ["Gorgonzola cheese provisioning. Correspondence, 1918 and 1920"].

- Folder 2, files 9 and 10: Approvvigionamento di granoturco e farina. Corrispondenza (1918 e 1920) ["Corn and flour provisioning. Correspondence, 1918 and 1920"].
- Folder 2, file 11: Approvvigionamento di lardo. Corrispondenza (1918) ["Bacon provisioning. Correspondence, 1918"].
- Folder 2, files 12 and 13: Approvvigionamento di latte. Corrispondenza (1918 e 1920) ["Milk provisioning. Correspondence, 1918 and 1920"].
- Folder 2, files 14–16: Approvvigionamento di legna. Corrispondenza (1918, 1919, 1920) ["Wood provisioning. Correspondence, 1918, 1919, 1920"].
- Folder 3, file 1: Approvvigionamento di macellazione (urgenza). Corrispondenza (1918) ["Slaughter provisioning (urgency). Correspondence, 1918"].
- Folder 3, file 2: Approvvigionamento di macina. Corrispondenza (1918) ["Grinded food provisioning. Correspondence, 1918"].
- Folder 3, file 3: Approvvigionamento di melica. Corrispondenza (1919) ["Melica provisioning. Correspondence, 1919"].
- Folder 3, files 4–6: Approvvigionamento di merluzzo. Corrispondenza (1918, 1919, 1920) ["Codfish provisioning. Correspondence, 1918, 1919, 1920"].
- Folder 3, files 7–9: Approvvigionamento di olio. Corrispondenza (1918, 1919, 1920) ["Olive oil provisioning. Correspondence, 1918, 1919, 1920"].
- Folder 3, file 10: Approvvigionamento di olio. Elenchi di distribuzione (1919) ["Olive oil provisioning. List of distribution, 1919"].
- Folder 3, files 11 and 12: Approvvigionamento di pasta. Corrispondenza (1918 e 1920) ["Pasta provisioning. Correspondence, 1918 and 1920"].
- Folder 3, files 13 and 14: Approvvigionamento di patate. Corrispondenza (1918 e 1919) ["Potatoes provisioning. Correspondence, 1918 and 1919"].
- Folder 3, file 15: Approvvigionamento di pesce. Corrispondenza (1919) ["Fish provisioning. Correspondence, 1919"].
- Folder 3, files 16 and 17: Approvvigionamento di petrolio. Corrispondenza (1918 e 1919) ["Petroleum provisioning. Correspondence, 1918 and 1919"].
- Folder 3, file 18; Folder 4, files 1 and 2: Approvvigionamento di riso. Corrispondenza (1918, 1919, 1920) ["Rice provisioning. Correspondence, 1918, 1919, 1920"].
- Folder 4, files 3 and 4: Approvvigionamento di sapone. Corrispondenza (1918 e 1919) ["Soap provisioning. Correspondence, 1918, 1919"].
- Folder 4, file 5: Approvvigionamento di scatole di carne. Corrispondenza (1918) ["Tins of meat provisioning. Correspondence, 1918"].
- Folder 4, file 6: Approvvigionamento di stracchino. Corrispondenza (1919) ["Stracchino cheese provisioning. Correspondence, 1919"].
- Folder 4, files 7 and 8: Approvvigionamento di suini. Corrispondenza (1918 e 1919) ["Pigs provisioning. Correspondence, 1918, 1919"].
- Folder 4, file 9: Approvvigionamento di tessuti. Corrispondenza (1920) ["Drapes provisioning. Correspondence, 1920"].
- Folder 4, files 10 and 11: Approvvigionamento di tonno e salmone. Corrispondenza (1919 e 1920) ["Tuna and salmon provisioning. Correspondence, 1919 and 1920"].
- Folder 4, files 12–14: Approvvigionamento di uova. Corrispondenza (1918, 1919, 1920) ["Eggs provisioning. Correspondence, 1918, 1919, 1920"].
- Folder 4, files 15–17: Approvvigionamento di zucchero. Corrispondenza (1918, 1919, 1920) ["Sugar provisioning. Correspondence, 1918, 1919, 1920"].

- Folder 5, file 1: Approvvigionamento di zucchero. Assegnazione delle licenze (1918) ["Sugar provisioning. License allocation, 1918"].
- Folder 5, file 2: Approvvigionamento di zucchero. Elenchi nominativi degli esercenti per la distribuzione di zucchero (1919) ["Sugar provisioning. Retailers list, 1918"].
- Folder 5, file 3: Assicurazioni (1915–1921) ["Insurances, 1915–1921"].
- Folder 5, file 4: Autosufficienti. Pane e generi da minestra. ["Self-sustaining families. Bread and vegetables"].
- Folder 5, file 5: Carne congelata, calzature, depositi e sequestri (1920) ["Frozen meat, shoes, deposits and requisitions, 1920"].
- Folder 5, file 6: Consorzio ortaggi. Corrispondenza (1918) ["Vegetables consortium. Correspondence, 1918"].
- Folder 5, files 7 and 8; Folder 6, files 1 and 2: Consorzio provinciale di approvvigionamento. Corrispondenza per farina e grano (1916–1918) ["Provincial provisioning consortium. Correspondence for flour and bread, 1916–1918"].
- Folder 6, file 3: Contratti con fornitori (1915–1920) ["Agreements with suppliers, 1915–1920"].
- Folder 6, files 4–8: Corrispondenza (1917–1921) ["Correspondence, 1917–1921"].
- Folder 6, file 9: Distribuzione di beni (1917–1921) ["Goods distribution, 1917–1921"].
- Folder 7, file 1: Giunta municipale. Corrispondenza (1918) ["Vigevano Municipality Executive board. Correspondence, 1918"].
- Folder 7, file 3: Macinazione di granturco. Corrispondenza (1919) ["Corn grinding. Correspondence, 1919"].
- Folder 7, file 4: Mulini. Corrispondenza (1919) ["Mills. Correspondence, 1919"].
- Folder 7, file 5: Mulini e latte. Corrispondenza (1921) ["Mills and milk. Correspondence, 1921"].
- Folder 7, file 6: Prefettura. Corrispondenza (1918) ["Local delegate of central government (Prefetto). Correspondence, 1918"].
- Folder 8, file 1: Libretti dei fornitori di pane (1917–1921) ["Books of bread suppliers lists, 1917–1921"].
- Folder 9, file 1: Situazione dell'Azienda Annonaria (1918–1921) ["Azienda Annonaria situation, 1918–1921"].
- Folder 9, file 2: Varie questioni di approvvigionamento. Corrispondenza (1920) ["Some provisioning issues. Correspondence, 1920"].
- Folder 9, file 3: Approvvigionamenti di carne alla popolazione civile. Verbali di requisizione (1918–1919) ["Meat provisioning to the civil population. Requisition minutes, 1918–1919"].

Main Accounting Documents

- 120 folder 15: Bilanci (1917 al 1920) ["Financial Statement, 1917–1920"].
- 121 folder 16: Conto approvvigionamento generi di prima necessità. Ordinativi di pagamento in conto corrente e pagamento (1917) ["Food Provisioning Accounts. Payment orders on the current account, 1917"].
- 122 folder 16: Conto approvvigionamento generi di prima necessità. Reversali (1917–1918) ["Food Provisioning Account. Receipt orders on the current account, 1917–1918"].

- 129 folder 18: Carico e scarico di generi alimentari (1916–1917) ["Loading and unloading food accounts, 1916–1917"].

Auxiliary Accounting Documents

- 100 folder 10: Allegati di bilancio (1917) ["Notes to the Financial Statement, 1917"].
- 101–106 folders 10, 11: Banca popolare di Vigevano. Mandato di pagamento (1917, 1918, 1919, 1920) ["Cooperative Bank of Vigevano. Payment order, 1917, 1918, 1919, 1920"].
- 107–112 folders 11–13: Mandati di pagamento interni (1918, 1919, 1920, 1921) ["Payment order within the internal provisioning, 1918, 1919, 1920, 1921"].
- 113–119 folders 13, 14: Banca popolare di Vigevano. Reversali di incasso relative al conto corrente L.200.000 grani e farine ed altri generi alimentari (1915–1921) ["Cooperative Bank of Vigevano. Receipt orders on the current account of 200,000 lire for grains and flour and other foods, 1915–1921"].
- 123 folder 17: Fatture e corrispondenza contabile (1917) ["Invoices and accounting correspondence, 1917"].
- 124 folder 17: Versamenti alla banca (1921) ["Bank payments, 1921"].
- 125–127 folder 17: Biscotti latte (1917)—Bollettario ["Milk biscuit, 1917—Invoice Book"].
- 128 folder 17: Carico crusca (1917)—Bollettario ["Bran load, 1917—Invoice Book"].
- 130–131 folder 18: Carico farina (1917) ["Flour load, 1917"].
- 132 folder 18: Carico grano e riso (1917) ["Wheat and rice load, 1917"].
- 133–134 folder 18: Carico latte (1917) ["Milk load, 1917"].
- 135 folder 18: Carico pasta (1917) ["Pasta load, 1917"].
- 136 folder 18: Carico grano e riso (1917) ["Wheat and rice load, 1917"].
- 137–138 folder 18: Carico zucchero (1917) ["Sugar load, 1917"].
- 139–145 folder 19: Carico farina (1917) ["Flour load, 1917"].
- 146 folder 19: Frumento crusca (1917)—Bollettario ["Wheat bran, 1917—Invoice Book"].
- 147–148 folder 19: Lardo, pasta, olio e farina di meliga (1917)—Bollettario ["Bacon, pasta, olive oil, corn flour, 1917—Invoice Book"].
- 149 folder 19: Olio (1917)—Bollettario ["Olive oil, 1917—Invoice Book"].
- 150–158 folder 20: Riso (1917)—Bollettario ["Rice, 1917—Invoice Book"].
- 159 folder 20: Scarico grano frumento ["Wheat bran unload, 1917—Invoice Book"].
- 160 folder 20: Scarico granturco ["Corn unload, 1917—Invoice Book"].
- 161 folder 20: Schedario con i dati dei beneficiari (1918–1920) ["Beneficiaries data-set, 1918–1920"].
- 162–163 folder 20: Zucchero (1917)—Bollettario ["Sugar, 1917—Invoice Book"].

Secondary Sources

Andrei, P. (2010) L'amministrazione economica dello Stato nel pensiero scientifico di Fabio Besta. *Contabilità e Cultura Aziendale* 10(2): 57–73.

Antonelli, V., D'Alessio, R. and Rossi, R. (2014) Budgetary practices in the Ministry of War and the Ministry of Munitions in Italy, 1915–1918. *Accounting History Review* 24(2–3): 139–160.

Baics, G. (2013) Is access to food a public good? Meat provisioning in early New York City, 1790–1820. *Journal of Urban History* 39(4): 643–668.

Baker, C.R. (2011) A genealogical history of positivist and critical accounting research. *Accounting History* 16(2): 207–221.

Belkaoui, A. (1989) Accounting as language. *Journal of Accounting Literature* 8: 281–292.

Besta, F. (1932) *La Ragioneria*, Vol. I, II e III, (II ed.). Milan: Vallardi.

Blank, A. (1999) Why do new meanings occur?: A cognitive typology of the motivations for lexical semantic change. In: Blank, A. and Koch, P. (eds.), *Historical semantics and cognition*. Berlin and New York: Mouton de Gruyter, pp. 61–89.

Bower, J. (1970) *Managing the resource allocation process*. Boston: Harvard Business School Press.

Burchell, S., Clubb, C., Hopwood, A.G., Hughes, J. and Nahapiet, N. (1980) The roles of accounting in organizations and society. *Accounting, Organizations and Society* 5(1): 5–27.

Burke, P., (1987) Introduction. In: Burke, P. and Porter, R. (eds.), *The social history of language*. Cambridge: Cambridge University Press, pp. 1–20.

Carmona, S. (2004) Accounting history research and its diffusion in an international context. *Accounting History* 9(3): 7–23.

Carnegie, G.D. and Napier, C.J. (1996) Critical and interpretive histories: Insights into accounting's present and future through its past. *Accounting, Auditing & Accountability Journal* 9(3): 7–39.

Carnegie, G.D. and Napier, C.J. (2012) Accounting's past, present and future: The unifying power of history. *Accounting, Auditing & Accountability Journal* 25(2): 328–369.

Catturi, G. (2005) Dato contabile, sistema di scritture del valore aggiunto e dimensione "politica" dell'azienda. *Contabilità e Cultura Aziendale* 5(2): 34–66.

Cavalleri, A. (Municipio di Brescia) (1918) *Relazione della giunta sulla gestione dell'Azienda Annonaria Comunale corredata da recenti pubblicazioni dell'avv. Attilio Cavalleri*. Available at: http://www.europeana.eu/portal/record/9200214/BibliographicResource_3000094622561.html?start=29&query=annonaria&startPage=25&qt=false&rows=24

Città di Mondovì. (1917) *Istruzioni per la commissione annonaria e per le squadre di vigilanza per l'applicazione dei provvedimenti relativi agli approvvigionamenti e consumi*. Available at: http://www.europeana.eu/portal/record/9200214/BibliographicResource_3000094622597.html?start=30&query=annonaria&startPage=25&qt=false&rows=24

Clark, G.K. (1967) *The critical historian*. London: Heinemann.

Comune di San Secondo Parmense, Azienda annonaria. (1919) *Bilancio al 31 maggio 1919*. Available at: http://www.europeana1914–1918.eu/en/europeana/record/9200214/BibliographicResource_3000094622613

Cooper, D.J. (1980) Discussion of towards a political economy of accounting. *Accounting, Organizations and Society* 5: 161–166.

Cooper, D.J. and Sherer, M.J. (1984) The value of corporate accounting reports: Arguments for a political economy of accounting. *Accounting, Organizations and Society* 9(3/4): 207–232.

Crystal, D. (2003) *The Cambridge encyclopaedia of language*, second edition. Cambridge: Cambridge University Press.

Davidson, D. (1997) Seeing through language. In: Preston, J. (ed.), *Thought and language*. Cambridge: Cambridge University Press, pp. 15–27.

Doni, F. (2008) L'evoluzione del personalismo contabile: la transizione da Francesco Marchi a Giuseppe Cerboni. *Contabilità e Cultura Aziendale* 8(2): 57–95.

Edwards, J.R. and Walker, S.P. (2009) *The Routledge companion to accounting history*. Abingdon: Routledge.

Evans, L. (2010) Observations on the changing language of accounting. *Accounting History* 15(4): 439–462.

Fairclough, N. (1995) *Critical discourse analysis: The critical study of language*. London: Longman.

Forson, P.W. and Counihan, C. (eds.) (2012) *Taking food public: Redefining foodways in a changing world*. New York: Routledge.

Foucault, M. (1972) *The archaeology of knowledge*. New York: Pantheon Books.

Foucault, M. (1979) Governmentality. *Ideology & Consciousness* 6: 5–21.

Francis, J. (1990) After virtue? Accounting as a moral and discursive practice. *Accounting, Auditing & Accountability Journal* 3(3): 5–17.

Frugatti, D., Lanza, D. and Merluzzi, D. (2014) *L'armonizzazione dei sistemi contabili negli enti locali*. Matelica, Italy: Hallay Informatica.

Funnell, W. (1996) Preserving history in accounting: Seeking common ground between "new" and "old" accounting history. *Accounting, Auditing & Accountability Journal* 9(4): 38–64.

Gaffikin, M. (1998) History is dead, long live history. *Critical Perspectives on Accounting* 9(6): 631–39.

Gerboth, D.L. (1972) Muddling through' with the APB. *The Journal of Accountancy* 133(May): 42–49.

Goldberg, L. (1956) The word 'stock'. *The Australian Accountant* 26(1): 11–5.

Goodman, D., DuPuis, E.M. and Goodman, M.K. (2012) *Alternative Food Networks: Knowledge, Practice, and Politics*. Abingdon, UK: Routledge.

Guthrie, J. and Parker, L. (1991) *Performance auditing in the Australian federal public sector: a mutable masque*. Paper presented at the Second Interdisciplinary Conference in Accounting, Manchester.

Habermas, J. (1984) *Theory of communicative action, Vol. 1: Reason and the rationalisation of society*. Oxford: Beacon Press and Cambridge: Polity Press in association with Basil Blackwell.

Habermas, J. (1987) *Theory of communicative action Vol. 2: Lifeworld and system: A critique of functionalist reason*. Oxford: Beacon Press and Cambridge: Polity Press in association with Basil Blackwell.

Habermas, J. (1968) *Knowledge and human interests*. London: Polity.

Handlin, O. (1979) *Truth in History*. Cambridge, MA: Harvard University Press.

Hines, R.D. (1988) Financial accounting: In communicating reality we construct reality. *Accounting, Organizations and Society* 13(3): 251–261.

Hopwood, A.G. (1976) Editorial: The path ahead. *Accounting, Organizations and Society* 1: 1–4.

Hopwood, A.G. (1977) Editorial. *Accounting, Organizations and Society* 2: 277–278.

Hopwood, A.G. (1987) The archaeology of accounting systems. *Accounting, Organizations and Society* 12(3): 207–234.

Hopwood, A.G. (1992) Accounting calculation and the shifting sphere of the economic. *The European Accounting Review* 1(1): 125–143.

Hoskin, K.W. and Macve, R.H. (1986) Accounting and the examination: A genealogy of disciplinary power. *Accounting, Organizations and Society* 11: 105–136.

Jack, L. (2007) Accounting, post-productivism and corporate power in UK food and agriculture. *Critical Perspectives on Accounting* 18(8): 905–931.

Johnson, S. (2006) Early socialization and language. In: Brown, K. (ed.), *Encyclopedia of language & linguistics*. Vol. 4, second edition, Amsterdam and Boston: Elsevier, pp. 51–53.

Johnsson, MacIntosh (1997) CATS, RATS, and EARS: Making the case for ethnographic accounting research. *Accounting, Organization and Society* 22(3/4): 367–86.

Laughlin, R. (1999) Critical accounting: Nature, progress and prognosis. *Accounting, Auditing & Accountability Journal* 12(1): 73–78.

Law, J. (1996) Organizing accountabilities: ontology and the mode of accounting. In: Munro R and Mouritsen, J. (eds.), *Accountability: Power, ethos and the technologies of managing*. London: International Thompson Publishing, pp. 283–306.

Lehman, G. (2006) Perspectives on language, accountability and critical accounting: An interpretative perspective. *Critical Perspectives on Accounting* 17(6): 755–779.

Marsden, T. and Morley, A. (eds.) (2014) *Sustainable food systems: Building a new paradigm*. Abingdon, UK: Routledge.

McKernan, J.F. (2007) Objectivity in accounting. *Accounting, Organizations and Society* 32(1–2): 155–180.

Miley, F. and Read, A. (2013) After the quake: The complex dance of local government, national government and accounting. *Accounting History* 18(4): 447–471.

Miller, P. and Napier, C. (1993) Genealogies of calculation. *Accounting, Organizations and Society* 18: 631–647.

Miller, P. and O'Leary, T. (1987) Accounting and the construction of the governable person. *Accounting, Organizations and Society* 12: 235–265.

Miller, P. and O'Leary, T. (1993) Accounting expertise and the politics of the product: Economic citizenship and the modes of corporate governance. *Accounting, Organizations and Society* 18: 187–206.

Miller, P. and Rose, N. (1990) Governing economic life. *Economy and Society* 19(1): 1–31.

Miller, P. and Rose, N. (2008) *Governing the present: Administering economic, social and personal life*. Cambridge: Polity Press.

Mills, P.A. (1989) Words and the study of accounting history. *Accounting, Auditing & Accountability Journal* 2(1): 21–35.

Milne, M., Guthrie, J. and Parker, L. (2008) Editorial: Into the light and engagement: Two decades of interdisciplinary perspectives on accounting, auditing and accountability research. *Accounting, Auditing & Accountability Journal* 21(2): 117–128.

Morgan, K., (2011) The green state. Sustainability and the power of purchase. In: Pike, A., Rodriguez-Pose, A. and Tomaney, J. (eds.), *Handbook of local and regional development*. Abingdon, UK: Routledge, pp. 89–96.

Morgan, K. (2014) The politics of the public plate: School food and sustainability. *International Journal of Sociology of Agriculture and Food* 21(3): 253–260. Morgan, K. and Sonnino, R. (2007) Empowering consumers: The creative procurement of school meals in Italy and the UK. *International Journal of Consumer Studies* 31(1): 19–25.

Morgan, K. and Sonnino, R. (2008) *The school food revolution: Public food and the challenge of sustainable development*. Oxford: Earthscan.

Munroe, R. and Mouritsen, J. (eds.) (1996) *Accountability: Power, ethos and the technologies of managing*. London: International Thompson Business Press.

Nagothu, U.S. (ed.) (2015) *Food security and development: Country case studies*. Abingdon, UK: Routledge.

Napier, C.J. (1989) Research directions in accounting history. *The British Accounting Review* 21(3): 237–254.

Napier, C.J. (2006) Accounts of change: 30 years of historical accounting research. *Accounting. Organizations and Society* 31(4–5): 445–507.Neu, D. (2006) Accounting for public spaces. *Accounting, Organizations and Society* 31(4/5): 391–414.

Neu, D., Cooper, D.J. and Everett, J. (2001) Critical accounting interventions. *Critical Perspectives on Accounting* 12(6): 735–762.

Neu, D. and Graham, G. (2005) Accounting and the public interest: An introduction. *Accounting, Auditing and Accountability Journal* 18(5): 585–591.

Pfeffer, J. (1981) *Power in organizations*. Marshfield, MA: Pitman Publishing.

Potter, B. (1999) The power of words: Explaining recent accounting reforms in the Australian public sector. *Accounting History* 4(2): 43–72.

Renting, H., Schemer, M. and Rossi, A. (2012) Building food democracy: Exploring civic food networks and newly emerging forms of food citizenship. *International Journal of Sociology of Agriculture and Food* 19(3): 289–307.

Ricci, U. (1921) *Il fallimento della politica annonaria: lezioni tenute nella Università Commerciale Bocconi*. Soc. an. ed. La Voce, Firenze. Available at: http://www.europeana.eu/portal/record/2023873/fedora_repository_openbess_TO043_00769.html?query=politica+annonaria&startPage=1&start=4&qt=false

Ryan, R.J., Scapens, R.W. and Theobald, M. (2002) *Research methods and methodology in accounting and finance*, second edition. London: Thomson Learning.

Sargiacomo, M. and Gomes, D. (2011) Accounting and accountability in local government: Contributions from accounting history research. *Accounting History* 6(3): 253–290.

Sargiacomo, M. and Gomes, D. (2013) Accounting and accountability in local government: An introduction. *Accounting History* 18(4): 439–446.

Sargiacomo, M., Servalli, S. and Andrei, P. (2012) Fabio Besta: Accounting thinker and accounting history pioneer (con Stefania Servalli e Paolo Andrei). *Accounting History Review* 22(3): 249–267.

Solomons, D. (1978) The politicization of accounting. *The Journal of Accountancy* 146(5): 65–72.

Solomons, D. (1991) Accounting and social change: A neutralist view. *Accounting Organizations and Society* 16(3): 287–295.

Stewart, R.E. (1992) Pluralizing our past: Foucault in accounting history. *Accounting, Auditing, & Accountability Journal* 5(2): 57–73.

Suzuki, T. (2003) The accounting figuration of business statistics as a foundation for the spread of economic ideas. *Accounting, Organizations and Societies* 28(1): 65–95.

Taylor, C. (1991) Language and society. In: Honneth, A. and Joas, H. (eds.), *Communicative action*. Cambridge, MA: MIT Press, pp. 23–36.

Thornborrow, J. (1999) Language and identity. In: Thomas, L. and Wareing, S. (eds.), *Language, society and power*. London and New York: Routledge, pp. 135–149.

Tinker, T. and Neimark, M. (1988) The struggle over meaning in accounting and corporate research: A comparative evaluation of conservative and critical historiography. *Accounting, Auditing & Accountability Journal* 1(1): 55–74.

United Nations, Department of Economic and Social Affairs, Population Division. (2014) *World Urbanization Prospects: The 2014 Revision, Highlights* (ST/ESA/SER.A/352).

Walker, S. (2008) Innovation, convergence and argument without end in accounting history. *Accounting, Auditing & Accountability Journal* 21(2): 296–322.

Yin, K. (1984) *Case study research: Design and methods, applied social research methods series*, Vol. 5. Beverly Hills, CA: Sage Publications.

16 Cereals, Politics and Accounting

The Bergamo Municipality Case (Sixteenth and Seventeenth Centuries)

Stefania Servalli and Antonio Gitto

INTRODUCTION

Cereals have always had a central role in human nutrition. Nowadays if scientists remind us the importance of their nutrients and the aid that unrefined cereals give in the prevention of certain diseases to stimulate us in consuming them, the governments remain alert to the food price volatility, as unpredictable climatic conditions have generated an intensification in droughts, floods and hurricanes. Dealing with the current cereals supply situation, the *Financial Times* has recently reported that "in 2007–08 low stocks ignited furious price rises and food riots in dozens of countries from Haiti to India" (Meyer, 2014).

In the past cereals were often the main or the only food available. For this reason, during the Renaissance cereals were inseparably linked to politics: the provisioning of the town (and its countryside) was a constant preoccupation for rulers. Indeed, the ensuring of a regular and sufficient cereals supply was one of the most important task of government (Dursteler, 2012). Indeed, "urban governments became more deeply and extensively involved in grain administration than any other area of city life" (Bullard, 1982, p. 280). Embedded in this scenario, the chapter explores the case of Bergamo, during the period of the Venetian domination, considering the sixteenth and seventeenth centuries. The geographical characteristics of the area and critical situations of different kinds, such as wars and famines, generated food scarcity, contributing to a diffuse poverty and alteration in the social equilibrium of the town (Pegrari, 2000). The lack of food and its social consequences required a control on cereals that Bergamo Municipality exercised by a specific body, named Collegio delle Biade (hereinafter Cereals Board).

The motivation for this work comes from the observation that this involvement of government in cereals administration has been studied by different scientists, included economists and historians (Tilly, 1975; Bohstedt, 2010). But despite the fact that accounting had a fundamental role in the achievement of political aims referred to cereals provisioning, this topic is still largely underexplored in the accounting history literature.

In exploring an Italian case of cereals control adopted by a Municipality, this chapter intends to addresses a series of areas that results overlooked in the accounting history domain. Indeed, this study contributes to the accounting history literature investigating an underexplored topic (politics of cereals provisioning), an often neglected field (local government), in a time (ancien régime) and space (Italy) dimension not yet highlighted by the existing literature.

The case analysis of this work will be informed through the application of the Foucauldian "governmentality" framework. The time span of this investigation corresponds to the period identified by Foucault (2009) as the start of the blooming of governmentality ideas (Sargiacomo, 2008, p. 669; Sargiacomo, 2009). In particular, in the light of this framework our work intends to explore the role of accounting as a technology of government in the control of cereals in the town of Bergamo, considering a number of financial and nonfinancial archival sources.

In particular, considering the role assumed by archival records, we can locate this study within the researches firmly set in the archive (Carnegie and Napier, 1996, 2012), considered in its wide notion "as comprehending not just records of profit-oriented businesses but also those of individuals, not-for-profit organizations, the public sector and other entities" (Carnegie and Napier, 1996, p. 30).

The rest of the chapter is organized as follows. The next section illustrates the methodological aspects and explores the theoretical perspective adopted. Then we consider the economic and political scenario referred to Bergamo in its geopolitical location within the Venetian Republic. The following sections explore the Cereals Board in Bergamo and discuss the findings, highlighting the role of accounting in the politics of food provisioning. The chapter concludes by suggesting possible future developments.

METHODOLOGICAL ASPECTS AND THEORETICAL PERSPECTIVE

In our exploration, the use of regulations in order to guarantee food access to the population, combined with the availability of primary sources attesting cereals registrations referred to the town of Bergamo during the sixteenth and seventeenth centuries, has permitted reflections upon the role of accounting in one of the most important roles of government: to ensure regular and sufficient food provision for urban and rural subjects (Dursteler, 2012, p. 83).

The study is based on a range of different primary and secondary sources. Primary sources include Venetian authorities orders and reports (VRP, VRR, VSD), municipality actions (MA) and specific permissions/licences (MP). These sources contain a wide variety of deliberations, which have been helpful for indicating the concern of the Bergamo Municipality for food uncertainty of the time, as well as the related politics and operations to contrast the paucity of cereals. In this regard, specific financial and nonfinancial records referred to cereals control have been investigated (CBA, CBAR, CDSP). Secondary sources have also been examined to provide historical contextualization for the study.

In our exploration, the concern with records of account is not centred on accounting techniques, but rather is focused on the recording of cereals as part of a wider information set that was prepared for underlying government purposes. A broad interpretation of accounting is here considered to embrace registrations of different kind, which typically use numbers and text in structured or unstructured ways to provide information on people and cereals and their movements/transactions.

Considering the aim of this investigation, the explored primary sources and their use in our analysis, this study may be located in the research stream firmly set in the archive (Carnegie and Napier, 1996, 2012) and regarded in the genre of "genealogies of calculation" (Miller and Napier, 1993).

Indeed, the exploration is mainly based on the aforementioned primary sources, mostly referring to the Bergamo Municipality Historical Archive (BMHA) located in the Angelo Mai Library in Bergamo.

At the same time the "focus on the outcomes of the past, rather than a quest for the origins of the present" (Miller and Napier, 1993, p. 631) and the absence of attempts to offer an "unbroken teleological narrative that begins with the 'invention' of double-entry bookkeeping" (p. 633), consent to consider this work within the "genealogies of calculation" ambit.

The analysis presented in this chapter is informed through the application of Foucauldian theoretical concepts. Indeed, the time span of our investigation can be set in the period identified by Foucault (2009, p. 88) as the beginning of the blooming of governmentality ideas.

Governmentality is intended by Foucault as the complex of

> institutions, procedures, analyses and reflections, calculations, and tactics that allow the exercise of this very specific, albeit very complex, power that has the population as its target, political economy as its major form of knowledge, and apparatuses of security as its essential technical instrument.
>
> (Foucault, 2009, p. 108)

In general, government is a problematizing activity, linked to creating ways to seek to remedy problems (Miller and Rose, 2008, p. 15). Indeed, it poses the obligations of rulers in relation to the problems they try to address (Rose and Miller, 1992, p. 181). The identification and examination of specific situations that call into question the activity of governing, that is, the problematization is fundamental to understand the context where government, in its "conduct of conduct" (Foucault, 1982, pp. 220–221), emerges. The idea of government also includes adverse situations, which require a government of "men in their relation to that other kind of things, accidents and misfortune such as famine, epidemics, death, etc." (Foucault, 1991, p. 93). Since the reality is a domain where the authorities can intervene by calculating and normalizing activities (Rose and Miller, 1992, p. 183), programmes of government are elaborated around these difficulties (p. 181).

Governmentality is also linked to the line of force that led towards the affirmation of government as a type of power. The consequent development of a series of apparatuses and knowledge arises. Administrative mechanisms and knowledge structures contribute to create the apparatus (*dispositif*) whose aim is to maintain and enhance the exercise of power in the social body (the town in our analysis). Power mechanisms and form of knowledge are strictly interrelated within Foucauldian governmentality approach. In this regard, governmentality involves specific forms of both representation and intervention. Indeed, it outlines a discursive area in which power is rationalized, enabling a government issue to be addressed (representation) and offering solving strategies (intervention) (Lemke, 2001). Programmes of government, elaborated around government problems, aim at the transformation of regimes of practices, reorienting them towards specific objectives. In so doing these programmes use "technologies of government" to direct the conduct. These technologies are represented by those mechanisms "through which authorities of various sorts have sought to shape, normalize and instrumentalize the conduct, thought, decisions and aspirations of others in order to achieve the objectives they consider desirable" (Miller and Rose, 1990, p. 8). In particular, authorities seek to instantiate government through technologies like techniques of notation, computation and calculation of different kinds (Rose and Miller, 1992, p. 183). It follows that programmes represent schema for the ordering of the social and the economic dimensions of life (Miller and Rose, 1990), where calculative activities have a fundamental role.

SCENARIO OF THE INVESTIGATION

In the time span of our investigation, Bergamo was a Dryland Dominion of the Venetian Republic. Indeed, Bergamo passed from Milan to Venice domination in 1427. In this new geopolitical context, Bergamo was an extremely important border area for commercial and military reasons. In this regard, it represented the only passage for commercial movements towards Western Europe and contemporary it had a strategic military role as the last western defense of the Venetian Republic deeply embedded in continuous wars (Sargiacomo et al., 2012).

In particular, Bergamo was a fortified town set on a hill, whose geography was characterized by a limited plain at its feet and mountain valleys at its back. This geography conditioned its economy, distinguishing three different kinds of activities: a strong commercial tradition in town, a woolen textile manufacturing economy in the valleys and an agricultural vocation on the plain (Cattini and Romani, 1998, p. 5).

The above illustrated economic and political geography of Bergamo and the surrounding territories was often at the origin of situations generating a diffuse poverty. Indeed, the limited agricultural area was often unable to produce cereals for the all population, and this situation frequently generated food crises, which exploded when there were famines.

In this regard, because of its central role in people feeding, wheat and other cereals were object of control by power. In Italy the cereals provisioning issue assumes a particular gravity with regard to towns, claiming public authorities attention (problematization). Indeed, starting from the tenth century the economic and demographic growth is coupled with an increase of urban population (Franco et al., 1991). Situations of towns with a lot of population, mainly devoted to trades, and country areas rarely able to support the towns with enough food emerge, requiring forms of interventions. Considering the Venetian Republic, which Bergamo was part of, the problem emerged both considering Venice and some its Dryland Dominations. Indeed, because of its lagoon isolation, Venice depended on external provisioning of food (Cacciavillani, 2010). In Venice this kind of problems were already faced in the twelfth century, when Doge Sebastiano Ziani created a specific body to surveil cereals trades (Franco et al., 1991, p. 6).

The acquisition of Dryland Dominations implied changes in the Venetian food rationing policy. Starting from the fifteenth century there was an increase in restrictions about cereals, and the relations between Venice and its Dominations were organized to favor the flow of cereals to Venice. The Rectors of the Venetian Dominations were often required to send out of their territory just the cereals directed to Venice and, in case of Venice urgent needs, local cereals surplus could not be kept in the area of production (Dal Pane, 1946).

All the process regarding cereals was object of a strict control by central authority and local government in Venice and its Dominations. The government interventions implied:

- Fighting against cornering
- Quota restrictions
- Regulations of the cereals' trade and production.

A severe discipline referred to cereals and flour trade was adopted. Indeed, the public authority had the need to fight the cornering of cereals, that is, an activity that created artful food crisis, mainly due to speculations (Cacciavillani, 2010).

A rigid quota restriction policy was also applied. This government policy involved controls on cereals production, including mandatory harvest bills, forms of exclusivity in cereals trade reserved to local operators, a ban on the import of undeclared cereals and flour, and the introduction of controlled prices for bread.

The Venetian authorities intervened against cereals and flour stocking. An extract of a Venetian Pregadi Council (Senate) decision shows that

> all the inhabitants of this Town (Venice), as well as all the ones of all our Dominations, that have stocked cereals and flours, must declare (personally, by letters or other instruments) to Cereals Office the right quantity of cereals or flour they have stocked by eight days for Venice inhabitants and fifteen days for inhabitants of our Dominations after the publication of the present deliberation. In addition, by one month they must take to this town the cereals (or flour) in order to sell them or to do what they will prefer (VSD, 1600).
>
> (VSD for Venetian Senate Deliberations)[1]

A punishment mechanism was also comprised in the deliberation, combined with a system of secret denunciations, particularly popular in Venice (Sargiacomo et al., 2012). Cash (or cereals) prizes and the possibility to free a bandit were provided by the deliberation to encourage the secret denunciations. Indeed, if a person was found guilty, the accuser received half of the goods or their cash equivalent and he had the faculty to free a person banned by one of the Venetian authority, except the Council of Ten (VSD, 1600).

In the context of the Venetian Dryland Dominations, its turn Bergamo was a town with cereals provisioning criticalities, as underlined by Venetian Rectors in their reports to the central government too. In this excerpt, Pizzamano Rector emphasizes the paucity of wheat production:

> In my opinion the most important thing is that because of the restricted flat area in this territory, there is a limited production of wheat (no more than IV months a year), and all the rest comes from Cremona, Gera d'Adda and the State of Milan.
>
> (VRR, 1560) (VRR for Venetian Rectors Reports)[2]

He proceeds to report that despite the prohibitions imposed by neighboring states with death penalty and the borders controlled by cavalry, smugglers, exhorted and persuaded by Rectors, were able to guarantee the cereals' provisioning of the town.

The cereals paucity of Bergamo (and its lands)—principally due to its geographical structure—became particularly problematic in situations such as wars involving the bellicose Venetian Republic, plagues and mainly famines. These circumstances represented elements able to alter social equilibrium of Bergamo (Pegrari, 2000, p. 258) and the consequent lack of food was at the origin of riots that constituted a danger for the public authorities.[3]

In particular, in the time span of our investigation (sixteenth and seventeenth centuries) Bergamo was strongly affected by misfortunes such as plagues and famines, which contributed to cereals paucity and determined a widespread poverty (Servalli, 2013). A government activity need arises for

Bergamo Municipality due to the dangers posed by these adverse situations (Foucault, 1991, p. 93) and the consequent social unrest in town (Rose and Miller, 1992, p. 181).

In the next section we will show as in Bergamo the cereals policies were operationalized through a specific body (Cereals Board) and the role of "technologies of government" assumed by financial and nonfinancial information.

CASE ANALYSIS

As underlined in the previous section, the scarcity of cereals and frequent famines constituted a problem for Bergamo authorities. These conditions were at the origins of programmes aiming to guarantee a sufficient cereals provision for the public interest. Specific interventions—regarding actions to fight cornering, quota restrictions, cereals trade and transport limitations—were realized (e.g., Venetian Rectors Proclamations: VRP, 1639; VRP 1649a; VRP 1649b; VRP 1661; VRP 1663; VRP 1669; VRP 1675).

It was prohibited to bring cereals towards a 5-mile area from the border (without a specific written permission from the Rector) and to store any kind of cereals in town (VRP, 1639). Orders to forbid the exportation of cereals (and in some cases wine or chestnuts) were also issued with the aim to keep cereals in Bergamo (VRP 1649a; VRP 1649b; VRP 1661; VRP 1663; VRP 1669; VRP 1675). Punishment mechanisms were adopted. The sanction could be fine, imprisonment, banishment and even capital punishment (VRP, 1649a).[4]

Within the complex of Muncipality actions adopted to remedy to cereals paucity, a specific body, the Cereals Board (Collegio delle Biade), was also instituted by Bergamo Major Council (MA, 1559). In the institutive deliberation is specified that Venetian Rectors and Bergamo Major Council decided to create this body "for the sake of the public interest and especially for poor" in order to find every possible instrument to remedy to cereals scarcity.

The Cereals Board was composed of 12 members:

- Two Rectors
- Two Members of the Minor Council
- Two Victuals Judges
- Two Ministers of MIA charity
- One Minister of Bergamo hospital
- One Minister of Prisoners charity
- One Pawnshop member
- One Monte dell'Abbondanza[5] member.

The Cereals Board had the power to do every activity required to supply the town and its territory with cereals. To reach this aim, it could procure any necessary funding or loans. In particular, to guarantee the cereal supply, the

Board could also ask loans either to charity institutions or private people. In this regard, to favour funding from these subjects, the Municipality Council specified that these funding operations had to be guaranteed by the "Monte dell'Abbondanza".

The recording of financial and non financial information about cereals was considered fundamental by the Municipality. Indeed, a Treasurer was appointed not only with the task to manage all the movements of money, but also to keep records of the cereals "in order to be always able to see the accounts of the above-mentioned cereals, and to keep memory of the beloved citizens and charities helping their homeland" (MA, 1559). Indeed all the cash movements were recorded (e.g., Cereals Board Accounting Records, CBAR, 1612) (Figure 16.1), and the Treasurer kept also buying and selling records, with the indication of the cereals, the sellers, the buyers (often bakers) and the relative monetary amount (Cereals Board Actions, CBA, 1598–1603) (Figure 16.2).

The Cereals Board also prepared meticulous registrations about different cereals (millet, wheat, rye, broomcorn) with details about the amounts sold on the local market, come out from shops, sold abroad or stocked (cereals deliveries, sales, possessions, CDSP, 1570a; 1570b[6]) (Figure 16.3). These latter kind of registration allowed Cereals Board and Rectors to know the situation referred to every type of cereals, considering what remained in town (sold or stocked) and what went abroad. Because of the need to control cereals' internal and external movements to guarantee the provisioning, this instrument was particularly important.

If a macro-knowledge was central to reach the government aims, a micro-knowledge was fundamental as well. In this regard, there were registrations referred to the presence of cereals in the houses of Bergamo and its lands (CDSP, 1591) and the ones located in bakers' shops and mills (CDSP, 1631) (Figure 16.4).

In this micro-perspective we can also position the analytic tables prepared to identify places and neighborhoods were cereals were located. These tables consider both the neighborhoods of the town and villages of its territory. A detailed registration identifies for each neighborhood (or villages) the name of the person, the number of people of his family (*bocche*, or mouths) and the amount of different kinds of cereals in his house. An example of this table is presented in Figure 16.5 (CDSP, 1569).

Concluding this section, it is worth noting that the Cereals Board also supported the government in relation to specific interventions about cereals transport, mentioned earlier. Indeed, likewise Venice, Bergamo required specific licenses to transport cereals. For example, considering a critical period such as 1569–1570, when a strong famine affected the area, permissions/licenses were issued to transport goods in Milan with the obligation to bring back cereals in Bergamo. Records of these permissions were kept by the Cereals Board with the indication of the name of the authorized persons and their locations. There were permissions/licenses to transport cows or wine

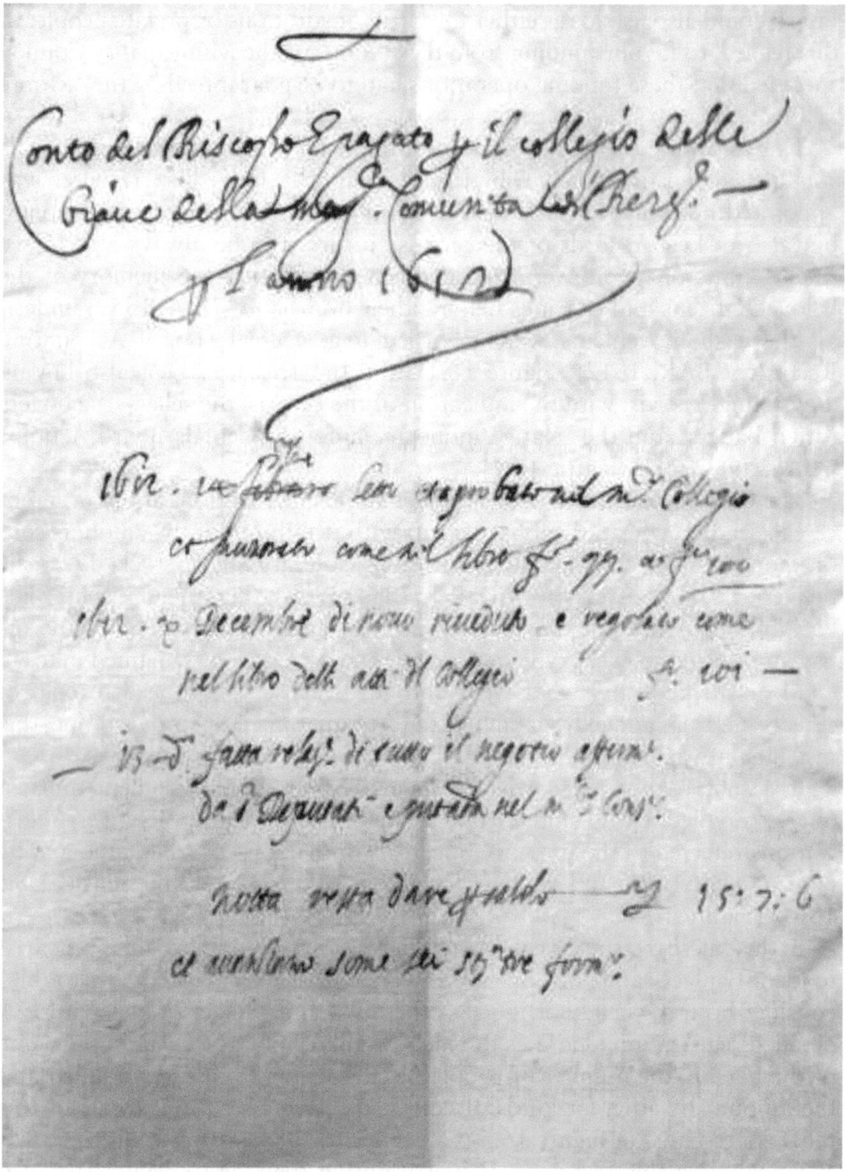

Figure 16.1 Cash account (CBAR, 1612)

in Milan with the obligation to bring back cereals in Bergamo (Permissions 1569–70a, Permissions 1569), as well as the permissions/licenses to receive cereals to take to Milan with the obligation to bring back the same amount within a time limit (e.g., 15 days, 1 month) (Permissions 1569–70b). These registrations allowed a complete view of the authorized subjects, the cereals, the area of transport and the linked obligations of cereals' imports.

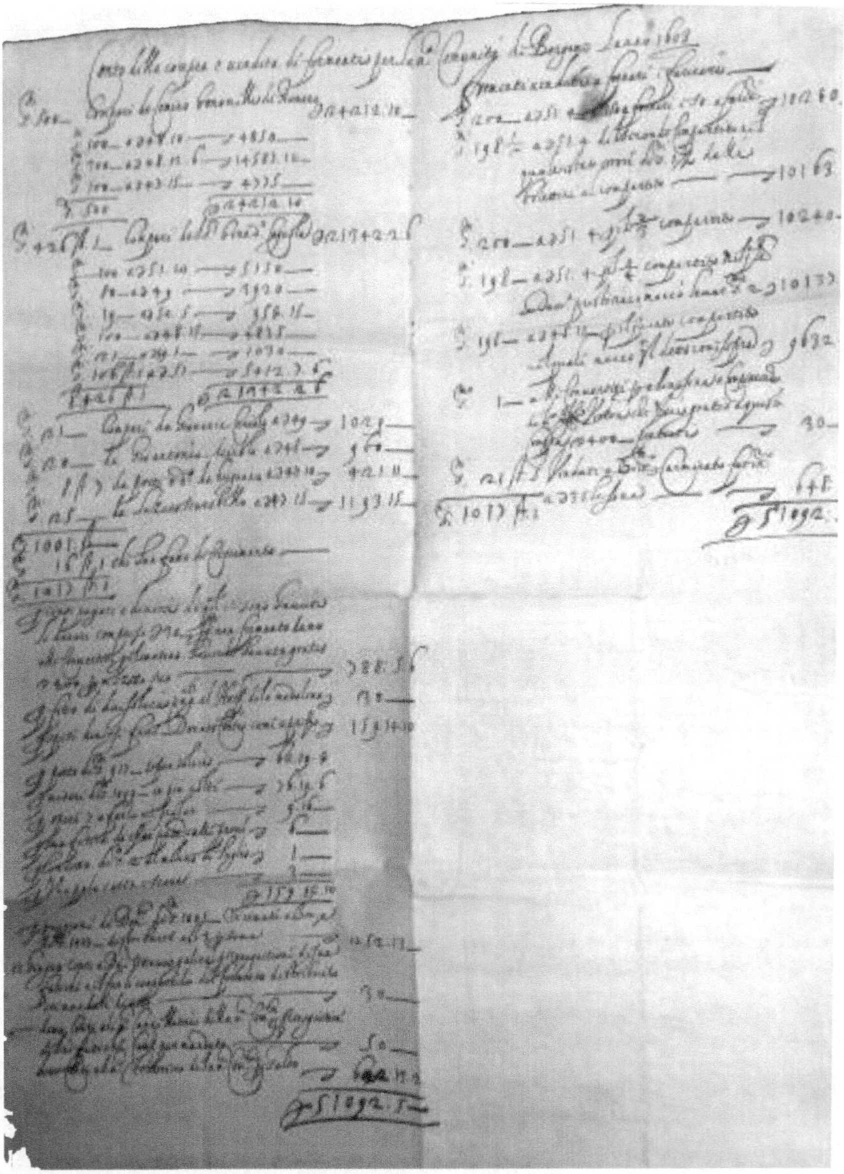

Figure 16.2 Buying and selling cereals account (1603) (CBA, 1598–1603)

DISCUSSION AND CONCLUSIONS

In this work a series of areas still overlooked in the accounting history domain have been addressed. Indeed, this study contributes to the accounting history debate investigating, one of the most important task of government

Figure 16.3 Cereals (millet, wheat, rye, broomcorn) with details about the amounts sold on the local market, come out from shops, sold abroad or stocked (1570) (CDSP, 1570a)

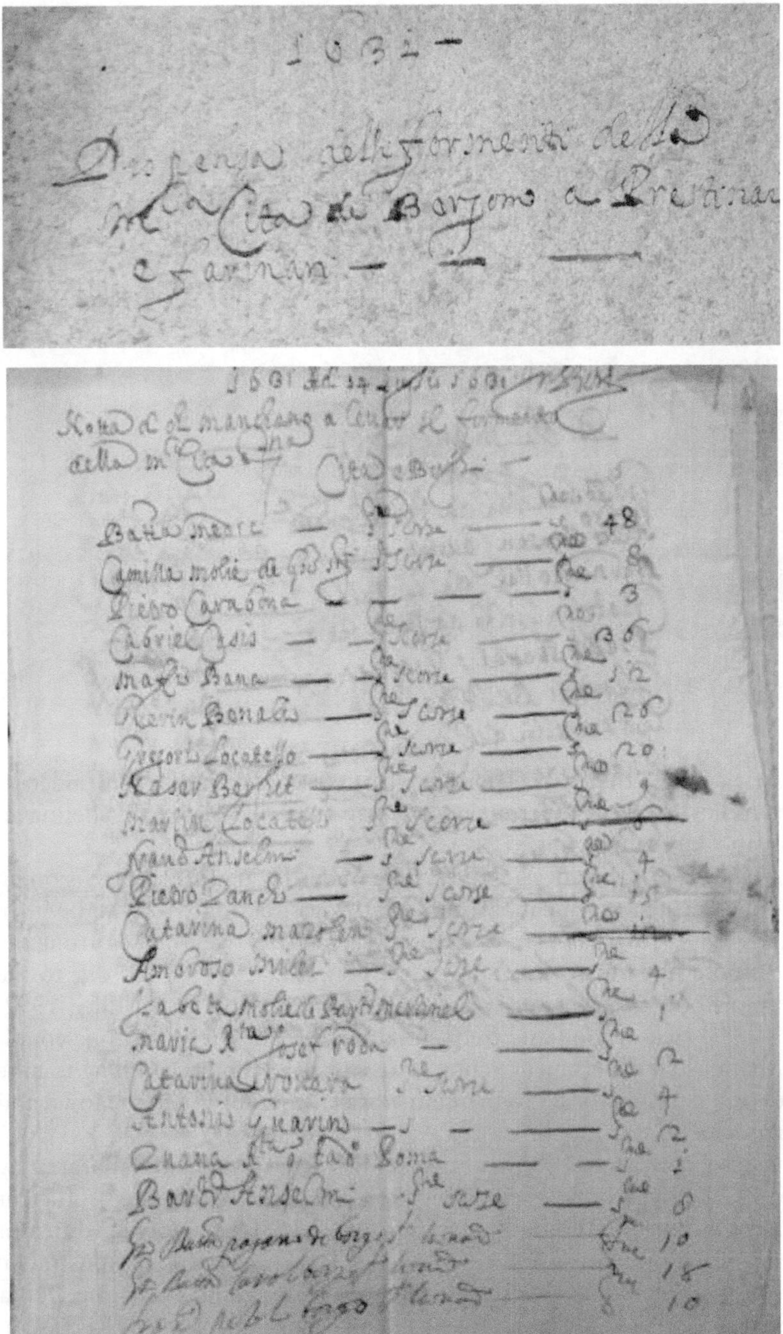

Figure 16.4 Cereals in bakeries and mills (1631) (CDSP, 1631)

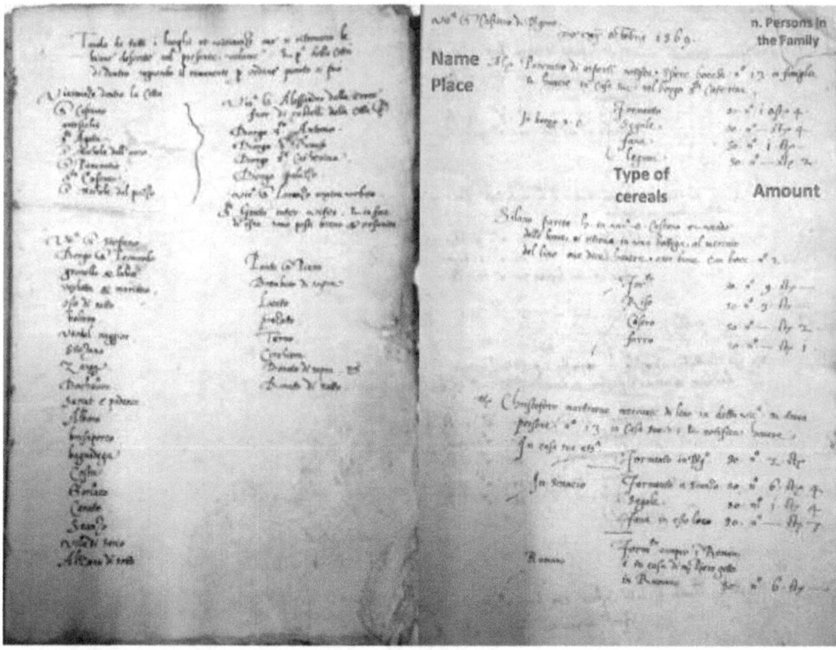

Figure 16.5 Table of cereals (1569) (CDSP, 1569)

(Dursteler, 2012) that is the politics of cereals provisioning (an underexplored topic) in a local government (an often neglected field), considering an Italian ancient regime context.

In the period of this investigation, Bergamo is facing cereals provisioning criticalities, which represents a problematizing situation (Rose and Miller, 1992, p. 181). In particular, a government activity need arises from the dangers posed by the adverse situations (Foucault, 1991, p. 93) due to the paucity of food and the consequent urban unrest (Rose and Miller, 1992, p. 181). The lack of food and frequent famines represent misfortune conditions that need a government action (Foucault, 1991, p. 93), aiming to take care of population in order to maintain a social equilibrium in the town and its territories.

The case analysis has shown programmes of government elaborated by the Municipality around these difficulties, aiming to guarantee sufficient cereals provision for the public interest (MCA, 1559), involving different administrative mechanisms and knowledge structures. The administrative mechanisms adopted include interventions to fight against cornering, quota restrictions, cereals trade and transport regulations (VRP, 1639; VRP 1649a; VRP 1649b; VRP 1661; VRP 1663; VRP 1669; VRP 1675), but also the creation of a specific body, the Cereals Board (MA, 1559), to achieve a government intended as the "conduct of conduct" (Foucault, 1982, pp. 220–221). In this regard, a central function of the Cereals Board is in offering a "specialist knowledge" referred both to cereals and people, as fundamental elements in order to intervene by calculating and normalizing activities (Rose and Miller, 1992, p. 183). In particular, financial and nonfinancial information of different kind arise as "technologies of government" to direct the conduct. Indeed, a wide range of information referred to macro and micro-knowledge of cereals and people are offered. Macro-knowledge is refereed to cash movements (CBAR, 1612), buying and selling records (CBA, 1598–1603), detailed registrations about cereals sold in town and abroad (CDSP, 1570a; 1570b[7]). Micro-knowledge regards registrations referred to the presence of cereals in houses (CDSP, 1591), in bakers' shops and mills (CDSP, 1631), permissions to transport cereals (MP 1569; 1569–70a, 1569–70b) and analytical tables identifying people and cereals available in the families for each neighborhood (or villages).

The analysis has unveiled how accounting, in the broad interpretation adopted in this work—that is, embracing registrations of different kinds, which typically use numbers and text in structured or unstructured ways to provide information on people and cereals—operates in its role of technology enabling the government issue of cereals' paucity to be addressed (representation) and offering the municipality a macro- and micro-knowledge for reshaping actions (interventions) (Lemke, 2001). In so doing accounting, as a technology of government, contributes to the maintenance of the social order.

The investigation presented in this work, in the novelty of its topic, referred to the politics of cereals provisioning, shows the need for further analysis in different time and space dimensions to increase an understanding of the role of accounting as calculative device reshaping the conduct towards desirable government aims and contributing to enhance the exercise of power in the social body.

NOTES

1. Similar deliberations are VSD, 1637 and VSD, 1649.
2. Similar observations are included in other Venetian Rectors Reports too (VRR, 1561; 1565).
3. Montanari underlines that "tensions exploded above all in time of food shortage or famine, when the inhabitants of the countryside crowded at the gates of the city in search of food and, in the most dramatic cases were violently driven away from the portals" (Montanari, 2006, p. 24).
4. It is worth noting that Dean (2001, p. 49) underlines that regulations backed up by coercive sanctions based on the right of death exercised by the authority were the instruments adopted in the earlier expressions of sovereignty.
5. The Monte dell'Abbondanza was instituted 1 May 1539 by Lorenzo da Bergamo, with the aim to collect victuals to locate on the market during famines (Giordano, 2006).
6. A distinction based on the gates of the town was also included.
7. A distinction based on the gates of the town was also included.

REFERENCES

Primary Sources

CBA (Cereals Board Actions) [Collegio delle Biade Azioni]:

- CBA 1598–1603 [Conto delle compere e delle vendite dei formenti—Buying and selling cereals account].

CBAR (Cereals Board Accounting Records) [Contabilità Collegio delle Biade]:

- CBAR (1612) [Conto del riscosso et pagato 1612—Cash account 1612].

CDSP (Cereals delivers, sales, possessions) [Consegna, vendita, dichiarazioni di possesso di cereali]:

- CDSP 1570a [Cereali venduti nel mercato cittadino e usciti dalla città—Cereals sold on the local market and exported cereals].
- CDSP 1570b [Cereali entrati e venduti in città—Imported cereals and cereals sold on the local market].
- CDSP 1591 [Cereali presenti nelle abitazioni di abitanti del territorio—Cereals in houses of Bergamo territory].
- CDSP 1631 [Dispensa delli formenti della Magnifica Città di Bergomo a prestinari e farinari—Cereals of the town of Bergamo to millers and bakers].
- CDSP 1569 [Tavola di tutti i luoghi e vicinanze dove si trovano le biave—Table of neighborhoods and villages where cereals are located].

MA (Municipality Actions) [Azioni del Comune]:

- MA (1559), Municipality Action 1559, 31 July.

MP (Municipality Permissions) [Autorizzazioni]:

- MP 1569 [Autorizzazioni al "trasporto" di vino nel milanese con l'obbligo di portare cereali in città—Permissions to transport wine in Milan with the obligation to bring back cereals in Bergamo].
- MP 1569–70a [Autorizzazioni al "trasporto" di bovini nel milanese con l'obbligo di portare cereali in città—Permissions to transport cows in Milan with the obligation to bring back cereals in Bergamo].
- MP 1569–70b [Autorizzazioni a ricevere cereali con l'obbligo di portarne altrettanti in città per la vendita—Permissions to receive cereals with the obligation to bring back the same amount for sale].

VRP (Venetian Rectors Proclamations) [Proclami Rettori Veneti]:

- VRP 1639, Rector Girolamo Michiel, 1639, 28 February.
- VRP 1649a, Rector Gasparo Zane, 1649, 18 January.
- VRP 1649b, Rector Paolo Lion, 1649, 20 November.
- VRP 1661, Rector Alvise Mocenigo Terzo, 1661, 19 February.
- VRP 1663, Cereal Officer Marco Ruzini, 1663, 24 July.
- VRP 1669, Rector Angelo Da Mosto, 1669, 24 August.
- VRP 1675, Rectors Carlo Belogno and Gio Micheli, 1675, 2 October.

VRR (Venetian Rectors Reports) [Relazioni Rettori Veneti]:

- VRR (Venetian Rectors Reports) (1560) [Pietro Pizzamano Report, 7 July 1560].

- VRR (Venetian Rectors Reports) (1561) [Francesco Venier Report, 6 November 1561].
- VRR (Venetian Rectors Reports) (1565) [Lorenzo Donato Report, 31 December 1565].

VSD (Venetian Senate Deliberations) [Delibere del Senato di Venezia]:

- VSD, 1600 [Consiglio de Pregadi in materia di incanevare formenti o farine—Pregadi Council (Senate) deliberation about stocking cereals and flour, 26 October 1600].
- VSD, 1637 [Senate in materia che non si possi condurre farine—Senate deliberation about prohibitions in flours transportations, 7 October 1637].
- VSD, 1649 [Consiglio de Pregadi in materia di formenti—Pregadi Council (Senate) deliberation about cereals and flour, 2 August 1649].

Secondary Sources

Bohstedt, J. (2010) *The politics of provisions: Food riots, moral economy, and market transition in England, c. 1550–1850*. Farnham, UK: Ashgate.

Bullard, M.M. (1982) Grain supply and urban unrest in Renaissance Rome. The crisis of 1533–34. In: Ramsey, P.A. (ed.), *Rome in the Renaissance: The city and the myth*. Binghamton: Center for Medieval and early Renaissance Study, pp. 136–165.

Cacciavillani, I. (2010) *La sanità pubblica nell'ordinamento veneziano*. Venice: ARPAV.

Carnegie, G.D. and Napier, C.J. (1996) Critical and interpretive histories: Insights into accounting's present and future through its past. *Accounting, Auditing & Accountability Journal* 9(3): 7–39.

Carnegie, G.D. and Napier, C.J. (2012) Accounting's past, present and future: The unifying power of history. *Accounting, Auditing & Accountability Journal* 25(2): 328–369.

Cattini, M. and Romani, M. (1998) Bergamo e la sua economia fra Quattrocento e Seicento. In: Cattini, M. and Romani, M. (eds.), *Storia economia e sociale di Bergamo, Il lungo Cinquecento*. Bergamo: Fondazione per la storia economica e sociale di Bergamo, pp. 5–48.

Dursteler, E.R. (2012) Food and politics. In: Albala, K. (ed.), *A cultural history of food, Vol. 3, The Renaissance, c. 1300–1600*. Oxford: Berg, pp. 83–100.

Corradi, A. (1973) *Annali delle epidemie occorse in Italia dalle prime memorie fino al 1850*. Bologna: Ed. Forni.

Dal Pane, L. (1946) La politica annonaria di Venezia. *Giornale degli economisti e Annali di economia* 5(1–2, maggio-giugno): 331–353.

Dean, M. (2001) Demonic societies: Liberalism, biopolitics and sovereignty. In: Hansen, T.B. and Stepputat, F. (eds.), *States of imagination*. Durham, NC: Duke University Press, pp. 41–64.

Foucault, M. (1982) The subject and power. In: Dreyfus, H.L. and Rabinow, P. (eds.), *Michel Foucault: Beyond structuralism and hermeneutics*. Brighton: Harvester Press, pp. 208–226.

Foucault, M. (1991) Governmentality. In: Burchell, G., Gordon, C. and Miller, P. (eds.), *The Foucault effects: Studies in governmentality*. Hemel Hempstead: Wheatsheaf, pp. 87–104.

Foucault, M. (2009) *Security, territory, population*. New York, NY: Palgrave Macmillan.

Franco, V., Lanconelli, A. and Quesada, M.A. (eds.) (1991) *Pane e potere. Istituzioni e società in Italia dal Medioevo all'età moderna*. Rome: Ministero per i Beni culturali e ambientali.

Giordano, S. (2006) *Lorenzo da Bergamo. Dizionario Biografico degli Italiani*, Vol. 66. Rome: Treccani.

Lemke, T. (2001) 'The birth of bio-politics': Michel Foucault's lecture at the Collège de France on neo-liberal governmentality. *Economy and Society* 30(2): 190–207.

Meyer, G. (2014) Commodities: Cereal excess, *Financial Times*, September 23, 2014. Available at: http://www.ft.com/intl/cms/s/2/42403074–3fe0–11e4-a381–00144feabdc0.html#axzz3asY2bSwW

Miller, P. and Napier, C. (1993) Genealogies of calculation. *Accounting, Organizations and Society* 18(7–8): 631–47.

Miller, P. and Rose, N. (1990) Governing economic life. *Economy and Society* 19(1): 1–31.

Miller, P. and Rose, N. (2008) *Governing the present: Administering social and personal life*. Cambridge: Polity.

Montanari, M. (2006) *Food is culture*. New York: Columbia University Press.

Pegrari, M. (2000) Pauperismo e carità pubblica a Bergamo in età moderna. In: De Maddalena, A., Cattini, M. and Romani, M. (eds.), *Storia economia e sociale di Bergamo, Un Seicento in controtendenza*. Bergamo: Fondazione per la storia economica e sociale di Bergamo, pp. 237–265.

Rose, N. and Miller, P. (1992) Political power beyond the state: Problematic of government. *The British Journal of Sociology* 43(2): 174–205.

Sargiacomo, M. (2008) Accounting and the 'Art of Government': Margaret of Austria in Abruzzo (1539–86). *European Accounting Review* 17(4): 667–695.

Sargiacomo, M. (2009) Accounting for the 'good administration of justice': The Farnese state of Abruzzo in the sixteenth century. *Accounting History* 14(3): 235–267.

Sargiacomo, M., Servalli, S. and Carnegie, G. (2012) Accounting for killing: Accountability for death. *Accounting History* 17(3/4): 393–413.

Servalli, S. (2013) The interface of power and charity in the government of poor. A case from the Italian context in the sixteenth-seventeenth centuries. *Accounting, Auditing & Accountability Journal* 26(8): 1306–1341.

Tilly, C. (1975) Food supply and Public order in Modern Europe. In: Tilly, C. (ed.), *The formation of national states in Western Europe*. Princeton: Princeton University Press, pp. 392–420.

17 State Audit in Public Organizations Supporting Agri-Food Business Development

The Ente Nazionale Risi after World War II (1945–1980)

Mara Zuccardi Merli and Elisa Bonollo

INTRODUCTION

Postwar Italy inherited from fascism a highly regulated private sector and large State stakes in agriculture, manufacturing, utilities and banking. Rather than being privatized, public organizations and State enterprises came to be seen as a tool for economic development. In other words, since the second postwar period, the State has become both an actor (the so-called Entrepreneurial State) and a regulator of the social and economic system, with the purpose of ensuring collective wellbeing and an orderly development of the economy (Anselmi, 1990; Borgonovi, 1996).

As specifically regards the production sectors, the economic recovery downsized the role of agriculture. Regardless of this decline, the agricultural sector remained socially and politically important, so the Italian government, and later the European Economic Community, started developing policies in support of the prices of agricultural products (Rossi Doria, 1969; Fabiani, 1995; Rossi and Toniolo, 1996).

Price support policies had already been developed for Italian rice production since the end of the nineteenth century (Brianta, 1991), leading to the foundation of Ente Nazionale Risi (National Rice Institution) in 1931 (with Royal Decree n. 1237/1931). This public organization is largely autonomous and audited by the State (Law 129/1939, Law 259/1958). Since its foundation, it has promoted strong protectionist policies against foreign competition and developed actions to support exports, because rice production in Italy has always exceeded domestic consumption (Boggeri, 1932). Later, all this was reconfirmed in the agricultural policies of the European Economic Community (Brianta, 1991; Fanfani, 1998).

This chapter focuses on the 1945–1980 period and aims to analyze how the State monitored the activities of Ente Nazionale Risi (ENR), a key public organization for the survival of Italian rice production. The State audit is carried out through the Supreme Audit Institution (SAI). According to different authors, the SAI may carry out mere compliance auditing or performance auditing or could be a "modernizer," offering suggestions to improve the management of public organizations (Pollitt et al., 1999; Morin, 2003; Bourn, 2007).

To investigate the role of the SAI, a historical case study will be analyzed: the State audit of ENR during the 1945–1980 period. Our analysis is based on the examination of both primary sources (the regulatory framework and SAI's Audit Reports) and secondary sources (to define the socioeconomic context and theoretical framework of the State audit).

This study contributes to the literature on SAI audits of public organizations supporting various sectors of the economy. SAI auditing on public organizations in the 1945–1980 period has been little explored in the historical accounting literature (Radcliffe, 1997). In details, while to date there has been a growing interest on the investigation of the State government apparatus (e.g., Sargiacomo, 2008, 2009), few Italian authors have focused on the aim of SAI auditing activities (Cassandro, 1963, 1975; Bennati, 1965; Giannessi, 1969) or on the SAI audits referred to the State subsidized entities (Cuomo, 1963; Coltelli, 1970; Colasanti, 1979). Non-Italian authors have also paid very little attention to the development of State audit during the 1945–1980 period (for an exception, see Radcliffe, 1998, 2009). Most of them have discussed other issues, such as the independence of public auditors (Funnell, 1994; Gendron et al., 2001), or have focused on other historical periods or other public organizations, such as the local governments (Funnell, 1997, 2004; Coombs and Edwards, 2004; Bunn and Gilchrist, 2013; Colquhoun, 2013).

In this context, the chapter investigates the content of the SAI audit on the ENR in the 1945–1980 period. In this regard, it offers a further contribution to the historical accounting literature not only on the State audit, but also on the Italian accounting in the agricultural sector (e.g., Mussari and Magliacani, 2007; Sargiacomo et al., 2014) with a study on the ENR and on its connections with the social, political and economic context of the period researched (Sargiacomo and Gomes, 2011).

The remainder of this chapter is structured as follows. The next two sections analyze the social, political and economic context of the 1945–1980 period and the role played by ENR in the Italian rice production. Then the following section focuses on the content of the Audit Reports completed by SAI after auditing ENR over the period specified, and the final section outlines the conclusions.

THE ITALIAN ECONOMIC SITUATION AFTER WORLD WAR II UNTIL 1980

After the economic and social crisis that characterized the periods of the First and Second World War, Italian economic recovery began in the 1950s (Rossi et al., 1992). This recovery was accompanied by a progressive evolution of public needs and required a response by the State, which expanded and diversified its intervention in the economic system. The Entrepreneurial State, that dated back to the years immediately preceding World War I, increasingly extended its scope starting from the 1950s, also by developing the so-called system of State-controlled enterprises.

More specifically, as regards the role of the State in the economy, we may distinguish three periods from years after World War II to 1980 (Graziani, 1998; Toniolo, 2013; Cafferata, 2010):

- The postwar period of industrial reconstruction (1945–1953), during which the State supported the reconstruction of the industry in the northern regions and started programmes of agricultural reform and extraordinary public works in southern Italy.
- The so-called Golden Age (1953–1973), when the State made huge investments in the industrial sector and price stability was reached together with a balance of payments' equilibrium.
- The period of oil crisis and decline of the system of State-controlled enterprises (1973–1980), when the State had to face a worsening of industrial relations, salary explosion and external economic shocks due to oil price increases.

In detail, since the first years after World War II, Italy worked hard for a progressive economic integration with the other European countries by concentrating all its strength in the attempt at conquering an increasingly higher degree of efficiency and competitiveness, in order to push its industry in the international markets (Graziani, 1998). In 1947, the State created the Fondo Industrie Meccaniche, a fund for the mechanical industry that had the purpose of favouring, with special funding, a redevelopment of mechanical enterprises that were having difficulties in reconverting their operations after the war. Subsequently, in 1948, new bylaws were approved in I.R.I. (Istituto per la Ricostruzione Industriale, or the Institute for Industrial Reconstruction) to allow the institute to develop different plans by sector and conclude the discussions on the possible privatization of its stakes (Anselmi, 1990; Zamagni, 1993). Therefore, the first Republican governments clearly showed a preference for industrial development.

When the postwar industrial reconstruction period ended, more favourable conditions emerged for a fast economic development (1945–1953). With the beginning of the "Golden Age," the rapid expansion of exports, favourable trends in exchange rates, low salaries, a low level of labour conflict and the reduction of the technological gap led to fast industrialization without inflation or foreign account deficit (Castronuovo, 1975; Grilli et al., 1982). The decisions made by government and parliament for the Italian economy during those years were based on openness towards foreign trade, extensive protection of domestic manufacturers and, most of all, an important role of the Entrepreneurial State. They proved to be appropriate to support the rapid growth of an economy that had started from a position of deep backwardness (Toniolo, 2013). In particular, the Entrepreneurial State became the main player of the history of the country by expanding the so-called system of State-controlled enterprises. During this period, public enterprises were proved to be good at accelerating investments and technical progress, and became the real promoters of the convergence of the Italian industrial structure towards the European industry (Barca and Trento, 1997). The rapid transformation of the Italian economy was also witnessed by the changes in the composition of exports, which were then essentially based on medium-technology productions, and by the fact that employment in the manufacturing sector was mostly concentrated in high-capital intensity industries, that is, the automobile, chemical, iron and steel, heavy engineering and shipbuilding industries (Amatori et al., 2013).

The situation began to change around the mid-1960s, when northern Italian regions almost reached full employment rates and it became increasingly difficult for the enterprises to support high levels of investment and simultaneously meet salary increase demands. Furthermore, while in the 1950s and 1960s public banks (owned by I.R.I.) had provided the access to credit efficiently, in the subsequent years the growing influence of lobbies hindered an adequate selection of the innovative enterprises that deserved funds. In other words, public banks, as well as public enterprises in general, began to be used as instruments for political power (Posner and Woolf, 1967; Woods, 1998). At the end of the 1960s, a clear need emerged for the country to adapt its institutions, financial markets, education and training, research and public intervention to an economy that could no longer be defined as "backward" (Rossi and Toniolo, 1996). However, not much was done in this direction, and this would negatively affect subsequent growth (Crafts and Magnani, 2013).

Starting from 1973 (during the period of the oil crisis and the decline of the system of State-controlled enterprises), the need to address the imbalances due to oil price increases, an increased inflation and numberless social needs caused a stunning growth in public spending, which was financed with a massive use of indebtedness. In this regard, just think, for example, of the resources needed for the reform of the Cassa Integrazione Guadagni (fund for temporary unemployment), of the creation of the National Healthcare System and the Gestione Partecipazioni Industriali, a public company aimed at rescuing industrial enterprises (which were having temporary troubles) by buying stakes of their capitals and granting low-interest rate loans (Zamagni, 1993; Battilani and Fauri, 2008). In addition to that, the persistence of direct public intervention in the economy progressively led to a degeneration of the Entrepreneurial State due to its systematic parcelling-out by political parties, to the use of public enterprises as instruments for contingent rescue policies and the spreading of corruption (Barca and Trento, 1997).

During these three periods (1945–1980), the role of agriculture in the economy rapidly decreased (Malanima and Zamagni, 2010): the employment rate in agriculture was about 44% in 1951, 18% in 1973, and 12%

in 1980 (Fabiani, 1995; Crafts and Magnani, 2013), while the portion of value-added agriculture was reduced by almost four times, that is, from its previous level of one-fourth of the total (25.3%) in 1950 to slightly less than 7% in 1980 (Pellegrini, 2002).

In detail, the weight of the agricultural sector in the postwar period was still significant in terms of labour (slightly less than 9 million workers over about 20 million workers in 1951) and political influence. Furthermore, the interests of the relative majority party led to the creation, inter alia, of a fund for the foundation of small farmers (Cassa per la formazione della piccola proprietà contadina) in 1948 and to a Southern Development Fund (Cassa per il Mezzogiorno) in 1950. The latter was founded for the implementation of special actions in favour of southern Italy, initially to support agriculture and the infrastructures, and then also extended to the industry. Moreover, agrarian consortia (Consorzi Agrari) were established and a federation of consortia called Federconsorzi was created to develop stockpile policies and relationships between farmers and the manufacturers of technical equipment. In addition to this, a number of sector laws, approved during the 1950s, had the consequence, inter alia, of causing the progressive disappearance of large estates or *latifundia* (Zamagni, 1993; Petri, 1997; Fanfani, 1998).

However, when Italy became a member of the European Community, its agriculture was still characterized by backwardness due to its low productivity and the lack of links with the industry supplying factors of production, as well as with the food processing industry, that represents the basis for the development of a modern agro-industrial system (Fabiani, 1995).

The agricultural sector was still considered important from both social and political viewpoints, at the national and European levels. More specifically, at national level, the 5-year plans for agricultural development (the so-called Green Plans) of 1961 and 1966 were prepared to establish a policy aiming at supporting agricultural income with facilitations on tax and social security contributions and with interventions on prices of agricultural products (Fanfani, 1998). At the same time, the mechanization of production processes was favoured with the objective not only of improving the productivity of agricultural enterprises (thus freeing up the labour force for the other sectors of the economy), but also of creating a protected market for the mechanical (tractors and agricultural machines) and chemical (fertilizers) industries.

At the European level, the agricultural policy of the European Community, which, starting from the 1960s, gradually prevailed over the national component, as a matter of fact went into the same direction, as it was essentially based on the establishment of support prices for the various products valid for the entire territory of the European Community. However, that policy was no longer uniformly implemented for all crops (Fabiani, 1995; Graziani, 1998): some crops, such as cereals and fodder (typically produced in northern European regions), used very high European Community support prices, while most of the other typical crops of Mediterranean regions (i.e., fruits and vegetables, oil and wine) received poor protection (De Filippis and Salvatici, 1991). This caused, inter alia, a change in the portions of surfaces dedicated to each kind of crop, with many farms also reconverting their operations into more remunerative varieties, such as corn and rice (Signorini and Zen, 1986).

Notwithstanding these contradictory aspects, the European Community price support policy ended up by being the main lever of a structural and manufacturing reorganization of the primary sector in all the member states of the European Community, thus leading to the specialization of enterprises and the most advanced areas, to a substantial increase in the level of mechanization, and to the growth of yields per unit.

THE ROLE OF THE ENTE NAZIONALE RISI AFTER WORLD WAR II UNTIL 1980

Within the Italian agricultural sector, rice production has always played a particularly significant role. In fact, Italy is not only the first European rice grower, but also the European main processor of paddy, brown and processed rice, with annual amounts constantly higher than the actual possibilities of absorption by the domestic market.

The excess of production over domestic demand, which calls for a necessary placement of products in foreign markets, combined with higher production costs compared to non-European competitor countries, makes it absolutely necessary to design support policies for the survival of the sector. In this regard, we should point out that the efforts of the State in support of rice characterized the agricultural policies of the first decades of the Kingdom of Italy, of the fascist regime, of the first Republican governments and, although in different ways, of the governments that came after the entrance of the Italian agriculture in the Common European Market (Brianta, 1991).

After the negative experience of the National Rice Consortium created in 1919 and dissolved in 1921, the ENR was created about a decade later, in 1931, in the form of a largely autonomous public entity supervised by the Ministry of Agriculture (with Royal Decree Law n. 1237 of 2 October 1931). According to the Decree, which was only slightly amended in the 1930s, the objectives of ENR are to "protect the national production of rice and the related industrial and commercial activities by facilitating the distribution and consumption of the product and promoting and supporting initiatives aimed at improving rice growing, processing and consumption" (Art. 1).

ENR carried out promotion and development actions in support of rice growing, but most of all became the tool for a permanent protectionist policy for the Italian rice production, aimed at taking the rice price in the domestic market to such a level as to be able to cover production costs and simultaneously ensuring the placement of the surplus that cannot be absorbed by the domestic market (Boggeri, 1932).

An essential characteristic of ENR is its strong link with the production chain, which led to its definition as a cartel within which "under the protection of the State, the players of the same sector agree a common policy regarding the quantity and quality produced, pricing and, in general, any regulation capable of affecting the offer" (Acerbi, 1980). In fact, the board of directors of ENR also includes representatives of the rice production chain: rice growers and the processing industry. Furthermore, the main source of funding of ENR is not the State, but rather the same players of the production chain: it is the so-called contract fee, which is paid by the purchaser (industrial buyer or trade intermediary) on each purchase and sale agreement of paddy rice. The amount of this fee, which is determined by the ENR's board of directors on an annual basis and submitted for ministerial approval, until the 1960s mostly fed a fund used to indemnify exporters, who are often forced to sell below cost (Brianta, 1985). Subsequently, after the development of European Community agricultural policies, this contract fee continued to be paid and, in 1994, was defined by the Court of Justice as a "payment made to offset the services provided to rice operators by ENR."

With specific reference to the 1945–1980 period considered in this chapter, we should specify that, in the first years after the war (1945–1948) supporting prices was a direct priority of ENR, while in the 1960s this institution implemented European agricultural policies, supporting the management of the rice surplus and playing the role of payer of the subsidies allocated to this sector by the European Community (Brianta, 1991).

In particular, in the years from 1945 to 1948, ENR focused on finding a compromise between the need to recognize sufficiently remunerative prices for rice growers (to face the continuous increases in the costs of labour and fertilizers) and that of supporting the government's retail price control policy. In addition to supporting rice prices, ENR supported production by granting growers significant advances on prices and ensuring an adequate technical-administrative support with the supply of selected seeds and chemical fertilizers at official prices.

The period from 1949 to 1953 was rather favourable for the rice production. The plan for the defence of the rice economy, based on traditional price support measures, implemented at domestic level, was accompanied by favourable trends in exchanges in the international market due to the gradual return to the free movement of goods, to the imbalance still existing between demographic growth and decrease in the global rice production, and by the Korean war (Korea was one of the most important Asian rice markets). As a consequence, Italy saw increases in crop surfaces, a greater annual production and higher prices in both the domestic and international markets. And precisely the high prices traded in foreign markets allowed ENR to use the contract fee not only to indemnify exporters, as in the past, but also to make new investments.

When the Korean war ended and rice prices consequently collapsed, a very difficult decade (1953–1963) started for the rice industry, with a progressive reduction of crop surfaces, a replacement of the labour factor with the technological factor (a compulsory transition, also due to the social phenomenon of rural depopulation in those years), a decrease in average costs (as a consequence of mechanization) and in the number of rice growers (Acerbi, 1978).

The European agricultural policy implemented in 1964 recognized the role of ENR in the negotiations for the definition of community rice prices, while, at national level, ENR was defined as the entity required to pay for the European Community interventions in support of rice production.

The European policy, although in different forms, followed the price support system that already existed at national level and created a system protected from non-European competition (Brianta, 1991). In summary, from the 1960s to the 1980s, ENR played the role of an intervention agency, obliged to purchase paddy rice upon request of the growers in exchange for the "intervention price" annually fixed by the European Community for all member states. Clearly, if the free market price is higher than the intervention price, the rice produced is sold by producers to private operators, and therefore ENR is not called to intervene. On the contrary, if the product is not absorbed, the players have the option of selling their crops to ENR in one of the general storehouses arranged by the institution for this need. In order to make the domestic market difficult to penetrate, a duty is applied on non-European rice, while exports can be supported by granting a refund to the exporter equal to the difference between the internal price and the lowest price of the global market.

Finally, we should point out that ENR does not only play the role of intervention agency on behalf of the European Community, but also supports rice production through the development of training, consulting and research activities. The latter is carried out through ENR's Research and Experimentation Centre (formally established in the 1970s), which plays a significant role for the improvement of rice varieties and seed supplies made available for the entire production chain.

THE STATE AUDIT THROUGH THE SUPREME AUDIT INSTITUTION

A Brief Overview on Law and Literature

Public intervention, at various levels, in support of the agricultural sector in general and therefore of rice (in the form of government actions for the sector and allocation of financial incentives) is certainly one of the distinctive features of the period following World War II. On the other hand, allocating huge public resources, in various forms, also requires a focus on the control of the actual use of said resources. In Italy, this kind of control is one of the task of the Supreme Audit Institution (SAI). The Italian SAI is the highest external body, independent of the Executive, that has the power to audit and control the public organizations.

At present, the literature (Barzelay, 1996; Power, 1997; Pollitt et al., 1999; Morin, 2003; Pollitt, 2003; Bourn, 2007; Skaerbaek, 2009) recognizes the following different roles of the SAI:

- *Supervisor*—independent of the government and external with respect to the audited public organizations, it has the purpose of auditing the compliance of public organization actions with the applicable legislation and ensuring parliament the necessary support in the exercise of its control function on the action of the executive power.
- *Support for change*—as body with the task of monitoring, *in itinere* and ex post, the achievement of objectives of efficiency and effectiveness of management in the audited public organizations, but without any power to impose its decisions.
- *Modernizer*—as body capable of actively guiding public organizations towards the introduction of the managerial government model.

All these roles, not necessarily opposed to one another, highlight the evolution of the activity of the SAI. The role of supervisor consists in conducting traditional financial or compliance auditing processes (consisting in a verification of the correct use of public resources and correct preparation of financial reports, in compliance with the applicable legislation); this is the activity that characterized the SAI since its origin. This activity may be integrated with performance auditing, that is, the evaluation of the economy, efficiency and effectiveness of the entire management of the audited public organization and its internal audit system (role of support for change), or even by with actions aimed at guiding change (role of modernizer) (Behn, 2001; Gendron et al., 2007; Skaerbaek, 2009; Gronlund et al., 2011; Lonsdale et al., 2014).

As regards the postwar period, the functions of the SAI were recognised by the Republican Constitution in 1948. According to the Constitution, the SAI, inter alia, "participates, in the cases and forms established by the legislation, in the control of the financial management of the entities ordinarily supported by the State. It directly reports the result of the audits conducted to the Parliament" (Art. 100).

The final audit of the financial management of the entities that normally use the public resources provided by the State was already required by the previous legislation (Royal Decree n. 129 of 1939), but had remained substantially unimplemented. Said auditing activity became particularly important in the years after World War II, which were characterized, as we have already pointed out, by a growing intervention of the State in the economic life of the country, including through its own entities and associated enterprises.

The auditing activity of the SAI was implemented only starting from 1958 with Law n. 259, which identified the types of "entities ordinarily supported by the State" and regulated the control of the SAI on their management. This provision would remain unchanged until the end of the 1980s. More specifically, the subsidized entities mentioned in the provisions of Law n. 259 of 1958 were:

- Entities benefiting from State financial assistance on a continuous basis;
- Entities authorized to levy taxes or, in any case, identified as beneficiaries;
- Public entities that received all or part of their assets (in the form of a capital, services or goods) from the State or any autonomous State agency;
- Public entities that benefit from a financial guarantee granted by the State in connection with their institutional tasks, with the exclusion of specific guarantees for individual transactions.

The audit may be implemented with different methods, depending on the nature of the relationship existing between the State and each entity. In the event of a periodic disbursement of financial resources and/or authorization to levy taxes, which are legally considered as an ordinary contribution, the audit will be merely formal, involving documents, and of an external nature. This control is exercised by a special section of the SAI called *Sezione controllo enti* (agency control section), which reviews the financial reports the entities are required to submit, together with the reports of the respective board of directors and internal auditors, within 15 days after their approval. Conversely, if the State contributes with capital or by granting a financial guarantee, the SAI may audit the entity through its magistrates, who are required to attend the meetings of the board of directors and internal auditors.

Based on a restrictive interpretation of the law, SAI's activity consists in a mere financial/compliance auditing of the regularity of the financial reports submitted for approval, without considering issues like the measurement and assessment of the economy, efficiency and effectiveness of management (performance auditing).

The more or less extensive scope of the SAI's auditing activity has been discussed in the research community after World War II starting from the 1960s. According to Bennati, the audit should not be limited to mere legal compliance, but should also concern management issues, even though not supported by penalty system (Bennati, 1965). In Cassandro's opinion, instead, the SAI's audit on these entities, as established by Law n. 259 of 1958, should be limited to a legal compliance audit and may not be extended to a control of the substance of actions aimed at judging the economic convenience and appropriateness of the actions implemented (Cassandro, 1975). On the other hand, this author believed that, for a control on the substance to be effective, the audit should be conducted ex ante rather than ex post, because only in advance could economically inappropriate, albeit lawful, actions be prevented. Cassandro highlighted the need for the lawmaker to develop further measures precisely for combining formal compliance audits with an audit of the cost-effectiveness of the public organization's actions.

The need to integrate mere formal compliance and accounting audits with performance auditing was also felt by Giannessi. Compliance audits may be deemed sufficient if the public organization delivers only essential services, but becomes inadequate when the State takes more extensive actions and intervenes in the economy. According to Giannesi, we need "a new Supreme Audit Institution empowered to control the use of public money in any manner and under any aspect" (Giannessi, 1969). He points out the consequent need to adapt the legislation to the new economic and social situation of the country, primarily by overcoming the notion of mere compliance audits and then establishing the extension to public enterprises of a "new" control by the SAI that, precisely as "supreme body for the control of the State, should intervene every time public money is used" (Giannessi, 1969).

In summary, in the postwar era, the lawmaker substantially required mere audits of the legal compliance of these entities with laws, regulations and bylaws, thus limiting the role of the SAI to that of a supervisor, while the literature proposed further changes in order to extend the content of these audits to the cost-effectiveness of management.

The State Audit on the Ente Nazionale Risi

In order to understand how the State, through the SAI, monitored the activity of ENR, we analyzed the content of the Reports on Financial Management of ENR submitted by the SAI to parliament over the period after World War II and until 1980. The analysis was conducted to see whether the SAI restricted its action to the monitoring of compliance with laws and regulations, thus playing a traditional financial/compliance auditing role, or interpreted the law more extensively and assessed the economy, efficiency and effectiveness of the management of ENR.

Then we examined the nature and extent of the information transmitted by SAI to the parliament over a period of approximately 30 years. In detail, the analysis is based on the examination of the SAI's Reports on State-Subsidized Entities concerning the years from 1942 to 1980. These documents are gathered from Italian Parliament archives (nowadays mainly available online).

In the period after World War II, the SAI submitted to Parliament the first Report on State-Subsidized Entities on 26 August 1950. This report concerned the years 1942–1950, but no analysis of ENR management (and no information on this topic).

Only in January 1962 the SAI submitted to parliament the first Report that also included the ENR and concerned the years 1951–1960. On that occasion, although Law n. 259 of 1958 had not yet been implemented with decrees, in the introduction section of the document concerning all the "entities ordinarily supported by the State," the SAI announced that it had carefully reviewed the main aspects of the management of subsidized entities, such as the use of capitals, the collection of revenues, the expenditure, the relationship between operating expenses and the results achieved, in order to allow for a global assessment of the compliance of the activity of the entities with their institutional nature.

With specific reference to the part dedicated to ENR, we used the content analysis method (Krippendorff, 1980) to classify text units into categories, a method that is considered to be appropriate for the study of narrative information (like the Reports on Financial Management prepared by the SAI).

The information was classified into the following categories: introduction of the document, history of the ENR and regulatory references, context, ENR activities, State-ENR relationships, organizational layout, financial reporting (revenues, expenses and balance sheet items and operating results), SAI's observations.

As far as coding and measuring units are concerned, our content analysis considered the "sentence" as the coding unit, for a better understanding of the message, and the "line" as a measuring unit, to quantify the space devoted to each individual information category (Milne and Adler, 1999). In addition to the body of the text, the analysis also concerned tables and diagrams, and identified the information category of each diagram and table by considering their lines as measuring units. The dominance principle was applied to the analysis, which was conducted without using any software by one of the co-authors of the chapter.

The content analysis carried out showed that the Reports examined devote almost all the space to information concerning financial/compliance auditing (Table 17.1).

In fact, the importance of the traditional legal compliance auditing of accounting documents is clear, hence the prevalence of the role of supervisor played by the SAI. However, it should be noted that the SAI did not merely pronounce an opinion of compliance or noncompliance of the resolutions approved by the ENR boards or of certain accounting practices. On the contrary, in many instances (and often repeatedly in multiple Reports), it gave suggestions and recommendations for a better management. Nevertheless, only in two cases, in the Report on Financial Management 1951–1960, the SAI's Observations can be associated with suggestions aimed at improving the cost-effectiveness of the ENR: these are the invitation to invest a portion of liquid assets in government securities, not to leave an excessive amount of liquid assets in stock, and the remark concerning the use of surplus income that, according to the SAI, should have been used more cautiously to create a reserve for future unfavourable conditions (Figure 17.1).

On the other Reports regarding the period between 1961 and 1980, the SAI's Observations discussed the lack of compliance with laws, regulations

Table 17.1 Content distribution (no. lines per IC/no. lines of content) (%)

	Introduction	History of ENR with indication of regulatory references, legal nature, institutional purposes	Context	ENR activities	State/ENR relationships	Organizational layout	Financial reporting			SAI's observations	
SAI Report	Presentation of the report	Decree issued to create ENR, national and EU laws, ENR bylaws and regulations, other ENR-related provisions	National, European and international situation; national rice production	Activities carried out in period considered in report	State financial support received by ENR; ad-hoc State intervention; document flow between ENR and State	ENR boards, offices, staff (composition and contractual issues); ENR associated companies	Revenues ("contract fee," indebtedness, interests, sale of paddy rice, etc.)	Expenditure (staff, promotion, administration, purchase of paddy rice, etc.)	Balance sheet items and operating result	Observations and suggestions to improve management	Observations and suggestions to improve accounting records of management facts and disclosures in financial reports
1942–1950	NA	NA	NA	NA	NA	NA	NA	NA	NA	NA	NA
1951–1960	0.50%	21.41%	3.17%	6.84%	20.42%	4.66%	11.30%	8.13%	22.79%	0.79%	0.00%
1961–1965	0.36%	4.22%	4.04%	1.71%	11.58%	12.39%	10.77%	30.79%	24.15%	0.00%	0.00%
1966–1968	0.33%	4.23%	1.35%	1.06%	0.53%	3.96%	6.60%	13.50%	66.72%	0.00%	1.72%
1969–1972	0.90%	7.90%	0.00%	0.00%	5.57%	18.31%	9.16%	17.24%	28.37%	0.00%	12.57%
1973–1974	2.80%	11.98%	0.93%	0.00%	11.66%	17.42%	6.07%	10.42%	20.53%	0.00%	18.20%
1975–1976	0.91%	14.78%	4.35%	0.00%	5.57%	14.27%	9.41%	11.23%	24.70%	0.00%	14.78%
1977–1978	0.70%	13.90%	4.79%	0.00%	4.67%	12.97%	11.10%	18.22%	30.14%	0.00%	3.50%
1979–1981	0.49%	22.50%	3.45%	7.88%	4.15%	7.74%	9.07%	16.03%	18.57%	0.00%	10.13%
Mean	*0.87%*	*12.61%*	*2.76%*	*2.18%*	*8.02%*	*11.46%*	*9.18%*	*15.70%*	*29.50%*	*0.10%*	*7.61%*

Note: NA = not available.

a) Le *banche correntiste* sono piuttosto numerose (21), anche se i depositi più consistenti riguardano la Popolare di Novara, la Nazionale del lavoro, la Banca dell'agricoltura.

Le variazioni sono in dipendenza degli impegni che si sono manifestati durante l'esercizio. In linea di principio sembrerebbe doversi raccomandare di investire una parte delle disponibilità in Buoni del Tesoro, lasciando presso gli Istituti di credito la disponibilità per fronteggiare i pagamenti urgenti.

[...]

L'avanzo risultato alla chiusura dell'esercizio 1957-58 è stato destinato (delibere Commissariali in data 27 ottobre 1958) a contribuire alla copertura del programma di nuovi investimenti in immobili ed impianti, di cui si è già trattato. È da rilevare che di fronte alla progressiva contrazione dell'utile sarebbe stato più opportuno costituire, con parte di tale cospicua rimanenza, un fondo di riserva capace di fronteggiare eventuali evenienze di gestioni non favorevoli.

Figure 17.1 Extract from SAI's Report on Financial Management 1951–1960

and accounting principles. In general, these cases dealt with the personnel's salaries, the composition of the boards and the accounting information system adopted by ENR. In the latter case, the observations expressed by the SAI can be summarized in a repeated invitation to pass to the traditional public accounting system and prepare the annual budget and the annual report consisting of traditional public accounting report, statement of assets and liabilities, and income statement. Actually ENR was merely presenting a summarized assessment of its financial needs at the beginning of each year, when the amount of the contract fee had to be determined, and, at year-end, it disclosed its management results in an annual report totally detached from the previous budget. The SAI repeatedly suggested ENR to prepare an annual budget with specifications of the priorities of the various interventions planned by the entity. Furthermore, the SAI recommended ENR to comply with traditional public accounting rules and principles in order to improve the clarity of its disclosures on management facts—an indispensable transparency that was needed to ensure "a responsible and sensible auditing" of the activity of a public organization. To offer an example, we are providing, in Figure 17.2, the criticism expressed by the SAI about certain accounting practices deemed to be incorrect and the respective answers of the ENR to said observations, reported by the same SAI in subsequent Reports.

Figure 17.2 clearly shows how the observations on the substance of the documents (change in the accounting information system) have remained disregarded, while those regarding a more transparent disclosure of management facts seem to have been accepted.

As regards the space dedicated to the individual information categories, other than the SAI's Observations, there is a prevalence of those concerning the balance sheet items and operating results (mean 29.50%), which underlines the importance attributed to the protection of the integrity of ENR assets. A good deal of attention is also paid to revenues, essentially from the contract fee (mean 9.18%) and to the annual operating expenses

SAI's observations (Parliamentary Act, 5th Legislature, Doc. XV, n. 91_1966-68)

Per quanto riguarda gli aspetti puntuali delle esaminate contabilità, non si può, in primo luogo, fare a meno di prospettare l'esigenza che l'Ente, allo scopo di pervenire ad una più chiara esposizione contabile ed al fine, soprattutto, di graduare in base all'importanza, le priorità dei vari interventi, i quali necessariamente non possono che essere limitati dalle disponibilità di bilancio, proceda alla predisposizione di annuali stati di previsione delle entrate e delle spese.

ENR's answer (Parliamentary Act, 6th Legislature, Doc. XV, n. 49_1969-72)

Al riguardo il Ministero vigilante, in risposta alla Presidenza del Consiglio, che aveva ad esso rappresentato la necessità dell'adozione di idonee iniziative dirette ad indurre l'Ente ad uniformarsi alle esigenze prospettate dalla Corte, e riportando le osservazioni in merito espresse dall'Ente medesimo, ha fatto presente che l'esigenza di un preventivo, pur essendo stata presa in esame, nelle riunioni tenutesi nel 1959-1960 per la predisposizione del nuovo statuto, non venne considerata preminente, in considerazione del fatto che l'Ente si trovava già nella necessità di formulare una previsione di spesa, ai fini della fissazione della misura del diritto di contratto per l'anno seguente.

ENR's answer (Parliamentary Act, 6th Legislature, Doc. XV, n. 49 1973-74)

Il comitato di presidenza dell'Ente ha trattato, nella propria relazione al consiglio per la fissazione del diritto di contratto 1974-75, quanto la Corte aveva fatto presente, nelle precedenti relazioni, riguardo alla contabilizzazione dei fatti gestori dell'Ente, ma non ha ritenuto di proporre l'adozione di modifiche al vigente assetto contabile, per numerosi motivi, che possono riassumersi nella difficoltà di preventivare la massima entrata dell'Ente, cioè il diritto di contratto, nonché di prevedere quelli che devono essere i necessari interventi di settore, e quindi le corrispondenti spese, a causa della mutevole e complessa realtà su cui l'Ente opera.

SAI's observations (Parliamentary Act, 6th Legislature, Doc. XV, n. 49 1973-74)

In merito la Corte, pur convenendo che la formulazione di stati di previsione di entrata e di spesa — i quali comportano poi la predisposizione di rendiconti finanziari, affiancati da conti economici dimostrativi dell'avanzo o del disavanzo di gestione — richiede una ponderata ed approfondita valutazione, non può che mantenere il proprio manifestato avviso, e riaffermare la viva esigenza che l'Ente provveda a predisporre un annuale bilancio di previsione, adeguando conseguentemente i propri interventi, e la loro esposiizone contabile, a quanto preventivato, salva la possibilità di deliberarne variazioni.

SAI's observations (Parliamentary Act, 6th Legislature, Doc. XV, n. 49 1973-74)

Il Ministero vigilante nel settembre 1974 ha provveduto, conclusivamente, ad effettuare il versamento all'Ente di un anticipo di 300 milioni di lire, perché questo potesse operare in favore degli operatori economici interessati.

Entro il 30 settembre 1974, l'Ente ha precisato di avere già corrisposto agli aventi diritto l'indennità in parola, con una complessiva erogazione alquanto superiore alle somme appena pervenute, ed ammontante a milioni 343,4 (13).

[...]

Si precisa, conclusivamente, che la sola che appaia nei documenti contabili dell'Ente per il 1974, è stata la citata maggiore erogazione di milioni 43,4 in quanto il relativo credito, appare esposto nella posta attiva patrimoniale « debitori diversi ».

Tutto ciò descritto, la Corte — nel censurare la detta mancata rendicontazione contabile di un fatto gestorio, la quale infrange i principi dell'universalità e dell'integrità del bilancio — deve riaffermare l'inderogabile esigenza, precedentemente espressa, che l'Ente provveda all'adozione di una idonea contabilizzazione finanziaria dei propri fatti gestori, ispirata ai principi regolatori della contabilità pubblica.

ENR's answer (Parliamentary Act, 7th Legislature, Doc. XV, n. 75_ 1975-76)

Il comitato di presidenza dell'Ente ha preso in esame, nella relazione per la fissazione del diritto di contratto 1976-77, il detto generale problema dell'adozione di modifiche al vigente assetto contabile, ma si è sostanzialmente limitato — senza menzionare il caso concreto su ricordato, il quale comprovava l'inadeguatezza del sistema contabile seguito — a precisare che nessuna norma ha mai finora previsto per l'Ente la predisposizione di bilanci di previsione, e che il vigente statuto dispone solo la stesura di un consuntivo annuale.

Figure 17.2 SAI's observations and ENR's answers—extracts

Circa le uscite, deve notarsi che gli importi più elevati sono quelli esposti nella voce « spese di amministrazione ». Gli aumenti retributivi concessi al personale (20) non potevano che provocare un aumento di tali spese, derivanti anche dalla connessa necessità di adeguare proporzionalmente l'entità del fondo di quiescenza: nell'ultimo esercizio in esame gli oneri per il personale hanno così comportato una spesa di milioni 1.327,7.

Deve, peraltro, precisarsi che in tale voce non è esposta la complessiva spesa che l'Ente sostiene per il proprio personale, in quanto — con un sistema che non può condividersi — il costo del personale, che è incaricato di svolgere funzioni operative, è contabilmente imputato — eventualmente anche per quote — sulle singoli voci di spesa, attinenti al compimento delle dette funzioni (21).

ENR's answer (Parliamentary Act, 7th Legislature, Doc. XV, n. 75_ 1975-76)

Riguardo alle uscite deve notarsi come gli importi più elevati siano esposti nella voce « oneri per il personale »: trattasi delle spese per stipendi, salari e indennità varie (1976: milioni 1.089,3), contributi sociali ed oneri previdenziali (1976: milioni 369,4), integrazione fondo quiescenza (1976: milioni 324,5), trasferte (1976: milioni 63,5) ed infine oneri esodo ex combattenti, in applicazione della legge n. 336/1970 (1976: milioni 43).

SAI's observations (Parliamentary Act, 6th Legislature, Doc. XV, n. 49 1973-74)

Passando ad esaminare le altre voci di entrata, deve notarsi che nel 1974 compare quella denominata « redditi diversi ». Nel verbale di una riunione del Collegio Sindacale (17), è precisato che in detta voce « trovano esplicita evidenza per la prima volta (...) le rendite diverse, che negli esercizi precedenti erano imputate in diminuzione ai rispettivi conti di spesa ».

Richiesto di chiarimenti, l'Ente ha precisato che in tutti gli esercizi precedenti il 1974, dette « rendite non figurano in voce propria, ma sono state conteggiate a diminuzione delle spese relative alla produzione delle rendite stesse, per cui le voci di spesa esposte nei bilanci precedenti risultano al netto delle rendite in questioni » (18).

La Corte non può che censurare siffatta esposizione contabile, attuata dall'Ente fino al 1973: due fondamentali principi regolanti la corretta esposizione di un pubblico bilancio, sono quelli della universalità e della integrità, in attuazioni dei quali ogni e qualsiasi entrata e spesa devono essere esposte, escludendosi così ogni possibilità di parziale e settoriale compensazione (19).

SAI's observations (Parliamentary Act, 6th Legislature, Doc. XV, n. 49 1973-74)

Come già precisato nelle precedenti relazioni, l'Ente è solito comprendere le perdite subite per condurre le varie campagne di commercializzazione — con impropria esposizione di bilancio — tra le poste attive del patrimonio, « in attesa che venga risolto il problema dei costi sostenuti » per il compimento di dette campagne. In applicazione di tale impostazione, le somme che rappresentano le eccedenze dei costi delle campagne, vengono dall'Ente esposte fra le attività patrimoniali in proprie e distinte voci.

In merito, peraltro, la Corte non può che ricordare come i decreti ministeriali disponenti la misura del diritto di contratto, che l'Ente è abilitato ad ottenere dai privati operatori, stabiliscono detta misura in base alle « effettive esigenze dell'Ente Nazionale risi per l'espletamento delle sue finalità istituzionali, e per gli interventi che esso è chiamato a svolgere quale organismo di intervento », senza quindi, differenziare detti fondamentali compiti dell'Ente dagli altri che allo stesso competono.

ENR's answer (Parliamentary Act, 7th Legislature, Doc. XV, n. 75_ 1975-76)

— Nel 1976 per la prima volta, l'Ente espone nella voce « organismo di intervento » gli oneri sostenuti per il funzionamento dei magazzini (16) tenuti a disposizione dei produttori di settore, nell'eventualità che gli stessi decidano, secondo la situazione di mercato, di vendere il proprio prodotto all'organismo di intervento, ricevendone in compenso il prezzo annualmente stabilito dagli organi della Comunità economica europea. In merito deve ricordarsi che l'Ente, così operando, ha tenuto conto delle osservazioni della Corte, la quale nel-

Figure 17.2 (Continued)

incurred for the personnel, for the purchase of paddy rice under the agricultural support policies, and for administration and promotion activities (mean 15.70%).

A considerable space is also devoted to historical highlights and the national and community legislation concerning the ENR activity (mean

12.60%), organizational layout (boards, offices, associated companies) and, to a lesser extent, national and international *context*, with a focus on national rice production trends. The purpose is to outline the context of the book values reported in the accounts. To offer an example, we are providing, in Figure 17.3, the table published in the Report on Financial Management 1961–1965 containing the main statistical data regarding the crop surface, production, number of producers, quantity of stockpiled products and quantities sold in the domestic and foreign markets.

A rather good deal of space is devoted to the description of the relationships between ENR and the State (mean 8.02%), while information on its activities (in terms of nature and volume of services provided) is poor (mean 2.18%), with the sole exception of the Reports on Financial Management 1950–1960 and 1978–1981, which contain a detailed descriptions of the actions implemented in support of prices and other promotion activities to increase rice consumption and incentives for technological progress.

The investigation conducted shows that the SAI prevalently plays a financial/compliance auditing role. Its activity essentially consists in conducting mere audits of the compliance of the entities with laws, regulations and bylaws, thus confirming its role of an independent supervisor.

In one of the Reports examined, we found some suggestions to improve the management of ENR, but they were only small changes and almost all the improvements proposed concerned accounting issues (accounting information system and accounting practices).

Therefore, in spite of the input of the scholars of the time, who suggested that compliance audits be combined with an auditing of the cost-effectiveness of the actions implemented by the public organization to be monitored, the SAI limits the exercise of its auditing function to traditional audits, without considering any issue regarding the management of the audited entity.

In other words, the audit conducted by the SAI is still focused on single actions (resolutions) and accounting documents, and not on the overall management in terms of efficiency and effectiveness; this trend, in fact, would be significantly developed only starting from the 1990s.

CONCLUSION

This study offers a contribution to the historical accounting literature in two significant areas: the food, in particular the rice production, framed in an analysis of the social, political and economic context (Sargiacomo and Gomes, 2011) of the 1945–1980 period and the SAI auditing activities that have been very little explored by historical accounting literature (Radcliffe, 1997, 1998, 2009).

More specifically, in the period after World War II (1945–1980), Italy has had a start-up phase of economic recovery. During these years, the State directly intervened in the economic life of the country, particularly through

	1961-1962		1962-1963		1963-1964		1964-1965	
Superficie coltivata . . . . Ha		127.777		122.628		120.970		124.930
Media unitaria di produzione ad Ha . . ql.		54.79		53,21		46,34		49,06
Numero aziende produttrici		21.592		20.014		18.735		17.766
Produzione dell'esercizio . . . . ql.		7.001.058		6.525.553		5.606.112		6.129.104
Rimanenza vecchio raccolto:								
a) presso ammasso . . . . ql.	531.463		158.386		6.645		85.935	
b) presso i produttori . . . . ql.	26.168	557.631	49.406	207.792	10.753	17.398	86.913	172.848
Disponibilita statistica . . . . ql.		7.558.689		6.733 345		5.623.510		6.301.952
Rimanenza a fine esercizio:								
a) presso ammasso . . . . ql.	158.386		6.645		82.656		32.436	
b) presso i produttori . . . . ql.	49.406	207.792	10.753	17.398	86.913	169.569	200.200	232.636
Conferimenti all'ammasso nell'esercizio ql.		6.626.206,61		6.204.122,33		5.196.940,62		6.015.817,—
Rimanenze presso l'ammasso di vecchio raccolto . . . . ql.		531.463,68		158.385,88		6.644,74		85.935,—
ql.		7.157.670,29		6.362.508,21		5.203.585,36		6.101.752,—
a) cali peso (1) . . . . — ql.	4.333,77		1.473,70		118,40		307.908,—	
b) superi peso . . . . + ql.	6.982,02	2.648,25	3.414,50	1.940,80	207,72	89,32	—	307.908,—
		7.160,318,54		6.364.449,01		5.203.674,68		5.793.844,—
Rimanenza a fine esercizio presso l'ammasso . . . . ql.		158.385,88		6.644,74		82.656,10		32.436,—
Prodotto venduto. . . . . ql.		7.001.932,66		6.357.804,27		5.121.018,58		5.761.408,—
Prodotto venduto:								
a) sul mercato interno. . . . . ql.		4.317.999,62		4.436.107,07		4.097.266,32		4.229.388,—
b) sul mercato estero . . . . ql.		2.683.933,04		1.921.697,20		1.023.752,26		1.532.020,—
		7.001.932,66		6.357.804,27		5.121.018,58		5.761.408,—
Esportazioni risone da seme . . . . . ql.		22.188,71		20.396,68		21.507,39		28.873,28

Nell'importo relativo al 1964-65 di tale voce sono compresi consumi per sementi e per uso zootecnico.

Figure 17.3 Extract from SAI's Report on Financial Management 1961–1965

the expansion of the system of State-controlled enterprises. In the 1950s, said system became a tool to accelerate investments and technical progress in the country, while, starting from the 1970s, Entrepreneurial State progressively declined.

The auditing of the financial management of the entities normally subsidized by the State became particularly important within the framework of the functions of the SAI precisely in the period after World War II, in connection with the role played by the State in the economy. ENR, which has been supporting rice production in Italy since 1931, is one of these entities.

Agricultural policies, first only at the national level and then, starting from the 1960s, even at the European Community level, could be defined as substantially focused on providing price support. In the rice production, ENR has always been the only institution to take care of the implementation of said policies. Since its activity, as public institution, involves the use of public funds, it is audited by the SAI.

Our analysis highlights that these audits did not change much over the 1945–1980 period. As a matter of fact, the SAI has merely played a role of supervisor of the ENR activities and substantially carried out financial/compliance auditing to ensure the correctness of the actions and procedures implemented by the entity, of its accounting records and related financial reports. This auditing, which produces annual Reports, sometimes contains assessments that go beyond the rigid compliance audit pattern and offer suggestions aimed at improving the transparency of management, even if only from the point of view of reporting and accounting. No clear evidence emerged of a performance auditing activity (with the SAI supporting change or playing the role of modernizer); in fact, this kind of activity will be undertaken by the SAI only starting from the 1990s.

REFERENCES

Primary Sources

Parliamentary Act, 1st Legislature, Doc. X, n. 1-ter, 1942–1950.
Parliamentary Act, 3rd Legislature, Doc. XIV, n. 1, 1951–1960.
Parliamentary Act, 4th Legislature, Doc. XIII, n. 1, 1961–1965.
Parliamentary Act, 5th Legislature, Doc. XV, n. 91, 1966–1968.
Parliamentary Act, 6th Legislature, Doc. XV, n. 49, 1969–1972.
Parliamentary Act, 6th Legislature, Doc. XV, n. 49, 1973–1974.
Parliamentary Act, 7th Legislature, Doc. XV, n. 75, 1975–1976.
Parliamentary Act, 8th Legislature, Doc. XV, n. 26, 1977–1978.
Parliamentary Act, 8th Legislature, Doc. XV, n. 26, 1979–1981.

Secondary Sources

Acerbi, S. (1978) L'azienda risicola italiana nel dopoguerra: un caso particolare di sostituzione dei fattori di produzione. *Rivista di storia dell'agricoltura* 1: 45–67.

Acerbi, S. (1980) La risicoltura e la formazione dell'Ente Nazionale Risi. *Rivista di storia dell'agricoltura* 1: 39–55.

Amatori, F., Bugamelli, M. and Colli, A. (2013) Technology, firm size, and entrepreneurship. In: Toniolo, G. (ed.), *The Italian economy since unification*. Oxford: Oxford University Press, pp. 455–484.

Anselmi, L. (ed.) (1990) *Il sistema delle partecipazioni statali: analisi delle condizioni di equilibrio*. Turin: Giappichelli.

Barca, F. and Trento, S. (1997) La parabola delle partecipazioni statali: una missione tradita. In: Barca, F. (ed.), *Storia del capitalismo italiano dal dopoguerra a oggi*. Rome: Donzelli, pp. 37–62.

Barzelay, M. (1996) Performance auditing and new public management: changing roles and strategies of central audit institutions. In: OECD (ed.), *Performance audit and the modernization of government*, Paris: PUMA/OECD, pp. 22–54.

Battilani, P. and Fauri, F. (2008) *Mezzo secolo di economia italiana*. Bologna: Il Mulino.

Behn, R.D. (2001) *Rethinking democratic accountability*. Washington: Brooking Institution Press.

Bennati, A. (1965) *Manuale di contabilità di Stato*, IV edizione. Naples: Casa editrice Novene.

Boggeri, M. (1932) *La crisi risicola e l'Ente nazionale risi*. Padua: Cedam.

Borgonovi, E. (1996) *Principi e sistemi aziendali per le amministrazioni pubbliche*. Milan: Egea.

Bourn, J. (2007) *Public sector auditing: Is it value for money*. London: John Wiley & Sons.

Brianta, D. (1985) *Amministrazione e mediazione degli interessi: l'Ente nazionaler risi*, Milan: Giuffrè.

Brianta, D. (1991) Il riso tra Stato e mercato. Un commercio agricolo padano. In: Bevilacqua, P. (ed.), *Storia dell'agricoltura italiana in età contemporanea*. Venice: Marsilio editori, pp.75–98.

Bunn, M. and Gilchrist, D.J. (2013) "A few good men": Public sector audit in the Swan River Colony 1828–1835. *Accounting History* 18(2): 193–209.

Cafferata, R. (2010) Dall'impresa strumento di politica economica all'attuale presenza di gruppi e società pubbliche nell'economia italiana. In: AA. VV. (ed.), *Contabilità e bilanci per l'amministrazione economica*. Milan: Atti X Convegno Nazionale SISR 2009, pp.148–176.

Cassandro, P.E. (1963) L'economicità dell'azienda statale e il controllo della Corte dei conti. In: AA. VV. (ed.), *Studi in occasione del primo centenario della Corte dei conti nell'unità d'Italia*. Milan: Giuffrè, pp. 98–121.

Cassandro, P.E. (1975) *Le gestioni erogatrici pubbliche*, III edizione riveduta ed aggiornata. Turin: Utet.

Castronuovo, V. (1975) La storia economica. In: AA. VV. (ed.), *Storia d'Italia*, Vol. 4/1. Turin: Giulio Einaudi Editore, pp. 1123–1129.

Colasanti, E. (1979) Vent'anni di controllo sugli enti sovvenzionati dallo Stato. In: AA. VV. (ed.), *La Corte dei conti strumento di attuazione della Costituzione nella materia della finanza pubblica* Rome: Edizioni Scientifiche italiane, pp. 35–76.

Colquhoun, P. (2013) Political and organizational legitimacy of public sector auditing in New Zealand local government. *Accounting History* 18(4): 473–489.

Coltelli, R. (1970) La valutazione della Corte dei conti sulle gestioni finanziarie degli enti sovvenzionati dallo Stato. In: AA. VV. (ed.), *Ricerca delle regole organizzative di buon andamento dell'amministrazione pubblica*. Milan: Giuffrè, pp. 67–85.

Coombs, H.M. and Edwards, J.R. (2004) The audit of municipal corporations—A quest for professional dominance. *Managerial Auditing Journal* 19(1): 68–83.

Crafts, N. and Magnani, M. (2013) The golden age and the second globalization in Italy. In: Toniolo, G. (ed.), *The Italian economy since unification*. Oxford: Oxford University Press, pp. 154–179.

Cuomo, G. (1963) Osservazioni sui limiti del controllo della Corte dei conti sugli enti sovvenzionati dallo Stato. In: AA. VV. (ed.), *Studi in occasione del primo centenario della Corte dei Conti nell'unità d'Italia*. Milan: Giuffrè, pp. 123–138.

De Filippis, F. and Salvatici, L. (1991) L'Italia e la politica agricola del Mercato Comune Europeo. In: Bevilacqua, P. (ed.), *Storia dell'agricoltura italiana in età contemporanea*. Venice: Marsilio, pp. 19–34.

Fabiani, G. (1995) L'agricoltura italiana nello sviluppo dell'Europa comunitaria. In: Barbagallo, F. (ed.), *Storia dell'Italia Repubblicana*, Vol. II, *La trasformazione dell'Italia: sviluppi e squilibri*. Turin: Giulio Einaudi Editore, pp. 56–87.

Fanfani, R. (1998) *L'agricoltura in Italia*. Bologna: Il Mulino.

Funnell, W. (1994) Independence and the State Auditor in Britain: A constitutional keystone or a case of reified imagery? *Abacus* 30(2): 175–195.

Funnell, W. (1997) Military influences on the evolution of public sector audit and accounting 1830–1880. *Accounting History* 2(2): 9–29.

Funnell, W. (2004) Victorian parsimony and the early champions of modern public sector audit. *Accounting History* 9(1): 25–60.

Gendron, Y., Cooper, D.J. and Towley, B. (2001) In the name of accountability. State auditing, independence and new public management. *Accounting, Auditing and Accountability Journal* 14(3): 278–310.

Giannessi, E. (1969) Il controllo della Corte dei conti sul bilancio dello Stato: In: AA. VV. (ed.), *Saggi in onore del centenario della Ragioneria generale dello Stato*. Rome: Ministero del Tesoro, pp. 76–102.

Graziani, A. (1998) *Lo sviluppo dell'economia italiana*. Turin: Bollati Boringhieri.

Grilli, E., Kregel, J.A. and Savona, P. (1982) Ragioni di scambio e crescita economica in Italia. *Moneta e credito* 4: 391–412.

Gronlund, A., Svardsten, F. and Ohman, P. (2011) Value for money and the rule of law: The (new) performance audit in Sweden. *International Journal of Public Sector Management* 24(2): 107–121.

Krippendorff, K. (1980) *Content Analysis. An Introduction to Its Methodology*. Beverly Hills, CA: Sage Publications.

Lonsdale, J., Wilkins, P. and Ling, T. (eds.) (2011) *Performance auditing contributing to accountability in democratic government*. Cheltenham, UK: Edward Elgar Pub.

Malanima, P. and Zamagni, V. (2010) 150 years of Italian economy 1861–2010. *Journal of modern Italian studies* 15(1): 1–20.

Milne, M.J. and Adler, R.W. (1999) Exploring the reliability of social and environmental disclosures content analysis. *Accounting, Auditing and Accountability Journal* 12(2): 237–256.

Morin, D. (2003) Controllers or catalysts for change and improvement: Would the real value for money auditors please stand up? *Managerial Auditing Journal* 18(1): 19–30.

Mussari, R. and Magliacani, M. (2007) Agricultural accounting in the nineteenth and early twentieth centuries: The case of the Noble Rucellai Family Farm in Campi. *Accounting, Business and Financial History* 17(1): 87–103.

Pellegrini, G. (2002) Lo sviluppo strutturale dell'economia italiana dal dopoguerra al nuovo secolo. In: Ciocca, P. and Toniolo, G. (eds.), *Storia economica d'Italia*. Roea: IntesaBci-Laterza, pp. 123–153.

Petri, R. (1997) Dalla ricostruzione al miracolo economico. In: Sabbatucci G, Vidotto V. (a cura di), *Storia d'Italia. La Repubblica*. Bari: Laterza, pp. 176–198.

Pollitt, C. (2003) Performance audit in Western Europe: Trends and choices. *Critical Perspectives on Accounting* 14(1–2): 157–170.

Pollitt, C., Girre, X., Lonsdale, J., Mul, R., Summa, H. and Waerness, M. (1999) *Performance or compliance? Performance audit and public management in five countries*. Oxford: Oxford University Press.

Posner, M. and Woolf, S. (1967) *Italian public enterprise*. Cambridge: Cambridge University Press.

Power, M. (1997) *The Audit society. Rituals of verification*. Oxford: Oxford University Press.

Radcliffe, V. (1997) Competing rationalities in "special" government audits: The case of NovAtel. *Critical Perspective on Accounting* 8(4): 343–366.

Radcliffe, V. (1998) Efficiency audit: An assembly of rationalities and programmes. *Accounting, Organizations and Society* 23(4): 377–410.

Radcliffe, V. (2009) Accountability in crisis: The sponsorship scandal and the Office of the Comptroller General in Canada. *Journal of Business Ethics* 84: 189–208.

Rossi Doria, M. (1969) *L'analisi zonale dell'agricoltura italiana*. Rome: Inea.

Rossi, N., Sorgato, A. and Toniolo, G. (1993) I conti economici italiani: una ricostruzione statistica 1890–1990. *Rivista di Storia Economica* 10: 1–47.

Rossi, N. and Toniolo, G. (1996) Italy. In: Crafts, N. and Toniolo, G. (eds.), *Economic growth in Europe since 1945*. Cambridge: Centre for Economic Policy Research, pp. 24–47.

Sargiacomo, M. (2008) Accounting and the 'Art of Government': Margaret of Austria in Abruzzo (1539–86). *European Accounting Review* 17(4): 667–695.

Sargiacomo, M. (2009) Accounting for the 'good administration of justice': The Farnese state of Abruzzo in the sixteenth century. *Accounting History* 14(3): 235–267.

Sargiacomo, M. and Gomes, D. (2011) Accounting and accountability in local government: Contributions from accounting history research. *Accounting History* 16(3): 253–290.

Sargiacomo, M., Ianni, L. and D'Andreamatteo, A. (2014) Contabilità e governo dell'economia agricola della Nazione: Arrigo Serpieri e la riforma dei Consorzi di Bonifica. *Contabilità e cultura aziendale* 1: 85–111.

Shaerbaek, P. (2009) Public sector audit identities in making efficiency auditable: The National Audit Office of Denmark as independent auditor and modernizer. *Accounting, Organization and Society* 34(8): 971–987.

Signorini, L.F. and Zen, G. (1986) *Modifiche strutturali e tendenze dell'agricoltura italiana (1961–1982)*. Temi di discussione del Servizio Studi, 79, Banca d'Italia.

Toniolo, G. (2013) An overview of Italy's economic growth. In: Toniolo, G. (ed.), *The Italian economy since unification*. Oxford: Oxford University Press, pp. 54–86.

Woods, D. (1998) The crisis (collapse) of Italy's public enterprises system: A revised property rights perspective. *Journal of modern Italian studies* 3(1): 22–41.

Zamagni, V. (1993) *The economic history of Italy 1860–1990*. Oxford: Clarendon Press.

Index

Note: figures and tables are denoted with italicized page numbers; end note information is denoted with an n and note number following the page number.